Cognitive Processes in Depression

COGNITIVE PROCESSES
IN DEPRESSION

Edited by
Lauren B. Alloy
Northwestern University

THE GUILFORD PRESS
New York London

This book is dedicated to
  my husband, Daniel
    my parents, Jacqueline and Philip
      and my sister, Marilyn

© 1988 The Guilford Press
A Division of Guilford Publications, Inc.
72 Spring Street, New York, NY 10012

Printed in the United States of America

Last digit is print number: 9 8 7 6 5 4 3 2 1

Library of Congress Cataloging in Publication Data
  Cognitive processes in depression.

  Includes index.
  1. Depression, Mental—Etiology. 2. Cognition.
I. Alloy, Lauren B. [DNLM: 1. Cognition. 2. Depressive
Disorder. WM 171 C6755]
RC537.C62 1988   616.85'27071   87-8696
ISBN 0-89862-706-0

Contributors

Lyn Y. Abramson, Ph.D., Department of Psychology, University of Wisconsin at Madison, Madison, Wisconsin.

Lauren B. Alloy, Ph.D., Department of Psychology, Northwestern University, Evanston, Illinois.

Pamela M. Cole, Ph.D., Department of Psychology, University of Houston, Houston, Texas.

Mark D. Evans, Ph.D., University of Minnesota, St. Paul, Minnesota; St. Paul-Ramsey Medical Center, St. Paul, Minnesota.

Michael S. Greenberg, Ph.D., Director, Florida Center for Cognitive Therapy, Clearwater, Florida.

Shirley Hartlage, M. S., Department of Psychology, Northwestern University, Evanston, Illinois.

Constance Hammen, Ph.D., Department of Psychology, University of California at Los Angeles, Los Angeles, California.

Bernard Hecker, Ph.D., Department of Psychology, University of Massachusetts at Amherst, Amherst, Massachusetts.

Steven D. Hollon, Ph.D., Department of Psychology, Vanderbilt University, Nashville, Tennessee.

Ronnie Janoff-Bulman, Ph.D., Department of Psychology, University of Massachusetts at Amherst, Amherst, Massachusetts.

Nadine J. Kaslow, Ph.D., Department of Psychiatry, Child Study Center, and Psychology, Yale University, New Haven, Connecticut.

Nicholas A. Kuiper, Ph.D., Department of Psychology, University of Western Ontario, London, Ontario, Canada.

Michael R. MacDonald, Ph.D., St. Mary's Hospital, London, Ontario.

Gerald I. Metalsky, Ph.D., Department of Psychology, University of Texas at Austin, Austin, Texas.

Dale T. Miller, Ph.D., Department of Psychology, Princeton University, Princeton, New Jersey.

Marlene M. Moretti, Ph.D., Department of Psychology, University of Waterloo, Waterloo, Ontario, Canada.

Robert F. Musson, Ph.D., Department of Psychology, Northwestern University, Evanston, Illinois.

L. Joan Olinger, Ph.D., Brescia College at the University of Western Ontario, London, Ontario, Canada.

Lynn P. Rehm, Ph.D., Department of Psychology, University of Houston, Houston, Texas.

Carmelo V. Vazquez, Ph.D., Departamento de Psicología, Universidad Complutense de Madrid, Madrid, Espagne.

Preface

Despite the fact that depression has been recognized as an important form of psychopathology for centuries, investigators have only recently begun to make major progress in discovering the causes of this complex disorder. Among psychological approaches to the study of psychopathology, the cognitive perspective has been dominant over the past decade and has contributed significantly to the recent advances in our understanding of depression. Cognitive theories of depression highlight the importance of the idiosyncratic meanings or inferences individuals derive from life experiences in producing and maintaining depressive symptomatology. These maladaptive inferences, in turn, are hypothesized to be the result of the operation of pervasive negative schemata or cognitive styles. Thus, from the cognitive perspective, dysfunctional schema-based interpretations of the self and the environment play a fundamental role in the etiology, course, and treatment of depression.

Several factors may account for the widespread impact of the cognitive models of depression. First, the demonstrated efficacy of cognitive therapy programs for at least some forms of depression underscores the valuable clinical implications of the cognitive approach. Second, the cognitive perspective has contributed to a fruitful cross-fertilization of clinical and experimental psychology. Studies derived from the cognitive perspective on depression have enriched our understanding of basic processes of human inference, and work in contemporary cognitive and social psychology, in turn, has had direct implications for the cognitive theories of depression. Third, cognitive models of depression may be particularly intriguing to researchers because they not only emphasize that depressed and depression-prone people think negatively but also that such individuals may systematically misinterpret and distort reality. Finally, the cognitive theories of depression may be attractive to researchers because they generate powerful etiological and therapeutic predictions that are empirically testable.

The goal of this volume is to present an up-to-date review of recent theoretical and empirical developments in the cognitive psychology of depression. In their chapters, the authors integrate conceptual and methodological advances in the fields of cognitive, personality, and social psychology for understanding the sorts of schema-based inference processes featured in the cognitive theories of depression with clinical knowledge about the psychopathology of the depressive disorders. The contributions reflect the creative application of these concepts and methods from experimental psychology to the understanding of the dynamic interaction between dysfunctional cognitive styles and the psychosocial environment in producing depressive information processing. The volume is divided into four broad sections. In Part I, the authors introduce the cognitive perspective by presenting the latest revisions of the two major cognitive diathesis-stress theories of depression. In Chapter 1, Lyn Abramson, Lauren Alloy, and Gerald Metalsky suggest that Beck's theory and the hopelessness theory (formerly called the reformulated helplessness theory) of depression postulate the existence in nature of a cognitive subtype of depression—"negative cognition depression." In Chapter 2, Lauren Alloy, Shirley Hartlage, and Lyn Abramson present a research strategy for searching for and validating this hypothesized subtype of depression and for conceptualizing and assessing the constructs featured in the cognitive theories of depression.

Part II focuses on the nature of the maladaptive personal and causal inference processes exhibited by depressed individuals and the psychological mechanisms underlying such processes. In Chapter 3, Constance Hammen integrates the major cognitive theories of depression with the broader cognitively oriented models of stress and coping in discussing the cognitive mediators of individuals' affective and behavioral reactions to personally stressful life events. She emphasizes the importance of a transactional approach between person and environment in understanding the meanings individuals assign to stressful circumstances. Michael Greenberg, Carmelo Vazquez, and Lauren Alloy in Chapter 4 provide evidence for the specificity of self-referent schematic processes in depression versus anxiety. Lynn Rehm reviews research on a variety of maladaptive self-management, inference, and memory processes in depression and proposes a new, integrative cognitive model of depression in Chapter 5. In Chapter 6, Ronnie Janoff-Bulman and Bernard Hecker discuss the role of people's assumptions about the world and their own personal vulnerability in the world in mediating pessimism and depressive responses to life stresses. In Chapter 7, Robert Musson and Lauren Alloy present several striking parallels between the effects of self-focused attention and the characteristics of depression and suggest that excessive self-focus may contribute to the onset and maintenance of depression.

Part III addresses the issue of realism versus distortion in depressive inference. In Chapter 8, Lauren Alloy and Lyn Abramson review empirical evidence on depressive realism, suggest cognitive and motivational mechanisms contributing to realism versus distortion in personal inference, and discuss the implications of the findings of depressive realism for understanding the psychopathology of depression. In Chapter 9, Dale Miller and Marlene Moretti specifically examine biases in depressed and nondepressed persons' causal attributions and discuss the relative accuracy and rationality of the two groups' causal attributions.

Finally, in Part IV, the contributors consider the development and remediation of cognitive styles and patterns of inference that may act as vulnerability factors for depression. Nicholas Kuiper, Joan Olinger, and Michael MacDonald in Chapter 10 distinguish between self-schemata that provide vulnerability to depression and self-schemata that only become activated following onset of a depressive episode but that may contribute to the maintenance of depression. In Chapter 11, Pamela Cole and Nadine Kaslow review evidence on the normal development of affect regulation processes in infancy and childhood. Cole and Kaslow examine the role of both intrapsychic and interpersonal resources for affect regulation at various points in development and the consequences of dysfunction in these affect regulation strategies for childhood, and later adult, depression. Finally, in Chapter 12, Mark Evans and Steven Hollon consider the implications of the research on depressive and nondepressive inference processes for the cognitive therapy of depression. They argue that cognitive therapy works by training depressed persons to be more systematic and normative in their information processing than are most other people.

I would like to express my appreciation to the contributing authors for the thought and effort that went into each chapter as well as for their patience in seeing this volume through to completion. I would also like to thank the editorial and production staffs at Guilford Publications for their assistance in the publication of this volume. And finally, special thanks go to Lyn Abramson for encouraging me to edit this book in the first place and for her continuing support throughout its preparation.

Lauren B. Alloy

Contents

THE COGNITIVE DIATHESIS–STRESS MODELS OF DEPRESSION

1

The Cognitive Diathesis–Stress Theories of Depression: Toward an Adequate Evaluation of the Theories' Validities

LYN Y. ABRAMSON
University of Wisconsin-Madison

LAUREN B. ALLOY
Northwestern University

GERALD I. METALSKY
University of Texas–Austin

Depression is one of the most common psychological disorders. During any given year, about 15% of all adults between ages 18 and 74 may suffer significant depressive symptoms (Secunda, Katz, & Friedman, 1973). Many people recover from depression, but unlike most other forms of psychopathology, it can be lethal. One out of every 100 people with a depressive disorder dies by suicide (Williams, Friedman, & Secunda, 1970). The economic cost of depression also is great. In the United States alone, the annual financial cost of depression has been estimated to be between 300 million and 900 million dollars (Secunda *et al.*, 1973).

Although depression has been recognized as an important form of psychopathology for centuries, researchers are just beginning to make progress in understanding this disorder. Within experimental psychopathology, it is only in the past 15 years that research on depression has burgeoned. During this time, a wide variety of investigators have emphasized the importance of cognitive processes in the etiology, maintenance, and treatment of depression (e.g., Abramson & Martin, 1981; Abramson, Seligman, & Teasdale, 1978; Alloy, 1982; Alloy & Abramson, 1979; Beck, 1967, 1976; Beck, Rush, Shaw, & Emery, 1979; Derry & Kuiper, 1981; Kovacs, Rush, Beck, & Hollon, 1981; Krantz & Hammen, 1979; Peterson & Seligman, 1984; Seligman, 1975). The two major cognitive theories of depression, Beck's (1967) theory and the hopelessness theory (Abramson, Metalsky, & Alloy, 1987; Abramson, Seligman, & Teasdale, 1978; previously referred to as the reformulated theory of helplessness and depression), have guided much of the psychological research on depression.

At least four factors may help explain why the cognitive theories of depression have captured the attention of a wide variety of researchers. First, the demonstrated efficacy of cognitive therapy for at least some forms of depression underscores the clinical implications of the cognitive theories of depression (e.g., Beck *et al.*, 1979; Blackburn, Bishop, Glen, Whalley, & Christie, 1981; Kovacs *et al.*, 1981; Shaw,

1977; Taylor & Marshall, 1977). Second, a striking similarity exists between work in contemporary cognitive and social psychology on the one hand, and concepts developed within the cognitive theories of depression on the other (e.g., Abramson & Martin, 1981; Alloy, 1982; Alloy & Tabachnik, 1984; Greenberg & Alloy, 1987; Metalsky & Abramson, 1981). Studies testing the cognitive theories of depression may enrich basic theory and research in psychology, and work in contemporary cognitive and social psychology has direct implications for the cognitive theories of depression. Third, Beck's theory may have been particularly intriguing to researchers because he emphasized not only that some hypothetically depression-prone individuals think negatively but also that such individuals systematically misinterpret and distort reality. Finally, the cognitive theories of depression, particularly the hopelessness theory, may have been attractive to researchers because they are empirically testable.

Recently, depression researchers have begun to evaluate the validity of the cognitive theories of depression on the basis of the empirical work conducted to date. Peterson and Seligman (1984) reviewed studies conducted since 1978 that were designed to test the hopelessness theory and concluded that these studies converged in their support for the theory. Surprisingly, Coyne and Gotlib (1983) reviewed many of the same studies and concluded that the hopelessness theory and Beck's theory did not have strong empirical bases. For example, in their abstract, Coyne and Gotlib stated that "depressed persons present themselves negatively on a variety of measures, but less consistently than either (cognitive) model suggests" (p. 472). Similarly, later in their article they stated:

> Our review of the literature suggests that depressed persons, whether drawn from patient or from student populations, tend to make negative and self-depreciating responses to laboratory tasks and to hypothetical and actual life situations. Although this tendency has been demonstrated with a variety of verbal self-report measures, it is not as strong or consistent as proponents of the learned helplessness and Beck's models have assumed. (p. 495)

Apparently Coyne and Gotlib believe that the magnitude and consistency of differences between depressed and nondepressed people with regard to the likelihood of displaying negative cognitive patterns is an important criterion against which to evaluate the validity of the cognitive theories of depression. Similar to Coyne and Gotlib, some other investigators have questioned the empirical validity of the cognitive theories' etiological account of depression (e.g., Lewinsohn, Steinmetz, Larson, & Franklin, 1981) or have expressed disappointment with the magnitude or robustness of the results of studies designed to test one or both of these theories (e.g., Blaney, Behar, & Head, 1980; Feather & Barber, 1983; Hammen, 1981).

In contrast to reviewers who argue that the existing empirical data corroborate the cognitive theories of depression as well as to reviewers who argue to the contrary, we believe it is *premature* to evaluate the validity of the cognitive theories of depression on the basis of studies conducted to date (Abramson *et al.*, 1986; Alloy, Clements, & Kolden, 1985; Halberstadt, Andrews, Metalsky, & Abramson, 1984; Kayne, Alloy, Romer, & Crocker, 1987; see also Brewin, 1985). Indeed, in evaluating this body of research, we have arrived at a very disturbing conclusion: The various *research strategies* utilized to test the cognitive theories of depression *do not provide an adequate test* of the theories' basic postulates. Furthermore, if investigators rely on the robustness and consistency of results obtained with these research strategies as the criterion against which to evaluate the validity of the cognitive theories, they may be seriously misled (Abramson *et al.*, 1987).

We (Abramson *et al.*, 1987) have suggested that the problems associated with research designed to test the cognitive theories of depression result, in part, from investigators' failure to appreciate the full methodological implications of the kinds of causal relations specified in the theories (e.g., sufficient but not necessary proximal cause; diathesis–stress). As a corollary, in research designed to test the cognitive theories, investigators' failure to appreciate these methodological implications also may have contributed to their failure to appreciate the heterogeneity that may exist among the depressive disorders. Consequently, one purpose of this chapter is to restate, clarify, expand, and, in some cases, modify the basic postulates of the cognitive theories of depression and to place these theories more explicitly in the context of work in descriptive psychiatry on the heterogeneity among the depressive disorders (see Depue & Monroe, 1978). Modifications of one of the theories will be described in accompanying notes. A second purpose of this chapter is to critique the work conducted to date that tests the cognitive theories of depression and to explicate the limitations in research strategy associated with this work. Although we have expanded and modified the hopelessness theory of depression, it is important to emphasize that our critique applies to work conducted in order to test Abramson, Seligman, & Teasdale's 1978 statement of the hopelessness theory of depression. Finally, we conclude by discussing the general implications of our analysis for research on other forms of psychopathology.

PRELIMINARY CONCEPTS

Before presenting our restatement and clarification of the cognitive theories of depression, we want to distinguish among the concepts of *necessary* cause, *sufficient* cause, and *contributory* cause with regard to the occurrence of symptoms. Although the reader may be familiar with these concepts, it is important to illustrate their defining features because the methodological implications of these concepts often have not been fully appreciated in research on the hopelessness theory of depression.

A necessary cause of some set of symptoms is an etiological factor that must be present or must have occurred in order for the symptoms to occur. In terms of formal logic, if the presence or occurrence of the etiological factor E is necessary for the occurrence of the set of symptoms S, this means the following: If S, then E, or, mathematically speaking, Probability $(E/S) = 1.00$.[1] An additional feature of such a necessary causal relationship is that the symptoms cannot occur if the etiological factor is absent or has not occurred (i.e., if $\bar{E}$, then $\bar{S}$; Probability $(S/\bar{E}) = 0.00$). It is important to note that such a necessary causal relationship does not require the symptoms always to occur when the etiological factor is present or has occurred.

A sufficient cause of some set of symptoms is an etiological factor whose presence or occurrence guarantees the occurrence of the symptoms. In terms of formal logic, if the presence or occurrence of the etiological factor E is sufficient for the occurrence of the set of symptoms S, this means the following: If E, then S, or, mathematically speaking, Probability $(S/E) = 1.00$. An additional feature of such a sufficient causal relationship is that if the symptoms do not occur, then the etiological factor cannot be present or have occurred (i.e., if $\bar{S}$, then $\bar{E}$; Probability $(E/\bar{S}) = 0.00$). It is important to note that such a sufficient causal relationship does not require the etiological factor always to have occurred or to be present for the symptoms to occur.

A contributory cause of some set of symptoms is an etiological factor that increases the likelihood of the occurrence of the symptoms but that is neither necessary nor sufficient for their occurrence. Mathematically speaking, if the presence or occurrence of the etiological factor E contributes to the occurrence of the set of symptoms S, this means the following: Probability $(S/E) >$ Probability $(S/\bar{E})$, where Probability $(E/S) < 1.00$ (i.e., not necessary) and Probability $(S/E) < 1.00$ (i.e., not sufficient).

There are various possible relationships among the three types of causes described. Of course, by definition, if a cause is contributory, it cannot be necessary or sufficient. Similarly, if a cause is necessary or sufficient, it cannot be contributory. In contrast, a particular etiological factor E may be necessary and sufficient, necessary but not sufficient, or sufficient but not necessary for the occurrence of the set of symptoms S.

In addition to varying in their formal relationship to the occurrence of symptoms (necessary, sufficient, or contributory), causes also may vary in their sequential relationship to the occurrence of symptoms. If one thinks of an etiological chain or sequence of events culminating in the occurrence of a set of symptoms, then some causes may operate toward the end of the chain, proximate to the occurrence of symptoms, whereas other causes may operate toward the beginning of the chain, distant from the occurrence of symptoms. We characterize the former as *proximal* causes, and the latter as *distal* causes. It is important to recognize that, strictly speaking, the formal and sequential relationships of causes and symptoms are not orthogonal, because a cause cannot be both sufficient and distal.[2]

It is useful to classify causes in terms of both their formal and their sequential relationships to a set of symptoms. Of course, the concepts of necessary, sufficient, and contributory in conjunction with the concepts of proximal and distal do not exhaust the possible kinds of relationships that may obtain between causes and symptoms. For example, complex causal feedback loops involving threshold effects may be involved in the production of a set of symptoms. However, at a minimum, the reader must have mastered the concepts of necessary, sufficient, and contributory cause as well as proximal and distal cause in order to understand the postulates of the cognitive theories of depression and our critique of the work conducted to test these theories. If future work using more adequate research strategies to test the cognitive theories of depression fails to corroborate the current statements of these theories, then further revisions involving more complex (e.g., nonlinear) causal chains may be in order.

CLARIFICATION AND REVISION OF THE HOPELESSNESS THEORY OF DEPRESSION

The hopelessness theory of depression can be understood best in terms of the concepts about causes just discussed. Overall, the theory specifies a chain of distal and proximal contributory causes hypothesized to culminate in a proximal sufficient cause of depression.

A Proximal Sufficient Cause of Depression

According to Abramson, Seligman, and Teasdale (1978), a proximal sufficient cause of depression is an expectation that highly desired outcomes are unlikely to occur or that highly aversive outcomes are likely to occur and that no response in one's repertoire will change the likelihood of occurrence of these outcomes.[3] We view this theory as a *hopelessness* theory of depression because the term "hopelessness" captures the core elements of the proximal sufficient cause featured in the theory: negative expectations about the occurrence of highly valued outcomes, and feelings of helplessness about changing the likelihood of occurrence of these outcomes. Throughout the remainder of this chapter, we use the phrase "hopelessness" to refer to this proximal sufficient cause.

It is important to emphasize that Abramson, Seligman, and Teasdale (1978) hypothesized hopelessness as a proximal sufficient, but not a necessary, cause of depression. Explicitly recognizing that depression may be a heterogeneous disorder, they allowed for the possibility that other factors, such as genetic vulnerability, norepinephrine depletion, or loss of interest in reinforcers, may be sufficient to cause depression (see Alloy, 1982, for a similar analysis of the learned helplessness phenomenon). Thus Abramson, Seligman, and Teasdale presented an etiological account of one hypothesized subtype of depression, defined in part by its cause, which we term "hopelessness depression."[4] In a later section of this chapter (Negative Cognition Depression: A Theory-Based Subtype of Depression), we more fully elaborate the concept of hopelessness depression and place it in the context of work in descriptive psychiatry about the heterogeneity among the depressive disorders.

One Hypothesized Causal Pathway to Depression

An important advantage of the hopelessness theory compared to the original helplessness theory is that it specifies not only a proximal sufficient cause of depression but also a sequence of events in a causal chain hypothesized to culminate in this proximal sufficient cause.[5] As can be seen in Figure 1-1, the hypothesized causal chain begins with the occurrence of negative life events (or the nonoccur-

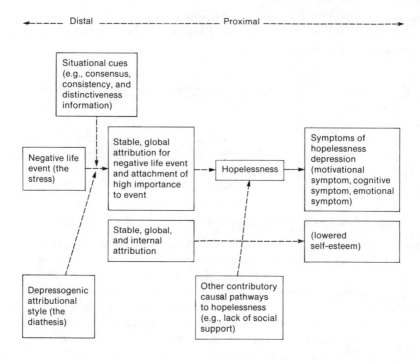

Figure 1-1. Causal chain specified in the hopelessness theory of depression. (The arrows with a solid line indicate a sufficient cause. Arrows with broken lines indicate contributory causes.)

rence of positive life events) and ends with the production of depressive symptoms (specifically, hopelessness depression).[6] Each event in the chain leading to the proximal sufficient cause is a contributory cause of depression because it increases the likelihood of, but is neither necessary nor sufficient for, the occurrence of depressive symptoms. In addition, these contributory causes vary in how proximal they are to the occurrence of depressive symptoms.

Proximal Contributory Causes

According to Abramson, Seligman, and Teasdale (1978), once people perceive that particular negative life events have occurred, the kinds of causal attributions they make for these events and the degree of importance they attach to them are important factors contributing to the development of hopelessness and, in turn, depressive symptoms. In brief, these investigators suggested that hopelessness and subsequent depressive symptoms are more likely to occur when negative life events are attributed to stable (i.e., enduring) and global (i.e., likely to affect many outcomes) factors and are viewed as important than when they are attributed to unstable, specific factors and are viewed as unimportant. Moreover, when negative life events are attributed to internal, stable, and global factors, Abramson, Selig- man, and Teasdale hypothesized that hopelessness will be accompanied by lowered self-esteem.[7]

Distal Contributory Causes

Abramson, Seligman, and Teasdale (1978) identified a relatively distal causal factor that may constrain the attribution process and influence the content of people's causal attributions for a particular event: individual differences in attributional style (see also Ickes & Layden, 1978). Abramson and colleagues speculated that some individuals exhibit a general tendency to attribute negative events to internal, stable, and global factors and to view these events as very important (i.e., "hypothesized depressogenic attributional style" or "attributional diathesis"), whereas other in- dividuals do not.

According to Abramson, Seligman, and Teasdale (1978), individuals who exhibit the hypothesized depressogenic attributional style should be more likely than individuals who do not exhibit this style to attribute any particular negative event they confront to internal, stable, and global factors and to view the event as very important, thereby increasing the likelihood of developing hopelessness and, in turn, depressive symptoms. However, in the presence of positive life events, or in the absence of negative life events, people exhibiting the hypothesized de- pressogenic attributional style should be no more likely to develop hopelessness, and therefore depression, than people not exhibiting this attributional style. This aspect of Abramson, Seligman, and Teasdale's theory is conceptualized usefully as a diathesis–stress component (Abramson *et al.*, 1987; Kayne *et al.*, 1987; Metal- sky, Abramson, Seligman, Semmel, & Peterson, 1982; Metalsky, Halberstadt, & Abramson, 1987): that is, the tendency to exhibit a style of attributing negative events to internal, stable, and global factors and to view these events as very important is a distal contributory cause of depression that operates in the presence, but not in the absence, of negative life events.

CLARIFICATION OF BECK'S COGNITIVE THEORY OF DEPRESSION

Although Beck's cognitive theory of depression is much less explicit than the hopelessness theory, we have suggested that its formal structure is similar to that of the hopelessness theory (Abramson *et al.*, 1987; Alloy *et al.*, 1985). Given this view, Beck's theory also is best understood as postulating a sequential causal pathway culminating in a proximal sufficient cause of depressive symptoms, as illustrated in Figure 1-2.

A Proximal Sufficient Cause of Depression

We suggest that Beck's cognitive theory of depression is best interpreted as postulating a negative view of the self, the world, and the future (i.e., the "negative

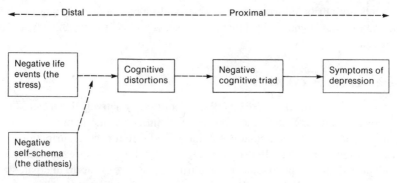

Figure 1-2. Causal chain implied in Beck's cognitive theory of depression. (The arrow with a solid line indicates a sufficient cause. Arrows with broken lines indicate contributory causes.)

cognitive triad") as a proximal sufficient cause of depression. The negative view of the self consists of the belief that one is deficient, inadequate, or unworthy. In the negative view of the world, one construes his or her experiences in terms of defeat, deprivation, or disparagement. The negative view of the future consists of the expectation that one's current difficulties will persist in the future, this concept is very similar to the concept of hopelessness featured in the hopelessness theory.

Although Beck and his colleagues have discussed the heterogeneity that may exist among the depressive disorders (Beck *et al.*, 1979), Beck has been less explicit about whether or not his theory postulates, as does the hopelessness theory, a distinct subtype of depression. Given the apparent formal structure of Beck's theory, we suggest that this theory is best construed as postulating a subtype of depression, defined in part by its cause: negative cognitive triad depression. Unfortunately, the theoretical development of the concept of negative cognitive triad depression is more primitive than that of the concept of hopelessness depression. We believe, however, that the hypothesized subtype of negative cognitive triad depression overlaps greatly with the subtype of hopelessness depression proposed in the hopelessness theory and that both theories are, for the most part, referring to the same group of individuals.

Proximal Contributory Causes

According to Beck (1967), the negative cognitive triad and subsequent depressive symptoms are more likely to occur when negative life events are interpreted in a negatively distorted fashion. Beck argues that some (if not all) depression-prone individuals make inferences about themselves and their environments that are unrealistic, extreme, and illogical. These cognitive distortions are hypothesized to consist of the following types of logical "errors": (1) arbitrary inference, (2) selective abstraction, (3) overgeneralization, (4) magnification and minimization, (5) personalization, and (6) absolutistic, dichotomous thinking (see Beck *et al.*, 1979, for a more complete explication of these cognitive errors).

Distal Contributory Causes

Beck (1967) suggested that relatively consistent individual differences exist in the tendency to exhibit evaluatively negative cognitive distortions about the self, the world, and the future. Schemata with negative content about loss, failure, inadequacy, and so forth constitute the cognitive "diathesis" in Beck's theory of depression (Alloy *et al.*, 1985; Beck *et al.*, 1979; Kuiper, Olinger, & MacDonald, Chapter 10, this volume). In line with cognitive psychologists (e.g., Neisser, 1967), Beck defined a "schema" as an organized representation of prior knowledge that guides the processing of current information. Beck (1967) hypothesized that when activated by stress (negative life events), depressogenic schemata lead to negative cognitive distortions because incoming information is assimilated to the schemata. The cognitive distortions are viewed as relatively automatic and involuntary products of depressogenic schematic processing.

COGNITIVE ETIOLOGICAL THEORIES AS COGNITIVE DIATHESIS–STRESS MODELS

We argue that the two major cognitive etiological theories of depression (Beck's theory and the hopelessness theory) are best conceptualized as cognitive *diathesis–stress* models. These theories postulate that when confronted with equivalent stress (similar negative life events), people who display the relevant cognitive diathesis should be more likely to experience a depressive reaction than people who do not display this predisposition. On the other hand, in situations in which stress is relatively nonexistent (in the presence of positive life events and/or in the absence of negative life events), people possessing the hypothesized cognitive diathesis should be no more likely to develop depressive symptoms than people not possessing this risk factor. Moreover, the cognitive diathesis–stress theories of depression are *sufficiency* models and not necessity models. They acknowledge the possibility, either explicitly (hopelessness theory) or implicitly (Beck's theory), that people might become depressed for reasons other than those specified in the cognitive theories, and thus recognize the heterogeneity of the depressive disorders (Craighead, 1980; Depue & Monroe, 1978).

NEGATIVE COGNITION DEPRESSION: A THEORY-BASED SUBTYPE OF DEPRESSION

Over the past 75 years, clinicians have suggested that depression probably is not a single disorder but instead a group of disorders heterogeneous with respect to symptoms, cause, course, therapy, and prevention (e.g., Abramson *et al.*, 1987; Beck, 1967; Craighead, 1980; Depue & Monroe, 1978; Fowles & Gersh, 1979; Gillespie, 1929; Kendell, 1968). Consequently, within the clinical tradition, much controversy has centered on which classification system most meaningfully subdivides the depressive disorders, or best "carves depression at its joints." Historically, a wide variety of nosological distinctions have been proposed for the purpose of classifying the depressive disorders, such as bipolar–unipolar, endogenous–neurotic, psychotic–neurotic, major–minor, and character spectrum–pure dysthymic disorder. In the main, the various classifications have arisen from insights gleaned in clinical practice or from numerical taxonometric procedures such as cluster analysis (Kendell, 1968; Skinner, 1981). Both the clinical and the numerical approaches to subdividing depression group people together on the basis of similar symptoms, with the *hope* that these similar symptoms will represent a syndrome having a common underlying cause, associated features, and similar treatment. Unfortunately, similar symptoms may represent only a final common pathway, and individuals grouped solely on the basis of symptom resemblance may represent heterogeneous subtypes with distinct underlying etiologies and treatments (cf. Akiskal & McKinney, 1975).

In contrast to these empirically based approaches to the classification of depression, the cognitive theories of depression represent a *theory-based* approach to the classification of a subset of the depressive disorders (see also Seligman, 1978). A theory-based approach specifies an etiological chain of events leading to the development of the cause(s) of the subtype. This approach then predicts (1) which symptoms should cohere in representing a syndrome as a result of the cause(s), (2) the course of the subtype, and (3) treatment and prevention strategies that are likely to be successful for the subtype.

At this point, a note on our terminology is in order. Henceforth we will use the term "hopelessness depression" to refer specifically to the cognitive subtype of depression postulated by the hopelessness theory, and the term "negative triad depression" to refer to the depressive subtype suggested by Beck's theory. However, we believe that these two subtypes of depression are similar and overlapping and that, for the most part, they refer to the same group of individuals, although they may not be identical to each other. Consequently, we will use the term "negative cognition depression" for the subtype of depression defined by the intersection of hopelessness depression and negative triad depression.

In essence, then, the cognitive theories of depression postulate the existence in nature of an as yet unidentified subtype of depression, negative cognition depression, defined in part by its proximal sufficient causes (hopelessness and the negative cognitive triad). Thus, to identify and validate the negative cognition subtype of depression, one must actually test the predictions of the cognitive theories of depression that form the nomological network within which the concept of negative cognition depression is embedded. That is, a test of any prediction in the etiological chains postulated by the cognitive theories (e.g., that negative causal schemata or negative self-schemata in interaction with stressors leads to particular negative interpretations of the stressors) is as important for validating negative cognition depression as is an examination of the particular symptom clusters hypothesized by the theories to constitute the manifestation of this subtype of depression. As an example, the subtype of mental retardation known as phenylketonuria (PKU) was validated not only by examining the coherence of its manifest symptoms (e.g., intellectual retardation, lack of pigmentation, musty odor, convulsions in early life) but also by testing the causal pathway hypothesized to culminate in this symptom cluster (i.e., deficiency of phenylalanine hydroxylase in combination with early exposure to phenylalanine in the diet leads to the buildup of phenylalanine and phenylpyruvic acid in the brain, which causes brain damage) and the treatment strategies hypothesized to remediate the disorder (e.g., restricted intake of phenylalanine; see Stanbury, Wyngaarden, Fredrickson, Goldstein & Brown, 1983).

Consistent with Skinner (1981), we utilize a construct validation approach, which emphasizes a continual interplay between theory development and empirical analyses, as an organizational framework for elaborating the concept of negative cognition depression. We emphasize that negative cognition depression is an open concept (Cronbach & Meehl, 1955; Hempel, 1952; Meehl, 1972; Pap, 1953) that is defined in terms of the laws or nomological network in which it is embedded. The concept of negative cognition depression is open rather than closed because we have not defined it exhaustively. Borrowing Cronbach and Meehl's (1955) terminology, we will be able to say "what negative cognition depression is" (i.e., define it exhaustively) when we know all of the laws involving it. Until then, negative cognition depression will remain an open concept and must be validated by testing the predictions of the cognitive theories of depression that already have been specified. Consequently, in utilizing a theory-based construct validation approach, one needs to test the causal pathways postulated by the cognitive theories to culminate in negative cognition depression as well as the symptom manifestations, course, and relationship to other forms of depression of this cognitive subtype of depression.

Perhaps the reader who appreciates the superiority of the descriptively based DSM-III (*Diagnostic and Statistical Manual of Mental Disorders–Third Edition;* American Psychiatric Association [APA], 1980) to the theory-based DSM-II with respect to diagnostic reliability and, possibly, treatment is concerned that the theory-based category of negative cognition depression will be plagued by many of the problems associated with DSM-II. We do not believe this concern is justified. In our view, the problems besetting DSM-II arose not because it was theory-based *per se* but rather because the underlying organizational theoretical principles were not confronted with empirical tests and perhaps were not formulated in a testable fashion. In contrast to DSM-II, our theory-based construct validation approach emphasizes the importance of and need for repeated subjection of the cognitive theories of depression to "severe" (Popper, 1959) empirical tests. More generally, Hempel (1965) has argued that theory-based classification systems in a field represent an advance over more descriptively based classification systems.

The Nomological Network of Negative Cognition Depression

CAUSE

In contrast to the majority of approaches to the classification of the depressive disorders that are based on differences in symptom clusters among depressed individuals (see Kendell, 1968), *cause* figures prominently in the definition of negative cognition depression. Few would disagree that when possible, classification of psychopathologies by etiology in addition to other factors is more desirable than classification by symptoms alone insofar as the former generally has more direct implications for cure and prevention than the latter.

It is important to emphasize that whereas the cognitive theories view hopelessness and the negative cognitive triad as proximal sufficient causes of *depression,* we view them as proximal sufficient *and* necessary causes of the hypothesized *negative cognition subtype of depression.* An analogy from work on mental retardation helps to illustrate this point. Whereas extreme hypothyroidism is sufficient but not necessary to produce mental retardation, this deficiency is a sufficient *and* necessary cause of cretinism, a relatively well defined subtype of mental retardation. In general, the history of medicine suggests that whereas the proximal causes of a heterogeneous disorder often are stated in terms of sufficiency but not necessity, the proximal causes of well-defined subtypes of the heterogeneous disorder often are stated in terms of both sufficiency and necessity.

The cognitive theories of depression postulate not only proximal sufficient and necessary causes of the hypothesized subtype of negative cognition depression but also more distal contributory causes of this subtype, namely, negative cognitive diatheses, negative life events, and the personal and causal interpretations of these negative life events. Although each of these theories identifies a contributory causal pathway hypothesized to culminate in hopelessness or the negative cognitive triad and, in turn, negative cognition depression, these pathways are not viewed as necessary for the formation of negative views of the self, the world, and the future (hopelessness). Therefore it is important to elaborate further that aspect of the nomological network of the theories involving the contributory causal pathways hypothesized to culminate in hopelessness or the negative cognitive triad. Along these lines, Hammen and her colleagues (e.g., Gong-Guy & Hammen, 1980; Hammen & Cochran, 1981; Hammen & de Mayo, 1982) have argued that the *inferred consequences* of negative life events, independently of causal attributions or other personal inferences for these events, may modulate the likelihood that people will become depressed when confronted with such events. "Inferred consequences" refer to an individual's assessment of the impact of a negative event on his or her life, either currently or in the future. Thus inferred consequences may moderate the relationship between negative life events and depressive symptoms by affecting the likelihood of formation of hopelessness (hopelessness theory) or negative views of the world *and* the future (Beck's theory).

SYMPTOMS

The nomological network surrounding the concept of hopelessness depression presented in the hopelessness theory of depression (Abramson, Seligman, & Teasdale, 1978; Abramson *et al.,* 1987) suggests that this subtype of depression should be characterized by at least three major symptoms: retarded initiation of voluntary responses *(motivational symptom),* difficulty in seeing that one's responses control outcomes related or similar to the outcomes about which one feels hopeless *(cognitive symptom),* and sad affect *(emotional symptom).* In addition, hopelessness depression should include a fourth symptom, lowered self-esteem, when individuals expect that other people can or could attain the important outcomes that they themselves feel hopeless about attaining (i.e., when individuals make internal, stable, and global attributions for negative outcomes; see Abramson, Seligman, & Teasdale, 1978).

In addition to these symptoms of hopelessness depression enumerated in the hopelessness theory, other symptoms may characterize this hypothesized subtype of depression. In particular, Beck and others have demonstrated that hopelessness is a key factor in serious suicide attempts and in suicidal ideation (Beck, Kovacs, & Weissman, 1975; Kazdin, French, Unis, Esveldt-Dawson, & Sherick, 1983; Minkoff, Bergman, Beck, & Beck, 1973; Petrie & Chamberlain, 1983). Thus it is possible that serious suicide attempts and suicidal ideation are core symptoms of hopelessness depression. Similarly, if lack of energy, apathy, and psychomotor retardation are concomitants of a severe decrease in the motivation to initiate voluntary responses (see Beck, 1967), then these symptoms also may be components of hopelessness depression.

Because Beck's model (1967; 1976) includes hopelessness as part of the negative cognitive triad, all of the symptoms just described that should be manifestations of hopelessness depression also should be expected to be components of negative triad depression. Beck (1967) suggests, however, that negative triad depression also will include self-blame, guilt, and increased dependency as consequences of the negative view of the self and the world. According to Beck (1967), negative triad depressives not only see themselves as inferior but also blame themselves for their inadequacies and believe that they could do or be otherwise (guilt). Similarly, the negative triad depressives' increased dependency is attributable to their negative evaluations of both the self and the world. Increased dependency on others is a likely result of the joint beliefs that one is inept, inadequate, and undesirable and that the world is complex, burdensome, and overwhelming. Finally, because in Beck's model a negative view of the self is viewed as one of the *causes* of negative triad depression, in order to avoid tautology, we will not include low self-esteem as one of the *symptoms* of this subtype of depression when testing the predictions of Beck's model.

Two aspects of the nomological network concerning the symptoms of negative cognition depression should be noted. First, some of the symptoms hypothesized to characterize the negative cognition subtype of depression (e.g., sad affect, dependency, guilt, suicidal ideation, lack of energy, psychomotor retardation) completely overlap with symptoms currently described in DSM-III as characterizing the syndrome of depression, whereas others (e.g., motivational and cognitive deficits) only partially overlap with symptoms currently described as part of the depressive syndrome. Second, the cognitive theories of depression postulate that certain specific symptoms (e.g., motivational and cognitive symptoms, sadness, suicidal ideation) will be a part of negative cognition depression. However, a second class of symptoms (e.g., worry, difficulty in concentrating, sleep disturbance), although not postulated to be part of negative cognition depression, may possibly be related to this syndrome. In contrast, it seems less plausible that a third class of symptoms (e.g., inability to experience pleasure, appetite disturbance) would be related to negative cognition depression, given our current understanding of the kinds of psychological processes featured by the cognitive theories of depression. Because negative cognition depression is still an open concept, several members of this second or third class of symptoms may be incorporated into the nomological network surrounding the definition of negative cognition depression if they are discovered to be empirically related to this subtype of depression.

COURSE: DURATION OF A GIVEN EPISODE

Insofar as hopelessness and/or the negative cognitive triad are hypothesized to be proximal sufficient and necessary causes of negative cognition depression, the course or duration of any given episode of negative cognition depression should be influenced by how long these beliefs are present. The longer the time during which an individual exhibits hopelessness and negative views of the self and the world, the longer the duration of the episode of negative cognition depression triggered by these expectations.

What, in turn, influences the duration of hopelessness and the negative views of the self and the world? In the hopelessness theory (Abramson, Seligman, & Teasdale, 1978; Abramson *et al.*, 1987), the chronicity of hopelessness is predicted by the relative stability of an individual's attributions for the negative life events or stressors he or she is experiencing. If an individual attributes the causes of negative life events to stable factors, he or she will expect those causes to again be present in the future and thus to again produce negative events, hence maintaining hopelessness. Although it is not a clear-cut prediction of the hopelessness theory, we speculate that the globality (cross-situational generality) of individuals' attributions for stressful events would also influence the duration of hopelessness and hence the duration of the episode of hopelessness depression. In Beck's model, the duration of activity of biased and distorted personal inferences about negative life events (e.g., selective abstractions, arbitrary inferences) will predict the chronicity of people's negative views of the self, the world, and the future, and thus the duration of an episode of negative triad depression. Similarly, the stability with which individuals infer negative consequences from the occurrence of negative life events should modulate the duration of negative expectations of self, world, and future. More generally, then, it is the duration of negatively biased (and plausible) personal and causal inferences that modulates the chronicity of negative expectations about the self, the world, and the future, and hence the duration of an episode of negative cognition depression.

Finally, it is important to note that the duration of hopelessness and the negative cognitive triad should be influenced not only by the duration of activity of negatively biased personal and causal interpretations of the *original* negative life events that "triggered" the onset of a given episode of negative cognition depression but *also* by the chronicity of negatively biased inferences for *newly occurring* life stressors. Indeed, Lloyd, Zisook, Click, and Jaffe (1981) and Brown and Harris (1978) found that concurrent negative life events are important predictors of the course of an acute episode of depression. The cognitive theories of depression would suggest that it is individuals' negatively biased interpretations for these concurrent events that modulate the course of the negative cognition subtype of depression, in particular.

All of the preceding hypothesized predictors of the duration of a given episode of negative cognition depression follow directly from the logic of the cognitive theories of depression. However, there may be other variables that also relate empirically to the duration of an episode of negative cognition depression. For example, prior episodes of depression (Angst *et al.*, 1973; Zis & Goodwin, 1979), a family history of depression (Boyd & Weissman, 1982; Coryell & Winokur, 1982), and the availability of social support (Brown & Harris, 1978; Monroe, 1983; Monroe, Imhoff, Wise, & Harris, 1983) have all been found to predict the course of depressive symptoms during a particular episode. It is possible that these additional predictors of the course of depressive symptoms—in particular, the course of a negative cognition depression episode—operate, in part, through the constructs featured in the cognitive theories of depression. For example, a personal or family history of depression may influence the likelihood and duration with which an individual makes negatively biased personal and causal interpretations of stressful events, and thus the chronicity of negative beliefs about the self, the world, and the future. The availability of social support may lessen hopelessness or provide significant others who may "correct" or "countermand" the negative personal and causal inferences of the depressive individual. If such variables influence hopelessness and the negative cognitive triad, it will be important to eventually include them in the nomological network defining negative cognition depression.

COURSE: RELAPSE AND RECURRENCE

A second aspect of the course of a disorder is the likelihood with which, and the time at which, individuals who have exhibited a past episode of the disorder succumb to relapses or recurrences of the disorder. Technically speaking, one should distinguish between incidences of relapse (a return of clinically significant symptoms within a relatively short period following remission from an acute episode) and recurrence (onset of a new episode following a prolonged interval of remission from the index episode; (Klerman, 1978).

As in our discussion of the duration of a given episode of negative cognition depression, the likelihood and timing of a relapse or recurrence of negative cognition depression should be predicted by the causal pathways featured in the cognitive theories of depression (i.e., cognitive diathesis in combination with stress → negative attributions or interpretations → hopelessness and negative cognitive triad → negative cognition depression), because, by definition, a relapse or a recurrence is a new onset of negative cognition depression. Hence individuals with depressogenic attributional styles or negative self-schemata will be more likely to have relapses or recurrences of depression when confronted with stressful events than individuals who do not possess these cognitive styles. In other words, people who are vulnerable to the negative cognition subtype of depression should be repeatedly vulnerable to such episodes. In line with the cognitive theories, Paykel and Tanner (1976) reported that among a sample of patients who had recovered from a depressive episode, those who relapsed experienced more undesirable events in the preceding 3-month period than those who did not exhibit symptom return. The cognitive models would suggest that the particular interpretations these "recovered" depressed patients made for those negative life events would provide even greater power for predicting the likelihood of relapse. Finally, a personal and/or family history of depression and the availability of social support may also influence the probability and timing of relapse or recurrence of negative cognition depression.

HYPOTHESIZED RELATIONSHIP OF NEGATIVE COGNITION DEPRESSION TO OTHER CATEGORIES OF DEPRESSION

It is useful to ask which diagnostic categories of unipolar depression, if any, involve etiological processes, and perhaps symptoms and therapy, different from those involved in negative cognition depression. Klein's (1974) concept of endogenomorphic depression may be fundamentally distinct from the concept of negative cognition depression. The hypothesized core process in endogenomorphic depression is impairment in the capacity to experience pleasure, leading to a profound lack of interest and investment in the environment (e.g., inability to enjoy food or sex). Klein's concept of endogenomorphic depression appears to be very similar to Costello's (1972) concept of reinforcer ineffectiveness and maps closely onto the DSM-III category of major depressive episode, with melancholia. It is of interest for our purposes that Klein distinguishes endogenomorphic depression, hypothesized to be responsive to imipramine drug therapy, from the categories of acute dysphoria and chronic overreactive dysphoria, which he believes are fundamentally different depressive disorders. A close reading of Klein's article suggests that the categories of acute dysphoria and chronic overreactive dysphoria correspond quite closely to our category of negative cognition depression. Other types of depression, such as character spectrum disorder (e.g., Akiskal, 1983; Rosenthal, Akiskal, Scott-Strauss, Rosenthal, & David, 1981), also may involve processes that are different from those involved in negative cognition depression.

Our elaboration on the concept of negative cognition depression suggests, as Seligman (1978) speculated, that this category may not map directly in a one-to-one fashion onto any existing nosological category of depression. Instead, the category of negative cognition depression may cut across traditional categories of depression and perhaps even include psychological phenomena not previously covered by the existing nosologies of depression. If this speculation is correct, then an integration of the cognitive theories with descriptive psychiatry would not simply involve designating the current nosological categories of depression to which the cognitive theories apply. Instead, such an integration would require a reorganization of the existing classification systems, to accommodate the inclusion of the category of negative cognition depression.

HYPOTHESIZED CURE AND PREVENTION

An important function of the cognitive theories of depression is to serve as organizing rationales for the derivation of predictions about therapeutic interventions for negative cognition depression (Alloy *et al.*, 1985; Beach, Abramson, & Levine, 1981; Halberstadt *et al.*, 1984). Because each theory specifies a chain of events that is hypothesized to contribute to the development of hopelessness or the negative cognitive triad and, in turn, the syndrome of negative cognition depression, each link in the chain suggests a point for clinical intervention (Alloy *et al.*, 1985; Beach *et al.*, 1981; Halberstadt *et al.*, 1984). A major advantage of using the proximal–distal continuum to order the events that cause negative cognition depression is that these hypothesized causal pathways suggest not only points of intervention for reversing current episodes of negative cognition depression but also points of intervention for decreasing vulnerability both to depressive episodes and to the development of depression proneness. We do not present the therapeutic and preventive implications of the cognitive models here because we have detailed them elsewhere (Alloy *et al.*, 1985; Beach *et al.*, 1981; Halberstadt *et al.*, 1984) and because they are beyond the scope of this chapter.

CRITIQUE OF RESEARCH STRATEGIES USED TO TEST THE COGNITIVE THEORIES

A useful way to begin our critique is by delineating the defining features of the cross-sectional and prospective research strategies typically used for assessing the validity of the cognitive theories of depression. In the cross-sectional studies, investigators often have attempted to test the cognitive theories by examining the magnitude and consistency across studies of the difference in cognitive patterns between groups of depressed and nondepressed individuals selected from various populations. In the main, investigators have compared depressed and nondepressed individuals with respect to the likelihood of their displaying the hypothesized cognitive diatheses featured in the cognitive theories (attributional style for the hopelessness theory; dysfunctional attitudes and negative schemata for Beck's theory) rather than the hypothesized proximal sufficient causes featured in these theories (hopelessness for the hopelessness theory; negative cognitive triad for Beck's theory). For example, to test the hopelessness theory, various investigators have examined attributional styles in depressed versus nondepressed people drawn from samples of college students (e.g., Barthe & Hammen, 1981; Blaney *et al.*, 1980; Hammen & Cochran, 1981; Hammen, Krantz, & Cochran, 1981; Harvey, 1981; Peterson, Schwartz, & Seligman, 1981; Seligman *et al.*, 1979), samples of patients (Eaves & Rush, 1984; Gong-Guy & Hammen, 1980; Hamilton & Abramson, 1983; Hollon, Kendall, & Lumrey, 1986; Miller, Klee, & Norman, 1982; Persons & Rao, 1985; Raps, Reinhard, Peterson, Abramson, & Seligman, 1982), and other samples (e.g., Feather & Barber, 1983; Hammen & de Mayo, 1982; Seligman *et al.*, 1984). Only a few investigators have examined hopelessness in depressed and nondepressed individuals (e.g., Abramson, Garber, Edwards, & Seligman, 1978; Greenberg & Alloy, 1986; Hamilton & Abramson, 1983).

Investigators using prospective research strategies have attempted to assess the validity of the cognitive theories of depression by examining the magnitude and consistency across studies of the difference in cognitive styles measured at one point in time (Time 1) between two groups of individuals: (1) a group that was not depressed at Time 1 but that became depressed later, at Time 2 (the currently nondepressed/future depressed group), and (2) a group that was not depressed at Time 1 and that did not become depressed at Time 2 (the currently nondepressed/ future nondepressed group). A prototypical study of this type was conducted by Lewinsohn, Steinmetz, Larson, & Franklin (1981), who asked whether cognitions known to be correlated with depression (e.g., expectancies of positive and negative outcomes, irrational beliefs) precede, accompany, or follow an episode of depression. A variation on the basic prospective research strategy consists of administering measures of cognitive styles and depression at two points in time and using cross-lagged panel correlational analysis to test hypotheses about temporal precedence (e.g., Golin, Sweeney, & Shaeffer, 1981). A second variant of the prospective research strategy consists of examining cognitive patterns in individuals while they are suffering from a depressive episode and after they recover from the episode. In this regard, Hamilton and Abramson (1983) and Eaves and Rush (1984) examined attributional styles and dysfunctional attitudes in patients while they were depressed as well as after they had recovered.

Other investigators have argued that the prospective research strategies used to test the hopelessness theory provide an important improvement over the cross-sectional strategies because an observed difference in attributional style between currently nondepressed/future depressed and currently nondepressed/future nondepressed individuals at Time 1 or correlation between attributional style at Time 1 and depression at Time 2 cannot be attributed to depressed subjects' acquiring the hypothesized depressogenic attributional style as a consequence of being in the depressed state (Golin *et al.*, 1981; Lewinsohn *et al.*, 1981; Seligman *et al.*, 1979). However, with respect to our critique, the cross-sectional and prospective strategies are fundamentally similar in that they rely on the same criterion against which to assess the validity of the cognitive theories of depression: *The apparent validity of the theories rises and falls on the basis of the magnitude and consistency across studies of the difference in likelihood, between depressed and nondepressed individuals, of displaying the hypothesized cognitive diatheses (or proximal sufficient causes).* That in one case cognitive patterns and depression are measured at the same point in time (cross-sectional method), whereas in the other case the patterns are measured prior to the development of depression (prospective method), has no relevance for our critique.

Fundamental Problems in the Research Strategies

Our critique does not cover all of the conceptual and methodological problems associated with work designed to test the cognitive theories of depression (e.g., the use of measures of unknown reliability and validity; see Peterson & Seligman, 1984, and Raps *et al.*, 1982, for this criticism). Instead, we focus on the basic flaws in research strategy and design that make it difficult to assess meaningfully the validity of the cognitive theories of depression.

The essence of our critique is that it is possible to obtain strong, modest, weak, or no differences in cognitive patterns between depressed and nondepressed (or currently nondepressed/future depressed and currently nondepressed/future nondepressed) subjects in the typical research designs when the cognitive theories are correct. Therefore, contrary to the assumptions of recent reviewers (e.g., Coyne & Gotlib, 1983), the magnitude and consistency across studies of results from these research strategies does not provide an appropriate criterion against which to evaluate the validity of the cognitive theories of depression. In fact, assuming error-free measurement, with the possible exception of the finding that nondepressives (or currently nondepressed/future nondepressed individuals) are more likely to exhibit the hypothesized depressogenic cognitive patterns than are depressives (or currently nondepressed/future depressed individuals), no set of results from the typical cross-sectional or prospective research strategies can "disconfirm" or challenge the cognitive theories. Moreover, inconsistency in results across studies utilizing these research strategies does not embarrass the cognitive theories. If one's preferred mode of testing theories is to subject them to "grave danger of refutation" (Meehl, 1978; Popper, 1959, 1962, 1972), then these research strategies are wholly inadequate, and a most unsatisfactory state of affairs exists in work on the cognitive theories of depression. A central theme in our critique is that the basic problems in research strategy associated with work designed to test the cognitive theories result, in part, from a failure to appreciate the full methodological implications of the kinds of causal relationships among variables specified in the theories, and, as a corollary, the heterogeneity that may exist among the depressive disorders.

Assessing the Validity of the Hypothesized Proximal Sufficient Cause

It is inappropriate to assess the validity of the statements of the proximal sufficient causes in the cognitive theories of depression on the basis of the magnitude and consistency across studies of the difference in the likelihood of displaying hopelessness or the negative cognitive triad between depressed and nondepressed (or currently nondepressed/future depressed and currently nondepressed/future nondepressed) subjects. Because the cognitive theories specify sufficient, but not necessary, proximal causes of depression, the existence of subtypes of depression not associated with hopelessness or the negative cognitive triad (e.g., biochemical depressions) does not challenge the validity of the proximal sufficient cause component of the cognitive theories. However, the existence of such other subtypes of depression would weaken the magnitude of differences in the likelihood of displaying hopelessness or the negative cognitive triad between depressed and nondepressed (or currently nondepressed/future depressed and currently nondepressed/future nondepressed) subjects. Moreover, if the proportion of individuals displaying other subtypes of depression varied across the subject samples used in different studies, then the magnitude of differences in the likelihood of displaying hopelessness or the negative cognitive triad between depressed and nondepressed (or currently nondepressed/future depressed and currently nondepressed/future nondepressed) subjects also would vary if the cognitive theories were correct. Of course, the finding that nondepressed (or currently nondepressed/future nondepressed) subjects display hopelessness or the negative cognitive triad would challenge the cognitive theories of depression. Thus, if depression is, in fact, a heterogeneous disorder with many subtypes, then it is inappropriate to simply lump all depressives together and examine their expectations about the self, the world, and the future in order to test the cognitive theories of depression. That is, these models may be correct in hypothesizing the existence of the subtype of negative cognition depression, but the subtype would go undetected with current research methods unless a sufficiently large number of depressives suffered from negative cognition depression (see also Abramson *et al.,* 1987; Buchsbaum & Rieder, 1979; Craighead, 1980; Depue & Monroe, 1983; Hamilton & Abramson, 1983).

Assessing the Validity of the Hypothesized Diathesis–Stress Component

Given the kinds of causal relations specified in the cognitive theories of depression, it would be inappropriate for the apparent validity of these theories to rise or fall on the basis of the magnitude and consistency across studies of the difference in likelihood of displaying the hypothesized cognitive diatheses between depressed and nondepressed (or currently nondepressed/future depressed and currently nondepressed/future nondepressed) subjects. Of course, two conditions must be met in order to actually obtain "big empirical effects" with these typically used research strategies: (1) A high proportion of depressed (or currently nondepressed/future depressed) subjects in the sample must display the hypothesized cognitive diatheses; and (2) a high proportion of the nondepressed (or currently nondepressed/future nondepressed) subjects in the sample must not display the hypothesized cognitive diatheses. However, neither of these conditions needs to be met for the diathesis–stress components of the cognitive theories to be correct.

The validity of the cognitive theories does not require the first condition (i.e., that a high proportion of depressed, or currently nondepressed/future depressed, subjects in a sample must display the hypothesized cognitive diatheses) for two major reasons. First, because the cognitive theories involve proximal sufficient, but not necessary, cause components (i.e., hopelessness and negative cognitive triad), other subtypes of depression may exist that do not involve the cognitive theories' hypothesized cognitive diatheses in their causation. Second, because the cognitive theories involve a diathesis–stress component, in cases in which there is a low base rate of negative life events in a given sample, few cases of negative cognition depression will exist that involve the hypothesized cognitive diatheses in their causation, and hence only a relatively small proportion of depressed (or currently nondepressed/future depressed) individuals will display the hypothesized cognitive diatheses.

The validity of the cognitive theories does not require the second condition (i.e., that a high proportion of the nondepressed, or currently nondepressed/future nondepressed, subjects in a sample must not display the hypothesized cognitive diatheses) for the major reason that when the base rate of negative life events is low in a given sample, a relatively large proportion of nondepressed (or currently nondepressed/future nondepressed) subjects may display the hypothesized cognitive diatheses. In the limiting case of a 0% base rate of negative life events, the nondepressed (or currently nondepressed/future nondepressed) subjects will be just as likely as the depressed (or currently nondepressed/future depressed) subjects to display the hypothesized cognitive diatheses. Clearly, then, it is inappropriate, and even misleading, to evaluate the validity of the cognitive theories of depression on the basis of magnitude and consistency across studies of the difference in likelihood of displaying the hypothesized cognitive diatheses between depressed and nondepressed (or currently nondepressed/future depressed and currently nondepressed/future nondepressed) subjects in the absence of additional information about the base rates of negative life events and other subtypes of depression.

In addition, it is important to note that in the main, even investigators who have assessed stress in their studies of the cognitive theories of depression (e.g., Cutrona, 1983; Hammen, *et al.*, 1981; O'Hara, Rehm, & Campbell, 1982; O'Hara, Neunaber, & Zekoski, 1984; but see Metalsky et al., 1987 and Kayne et al., 1987 for exceptions) have not provided an appropriate test of the diathesis–stress component of the theories (cf. Kayne *et al.*, 1987; Metalsky *et al.*, 1987). Most of these investigators who have examined stress simply have asked whether hypothesized cognitive diatheses increased the prediction of the level of depression beyond knowledge of stress alone in hierarchical regression analyses. Such a test does *not* provide an adequate translation into statistical language of the logic of the diathesis–stress component of the cognitive theories of depression. Instead, an appropriate translation into statistical language would involve examining the *interaction* of the hypothesized cognitive diatheses and life stresses in predicting depression (see Kayne, *et al.*, 1986; Metalsky *et al.*, 1987). Of course, ideally, it is crucial to examine the interaction of the hypothesized cognitive diatheses and life stresses in predicting *negative cognition depression*.

The preceding analysis suggests that an adequate test of the cognitive theories of depression involves a "search" for negative cognition depression. In Chapter 2 of this volume, Alloy, Hartlage, and Abramson outline more adequate tests of the cognitive theories of depression and address the issues of conceptualization, assessment, and research design that will arise in such tests.

THEORETICAL AND CLINICAL IMPORTANCE OF PROVIDING AN ADEQUATE TEST OF THE COGNITIVE THEORIES OF DEPRESSION

We believe that for at least five reasons it is crucial to provide an adequate test of the cognitive theories of depression. First, although depression has long been recognized as a major form of psychopathology, investigators are only just beginning to amass cumulative knowledge about the cause of this disorder (Klerman, 1978). Despite the flurry of experimental studies designed to test the cognitive theories of depression, our preceding critique suggests that as yet these theories remain untested in very important respects. Thus adequately testing *causal theories* of depression, such as the cognitive theories, may increase significantly our scientific understanding of this not yet well understood form of psychopathology.

Second, from the standpoint of clinical description, one of the most intriguing speculations of Abramson, Seligman, and Teasdale (1978) is their proposal of a hopelessness subtype of depression. Similarly, Beck's (1967) theory, in our view, implies the existence of negative cognitive triad depression. Insofar as *causal processes* figure prominently in the definition of negative cognition depression, from the perspective of both the clinical description of depression and the scientific understanding of this disorder, a search for the negative cognition subtype(s) may prove fruitful.

A third reason for adequately testing the cognitive theories of depression is that they have clear-cut *therapeutic and preventive implications* for depression. In addition, an adequate test of the theories may aid in understanding the causal mechanisms responsible for the success of cognitive therapy for depression.

A fourth reason for adequately testing the hopelessness theory, in particular, is that it explicitly specifies *invulnerability* factors for depression. For instance, a clear-cut prediction of the hopelessness theory is that individuals who exhibit a style to attribute negative life events to unstable, specific causes should be relatively invulnerable to depression, specifically, to hopelessness depression. We believe that an accurate understanding of factors that protect against depression is crucial for a comprehensive theory of depression. Yet, little work has been conducted to uncover invulnerability factors for depression (but see Brown & Harris, 1978, for an exception).

A final reason for providing a more adequate test of the cognitive theories of depression is that increased understanding of depression and nondepression from a cognitive perspective will help build a bridge between clinical and *experimental psychology*. Although researchers in several areas of psychology (e.g., neuropsychology and visual perception) have utilized the strategy of studying abnormal individuals as a means of developing principles of normal psychological functioning, clinical psychologists rarely have pursued this line of inquiry. Clinical investigators typically conduct research on depression simply in order to understand this disorder. We believe that such research also can illuminate the functions of pervasive optimistic biases in normal cognition. These biases may be highly robust and have adaptive and/or evolutionary significance (e.g., Abramson & Alloy, 1981; Alloy & Abramson, 1979; Freud, 1917/1957; Greenwald, 1980; Martin, Abramson, & Alloy, 1984; Tiger, 1979).

GENERAL IMPLICATIONS

Our discussion of basic inadequacies in prior research strategies used to test the cognitive theories of depression has implications for other work in the field of depression. Many so-called competing theories of depression may not be competing at all (see also Akiskal & McKinney, 1975). These theories simply may be describing different points along a particular causal pathway to depression, with some theories focusing on more distal causes than others. In this vein, Brown and Harris (1978) have integrated their work on the social origins of depression with the cognitive theories of depression by suggesting that the presence of particular social factors modulates the likelihood that an individual will become hopeless when confronted with a negative life event. Alternatively, various theories of depression may be describing equally proximal complementary contributory causes in a particular causal pathway culminating in depression. For example, as we argued earlier, inferred consequences of negative life events may have such a status in relation to causal attributions for negative life events. Of course, we do not mean to imply that all current or future theories of depression can be reconciled with one another. Some of these theories indeed may compete with one another.

Historically, work on depression conducted by psychologists has had little influence on formal nosological systems such as DSM-III. No doubt there are many reasons for this disappointing state of affairs. We suspect that one cause is the apparent lack of cumulative progress in psychopathology research. If theories simply come and go in clinical psychology (cf. Meehl, 1978), why incorporate them into formal nosological systems? A second cause may be that research on psychopathology by psychologists has not had clear-cut therapeutic and preventive implications. We conclude by speculating that when psychopathologists propose theories of depression that specify clearly the formal and sequential relationships between causes and symptoms, and that when they heed the methodological implications of the specified causal relations in testing the theories, their work will significantly influence formal nosological systems.

NOTES

1. This conditional probability should read, "The probability of the presence (or occurrence) of the etiological factor given the presence (or occurrence) of the set of symptoms is equal to 1.00." In this paper, we denote the *absence* (or lack of occurrence) of the ctiological factor and the set of symptoms as $\bar{E}$ and $\bar{S}$, respectively.
2. For simplicity of exposition, we have presented the proximal–distal distinction in terms of a dichotomy: proximal versus distal. Strictly speaking, however, it is more appropriate to think in terms of a proximal–distal continuum.
3. Abramson, Seligman, and Teasdale (1978) cautioned that a basic problem existed in their statement of the proximal sufficient cause of depression featured in the hopelessness theory. They illustrated the problem as follows: "It is a 'highly desired' outcome that the editor of this journal give us each one million dollars, and we believe this outcome has a very low probability and that there is nothing we can do to increase its probability. Yet, we do not become depressed upon realizing this" (p. 65). Abramson, Seligman, and Teasdale suggested that some notion such as Klinger's (1975) "current concerns" is needed in this statement of the proximal sufficient cause. "We feel depressed about the nonoccurrence of highly desired outcomes that we believe we cannot obtain only when they are 'on our mind,' 'in the realm of possibility,' 'troubling us now,' and so on" (p. 65). Although Abramson, Seligman, and Teasdale found Klinger's concept heuristic, they felt it was not sufficiently well defined to be incorporated into the hopelessness theory. We emphasize that the problem of current concerns still remains to be solved.
4. Note that Abramson, Seligman, and Teasdale (1978) and Seligman (1978) referred to this subtype as "helplessness depression." We prefer the term "hopelessness depression" because it better describes the hypothesized cause of this disorder.
5. The 1978 statement of the hopelessness theory of depression was unclear about whether or not certain events (i.e., causal attributions) in the hypothesized causal chain contributed to

the onset of depressive symptoms as well as to their chronicity and generality or only to their chronicity and generality. We believe the underlying logic of the 1978 statement suggests that the causal events in question contribute to the onset, chronicity, and generality of depressive symptoms, and present the theory accordingly. Consistent with our interpretation of the underlying logic of the 1978 statement, Seligman, Abramson, Semmel, and von Baeyer (1979) wrote, "According to the reformulated hypothesis, a certain attributional style, when combined with bad outcomes, causes depression" (p. 247).

6. For the sake of brevity, we will henceforth use the phrase "negative life events" to refer to both the occurrence of negative life events *and* the nonoccurrence of positive life events. Note that Abramson, Seligman, and Teasdale (1978) began the causal chain with the occurrence of uncontrollable events rather than with the occurrence of negative life events. However, because the majority of subsequent studies focused on the occurrence of negative life events rather than uncontrollable events, we chose to begin the causal chain with the former. Moreover, the logic of the hopelessness theory requires only the occurrence of a negative event, rather than the occurrence of an uncontrollable event, to initiate the series of inferences hypothesized to culminate in hopelessness.

7. This statement represents a revision of the 1978 statement of the theory. Whereas Abramson, Seligman, and Teasdale (1978) postulated that all internal attributions for negative life events contribute to lowered self-esteem, we suggest that only internal, stable, and global attributions for negative life events contribute to lowered self-esteem.

ACKNOWLEDGMENT

Preparation of this chapter was supported by a grant from the MacArthur Foundation.

REFERENCES

Abramson, L. Y., & Alloy, L. B. (1981). Depression, nondepression, and cognitive illusions: A reply to Schwartz. *Journal of Experimental Psychology: General, 110,* 436–447.

Abramson, L. Y., Garber, J., Edwards, N. B., & Seligman, M. E. P. (1978). Expectancy changes in depression and schizophrenia. *Journal of Abnormal Psychology, 87,* 102–109.

Abramson, L. Y., & Martin, D. (1981). Depression and the causal inference process. In J. Harvey, W. Ickes, & R. Kidd (Eds.), *New directions in attribution research* (pp. 117–168). Hillsdale, NJ: Erlbaum.

Abramson, L. Y., Metalsky, G. I., & Alloy, L. B. (1987). *The hopelessness theory of depression: A metatheoretical analysis with implications for psychopathology research.* Manuscript submitted for publication.

Abramson, L. Y., Seligman, M. E. P., & Teasdale, J. (1978). Learned helplessness in humans: Critique and reformulation. *Journal of Abnormal Psychology, 87,* 49–74.

Akiskal, H. S. (1983). Dysthymic disorder: Psychopathology of proposed chronic depressive subtypes. *American Journal of Psychiatry, 140,* 11–20.

Akiskal, H. S., & McKinney, W. T. (1975). Overview of recent research in depression: Integration of ten conceptual models into a comprehensive clinical frame. *Archives of General Psychiatry, 32,* 285–305.

Alloy, L. B. (1982). The role of perceptions and attributions for response–outcome noncontingency in learned helplessness: A commentary and discussion. *Journal of Personality, 50,* 443–479.

Alloy, L. B., & Abramson, L. Y. (1979). Judgment of contingency in depressed and nondepressed students: Sadder but wiser? *Journal of Experimental Psychology: General, 108,* 441–485.

Alloy, L. B., Clements, C., & Kolden, G. (1985). The cognitive diathesis–stress theories of depression:

Therapeutic implications. In S. Reiss & R. Bootzin (Eds.), *Theoretical issues in behavior therapy*. New York: Academic Press.

Alloy, L. B., & Tabachnik, N. (1984). The assessment of covariation by humans and animals: The joint influence of prior expectations and current situational information. *Psychological Review, 91,* 112–149.

American Psychiatric Association. (1980). *Diagnostic and statistical* manual of mental disorders (3rd ed.). Washington, DC: Author.

Angst, J., Baastrup, P., Grof, P., Hippius, H., Poldinger, W., & Weis, P. (1973). The course of monopolar depression and bipolar psychoses. *Psychiatrica, Neurologica, et Neurochirurgia, 76,* 489–500.

Barthe, D., & Hammen, C. (1981). A naturalistic extension of the attributional model of depression. *Personality and Social Psychology Bulletin, 7,* 53–58.

Beach, S. R. H., Abramson, L. Y., & Levine, F. M. (1981). Attributional reformulation of learned helplessness and depression: Therapeutic implications. In J. F. Clarkin & H. I. Glazer (Eds.), *Depression: Behavioral and directive intervention strategies* (pp. 131–165). New York: Garland Press.

Beck, A. T. (1967). *Depression: Clinical, experimental, and theoretical aspects.* New York: Harper & Row.

Beck, A. T. (1976). *Cognitive therapy and the emotional disorders.* New York: International Universities Press.

Beck, A. T., Kovacs, M., & Weissman, A. (1975). Hopelessness and suicidal behavior: An overview. *Journal of the American Medical Association, 234,* 1146–1149.

Beck, A. T., Rush, A. J., Shaw, B. F., & Emery, G. (1979). *Cognitive therapy of depression.* New York: Guilford Press.

Blackburn, I. M., Bishop, S., Glen, A., Whalley, L. J., & Christie, J. E. (1981). The efficacy of cognitive therapy in depression: A treatment trial using cognitive therapy and pharmacotherapy, each alone and in combination. *British Journal of Psychiatry, 139,* 181–189.

Blaney, P. H., Behar, V., & Head, R. (1980). Two measures of depressive cognitions: Their association with depression and with each other. *Journal of Abnormal Psychology, 89,* 678–682.

Boyd, J. H., & Weissman, M. M. (1982). Epidemiology. In E. S. Paykel (Ed.), *Handbook of affective disorders* (pp. 109–125). New York: Guilford Press.

Brewin, C. R. (1985). Depression and causal attributions: What is their relation? *Psychological Bulletin, 98,* 297–309.

Brown, G. W., & Harris, T. (1978). *Social origins of depression.* New York: Free Press.

Buchsbaum, M. S., & Rieder, R. (1979). Biologic heterogeneity and psychiatric research. *Archives of General Psychiatry, 36,* 1163–1169.

Coryell, W., & Winokur, G. (1982). Course and outcome. In E. S. Paykel (Ed.), *Handbook of affective disorders* (pp. 93–106). New York: Guilford Press.

Costello, C. G. (1972). Depression: Loss of reinforcers or loss of reinforcer effectiveness? *Behavior Therapy, 3,* 240–247.

Coyne, J. C., & Gotlib, I. H. (1983). The role of cognition in depression: A critical appraisal. *Psychological Bulletin, 94,* 472–505.

Craighead, W. E. (1980). Away from a unitary model of depression. *Behavior Therapy, 11,* 122–128.

Cronbach, L. J., & Meehl, P. E. (1955). Construct validity in psychological tests. *Psychological Bulletin, 52,* 281–302.

Cutrona, C. E. (1983). Causal attributions and perinatal depression. *Journal of Abnormal Psychology, 92,* 161–192.

Depue, R. A., & Monroe, S. M. (1978). Learned helplessness in the perspective of the depressive disorders. *Journal of Abnormal Psychology, 87,* 3–20.

Depue, R. A., & Monroe, S. M. (1983). Psychopathology research. In M. Hersen, A. E. Kazdin, & A. S. Bellack (Eds.), *The clinical psychology handbook* (pp. 239–263). New York: Pergamon Press.

Derry, P. A., & Kuiper, N. A. (1981). Schematic processing and self-reference in clinical depression. *Journal of Abnormal Psychology, 90,* 286–297.

Eaves, G., & Rush, A. J. (1984). Cognitive patterns in symptomatic and remitted unipolar major depression. *Journal of Abnormal Psychology, 93,* 31–40.

Feather, N. T., & Barber, J. G. (1983). Depressive reactions and unemployment. *Journal of Abnormal Psychology, 92,* 185–195.

Fowles, D., & Gersh, F. (1979). Neurotic depression: The endogenous–neurotic distinction. In R. Depue (Ed.), *The psychobiology of the depressive disorders: Implications for the effects of stress* (pp. 55–80). New York: Academic Press.

Freud, S. (1957). Mourning and melancholia. In J. Strachey (Ed. and Trans.), *The standard edition of the complete psychological works of Sigmund Freud* (Vol. 14, pp. 243–133). London: Hogarth Press. (Original work published 1917)

Gillespie, R. D. (1929). Clinical differentiation of types of depression. *Guy Hospital Reports, 79,* 306–344.

Golin, S., Sweeney, P. D., & Shaeffer, D. E. (1981). The causality of causal attributions in depression: A cross-lagged panel correlational analysis. *Journal of Abnormal Psychology, 90,* 14–22.

Gong-Guy, E., & Hammen, C. (1980). Causal perceptions of stressful life events in depressed and nondepressed clinic outpatients. *Journal of Abnormal Psychology, 89,* 662–669.

Greenberg, M. S., & Alloy, L. B. (1987). *Depression versus anxiety: Schematic processing of self- and other-referent information.* Manuscript submitted for publication.

Greenwald, A. G. (1980). The totalitarian ego: Fabrication and revision of personal history. *American Psychologist, 35,* 603–618.

Halberstadt, L. J., Andrews, D., Metalsky, G. I., & Abramson, L. Y. (1984). Helplessness, hopelessness, and depression: A review of progress and future directions. In N. S. Endler & J. Hunt (Eds.), *Personality and behavior disorders* (pp. 373–411). New York: Wiley.

Hamilton, E. W., & Abramson, L. Y. (1983). Cognitive patterns in major depressive disorder: A longitudinal study in a hospital setting. *Journal of Abnormal Psychology, 92,* 173–184.

Hammen, C. (1981, August). *Issues in cognitive research on depression: Attributional models.* Paper presented at the meeting of the American Psychological Association, Los Angeles.

Hammen, C., & Cochran, S. (1981). Cognitive correlates of life stress and depression in college students. *Journal of Abnormal Psychology, 90,* 23–27.

Hammen, C., & de Mayo, R. (1982). Cognitive correlates of teacher stress and depressive symptoms: Implications for attributional models of depression. *Journal of Abnormal Psychology, 91,* 96–101.

Hammen, C., Krantz, S., & Cochran, S. (1981). Relationships between depression and causal attributions about stressful life events. *Cognitive Therapy and Research, 5,* 351–358.

Harvey, D. (1981). Depression and attributional style: Interpretations of important personal events. *Journal of Abnormal Psychology, 90,* 134–142.

Hempel, C. G. (1952). *Fundamentals of concept formation in empirical science.* Chicago: University of Chicago Press.

Hempel, C. G. (1965). *Aspects of scientific explanation.* New York: Free Press.

Hollon, S. D., Kendall, P. C., & Lumrey, A. (1986). Specificity of depressotypic cognitions in clinical depression. *Journal of Abnormal Psychology, 95,* 52–59.

Ickes, W., & Layden, M. A. (1978). Attributional styles. In J. Harvey, W. Ickes, & R. Kidd (Eds.), *New directions in attribution research* (Vol. 2, pp. 119–152). Hillsdale, NJ: Erlbaum.

Kayne, N. T., Alloy, L. B., Romer, D., & Crocker, J. (1987). *Predicting depressive reactions in the classroom: A test of a cognitive diathesis–stress theory of depression with causal modeling techniques.* Manuscript submitted for publication.

Kazdin, A. E., French, N. H., Unis, A. S., Esveldt-Dawson, K., & Sherick, R. B. (1983). Hopelessness, depression, and suicidal intent among psychiatrically disturbed inpatient children. *Journal of Consulting and Clinical Psychology, 51,* 504–510.

Kendell, R. E. (1968). *The classification of depression illness.* London: Oxford University Press.

Klein, D. F. (1974). Endogenomorphic depression: Conceptual and terminological revision. *Archives of General Psychiatry, 31,* 447–454.

Klinger, E. (1975). Consequences of commitment to and disengagement from incentives. *Psychological Review, 82,* 1–25.

Kovacs, M., Rush, A. J., Beck, A. T., & Hollon, S. D. (1981). Depressed outpatients treated with cognitive therapy or pharmacotherapy. *Archives of General Psychiatry, 38*, 33–39.

Krantz, S., & Hammen, C. (1979). Assessment of cognitive bias in depression. *Journal of Abnormal Psychology, 88*, 611–619.

Lewinsohn, P. M., Steinmetz, J. L., Larson, D. W., & Franklin, J. (1981). Depression-related cognitions: Antecedent or consequence? *Journal of Abnormal Psychology, 90*, 213–219.

Lloyd, C., Zisook, S., Click, M., Jr., & Jaffe, K. E. (1981). Life events and response to antidepressants. *Journal of Human Stress, 7*, 2–15.

Martin, D., Abramson, L. Y., & Alloy, L. B. (1984). The illusion of control for self and others in depressed and nondepressed college students. *Journal of Personality and Social Psychology, 46*, 125–136.

Meehl, P. E. (1972). Specific genetic etiology, psychodynamics and therapeutic nihilism. *International Journal of Mental Health, 1*, 10–27.

Meehl, P. E. (1978). Theoretical risks and tabular asterisks: Sir Karl, Sir Ronald, and the slow progress of soft psychology. *Journal of Consulting and Clinical Psychology, 46*, 806–834.

Metalsky, G. I., & Abramson, L. Y. (1981). Attributional styles: Toward a framework for conceptualization and assessment. In P. C. Kendall & S. D. Hollon (Eds.), *Cognitive–behavioral interventions: Assessment methods* (pp. 13–58). New York: Academic Press.

Metalsky, G. I., Abramson, L. Y., Seligman, M. E. P., Semmel, A., & Peterson, C. (1982). Attributional styles and life events in the classroom: Vulnerability and invulnerability to depressive mood reactions. *Journal of Personality and Social Psychology, 43*, 612–617.

Metalsky, G. I., Halberstadt, L. J., & Abramson, L. Y. (1987). Vulnerability and invulnerability to depressive mood reactions: Toward a more powerful test of the diathesis–stress and causal mediation components of the reformulated theory of depression. *Journal of Personality and Social Psychology, 52*, 386–393.

Miller, I. W., Klee, S. H., & Norman, W. H. (1982). Depressed and nondepressed inpatients' cognitions of hypothetical events, experimental tasks, and stressful life events. *Journal of Abnormal Psychology, 91*, 78–81.

Minkoff, K., Bergman, E., Beck, A. T., & Beck, R. (1973). Hopelessness, depression and attempted suicide. *American Journal of Psychiatry, 130*, 455–459.

Monroe, S. M. (1983). Social support and disorder: Toward an untangling of cause and effect. *American Journal of Community Psychology, 11*, 81 97.

Monroe, S. M., Imhoff, D., Wise, B. D., & Harris, J. E. (1983). Prediction of psychological symptoms under high-risk psychosocial circumstances: Life events, social support, and symptom specificity. *Journal of Abnormal Psychology, 92*, 338–350.

Neisser, U. (1967). *Cognitive psychology.* New York: Appleton-Century-Crofts.

O'Hara, M. W., Neunaber, D. J., & Zekoski, E. M. (1984). Prospective study of postpartum depression: Prevalence, course, and predictive factors. *Journal of Abnormal Psychology, 93*, 158–171.

O'Hara, M. W., Rehm, L. P., & Campbell, S. B. (1982). Predicting depressive symptomatology: Cognitive–behavioral models and postpartum depression. *Journal of Abnormal Psychology, 91*, 457–461.

Pap, A. (1953). Reduction-sentences and open concepts. *Methodos, 5*, 3–30.

Paykel, E. S., & Tanner, J. (1976). Life events, depressive relapse and maintenance treatment. *Psychological Medicine, 6*, 481–485.

Persons, J. B., & Rao, P. A. (1985). Longitudinal study of cognitions, life events, and depression in psychiatric inpatients. *Journal of Abnormal Psychology, 94*, 51–63.

Peterson, C., Schwartz, S. M., & Seligman, M. E. P. (1981). Self-blame and depressive symptoms. *Journal of Personality and Social Psychology, 41*, 253–259.

Peterson, C., & Seligman, M. E. P. (1984). Causal explanations as a risk factor for depression: Theory and evidence. *Psychological Review, 91*, 347–374.

Petrie, K., & Chamberlain, K. (1983). Hopelessness and social desirability as moderator variables in predicting suicidal behavior. *Journal of Consulting and Clinical Psychology, 51*, 485–487.

Popper, K. R. (1959). *The logic of scientific discovery.* New York: Basic Books.

Popper, K. R. (1962). *Conjectures and refutations*. New York: Basic Books.

Popper, K. R. (1972). *Objective knowledge*. Oxford, England: Oxford University Press.

Raps, C. S., Reinhard, K. E., Peterson, C., Abramson, L. Y., & Seligman, M. E. P. (1982). Attributional style among depressed patients. *Journal of Abnormal Psychology, 91*, 102–108.

Rosenthal, T. L., Akiskal, H. S., Scott-Strauss, A., Rosenthal, R. H., & David, M. (1981). Familial and developmental factors in characterological depressions. *Journal of Affective Disorders, 3*, 183–192.

Secunda, S., Katz, M. M., Friedman, R., & Schuyler, D. (1973). *The depressive disorders in 1973* (National Institute of Mental Health). Washington, DC: U.S. Government Printing Office.

Seligman, M. E. P. (1975). *Helplessness: On depression, development, and death*. San Francisco: W. H. Freeman.

Seligman, M. E. P. (1978). Comment and integration. *Journal of Abnormal Psychology, 87*, 165–179.

Seligman, M. E. P., Abramson, L. Y., Semmel, A., & von Baeyer, C. (1979). Depressive attributional style. *Journal of Abnormal Psychology, 88*, 242–247.

Shaw, B. F. (1977). Comparison of cognitive therapy and behavior therapy in the treatment of depression. *Journal of Consulting and Clinical Psychology, 45*, 543–551.

Skinner, H. A. (1981). Toward the integration of classification theory and methods. *Journal of Abnormal Psychology, 90*, 68–87.

Stanbury, J. B., Wyngaarden, J. B., Fredrickson, D. S., Goldstein, J. L., & Brown, M. S. (1983). *The metabolic basis of inherited disease* (5th ed.). New York: McGraw-Hill.

Taylor, F. C., & Marshall, W. L. (1977). Experimental analysis of a cognitive–behavior therapy for depression. *Cognitive Therapy and Research, 1*, 59–72.

Tiger, L. (1979). *Optimism: The biology of hope*. New York: Simon & Schuster.

Williams, T. A., Friedman, R. J., & Secunda, S. K. (1970). *The depressive illness* (National Institute of Mental Health). Washington, DC: U.S. Government Printing Office.

Zis, A. P., & Goodwin, F. K. (1979). Major affective disorder as a recurrent illness: A critical review. *Archives of General Psychiatry, 36*, 835–839.

2

Testing the Cognitive Diathesis–Stress Theories of Depression: Issues of Research Design, Conceptualization, and Assessment

LAUREN B. ALLOY
SHIRLEY HARTLAGE
Northwestern University

LYN Y. ABRAMSON
University of Wisconsin-Madison

In this chapter, we present a detailed outline of a research strategy for adequately evaluating the validity of the cognitive diathesis–stress theories of depression and discuss issues of conceptualization and assessment that will arise in carrying out this research strategy. As pointed out by Abramson, Alloy, and Metalsky (Chapter 1, this volume), the major problem associated with earlier research strategies designed to test the cognitive theories of depression is that they fail to take into account the full methodological implications of the kinds of causal relations specified in the cognitive models and the heterogeneity that may exist among the depressive disorders. Although there are a number of possible approaches one may take in attempting to address these basic issues in a given research context, a discussion of all such approaches would take us far afield (see Skinner, 1981, for a recent discussion). Instead, we develop a general strategic framework that we believe may be most suitable for testing the theories and discuss some of the tough conceptual and methodological issues that arise in conducting such tests. Before outlining our proposed research strategy and our suggestions for assessment, we first briefly review the formal properties and postulates of the cognitive theories of depression.

THE COGNITIVE DIATHESIS–STRESS THEORIES OF DEPRESSION

The two major cognitive theories of depression, the hopelessness theory (Abramson, Metalsky, & Alloy, 1987; Abramson, Alloy, & Metalsky, Chapter 1, this volume), previously called the reformulated helplessness theory (Abramson, Seligman, & Teasdale, 1978), and Beck's (1967, 1976) cognitive model, may both be conceptualized as cognitive diathesis–stress theories. In each, individuals with particular cognitive styles are hypothesized to be vulnerable to depression when confronted with negative life experiences. The theories also share similar formal properties regarding the logical and sequential relationships between cognitions featured as causes in the theories and resulting depressive symptomatology.

In reviewing the theories, it is useful to differentiate among the logical concepts of necessary, sufficient, and contributory causes in regard to depressive symptoms (see Abramson *et al.*, 1987). "Necessary causes" are etiological factors that must be present in order for depressive symptomatology to become manifest. "Sufficient causes" are etiological factors that, if present, ensure the manifestation of symptoms of depression. "Contributory causes" increase the probability that depressive symptoms will occur but are neither necessary nor sufficient for their occurrence. Causes may also be distinguished according to their sequential relationships to symptom onset. "Distal causes" occur early in the etiological sequence, when there is little or no manifestation of depressive symptomatology. "Proximal causes," on the other hand, operate late in the causal pathway, occurring immediately prior to or concurrent with the onset of depression.

In the hopelessness theory of depression (Abramson *et al.*, 1987; Abramson, Alloy, & Metalsky, Chapter 1, this volume), the expectation of hopelessness—that is, that highly desired outcomes are unlikely to occur, or that highly aversive outcomes are probable, and that no response one can make will change the probability of these outcomes—is viewed as a proximal sufficient cause of depression. According to Abramson *et al.* (1978; 1987), the attribution of negative life events to internal, stable, and global causes and the attachment of high importance to these events are proximal contributory causes of depression that increase the likelihood of developing hopelessness and thus depressive symptoms. Further, Abramson *et al.* (1978) hypothesized that some people possess a depressogenic attributional style, that is, a general tendency to attribute negative events to internal, stable, and global factors and to view these events as very important. These people are thought to be more likely than people who do not exhibit this style to develop hopelessness, and thus depressive symptoms, when confronted with negative outcomes. Hence a depressogenic attributional style may be viewed as a distal contributory cause of depression.

Although Beck's model is much less explicit than the hopelessness theory, we believe its formal structure is similar to that of the hopelessness theory (Alloy, Clements, & Kolden, 1985). In Beck's model, the proximal sufficient causes of depression are negative views of the self, the world, and the future—the negative cognitive triad. The formation of the negative cognitive triad is made more probable by the occurrence of cognitive distortions or errors (proximal contributory causes of depression). These consist of personally relevant perceptions and inferences that are unrealistic, extreme, and distorted in a negative fashion. These cognitive distortions are, in turn, typically produced by the operation of negative, maladaptive cognitive schemata (distal contributory causes of depression). According to Beck (1967), depressogenic schemata are negative in content and consist of immature and absolutistic attitudes concerning the self and its relation to the world. They influence the way situations are interpreted and predispose individuals to the development of depressive symptoms when confronted with stress.

It is important to note that the cognitive diathesis–stress theories acknowledge the possibility, either explicitly (the hopelessness theory) or implicitly (Beck's theory), that people can become depressed for reasons other than those specified in the theories, and that they thus recognize the heterogeneity of the depressive disorders (e.g., Craighead, 1980; Depue & Monroe, 1978). In essence, it could be said that the cognitive theories posit the existence of a *subtype* of depression— negative cognition depression—defined, in part, by its proximal sufficient causes (negative views of the self, the world, and the future). This subtype may cut across current diagnostic categories of clinical depression (e.g., major, intermittent, endogenous) and may be found in subsyndromal form in nonclinical populations as well (Akiskal, 1983; Depue *et al.*, 1981; Seligman, 1978). Abramson, Alloy, and Metalsky (Chapter 1, this volume) describe in detail the cognitive theories' predictions regarding the symptoms, course, relation to other subtypes of depression, and treatment of negative cognition depression.

A RESEARCH STRATEGY FOR ADEQUATELY TESTING THE THEORIES

In essence, assessing the validity of the cognitive theories of depression involves validating the laws or nomological network in which the concept of negative cognition depression is embedded. Specifically, to provide an adequate test of the theories, we believe investigators need to address two basic questions. First, do the contributory causal chains described in the theories actually culminate in hopelessness (hopelessness theory) or the negative cognitive triad (Beck's theory), and is hopelessness or the negative cognitive triad, in turn, sufficient for depression (specifically, necessary and sufficient for negative cognition depression)? Second, if there *are* depressions existing in nature caused by the etiological chains described in the cognitive models, do their symptoms, course, treatment, prevention, and relation to other types of depression actually conform to the specifications of the concept of negative cognition depression as elaborated in the theories?

How can we identify negative cognition depression in nature? There are various possible methodological approaches one may take in attempting to distinguish negative cognition depressions from other types of depression. For example, a *symptom-based* approach would involve identifying depressives who exhibit the symptoms hypothesized to be associated with negative cognition depression (see Abramson, Alloy, & Metalsky, Chapter 1, this volume) and depressives who do not. Such an approach commonly has been used by workers in descriptive psychiatry, where categories of depression traditionally have been formed on the basis of symptom similarity (e.g., environmental responsivity in "reactive" depressions versus unresponsivity in "endogenous" depressions; see Gillespie, 1929). However, we believe a symptom-based approach alone would be unsatisfactory in the context of work on the cognitive theories of depression. The basic problem is that some or all of the symptoms hypothesized to be characteristic of negative cognition depressions may be present in other types of depression as well.

Instead of the symptom-based approach, the cognitive theories of depression point to an alternative strategy for differentiating between negative cognition depressions and other types of depression: *a process-oriented,* etiology-based approach. We believe an etiological approach is better suited for work on the cognitive theories because the theories explicate a necessary and sufficient final common pathway to negative cognition depression. That is, the models suggest that negative cognition depressions may best be distinguished from other types of depression on the basis of causal mechanism.

In the context of the cognitive theories, an etiological approach would involve following people along the causal chains described in the models and identifying both depressives who develop the disorder as a consequence of these causal sequences and depressives who do not. Because the theories view hopelessness and/or the negative cognitive triad as sufficient for negative cognition depression, any person who follows the specific causal chains in becoming depressed may be properly regarded as a negative cognition depressive. Moreover, because hopelessness and/or the negative cognitive triad are viewed as necessary for negative cognition depression, any person who becomes depressed without following the specified causal chains cannot be exhibiting negative cognition depression and therefore must be viewed as exhibiting some "other" form of depression. It is of interest that the history of medicine suggests that classification by causal process often yields more meaningful categories with respect to treatment and prevention than classification by symptoms alone.

OUTLINE OF AN ADEQUATE TEST OF THE COGNITIVE THEORIES OF DEPRESSION

With these considerations in mind, we now present a detailed outline of what would constitute an adequate test of the cognitive theories of depression. We believe that such a test involves five components: (1) a test of the cognitive diathesis–stress component of the theories, (2) a test of the mediational processes specified by the theories to culminate in hopelessness or the negative cognitive triad, (3) identification of the negative cognition subtype of depression, (4) a test of the cognitive theories' predictions regarding the course of negative cognition depression, and (5) delineation of the place of negative cognition depression in the context of descriptive psychiatry. In describing what would constitute adequate tests of each of these components of the cognitive theories, we distinguish between tests that are *necessary* for evaluating the empirical validity of theoretical statements contained in the cognitive theories and tests that *elaborate* the nomological network relevant to each component of the theories but about which the theories currently make no explicit predictions.

Necessary Test of the Diathesis–Stress Component

The cognitive theories of depression explicitly predict that a negative attributional style or self-schema (cognitive diathesis) *interacts* with the occurrence of negative life events (stress) to increase the probability of onset of depression, specifically, the negative cognition subtype of depression. Hence an adequate test of the diathesis–stress component of the cognitive theories involves at least two parts: (1) a demonstration that the *interaction* between the hypothesized cognitive diatheses and negative life events predicts future depression, specifically negative cognition depression, over and above its association with past or current depression (cf. Kayne, Alloy, Romer, & Crocker, 1987; Metalsky, Halberstadt, & Abramson, 1987); and (2) a demonstration that the interaction between the hypothesized cognitive diatheses and negative life events predicts the complete constellation of features hypothesized to constitute the negative cognition subtype of depression (see Abramson, Alloy, and Metalsky, Chapter 1, this volume) as opposed to only a subset of these features or to features that constitute other subtypes of depression.

In addition, the logic of the etiological sequences postulated by the cognitive theories implies that a depressogenic attributional style or self-schema in a particular content domain (e.g., for interpersonal events) provides "specific vulnerability" to negative cognition depression when an individual is confronted with negative life events in that same content domain (e.g., social rejection). This specific-vulnerability hypothesis of the diathesis–stress component of the cognitive models requires that there be a *match* between the content areas of an individual's cognitive diatheses and the negative life events he or she encounters for the cognitive diathesis–stress interaction to predict future negative cognition depression (Alloy *et al.*, 1985; Hammen, Marks, Mayol, & de Mayo, 1985; Riskind & Rholes, 1984).

Elaborative Test of the Diathesis–Stress Component

One issue that is relevant to elaborating the cognitive theories of depression is the relative stability of the hypothesized depressogenic attributional style or self-schema. Although it is often assumed that the cognitive theories predict that the depressogenic attributional style or self-schema is traitlike, in fact, nothing in the logic of the theories requires that the cognitive diatheses be enduring. For example, even if the hypothesized depressogenic causal schema or self-schema is relatively statelike, as long as the interaction of this style and negative life events increases risk for depression, specifically, negative cognition depression, the cognitive theories would be corroborated. Among the questions that need to be addressed in examining the stability of the depressogenic cognitive diatheses are the following: (1) In the natural course of negative cognition depression, does a depressogenic attributional style or self-schema persist beyond remission of a current depressive episode (cf. Eaves & Rush, 1984; Hamilton & Abramson, 1983; Persons & Rao, 1985)? (2) To what degree does a depressogenic attributional style or self-schema fluctuate over time in synchrony with environmental circumstances? That is, do challenges to an individual's cognitive system by environmental stressors (negative life events) "activate" or "prime" a depressogenic causal schema or self-schema (cf. Alloy *et al.*, 1985; Riskind & Rholes, 1984)?

A second elaborative issue concerns the specific kinds of negative life events that contribute to negative cognition depression–proneness in interaction with the hypothesized cognitive diatheses. Although the cognitive models make no explicit predictions about particular types of negative events, some kinds may be especially likely to induce hopelessness or the negative cognitive triad in cognitively vulnerable individuals (e.g., uncontrollable events, exits from the social field, chronic stressors; cf. Alloy *et al.*, 1985).

Finally, it would be useful to examine whether or not there is a feedback loop among the hypothesized cognitive diatheses, negative life events, and depression such that current depression alone or current depression in interaction with stress predicts the development of a depressogenic attributional style or self-schema as well as the depressogenic causal schema or self-schema–stress interaction predicting the development of depression. Such an examination would significantly increase our understanding of the interplay among these factors in negative cognition depression (cf. Beck, 1967; Hamilton & Abramson, 1983).

Necessary Test of the Mediational Processes Component

The cognitive theories of depression not only postulate distal diathesis–stress and proximal sufficient cause components but also specify a causal chain of events hypothesized to mediate these two components. Thus it is necessary to determine whether the *probability linkages* delineated in the theories actually obtain in nature. Is the likelihood of occurrence of each causal component in the hypothesized etiological chains increased by the occurrence of the next most distal causal component in the chains?

Specifically, an investigation of the empirical status of three probability linkages is required for an adequate test of the mediational processes component of the cognitive theories:

1. The interaction of the hypothesized cognitive diatheses and negative life events should increase the likelihood that individuals will make negative interpretations (i.e., internal, stable, and global attributions or biased personal inferences) for the particular negative events they encounter. Because in both theories cognitive diatheses and stress contribute to, but are not sufficient for, the particular interpretations a person makes, this probability linkage should be greater than 0 but less than 1.0 (Kayne *et al.*, 1987; Metalsky *et al.*, 1987).

2. The negative interpretations for particular negative life events (attributions or biased inferences) that a person makes should, in turn, increase the likelihood of forming the expectation of hopelessness or the negative cognitive triad. Again, because the particular interpretations an individual makes for negative events are hypothesized to contribute to, but not be sufficient for, the formation of hopelessness or the negative cognitive triad, this probability linkage should also be greater than 0 but less than 1.0 (Alloy, 1982).

3. The occurrence of hopelessness or the negative cognitive triad should increase the likelihood of the development of depression (particularly, negative cognition depression). Because hopelessness or the negative cognitive triad are hypothesized to be sufficient causes of depression, this probability linkage should equal 1.0.

Elaborative Test of the Mediational Processes Component

Although the cognitive theories clearly specify the probability linkages among the hypothesized causal components in the etiological chains culminating in negative cognition depression, the theories are silent about the temporal intervals between pairs of these causal components (Cochran & Hammen, 1985; Kayne *et al.*, 1987; Metalsky *et al.*, 1987). That is, what is the time lag experienced by a cognitively vulnerable person between the occurrence of negative events and the occurrence of negative interpretations for these events, or between the occurrence of negative inferences for particular negative events and the formation of hopelessness or the negative cognitive triad? Consideration of the temporal issue is important because attempts to test the probability linkages predicted by the theories could conclude mistakenly that the models are invalid if the relevant causal components are assessed with inappropriate time lags (Metalsky *et al.*, 1987).

Necessary Test of the Negative Cognition Depression Component

The hopelessness theory (and the negative view of the future portion of the negative cognitive triad in Beck's theory) predicts that the negative cognition subtype of depression will be characterized by at least three major symptoms, including retarded initiation of voluntary responses (motivational symptom), difficulty in seeing that one's responses control outcomes similar to the outcome about which one feels hopeless (cognitive symptom), and sad affect (emotional symptom), as well as by a fourth symptom, low self-esteem, when individuals expect that other people can attain the outcomes about which they feel hopeless. The negative view of the self and the world in Beck's theory also predicts that guilt and increased dependency should be symptoms of negative cognition depression (see Abramson, Alloy, & Metalsky, Chapter 1, this volume, for greater elaboration of the basis of these predictions). Thus a necessary condition for the validity of the negative cognition depression component of the cognitive theories would include (1) that these symptoms be intercorrelated with one another (convergent validity) but not be as highly correlated with other symptoms found in depression and in other psychopathologies (divergent validity); (2) that this constellation of symptoms be correlated (in fact, perfectly correlated) with the hypothesized proximal sufficient causes of these symptoms (hopelessness, negative cognitive triad); and (3) that hopelessness and/or the negative cognitive triad not only be correlated with the motivational, cognitive, and affective symptom complex but that it temporally precede the formation of this symptom constellation.

The cognitive theories of depression also serve as organizing rationales for the derivation of predictions about therapeutic interventions for negative cognition depression. We do not present here the therapeutic and preventive implications of the cognitive theories, or the strategies for adequately testing these predictions, because they are beyond the scope of our chapter (but see Alloy *et al.*, 1985; Halberstadt, Andrews, Metalsky, & Abramson, 1984). However, testing the therapeutic and preventive implications of the cognitive theories of depression would be an important goal of a long-term research strategy.

Elaborative Test of the Negative Cognition Depression Component

As indicated by Abramson, Alloy, and Metalsky (Chapter 1, this volume), we view the concept of negative cognition depression as open, and therefore exploratory work is needed in order to further characterize this subtype of depression. The concept of negative cognition depression could be elaborated more fully by an examination of the following issues: (1) determination of other symptoms and clinical characteristics that may cohere with the predicted symptom constellation of negative cognition depression (e.g., suicide potential, psychomotor retardation); (2) examination of demographic (e.g., sex ratio, socioeconomic class, age, and race) and family history correlates of negative cognition depression; and (3) determination of whether individuals experiencing a current episode of negative cognition depression also exhibit an elevated number of past or future episodes of this subtype of depression.

Necessary Test of the Course Component

A basic prediction from the cognitive theories is that the duration of the proximal sufficient causes featured in these theories should predict the course or chronicity of the negative cognition subtype of depression. In addition, the theories make predictions about what variables should influence the duration of the featured proximal sufficient causes. For example, a key prediction of the hopelessness theory is that the more stable a person's attribution for a negative life event, the longer the person will be hopeless and, consequently, depressed. The etiological chain hypothesized to culminate in the onset of negative cognition depression also should predict relapse and recurrence of this subtype of depression. Thus, an adequate test of the course component of the cognitive theories of depression involves the following: (1) examination of whether the duration of time over which individuals are hopeless and/or hold negative views of the self, world, and future determine the duration of an episode of negative cognition depression; (2) examination of whether the content (e.g., stable versus unstable attribution) and duration of the personal and causal inferences individuals make for the *original* negative life events that "triggered" an episode of negative cognition depression or for any *newly occurring* negative life events (i.e., events that occur after the events that "trigger" an episode) influence the duration of an episode of negative cognition depression; and (3) examination of whether the likelihood of and time to a relapse or recurrence of negative cognition depression is predicted by the reappearance of hopelessness and/or the negative cognitive triad (which, in turn, should be predicted by the entire etiological sequences featured in the cognitive theories of depression).

Elaborative Test of the Course Component

The major issue relevant to elaborating the course component of the cognitive theories involves an investigation of whether there are additional predictors of the duration of an episode of negative cognition depression or of relapses or recurrences of negative cognition depression that do not follow directly from the logic of the cognitive theories. Additional predictors of the course of negative cognition depression may include prior episodes of depression (e.g., Klerman, 1978; Zis & Goodwin, 1979), family history of depression (Boyd & Weissman, 1982; Coryell & Winokur, 1982) and past or concurrent dysthymia (Keller & Lavori, 1984; Keller & Shapiro, 1982). An examination of whether some or all of these variables do, in fact, influence the course of negative cognition depression and whether they do so, in part, through the constructs featured in the cognitive theories of depression would serve to elaborate more fully these theories.

Negative Cognition Depression in the Context of Descriptive Psychiatry

By postulating the existence of an etiological subtype of depression—negative cognition depression—the cognitive theories explicitly (the hopelessness theory) or implicitly (Beck's theory) recognize the heterogeneity of the depressive disorders. Thus an important component of an adequate test of the cognitive theories is a determination of the relationship between negative cognition depression and other subtypes of depression. Before outlining research suggestions for placing the negative cognition subtype in the context of descriptive psychiatry, we note that negative cognition depression consists of at least two parts: the constellation of symptoms hypothesized to cohere by the cognitive theories (e.g., reduced initiation of voluntary responses, sad affect) and the causal chain of events postulated by the theories to culminate in this symptom complex. For example, the hypothesized symptom constellation may, in fact, cohere in nature but may not be caused by the chain of events specified in the theories. Alternatively, the etiological sequences described by the theories may produce an outcome that would be recognized as a case of depression but not the specific aggregate of symptoms hypothesized to constitute the negative cognition subtype of depression. Consequently, in delineating the issues involved in determining the place of negative cognition depression in descriptive psychiatry, we distinguish between the causal chain component and the symptom component.

The nosological questions that need to be addressed include the following:

1. Does the concept of negative cognition depression (either the symptom or the causal chain component) *map onto* any nosological category of affective disorders that is currently diagnosed (e.g., dysthymic disorder, unipolar major depression, intermittent depression)?

2. Does the concept of negative cognition depression (either the symptom or the causal chain component) *cut across* the various nosological categories of affective disorders that currently are diagnosed (cf. Abramson *et al.*, 1987; Seligman, 1978)?

3. Does the concept of negative cognition depression (either the symptom or the causal component) *include* subsets or components of disorders not currently included among the affective disorders (e.g., generalized anxiety, borderline conditions)?

If the empirical facts suggest that the answers to questions 2 and 3 are yes, then an integration of the cognitive theories with descriptive psychiatry may require a reorganization of the existing nosology, to accommodate the inclusion of the category of negative cognition depression (Abramson *et al.,* 1987; Seligman, 1978).

CONCEPTUALIZATION AND ASSESSMENT OF THE COMPONENTS IN THE COGNITIVE THEORIES OF DEPRESSION

In this section, we describe conceptualizations of each of the hypothesized causal components (e.g., diathesis, stress) and outcomes (e.g., negative cognition subtype of depression) in the etiological sequences postulated by the cognitive theories of depression and the methodological issues involved in assessing each component.

Cognitive Diatheses

GENERAL ISSUES

Recall that in the hopelessness theory, attributional style serves as the cognitive diathesis for depression, whereas in Beck's theory, schemata containing negative attitudes about the self and its relation to the world are postulated to act as cognitive diatheses. We believe four general issues are critical to the assessment of both types of cognitive styles.

First, a striking similarity exists between work in contemporary cognitive, social, and personality psychology on the one hand, and the concepts of cognitive diatheses developed within the cognitive theories of depression on the other (cf. Alloy *et al.,* 1985; Kihlstrom & Nasby, 1981; Kuiper & Derry, 1980; Metalsky & Abramson, 1981). Both perspectives emphasize the role of prior knowledge or schemata about causality, the self, and the world in guiding the interpretation and comprehension of environmental events. In addition, both perspectives emphasize the cognitive biases inherent in style- or schema-based processing. Thus contemporary work in cognitive, social, and personality psychology has much to offer the cognitive theories of depression in terms of refined and powerful concepts and sophisticated methods for assessing the kinds of cognitive styles featured by these depression theories. An important critique of many prior studies that have attempted to test the causal role of attributional styles or schemata in depression (e.g., Lewinsohn, Steinmetz, Larson, & Franklin, 1981; Weintraub, Segal, & Beck, 1974; Wilkinson & Blackburn, 1981) is that they have not incorporated advances in contemporary experimental psychology for measuring these cognitive diatheses. (For recent studies that do, see Hammen, Marks, de Mayo, & Mayol, 1985; Hammen, Marks, Mayol, & de Mayo, 1985; Kayne *et al.,* 1987; Kuiper, Olinger, & MacDonald, Chapter 10, this volume; and Metalsky *et al.,* 1987.) We suggest that the application of some of the sophisticated methods developed within cognitive, social, and personality psychology to the assessment of the hypothesized depressogenic attributional styles and schemata will allow for more adequate tests of the diathesis–stress components of the cognitive theories of depression.

Second, the logic of the cognitive theories of depression implies that there needs to be a match between the content of an individual's cognitive style and the content of the negative life events he or she confronts for the interaction between cognitive diathesis and stress to contribute to the onset of depression (Alloy *et al.,* 1985; Riskind & Rholes, 1984). Consequently, we suggest the assessment of depressogenic attributional styles and schemata in different content domains in order to test whether congruence between the content of an individual's experienced life events and his or her cognitive patterns provides *specific vulnerability* to depression, particularly, negative cognition depression (see Hammen, Marks, Mayol, & de Mayo, 1985; Metalsky *et al.,* 1987).

Third, to tap cognitive styles that provide specific vulnerability to depression for particular individuals, it is important to assess content domains of personal relevance to these individuals. A shortcoming of empirical studies designed to test the cognitive theories of depression is that they have failed to employ a more idiographic approach with respect to the content of people's inferential styles. For example, recent work has indicated that problems and/or concerns in the interpersonal area are at least as important as achievement concerns for depressives (e.g., Coates & Wortman, 1980; Coyne, 1976a, 1976b; Gotlib & Robinson, 1982; Howes & Hokanson, 1979; Siegel & Alloy, 1987; Youngren & Lewinsohn, 1980) and may be even more important for certain populations of depression-prone individuals (e.g., women; Brown & Harris, 1978; Weissman & Paykel, 1974). Yet, research examining cognitive styles associated with depression has often focused on such styles in the achievement domain to the relative exclusion of other content domains. Belief-based information processing may not be identical for personally significant versus insignificant content (see Gong-Guy & Hammen, 1980; Hammen & Cochran, 1981; Klinger, 1975; Klinger, Barta, & Maxeiner, 1981). In fact, differences in the schema-based interpretation of events along this continuum of personal relevance may help to resolve the paradox between Beck's (1967) predicted cognitive distortions in depressive inference and the empirical failures to find such distortions (e.g., Alloy & Abramson, 1979, and Chapter 8, this volume; Lewisohn, Mischel, Chaplain, & Barton, 1980). Beck's theory is based on clinical observations of people in therapy for depression who report cognitions and behaviors in areas of high personal relevance, whereas the empirical studies of cognitive biases and distortions in depression are based primarily on achievement and/or problem-solving situations that may or may not have high personal relevance to the subjects involved. We believe that tests of the diathesis–stress components of the cognitive theories of depression would benefit from an assessment of attributional styles and schemata in content domains with high personal meaning to subjects.

Finally, in the cognitive theories of depression, negative life events act as triggers of depressive symptoms by initiating a causal sequence leading to symptom onset in individuals predisposed to this disorder by virtue of possessing depressogenic self-schemata (Beck, 1967) or causal schemata (Abramson *et al.,* 1978;

1987). In this context, stressful life events may be viewed as occupying two roles in the cognitive theories: a passive role and an active role (cf. Alloy *et al.*, 1985). In their passive role, life experiences provide the occasion for the operation of the cognitive diatheses in the models. That is, they constitute the situational information that is filtered through and interpreted by the negative depressogenic schemata or attributional styles. In their active role, negative life events may "activate" or "prime" depressogenic self-schemata or causal schemata, so that they become accessible in memory and can bias the processing of situational information (cf. Alloy *et al.*, 1985; Riskind & Rholes, 1984). Negativistic schema-based attitudes may be enduring, but latent, characteristics of depression-prone persons that are not always more dominant or cognitively accessible than other neutral or positive content patterns of thinking and therefore not always easily assessed with baseline, static measures. Instead, these latent schemata or attributional styles may be cognitively activated or primed in stressful situations (situations of negative life events), and once activated and thus accessible, they will tend to produce negative attributions and inferences, and hence the symptoms of negative cognition depression.

An analogous line of reasoning has been espoused by investigators concerned with biologic risk factors for depression (e.g., Depue & Monroe, 1983). Numerous biologic dysfunctions have been postulated to characterize individuals at "high risk" for depression, including deficits in noradrenergic, serotonergic, and cortisol functioning (Depue & Monroe, 1983). Yet, individuals identified as biologically vulnerable often exhibit no psychobiologic disturbance, or only mild disturbance, with either baseline or dynamic measures (Depue & Monroe, 1983). Instead, researchers of biologic diatheses to depression have argued for the use of "challenge" protocols, in which the adaptive capacity of the functional system of interest is challenged pharmacologically or environmentally (laboratory stress) in order to evoke an underlying, latent disturbance that would otherwise be undetectable (Depue & Kleiman, 1979; Depue & Monroe, 1983; Gershon, 1978). The dexamethasone suppression test (DST) represents an example of a recent application of such a challenge protocol.

Similar to the recognized need for challenge protocols in studies of biologic diatheses to depression, the cognitive diatheses postulated by the cognitive theories may also be more readily and reliably measured following a stress challenge. Research in cognitive and social psychology offers some support for the view that a person's mode of thinking can differ across situations as a function of cognitive priming or activation (e.g., Geller & Shaver, 1976; Isen, Shalker, Clark, & Karp, 1978; Pryor & Kriss, 1977). Measures of attributional styles or schemata may possess the capacity to predict future symptoms of depression to the extent that the cognitive styles have been activated appropriately. This would be most likely in a situation in which the person has recently experienced a life event that is in some way analogous to past situations that engendered the depressogenic cognitive style (Riskind & Rholes, 1984). Consequently, we suggest examining whether a *challenge protocol* for measuring schemata and attributional styles improves the ability of these cognitive diatheses to predict future depressive episodes (particularly, negative cognition depression episodes) in interaction with *subsequently* occurring negative life events. Because one cannot assume that individuals will have experienced a stressful life event that is analogous to the events that originally contributed to the formation of negative cognitive styles immediately prior to the current assessment of these styles, it may be necessary to adopt a measurement strategy involving the use of situational manipulations, to increase accessibility of negative cognitive diatheses.

ATTRIBUTIONAL STYLES

Definition and Conceptualization. In line with other investigators (e.g., Ickes & Layden, 1978; Rotter, 1966; Weiner, 1974), we define an "attributional style" as a tendency to make particular kinds of causal inferences, rather than others, across different situations and over time (Metalsky & Abramson, 1981). It is important to distinguish between attributional *content* and attributional *style*. Attributional content simply refers to the particular attribution an individual makes, such as "ability" or "task difficulty." In contrast, attributional style refers to the *consistency* in attributional content across situations and time. It is also important to distinguish between attributions for *specific events* and attributional *style*. Attributions for specific events are the particular causes an individual assigns to a specific life event occurring in one situation at one point in time, whereas attributional style refers to the individual's consistent tendency to provide similar attributions for many different specific life events.

When will a person make similar causal inferences in different situations and over time? Metalsky and Abramson (1981) suggest that an individual will display an attributional style to the extent that he or she relies on and utilizes the same or similar information to resolve causal ambiguity across different situations and time. According to Metalsky and Abramson (1981) and Alloy and Tabachnik (1984), two sources of information are relevant to resolving causal ambiguity: (1) generalized beliefs about the self and the world, and (2) situational information about the extent to which an event occurs across people, situations, and time (consensus, distinctiveness, and consistency information, respectively; Kelley, 1967). This suggests that at least two different classes of attributional styles may exist: belief-based and evidence-based styles.

A belief-based attributional style is a tendency to make particular causal inferences, rather than others, by consistently relying on the same or similar generalized beliefs to resolve causal ambiguity. Individual differences in belief-based attributional styles may occur as a function of differences in the content ("I am competent" vs. "I am incompetent"), degree of differentiation ("I lack ability" vs. "I lack math ability"), and strength ("I am certain of my incompetence" vs. "I suspect I may be incompetent") of generalized beliefs. An evidence-based attributional style consists of the tendency to make particular causal inferences, rather than others, by consistently relying on the same or similar patterns of situational information to resolve causal ambiguity. For example, a person may be likely to display cross-situational consistency in the attributions he or she makes because the situational information contained in each event points to the same causal inference as being most plausible (i.e., lack of ability). Individuals may confront similar configurations of information in different situations at different times either "by chance" or because they generate such consistent information by their own actions (Metalsky & Abramson, 1981).

Issues in Assessing Attributional Styles. A self-report questionnaire is frequently used for assessing individuals' attributional styles (e.g., Seligman, Abramson, Semmel, & von Baeyer, 1979). Two methodological issues are relevant to measuring attributional styles in this manner.

The first issue is whether to require individuals to make causal inferences about hypothetical events or about real-life events that they have experienced in the past. Prior studies of the role of attributional style in depression have utilized assessment procedures for both hypothetical (e.g., Eaves & Rush, 1984; Hamilton & Abramson, 1983; Kayne *et al.*, 1987; Metalsky, Abramson, Seligman, Semmel, & Peterson, 1982; Metalsky *et al.*, 1987; Seligman *et al.*, 1979) and real-life events (e.g., Gong-Guy & Hammen, 1980; Hammen & Cochran, 1981; Harvey, 1981; Miller, Klee, & Norman, 1982). Some authors (e.g., Gong-Guy & Hammen, 1980; Hammen & Cochran, 1981; Harvey, 1981; Miller *et al.*, 1982) have argued that attributional styles for hypothetical events may not reflect attributional styles for actual life events and thus may not predict the onset of depression following a naturally occurring life stressor. In fact, however, attributional styles assessed with a procedure for hypothetical events have proved to be good predictors of depressive reactions following actual negative life events (e.g., Cutrona, 1983; Kayne *et al.*, 1987; Metalsky *et al.*, 1982, 1987; O'Hara, Neunaber, & Zekoski, 1984; O'Hara, Rehm, & Campbell, 1982).

We believe that a procedure for hypothetical events has three distinct advantages over one utilizing real events from subjects' pasts. First, hypothetical events tend to be ambiguous with respect to the particular causal inferences that are most plausible. Real events, in contrast, tend to occur in specific contexts that provide more clear-cut consensus, consistency, and distinctiveness information. Because hypothetical outcomes are relatively causally ambiguous, respondents are required to make their own "cognitive contributions" to the situation in order to provide a causal attribution. Consequently, measures that use hypothetical events are unlikely to force individuals toward one particular type of attribution for each outcome because of overpowering situational information; instead, they are more likely to allow any stable, cross-situational styles to operate. A second advantage of hypothetical outcomes is that it is possible to present individuals with the wide range of events in different content domains that is necessary for assessing an attributional style. One cannot guarantee that individuals will have experienced a sufficiently extensive set of real events in their own lives. Finally, each person can be presented with the same set of events, and thus situational information can be controlled and equated across individuals.

The second issue relevant to assessing attributional styles with a questionnaire concerns the best format for the instrument. A number of different techniques have been developed for assessing people's causal attributions (see Elig & Frieze, 1979, for a review and comparative analysis). Overall, the various techniques may be categorized as employing either an unstructured or a structured response format. In the open-ended, unstructured approach, respondents are asked to state why a particular event occurred. Subjects' responses may be coded by raters into those attributional dimensions of interest to the investigator (e.g., internal–external). Ross's (1977) observation that the coding of causal attributions into abstract attributional dimensions may depend more on the grammatical form of the attribution than on its actual meaning argues against the use of completely open-ended questionnaires. In the structured response format, subjects are provided with possible causal factors and are asked to rate the extent to which each factor is a cause for the event in question (e.g., ability, effort). The potential problem with structured formats is that they confine subjects to a limited set of factors, defined in advance by the investigator as relevant. This set may not include the factors of importance for some subjects. A major distinction among various structured attribution measures is whether they involve ipsative or independent judgments (Elig & Frieze, 1979). In ipsative measures, the rating of one causal factor must influence the rating of other factors (e.g., percent due to ability, percent due to effort), thus inducing negative correlations. Independent ratings do not force negative correlations among different causal factors and typically involve the use of within-dimension bipolar scales (e.g., internal–external).

Elig and Frieze (1979) compared the efficacy of unstructured and structured approaches to assessing people's causal attributions for success and failure. The structured format was found to have greater convergent and discriminant validity and reliability than the open-response, unstructured format. Among the structured approaches, Elig and Frieze argued that the dimensional bipolar scale format was superior to the percentage measure because it had greater face validity for subjects and was easier to respond to. Taken together, these results argue for the relative psychometric superiority of a structured approach, particularly a dimensional rating scale format, to assessing people's attributional styles.

SELF-SCHEMATA

Definition and Conceptualization. According to Beck, depression-prone individuals possess enduring maladaptive cognitive schemata that contain specific negative attitudes about the self and its relation to the environment. In Beck's view, schemata are structural constellations of negative beliefs stored in memory that serve as a framework against which current information is perceived and evaluated. These schemata become activated by environmental stress and then dominate the cognitions of the depression-prone individual, leading to systematic biases and distortions in the perception and interpretation of self-relevant information. Although Beck's theory is clinically rich and descriptive, it lacks conceptual clarity and precision because many of the concepts are difficult to operationalize. In many ways, the cognitive model of depression simply was "ahead of its time" when Beck first proposed it in 1967. At that time, experimental cognitive psychologists were just beginning to develop concepts and methods for understanding and measuring the sorts of schemata and schema-based inferential processes featured in Beck's model (cf. Abramson & Martin, 1981; Kihlstrom & Nasby, 1981). Given this historical context, it is not surprising that depression researchers have only just begun to develop techniques capable of assessing the hypothesized depressogenic self-schemata featured in Beck's model (cf. Derry & Kuiper, 1981; Greenberg & Alloy, 1987; Greenberg, Vazquez & Alloy, Chapter 4, this volume; Kuiper & Derry, 1980; Kuiper, Olinger, & MacDonald, Chapter 10, this volume).

Beginning with Bartlett (1932), cognitive psychologists have emphasized the importance of cognitive structures, or schemata, in guiding the interpretation or comprehension of information (Abelson, 1975; Bobrow & Norman, 1975; Bower, Black, & Turner, 1979; Bransford & McCarrell, 1975; Minsky, 1975). Although cognitive psychologists have defined "schemata" in a number of ways (Hastie, 1980), the common theme running through the various usages is that of organized representations of prior knowledge that guide the processing of current information. Because information-processing capacity is limited, individuals must be selective in what they notice, learn, remember, or infer in any situation (Neisser, 1967). Cognitive knowledge structures, or schemata, facilitate perception, comprehension, recall, and problem solving, but an inevitable consequence of their operation is bias and distortion (Alloy & Tabachnik, 1984; Taylor & Crocker, 1980).

Recently, a number of social psychologists have applied the concept of schemata to the processing and interpretation of information in the social world (e.g., Cantor & Mischel, 1977; Markus, 1977; Rogers, 1981; Taylor & Crocker, 1980). The concept of self-schemata is particularly relevant to Beck's theory. Several social psychologists suggest that an individual's self-concept is composed of numerous interrelated prototypes in different content domains, with each schema containing both structural and processing components (Kuiper & Derry, 1980; Markus, 1977). The structural component is defined as a list of "features" that have been established through a lifetime of experience with personal information. This list of features includes both general terms, conceptualized as similar to personality traits, and specific terms, representing situation-specific aspects of self-perception and specific behaviors. With respect to the processing components of self-schemata, the generalized traits and specific exemplars contained in each self-schema serve as a "background" or setting against which incoming information is evaluated and interpreted. Self-schemata thus function to enhance and bias the processing of self-relevant information. Compared to Beck's theory of depression, contemporary work in cognitive and social psychology provides more refined and powerful concepts and methods for understanding the kinds of self-schemata featured in Beck's model. Consequently, we advocate the application of these concepts and methods to the assessment of depressogenic self-schemata.

Issues in Assessing Self–Schemata. Several methodological issues should be considered in measuring self-schemata.

A critical aspect of Beck's (1967) theory is that depressives process situational information in a biased way because they assimilate incoming information to their negative self-schemata. Although this *dynamic interaction* between schemata and incoming information is a cornerstone of Beck's theory, some investigators studying cognitive processes in depressed and nondepressed people have ignored it in their work. Instead, these investigators have focused on attempting to measure the content of beliefs and attitudes in the schemata of depressives (e.g., Hollon & Kendall, 1980; Weissman & Beck, 1979), without assessing the information-processing effects of these schemata. Similarly, as discussed earlier, inherent in the concept of schemata utilized by experimental psychologists is the idea that schemata guide and also bias the perception and interpretation of situational information. Those individuals who exhibit *both* facilitated processing of schema-congruent information and biased processing of schema-incongruent information across a range of tasks are most likely to possess stable, situationally general self-schemata. Consequently, an *adequate* assessment of depressogenic self-schemata requires an examination of the specific information-processing effects associated with negative self-perceptions contained in the schemata as well as a measurement of the content of the negative beliefs themselves.

Several experimental paradigms have been employed within cognitive and social psychology for detecting schemata and their biasing effects on information processing. These include reaction-time studies (e.g., Derry & Kuiper, 1981; Markus, 1977; Rogers, 1981; Rosch, 1975), false-recognition paradigms (e.g., Bransford & McCarrell, 1975; Cantor & Mischel, 1977; Owens, Bower, & Black, 1979), and recall paradigms (e.g., Derry & Kuiper, 1981; Ingram, Smith, & Brehm, 1983; Rogers, Kuiper, & Kirker, 1977). We believe that a critical short-coming of many of the previous investigations that have attempted to assess negative self-schemata associated with depression is that they have employed only one or two measures of schematic processing (e.g., Davis, 1979a, 1979b; Davis & Unruh, 1981; Derry & Kuiper, 1981; Ingram *et al.*, 1983; Kuiper & Derry, 1982; Kuiper & MacDonald, 1982). Instead, we believe that in order to identify individuals who are cognitively vulnerable to depression by virtue of possessing depressogenic self schemata, it is important to employ *multiple converging measures* of schematic information processing. We suggest the examination of several information-processing effects that cognitive, social, and personality psychologists have considered critical in demonstrating that an individual has a well-developed self-schema in a particular content domain. These effects may include (1) judgments that schema-congruent stimuli are self-descriptive, (2) more rapid processing (faster reaction times) of schema-congruent than schema-incongruent stimuli, (3) the ability to easily recall many relevant behavioral instances from one's past experiences in the schema content domain, (4) the prediction of schema-congruent future behaviors or events in the schema content domain, (5) better recall of schema-congruent than schema-incongruent stimuli, (6) better recognition of schema-congruent than schema-incongruent stimuli, and (7) false recognition of schema-congruent distractors that were not actually seen before (e.g., Cantor & Mischel, 1977; Derry & Kuiper, 1981; Greenberg & Alloy, 1987; Ingram *et al.*, 1983; Markus, 1977; Vazquez & Alloy, 1987).

According to Beck (1967, 1976), depressogenic self-schemata may be distinguished from the negative self-schemata characterizing individuals with other emotional disorders (e.g., anxiety) on the basis of the specific content of the beliefs that they contain. The self-schemata of depression-prone persons are hypothesized to involve the depressive themes of personal deficiency, worthlessness, lack of motivation, self-blame, deprivation, and rejection. According to Beck's content-specificity hypothesis, the schematic processing effects just enumerated should be limited to stimulus material congruent with the content embodied in the self-schemata (Derry & Kuiper, 1981; Greenberg & Alloy, 1987). Previous research on self-schemata associated with depression (e.g., Davis, 1979a, b; Davis & Unruh, 1981; Derry & Kuiper, 1981; Ingram et al., 1983; Kuiper & Derry, 1982; Kuiper & MacDonald, 1982) has paid insufficient attention to the content of the stimuli used and has often incorrectly assumed that depressed or depression-prone individuals will exhibit more efficient processing and recall of *any* negatively valenced information. Thus we suggest that assessments of the depressogenic self-schemata featured in Beck's model include positively and negatively valenced stimuli that are relevant both to depressive themes and to other disorders (e.g., anxiety), to demonstrate the specificity of content for depression (see Greenberg & Alloy, 1987; Greenberg, Vazquez, & Alloy, Chapter 4, this volume; Vazquez & Alloy, 1987).

Stress

As we argued earlier (see also Abramson, Alloy, & Metalsky, Chapter 1, this volume; Alloy *et al.*, 1985), the cognitive theories of depression are diathesis–stress theories. Unfortunately, however, the theories are less articulate about the hypothesized stress component than about the cognitive style component. Indeed, these theories have been misunderstood by some investigators (e.g., Coyne & Gotlib, 1983) as postulating only a minimal role, or no role, for the environment in causing depression. Consistent with this misunderstanding, most studies designed to test the cognitive theories of depression have, to date, focused almost exclusively on cognitive style (e.g., attributional style) as a contributory cause of depression and have ignored stress (for exceptions see Hammen, Marks, de Mayo, & Mayol, 1985; Hammen, Marks, Mayol, & de Mayo, 1985; Kayne *et al.*, 1987; Metalsky *et al.*, 1982, 1987). To remedy the relative neglect of the stress component by research designed to test the cognitive theories of depression, we spell out the implications of these theories for the conceptualization and assessment of their stress components. In addition, we draw on prior work on the relationship between life events and psychiatric disorder in developing a more adequate conceptualization and assessment of stress for testing these models.

GENERAL ISSUES

Contributions from the Cognitive Theories of Depression. What constitutes "stress" in the cognitive theories of depression? Although not directly asserted in the theories, an implication of these models is that life events whose occurrence contributes to the formation of hopelessness (the hopelessness theory) or the negative cognitive triad (Beck's theory), the proximal sufficient causes of depression in the theories, are the "stressors" featured in these theories. A second implication of the theories is that life events whose occurrence induces spontaneous attributional processing or inference making are theoretically relevant stressors in the cases in which such causal and personal inferences contribute to the formation of hopelessness or the negative cognitive triad, respectively. A third implication is that an adequate test of these theories would require as *comprehensive* or exhaustive an assessment as possible of potential stressors. In the theoretically ideal, but practically impossible, case, one would want to know to which of *all* possible stressors individuals with and without the hypothesized cognitive diatheses had been exposed.

The concept of specific vulnerability in the cognitive theories of depression has a final implication for the characterization of the stressor in these models. For a given individual, stressors will be those events that have the aforementioned properties (e.g., contributing to the formation of hopelessness) and whose content (e.g., interpersonal-related) matches the content of the person's cognitive diatheses.

Contributions from Work on the Relationship between Life Events and Psychiatric Disorder. Recently, investigators have begun to raise various conceptual and methodological issues pertinent to research on life events and psychiatric disorder in general that are relevant to conceptualizing and assessing the stressors featured in the cognitive theories of depression (e.g., Brown, 1974; Dohrenwend & Dohrenwend, 1978; Jenkins, Hurst, & Rose, 1979; Kanner, Coyne, Schaefer, & Lazarus, 1981; Lei & Skinner, 1980; Lloyd, 1980; Monroe, 1982a, 1982c; Neugebauer, 1981; Sarason, de Monchaux, & Hunt, 1975; Tennant, Bebbington, & Hurry, 1981; Zimmerman, 1983).

First, a controversy exists in the field of life stress and disorder about whether *weighted* summary scores are more highly correlated with illness or impairment than is a simple count of the number of life events with which a person has been confronted (e.g., Lei & Skinner, 1980; Zimmerman, 1983). Zimmerman (1983) recently reviewed studies reporting the intercorrelations between unweighted and weighted life-event indices and concluded that the use of group-derived weights generally has not been found to improve the stress–illness relationship. However, in assessing stress, we suggest comparison of a weighted versus an unweighted summary score, to see which, if either, interacts with the cognitive diatheses to predict negative cognition depression.

A second, related controversy is whether or not to use *subjective weights* in life-event indices (i.e., the subject provides the stress rating rather than a judge). Advocates of "objective" weights (a judge provides *a priori* stress ratings of the events) argue that "circularity" is involved when the subject rates *a posteriori* the degree of stressfulness of an event he or she confronts (Brown, 1974; Brown & Harris, 1978; Dohrenwend & Dohrenwend, 1978). These writers contend that people who develop psychiatric illnesses might magnify their ratings of the stressfulness of events they confronted in order to explain or rationalize their illness (a putative response bias called "effort after meaning"). However, a number of investigators have suggested that the amount of stress produced by a life event cannot be determined accurately without assessing the meaning of the event to the individual who experiences it (e.g., Lazarus, 1966; Hammen, Chapter 3, this volume). Although we agree with this view, it is important to recognize that it would be inappropriate to use subjective weights in tests of the diathesis–stress component of the cognitive theories of depression. To test this diathesis–stress component, adequately, it is necessary to know whether people with different cognitive styles are differentially likely to develop depression, given a *standard* stimulus event or the same level of stress. According to the logic of the theories, people's cognitive styles would predict the subjective weights they assigned to events. Thus we suggest asking subjects to provide subjective ratings of stressful life events they confront and testing whether their cognitive styles predict such ratings.

A third major issue in work on life events and disorder is on what *dimensions* events should be scaled. For example, Holmes and Rahe (1967) suggested that the magnitude of the change or readjustment that the occurrence of an event entails, irrespective of its desirability, determines the degree of stressfulness of the event. However, work on life stress and disorder strongly suggests that undesirable or negative events are more strongly related to disorder than are desirable or positive events (Monroe, 1982b; Zimmerman, 1983). An examination of work on life events and disorder suggests that it is useful to classify events along the following dimensions: (1) desirable versus undesirable (Zimmerman, 1983), (2) daily hassles versus major life events (Kanner *et al.,* 1981; Monroe, 1983a), (3) episodic versus chronic events (Monroe, 1983b), (4) entrances versus exits (Paykel, 1979; Paykel *et al.,* 1969), and (5) controllable versus uncontrollable events (Folkman, 1984; Monroe, Imhoff, Wise, & Harris, 1983).

A fourth issue in work on life events and disorder is the *temporal relationship* between the occurrence of life events and the development of disorder (e.g., Lloyd, 1980; Zimmerman, 1983). Over what time interval do events act to contribute to the development of disorder? A corollary question for assessing life events is, How far back in time should one sample in order to assess events that may contribute to the production of a current disorder? Lloyd's (1980) review of work on life events and depression suggests that events occuring during the 3-month interval prior to the onset of depression may have contributed to its onset. Thus, in testing the diathesis–stress component of the cognitive theories of depression, we suggest determining whether or not life events interact with cognitive styles to predict depression, specifically negative cognition depression, any time during the 3 months prior to the occurrence of the depression.

In relation to the temporal issue, Dohrenwend and Dohrenwend (1978) cautioned that many life-event scales contain items that may be symptoms or consequences of a disorder (i.e., "symptom contamination" of life-event scales). Similarly, Brown (1972) suggested that some negative life events may be due to the insidious onset of a disorder itself and in no way cause it. Thus a positive relationship between experiencing stressful life events and developing depression does not necessarily imply that the stressful events caused the disorder; they may be symptoms or consequences of the disorder. We will soon discuss how this problem in interpretation can be remedied.

The work on life events and disorder suggests two final issues relevant to the conceptualization and assessment of the stressors specified in the cognitive theories of depression. First, do different kinds of events predict the onset, maintenance, and relapse of depression (Monroe, 1982b; Monroe, Bellack, Hersen, & Himmelhoch, 1983)? Second, do different kinds of events predict different aspects of the depressive syndrome (Monroe, Imhoff, Wise, & Harris, 1983)? In this regard, Monroe, Imhoff, Wise, and Harris (1983) reported that in a sample of unipolar depressives, event categories were related mainly to depressive mood and not to more behavioral or somatic features of the disorder.

Implications for the Assessment of Stress. The preceding discussion has a number of straightforward implications for the assessment of life events in research designed to test the cognitive theories of depression. First, it is necessary to assess negative, rather than positive, life events because prior research has shown that it is undesirable events that are associated with the production of disorder. Common sense itself suggests that the occurrence of negative, rather than positive, events will contribute to the formation of hopelessness or the negative cognitive triad. Similarly, social psychologists (e.g., Pittman & Pittman, 1980; Pyszczynski & Greenberg, 1981; Wong & Weiner, 1981) have found that major determinants of the onset of spontaneous causal analyses include the occurrence of negative events, uncontrollable events, and events involving failure.

Second, to investigate specific vulnerability, it is necessary to examine negative life events from all the possible domains for which a person may have depressogenic cognitive styles. Insofar as clinical theorists and everyday people view love and work as important areas of life, it is crucial to examine both interpersonally oriented and achievement-oriented life events. Moreover, such events should be sampled as exhaustively as possible over a given period of time. The measurement of life stress should include major and minor events as well as episodic and chronic events; the number of times a given episodic event occurs and the duration of more chronic events should also be assessed.

Third, the accurate dating of events is crucial for testing the cognitive theories of depression for at least three reasons: (1) Accurate dating of events allows resolution of the temporal aspects of the hypothesized causal chains in the cognitive theories (see also Brown, 1972); (2) accurate dating is necessary for testing the mediational processes featured in the theories (e.g., the stressful life event needs to occur before an interpretation is made for it) and, in particular, the causal contribution of negative life events; and (3) accurate dating of the event in conjunction with accurate dating of the onset of a depressive episode allows one to determine whether or not a given event is best viewed as a cause, symptom, or consequence of the depression (Dohrenwend & Dohrenwend, 1978; Zimmerman, 1983).

In addition to the accurate dating of events, two other procedures may help address the issue of possible symptom contamination of life-event measures: (1) Clinical judges can make normative ratings of the degree to which events are independent of a person's depression; and (2) in rating stressors in their lives, people can provide contextual information so that raters may judge whether or not a given event is independent of that particular individual's depression.

Finally, life events need to be rated along all of the dimensions previously discussed (e.g., desirability, change, controllability). To test the diathesis–stress component of the cognitive theories, both judges and subjects would need to rate the events along these dimensions.

Format, Dating, and Timing of Assessments of Stress. An important methodological issue in the assessment of stress is the use of self-report scales versus interviews (e.g., Brown & Harris, 1978). We believe that each method of assessment has special advantages and disadvantages. Among the advantages of self-report scales are (1) efficient and low-cost administration; (2) the presentation of precisely the same stimuli to all subjects; (3) an increase in the likelihood of subjects' reporting of embarrassing or troubling events, given the anonymity of self-report scales; and (4) the lack of interview bias. The disadvantages of these scales include (1) the lack of a guarantee that subjects are interpreting a given life event (e.g., a serious argument with close friend) in the same way and/or in the manner intended by the developer of the scale and (2) a lack of probes to help subjects remember if and when they experienced a particular kind of event. In contrast, the advantages of an interview format are the reduction of variance in subjects' definitions of what counts as an event (the interviewer explains the items) and the inclusion of probes. But the disadvantages of this format include the possibility of interviewer bias, the high cost of administration, and the possible reticence of subjects to report more embarrassing or troubling events to the interviewer. To capitalize on the advantages and reduce the disadvantages of each format, we suggest the use of a self-report scale combined with brief, follow-up interviews. The interviews may serve as a check on the validity and reliability of the scale.

The accurate dating of stressful life events may be facilitated in several ways. Subjects can be provided with a calendar to help them determine when particular events occurred. In addition, following Brown, Sklair, Harris, and Birley (1973), subjects may be instructed to "anchor" events to special dates, such as holidays and birthdays, to help them date those events about which they are not confident. "Cross-referencing" and double-checking of the dates of events can also be carried out in follow-up interviews. Finally, subjects can be asked to provide the names of people who may be able to date accurately events about which subjects are not completely confident.

Another important methodological issue is how far back in time subjects should be asked to recall life events on any given assessment. With regard to this issue, Monroe (1982a) has presented evidence suggesting that people may "underreport" events from even the most recent 4-month period. These data suggest the use of event assessment intervals of less than 4-months. However, the use of extremely recent intervals may also be problematic. Insofar as subjects will be asked to make a number of personal and causal inferences about particular events they experienced over a given period, it is useful to note that Moore, Sherrod, Liu, and Underwood (1979) reported that causal attributions change with the passage of time. Thus, to guard against the underreporting that may be associated with too infrequent assessments of life events, and against the premature beliefs that may be associated with too frequent assessments of life events, we suggest the assessment of life events occurring over intermediate time intervals (e.g., from 1 week to 3 months), with the exact interval depending upon the design of the particular study and upon whether one is testing predictions of the cognitive models with regard to the onset or the course of depression.

Finally, in constructing a life-event measure, it is useful to construe it partly as a memory task, because one can then borrow methods from cognitive psychology to facilitate subjects' recall. In this vein, we suggest two methods to help subjects recall events and reduce variance in the interpretation of different event categories. First, rather than asking subjects to freely recall stressful events in their lives over a given period, subjects can be presented with clearly specified event categories and then be asked if they have experienced the given event. Second, for each event category that may be associated with any variance in interpretation, subjects may be provided with examples of what would "count" as an instance of the event category. Note that our approach here constitutes a recognition, rather than a recall, task and therefore should facilitate accurate memory for events (e.g., Brown, 1976).

Report Biases in the Assessment of Stress. To adequately test the diathesis–stress component of the cognitive theories of depression, two potential report biases in assessing life events must be minimized: effort after meaning (Bartlett, 1932) and telescoping events (Duncan-Jones, 1981). "Effort after meaning" refers to the hypothesis that individuals in a disordered state may "try harder" to recall stressful life events in order to explain the onset of their disorder. This response bias may operate by reducing the criteria for deciding that a given event qualifies as a stressor and/or by increasing the significance that disordered individuals attach to stressors they actually have experienced (Brown *et al.*, 1973). Although, to our knowledge, no studies have actually corroborated that depressed individuals succumb to the effort-after-meaning bias, it is important to address this issue in studies of the diathesis–stress component of the cognitive theories of depression. First, the effort-after-meaning bias will not undermine any etiological inferences if one uses a longitudinal, prospective design and determines whether stressors reported *prior to the onset of depression* interact with cognitive styles to predict the onset of the depression. Second, two aspects of the stress assessment procedures we have suggested can greatly reduce the likelihood of recently depressed subjects' reporting an inappropriately high number of stressors to justify their disorder. By employing clearly defined event categories with specific examples, one may prevent subject variance in the interpretation of event definitions and thus in decisions about what counts as an event. In addition, probing in follow-up interviews may greatly facilitate uniformity in event definitions and decision making about whether or not various experiences "count" as instances of event categories.

"Telescoping" events refers to the hypothesis that individuals may report temporally distant events as happening more recently, especially to justify the onset of a disorder (effort after meaning). Similar to the logic applied for the case of effort-after-meaning bias, by using a longitudinal, prospective design, the telescoping bias also will not undermine any etiological inferences about the causal significance of a life event. In addition, by providing subjects with the various aids to accurately dating events described previously, the likelihood of telescoping may be decreased.

In addition to decreasing the likelihood of report biases in assessing life events, it also is important to examine the possibility that mood states, particularly depression, will influence the recall of negative life events (Blaney, 1986). Again, by using prospective assessments of life events, even if subjects' recall of events were influenced by being in a depressed state, no etiological inferences would be undermined. In addition, three aspects of our suggested stress assessment procedures greatly reduce the likelihood of subjects' mood states influencing their recall of events. First, the stress assessment scale and follow-up interviews can employ a "recognition" rather than a "free recall" memory-for-events task. Recognition memory should be less influenced by current mood state than free recall (see Blaney, 1986). Second, the use of clearly defined event categories with specific examples should facilitate accurate reporting of life events despite mood state. Finally, the follow-up interviews should serve as additional prompts for the accurate remembering of events.

Proximal Contributory Causes

GENERAL ISSUES

Recall that the proximal contributory causes of the cognitive theories of depression are the negative personal (Beck's theory) and causal (hopelessness theory) inferences people make when they experience a negative life event. These negative inferences about particular life events are hypothesized to mediate between the cognitive diatheses postulated to act as vulnerability factors in the theories (i.e., the depressogenic attributional style or self-schema) and the development of hopelessness or the negative cognitive triad (the proximal sufficient causes of depression in the theories). Interestingly, very little work has been conducted to date in order to test whether particular personal or causal inferences for negative events mediate the impact of attributional styles or self-schemata on the development of depression, as the cognitive theories predict (but see Kayne *et al.*, 1987 and Metalsky *et al.*, 1987, for exceptions). Perhaps the dearth of research on the role of personal and causal inferences as contributory causes of hopelessness or the negative cognitive triad, and thus of depression (negative cognition depression), may be due, in part, to inadequate conceptualization and assessment strategies for measuring these types of inferences. Thus, in this section, we discuss three issues common to the operationalization and assessment of both personal and causal inferences and then present suggestions for measuring these cognitions.

Pragmatic Inferences. Although both cognitive theories of depression highlight the role of negatively biased, maladaptive inference processes as contributory causes of negative cognition depression, conceptual and methodological advances in cognitive psychology about human inference have not been incorporated in research testing these theories' predictions. Yet, it would seem that contemporary work in cognitive psychology, particularly psycholinguistics, would have much to offer the cognitive theories of depression with respect to sophisticated concepts and powerful strategies for assessing the personal and causal inference processes featured in these theories.

A core postulate of the cognitive theories of depression is that a person's emotional response to a situation is determined by the *meaning* the person assigns to the situation (Hammen, Chapter 3, this volume). According to Beck (1967, 1976), depression-prone individuals derive different and more deviant meanings from situations than do non-depression-prone people because depressives systematically distort the perception and interpretation of information about themselves and their experiences. Although Beck described a number of different types of distortions hypothesized to characterize depressive cognition (e.g., selective abstraction, arbitrary inference), Abramson and Martin (1981) noted that a common theme runs through many of the types. Depression-prone individuals are hypothesized to make negative inferences about themselves, their experiences, and their futures when the current situational information, by itself, seems insufficient to justify such inferences. According to Beck's theory, the mechanism underlying depressives' propensity to make apparently unwarranted negative inferences is the operation of pervasive negative self-schemata about loss, failure, and inadequacy that bias the interpretation of current information. Similarly, according to the hopelessness theory (Abramson *et al.*, 1978, 1987), depression-prone people make maladaptive inferences about the causes of ambiguous negative situations (i.e., internal, stable and global attributions) that are constrained by their generalized depressogenic attributional styles.

Although many studies have examined the *content* of inferences that depressed people were explicitly asked to make in interpreting a situation (e.g., causal attributions—Gong-Guy & Hammen, 1980; Seligman *et al.*, 1979; personal inferences—Hollon & Kendall, 1980; Weissman & Beck, 1979), few adequate tests of the cognitive theories' hypotheses about the depressive inference *process* have been conducted. Fortunately, recent work in psycholinguistics has direct implications for more adequately conceptualizing and, in turn, operationalizing the cognitive theories' hypotheses about the depressive inference process (see Halberstadt, Mukherji, & Abramson, 1986). In the tradition of Bartlett (1932), many contemporary cognitive and social psychologists emphasize that people in general, not just individuals prone to depression or other psychological disorders, often "go beyond the information given" (Bruner, 1957) in comprehending and interpreting that information (Johnson, Bransford, & Solomon, 1973; Owens, *et al.*, 1979). An application of psycholinguistic theory to environmental situations suggests that the meaning of a situation comprises what events actually happen in the situation *and* the sum total of inferences that can be derived from the situation (Harris & Monaco, 1978). A "logical inference" follows as a logical or necessary consequence of the events in a situation (e.g., the inference that one can't use the keys to start the car following from the event of lost car keys). In contrast, a "pragmatic inference" is one that is very plausible, given people's knowledge of the world, but one that does not follow logically (i.e., of necessity) from a situation (e.g., the inference that one will be late for work following from the event of lost car keys). In this view, the meaning of an event is not an invariant; people with different knowledge bases or schemata will make different pragmatic inferences when confronted with the same situational information and thereby derive different meaning from the information (Owens *et al.*, 1979).

The cognitive theories' hypothesis that for depression-prone individuals certain negative personal and causal inferences are highly plausible given the occurrence of particular life events can be translated into the more precise and methodologically well grounded concept of pragmatic inferences (see Halberstadt *et al.*, 1987). Thus, to assess personal and causal inferences hypothesized by the cognitive theories of depression to contribute to hopelessness and the negative cognitive triad, we suggest use of a modification of prototypical methodology from cognitive research on pragmatic inference (Harris & Monaco, 1978; Johnson *et al.*, 1973; Owens *et al.*, 1979). Specifically, on a pragmatic-inference type of task, individuals with negative causal schemata or self-schemata should go beyond the information available in a situation and judge that inference statements that do not follow logically from the occurrence of a particular negative life event they have experienced, but that are consistent with their negative schemata, do follow pragmatically (plausibly) from the occurrence of the event (e.g., "I am flawed in some way" following a failure on an exam). Similarly, individuals with negative cognitive schemata should judge that inference statements inconsistent with their schemata are likely to be false (e.g., "I am not blameworthy" following a failure on an exam).

Depressive Realism versus Distortion. Both cognitive theories of depression hypothesize that negatively biased and maladaptive inferences contribute to the cause of depression (particularly, the negative cognition subtype) through their influence on the development of hopelessness and the negative cognitive triad. In Beck's model, depression-prone people are hypothesized to make inferences about themselves, their worlds, and their futures that are negative in content, that are distorted from reality, and that "go beyond the information given" in particular situations. Moreover, implicit in Beck's theory is the idea that nondepressive persons are rational information processors—who are logical, who draw conclusions that do not go beyond available information, and who do not exhibit systematic distortions in their inferences (but see Beck, 1986, for a recent revision of his views on nondepressive inferences). The hopelessness theory is silent about the degree of distortion in depression-prone people's causal inferences, but it does predict that depressives' causal attributions are negatively biased (e.g., toward internal, stable, and global causes for negative events) by virtue of their generalized attributional styles.

Surprisingly, in recent years a growing body of empirical research has suggested that depressed people's perceptions and inferences in situations relevant to the self are often more accurate or realistic than those of nondepressed people (e.g., Abramson & Alloy, 1981; Alloy, 1982; Alloy & Abramson, 1979, 1982; Alloy, Abramson, & Viscusi, 1981; Alloy & Ahrens, 1987; Alloy, Albright, & Clements, 1987; Golin, Terrell, & Johnson, 1977; Golin, Terrell, Weitz, & Drost, 1979; Lewinsohn *et al.*, 1980; Martin, Abramson, & Alloy, 1984; Nelson & Craighead,

1977; Raps, Reinhard, Peterson, Abramson, & Seligman, 1982; Rozensky, Rehm, Pry, & Roth, 1977; Tabachnik, Crocker, & Alloy, 1983; Wenzlaff & Berman, 1985; see Alloy & Abramson, Chapter 8, this volume, for a review). These studies have documented pervasive self-enhancing biases and optimistic illusions in non-depressives' personal and causal inferences. Moreover, they suggest that an important property of depressives' self-relevant judgments is the relative absence of biases and distortions that would allow depressives to perceive themselves, their worlds, and their futures optimistically.

The work on "depressive realism" (Mischel, 1979) and nondepressive biases and illusions suggests three implications that may bear significantly on the approach adopted for conceptualizing and measuring the personal and causal inferences featured in the cognitive theories of depression. First, individuals who are not vulnerable to depression (specifically, negative cognition depression) by virtue of their positive attributional styles and self-schemata should also go beyond the information available in a situation and make personal and causal inferences about the occurrence of negative life events that are logically unwarranted and biased in a positive direction. Second, depression-prone individuals' personal and causal inferences may be characterized more by the absence of positively biased pragmatic inferences than by the presence of strong negatively biased pragmatic inferences. For both of these reasons, then, it may be important to use an instrument for measuring personal and causal inferences in response to negative life events that allows for the assessment of *degrees of positive bias* as well as degrees of negative bias.

Third, the findings of work on depressive realism and nondepressive distortion emphasize the importance of distinguishing among the concepts of "error" or "distortion," "bias," and "plausibility" in assessing personal and causal inferences (see Abramson & Alloy, 1981, and Alloy & Tabachnik, 1984, for more detailed discussion of some of these concepts and their implications). An "erroneous" or "distorted" inference would consist of a conclusion or judgment that violates some commonly accepted measure of objective reality. Thus, to determine the accuracy of a causal or personal inference for an event, one would need to know the actual cause of the event or the objective implications of the event for the individual. Because a number of the aforementioned studies documenting depressive realism employed tasks in which the reality of the situation was clear (see Alloy & Abramson, Chapter 8, this volume), it was possible to show that depressives' judgments were often more accurate or realistic than those of nondepressives. However, the objective causes or implications of most naturally occurring life events are unknown, and thus the degree of error or distortion in individuals' inferences for such events is likely to be indeterminate.

The concept of "bias" refers to the tendency of an individual to respond in a systematic and consistent fashion across specific times and situations (e.g., to always make internal, stable, and global attributions for negative events across particular occasions and circumstances). Thus an inferential bias will lead to accurate judgments when the objective circumstances happen to match the content of the bias and to erroneous or distorted conclusions when the objective circumstances are at odds with the content of the bias. Inferential biases can differ in both degree (strength) and valence, that is, whether they are positive or negative. The studies of depressive realism suggest that depressives' inferences are often not only more accurate than those of nondepressives but also less optimistically biased. It may be that a systematic tendency to make negative inferences or to fail to make positive inferences consistently across situations and occasions (i.e., bias) contributes more to the development of hopelessness or the negative cognitive triad than does the degree of negativity or distortion of an inference for any particular negative event. Hence we suggest measurement of the degree and the valence (positive or negative) of individuals' biases in making inferences for negative life events.

The "plausibility" of an inference refers to the degree to which an individual is willing to go beyond the information given (Bruner, 1957) and actually make an inference. Individuals may differ not only in the strength and valence of their inferential biases but also in their willingness to jump to conclusions and make any inferences at all about particular life events. Because studies of depressive and nondepressive inference have essentially forced subjects to make inferences (i.e., subjects had no opportunity to refrain from making a judgment), no information is currently available on the relative plausibility of positive and negative inferences to depressive and nondepressive individuals. Thus, in assessing the personal and causal interpretations of particular negative events featured in the cognitive theories, it will be important to measure inference plausibility as well as inferential bias and valence.

Hypothetical versus Real Events. Whereas we have argued that "styles" are more validly assessed with hypothetical events because hypothetical outcomes are less constrained by contextual information, in contrast, real-life events are necessary for adequately assessing the particular attributions and inferences people make for the outcomes they actually encounter. In addition, to address the specific-vulnerability hypothesis of the cognitive theories, namely, that negative life events in the same content area as people's depressogenic causal schemata and self-schemata are more apt to lead to maladaptive causal and personal inferences for the events, we suggest the assessment of people's inferences for negative events in both the achievement and interpersonal domains to go along with the assessment of attributional styles and self-schemata in these two domains.

DEFINITION AND REFORMULATION OF PERSONAL AND CAUSAL INFERENCES

Personal inferences in Beck's theory are defined here as the specific conclusions an individual draws, given the occurrence of particular negative life events. Beck (1967, 1976) discusses the content, types, and formal characteristics of personal inferences hypothesized to contribute to the cause of depression. The disturbance in depression, according to Beck, may be viewed in terms of the activation of a set of three cognitive patterns that cause the individual to view negatively the self, the world, and the future. In addition, a crucial characteristic of depressive inferences is that they are systematically biased against the self. Finally, the formal characteristics of depressive inferences in Beck's model are that they are highly plausible to the individual, they have a perseverative quality about them, and they occur automatically, without the individual's direct awareness or intention (Hartlage, Alloy, & Vazquez, 1987).

Although Beck's (1967, 1976) delineation of the nature of depressive inference is clinically rich and descriptive, it is not precise enough to generate specific measurement strategies. However, as discussed previously, if Beck's ideas about depressive personal inferences are reformulated in the language of cognitive psychology, and psycholinguistics in particular, then one can clarify the conceptualization and operationalization of such inferences. Depressive inferences that are systematically biased against the self may be reformulated as negative pragmatic inferences, in which individuals go beyond the information available in a situation and draw conclusions that are plausible to them, given their self-schemata, but that do not follow logically (of necessity) from the actual events in the situation.

In the hopelessness theory, causal inferences are defined as the particular attributions an individual makes for specific life events along the internal–external, stable–unstable, and global–specific dimensions. The degree of importance individuals attach to specific life events they experience is also hypothesized to be a critical inference in the theory. The attributions people make for specific life events and the degree of importance they attach to these events may also reasonably be viewed as pragmatic causal inferences, which may or may not be negative and/or biased and may or may not go beyond the information available.

SPECIFIC ISSUES IN ASSESSING PERSONAL AND CAUSAL INFERENCES

As discussed previously, we suggest the use of a pragmatic-inference measure for assessing individuals' personal and causal inferences. Several methodological issues are relevant to measuring inferences in this manner.

Content. Because the cognitive theories postulate that personal and causal inferences in particular content areas are critical in the development of depression (the negative cognition subtype), it will be necessary to measure inferences in these content domains. Specifically, to adequately test the hopelessness theory of depression, we must assess causal inferences for events along the internality, stability, and globality dimensions and must measure the degree of importance attached to the events. To test Beck's theory, we need to assess personal inferences that are relevant to the self (e.g., inferred social comparison, self-characteristics, guilt or blameworthiness), the world (e.g., inferred world characteristics, consequences, overshadowing of the positive), and the future (e.g., inferred future consequences, impact on goals).

Format. Three specific issues arise with respect to the format of a pragmatic-inference measure. First, as discussed previously, one needs to assess the nature (positive or negative) of the inference made, the degree of bias associated with the inference, and the readiness or willingness of the individual to make any inference at all for each of the content areas (i.e., internality, stability, globality, importance; self, world, future) deemed important by the cognitive theories of depression. The second issue concerns the types of negative life events for which personal and causal interpretations should be obtained. To test the specific-vulnerability hypothesis of the cognitive theories, it will be necessary to assess people's inferences for negative events they have experienced in both achievement and interpersonal areas. Finally, there is controversy in the literature on depression and life events as to which events are more important contributors to the onset of depressive episodes: events that are most stressful for, or that have the most impact on, individuals, or events that have occurred most recently in individuals' lives (e.g., Monroe, 1982a; Zimmerman, 1983; see the Stress section in this chapter). Because the relative contribution of different types of negative life events for the onset of depression, and for the onset versus maintenance of depression, may differ (e.g., Monroe, 1982c; Monroe, Bellack, Hersen, & Himmelhoch, 1983), we believe it is prudent to assess people's personal and causal inferences for both highly stressful and highly recent negative events. Alloy and Abramson (1986) have recently developed an inference questionnaire, using a pragmatic-inference format, that assesses the nature (positive or negative) of bias, degree of bias, and willingness to go beyond the information available in making inferences for actual negative life events in the causal, self, world, and future content areas.

Proximal Sufficient Causes

Interestingly, investigators of the cognitive theories of depression have given considerably less effort to conceptualizing and assessing the proximal sufficient cause component than to conceptualizing and assessing the cognitive diathesis component (cf. Peterson & Seligman, 1984). Indeed, we know of no work to date that tests whether hopelessness and the negative cognitive triad are, in fact, sufficient causes of depression or whether they mediate the effects of the more distal diathesis and stress components of the theories.

CONCEPTUALIZATION OF THE NEGATIVE COGNITIVE TRIAD

The Expectation of Hopelessness/Negative View of the Future. The phrase "expectation of hopelessness," or "negative view of the future," captures the common language belief that negative outcomes are highly likely to occur and that one is helpless to do anything about it. It is useful to compare this proximal sufficient cause of depression, which is featured in the hopelessness theory (Abramson *et al.*, 1978; 1987) and in Beck's (1967) theory, with that featured in the original learned helplessness theory of depression (Seligman, 1975). According to the original model, a proximal sufficient cause of depression was the expectation that one could not control outcomes, regardless of their hedonic valence or their likelihood of occurrence. In essence, Abramson *et al.* (1978) viewed only a subset of cases of expected lack of control—those involving negative expectations about the occurrence of highly valued or important events—as resulting in depression. This revision makes the hopelessness theory more similar to other cognitive theories of depression (e.g., Beck, 1967; Brown & Harris, 1978; Lichtenberg, 1957; Melges & Bowlby, 1969) than was the original helplessness model.

The Negative View of the Self. Beck's notion of a negative view of the self refers to depression-prone persons' beliefs that they are deficient, inadequate, unworthy, and unlovable. Moreover, depression-prone individuals are hypothesized to believe that they are to blame for all of the hardships and negative outcomes that they experience. In short, the self component of Beck's negative cognitive triad overlaps completely with more traditional notions of low self-esteem as a causal factor in depression (e.g., Bibring, 1953; Freud, 1917/1957).

The Negative View of the World. Beck's idea that a negative view of the world is a sufficient cause of depression is rather novel among depression theories but may have some counterparts in selected portions of other theoretical models. When Beck posits that depression-prone people see the world in a pessimistic fashion, he appears to mean that they believe that their life experiences are characterized by defeat, deprivation, and hardship. The hypothesis that a reduction in, or an absence of, positive reinforcement is a causal factor in depression, characteristic of the behavioral theories (e.g., Eastman, 1976; Lewinsohn, 1974), appears to capture part of Beck's concept of the negative view of the world. Similarly, the original helplessness theory's (Seligman, 1975) view that depression-prone people believe that the world is uncontrollable and that life is filled with unsolvable problems is also consistent with the negative view of the world of Beck's negative cognitive triad.

ISSUES IN ASSESSING HOPELESSNESS AND THE NEGATIVE COGNITIVE TRIAD

As discussed before, an important hypothesis of the cognitive theories of depression is that there needs to be a match between the content of individuals' cognitive styles and the content of the negative life events they confront for the interaction between cognitive diathesis and stress to contribute to the onset of depression. Because the etiological sequences proposed in the cognitive theories suggest that the interaction of cognitive diathesis and stress increases the probability of negative attributions or self-referent inferences (proximal contributory causes), which, in turn, increase the likelihood of hopelessness or the negative cognitive triad (proximal sufficient causes), the logic of these causal chains implies that manifestations of hopelessness or the negative cognitive triad in individuals will also occur in the same content domains as the individuals' cognitive styles and experienced stressors. Consequently, in measuring hopelessness and the negative cognitive triad, one should examine individuals' cognitions in both the achievement and interpersonal areas.

An important distinction between the cognitive diatheses and the proximal sufficient causes specified in the cognitive theories of depression is that attributional styles and self-schemata are expected to be relatively stable characteristics of individuals, whereas negative views of the self, the world, and the future describe cognitions that are more state dependent. Because perceptions of the self, the world, and the future are hypothesized to be influenced both by people's cognitive styles and by current sources of situational information, such perceptions will not necessarily be consistent over time or across situations. Thus, in assessing the proximal sufficient causes of the cognitive theories, it would be important to ensure the measurement of people's *current views* rather than their enduring beliefs. Note that by assessing people's current views at frequent intervals, the duration of these beliefs can be assessed and hence predictions may be made about the duration of an episode of negative cognition depression.

Negative Cognition Depression

As discussed in detail at the beginning of this chapter, the cognitive theories of depression represent a *theory-based* approach to the classification of a subset of the depressive disorders (see also Seligman, 1978) as opposed to the symptom-based approach characteristic of most clinical or empirical studies (Kendell, 1968; Skinner, 1981). Thus, to identify and validate the negative cognition subtype of depression, one must actually test the predictions of the cognitive theories of depression that form the nomological network within which the concept of negative cognition depression is embedded. That is, a complete test of the negative cognition subtype of depression would include an examination of the causal pathways postulated by the cognitive theories to culminate in negative cognition depression as well as the symptom manifestations, course, relationship to other forms of depression, and treatment of this subtype of depression.

ISSUES IN ASSESSMENT

Cause. The cognitive theories of depression postulate not only proximal sufficient and necessary causes of the hypothesized subtype of negative cognition depression but also more distal contributory causes, namely, negative cognitive diatheses, negative life events, and personal and causal interpretations of these negative events. We already have proposed research strategies for testing the causal pathways of the cognitive theories (see section on A Research Strategy for Adequately Testing the Theories) and have described some of the conceptual and methodological issues surrounding the assessment of each component (cognitive diatheses, stress, personal and causal inferences, hopelessness/negative cognitive triad) in these pathways. Thus, by using research designs and assessment methods such as those advocated here, one could adequately test the cognitive theories' hypotheses regarding the etiology of negative cognition depression.

Symptoms. According to the hopelessness theory (Abramson *et al.*, 1987; in press), the negative cognition subtype of depression should be characterized by at least three major symptoms (see Abramson, Alloy, & Metalsky, Chapter 1, this volume, for the logic of these predictions): retarded initiation of voluntary responses (motivational symptom); difficulty in seeing that one's responses control outcomes similar to the outcomes about which one feels hopeless (cognitive symptom); and sad affect (emotional symptom). In addition, when individuals expect that other people can or could attain important outcomes that they feel hopeless to attain themselves (i.e., when individuals make internal attributions for these outcomes), negative cognition depression is predicted to include lowered self-esteem as a fourth symptom. Because Beck's theory (1967, 1976) includes hopelessness as part of the negative cognitive triad, these four symptoms would also be expected to be manifestations of negative cognition depression in Beck's theory. Beck's (1967) theory also suggests that negative cognition depression will include guilt and increased dependency as consequences of the negative view of the self and the world. Although not explicitly postulated by the cognitive theories, the negative cognition subtype of depression may be characterized by other symptoms as well. In particular, researchers have demonstrated that suicidal ideation and behaviors are a consequence of hopelessness (Beck, Kovacs, & Weissman, 1975; Kazdin, French, Unis, Esveldt-Dawson, & Sherick, 1983; Minkoff, Bergman, Beck, & Beck, 1973; Petrie & Chamberlain, 1983). Similarly, lack of energy, apathy, and psychomotor retardation may be concomitants of a severe decrease in the motivation to initiate voluntary responses (see Beck, 1967) and thus may also be symptoms of negative cognition depression. Consequently, in order to test the cognitive theories' hypotheses regarding the symptoms of negative cognition depression, one should assess at least these nine symptoms and determine whether they are predicted by hopelessness and/or the negative cognitive triad.

In conducting these symptom assessments, two major issues are likely to arise. First, some of the symptoms hypothesized to characterize the negative cognition subtype of depression completely overlap with symptoms currently described as characterizing the syndrome of depression in DSM-III (e.g., sad affect, dependency, guilt, suicidal ideation, lack of energy, psychomotor retardation), whereas others only partially overlap with symptoms described as part of the depressive syndrome (e.g., motivational and cognitive deficits). In assessing the first group of symptoms, one could readily use the self-report (e.g., Beck Depression Inventory—BDI—Beck, Ward, Mendelsohn, Mock, & Erbaugh, 1961; Symptom Checklist 90—SCL—Derogatis, 1977) and clinician-rated (Hamilton Rating Scale for Depression—HRSD—Hamilton, 1960; Schedule for Affective Disorders and Schizophrenia—SADS—Endicott & Spitzer, 1978) instruments that are currently available for rating the presence and severity of depressive symptoms. (Of course, to ensure the reliability and validity of these symptom assessments, it may be advisable to employ multiple converging measures of depressive symptoms.) However, because no instruments are currently available for measuring the core motivational and cognitive symptoms specifically postulated by the cognitive theories, it will be necessary to create new instruments or tasks for assessing these symptoms.

A second concern in adequately testing the symptom predictions of the cognitive theories is the need to avoid tautology. As discussed by Abramson, Alloy, and Metalsky (Chapter 1, this volume), in the past, many investigators have tested the cognitive theories of depression by examining whether particular kinds of negative cognitions predict symptoms of depression that include negative cognitions. It is important to recognize, however, that although hopelessness and negative perceptions of the self and the world have been traditionally viewed as symptoms of depression, the cognitive theories of depression remove these constructs from the symptom category and give them *causal status*. Thus, to test the symptom predictions of the cognitive theories adequately, one must determine whether hopelessness and negative views of the self and the world predict and temporally precede the hypothesized symptoms of negative cognition depression that do *not* include negative self, world, and future perceptions as part of these symptoms.

Relationship to Other Categories of Depression. As discussed previously (see section on A Research Strategy for Adequately Testing the Theories), an important component of an adequate test of the cognitive theories of depression is a determination of the place of negative cognition depression in the psychiatric nosology. That is, does negative cognition depression map onto or cut across nosological distinctions currently made within the depressive disorders, and does it include people who currently would receive diagnoses of other disorders (e.g., anxiety disorders)? In addressing this issue, one must assess numerous currently diagnosed subcategories of depression as well as other psychiatric disorders in order to examine the degree to which they overlap with the hypothesized subtype of negative cognition depression. Useful in this regard may be structured diagnostic interviews and diagnostic criteria that allow for the delineation of subtypes of affective and other disorders; an example of such a measure is the SADS (Endicott & Spitzer, 1978), with its accompanying Research Diagnostic Criteria (RDC; Spitzer, Endicott, & Robins, 1978).

Course: Maintenance, Relapse, and Recurrence. In considering the course of a disorder, we may distinguish among the concepts of maintenance, relapse, and recurrence. "Maintenance" refers to the duration of a given episode of a disorder, whereas "relapse" is a return of clinically significant symptoms within a relatively short period following remission from an acute episode, and "recurrence" is the onset of a new episode following a prolonged interval of remission from the index episode (Klerman, 1978). Because hopelessness and the negative cognitive triad are hypothesized to be proximal causes of negative cognition depression, the maintenance, or duration, of any given episode of negative cognition depression should be influenced by how long these beliefs are held by an individual. Similarly, the likelihood of a relapse or a recurrence of negative cognition depression, and the time from remission to relapse or recurrence, should also be predicted by the reappearance of hopelessness and/or the negative cognitive triad, because, by definition, a relapse or a recurrence is an exacerbation or a new onset of negative cognition depression. The occurrence and chronicity of hopelessness and negative views of the self and the world, in turn, are predicted by the cognitive theories to be modulated by the content (e.g., stable vs. unstable attribution) and duration of individuals' causal and personal interpretations of the negative life events they experience, both the original triggering events and newly occurring events (see Abramson, Alloy, & Metalsky, Chapter 1, this volume, for a detailed discussion of the cognitive models' predictions regarding the course of negative cognition depression).

Consequently, an adequate test of the predictions of the cognitive theories with respect to the course of negative cognition depression would involve two components. First, one must derive explicit, operational criteria for defining remission from an index episode of depression (in order to determine the episode's length) as well as relapses and recurrences. Such definitions should include criteria for the levels of symptom severity that must be present over specified time intervals. Second, one would need to assess carefully (1) the occurrence and duration of hopelessness and/or the negative cognitive triad, (2) the content of personal and causal inferences for the negative life events that "triggered" an index episode, (3) the duration of these inferences, (4) the content of personal and causal inferences for newly occurring negative life events, and (5) the duration of the inferences for the newly occurring events. Because we have already described issues and proposed methods for assessing the content and nature of people's personal and causal inferences for events and their views about the self, the world, and the future, the major methodological issue requiring elaboration here is a strategy for measuring the duration of inferences and of hopelessness and/or the negative cognitive triad. In brief, we suggest avoiding the use of largely retrospective measurements, with their attendant memory failures and report biases (see the Stress section for a discussion of these biases), and instead recommend *frequent prospective* assessments of these constructs (i.e., on a weekly basis), using measurement procedures similar to those discussed in this chapter.

CONCLUSION

Our goal in this chapter was to provide a brief outline of a research strategy for more adequately testing the cognitive theories of depression. In addition, we presented a proposed conceptualization of each component in the theories, a set of suggested assessment strategies for translating the conceptualizations into measured variables, and a discussion of methodological issues important to the development of the assessment strategies. The identification and validation of the negative cognition subtype of depression postulated by the cognitive theories is a tough problem, and it raises some of the most challenging questions facing any psychopathologist. For example: What is a meaningful psychopathological entity? How can one most meaningfully subdivide a heterogeneous disorder into its constituent subtypes? (cf. Meehl & Golden, 1982). How can one distinguish between a heterogeneous disorder with multiple etiologic subtypes and a disorder with multiple contributory causes that influence a final common pathway? We do not have the final answers to these questions, but we hope the issues and research strategies included here serve to point us in the right direction with respect to the subdivision of the depressive disorders.

ACKNOWLEDGMENT

Preparation of this chapter was supported by a grant from the John D. and Catherine T. MacArthur Foundation to Lauren B. Alloy and Lyn Y. Abramson.

REFERENCES

Abelson, R. P. (1975). Concepts for representing mundane reality in plans. In D. G. Bobrow & A. Collins (Eds.), *Representation and understanding: Studies in cognitive science* (pp. 273–309). New York: Academic Press.

Abramson, L. Y., & Alloy, L. B. (1981). Depression, nondepression, and cognitive illusions: A reply to Schwartz. *Journal of Experimental Psychology: General, 110,* 436–447.

Abramson, L. Y., & Martin, D. (1981). Depression and the causal inference process. In J. Harvey, W. Ickes, & R. Kidd (Eds.), *New directions in attribution research* (pp. 117–168). Hillsdale, NJ: Erlbaum.

Abramson, L. Y., Metalsky, G. I., & Alloy, L. B. (1987). *The hopelessness theory of depression: A metatheoretical analysis with implications for psychopathology research.* Manuscript submitted for publication.

Abramson, L. Y., Metalsky, G. I., & Alloy, L. B. (in press). The hopelessness theory of depression: Does the research test the theory? In L. Y. Abramson (Ed.), *Social cognition and clinical psychology: A synthesis.* New York: Guilford Press.

Abramson, L. Y., Seligman, M. E. P., & Teasdale, J. (1978). Learned helplessness in humans: Critique and reformulation. *Journal of Abnormal Psychology, 87,* 49–74.

Akiskal, H. S. (1983). Dysthymic disorder: Psychopathology of proposed chronic depressive subtypes. *American Journal of Psychiatry, 140,* 11–20.

Alloy, L. B. (1982). The role of perceptions and attributions for response–outcome noncontingency in learned helplessness: A commentary and discussion. *Journal of Personality, 50,* 443–479.

Alloy, L. B., & Abramson, L. Y. (1979). Judgment of contingency in depressed and nondepressed students: Sadder but wiser? *Journal of Experimental Psychology: General, 108,* 441–485.

Alloy, L. B., & Abramson, L. Y. (1982). Learned helplessness, depression and the illusion of control. *Journal of Personality and Social Psychology, 42,* 1114–1126.

Alloy, L. B., & Abramson, L. Y. (1986). *Negative cognition depression: Prospective/longitudinal validation of a theory-based subtype of depression.* Unpublished manuscript.

Alloy, L. B., Abramson, L. Y., & Viscusi, D. (1981). Induced mood and the illusion of control. *Journal of Personality and Social Psychology, 41,* 1129–1140.

Alloy, L. B., & Ahrens, A. H. (1987). Depression and pessimism for the future: Biased use of statistically relevant information in predictions for self versus others. *Journal of Personality and Social Psychology, 52,* 366–378.

Alloy, L. B., Albright, J. S., & Clements, C. M. (1987). Depression, nondepression, and social comparison biases. In J. E. Maddux, C. D. Stoltenberg, & R. Rosenwein (Eds.), *Social processes in clinical and counseling psychology* (pp. 94–112). New York: Springer-Verlag.

Alloy, L. B., Clements, C., & Kolden, G. (1985). The cognitive diathesis–stress theories of depression: Therapeutic implications. In S. Reiss & R. Bootzin (Eds.), *Theoretical issues in behavior therapy* (pp. 379–410). New York: Academic Press.

Alloy, L. B., & Tabachnik, N. (1984). Assessment of covariation by humans and animals: The joint influence of prior expectations and current situational information. *Psychological Review, 91,* 112–149.

Bartlett, F. C. (1932). *Remembering.* Cambridge, England: Cambridge University Press.

Beck, A. T. (1967). *Depression: Clinical, experimental, and theoretical aspects.* New York: Harper & Row.

Beck, A. T. (1976). *Cognitive therapy and the emotional disorders.* New York: International Universities Press.

Beck, A. T. (1986). Cognitive therapy, behavior therapy, psychoanalysis, and pharmacotherapy: The cognitive continuum. In J. B. W. William & R. L. Spitzer (Eds.), *Psychotherapy research: Where are we and where should we go?* (pp. 114–134). New York: Guilford Press.

Beck, A. T., Kovacs, M., & Weissman, A. (1975). Hopelessness and suicidal behavior: An overview. *Journal of the American Medical Association, 234,* 1146–1149.

Beck, A. T., Ward, C. H., Mendelsohn, M., Mock, J., & Erbaugh, J. (1961). An inventory for measuring depression. *Archives of General Psychiatry, 4,* 53–63.

Bibring, E. (1953). The mechanism of depression. In P. Greenacre (Ed.), *Affective disorders: Psychoanalytic contributions to their study* (pp. 13–48). New York: International Universities Press.

Blaney, P. H. (1986). Affect and memory: A review. *Psychological Bulletin, 99*, 229–246.

Bobrow, D. G., & Norman, D. A. (1975). Some principles of memory schemata. In D. G. Bobrow & A. Collins (Eds.), *Representation and understanding: Studies in cognitive science* (pp. 131–149). New York: Academic Press.

Bower, G. H., Black, J. B., & Turner, T. J. (1979). Scripts in memory for text. *Cognitive Psychology, 11*, 177–220.

Boyd, J. H., & Weissman, M. M. (1982). Epidemiology. In E. S. Paykel (Ed.), *Handbook of affective disorders* (pp. 109–125). New York: Guilford Press.

Bransford, J. D., & McCarrell, N. S. (1975). A sketch of a cognitive approach to comprehension: Some thoughts about what it means to comprehend. In W. B. Weimer & D. S. Palermo (Eds.), *Cognition and symbolic processes*. Hillsdale, NJ: Erlbaum.

Brown, G. W. (1972). Life-events and psychiatric illness: Some thoughts on methodology and causality. *Journal of Psychosomatic Research, 16*, 311–320.

Brown, G. W. (1974). Meaning, measurement, and stress of life events. In B. S. Dohrenwend & B. P. Dohrenwend (Eds.), *Stressful life events: Their nature and effects* (pp. 217–243). New York: Wiley.

Brown, G. W., & Harris, T. (1978). *Social origins of depression*. New York: Free Press.

Brown, G. W., Sklair, F., Harris, T. O., & Birley, J. L. T. (1973). LIfe events and psychiatric disorders. Part 1: Some methodological issues. *Psychological Medicine, 3*, 74–87.

Brown, J. (Ed.) (1976). *Recall and recognition*. New York: Wiley.

Bruner, J. S. (1957). Going beyond the information given. In *Contemporary approaches to cognition* (pp. 41–69). Cambridge, MA: Harvard University Press.

Cantor, N., & Mischel, W. (1977). Traits as prototypes: Effects on recognition memory. *Journal of Personality and Social Psychology, 35*, 38–48.

Coates, D., & Wortman, C. B. (1980). Depression maintenance and interpersonal control. In A. Baum & J. Singer (Eds.), *Advances in environmental psychology* (Vol. 2, pp. 149–182). Hillsdale, NJ: Erlbaum.

Cochran, S. D., & Hammen, C. L. (1985). Perceptions of stressful life events and depression: A test of attributional models. *Journal of Personality and Social Psychology, 48*, 1562–1571.

Coryell, W., & Winokur, G. (1982). Course and outcome. In E. S. Paykel (Ed.), *Handbook of affective disorders* (pp. 93–106). New York: Guilford Press.

Coyne, J. C. (1976a). Toward an interactional description of depression. *Psychiatry, 39*, 28–40.

Coyne, J. C. (1976b). Depression and the response of others. *Journal of Abnormal Psychology, 85*, 186–193.

Coyne, J. C., & Gotlib, I. H. (1983). The role of cognition in depression: A critical appraisal. *Psychological Bulletin, 94*, 472–505.

Craighead, W. E. (1980). Away from a unitary model of depression. *Behavior Therapy, 11*, 122–128.

Cutrona, C. E. (1983). Causal attributions and perinatal depression. *Journal of Abnormal Psychology, 92*, 161–172.

Davis, H. (1979a). Self-reference and the encoding of personal information in depression. *Cognitive Therapy and Research, 3*, 97–110.

Davis, H. (1979b). The self-schema and subjective organization of personal information in depression. *Cognitive Therapy and Research, 3*, 415–425.

Davis, H., & Unruh, W. R. (1981). The development of self-schema in adult depression. *Journal of Abnormal Psychology, 90*, 125–133.

Depue, R. A., & Kleiman, R. M. (1979). Free cortisol as a peripheral index of central vulnerability to major forms of polar depressive disorders: Examining stress–biology interactions in subsyndromal high-risk persons. In R. A. Depue (Ed.), *The psychobiology of the depressive disorders: Implications for the effects of stress* (pp. 177–204). New York: Academic Press.

Depue, R. A., & Monroe, S. M. (1978). Learned helplessness in the perspective of the depressive disorders. *Journal of Abnormal Psychology, 87*, 3–20.

Depue, R. A., & Monroe, S. M. (1983). Psychopathology research. In M. Hersen, A. E. Kazdin, & A. S. Bellack (Eds.), *The clinical psychology handbook* (pp. 239–264). New York: Pergamon Press.

Depue, R. A., Slater, J., Wolfstetter-Kausch, H., Klein, D., Goplerud, E., & Farr, D. (1981). A behavioral paradigm for identifying persons at risk for bipolar depressive disorder: A conceptual framework and five validation studies. *Journal of Abnormal Psychology, 90*, 381–438.

Derogatis, L. R. (1977). *SCL-90-R: Administration, scoring, and procedure manual 1*. Baltimore, MD: Clinical Psychometrics Research.

Derry, P. A., & Kuiper, N. A. (1981). Schematic processing and self-reference in clinical depression. *Journal of Abnormal Psychology, 90*, 286–297.

Dohrenwend, B. S., & Dohrenwend, B. P. (1978). Some issues in research on stressful life events. *The Journal of Nervous and Mental Disease, 166*, 7–15.

Duncan-Jones, P. (1981). The natural history of neurosis: Probability models. In J. K. Wing, P. Bebbington, & L. N. Robins (Eds.), *What is a case? The problem of definition in psychiatric community surveys*. London: Grant McIntyre.

Eastman, C. (1976). Behavioral formulations of depression. *Psychological Review, 83*, 277–291.

Eaves, G., & Rush, A. J. (1984). Cognitive patterns in symptomatic and remitted unipolar major depression. *Journal of Abnormal Psychology, 93*, 31–40.

Elig, T. W., & Frieze, I. H. (1979). Measuring causal attributions for success and failure. *Journal of Personality and Social Psychology, 37*, 621–634.

Endicott, J., & Spitzer, R. L. (1978). A diagnostic interview: The Schedule for Affective Disorders and Schizophrenia. *Archives of General Psychiatry, 35*, 837–844.

Folkman, S. (1984). Personal control and stress and coping processes: A theoretical analysis. *Journal of Personality and Social Psychology, 46*, 839–852.

Freud, S. (1957). Mourning and melancholia. In J. Strachey (Ed. and Trans.), *The standard edition of the complete psychological works of Sigmund Freud* (Vol. 14, pp. 239–258). London: Hogarth Press. (Original work published 1917)

Geller, V., & Shaver, P. (1976). The cognitive consequences of self-awareness. *Journal of Experimental Social Psychology, 12*, 438–445.

Gershon, E. S. (1978). The search for genetic markers in affective disorders. In M. A. Lipton, A. DiMascio, & K. F. Killam (Eds.), *Psychopharmacology: A generation of progress* (pp. 1197–1212). New York: Raven Press.

Gillespie, R. D. (1929). Clinical differentiation of types of depression. *Guy Hospital Reports, 79*, 306–344.

Golin, S., Terrell, F., & Johnson, B. (1977). Depression and the illusion of control. *Journal of Abnormal Psychology, 86*, 440–442.

Golin, S., Terrell, F., Weitz, J., & Drost, P. L. (1979). The illusion of control among depressed patients. *Journal of Abnormal Psychology, 88*, 454–457.

Gong-Guy, E., & Hammen, C. (1980). Causal perceptions of stressful life events in depressed and nondepressed clinic outpatients. *Journal of Abnormal Psychology, 89*, 662–669.

Gotlib, I. H., & Robinson, L. A. (1982). Responses to depressed individuals: Discrepancies between self-report and observer-rated behavior. *Journal of Abnormal Psychology, 91*, 231–240.

Greenberg, M. S., & Alloy, L. B. (1987). *Depression versus anxiety: Schematic processing of self- and other-referent information*. Manuscript submitted for publication.

Halberstadt, L. J., Andrews, D., Metalsky, G. I., & Abramson, L. Y. (1984). Helplessness, hopelessness, and depression: A review of progress and future directions. In N. S. Endler & J. Hunt (Eds.), *Personality and behavior disorders* (Vol. 1, pp. 373–411). New York: Wiley.

Halberstadt, L. J., Mukherji, B. R., & Abramson, L. Y. (1987). *Cognitive styles among college students: Toward an integration of the cognitive theories of depression with cognitive psychology and descriptive psychiatry*. Manuscript submitted for publication.

Hamilton, E. W., & Abramson, L. Y. (1983). Cognitive patterns in major depressive disorder: A longitudinal study in a hospital setting. *Journal of Abnormal Psychology, 92*, 173–184.

Hamilton, M. (1960). A rating scale for depression. *Journal of Neurology, Neurosurgery, and Psychiatry, 23*, 56–61.

Hammen, C., & Cochran, S. (1981). Cognitive correlates of life stress and depression in college students. *Journal of Abnormal Psychology, 90,* 23–27.

Hammen, C., Marks, T., de Mayo, R., & Mayol, A. (1985). Self-schemas and risk for depression: A prospective study. *Journal of Personality and Social Psychology, 49,* 1147–1159.

Hammen, C., Marks, T., Mayol, A., & de Mayo, R. (1985). Depressive self-schemas, life stress, and vulnerability to depression. *Journal of Abnormal Psychology, 94,* 308–319.

Harris, R. J., & Monaco, G. E. (1978). Psychology of pragmatic implication: Information processing between the lines. *Journal of Experimental Psychology: General, 107,* 1–22.

Hartlage, S., Alloy, L. B., & Vazquez, C. V. (1987). *Automatic and effortful processing in depression.* Manuscript submitted for publication.

Harvey, D. (1981). Depression and attributional style: Interpretations of important personal events. *Journal of Abnormal Psychology, 90,* 134–142.

Hastie, R. (1980). Schematic principles in human memory. In E. T. Higgins, C. P. Herman, & M. P. Zanna (Eds.), *Social cognition: The Ontario Symposium* (Vol. 1, pp. 39–88). Hillsdale, NJ: Erlbaum.

Hollon, S. D., & Kendall, P. C. (1980). Cognitive self-statements in depression: Development of an automatic thoughts questionnaire. *Cognitive Therapy and Research, 4,* 383–395.

Holmes, T. H., & Rahe, R. H. (1967). The Social Readjustment Rating Scale. *Journal of Psychosomatic Research, 11,* 213–218.

Howes, M. J., & Hokanson, J. E. (1979). Conversational and social responses to depressive interpersonal behavior. *Journal of Abnormal Psychology, 88,* 625–634.

Ickes, W., & Layden, M. A. (1978). Attributional styles. In J. Harvey, W. Ickes, & R. Kidd (Eds.), *New directions in attribution research* (Vol. 2, pp. 119–152). Hillsdale, NJ: Erlbaum.

Ingram, R. E., Smith, T. W., & Brehm, S. S. (1983). Depression and information processing: Self-schemata and the encoding of self-referent information. *Journal of Personality and Social Psychology, 45,* 412–420.

Isen, A. M., Shalker, T. E., Clark, M., & Karp, L. (1978). Affect, accessibility of material in memory, and behavior: A cognitive loop? *Journal of Personality and Social Psychology, 36,* 1–12.

Jenkins, C. D., Hurst, M. W., & Rose, R. M. (1979). Life changes: Do people really remember? *Archives of General Psychiatry, 36,* 379–384.

Johnson, M. K., Bransford, J. D., & Solomon, S. K. (1973). Memory for tacit implications of sentences. *Journal of Experimental Psychology, 98,* 203–225.

Kanner, A. D., Coyne, J. C., Schaefer, C., & Lazarus, R. S. (1981). Comparison of two modes of stress measurement: Daily hassles and uplifts versus major life events. *Journal of Behavioral Medicine, 4,* 1–39.

Kayne, N. T., Alloy, L. B., Romer, D., & Crocker, J. (1987). *Predicting depressive reactions in the classroom: A test of an attributional diathesis–stress theory of depression.* Manuscript submitted for publication.

Kazdin, A. E., French, N. H., Unis, A. S., Esveldt-Dawson, K., & Sherick, R. B. (1983). Hopelessness, depression, and suicidal intent among psychiatrically disturbed inpatient children. *Journal of Consulting and Clinical Psychology, 51,* 504–510.

Keller, M. B., & Lavori, P. W. (1984). Double depression, major depression, and dysthymia: Distinct entities or different phases of a single disorder? *Psychopharmacology Bulletin, 20,* 399–402.

Keller, M. B., & Shapiro, R. W. (1982). "Double depression." Superimposition of acute depressive episodes on chronic depressive disorders. *American Journal of Psychiatry, 139,* 438–442.

Kelley, H. H. (1967). Attribution theory in social psychology. In D. Levine (Ed.), *Nebraska Symposium on Motivation* (Vol. 15, pp. 192–238). Lincoln: University of Nebraska Press.

Kendell, R. E. (1968). *The classification of depression illness.* London: Oxford University Press.

Kihlstrom, J. F., & Nasby, W. (1981). Cognitive tasks in clinical assessment: An exercise in applied psychology. In P. C. Kendall & S. D. Hollon (Eds.), *Assessment, strategies for cognitive–behavioral interventions* (pp. 287–317). New York: Academic Press.

Klerman, G. L. (1978). The evolution of a scientific nosology. In J. C. Shershow (Ed.), *Schizophrenia: Science and practice* (pp. 99–121). Cambridge, MA: Harvard University Press.

Klinger, E. (1975). Consequences of commitment to and disengagement from incentives. *Psychological Review, 82*, 1–25.

Klinger, E., Barta, S. G., & Maxeiner, M. E. (1981). Current concerns: Assessing therapeutically relevant motivation. In P. C. Kendall & S. D. Hollon (Eds.), *Assessment strategies for cognitive–behavioral interventions* (pp. 161–196). New York: Academic Press.

Kuiper, N. A., & Derry, P. A. (1980). The self as a cognitive prototype: An application to person perception and depression. In N. Cantor & J. F. Kihlstrom (Eds.), *Personality, cognition, and social interaction* (pp. 215–232). Hillsdale, NJ: Erlbaum.

Kuiper, N. A., & Derry, P. (1982). Depressed and nondepressed content self-reference in mild depressives. *Journal of Personality, 50*, 67–79.

Kuiper, N. A., & MacDonald, M. R. (1982). Self and other perception in mild depressives. *Social Cognition, 1*, 223–229.

Lazarus, R. S. (1966). *Psychological stress and the coping process*. New York: McGraw-Hill.

Lei, H., & Skinner, H. (1980). A psychometric study of life events and social readjustment. *Journal of Psychosomatic Research, 24*, 57–65.

Lewinsohn, P. M. (1974). A behavioral approach to depression. In R. J. Friedman & M. M. Katz (Eds.), *The psychology of depression: Contemporary theory and research* (pp. 157–186). Washington, DC: Winston-Wiley.

Lewinsohn, P. M., Mischel, W., Chaplain, W., & Barton, R. (1980). Social competence and depression: The role of illusory self perceptions? *Journal of Abnormal Psychology, 89*, 203–212.

Lewisohn, P. M., Steinmetz, J. L., Larson, D. W., & Franklin, J. (1981). Depression-related cognitions: Antecedent or consequence? *Journal of Abnormal Psychology, 90*, 213–219.

Lichtenberg, P. (1957). A definition and analysis of depression. *Archives of Neurology and Psychiatry, 77*, 516–527.

Lloyd, C. (1980). Life events and depressive disorder reviewed: 2. Events as precipitating factors. *Archives of General Psychiatry, 37*, 542–548.

Markus, H. (1977). Self-schemata and processing information about the self. *Journal of Personality and Social Psychology, 35*, 63–78.

Martin, D. J., Abramson, L. Y., & Alloy, L. B. (1984). Illusion of control for self and others in depressed and nondepressed college students. *Journal of Personality and Social Psychology, 46*, 125–136.

Meehl, P. E., & Golden, R. R. (1982). Taxometric methods. In P. C. Kendall & J. N. Butcher (Eds.), *Handbook of research methods in clinical psychology* (pp. 127–181). New York: Wiley.

Melges, F. J., & Bowlby, J. (1969). Types of hopelessness in psychopathological process. *Archives of General Psychiatry, 20*, 690–699.

Metalsky, G. I., & Abramson, L. Y. (1981). Attributional styles: Toward a framework for conceptualization and assessment. In P. C. Kendall & S. D. Hollon (Eds.), *Cognitive behavioral interventions: Assessment methods* (pp. 13–58). New York: Academic Press.

Metalsky, G. I., Abramson, L. Y., Seligman, M. E. P., Semmel, A., & Peterson, C. (1982). Attributional styles and life events in the classroom: Vulnerability and invulnerability to depressive mood reactions. *Journal of Personality and Social Psychology, 43*, 612–617.

Metalsky, G. I., Halberstadt, L. J., & Abramson, L. Y. (1987). Vulnerability to depressive mood reactions: Toward a more powerful test of the diathesis–stress and causal mediation components of the reformulated theory of depression. *Journal of Personality and Social Psychology, 52*, 386–393.

Miller, I. W., Klee, S. H., & Norman, W. H. (1982). Depressed and nondepressed inpatients' cognitions of hypothetical events, experimental tasks, and stressful life events. *Journal of Abnormal Psychology, 91*, 78–81.

Minkoff, K., Bergman, E., Beck, A. T., & Beck, R. (1973). Hopelessness, depression and attempted suicide. *American Journal of Psychiatry, 130*, 455–459.

Minsky, M. (1975). A framework for representing knowledge. In P. H. Winston (Ed.), *The psychology of computer vision*. New York: McGraw-Hill.

Mischel, W. (1979). On the interface of cognition and personality: Beyond the person–situation debate. *American Psychologist, 34*, 740–754.

Monroe, S. M. (1982a). Assessment of life events: Retrospective versus concurrent strategies. *Archives of General Psychiatry, 39,* 606–610.

Monroe, S. M. (1982b). Life events and disorder: Event–symptom associations and the course of disorder. *Journal of Abnormal Psychology, 91,* 14–24.

Monroe, S. M. (1982c). Life events assessment: Current practices, emerging trends. *Clinical Psychology Review, 2,* 435–452.

Monroe, S. M. (1983a). Major and minor life events as predictors of disorder: Further issues and findings. *Journal of Behavioral Medicine, 6,* 189–205.

Monroe, S. M. (1983b). Social support and disorder: Toward an untangling of cause and effect. *American Journal of Community Psychology, 11,* 81–97.

Monroe, S. M., Bellack, A. S., Hersen, M., & Himmelhoch, J. M. (1983). Life events, symptom course, and treatment outcome in unipolar depressed women. *Journal of Consulting and Clinical Psychology, 51,* 604–615.

Monroe, S. M., Imhoff, D., Wise, B. D., & Harris, J. E. (1983). Prediction of psychological symptoms under high-risk psychosocial circumstances: Life events, social support, and symptom specificity. *Journal of Abnormal Psychology, 92,* 338–350.

Moore, B. S., Sherrod, D. R., Liu, T. J., & Underwood, B. (1979). The dispositional shift in attribution over time. *Journal of Experimental Social Psychology, 15,* 553–569.

Neisser, U. (1967). *Cognitive psychology.* New York: Appleton-Century-Crofts.

Nelson, R. E., & Craighead, W. E. (1977). Selective recall of positive and negative feedback, self-control behaviors, and depression. *Journal of Abnormal Psychology, 86,* 379–388.

Neugebauer, R. (1981). The reliability of life-event reports. In B. S. Dohrenwend & B. P. Dohrenwend (Eds.), *Stressful life events and their contexts.* New York: Prodist.

O'Hara, M. W., Neunaber, D. J., & Zekoski, E. M. (1984). Prospective study of postpartum depression: Prevalence, course, and predictive factors. *Journal of Abnormal Psychology, 93,* 158–171.

O'Hara, M. W., Rehm, L. P., & Campbell, S. B. (1982). Predicting depressive symptomatology: Cognitive–behavioral models and postpartum depression. *Journal of Abnormal Psychology, 91,* 457–461.

Owens, J., Bower, G., & Black, J. (1979). The "soap opera" effect in story recall. *Memory and Cognition, 7,* 185–191.

Paykel, E. S. (1979). Recent life events in the development of the depressive disorders. In R. A. Depue (Ed.), *The psychobiology of the depressive disorders: Implications for the effects of stress* (pp. 245–262). New York: Academic Press.

Paykel, E. S., Myers, J. K., Dienelt, M. N., Klerman, G. L., Lindenthal, J. J., & Pepper, M. P. (1969). Life events and depression: A controlled study. *Archives of General Psychiatry, 21,* 753–760.

Persons, J. B., & Rao, P. A. (1985). Longitudinal study of cognitions, life events, and depression in psychiatric inpatients. *Journal of Abnormal Psychology, 94,* 51–63.

Peterson, C., & Seligman, M. E. P. (1984). Causal explanations as a risk factor for depression: Theory and evidence. *Psychological Review, 91,* 347–374.

Petrie, K., & Chamberlain, K. (1983). Hopelessness and social desirability as moderator variables in predicting suicidal behavior. *Journal of Consulting and Clinical Psychology, 51,* 485–487.

Pittman, T. S., & Pittman, N. L. (1980). Deprivation of control and the attribution process. *Journal of Personality and Social Psychology, 39,* 377–389.

Pryor, J. B., & Kriss, M. (1977). The cognitive dynamics of salience in the attribution process. *Journal of Personality and Social Psychology, 35,* 49–55.

Pyszczynski, T. A., & Greenberg, J. (1981). Role of disconfirmed expectancies in the instigation of attributional processing. *Journal of Personality and Social Psychology, 40,* 31–38.

Raps, C. S., Reinhard, K. E., Peterson, C., Abramson, L. Y., & Seligman, M. E. P. (1982). Attributional style among depressed patients. *Journal of Abnormal Psychology, 91,* 102–108.

Riskind, J. H., & Rholes, W. S. (1984). Cognitive accessibility and the capacity of cognitions to predict future depression: A theoretical note. *Cognitive Therapy and Research, 8,* 1–12.

Rogers, T. B. (1981). A model of the self as an aspect of the human information processing system. In

N. Cantor & J. F. Kihlstrom (Eds.), *Personality, cognition, and social interaction* (pp. 193–214). Hillsdale, NJ: Erlbaum.

Rogers, T. B., Kuiper, N., & Kirker, W. (1977). Self-reference and the encoding of personal information. *Journal of Personality and Social Psychology, 35,* 677–688.

Rosch, E. (1975). Cognitive representation of semantic categories. *Journal of Experimental Psychology: General, 104,* 192–233.

Ross, L. (1977). The intuitive psychologist and his shortcomings. In L. Berkowitz (Ed.), *Advances in experimental social psychology* (Vol. 10, pp. 173–220). New York: Academic Press.

Rotter, J. B. (1966). Generalized expectancies for internal versus external control of reinforccement. *Psychological Monographs, 80* (1, Whole No. 609).

Rozensky, R. H., Rehm, L. P., Pry, G. G., & Roth, D. (1977). Depression and self-reinforcement behavior in hospitalized patients. *Journal of Behavior Therapy and Experimental Psychiatry, 8,* 35–38.

Sarason, I. G., de Monchaux, C., & Hunt, T. (1975). Methodological issues in the assessment of life stress. In L. Levi (Ed.), *Emotions—Their parameters and measurement* (pp. 499–509). New York: Raven Press.

Seligman, M. E. P. (1975). *Helplessness: On depression, development, and death.* San Francisco: W. H. Freeman.

Seligman, M. E. P. (1978). Comment and integration. *Journal of Abnormal Psychology, 87,* 165–179.

Seligman, M. E. P., Abramson, L. Y., Semmel, A., & von Baeyer, C. (1979). Depressive attributional style. *Journal of Abnormal Psychology, 88,* 242–247.

Siegel, S. J., & Alloy, L. B. (1987). *Interpersonal perceptions and consequences of depressive–significant other interactions: A naturalistic study of college roommates.* Manuscript submitted for publication.

Skinner, H. A. (1981). Toward the integration of classification theory and methods. *Journal of Abnormal Psychology, 90,* 68–87.

Spitzer, R. L., Endicott, J., & Robins, E. (1978). Research diagnostic criteria: Rationale and reliability. *Archives of General Psychiatry, 35,* 773–782.

Tabachnik, N., Crocker, J., & Alloy, L. B. (1983). Depression, social comparison, and the false-consensus effect. *Journal of Personality and Social Psychology, 45,* 688–699.

Taylor, S., & Crocker, J. (1980). Schematic bases of social information processing. In E. T. Higgens, P. Herman, & M. P. Zanna (Eds.), *Social cognition: The Ontario Symposium on Personality and Social Psychology* (Vol. 1, pp. 87–134). Hillsdale, NJ: Erlbaum.

Tennant, C., Bebbington, P., & Hurry, J. (1981). The role of life events in depressive illness: Is there a substantial causal relation? *Psychological Medicine, 11,* 379–389.

Vazquez, C. V., & Alloy, L. B. (1987). *Schematic memory processes for self- and other-referent information in depression versus anxiety: A signal detection analysis.* Unpublished manuscript, Northwestern University, Evanston, IL.

Weiner, B. (1974). *Achievement motivation and attribution theory.* Morristown, NJ: General Learning Press.

Weintraub, M., Segal, R. M., & Beck, A. T. (1974). An investigation of cognition and affect in the depressive experiences of normal men. *Journal of Consulting and Clinical Psychology, 42,* 911.

Weissman, A., & Beck, A. T. (1979, August). *The dysfunctional attitude scale.* Paper presented at the meeting of the American Psychological Association, New York.

Weissman, M. M., & Paykel, E. S. (1974). *The depressed woman: A study of social relationships.* Chicago: University of Chicago Press.

Wenzlaff, R. M., & Berman, J. S. (1985, August). *Judgmental accuracy in depression.* Paper presented at the meeting of the American Psychological Association, Los Angeles.

Wilkinson, I. M., & Blackburn, I. M. (1981). Cognitive style in depressed and recovered patients. *British Journal of Clinical Psychology, 20,* 283–292.

Wong, P. T. P., & Weiner, B. (1981). When people ask "why" questions, and the heuristics of attributional search. *Journal of Personality and Social Psychology, 40,* 650–663.

Youngren, M. A., & Lewinsohn, P. M. (1980). The functional relation between depression and problematic interpersonal behavior. *Journal of Abnormal Psychology, 89,* 333–341.

Zimmerman, M. (1983). Methodological issues in the assessment of life events: A review of issues and research. *Clinical Psychology Review, 3,* 339–370.

Zis, A. P., & Goodwin, F. K. (1979). Major affective disorder as a recurrent illness: A critical review. *Archives of General Psychiatry, 36,* 835–839.

PERSONAL AND CAUSAL INFERENCE PROCESSES IN DEPRESSION

3

Depression and Cognitions about Personal Stressful Life Events

CONSTANCE HAMMEN
University of California, Los Angeles

Research on the impact of stressful life events and circumstances has been reasonably consistent in establishing a significant association between events and depressive symptomatology in both patients and the general population (for reviews see Billings & Moos, 1982; Lloyd, 1980a; Paykel, 1978, 1979; Rabkin & Streuning, 1976). However, there is general agreement that the direct relationship is a weak one, apparently accounting for only 4%–15% of the variance in symptomatology. The low figure obtains even when stringent and diverse methodological and statistical controls are used to address various potential measurement problems (e.g., Tausig, 1982). The fact is that the majority of individuals who experience even severely stressful events do not become depressed. On the other hand, many people in stressful circumstances do suffer reactions, ranging from relatively mild demoralization to severe depressive episodes. The diversity of responses to stressors challenges researchers to understand the causes underlying this variation, so that ultimately we may predict which persons can be expected to have debilitating reactions and the conditions under which they may occur.

The large variability in individual responses and the small statistical impact of mere exposure to event occurrence are among the factors that have led to an almost universal current emphasis among stress researchers on considering cognitive appraisal processes and other psychosocial variables in predictions of illness outcome in response to stressful circumstances. Joining the early voice of Alexander (1950), whose attention to psychological conflict in the onset of disease presaged the current emphasis on personal "meaning," many researchers have given priority to appraisal processes as crucial mediating variables in stress reactions. Variously termed "perceptive sets," "cognitive sets," "depressive triad," "depressive attributional style," "cognitive processes," "symbolic meanings," "appraisal processes," and the like, a number of contemporary stress–illness models have attempted to capture in graphic form the apparently complex relationships between stressful events and illness outcomes, including depression, by depicting multiple variables (boxes) interacting in complex fashion (arrows). Although differing in their selection and sequencing of variables, and in the particular interactions specified among them, all of the models incorporate cognitive mediational factors that interact with event onset, event impact, personal coping responses, and adaptation/outcome. Some of these box-and-arrow theories are general stress–illness theories (e.g., Depue, Monroe, & Shackman, 1979; Dohrenwend & Dohrenwend, 1979; Lazarus & Launier, 1978; Rahe & Arthur, 1978), whereas others are more specific to depression (Billings & Moos, 1982; Brown & Harris, 1978b; Paykel, 1979; Warheit, 1979).

In view of the widespread inclusion of cognitive mediation variables in the relationship between stressors and illness outcomes, there is a need for empirical and conceptual evaluation of such factors as they apply to depression. This chapter will review three areas: major cognitive theories of depression, major cognitive approaches to stress and coping, and cognitions associated with stressful life events. The various approaches differ in the primacy to which they assign environmental or cognitive factors in predicting depressive outcomes. Many theories incorporate both of these ingredients and differ primarily in the level of specificity of their models. There is no doubt that many of the perspectives to be explored in the following pages are not incompatible; they merely differ in the level and emphasis of their analyses. Therefore the goal in reviewing several of these models is to identify the commonalities as well as the unique contributions of each to our understanding of how stressful events may eventuate in depressive reactions.

COGNITIVE THEORIES OF DEPRESSIVE REACTIONS TO STRESSFUL EVENTS

Causal Attributions about Stressful Life Events

One of the most clearly elaborated and best-researched cognitive theories of depression is the learned helplessness model and its revisions (e.g., Abramson, Seligman, & Teasdale, 1978; Peterson & Seligman, 1984; Seligman, Abramson, Semmel, & von Baeyer, 1979). Originally developed to explore performance decrements observed in animals exposed to uncontrollable outcomes, the learned helplessness theory was subsequently applied to explain human depression as a response to uncontrollable outcomes. Inconsistent findings and other criticisms eventually led to the notion that it isn't perceived uncontrollability as such that leads to helplessness effects, but rather it is the way in which the causes of the uncontrollability are construed. Attributional reformulations emphasized that uncontrollable outcomes that are construed as the result of internal, stable, and global causes lead to depressive symptoms (Abramson *et al.*, 1978; Miller & Norman, 1979; Weiner & Litman-Adizes, 1980). Subsequently, Seligman and colleagues (Seligman *et al.*, 1979; Peterson & Seligman, 1984) hypothesized that a traitlike tendency to view causes of negative outcomes as internal, global, and stable—a depressive attributional style—is a vulnerability factor in depression.

Although the learned helplessness model is clearly recognizable as a diathesis–stress model, the earliest tests of the model emphasized cognitions far more than negative events. Though there has continued to be an emphasis on the same cognitive constructs over time, the terminology for describing the stress portion of the model has shown considerable shifting, from noncontingent outcomes or uncontrollable outcomes (both positive and negative; Abramson *et al.*, 1978), to good and bad hypothetical events (Seligman *et al.*, 1979), to mostly a focus on "important negative life events" (Abramson, Metalsky, & Alloy, 1986). Also, most of the original studies supporting the attributional reformulation and attributional style version did not actually test individuals' reactions to real-life negative outcomes but relied instead on controlled laboratory paradigms typically manipulating success and failure or presenting hypothetical outcomes (see review by Abramson, Garber, & Seligman, 1980). A number of researchers have pointed out the difficulties of generalizing such studies to explain depressive reactions to stressful personal life events (Coyne & Lazarus, 1980; Gong-Guy & Hammen, 1980; Hammen & Cochran, 1981; Harvey, 1981). Among the difficulties noted are the overuse in such research of achievement situations to the neglect of other experiences of loss and disruption; the presentation of situations limited in personal relevance, significance, or complexity; and constraints or artifacts imposed by measuring instruments in capturing valid representations of actual cognitive processes.

Additional conceptual and methodological criticisms of the helplessness formulations are beyond the scope of this chapter (but see Coyne & Gotlib, 1983; Hammen, 1985; Wortman & Dintzer, 1978). Many of the criticisms have been addressed in more recent empirical studies; in particular, more attention has been devoted to attributions and actual stressful events as they affect depression. The following section reviews some of these studies in order to further clarify the empirical and conceptual basis of the role of attributional cognitions in mediating depressive reactions to stressful life events. Only those studies are included that involved actual, rather than hypothetical, negative outcomes.

CROSS-SECTIONAL STUDIES

The great majority of studies attempting to test the attributional reformulation shared a similar design: Samples of currently depressed and nondepressed persons were compared, or the correlations between depression and attributions were examined in a sample of persons with an array of depression scores. Several studies examined reactions to the same, single stressor, whereas others evaluated responses to several stressors unique to the individual.

Among the single-stressor studies are those in which investigators have examined individuals' reactions to unemployment, examination failure (or disappointment), kidney disease, teaching-related stress, the breakup of a romantic relationship, and starting college. Feather and Barber (1983) explored young adults' attributions for unemployment and found that depression was associated with perceived uncontrollability and ascriptions to internal causes. Situation-specific depressed mood about unemployment was associated with attributions to external causes. The authors noted that very small amounts of variance in either depression measure were accounted for by attribution variables (5%–7%). Barthe and Hammen (1981) studied students' attributions for perceived success and failure on an actual examination and found that perceived failure was associated with depression to the extent that attributions were made to lack of ability. When several specific causes were examined for internality and stability dimensions, however, there were no differences between relatively depressed and nondepressed groups.

Devins, Binik, Hollomby, Barre, and Guttmann (1981) examined the causal analyses made by patients with end-stage renal disease for the control of dialysis they experienced, and the general attributional style of these patients. The measure of depression was unrelated to specific attributions about treatment or to attributional style. Hammen and de Mayo (1982) assessed public secondary school teachers' causal analyses of teaching-related stress. Although many teachers were markedly depressed, their causal attributions for sources of stress in teaching were unrelated to depression. Instead, depression was strongly related to teachers' beliefs that neither they nor others could control the problems they faced.

Peterson, Rosenbaum, and Conn (1985) examined students' beliefs about the causes of romantic breakups and found no association between retrospectively assessed depressed mood and attributions to internal, stable, or global causes. Depression was associated, however, with perceptions that they had no control over the breakup and with expectations that they would have difficulties with future romantic relationships. Hammen, Krantz, and Cochran (1981) assessed current depression in students who had recently experienced romantic difficulties. They found no relationship between mood and attributions to internal and stable causes, but attributions to global causes of romantic difficulties were associated with depression. In the same study, students who identified starting college as their most stressful recent event did not display an association between depression and internal, stable, or global attributions; however, there was a significant relationship between depression and perceived lack of control over starting college.

Other studies have examined causal cognitions for several personally relevant stressors. Harvey (1981) and Hammen *et al.* (1981) examined the causal ascriptions of mildly depressed and nondepressed college students for events that they had experienced recently. Hammen *et al.* (1981) found that across all events, only uncontrollability and globability significantly distinguished the mildly depressed from the nondepressed group, whereas Harvey found that mildly depressed students made more internal attributions and perceived greater control over negative outcomes. Differences in the results of the two studies may stem from differences in composition of the samples and from the different methods employed for assessing attributions.

Hammen and Cochran (1981) compared questionnaire-rated attributions about recent stresses among three groups of college students: moderately depressed students, highly stressed but not depressed students, and nondepressed students. The three groups did not differ overall on attributions; the few *post hoc* differences on various cognition items suggested differences due to stress rather than to depression. In the case of the students' most extremely upsetting events, all groups reported that they experienced such events as relatively uncontrollable and as externally caused. When interview-assessed cognitions about their single most upsetting events were compared for depressed and nondepressed subsamples of the students, the moderately depressed students showed a tendency to assign causal responsibility more to themselves or to fate, whereas nondepressed but highly stressed students blamed others. There was also a tendency among depressed students to believe to a greater degree than the nondepressed students that their events were avoidable. This suggestion of self-blame among depressed persons generally agrees with Harvey's (1981) results.

Three additional studies with patient samples have similarly found only minimal support for the hypothesis that depression is accompanied by cognitions of internal, stable, and global causes of personally stressful events. Cochran and Hammen (1985) examined the causal beliefs of clinically depressed elderly patients about their recent stressful life events and observed that they typically viewed the events as uncontrollable and as having been caused by external factors (although within the patient sample, more depression was associated with less externality). Gong-Guy and Hammen (1980) examined the causal cognitions of relatively depressed and nondepressed clinic outpatients and found that when averaged across all recent major stressors, attributional cognitions did not differ between groups. For their single most upsetting events, however (for many, the event precipitating their seeking of help), depressed patients made significantly more internal attributions and tended toward more global ascriptions compared to nondepressed patients. Miller, Klee, and Norman (1982) found that composite questionnaire attributions of depressed inpatients were significantly different in the predicted direction from those of nondepressed patients, although the specific dimensions accounting for the effects were not reported. However, the attributions for personally stressful events were generally not correlated with attributions for failure on hypothetical and experimental tasks.

LONGITUDINAL STUDIES

Clearly, cross-sectional studies are limited in terms of the kinds of conclusions that can be drawn regarding the attributional theory. They do not test the causal portion of the theory; that is, they do not enable one to rule out the possibility that depression is the cause of the cognitions, that the two mutually affect each other, or that both are products of yet additional unspecified factors. Longitudinal studies that are more appropriate to tests of the causal hypotheses have been relatively rare in research on cognition and depression, and even more rare are those that have identified the occurrence of stressful life events after the preexisting level of depression was established.

Cutrona (1983) examined women's causal attributions for personally stressful life events and childcare stressors, as well as depressive attributional style, in a sample of women experiencing the birth of their first child. She found that attributional style in the prepartum period predicted the level of postpartum depression. Cutrona cautions, however, that the amount of variance in depression accounted for by attributional cognitions was small. Rather similar results and conclusions were reported by O'Hara, Rehm, and Campbell (1982) in their study of postpartum depression; however, Manly, McMahon, Bradley, and Davidson (1982) found no support for a link between explanatory style and depression after childbirth. Finally, Kayne, Alloy, Romer, and Crocker (1986) observed that the interaction of explanatory style and stress level, the latter being a measure derived from expected and actual grades on a midterm examination, predicted changes in depression after the exam. An especially noteworthy feature of this study, which is missing in every other investigation of attributional style, is the demonstration that effects were mediated by the actual attributions for the stressful event. Other studies have failed to demonstrate that explanatory style predicts actual causal appraisals of a negative event associated with depression, a step that is needed to support the theory of an attributional mechanism rather than simply a general negativistic self-presentational style.

OVERALL EVALUATION AND DISCUSSION

Taken as a whole, studies of individuals' cognitions about the causes of their personally stressful recent life events offer little consistent support that internal, stable, and global causal ascriptions about the events are associated with depressive outcomes. Results tend to vary considerably according to sample characteristics and types of events surveyed, and frequently the events appear to be associated with similar cognitions in both depressed and nondepressed samples (e.g., highly stressful events were often seen as uncontrollable and as having been externally caused). Hammen and Mayol (1982) have argued that, indeed, situations exert powerful influences on cognitions about causality and have urged that situational parameters involving the nature of the life events themselves be taken more fully into account in cognition–stress models.

Peterson and Raps (1983) and Peterson and Seligman (1984) have argued that many of the studies cited, especially those examining single events, do not adequately test the role of explanatory style and that multiple events need to be assessed in order to have a reliable measure of the tendency to attribute events to internal, stable, and global causes. The research of Seligman and colleagues on depressive attributional style assessed by their Attributional Style Questionnaire across six bad events and/or six good events has been more consistent in its support of the model (review by Peterson & Seligman, 1984) than was the research on personally relevant events cited previously. However, there are three problems with the argument.

First, although such research on explanatory style may have shown a link between explanatory style and depression, neither the research using the Attributional Style Questionnaire nor the very few studies of attributional style and actual stressors have tested the hypothesized mediator between explanatory style and depression, that is, attributions for specific negative events (Kayne *et al.*, 1986, is the single exception). A second problem is that although the explanatory style theory assumes cross-situational and temporal stability for this vulnerability trait, numerous investigators have challenged this assumption (e.g., Cutrona, Russell, & Jones, 1984; Hamilton & Abramson, 1983; Miller *et al.*, 1982; Persons & Rao, 1985). A third problem is that the argument implicitly assigns considerable significance to events, suggesting that features of stressful life events themselves may be important determinants of depression and cognition, so that only when the tendency to make depressive attributional analyses regardless of features of a particular event is evident would there be a fair test of the model. To show that the attributional model is more than just a prediction that persons with pervasive negativistic thinking will become depressed when stressed, it seems essential (1) to demonstrate in a longitudinal design that the actual causal cognitions about an event mediate its impact on depression and (2) to demonstrate the effect in naturalistic studies, in which a real event occurs, rather than in studies based on a questionnaire.

In recent articles, Peterson and Seligman (1984) and Abramson *et al*. (1986) have elaborated important clarifications and refinements that may help to resolve some of the discrepancies in the research results. These authors indicate that it is the expectation of uncontrollability over future outcomes that is the sufficient cause of depression, whereas explanatory style and its associated causal explanations for negative events are risk factors inasmuch as they affect the expectation. While knowledge of explanatory style usually helps predict expectations, there may not be an invariable relationship. The authors further clarify that specific explanations may be determined by both the explanatory style and the actual nature of the event; Abramson *et al*. (1986) and Kayne *et al*. (1986) particularly note the need to test the diathesis–stress *interaction*. Abramson *et al*. (1986) further specify in an important refinement of the attributional model that only some kinds of depressions are "hopelessness" depressions; hence different samples of depressed individuals may differ in their compositions such that what appear to be weak or nonsupportive results for the attributional model may actually reflect low proportions of hopelessness depressives in the sample. The most valid tests of the model, therefore, would require selection of an appropriate sample rather than unselected groups, although this step of course awaits further clarification as to how to define the applicable groups.

Beck's Cognitive Distortion Model

Probably the most widely influential psychological theory of depression of the past few decades is that of Aaron Beck (1967, 1976), a psychiatrist whose puzzlings over the phenomenology of his patients' depressive experiences led to his theorizing about depression as a disorder of thinking rather than primarily of affect. His theory has been significantly modified and refined over time but continues to give a primary role in symptom formation and maintenance to individuals' negative interpretations of themselves, the environment, and the future. According to the theory, persons who are vulnerable to depression characteristically exaggerate the significance of their misfortunes while simultaneously minimizing their positive capabilities for resolving problems or finding satisfaction. Such interpretations are believed to be distortions of reality in the sense that they are illogical inferences and/or are based on an arbitrary selection of negative information and neglect of available positive information. Such tendencies of thinking, or schemas, are thought to arise from early childhood experiences, possibly traumatic occurrences.

The schematic organization of information in memory directs the potentially biased encoding and retrieval of information so that dysfunctional schemas exert an ongoing effect on the interpretation of experiences.

The theory is a stress–diathesis model in that it is assumed that the occurrence of an event, particularly a negative one, or one of special significance to the person, will activate the negativistic thinking pattern, which in turn leads to the symptoms of the depression syndrome. In research applications, however, there has been little emphasis on events and nearly total focus on individual differences in negativistic thinking. In the past, scores of laboratory studies and investigations of clinical samples have been conducted, and results generally support the predicted pattern of relatively depressive interpretations among depressed samples compared to nondepressed controls (e.g., Coyne & Gotlib, 1983; Hammen & Krantz, 1985; Segal & Shaw, 1986). Cognitive–behavioral therapy for depression, with the goal of modifying depressive negative thinking, has been a highly popular and apparently effective treatment (Beck, Rush, Shaw, & Emery, 1979; Elkin *et al.*, 1986).

The most recent research on information-processing biases in depression has attempted to go beyond the descriptive designs of earlier research in order to address additional, interrelated components of Beck's model: explorations of the nature and function of cognitive vulnerability and the etiological role of depressive thinking.

VULNERABILITY COGNITIONS

Beck was in some ways ahead of his time in postulating the operation of schema mechanisms that direct the biased processing of information. Although his formulations have not been clearly defined and specified, contemporary research in cognitive psychology and social cognition have helped provide paradigms for exploring such processes.

For instance, Kuiper and colleagues have applied a levels-of-processing incidental recall procedure to the assessment of self-schemas. They have demonstrated that memory for self-descriptive adjectives is superior to memory for adjectives encoded by word length or semantic properties and, most critically, that relatively depressed persons recall more self-descriptions with negative content than do nondepressed persons (e.g., Derry & Kuiper, 1981; Kuiper & Derry, 1982). Kuiper has argued that the results support Beck's notion of depressive bias in that self-schemas facilitate the processing of congruent information—in this case, the recall of relatively negative trait adjectives. Subsequently, Hammen, Miklowitz, and Dyck (1986) demonstrated that additional measures of an inferred self-schema, such as decision times for judging self-relevant adjectives and recall of self-descriptive critical incidents (Markus, 1977), similarly showed content effects congruent with depressed or nondepressed mood status. Hammen, Marks, de Mayo, and Mayol (1985) showed that memory for recent events was consistent with mood, and Hammen and Zupan (1984) applied the levels-of-processing paradigm to children. All these studies support the hypothesis of a self-construct represented in memory that selectively directs attention and memory to information congruent with the dominant mood. Further research investigating the potential role of such schema processes in vulnerability to the onset of depression is reviewed in a later section.

Recently, Beck, Epstein, and Harrison (1982) argued that it is important to distinguish between negativistic "cognitions," which are immediately related to affective states but may be unstable and not detectable in normal mood states, and dysfunctional attitudes, which are stable beliefs that render a person vulnerable to depression because of their rigid and perfectionistic standards, engendering disappointment and failure. The Dysfunctional Attitude Scale (DAS; Weissman, 1979) has been found to help predict relapse in depressed patients (Simons, Murphy, Levine, & Wetzel, 1986) and has shown that dysfunctional attitudes persist even in remission in depressed patients (Eaves & Rush, 1984). The latter finding has not been replicated, however; Hamilton and Abramson (1983) and Silverman, Silverman, and Eardley (1984) found significant declines in DAS scores once patients showed symptom remission. Finally, Hollon, Kendall, and Lumry (1986) have shown that the DAS appears to be state dependent across subtypes of remitted depressed patients but that it does not appear to measure cognitions specific to depression. Nondepressed psychiatric patients also displayed elevated levels of dysfunctional attitudes, a finding consistent with previous conclusions drawn from the work of Hammen, Jacobs, Mayol, and Cochran (1980). Taken together, such studies cast doubt on the Beck *et al.* (1982) suggestion that such beliefs are stable depressogenic cognitions that mark vulnerability to developing depression.

COGNITIONS AS CAUSES OF DEPRESSION

Until relatively recently, few studies had tested the critical etiological component of Beck's theory: the extent to which characteristic depressive cognitions cause depression. Lewinsohn, Steinmetz, Larson, and Franklin (1981) measured cognitions about the self, the world, and the future in a large sample of depressed and nondepressed community residents and reassessed their depression status some months later. Persons who were initially nondepressed but who became depressed did not show evidence of depressogenic cognitions at the initial testing, thus failing to support the etiological role of negative thinking. Hammen, Miklowitz, and Dyck (1986) reasoned that depressive self-schemas should be stable and exert an ongoing influence on the interpretation of everyday events. However, they found no evidence of stable self-schema responding in students who became less depressed between first and second testings; moreover, additional measures of self-schema performance also demonstrated a strong mood-state-dependent effect that persons no longer depressed resembled nondepressed persons. Hammen, Marks, de Mayo, and Mayol (1985), in a further longitudinal study, also demonstrated that schema responding is related to current mood rather than representing a stable characteristic of cognition. Furthermore, Hammen, Marks, de Mayo, and Mayol (1985) and Hammen, Miklowitz, and Dyck (1986) found that initially high levels of depressive self-schema responding do not predict subsequent depression (apart from that predictable by previous depression). Taken together, these longitudinal studies clearly indicate that certain negative cognitions do not appear to be enduring qualities of an individual that predispose to later depression; instead, the cognitions appear to be either the *result* of the depressed mood or reciprocally related in a manner that confounds simple linear causality.

COGNITION–STRESSOR INTERACTION

Beck and others have argued, as have the recent reformulated attributional models, that a true test of the role of cognitive vulnerability models involves the *interaction* of cognitions with personally significant stressors. Riskind and Rholes (1984), for instance, postulated that negativistic cognitions may in fact be enduring but need to be "primed" by stressful situations in order to be accessible. Beck and Rush (1978) had speculated that schemas may be latent until activated by stressful situations analogous to the original experience "responsible for embedding a negative attitude." Relatively recently, Beck and colleagues (Beck, 1982; Beck *et al.*, 1982) amended the original theory to include personality organization as an ingredient in vulnerability to depression. Two types of personality organization, one involving central value systems organized around contact with others and the other involving such systems organized around autonomous achievement, are hypothesized to yield differences in etiology, symptomatology, and treatment response. To the degree that the sociotropic person experiences negative events that threaten the interpersonal realm, or the autonomous person experiences goal frustration or failure, depression will occur.

To date, only three empirical investigations are known that test the Stress × Cognition interaction hypothesized in Beck's model. Hammen, Marks, de Mayo, and Mayol (1985) employed the levels-of-processing procedure to identify students who varied in level of depressive self-schema and who were currently depressed or nondepressed. Following these students over time with periodic assessments of depression and stressful life events, multiple regression analyses indicated no significant Life Event × Schema interaction effect in the prediction of depression. That is, there did not appear to be a triggering effect of negative events on present or "latent" schemas to produce depression.

A second model of Life Event × Schema interaction was tested by Hammen, Marks, Mayol, and de Mayo (1985), who hypothesized the operation of self-schemas involving specific content vulnerability, such that encountering life events with congruent content would produce depression. The investigators employed the same sample as in their first study and characterized self-schemas in nearly 100 college students according to the extent to which memories of recent experiences about the self were organized in terms of dependency for satisfaction and worth either from relations with others or from accomplishment in the achievement domain. These dependent and self-critical schema types are similar not only to Beck's subtypes (Beck, 1982) but also to the psychodynamically construed "dominant goal" and "dominant other" depressive subtypes of Arieti and Bemporad (1980) and to the dependent and self-critical subtypes discussed by Blatt and colleagues (Blatt, D'Afflitti, & Quinlan, 1976; Blatt, Quinlan, Chevron, McDonald, & Zuroff, 1982). Participants were followed longitudinally and were assessed by interview and questionnaire for the occurrence of stressful life events and depression levels at four monthly intervals. As predicted, persons classified as being schematic for dependency themes experienced significantly more depression associated with negative interpersonal events than with negative achievement events; also, but to a less pronounced degree, self-critical persons experienced more depression associated with negative achievement events than with negative interpersonal events.

In a third study, Olinger, Kuiper, and Shaw (1986) hypothesized a stress–vulnerability model similar to that of Hammen, Marks, Mayol, and de Mayo (1985); Life events that impinge upon an individual's dysfunctional attitudes produce depression. Olinger *et al.* (1986) developed a scale for assessing life events relevant to attitudes on the DAS-Contractual Conditions. For example, "I don't have other people to lean on" is the life-event contractual condition corresponding to the attitude "If you don't have other people to lean on, you are bound to be sad." There was a significant interaction of DAS level and contractual condition score, such that attitudinally vulnerable and stressed subjects were most depressed. The model is more fully discussed by Kuiper, Olinger, and MacDonald in Chapter 10 of this volume.

These studies, along with research described earlier, suggest two important clarifications of Beck's model. First, as Hammen and colleagues have noted, along with Kuiper, Olinger, MacDonald, and Shaw (1985), it seems important to distinguish between "episode schemas," which are state dependent and are activated after the onset of depression, and true content "vulnerability" schemas, which play a causal role in some forms of depression. Second, Kuiper *et al.* (1985) and Hammen, Marks, Mayol, and de Mayo (1985) suggested that a match between stressful-life-event-type and specific vulnerable self-schema may lead to depression. Although the level of nonspecific stress may bear a relationship to depression, greater predictability is likely when the event is specifically construed as a loss or failure that reduces feelings of self-worth and the ability to cope with the negative consequences of the event now and in the future. Considerably more work is needed, however, to clarify this model's range of application and the mechanisms by which such processes exert their effects.

CONCLUSION

Just as the learned helplessness model has undergone major transformations over time, so, too, has Beck's model evolved. Included now are clearer articulations of differences between transitory, concomitant depressive cognitions and vulnerability cognitions. Nonetheless, a measure of relatively specific and stable vulnerability cognitions remains elusive. The model has always hypothesized a link between specific experiences that foster vulnerability to certain themes and later activation of such vulnerability in the face of similar events. The increased emphasis on personality subtypes that specify the dysfunctional attitudes–event domains represents an increased emphasis on personally significant stressors. Nevertheless, the utility of this formulation remains to be seen, and thus far, only Hammen and colleagues have actually tested the role of life events in interaction with cognitive vulnerability to predict depression over a prospective course. Attention to both personal cognitions and life-event characteristics in a cognitive–environmental perspective promises to bring greater clarity to Beck's formulations as well as to improve the predictability of depression from knowledge of stressful life events alone (Hammen, 1985; Segal & Shaw, 1986).

COGNITIVE PERSPECTIVES ON COPING
WITH STRESSFUL LIFE EVENTS

Both the reformulated attributional model and Beck's theory predict depressive reactions to negative events under specific conditions of cognitive appraisal. Both approaches also emphasize individual predisposition to negative interpretations and focus the bulk of their research efforts on individual differences in cognitions. In contrast, another perspective considers coping processes to be important mediators of responses to stressors. Although a consideration of coping behaviors as such is not germane to this review of cognitive mediators of depressive reactions to stressful life events, cognitions about coping are relevant. In particular, the recent theories of Lazarus and colleagues, though not limited to depression, provide important cognitive constructs for understanding emotional reactions to stress.

Coping Cognitions

STUDIES BY LAZARUS

The work of Richard Lazarus has long been associated with cognitive appraisal processes mediating emotional responses to stressful stimuli. The most recent contributions from his group provide a general framework for construing depressive (and other emotional) reactions to personally stressful events and circumstances (e.g., Coyne, Aldwin, & Lazarus, 1981; Folkman & Lazarus, 1986; Lazarus & Folkman, 1984).

The essential ingredients of the cognitive–phenomenological model include a transactional perspective with emphasis on person–environment reciprocal influences, cognitive appraisal processes, and coping. The transactional perspective emphasizes relational factors that are thought to "transcend the separate sets of person and environment variables of which they are comprised" (Lazarus & Launier, 1978, p. 2). In contrast to a transactional framework, according to Lazarus, ordinary interactional perspectives seek *determinants* of outcomes, typically use methods incapable of validly describing process, and frequently employ static variables and simplistic notions of linear causality (Coyne, 1982; Lazarus & Launier, 1978). In Lazarus's model, both environmental and personal factors are seen to be involved in an ongoing reciprocal relationship, studied as person–environment units. Transactions between person and environment are mediated by two processes: appraisals and coping.

According to Lazarus and Launier, "cognitive appraisal can be simply understood as the mental process of placing any event in one of a series of evaluative categories related either to its significance for the person's well-being (primary appraisal) or to the available coping resources and options (secondary appraisal)" (p. 24). Emotional responses are a direct outcome of appraisals of the meaning of an event for a person's well-being. The emotional response may be immediate and nonreflective, so that thoughts and feelings are simultaneous, but appraisal is an essential component of emotion (Lazarus, 1982). Primary appraisals may lead to judgments that a circumstance is irrelevant, benign-positive, or stressful. The stress can be classified as one of three types: harm/loss (the damage has already occurred), threat (anticipated harm or loss), and challenge. The outcome of the primary appraisal will be determined by the transaction between personal experiences and predisposition on the one hand and environmental factors on the other. Coping appraisals significantly affect primary appraisals. That is, secondary appraisals of perceived coping resources and options reciprocally interact with the primary appraisal of the nature and magnitude of the stressor and its effect on the person's well-being. Reappraisals occur throughout the process, incorporating information from one's own reactions, the environment's responses, and the like.

Like most models of depression, the cognitive–phenomenological approach assigns primacy to cognitive processes in provoking depressive reactions to stressful events. The transactional emphasis, however, differs from perspectives that emphasize either the qualities of events (e.g., Paykel, 1979; Brown & Harris, 1978b) or personal characteristics (Abramson *et al.,* 1978; Beck, 1967). In contrast to the perspective of life-event research, the Lazarus model views the individual as someone in a continuing state of appraising and negotiating stressful occurrences and everyday circumstances. That is, severely threatening episodic stressful events or ongoing chronic stressors are seen as important antecedents of emotional reactions, but so, too, may everyday hassles be associated with depressive and other symptomatology (Kanner, Coyne, Schaefer, & Lazarus, 1981). Indeed, Kanner *et al.* (1981) found in a community sample that daily hassles were more predictive of depression levels than were major life events.

Recently, in a further application of the model to everyday events and their relevance for depression, Folkman and Lazarus (1986), in several monthly follow-ups, studied individuals' reported coping experiences concerning stressors they had encountered during the previous week. Primary appraisal was operationalized according to six content areas of what was at stake in each encounter; secondary appraisal of coping options was measured by four items (e.g., the extent to which the situation was "one that you could change or do something about"). Coping was assessed with the Ways of Coping Questionnaire (Folkman & Lazarus, 1986), which contained eight factor-analytic subscales (e.g., Seeking Social Support). Relatively depressed and nondepressed community residents differed significantly on five primary appraisals (stakes) but on only one secondary appraisal (coping option; "had to hold back from doing what you wanted to do"). Groups did not differ on perceptions of ability to change the situation or on need to accept the situation. Five of the eight coping subscales yielded significant differences (e.g., Escape–Avoidance, Confrontive Coping), but there were no differences on Planful

Problem Solving, Positive Reappraisal, or Distancing). The groups did not differ on proportions of satisfactory or unsatisfactory outcomes of the stressful encounters. The authors conclude that certain appraisal and coping processes of relatively depressed persons are characterized by vulnerability to threat but not necessarily by negativity in all facets of their cognitive processes; they note that their results share some common features with Beck's model, with interpersonal models, and, to a more limited extent, with the reformulated attributional model.

Unfortunately, as other critics have noted in a different context (e.g., Dohrenwend & Shrout, 1985), the methods of analysis make it difficult to interpret confounding of the independent and dependent variables. Persons already depressed may gauge the "stakes" to be higher (e.g., self-esteem decrements are a *sign* of depression), and reported coping responses have been shown to be highly dependent on mood state (Parker & Brown, 1982).

The Lazarus model differs from the models of the attributional theorists and Beck, who focus primarily on individual differences, by incorporating environmental factors and coping resources more directly into the model. The emphasis on perceived coping resources (secondary appraisal) in mediating the outcome of perceived stress represents a significant difference from the attributional reformulation. The Lazarus model suggests that depression as an outcome is likely to occur when the person considers the stakes, coping options, and consequences, not just the causes, of a stressful event.

Although the appraisal model has considerable intuitive appeal and provides a language for linking together a variety of important personal and environmental factors operating over time, its adequacy and utility are difficult to evaluate. One reason is that mechanisms of appraisal processes have not been fully explained, nor are their temporal characteristics specified. Furthermore, there is not much discussion about possible determinants of appraisals, whether they are veridical or biased appraisals, and whether they reflect current mood, previous experience, or some other basis. The ways in which "depression-prone" persons may engage in appraisals are thus not considered, and there are no predictions in advance about who will become depressed and who will not. The transactional perspective is an important one theoretically and methodologically, but it is necessarily enormously difficult to test. Nevertheless, increasingly sophisticated studies of the coping process suggest that such variables add significantly to predicting depression over time (Parker, Brown, & Bignault, 1986; Pearlin, Lieberman, Menaghan, & Mullan, 1981).

OTHER APPROACHES TO STRESS AND COPING

The work of Wortman and her colleagues (e.g., Bulman & Wortman, 1977; Silver & Wortman, 1980; Wortman & Dintzer, 1978) has also explored mediators of responses to major stressors and their application to depression. A central feature of her work is the emphasis on ascription of meaning as a determinant of adjustment to serious personal events. "Ascribing meaning" in this context means finding purpose in one's misfortune; it is hypothesized to result in more successful adjustment. Support for such a hypothesis has been reported by Wortman (Bulman & Wortman, 1977; Silver & Wortman, 1980) and Taylor (1983). This process of finding meaning may be similar to Lazarus' ideas of stress reappraisal, in which some individuals may come to view an initial threat or harm/loss as a challenge to be mastered. The views of Wortman and Taylor also share Lazarus's emphasis on response to stress as an ongoing transactional process. Moreover, all of these perspectives, like that of the attributional theorists such as Abramson *et al.* (1978), portray the victim or target of personal stressors as an active, construing agent engaged in ongoing hypothesis generating and testing in order to make sense of misfortune and understand it in the broader context of one's life and well-being. In this view, those who can make self-esteem-enhancing constructions or adaptations (Taylor, 1983) are not likely to become depressed, whereas those whose interpretations, resources, and forecasts of the future fail to enhance self-esteem may become depressed or suffer another negative emotional reaction.

STRESSFUL-LIFE-EVENT THEORIES OF DEPRESSION

The early view that stressful life events occasioned illness responses in individuals because of the demands for change and adaptation they imposed at first led researchers to view the sheer number of events and their population-derived life-change-impact units as the predictors of illness or psychopathology (e.g., Holmes & Rahe, 1967). However, as noted previously, such a simple view has largely been discredited on both empirical and conceptual grounds. In recent years, a great deal of research has explored individuals' perceptions of events and the psychological properties of events that may be associated with depressive reactions. Such efforts have not, for the most part, been concerned with individual differences in perceptions and interpretations of events but rather with properties of events that are assumed to affect the ways in which events are construed.

The contributions of George Brown and E. S. Paykel are of particular importance in recent explorations of the meaning to individuals of stressful events. It should be noted at the outset, however, that although each investigator proposes a model of depressive reactions to stressful events that emphasizes cognitive appraisals, the actual research of each concerns the formal properties of events—not individuals' appraisals. For instance, Brown's model includes "cognitive sets," which affect interpretation and reaction to provoking agents, but these constructs are hypothetical and are not directly tested. His research has focused on the relatively objective assessment of the stressfulness of events, given the inferred meaning or significance of the event from each individual's unique perspective (Brown & Harris, 1978b). Similarly, Paykel presents a model that includes such cognitions as "symbolic significance" as well as vulnerability factors that encompass personal interpretations and reactions (Paykel, 1979), but like Brown, he merely asserts these factors while directly studying only objective properties of events.

The contributions of Brown, Paykel, and others relevant to cognitions about stressful events will be discussed in the context of the three aspects of interpretations of stressful events that have received the most attention: assessment of the subjective impact of events, assessment of the degree to which events can represent threats to individual values, and assessment of the impact of events construed as losses.

THE SUBJECTIVE IMPACT OF STRESSFUL EVENTS

Perhaps the most straightforward cognitive dimension of event appraisal is the degree to which the event is seen as stressful by the individual. The investigation of this issue was prompted less by a cognitive perspective than by methodological considerations: Should stressfulness be determined by "objective" weightings of events or by individuals' subjective evaluations? Some investigators who have compared objective weights, such as life-change units, with individual subjective ratings have found the latter to be more strongly correlated with dependent variables than are objective weights (Sarason, Johnson, & Siegel, 1978), whereas others have urged the use of subjective ratings because objective "normative" weights are not universal or independent of subject characteristics (Redfield & Stone, 1979). On the other hand, Dohrenwend (Dohrenwend, Kransoff, Askenasy, & Dohrenwend, 1978; Dohrenwend & Shrout, 1985) argues that use of subjective weights guarantees the confounding of dependent and independent variables. Thoits (1983) urges unit weighting (simple counts of recent events).

A related theoretical issue concerns the roles of change *per se* versus the undesirability of events as mediators of depressive reactions to stress. The data are clear and consistent in the finding that undesirable events, particularly those with moderate or severe impact, whether objectively or subjectively defined, are more closely associated with depression and suicide than are desirable or ambiguous events (Brown & Harris, 1978b; Costello, 1982; Monroe, 1982; Mueller, Edwards, & Yarvis, 1977; Slater & Depue, 1981; Tausig, 1982; see Paykel, 1979, for a review). Thus it is the psychological negative impact of an event, not the mere occurrence of any positive or negative event requiring adaptation, that appears to be associated with depressive reactions.

Although most research on stressful life events has not been concerned with individual differences in the appraisal of event undesirability, there are a few studies suggesting that relatively more depressed people do tend to ascribe greater negative impact, aversiveness, upset, and the like to their personal events than do nondepressed persons. This has been shown to occur for events in general (Hammen & Cochran, 1981; Hammen *et al.*, 1981; Lewinsohn & Amenson, 1978; Lewinsohn & Talkington, 1979) as well as for different individuals when experiencing the same event (Hammen et al., 1981). One implication of this work, consistent with Beck's cognitive bias formulations, is that certain individuals vulnerable to depression may exaggerate the impact of events. However, the correlational and retrospective nature of much of this research cannot rule out the opposite interpretation—that depression leads to more negative evaluations of the stressfulness of events.

CONTEXTUAL THREAT

A special case of the subjective impact of an event concerns "contextual threat," a term developed by Brown, a London sociologist, who expanded his original research on life events and schizophrenia to include studies of the social origins of depression (Brown & Harris, 1978b). In so doing, he moved away from the relatively simple view that events disrupt lives and lead to aversive consequences and moved toward a view that events occasion changes in people's lives that may produce illness to the degree that the changes affect people's assumptions and beliefs about themselves and life. "[Changes] focus our attention on the present and since this is the visible outcome of our past—our choices, commitments, and mistakes—we may come to question what our life might have been, what it is about, and what it will become" (Brown & Harris, 1978b, p. 84). Espousing a highly cognitive view, Brown continues: "Changes are important in so far as they alter assumptions a person has made about the world. . . . Indeed, a crisis or change is probably only ever significant if it leads to a change in thought about the world" (p. 85).

In their research on women in London, Brown and colleagues attempted to assess the meaning or impact of events by operationalizing meaning in the form of "contextual threat." That is, by thoroughly interviewing the respondent about the circumstances surrounding the event, and by drawing inferences about the woman's plans or goals relevant to the event, they attempted to "make a reasonable estimate of its meaning without taking into account how she felt about it" (Brown, 1979, p. 266). Indeed, Brown makes it clear that they specifically ignored what the respondent said was the meaning of the event for her in an attempt to minimize the methodological problem of "effort after meaning," in which individuals may attempt to explain their depression by attributing it to an event or circumstance of which it may, in fact, have been independent. Independent judges then evaluated the contextual threat of an event by judging what most persons would feel if they had experienced the same event in the same context. Thus, although contextual threat ratings attempt to capture personal meaning, it is actually the researchers' attributions of meaning that are studied, while personal appraisals are specifically ignored.

In sample and scope of measurement, Brown's Camberwell studies are virtually unparalleled in life-event research. Brown reports a significant etiological role for events with a moderate or severe contextual threat of long-term significance, finding 53% of depressed cases in the community sample to have recently experienced such events. Based on the data of nearly 500 respondents, he developed a three-factor model of the social origins of depression, including event-difficulty factors, vulnerability factors, and symptom-formation factors (Brown & Harris, 1978b). He further speculated, as did Beck (1967) and Becker (1979), that low self-esteem is a crucial ingredient of the various vulnerability factors, thus opening the door to a person-by-environment perspective. Although Brown disagrees with Beck in that he emphasizes realistic perceptions of threatening events as opposed to Beck's emphasis on idiosyncratic dysfunctional interpretations of events, his view of the role of poor self-esteem is explicitly cognitive:

> If self-esteem is low *before* the onset of any depression, a woman is less likely to be able to imagine herself emerging from her privation. We suggest that vulnerability factors play a crucial etiologic role because they limit a woman's ability to develop an

optimistic view about controlling the world in order to regain some source of value. Of course, an appraisal of hopelessness is often entirely realistic: the future for many women *is* bleak. But given a particular event or difficulty, ongoing low self-esteem will increase the chance of such an interpretation. (Brown, 1979, p. 283)

The emphasis on hopelessness is very similar to that of Beck (1967) and, more recently, to that of Abramson *et al.* (1986). Also, Brown's concept of self-esteem, while employing the traditional trait concept, is remarkably similar in implications to Bandura's notion of self-efficacy (Bandura, 1977, 1978, 1982). Bandura proposes that a sense of personal efficacy (belief that one can successfully execute the behavior required to produce desired outcomes) determines whether coping behaviors will be initiated and how much effort and persistence will be sustained in the face of obstacles. The implications of Bandura's theory for explaining depressive reactions to stressful events seem apparent, although as with Brown's views of self-esteem, no direct empirical investigation of this important cognitive construct has been undertaken.

In addition to the lack of direct investigation of some of Brown's key cognitive constructs, other conceptual, methodological, and statistical criticisms of this work have been explored in a lively and illuminating debate (Brown & Harris, 1978a; Dohrenwend, 1977; Everitt & Smith, 1979; Tennant & Bebbington, 1978; Tennant, Bebbington, & Hurry, 1981). Nevertheless, the central findings of Brown's work regarding the etiological role of severely threatening events in the onset of depression have been essentially replicated in a Canadian study using similar procedures (Costello, 1982).

EVENTS INVOLVING LOSS

Investigations of the formal properties of stressful life events, such as content, have been largely unproductive (see Paykel, 1979). On the other hand, the categorization of events according to their psychological meaning, such as exits from the social field, has been productively explored by Paykel. Social exits (object losses) have been found to be significantly associated with depression (Paykel review, 1979). Across several studies, depressives and persons who had attempted suicide had higher proportions of exit events than did other patient groups and controls from the general population. Warheit (1979) reported similar results from a large-scale survey using Paykel's list of object-loss events: Greater depression was associated with more exits and exit events contributed to the persistence of depression over time as well as to the greater use of health care services.

Using a much broader definition of loss than merely exits from the social field, Finlay-Jones and Brown (1981) included loss of valued others, loss of health, lost jobs or material possessions, and loss of cherished ideas. They studied more than 100 women who had consulted general practice physicians for any reason, with the purpose of learning whether events judged as losses predicted depressive symptoms as opposed to anxiety symptoms, which are associated with events suggesting future danger or threat. Using only participants who had experienced recent severe events as defined in the earlier Camberwell studies, the researchers found a significant excess of depressed women, as compared with anxious women, among those who reported a severe loss. Parallel results were obtained for those who reported events involving severe danger, with significantly more anxiety than depression reactions. This important study requires replication but suggests that the psychological impact of certain losses may be uniquely depression—a view that has been prevalent from Freud to Beck (1976).

There are enormous difficulties with the construct of loss. Even when limited to object loss, as in exits from the social field, the factors mediating the development of symptoms are unknown, since such events not only affect interpretations of oneself, life, and the future but also may affect social supports and other circumstances that influence well-being, such as finances, occupation and work status, and the like. When loss is expanded to include a variety of onsets, as in Finlay-Jones and Brown (1981), the diversity may undermine the utility of the concept. Moreover, Brown concluded elsewhere that it is not loss as such that is central to depression, but rather it is the hopelessness and threat to one's values that loss may occasion (Brown, 1979).

Though we are concerned here with the impact of current life stresses, it must be noted as well that the role of loss is made still more difficult to understand and evaluate by the enormous and conflicting body of research on early object loss in depressed patients. Lloyd's (1980b) review conveys some of the controversy, as do conflicting results from two similar studies by Brown (Brown & Harris, 1978b) and Costello (1982; see also Barnes & Prosen, 1985; Roy, 1985). Despite its long history in the etiological theories of depression, the concept of loss remains imprecise and poorly understood.

RESEARCH ON THE COGNITIVE CHARACTERISTICS OF STRESSFUL EVENTS

Several specific cognitive constructs have figured prominently in various formulations describing emotional reactions to stressful life events. Some have been touched on already as elements of major theories, while others have been studied more specifically. The constructs that have received the most attention include controllability, personal responsibility, meaning, anticipation or expectancy, and efficacy. Each of these has been described and investigated differently across various studies, making conclusions and generalizations difficult. The investigations also vary in terms of whether these constructs are ascribed to intraindividual characteristics or to properties of the events themselves, or whether this factor is considered at all. Despite such problems, however, it is clear that few cognitions have been found to have a universally significant impact in producing depressive reactions. Our review will be limited to studies of cognitions about actual stressful life events, although where possible, studies of situational or personal determinants of the cognitions will be noted.

Controllability

Perhaps the most extensively discussed cognitive dimension of stressful events is the perceived controllability of an event. A host of laboratory and naturalistic studies, guided by a myriad of theoretical formulations, have suggested that the uncontrollability of stressful stimuli is an important mediator of their aversiveness (e.g., Averill, 1973; Cohen, 1980; Glass & Singer, 1972; Miller, 1980; Seligman, 1975). Uncontrollability has figured prominently in depression research in the learned helplessness formulation (Seligman, 1975). It is clear that there is considerable divergence in the manner in which uncontrollability has been construed (see Dohrenwend & Martin, 1979; Novaco, 1979). Although a comprehensive review is beyond the scope of this work, two major issues warrant discussion.

One concerns the complexity of the construct of uncontrollability. The construct overlaps with, or requires the simultaneous consideration of, additional dimensions, such as predictability or expectation of an event, intentionality, avoidability, locus of causality, and personal responsibility; it refers variously to control over onset, cessation, or both. Uncontrollability may or may not refer to its independence of the behaviors of the person, depending on who does the judging. Even attribution researchers have had some difficulty in deciding how to construe the dimension of controllability and its role in depression (e.g., Harvey, 1981; Weiner & Litman-Adizes, 1980). In fact, in the Abramson *et al.* (1978) reformulation of the helplessness model of depression, and in subsequent research on "depressive attributional style" (Seligman *et al.*, 1979), perceived uncontrollability of outcomes is used virtually interchangeably with bad outcomes. Thus the complexity and imprecision of the term render its unique effects, if any, difficult to gauge.

The second issue regarding the construct of uncontrollability is equally troublesome. There is simply inconsistent empirical support in research on stressful life events for the construct of uncontrollability, and there is little evidence of any uniquely depressive consequences of uncontrollable events. Reviewing his research from several samples, Paykel (1979) reported that persons who had attempted suicide acknowledged more experimenter-defined uncontrollable recent events than did depressed patients, and both groups had more such events than did the general-population controls. However, the two patient groups did not differ in controllable events but reported significantly more such events than did the control group. Thus depressed patients showed an excess of both controllable and uncontrollable events. Paykel's definition of controllability includes the degree of choice the respondent might expect over the initiation of the event, and thus includes intentionality. In a prospective study, Grant, Sweetwood, Yager, and Gerst (1981) examined the stressful life events of outpatients at a Veterans Administration (VA) hospital and of controls and found that dysphoric symptoms were significantly associated with experimenter-defined uncontrollable events, although controllable events were also significantly, but more weakly, associated with depression.

In the Grant *et al.* (1981) study, uncontrollable negative events, such as major personal illness or injury and the death of a spouse, tended to be among the most distressing of all negative events. Additional studies reviewed by Thoits (1983) report inconsistent findings about controllability (independence) associated with various psychiatric outcomes. In other studies where subjects make their own ratings of perceived controllability over the causes of the events, it appears that low control is attributed to events that people experience as highly upsetting. However, perceptions of low control are not unique to depressives; Gong-Guy and Hammen (1980) and Hammen and Cochran (1981) found no differences in controllability ratings between depressed and nondepressed outpatients, nor between depressed and nondepressed but highly stressed students, respectively. Also, Hammen and Mayol (1982) found that the recent events that were seen both objectively and subjectively as the most uncontrollable were actually significantly less associated with depressive symptoms than were events that were at least partly controllable.

Perceived control over events has been viewed both as an intraindividual quality and as a property of certain events. As a trait, "locus of control" refers to a generalized belief in one's ability to affect the environment so as to maximize rewards and minimize negative outcomes (e.g., Lefcourt, 1976; Rotter, 1966). On the other hand, two studies suggest that perceptions of control over an *event* are strongly determined by the characteristics of the event itself (Dohrenwend & Martin, 1979; Hammen & Mayol, 1982). Indeed, Dohrenwend and Martin demonstrated statistically that situational difference exceeded individual difference in the determination of perceived control over events. Studies of person–situation interactions have not been done; thus the question of what happens to people who expect to be able to control events but who experience an objectively uncontrollable event, or the reverse, poses interesting predictive possibilities. Wortman (1976) reported that persons who expect to be able to control events found uncontrollable outcomes especially stressful. Johnson and Sarason (1978) found that persons with an internal locus of control showed no association between depression and negative life events, although there was no indication whether any of the events were objectively uncontrollable.

In sum, the effects of the uncontrollability of stressors seem to depend on how the term is defined and on a variety of additional cognitive and event characteristics. It appears that highly upsetting events are often perceived by subjects as relatively uncontrollable, and that uncontrollability is very upsetting. However, although individuals might be highly distressed, they may not necessarily experience depression, and depressed persons apparently experience high levels of both controllable and uncontrollable events.

Personal Responsibility

A construct that is closely related to uncontrollability is personal responsibility for the occurrence of an event. Beck (1967, 1976) has argued that depressives characteristically blame themselves for negative events, thereby intensifying dysphoria. Abramson *et al.* (1978) postulated that only when uncontrollable events are ascribed to internal causes, such as personal incompetence, do self-esteem deficits occur.

Both views argue that individual predispositions (depressive schemas, attributional style) determine self-blame for negative events.

In an entirely different approach to the issue of personal responsibility, life stress researchers such as Dohrenwend (1974), Fairbank and Hough (1979), and Brown and Harris (1978b) have reasoned that personal responsibility is a method-ological problem that confounds independent and dependent variables in stress–illness studies. That is, events that could be caused by the illness (depression) need to be ignored in order to assess the true relationship between symptoms and events. Several such measurement or assessment systems have been proposed that permit the analysis of the degree to which depression may be related to events for which there might be some personal responsibility or to events that are independent of the person. Brown and Harris (1978b) and Costello (1982) identified "independent" events (independent of a woman's personality or behavior on logical grounds) and "possibly independent" (i.e., possibly dependent) events. Brown and Harris (1978b) found that severe events of both types were associated equally with depression, whereas Costello (1982) found that severe "possibly dependent" events were much more strongly associated with depression than were independent events. Fairbank and Hough (1979) and Hammen and Mayol (1982), employing the Fairbank–Hough system of classification, found greater depressive symptomatolo-gy associated with "undesirable-responsible" events (those similar to Brown's and Costello's classification of possibly dependent).

All of these studies suggest that events for which the individual may be at least partly responsible, whether determined by properties of the events themselves or by subjective appraisal, are associated with depression. Thus it is clear that methods that would omit such events from studies of depressive reactions to stressful events would ignore an important factor in depression (see also Lazarus, DeLongis, Folkman, & Gruen, 1985). On the other hand, the mediators of such effects are unclear. As indicated earlier, findings of causal attributions to internal factors (self-blame) have not been unequivocally observed. Also, even when data do support a link between subjective self-blame and depression, the correlational methods do not permit certainty about the direction of causality. It is equally plausible, for instance, to believe that depression causes self-blame.

The finding of Costello (1982) and Hammen and Mayol (1982) that greatest depression was associated with events for which the person might be considered at least partly responsible raises various possibilities. One is that it would be normal to blame oneself for such events because they are actually partly attributable to one's actions or characteristics, and this self-blame then causes depression. Another possibility is that additional qualities of such events themselves (many are in-terpersonal or failure experiences) elicit depression. Yet another is that additional factors or the personal qualities of individuals cause both the events and the depression to occur.

Finally, it should be noted that self-blame for a negative event not only does not always lead to depression but may sometimes be associated with *less* distress. For instance, Bulman and Wortman (1977) found that accident victims with spinal cord injury who blamed themselves coped better then those who blamed others or who felt that the accident could have been avoided. The authors speculate that self-blame may be adaptive, however, only in cases where it may facilitate action to remedy the situation. In cases where no responses are available, self-blame may be maladaptive.

In sum, self-blame may be associated with depression, although the direction of responsibility is unclear, and in some cases self-blame may be adaptive. In all these instances, the effects appear to depend on additional factors. Also, self-blame may not be merely a characteristic distortion of depression-prone persons, as in the Beck and Abramson *et al.* formulations, but may reflect a veridical perception. Further, as a methodological issue, the research on "responsibility" demonstrates that considering only objectively independent events would obscure important questions about depression. Finally, as Costello (1982) has suggested, we must consider whether unknown personal qualities of individuals may actually cause both the events and the depression.

Meaning

Another cognition or cognitive process that surfaces frequently in research on life events or stress is meaning. Assessing the role of meaning in predicting reactions to stress is, of course, the quintessential cognitive approach. Unfortunately, however, there are several ways in which "meaning" is meant, thereby clouding its precision and utility.

In one definition, meaning appears to capture the sense of primary appraisals. The individual appraises the significance of an event for his or her well-being, that is, what is "at stake" (Lazarus & Folkman, 1984; Lazarus & Launier, 1978). Brown and Harris (1978b) also view meaning as the threat and implications imposed by a stressful event, although unlike Lazarus, they attempt to employ a nonsubjective assessment of personal meaning. In this formulation, mere knowledge of the occurrence of an event is not as predictive of emotional reaction as is knowledge of the likely impact of the event for the person—for example, a broken leg has vastly different "meaning" to a 30-year-old than to a 90-year-old. There seems to be universal agreement on the significance of meaning in this usage.

Another sense of the term, which is somewhat related, includes the more long-term consequences of an event for the person's definition of self and the world and for his or her expectations for the future. This version of "meaning" refers to interpretations, psychological consequences, and perhaps philosophical speculations that occur not at the stage of initial threat appraisals but rather at some point after the occurrence of the event. Brown and Harris (1978b) allude to the critical role of the impact of events in the way people's world views change. Although this process has not been studied directly, aspects of the attributional analysis of the causes of events may reflect portions of this process. Weiner (1979) has speculated that self-ascriptions for the causes of events lead to esteem-related affects that have "the greatest longevity and most significance to the individual" (p. 14). Thus "meaning" in this usage appears to affect expectations of future well-being; it is included in the characterization of the attributional learned helplessness reformulation as a theory of expectations about future uncontrollability (Abramson *et al.*, 1978, 1986).

Finally, attributing meaning has been used in the sense of a coping process or outcome, in which the person may attempt to find a positive purpose in misfortune. To the degree that individuals can formulate a philosophical theory of the cause or consequences of a stressful event, it is hypothesized that they will experience a more positive adjustment (Silver & Wortman, 1980). Taylor (1983) argues that individuals explicitly search for meaning after a threatening event and that their success in finding a positive meaning in the experience significantly affects success-ful adjustment. Clearly, such efforts are shaped by intraindividual and situational factors. As Silver and Wortman (1980) point out, for instance, the ability to find positive purposes in negative events is influenced by the nature of the event itself.

Expectancy

As with the other cognitive constructs discussed, the notion of expectancy has been variously conceptualized and applied to research on stress. In one version, theorists have speculated that unexpected (unanticipated) negative events will be more aversive than anticipated negative events (Dohrenwend & Martin, 1979). This view generally holds that the unpredictability of the onset of an event is an aspect of uncontrollability. Although laboratory and some field research supports the hypoth-esis that unpredictable and uncontrollable stressors are especially noxious (Cohen, 1980), few studies of personal life stresses are available that test this view. From the Camberwell study in London there appeared to be no evidence that depression was significantly associated with unanticipated events (Brown & Harris, 1978b). Also, Hammen and Mayol (1982) found that *less* depression was associated with un-expected events than with somewhat expected events. Hammen and Mayol also found that type of event appears to determine its expectedness, with negative events that are beyond one's responsibility seen as the most unexpected (as well as uncontrollable, unintended, etc.).

In another usage of the term, expectancy refers to views of the future as in the learned helplessness paradigm of expectations of future uncontrollability, and such expectations are regarded as determining helplessness deficits (Abramson *et al.*, 1980, 1986). Expectancy may refer not only to outcomes but also to personal efficacy, as will be discussed in the next section.

In sum, the pervasiveness of various expectancy formulations leads to the conclusion that in some fashion, apparently operating on both primary and second-ary levels, such processes affect reactions to stressful events. As Novaco (1979) puts it, "The essence of these variously labelled cognitive activities is some subjective probability about events and one's responses to them. Thus, expectation can usefully be designated in conjunction with appraisal as the cognitive determi-nants of stress responses" (p. 251). Unfortunately, this generalization does not clarify the mechanisms by which such processes lead to stress responses. The frequent usage of "expectancy" to refer both to a process and to specific content, and the apparent interdependence between expectation and other cognitive constructs, cloud the significance of this concept.

Efficacy

Cognitions about personal efficacy would appear to be important predictors of responses to stressful events. As noted elsewhere, Bandura's (1977, 1978, 1982) model predicts that coping and persistence will be affected by self-efficacy expectations, although the model has not made specific predictions about depression and has not been tested in real-life reactions to personal stressors. As with other cognitions, both individual and situational determinants of self-efficacy beliefs are relevant. Generalized beliefs about personal control (e.g., Lefcourt, 1976; Rotter, 1966) as well as personal experiences of mastery of previous stressors may affect self-efficacy expectations (Billings & Moos, 1982). Also, as noted, "self-esteem" may overlap with self-efficacy to the degree that it includes beliefs about personal competence. Similarly, efficacy expectations may be determined in part by actual resources and options available to the person for resolving particular stressful circumstances. Thus, although intuitively appealing as a useful construct in predicting distress, the parameters of self-efficacy are minimally developed.

Summary

A review of the various cognitive constructs viewed as mediating depressive reactions to stress reveals a confusing picture of highly interrelated, overlapping concepts. The meager data on the ways these constructs relate to actual personal stressors generally fail to support a singular role of simple concepts such as uncontrollability, unpredictability, self-blame, or self-efficacy. On the other hand, the data are congruent with the importance of the interrelated cognitions concerning meaning (impact, personal significance) and the ability to handle consequences (coping capability, self-efficacy). Such cognitions seem fundamentally embedded in a self-system of beliefs and capabilities regarding one's worth, requirements for fulfillment, and likelihood of obtaining, keeping, and replacing such supplies. As Thoits (1983) recently concluded, "In short, psychological symptoms may be the result of the meanings people attach to, or the cognitive interpretations people make of, events and their aftermaths with respect to the self" (p. 83). Nonetheless, the determinants and functions of these processes require considerable additional research.

CONCLUSION

It would appear that the singular contribution of both the multifactor and the unitary cognitive theory approaches to depression has been to highlight the complexity of the problem of predicting depressive reactions. The life-event researchers, who propose complex theories, have provided little empirical support for, or clarification of, their cognitive speculations and still largely focus not on individual appraisal but on relatively objective properties of events. The cognitive theorists, such as Beck, Abramson, Seligman, and their colleagues, have largely downplayed situational determinants of cognitions and instead continue to focus extensively on intraindividual "vulnerability" variables, using heuristically significant but narrow theories. Although the pursuit of individual differences on the one hand and the examination of normative reactions to objectively stressful events on the other represent different but equally valid research strategies, there is an obvious need for the kinds of person-by-situation interaction studies often heralded but rarely pursued (Coyne, 1982; Dohrenwend & Martin, 1979; Hammen & Mayol, 1982). It is notable that the level of theorizing about causes of depression has grown grander while the data have become less consistent. Thus the trade-off between highly precise theories that yield explanation for a small amount of variance, and broad but empirically untested theories, suggests a need for more modest, midrange formulations. We also need to consider that theories that may account for depressive onset may need to be different from theories of depression maintenance (Hammen, Mayol, de Mayo, & Marks, 1986).

Current research perspectives support a view of individuals as active constructionists, engaging in ongoing and shifting appraisals, reappraisals, hypothesis testing, planning, philosophizing, and the like. The appraisals of stressful events determine emotional reactions, such as depression, as well as the behaviors undertaken to remedy or resolve the stressful circumstances. Lazarus's stress–emotion coping model, though not specific to depression, probably best captures the fluid and transactional nature of this cognitive activity. The model captures two elements that are vital to effective prediction but that have been virtually ignored in other major theories: the temporal process and the interactive (or, more accurately, transactive) relations between the person and the environment. To put this in its simplest terms, future research must study processes over time, not just for methodological purposes of clarifying causation, but also because of the validity of this strategy for capturing the active and changing processes by which events are construed and coped with. Future research must also consider contextual factors regarding situational demands and actual personal resources in an effort to understand the mechanisms by which these exert any effects.

This review points out that there are few specific cognitive contributions to understanding depression that have universal applicability. Beliefs about the causes of negative events seem inconsistently or only weakly related to depression. Perceived uncontrollability may often be as linked with nondepression as with depression, while the self-blame that may exacerbate depression for some might be adaptive for others. In any case, the self-blame may be accurate; at least it must be considered that qualities of persons may contribute to the occurrence of events. The construct of loss that is so central to traditional formulations of depression seems so elusive as not to be a useful predictor of depression at present. On the other hand, the cognitive constructs of meaning and self-efficacy recur in the literature in many forms, and the available data are consistent with their potential mediating role in depressive responses to stress. The mere occurrence of undesirable events, or the mere presence or lack of coping resources, predicts depression far less adequately than does consideration of the meaning of the event for the person and the person's sense of personal efficacy. It continues to be the challenge for depression researchers to clarify the determinants and modes of operation of such self-related cognitive processes.

Little has been said in this review about methodological issues in research on life- stress and depression. Yet, the same concerns often voiced by others bear repeating: This research is plagued by imprecise definitions and measures of depression and specific cognitions and by overreliance on designs that obscure the direction of causality or that are inadequate to determining whether certain factors uniquely produce depression rather than other outcomes.

The combination of conceptual and methodological issues seems formidable. The cost of good research is great, and the yield of grand theorizing is small. Yet, the questions to be answered are important, and the human significance is substantial. There is much to be gained from past and current efforts, and the combined study of cognitions and stressful life events promises to reward the persistent efforts of painstaking researchers.

REFERENCES

Abramson, L., Garber, J., & Seligman, M. (1980). Learned helplessness in humans: An attributional analysis. In J. Garber & M. Seligman (Eds.), *Human helplessness: Theory and applications* (pp. 3–34). New York: Academic Press.

Abramson, L. Y., Metalsky, G. I., & Alloy, L. B. (1986). *The Hopelessness theory of depression: A metatheoretical analysis with implications for psychopathology research.* Manuscript submitted for publication.

Abramson, L., Seligman, M., & Teasdale, J. (1978). Learned helplessness in humans: Critique and reformulation. *Journal of Abnormal Psychology, 87,* 49–74.

Alexander, F. (1950). *Psychosomatic medicine.* New York: W. W. Norton.

Arieti, S., & Bemporad, J. (1980). The psychological organization of depression. *American Journal of Psychiatry, 137,* 1360–1365.

Averill, J. R. (1973). Personal control over aversive stimuli and its relationship to stress. *Psychological Bulletin, 80,* 286–303.

Bandura, A. (1977). Self-efficacy: Toward a unifying theory of behavioral change. *Psychological Review, 84,* 191–215.

Bandura, A. (1978). The self-system in reciprocal determinism. *American Psychologist, 33,* 344–358.

Bandura, A. (1982). Self-efficacy mechanism in human agency. *American Psychologist, 37,* 122–147.

Barnes, G. E., & Prosen, H. (1985). Parental death and depression. *Journal of Abnormal Psychology, 94,* 64–69.

Barthe, D., & Hammen, C. (1981). A naturalistic extension of the attributional model of depression. *Personality and Social Psychology Bulletin, 7,* 53–58.

Beck, A. T. (1967). *Depression: Clinical, experimental, and theoretical aspects.* New York: Harper & Row.

Beck, A. T. (1976). *Cognitive therapy and emotional disorders.* New York: International Universities Press.

Beck, A. T. (1982). Cognitive therapy of depression: New perspectives. In P. Clayton & J. Barrett (Eds.), *Treatment of depression: Old controversies and new approaches* (pp. 265–290). New York: Raven Press.

Beck, A. T., Epstein, N., & Harrison, R. (1982). *Cognitions, attitudes, and personality dimensions in depression*. Paper presented at the meeting of the Society for Psychotherapy Research, Smugglers Notch, VT.

Beck, A. T., & Rush, A. J. (1978). Cognitive approaches to depression and suicide. In G. Serban (Ed.), *Cognitive defects in the development of mental illness* (pp. 235–257). New York: Brunner/Mazel.

Beck, A., Rush, A. J., Shaw, B., & Emery, G. (1979). *Cognitive therapy of depression*. New York: Guilford Press.

Becker, J. (1979). Vulnerable self-esteem as a predisposing factor in depressive disorders. In R. A. Depue (Ed.), *The psychobiology of the depressive disorders: Implications for the effects of stress* (pp. 317–334). New York: Academic Press.

Billings, A., & Moos, R. (1982). Psychosocial theory and research on depression: An integrative framework and review. *Clinical Psychology Review, 2,* 213–237.

Blatt, S., D'Afflitti, J., & Quinlan, D. (1976). Experiences of depression in normal young adults. *Journal of Abnormal Psychology, 85,* 383–389.

Blatt, S., Quinlan, B., Chevron, E., McDonald, C., & Zuroff, D. (1982). Dependency and self-criticism: Psychological dimensions of depression. *Journal of Consulting and Clinical Psychology, 50,* 113–124.

Brown, G. (1979). The social etiology of depression—London studies. In R. A. Depue (Ed.), *The psychobiology of the depressive disorders: Implications for the effects of stress* (pp. 263–290). New York: Academic Press.

Brown, G., & Harris, T. (1978a). Social origins of depression: A reply. *Psychological Medicine, 8,* 577–588.

Brown, G., & Harris, T. (1978b). *Social origins of depression: A study of psychiatric disorders in women*. New York: Free Press.

Bulman, R. J., & Wortman, C. B. (1977). Attribution of blame and coping in the "real world": Severe accident victims react to their lot. *Journal of Personality and Social Psychology, 35,* 351–363.

Cochran, S., & Hammen, C. (1985). Perceptions of stressful life events and depression: A test of attributional models. *Journal of Personality and Social Psychology, 48,* 1562–1571.

Cohen, S. (1980). Aftereffects of stress on human performance and social behavior: A review of research and theory. *Psychological Bulletin, 88,* 82–108.

Costello, C. (1982). Social factors associated with depression: A retrospective community study. *Psychological Medicine, 12,* 329–339.

Coyne, J. (1982). A critique of cognitions as causal entities with particular reference to depression. *Cognitive Theory and Research, 6,* 3–13.

Coyne, J., Aldwin, C., & Lazarus, R. (1981). Depression and coping in stressful episodes. *Journal of Abnormal Psychology, 90,* 439–441.

Coyne, J. C., & Gotlib, I. H. (1983). The role of cognition in depression: A critical appraisal. *Psychological Bulletin, 94,* 472–505.

Coyne, J., & Lazarus, R. (1980). Cognition, stress and coping: A transactional perspective. In I. L. Kutash & L. B. Schlesinger (Eds.), *Handbook on stress and anxiety*. San Francisco: Jossey-Bass.

Cutrona, C. (1983). Causal attributions and perinatal depression. *Journal of Abnormal Psychology, 92,* 161–172.

Cutrona, C., Russell, D., & Jones, R. (1984). Cross-situational consistency in causal attributions: Does "attributional style" exist? *Journal of Personality and Social Psychology, 47,* 1043–1058.

Depue, R., Monroe, S., & Shackman, S. (1979). The psychobiology of human disease: Implications for conceptualizing the depressive disorders. In R. A. Depue (Ed.), *The psychobiology of the depressive disorders: Implications for the effects of stress* (pp. 3–22). New York: Academic Press.

Derry, P., & Kuiper, N. (1981). Schematic processing and self reference in clinical depression. *Journal of Abnormal Psychology, 90,* 286–297.

Devins, G. M., Binik, Y. M., Hollomby, D. J., Barre, P. E., & Guttman, R. D. (1981). Helplessness and depression in end-stage renal disease. *Journal of Abnormal Psychology, 90,* 531–545.

Dohrenwend, B. P. (1974). Problems in defining and sampling the relevant population of stressful life events. In B. P. Dohrenwend & B. S. Dohrenwend (Eds.), *Stressful life events: Their nature and effects* (pp. 275–310). New York: Wiley.

Dohrenwend, B. P., &: Dohrenwend, B. S. (1979). The conceptualization and measurement for stressful life events: An overview of the issues. In R. A. Depue (Ed.), *The psychobiology of the depressive disorders: Implications for the effects of stress* (pp. 105–121). New York: Academic Press.

Dohrenwend, B. S., Kransoff, L., Askenasy, A., & Dohrenwend, B. P. (1978). Exemplification of a method for scaling life events: The PERI Life Events Scale. *Journal of Health and Social Behavior, 19,* 205–229.

Dohrenwend, B. S., & Martin, J. (1979). Personal versus situational determination of anticipation and control of the occurrence of stressful life events. *American Journal of Community Psychology, 7,* 453–468.

Dohrenwend, B. P., & Shrout, P. E. (1985). "Hassles" in the conceptualization and measurement of life stress variables. *American Psychologist, 40,* 780–785.

Eaves, G., & Rush, J. A. (1984). Cognitive patterns in symptomatic and remitted unipolar major depression. *Journal of Abnormal Psychology, 93,* 31–40.

Elkin, I., Shea, T., Watkins, J. T., Collins, J. F., Docherty, J. P., & Shaw, B. F. (1986, May). *NIMH treatment of depression collaborative research program: Outcome findings and therapist performance.* Paper presented at the meeting of the American Psychiatric Association, Washington, DC.

Everitt, B., & Smith, A. (1979). Interactions in contingency tables: A brief discussion of alternative definitions. *Psychological Medicine, 9,* 581–583.

Fairbank, D., & Hough, R. (1979). Life event classifications and event–illness relationship. *Journal of Human Stress, 5,* 41–47.

Feather, N., & Barber, J. (1983). Depressive reactions and unemployment. *Journal of Abnormal Psychology, 92,* 185–195.

Finlay-Jones, R., & Brown, G. (1981). Types of stressful life events and the onset of anxiety and depressive disorders. *Psychological Medicine, 11,* 803–815.

Folkman, S., & Lazarus, R. S. (1986). Stress processes and depressive symptomatology. *Journal of Abnormal Psychology, 95,* 107–113.

Glass, D., & Singer, J. (1972). *Urban stress.* New York: Academic Press.

Gong-Guy, E., & Hammen, C. (1980). Causal perceptions of stressful life events in depressed and nondepressed clinic outpatients. *Journal of Abnormal Psychology, 89,* 662–669.

Grant, I., Sweetwood, H., Yager, J., & Gerst, M. (1981). Quality of life events in relation to psychiatric symptoms. *Archives of General Psychiatry, 38,* 335–339.

Hamilton, E., & Abramson, L. (1983). Cognitive patterns and major depressive disorder: A longitudinal study in a hospital setting. *Journal of Abnormal Psychology, 92,* 173–184.

Hammen, C. L. (1985). Predicting depression: A cognitive–behavioral perspective. *Advances in Cognitive–Behavioral Research and Therapy, 4,* 29–71.

Hammen, C., & Cochran, S. (1981). Cognitive correlates of life stress and depression in college students. *Journal of Abnormal Psychology, 90,* 23–27.

Hammen, C., & de Mayo, R. (1982). Cognitive correlates of teacher stress and depressive symptoms: Implications for attributional models of depression. *Journal of Abnormal Psychology, 91,* 96–101.

Hammen, C., Jacobs, M., Mayol, A., & Cochran, S. (1980). Dysfunctional cognitions and the effectiveness of skills and cognitive–behavioral assertion training. *Journal of Consulting and Clinical Psychology, 48,* 685–695.

Hammen, C., & Krantz, S. (1985). Measuring the crucial process in depression. In E. E. Beckham & W. R. Leber (Eds.), *Depression: Treatment, assessment, and research* (pp. 408–444). Homewood, IL: Dow Jones-Irwin.

Hammen, C., Krantz, S., & Cochran, S. (1981). Relationships between depression and causal attributions about stressful life events. *Cognitive Therapy and Research, 5,* 351–358.

Hammen, C. L., Marks, T., de Mayo, R., & Mayol, A. (1985). Self-schemas and risk for depression: A prospective study. *Journal of Personality and Social Psychology, 49*(5), 1147–1159.

Hammen, C., Marks, T., Mayol, A., & de Mayo, R. (1985). Depressive self-schemas, life stress, and vulnerability to depression. *Journal of Abnormal Psychology, 94,* 308–319.

Hammen, C., & Mayol, A. (1982). Depression and cognitive characteristics of stressful life-event types. *Journal of Abnormal Psychology, 91,* 165–174.

Hammen, C., Mayol, A., de Mayo, R., & Marks, T. (1986). Initial symptom levels and the life-event–depression relationship. *Journal of Abnormal Psychology, 95,* 114–122.

Hammen, C., Miklowitz, D., & Dyck, D. (1986). Stability and severity parameters of depressive self-schema responding. *Journal of Social and Clinical Psychology, 4,* 23–45.

Hammen, C., & Zupan, B. (1984). Self-schemas, depression, and the processing of personal information in children. *Journal of Experimental Child Psychology, 37,* 598–608.

Harvey, D. (1981). Depression and attributional style: Interpretations of important personal events. *Journal of Abnormal Psychology, 90,* 134–142.

Hollon, S. D., Kendall, P. C., & Lumry, A. (1986). Specificity of depressotypic cognitions in clinical depression. *Journal of Abnormal Psychology, 95,* 52–59.

Holmes, T. H., & Rahe, R. H. (1967). The Social Readjustment Rating Scale. *Journal of Psychosomatic Research, 11,* 213–218.

Johnson, J. H., & Sarason, I. G. (1978). Life stress, depression, and anxiety: Internal–external control as a moderator variable. *Journal of Psychosomatic Research, 22,* 205–208.

Kanner, A. D., Coyne, J. C., Schaefer, C., & Lazarus, R. (1981). Comparison of two modes of stress measurement: Daily hassles and uplifts versus major life events. *Journal of Behavioral Medicine, 4,* 1–39.

Kayne, N. T., Alloy, L. B., Romer, D., & Crocker, J. (1986). *Predicting depression and elation reactions in the classroom: A test of an attributional diathesis–stress theory of depression.* Manuscript submitted for publication.

Kuiper, N., & Derry, P. (1982). Depressed and nondepressed content self-reference in mild depressives. *Journal of Personality, 50,* 62–74.

Kuiper, N. A., Olinger, L. J., MacDonald, M. R., & Shaw, B. F. (1985). Self-schema processing of depressed and nondepressed content: The effects of vulnerability to depression. *Social Cognition, 3,* 77–93.

Lazarus, R. (1982). Thoughts on the relations between emotions and cognition. *American Psychologist, 37,* 1019–1024.

Lazarus, R. S., DeLongis, A., Folkman, S., & Gruen, R. (1985). Stress and adaptational outcomes: The problem of confounded measures. *American Psychologist, 40,* 770–779.

Lazarus, R. S., & Folkman, S. (1984). *Stress, appraisal, and coping.* New York: Springer.

Lazarus, R., & Launier, R. (1978). Stress-related transactions between person and environment. In L. Pervin & M. Lewis (Eds.), *Internal and external determinants of behavior.* New York: Plenum.

Lefcourt, H. (1976). *Locus of control.* Hillsdale, NJ: Erlbaum.

Lewinsohn, P., & Amenson, C. (1978). Some relations between pleasant and unpleasant mood-related events and depression. *Journal of Abnormal Psychology, 87,* 644–654.

Lewinsohn, P., Steinmetz, J., Larson, D., & Franklin, J. (1981). Depression-related cognitions: Antecedent or consequence? *Journal of Abnormal Psychology, 90,* 213–219.

Lewinsohn, P., & Talkington, J. (1979). Studies in the measurement of unpleasant events and relations with depression. *Applied Psychological Measurement, 3,* 83–101.

Lloyd, C. (1980a). Life events and depressive disorders reviewed. 2. Events as precipitating factors. *Archives of General Psychiatry, 37,* 541–548.

Lloyd, C. (1980b). Life events and depressive disorders reviewed. 1. Events as predisposing factors. *Archives of General Psychiatry, 37,* 529–537.

Manly, P. C., McMahon, R. J., Bradley, C. F., & Davidson, P. O. (1982). Depressive attributional style and depression following childbirth. *Journal of Abnormal Psychology, 91,* 245–254.

Markus, H. (1977). Self-schemata and processing of information about the self. *Journal of Personality and Social Psychology, 35,* 63–78.

Miller, I., Klee, S., & Norman, W. (1982). Depressed and nondepressed inpatients' cognitions of hypothetical events, experimental tasks and stressful life events. *Journal of Abnormal Psychology, 91,* 78–81.

Miller, I., & Norman, W. (1979). Learned helplessness in humans: A review and attribution theory model. *Psychological Bulletin, 86,* 93–118.

Miller, S. (1980). Why having control reduces stress: If I can stop the roller coaster, I don't want to get off. In J. Garber & M. Seligman (Eds.), *Human helplessness: Theory and applications* (pp. 71–96). New York: Academic Press.

Monroe, S. (1982). Life events and disorder: Event–symptom associations and the course of disorder. *Journal of Abnormal Psychology, 91,* 14–24.

Mueller, D., Edwards, D., & Yarvis, R. (1977). Stressful life events and psychiatric symptomatology: Change or undesirability? *Journal of Health and Social Behavior, 18,* 307–317.

Novaco, R. (1979). The cognitive regulation of anger and stress. In P. Kendall & S. Hollon (Eds.), *Cognitive–behavioral interventions: Theory, research and procedures.* (pp. 241–286). New York: Academic Press.

O'Hara, M., Rehm, L., & Campbell, S. (1982). Predicting depressive symptomatology: Cognitive–behavioral models and postpartum depression. *Journal of Abnormal Psychology, 91,* 457–461.

Olinger, L. J., Kuiper, N. A., & Shaw, B. F. (1986). *Dysfunctional attitudes and negative life events: A cognitive vulnerability to depression.* Manuscript submitted for publication.

Parker, G. B., & Brown, L. B. (1982). Coping behaviors that mediate between life events and depression. *Archives of General Psychiatry, 39,* 1386–1391.

Parker, G., Brown, L., & Bignault, I. (1986). Coping behaviors as predictors of the course of clinical depression. *Archives of General Psychiatry, 43,* 561–565.

Paykel, E. S. (1978). Contribution of life events to causation of psychiatric illness. *Psychological Medicine, 8,* 245–253.

Paykel, E. S. (1979). Recent life events in the development of the depressive disorder. In R. A. Depue (Ed.), *The psychobiology of the depressive disorders: Implications for the effects of stress* (pp. 245–262). New York: Academic Press.

Pearlin, L. I., Lieberman, M. A., Menaghan, E. G., & Mullan, J. T. (1981). The stress process. *Journal of Health and Social Behavior, 22,* 337–356.

Persons, J. B., & Rao, P. A. (1985). Longitudinal study of cognitions, life events, and depression in psychiatric inpatients. *Journal of Abnormal Psychology, 94,* 51–63.

Peterson, C., & Raps, C. S. (1983). *Depression, attributions, and attributional style.* Unpublished manuscript, Virginia Polytechnic Institute and State University, Blacksburg.

Peterson, C., Rosenbaum, A. C., & Conn, M. K. (1985). Depressive mood reactions to breaking up: Testing the learned helplessness model of depression. *Journal of Social and Clinical Psychology, 3,* 161–169.

Peterson, C., & Seligman, M. E. P. (1984). Causal explanations as a risk factor for depression: Theory and evidence. *Psychological Review, 91,* 347–374.

Rabkin, J., & Streuning, E. (1976). Life events, stress and illness. *Science, 194,* 1013–1020.

Rahe, R. H., & Arthur, R. J. (1978). Life change and illness studies: Past history and future directions. *Journal of Human Stress, 4,* 3–15.

Redfield, J., & Stone, A. (1979). Individual viewpoint of stressful life events. *Journal of Consulting and Clinical Psychology, 47,* 147–154.

Riskind, J., & Rholes, W. (1984). Cognitive accessibility and the capacity of cognitions to predict future depression: A theoretical note. *Cognitive Therapy and Research, 8,* 1–12.

Rotter, J. B. (1966). Generalized expectancies for internal versus external control of reinforcement. *Psychological Monographs, 80*(1, Whole No. 609).

Roy, A. (1985). Early parental separation and adult depression. *Archives of General Psychiatry, 42,* 987–991.

Sarason, I. G., Johnson, J. H., & Siegel, J. M. (1978). Assessing the impact of life changes: Development of the life experiences survey. *Journal of Consulting and Clinical Psychology, 46,* 932–946.

Segal, Z. V., & Shaw, B. F. (1986). Cognition in depression: A reappraisal of Coyne and Gotlib's critique. *Cognitive Therapy and Research, 10,* 671–693.

Seligman, M. E. P. (1975). *Helplessness: On depression, development and death*. San Francisco: W. H. Freeman.

Seligman, M., Abramson, L., Semmel, A., & von Baeyer, C. (1979). Depressive attributional style. *Journal of Abnormal Psychology, 88*, 242–247.

Silver, R., & Wortman, C. (1980). Coping with undesirable life events. In J. Garber & M. Seligman (Eds.), *Human helplessness: Theory and applications* (pp. 279–375). New York: Academic Press.

Silverman, J., Silverman, J., & Eardley, D. (1984). Do maladaptive attitudes cause depression? *Archives of General Psychiatry, 41*, 28–30.

Simons, A. D., Murphy, G. E., Levine, J. L., & Wetzel, R. D. (1986). Cognitive therapy and pharmacotherapy for depression. *Archives of General Psychiatry, 43*, 43–48.

Slater, J., & Depue, R. (1981). The contribution of environmental events and social support to serious suicide attempts in primary affective disorder. *Journal of Abnormal Psychology, 90*, 275–285.

Tausig, M. (1982). Measuring life events. *Journal of Health and Social Behavior, 23*, 52–64.

Taylor, S. E. (1983). Adjustment to threatening events: A theory of cognitive adaptation. *American Psychologist, 38*, 1161–1173.

Tennant, C., & Bebbington, P. (1978). The social causation of depression: A critique of the work of Brown and his colleagues. *Psychological Medicine, 8*, 565–575.

Tennant, C., Bebbington, P., & Hurry, J. (1981). The role of life events in depressive illness: Is there a substantial causal relation? *Psychological Medicine, 11*, 379–389.

Thoits, P. (1983). Dimensions of life events that influence psychological distress: An evaluation and synthesis of the literature. In H. B. Kaplan (Ed.), *Psychosocial stress: Trends in theory and research* (pp. 33–103). New York: Academic Press.

Warheit, G. (1979). Life events, coping, stress and depressive symptomatology. *American Journal of Psychiatry, 136*, 502–507.

Weiner, B. (1974). *Achievement motivation and attribution theory*. Morristown, NJ: General Learning Press.

Weiner, B., & Litman-Adizes, T. (1980). An attributional, expectancy-value analysis of learned helplessness and depression. In J. Garber & M. Seligman (Eds.), *Human helplessness: Theory and applications* (pp. 35–58). New York: Academic Press.

Weissman, A. N. (1979). *The Dysfunctional Attitude Scale: A validation study*. Unpublished doctoral dissertation, University of Pennsylvania, Philadelphia.

Wortman, C. B. (1976). Causal attributions and personal control. In J. H. Harvey, W. J. Ickes, & R. F. Kidd (Eds.), *New directions in attribution research*. Hillsdale, NJ: Erlbaum.

Wortman, C., & Dintzer, L. (1978). Is an attributional analysis of the learned helplessness phenomenon viable? A critique of the Abramson–Seligman–Teasdale reformulation. *Journal of Abnormal Psychology, 87*, 75–80.

4

Depression versus Anxiety: Differences in Self- and Other-schemata

MICHAEL S. GREENBERG
Florida Center for Cognitive Therapy

CARMELO V. VAZQUEZ
Universidad Complutense de Madrid

LAUREN B. ALLOY
Northwestern University

The phenomena of depression and anxiety have been closely related in clinical, empirical, and theoretical investigations. Among clinicians, a long-standing controversy has existed over whether anxious and depressive states are two separate disorders (Kraepelin, 1981/1883) or states belonging to different parts of a single continuum of affective disorders varying in severity (Lewis, 1934; 1938). By the mid-1970s, the consensus of opinion in psychiatry was that anxiety and depression were separate but related disorders. This opinion was largely shaped by a series of psychiatric studies suggesting that clinical samples of depressed and anxious patients could be discriminated with respect to symptomatology, personality, past history, and treatment response (e.g., Garber, Miller, & Abramson, 1980; Gersh & Fowles, 1979; Grinker, 1966; Gurney, Roth, Garside, Kerr, & Schapira, 1972; Klerman, 1977; Levitt & Lubin, 1975; Mathew, Swihart, & Weinman, 1982; Murray & Blackburn, 1974; Parkes, 1981; Prusoff & Klerman, 1974; Roth, Gurney, Garside, & Kerr, 1972; Roth & Mountjoy, 1982). However, several more recent clinical, family, and treatment studies have raised the possibility that depressive and anxiety disorders share a common diathesis (Barlow, 1985; Foa & Foa, 1982; Klein, 1980; Leckman, Merikangus, Pauls, Prusoff, & Weissman, 1983; Leckman, Weissman, Merikangus, Pauls, & Prusoff, 1983; Weissman, Leckman, Merikangus, Prusoff, & Gammon, 1983). In general, both sets of psychiatric studies have ignored theoretical processes that may account for both the differences and the similarities between the two affective phenomena.

In contrast, psychological investigations have presented more sophisticated theoretical accounts of depression and anxiety but have not considered the two phenomena within a single, unifying framework (e.g., Abramson, Seligman, & Teasdale, 1978; Epstein, 1972, 1976; Lazarus & Averill, 1972; Lewinsohn, 1974;

Mandler, 1972; Mandler & Watson, 1966; Sarason, 1975; Spielberger, 1972). Indeed, it appears that two parallel literatures exist within psychology, with many of the same paradigms and concepts used separately to account for depression and anxiety. For example, investigators have emphasized threats to self-esteem, fear of failure, negative cognitions, helplessness, and performance deficits as central to the understanding of both depression and anxiety (e.g., Abramson *et al.*, 1978; Beck, 1967, 1976; Garber *et al.*, 1980; Mandler, 1972; Sarason, 1975; Spielberger, 1972). Thus most relevant research on the relationship between depression and anxiety appears to fall into two separate literatures, with relatively few studies attempting to provide an integrated theoretical account of the two disorders.

In this chapter, we employ a cognitive "schema" framework for investigating the similarities and differences between depression and anxiety, and present findings from two studies (Greenberg & Alloy, 1987; Vazquez & Alloy, 1987) examining the self- and other-schemata of depressed and anxious individuals. Before presenting our rationale for adopting a schema approach to the integrated study of depression and anxiety, and our empirical findings with this approach, we first briefly discuss classificatory and diagnostic distinctions in these two disorders and review clinical, familial, and psychometric studies that investigate their interrelation.

CLASSIFICATORY AND DIAGNOSTIC DISTINCTIONS IN DEPRESSION AND ANXIETY

Depression is a heterogeneous concept, and many investigators have presented classification schemes for this disorder (e.g., Craighead, 1980; Depue & Monroe, 1979). Kendell (1976) reviewed some of the diagnostic schemes that have been formulated; a brief list of them conveys the complexity of the concept of depression: unipolar–bipolar (Depue & Monroe, 1979); primary–secondary; anxious, hostile, psychotic, and young depressives with personality disorders (Paykel, 1971, 1972a, 1972b); harried depression, pure melancholy, self-torturing depression, suspicious depression, nonparticipatory depression, hypochondriacal depression (Leonhard, 1979); endogenous–neurotic depression (Fowles & Gersh, 1979). The various classification schemes that have been proposed for depressive disorders typically describe fundamentally different clinical patterns of depression. However, the evidence for the validity of these subtypes varies, with minimal support found for specific categories, such as hypochondriacal and suspicious depression, but widespread acceptance for the broad distinctions of unipolar–bipolar (Depue & Monroe, 1979) and endogenous–nonendogenous depression (Fowles & Gersh, 1979).

The term "anxiety" has also been employed in a wide variety of contexts. For example, anxiety has been described as a protective signal, a drive, a conditioned form of fear, a trait, a state, an innate disposition, a syndrome, and a clinical diagnosis (Mandler, 1972). With respect to psychopathology, some of the more common distinctions include state–trait anxiety (Spielberger, 1972), acute–chronic anxiety (Gray, 1978; Schweitzer & Adams, 1979), and free-floating versus panic anxiety (Beck, 1967). Although distinctions among types of anxiety states have been offered, these distinctions represent relatively less complex classification schemes than those proposed for depression. Distinctions among anxiety states appear to be based upon unidimensional criteria, such as severity, temporal duration of the phenomena, the presence of panic attacks, and subjective perception of the source of threat (Barlow, 1985; Jablensky, 1985). However, it does seem that the phenomenological subtypes of anxiety featured in the DSM-III (APA, 1980), including agoraphobia, social phobia, simple phobia, panic disorder, generalized anxiety disorder, and obsessive–compulsive disorder, can be reliably distinguished from one another (Barlow, 1985).

What is the relationship between anxiety and the various clinical forms of depression? A large number of psychiatric and psychometric studies suggest that anxiety is differentially associated with various forms of clinical depression (e.g., Kiloh & Garside, 1963; Levitt & Lubin, 1975; Nelson & Charney, 1981; Rosenthal & Klerman, 1966). These studies suggest that overt anxiety is commonly found in reactive and neurotic depression (e.g., Grinker & Nunally, 1968; Prusoff & Klerman, 1974) but infrequently observed in psychotic, bipolar, and other more severe forms of depression (Depue & Monroe, 1979).

However, it would be simplistic and misleading to conclude that anxiety is of minimal importance in severe forms of depression (Leonhard, 1979; Lorr, Sonn, & Katz, 1967; Paykel, 1972a; Teja, Narang, & Aggarwal, 1971). Grinker (1966) argued that anxiety is often present in patients who appear withdrawn, retarded, and in "physiological hibernation." When these patients begin to recover from their depressive reactions, the appearance of behavioral anxiety and elevations in hormones related to activity and anxiety (adrenocortical hormones) become prominent. In agreement, Overall and Zisook (1980) suggested that anxiety usually accompanies depressed mood in all types of depression. Gersh and Fowles (1979) reviewed evidence suggesting that clinical agitation may be a severe but atypical manifestation of anxiety, although there is considerable disagreement on this issue. These writers suggested that anxiety may be present in all subtypes of depression, although it may be overshadowed by psychomotor retardation or neurovegetative signs, or may appear in atypical form as agitation in severe, psychotic, or endogenous depressions.

Not only is anxiety a common feature of depressive clinical presentations (Jablensky, Sartorius, Gulbinat, & Ernberg, 1981), but the differential diagnosis of depressive and anxiety disorders is also quite difficult. Both anxiety and depression are marked by feelings of dysphoria, apprehension, tension, excessive worrying, and self-preoccupation (Sarason, 1985; Spielberger, 1972), and the inclusion criteria for the two disorders in DSM-III are similar in a number of respects. Barlow (1985) reported that depressive diagnoses (either major affective disorder or dysthymic disorder) occurred as an additional diagnosis with high frequency among patients with anxiety disorders. Specifically, 66% of obsessive–compulsive, 39% of agoraphobic, 35% of panic-disordered, 21% of social-phobic, and 17% of generalized-anxiety-disordered patients also met DSM-III criteria for a depressive disorder. Indeed, in proposing revisions for DSM-III, Spitzer and Williams (1985) suggested the removal of the hierarchical principle by which a diagnosis of major depression excludes a concurrent diagnosis of an anxiety disorder.

CLINICAL AND FAMILIAL DISTINCTIONS BETWEEN DEPRESSION AND ANXIETY

Although depression and anxiety are difficult to differentiate, a series of studies by Roth and his colleagues suggested that the two disorders may be separate and distinctive (Gurney *et al.*, 1972; Kerr, Roth, & Schapira, 1974; Roth *et al.*, 1972; Schapira, Roth, Kerr, & Gurney, 1972). Patients admitted to a hospital with a diagnosis of either "depressive illness" or "anxiety state" were studied prospectively in terms of presenting symptoms, family history, premorbid personality characteristics, and outcome at an average of 3.8 years after the initial assessment. Although the two groups of patients showed a number of overlapping features, there were significant differences in clinical symptomatology, personality, family history, and clinical outcome. Panic attacks, vasomotor signs, dizziness, emotional lability, depersonalization, derealization, and agoraphobic experiences occurred with much higher frequency in the anxious patients, whereas worse depression in the morning, depressive mood reactive to change, psychomotor retardation, early waking, and suicidal acts were more common in the depressed patients. Depressive mood and tension were equally frequent in the two diagnostic groups; however, the combination of persistent depression and episodic tension was more common among patients with depressive illnesses, whereas the combination of episodic depression and chronic tension was characteristic of the patients with anxiety states. With respect to family history, neurotic and personality disorders were more frequent in the parents and siblings of patients with anxiety states than in the families of depressed patients. Anxiety patients also exhibited more social anxiety and maladjustment than their depressed counterparts. Finally, the patients with an initial diagnosis of depressive illness had a better prognosis than the patients with diagnoses of anxiety states, and symptomatological "crossover" during the course of the two groups' disorders was rare.

However, several recent family and treatment studies suggest that depressive and anxiety disorders may not be completely separate entities. Leckman, Weissman, and their colleagues (Leckman, Merikangus, Pauls, Prusoff, & Weissman, 1983; Leckman, Weissman, Merikangus, Pauls, & Prusoff, 1983; Weissman *et al.*, 1984a, 1984b) found that individuals with an anxiety disorder are at increased risk to develop either another anxiety disorder or major depression, and that first-degree relatives of probands with both major depression and an anxiety disorder showed higher rates of major depression *and* anxiety disorders than the relatives of patients with either one of the disorders alone. The highest rates of depression and anxiety were found in relatives of probands with both depression and panic disorder. On the basis of these studies, Weissman (1985) suggested that panic disorder (and perhaps agoraphobia) is more similar to depression than to other anxiety disorders and that it may be a manifestation of the same underlying diathesis.

Other family (Cloninger, Martin, Clayton, & Guze, 1981; Crowe, Noyes, Pauls, & Slyman, 1983) and genetic (Torgerson, 1983) studies are more supportive of the hypothesis that the two affective states are distinct. Pharmacological studies have also provided evidence for the similarity of panic states and depression. Klein (1980) reported that tricyclic antidepressants were effective in treating panic disorder and agoraphobia, whereas benzodiazepines, normally the drugs of choice for treating anxiety, did not work for these anxiety subgroups. Van Valkenburg, Akiskal, Puzantian, and Rosenthal (1984) also found that on most phenomenological, familial, treatment-response, and outcome measures, patients with primary panic, panic complicated by depression, depression complicated by panic, or primary depression formed a spectrum, with primary panic and primary depression constituting the extremes of a continuum joined by the two intermediate groups of anxious depressions.

PSYCHOMETRIC STUDIES OF DEPRESSION AND ANXIETY

In general, psychometric studies have had even less success in discriminating depression and anxiety than studies examining clinical, physiological, and genetic variables. For example, Mendels, Weinstein, and Cochrane (1972) attempted to discriminate between depression and anxiety in psychiatric patients by the use of several self-report measures and found that depression and anxiety scales loaded on the same (first) factor when the tests were factor analyzed. In addition, the anxiety scales correlated higher with the depression scales than they did with each other. Mendels *et al.* concluded that depression and anxiety scales could not be separated into two factors but instead represented a general dimension of psychological distress (see also Gotlib, 1984; Nezu, Nezu, & Nezu, 1986). Similar correlations have been reported in other psychometric investigations of depression and anxiety (e.g., Biglan & Dow, 1981; Gotlib, 1984; Meites, Lovallo, & Pishkin, 1980; Serra & Pollitt, 1975).

Psychometric studies that have not obtained differences between depression and anxiety have usually employed undiagnosed subject groups (e.g., Gotlib, 1984; Mendels *et al.*, 1972). It appears that studies of this type are less likely to differentiate depression and anxiety scales/symptoms because the two phenomena coexist in so many clinical states, medical conditions, and nonclinical mood variations (Jablensky, 1985). For example, studies examining college samples (Greenberg & Alloy, 1987; Miller, Seligman, & Kurlander, 1975) are usually unable to identify a substantial number of subjects who are depressed but not anxious.

In contrast to the preceding reports, several psychometric studies have been successful in discriminating between depression and anxiety (Costello & Comrey, 1967; Derogatis, Lipman, Covi, & Rickles, 1972; Riskind, Beck, Brown, & Steer, 1986; Tellegen, 1985). Costello and Comrey reported that it was the presence of depression and not anxiety that distinguished between preselected depression and anxiety groups (see also Gersh & Fowles, 1979; Roth *et al.*, 1972). Tellegen (1985) found that although both depressed and anxious subjects endorsed "unpleasant mood" items on a self-report personality questionnaire, anxious subjects loaded more heavily on High Negative Affect, whereas depressed subjects loaded more highly on Low Positive Affect. In general, studies that have obtained psychometric differences between depression and anxiety have often compared relatively carefully defined subgroups of depressed and anxious individuals. Further, group differences are maximized when the ratio of depressive to anxious symptoms is carefully considered before assigning a subject to a particular group (Riskind *et al.*, 1986).

In sum, the relationship between depression and anxiety remains quite unclear, and the majority of clinical, familial, and psychometric studies designed to investigate their association are characterized by a distinct element of "blind empiricism." Although psychological studies have been more concerned with conceptual issues (e.g., Abramson *et al.*, 1978; Lewinsohn, 1974; Sarason, 1975; Spielberger, 1972), these studies have failed to consider depression and anxiety in a single framework. Thus progress toward resolving the interrelation between these two disorders may depend on the development of an integrated theoretical framework.

A COGNITIVE-SCHEMA APPROACH TO DEPRESSION AND ANXIETY: RATIONALE

In line with recent cognitive–information-processing approaches to the study of psychopathology, we employ in this chapter the construct of cognitive schemata as mechanisms that may account for both the overlap and the differences between depression and anxiety. The term "schema" refers to an enduring cognitive organization that acts as a pattern for selecting, encoding, retrieving, and interpreting the stimuli that confront an individual. Cognitive schemata enable an individual to break down and filter the vast array of stimuli impinging upon him or her at any given moment, thus serving a function of "cognitive economy" (Rosch, 1975).

Because the quantity and variety of information available at any time is greater than what any person could process, individuals must be selective in what they notice, learn, remember, or infer in any situation (Neisser, 1967). Information that is inconsistent with the general organization of the schema is often ignored or forgotten; other aspects of the information are elaborated in ways that make them consistent with the schema (e.g., Bartlett, 1932; Bobrow & Norman, 1975; Bower, Black, & Turner, 1979; Bransford & Johnson, 1972, 1973; Minsky, 1975; Owens, Bower, & Black, 1979). Thus, although schemata facilitate perception, comprehension, recall, and problem solving, an important consequence of their operation is bias and distortion (e.g., Alloy & Tabachnik, 1984; Taylor & Crocker, 1980).

A major impetus for examining schematic processes in depression and anxiety is Beck's comprehensive theory of the emotional disorders (Beck, 1967, 1976; Beck & Emery, 1985). Beck's major premise is that affective responses are largely determined by a person's cognitive construction of his or her experiences. According to Beck, individuals suffering from each of the emotional disorders can be characterized as possessing enduring and maladaptive cognitive schemata that contain specific negative beliefs about the self and its relationship to the world and the future. Beck argues that these negative schemata dominate the cognitions of depressed or anxious individuals, leading to systematic biases and distortions in the perception and interpretation of self-relevant information (Alloy, Clements, & Kolden, 1985).

In Beck's (1976) model, the emotional disorders can be distinguished from one another on the basis of the specific content of their self-schemata. Depressed individuals are hypothesized to possess negative schemata involving the depressive themes of personal deficiency, worthlessness, self-blame, guilt, deprivation, and rejection. Anxious individuals also have negative beliefs about the self, but their schemata are organized around the themes of threat, danger, and uncertainty (Beck, 1976; Beck & Emery, 1985; see also Epstein, 1976; Mandler, 1972; Spielberger, 1972). Thus Beck's theory predicts that depressed and anxious individuals can be differentiated on the basis of the specific content of their self-schemata, whereas the operation of self-schemata is similar in the two groups.

Recently, a variety of empirical methods for detecting schemata and their effects on information processing have been developed by cognitive psychologists (e.g., Bower *et al.,* 1979; Bransford & Johnson, 1972, 1973; Owens *et al.,* 1979; Rogers, 1981). These various methods have converged on the general finding that although schemata facilitate perception and recall of schema-relevant information, their operation leads to biased processing because available data are assimilated by the schemata (Alloy & Tabachnik, 1984; Taylor & Crocker, 1980). Schema approaches have also recently influenced social and personality psychology as theorists have become increasingly interested in the role of enduring knowledge structures in complex social behaviors (e.g., Cantor & Mischel, 1977; Markus, 1977; Schank & Abelson, 1975). In particular, personality studies have supported the existence of a well-organized self-schema that influences a person's endorsement of trait adjectives as personally descriptive, increases the efficiency or speed of processing stimuli that match the self-schema content, and enhances the recall of schema-consistent information while at the same time producing erroneous recall and recognition of self-schema-congruent material that was never presented (e.g., Markus, 1977; Rogers, Kuiper, & Kirker, 1977).

Self-schemata in Depression and Anxiety

In the last few years, clinical investigators have applied methods developed within cognitive and social psychology to an examination of the content and operation of self-schemata in depressed and nondepressed people (Alloy, Greenberg, Clements, & Kolden, 1983; Davis, 1979a, 1979b; Davis & Unruh, 1981; Derry & Kuiper, 1981; Hammen, Marks, de Mayo, & Mayol, 1985; Hammen, Marks, Mayol, & de Mayo, 1985; Hammen, Miklowitz, & Dyck, 1986; Ingram, Smith, & Brehm, 1983; Kuiper & Derry, 1982; Kuiper & MacDonald, 1982; Kuiper, Olinger, & MacDonald, Chapter 10, this volume; Kuiper, Olinger, MacDonald, & Shaw, 1985; Ross

& Mueller, 1983; Ross, Mueller, & de la Torre, 1986). This research clearly demonstrates that normal, nondepressed individuals are characterized by strong, positive-content self-schemata that increase their endorsement of, processing efficiency for, and recall of positive self-referent information. The evidence regarding depressives' schematic processing is less clear cut. Some evidence suggests that consistent with the content-specificity hypothesis (Beck, 1967, 1976), clinically depressed patients may exhibit strong self-schema processing effects, parallel to those of nondepressives, with the exception that depressives' schemata are negative in content (Derry & Kuiper, 1981). In contrast, other studies suggest that depressed individuals may possess relatively unstable self-schemata containing mixed positive and negative content (e.g., Ingram *et al.*, 1983; Kuiper & Derry, 1982; Kuiper & MacDonald, 1982; Kuiper *et al.*, 1985).

Whether depressed individuals possess strong negative self-schemata or balanced, mixed-content schemata may depend on the severity (Kuiper & Derry, 1982; Kuiper & MacDonald, 1982) and/or chronicity of their symptoms (Davis, 1979a, 1979b; Davis & Unruh, 1981). Kuiper and MacDonald (1982) argued that mildly depressed people may be characterized by a period of uncertainty or confusion regarding their self-concepts and therefore show information processing characteristic of a mixed-content schema or inconsistent effects across schematic processing tasks. However, as depression either increases in severity or decreases to nondepressed levels, the relative balance of positive versus negative content is hypothesized to change, thereby giving rise to "content-specificity" effects.

Unfortunately, the role of anxiety has been ignored in these studies of depressed and nondepressed individuals' self-schemata. Inasmuch as depressive and anxious symptoms are closely related, particularly in milder forms of depression (e.g., Costello & Comrey, 1967; Gotlib, 1984; Mendels *et al.*, 1972; Miller *et al.*, 1975; Prusoff & Klerman, 1974), it is unclear whether the depressed–nondepressed differences in schematic processing obtained in these studies are attributable to subjects' differing levels of depression or to anxiety. In fact, the two experiments that have explicitly examined the self-schemata of test-anxious individuals (Lang, Mueller, & Nelson, 1983; Mueller & Curtois, 1980) have found increased endorsement and recall of negative-content trait adjectives for this group as well. To date, however, no one has adequately investigated the specificity of the content and operation of self-schemata in depressed versus anxious persons by specifically comparing the schematic processing of the two groups within a single study. Our two studies—Greenberg and Alloy (1987) and Vazquez and Alloy (1987)—which we report on later, address this issue (see also Clements, Alloy, Kolden, & Greenberg, 1987).

A second important feature of the studies reported here, relevant to testing Beck's content-specificity model, is that we employ positively and negatively valenced trait adjective stimuli whose contents are specifically related to depressive, anxious, and normal themes. The content-specificity hypothesis and basic schema research suggest that schematic processing effects should be limited to stimulus material congruent with the content embodied in the self-schema (Derry & Kuiper, 1981; Riskind & Rholes, 1984; Taylor & Crocker, 1980). This is because information that matches the content of the self-schema can be quickly and elaborately encoded and later readily retrieved (Rogers, 1981). The previous research on self-schemata in depression and anxiety has paid insufficient attention to the content of the stimuli used and has often incorrectly assumed that depressed or anxious subjects will exhibit more efficient processing and recall of any negatively valenced information.

Self- versus Other-schemata

A final way in which the studies we report here investigated the specificity of depressed and anxious persons' self-schemata was by also examining these subjects' processing of information encoded in reference to another person. It is possible that schematic effects observed for self-referent encoding are due merely to the accessing of any well-organized "person" schema rather than to a schema with content unique to the self (Bower & Gilligan, 1979; Kuiper & Rogers, 1979). A comparison of subjects' schemata for a well-known other person (a best friend) to their self-schemata provides a relatively stringent test of the content-specificity hypothesis.

Moreover, the "self–other" distinction is a critical feature of Beck's (1967, 1976) cognitive model. Beck (1967) has argued that depressed individuals' cognitions are characterized by a systematic "bias against the self" in which they compare themselves unfavorably to others. More generally, several social psychological theories hypothesize that people's self-esteem is influenced by their comparisons of themselves to others (e.g., Festinger, 1954; Morse & Gergen, 1970; Rosenberg, 1965; Schachter, 1959). That depressed and anxious people both typically exhibit low self-esteem (e.g., Beck, 1976; Beck & Emery, 1985; Bibring, 1953; Epstein, 1972; Nadich, Gargan, & Michael, 1975; Sarason, 1975; Spielberger, 1972) suggests that both groups may perpetuate or accentuate their negative self-images by perceiving others in highly positive terms (Alloy & Ahrens, 1987; Martin, Abramson, & Alloy, 1984; Tabachnik, Crocker, & Alloy, 1983). This line of theorizing and research suggests a social-comparison hypothesis (Alloy, Albright, & Clements, 1987; Kuiper & MacDonald, 1982) in which depressed and anxious subjects may exhibit negative self-schemata specific to depressive and anxious content, respectively, but schemata for others that contains positive content. Similarly, recent work documenting self-enhancing biases in nondepressive cognition (Abramson & Alloy, 1981; Alloy et al., 1987; Greenwald, 1980) suggests that normal subjects may maintain positive self-esteem by also exhibiting a social-comparison effect in which their other-schemata are more negative than their self-schemata. Because depressed and anxious persons are most likely to compare themselves negatively, and normal persons, to compare themselves positively, to an unfamiliar, generalized other (Alloy et al., 1987; Beck, 1976), in one of the two studies we report on here (Vazquez & Alloy, 1987), we used "people in general" as a comparison "other" in addition to subjects' best friends.

An alternative, self-consensus hypothesis is that self-schemata influence individuals' perceptions and judgments of others (Fong & Markus, 1982; Markus &

Smith, 1981). This hypothesis suggests that the presence of an organized self-schema may bias an individual to perceive others in a similar fashion. Along related lines, studies of the "false-consensus effect" (Ross, Greene, & House, 1977) suggest that people tend to perceive high consensus in others for their own attributes. This line of reasoning, therefore, predicts that differences among depressed, anxious, and normal subjects in their self-referent processing will be accompanied by similar differences in their processing of other-referent information.

SELF- AND OTHER-SCHEMATA IN DEPRESSION VERSUS ANXIETY: TWO EMPIRICAL STUDIES

In overview then, we present two studies, by Greenberg and Alloy (1987) and Vazquez and Alloy (1987), whose common goal was the investigation of depressed and anxious individuals' processing of information about themselves and others. Both studies used a "depth-of-processing" paradigm (Craik & Tulving, 1975; Derry & Kuiper, 1981) to provide a stringent test of Beck's content-specificity model of the emotional disorders. In both studies, we examined the self- and other-schemata (best friend and/or people in general) of depressed students, anxious but nondepressed students, and normal students for positive and negative depression-relevant, anxiety-relevant, and control content. In the depth-of-processing paradigm, subjects rate the descriptiveness of each of a series of adjectives on a semantic, self-referent, or other-referent orienting task. Following the orienting task, they are given a memory test (either recall or recognition) for the adjectives they rated in the encoding phase.

The typical findings in depth-of-processing experiments are recall enhancement of, and false recognition for, schema-congruent information encoded with reference to the self as well as faster processing and greater endorsement of self-schema-congruent stimuli (e.g., Cantor & Mischel, 1977; Derry & Kuiper, 1981; Rogers *et al.*, 1977). Thus Beck's content-specificity model of the emotional disorders suggests that depressed subjects will exhibit these typical effects only for negative, depression-relevant content encoded with reference to the self, whereas anxious subjects will exhibit these effects only for negative, anxiety-relevant content encoded in self-referent fashion. Given that the Greenberg and Alloy (1987) and Vazquez and Alloy (1987) experiments studied relatively mildly depressed individuals who were also anxious, a weaker version of the content-specificity hypothesis, in which depressed subjects exhibit evidence of self-schemata containing mixed positive and negative and depression-relevant and anxiety-relevant content, may be expected to receive support.

Although our two studies were quite similar in design and procedure, three differences should be mentioned. First, like most depth-of-processing studies in depression (e.g., Derry & Kuiper, 1981; Kuiper & Derry, 1982), Greenberg and Alloy (1987) used a free-recall test to evaluate subjects' memory for the trait adjectives processed with respect to different referents (self, other). In contrast, Vazquez and Alloy (1987) used a recognition test to examine subjects' abilities to discriminate between adjectives they rated in the encoding phase and "new," similar distractors (see Brown, 1976, and Gillund & Shiffrin, 1984, for conceptual differences between recall and recognition). An advantage of a recognition test is that it is sensitive to distortions, or "false alarms," in the retrieval of schema-congruent information (Hastie & Carlston, 1980). This consideration is important, because strong cognitive schemata (e.g., self-schemata) may be powerful devices for processing relevant information, but, by the same token, they may lead to the distortion of such information (Alba & Hasher, 1983; Taylor & Crocker, 1980). In addition, when using a recognition test, signal detection theory (e.g., Green & Swets, 1966; McNicol, 1972) provides a way of assessing subjects' "response biases" as well as their memory sensitivities. That is, two subjects may possess different response styles in retrieving information from memory (e.g., "risky" vs. "conservative"), even though both show the same level of memory sensitivity or discriminability.

A second difference between the two studies is that Vazquez and Alloy (1987) included "people in general," in addition to "best friends" (the only "other" used by Greenberg and Alloy, 1987), as a comparison target for assessing subjects' other-schemata. As noted previously, the inclusion of a generalized other as a comparison target contributes to a stronger test of the social-comparison versus self-consensus hypotheses of the relation between self- and other-schemata.

Finally, Vazquez and Alloy (1987) investigated the effects of the severity of depression on the schematic processing of self- and other-referent information by including a moderately depressed group as well as a mildly depressed group in their study.

Selection and Matching of Task Stimuli

As discussed previously, an important requirement for an adequate test of the content-specificity hypothesis is that subjects be provided with stimulus content for processing that is *specific* to their pathology. Activation of negative self-schemata is more likely to occur when individuals with affective disturbances are exposed to specific events or stimuli that are congruent with the content embodied in their schemata (Alloy *et al.*, 1985; Derry & Kuiper, 1981; Riskind & Rholes, 1984). This point has often been overlooked in studies (e.g., Davis & Unruh, 1981; Dobson & Shaw, 1987; Zuroff, Colussy, & Wielgus, 1983) that have examined the schematic processing of depressed subjects. Therefore we developed for use in our two studies a set of trait adjectives with depression-relevant, anxiety-relevant, and control content.

The selection of these adjectives involved two major phases (see Greenberg & Alloy, 1987, for details). First, a large sample of undergraduates were asked to rate their self-concepts on a questionnaire containing 53 bipolar semantic differential items (Self-Perception Questionnaire; Greenberg & Alloy, 1987). These items were designed to be relevant to either depression (e.g., incompetent–competent) or anxiety (e.g., nervous–calm), or to be irrelevant to both depression and anxiety (e.g., untrustworthy–trustworthy). From this original pool of items, three lists of adjectives—depression-relevant (DR), anxiety-relevant (AR), and control (C) adjectives—were empirically formed, based on their ability to discriminate among depressed, anxious but nondepressed, and nondepressed–nonanxious subjects within the sample. For instance, AR adjectives were those for which anxious subjects obtained higher mean ratings than nonanxious subjects and that correlated more strongly with subjects' scores on the Trait Anxiety Inventory (TAI; Spielberger, Gorsuch, & Luschene, 1970) than on the BDI (Beck, Ward, Mendelson, Mock, & Erbaugh, 1961).

In the second phase of adjective selection, we added synonymous adjectives of each type in order to increase the length of the three lists. Fifty subjects then rated these new adjectives for "conceptual similarity" with the original lists. An adjective was included as part of the final pool if it was significantly more related to its designated concept (e.g., depression-relevant) than to the alternative (i.e., anxiety-relevant or control) concepts. The adjectives were then equated on social desirability, word frequency, and word length, and the valence of each list was balanced, so that half of the adjectives of each content type were positive and half were negative. The final pool of 72 adjectives (24 DR, 24 AR, and 24 C), shown in Table 4-1, served as the stimuli in both of our studies.

Subjects and Assessment

Sixty undergraduates (16 depressed, 17 anxious but nondepressed, and 27 nondepressed–nonanxious, or normal) participated in the Greenberg and Alloy (1987) study. Subjects were classified into the three groups on the basis of their scores on the BDI (Beck et al., 1961) and the TAI (Spielberger et al., 1970). Individuals scoring 9 or above on the BDI were classified as depressed, regardless of their anxiety scores. Subjects scoring 38 or above on the TAI but 8 or below on the BDI were classified as anxious but nondepressed.[1] Subjects were assigned to the normal group if they scored 8 or below on the BDI *and* 37 or below on the TAI. It

Table 4-1. Trait Adjectives Used in the Experimental Tasks

	Control		Depression-relevant		Anxiety-relevant	
Positive	Tactful	Cordial	Worthy	Energetic	Relaxed	Competent
	Congenial	Honest	Outgoing	Ambitious	Serene	Graceful
	Cooperative	Ethical	Potent	Enthusiastic	Calm	Assured
	Scrupulous	Nice	Valuable	Praiseworthy	Secure	Comfortable
	Genuine	Mannered	Loveable	Lively	Unruffled	Invulnerable
	Polite	Amiable	Motivated	Eager	Confident	Consistent
Negative	Thoughtless	Obnoxious	Withdrawn	Shameful	Tense	Shaky
	Uncivil	Ungrateful	Inadequate	Uninspired	Nervous	Unsafe
	Phony	Rude	Powerless	Insignificant	Jittery	Edgy
	Nosy	Immoral	Lazy	Sluggish	Anxious	Inconsistent
	Crude	Disrespectful	Weak	Ineffective	Touchy	Unsteady
	Discourteous	Unprincipled	Deficient	Lowly	Irritable	Offensive

should be noted that the depressed group was as anxious as the anxious group on the TAI, but was significantly more depressed than the anxious group on the BDI. This is not surprising, given our preceding review of clinical and psychometric studies suggesting that it is almost impossible to find depressed subjects who do not also exhibit symptoms of anxiety. Finally, to increase the reliability of subjects' group classification, subjects were required to meet these criteria on two different testing occasions separated by a 1-week interval.

Identical subject groups and selection criteria were employed in the Vazquez and Alloy (1987) study, with one exception. Because some investigators have suggested that schematic processes in depression depend upon the severity of depressive symptoms (e.g., Kuiper & Derry, 1982; Kuiper & MacDonald, 1982), two different groups of depressed subjects were formed. Based on Beck's norms (Beck *et al.,* 1961), subjects were assigned to a mildly depressed group if they scored between 9 and 15 on the BDI, and to a moderately depressed group if they scored 16 or above on the BDI. A total of 64 undergraduates (16 mildly depressed, 16 moderately depressed, 16 anxious but nondepressed, and 16 nondepressed–nonanxious) participated in Vazquez and Alloy's study.

Experimental Design and Procedure

In Greenberg and Alloy's study, subjects were exposed to a typical incidental learning task, in which the 72 trait adjectives of six different content-by-valence combinations (DR+, DR–, AR+, AR–, C+, C–) were presented randomly following one of three different orienting questions (self-referent, best-friend-referent, and semantic).[2] The subjects' task was to respond "yes" or "no" to each orienting question by pressing the appropriate button on a computer keyboard ("Describes you?" for the self-referent question, "Describes your best friend?" for the other-referent question, or "Means the same as ____?" for the semantic question).[3] Subjects' responses and reaction times were recorded by the microcomputer (see Greenberg & Alloy, 1987, for details of the design and procedure). After all adjectives were presented twice, subjects were given an unexpected 5-minute free-recall test in which they were to write down all of the adjectives they could remember, in any order.

The incidental learning task in Vazquez and Alloy's study was identical, with two exceptions. Instead of using six different types of adjectives (resulting from the combination of the three adjective contents by their valence), Vazquez and Alloy regrouped these six categories into just four types of trait adjectives: 16 depressed-type (i.e., DR negative) adjectives, 16 anxious-type (i.e., AR negative) adjectives, 16 nondepressed–nonanxious-type (i.e., a combination of positive AR and positive DR) adjectives, and 16 control-type (i.e., a combination of positive and negative C) adjectives. In addition, four different orienting questions were used; three of them (self-referent, best-friend-referent, and semantic) were the same as in Greenberg and Alloy (1987), and a new question (people-referent: "Describes people in general?") was added. Each of the 16 adjectives of the four types was presented once, following one of the four kinds of cue questions. The order of presentation was randomized for each subject. A surprise recognition test followed. For this purpose, a list of 64 new adjectives was constructed; a synonym was found for each of the original adjectives so that each old adjective had a corresponding distractor in the recognition test. Thus, in the recognition test, 128 adjectives were presented randomly, and the subjects' task was to decide, for each one, whether or not it was presented in the earlier judgment task.[4]

Content of Schemata

Analyses of the number of "yes" responses to the cue questions provided a way of assessing the content of subjects' self- and other-schemata. Results from both studies suggested that nondepressed–nonanxious subjects are characterized by a highly positive self-schema, anxious subjects by a more negative self-schema only somewhat specific to anxiety-relevant content, and depressed subjects by a balanced, mixed-content self-schema containing both positive and negative content.

In Greenberg and Alloy's study, as predicted, there were no group differences for the number of "yes" responses to C content stimuli. However, the group effects for the DR and AR adjectives were significant (see Figure 4-1). Depressed and anxious students both judged fewer positive DR and AR adjectives as self-descriptive than did normal (nondepressed–nonanxious) students, but there were no differences between the depressed and anxious groups. For the negative DR stimuli, the normal group endorsed fewer items than both the depressed and anxious groups, and the anxious subjects endorsed fewer items than the depressed group. For the negative AR stimuli, there were no differences between the depressed and anxious groups, replicating the pattern for the positive AR stimuli. However, the normal group judged fewer negative AR items as self-descriptive than did the anxious and depressed students. Thus, for negative adjectives, the depressed group could be differentiated from the anxious group by their greater endorsement of DR adjectives, but the two groups rated an equally high number of AR adjectives as self-descriptive.

An examination of adjective endorsement patterns within each group revealed that normal students endorsed more positive than negative items for each of the three content types, suggesting an overall positive view of the self for these subjects. However, depressed students endorsed an equal number of positive and negative DR and AR adjectives, suggesting that their self-concepts contain both positive and negative content. The anxious students rated more positive than negative items as self-descriptive for the C and DR stimuli, but more negative than positive AR adjectives. This finding was unique to this group, although a similar but nonsignificant trend was noted for depressed subjects.

Vazquez and Alloy obtained a similar pattern of endorsements for the self-referent orienting task,[5] including the finding that depressed students' responses were again more balanced than those of normal and anxious students. In fact, Vazquez and Alloy's results suggested that this positive–negative "evenhandedness" may depend on the severity of depressive symptoms. Rating differences between positive and negative adjectives were smaller for moderately depressed

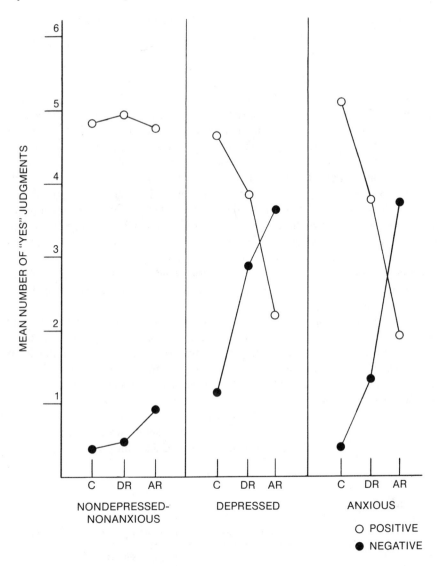

Figure 4-1. Self-schema: Mean number of "yes" judgments of positive and negative control (C), depression-relevant (DR), and anxiety-relevant (AR) adjectives for nondepressed–nonanxious (normal), depressed, and anxious subjects.

subjects than for mildly depressed subjects, whose positive–negative rating differences were, in turn, smaller than for either normal or anxious subjects.

In addition, Vazquez and Alloy (1987) conducted an analysis of the "extremity" of subjects' self-referent judgments. That is, we examined the number of subjects within each group who failed to give at least one "yes" response to each particular type of adjective, and the number who responded affirmatively to all the adjectives belonging to that particular content type. As can be seen in Table 4-2, 78% of the normal subjects selected all of the nondepressed–nonanxious adjectives as self-descriptive, whereas this was the case for only 36% of the anxious and 20% of the depressed subjects (18% of the mildly depressed and 25% of the moderately depressed subjects). Yet, 80% of the normal and 75% of the anxious subjects rejected all the depressed-content adjectives as self-descriptive, whereas only 54% of mildly depressed and 25% of moderately depressed subjects did so. Thus it is interesting that in a situation in which subjects *must* make a decision ("yes" or "no"), clear differences emerge in the content of the self-referent judgments of all the participating groups. Under such conditions, normal subjects systematically endorse positive adjectives and reject negative ones. That there was no depressed subject who rated as self-descriptive all of the presented depressive adjectives is not surprising. In fact, even clinically depressed subjects may *not* be characterized by having an extreme negative view of themselves (e.g., Dobson & Shaw, 1987; Derry & Kuiper, 1981). However, taken together, our two studies suggest that as the severity of depressive symptoms increases from nondepressed to mild to moderate depression, the ratio of negative to positive depression-relevant adjectives endorsed as self-descriptive also increases.

With respect to the content of other-schemata, both of our studies found that students' schemata for their best friends were, in general, very positive. Subjects consistently ascribed many positive and very few negative adjectives of all content types to their best friends. Obviously, given this pattern of responses, it is clear that depressed and anxious subjects' best-friend schemata were more positive than their self-schemata. In contrast, normal subjects' self-schemata and best-friend schemata were similar, and both were highly positive.

However, subjects' concepts of "people in general" were not as uniformly positive as their concepts of "best friend" in Vazquez and Alloy's study. In general,

Table 4-2. Extremity of Self-referent Judgments (Vazquez & Alloy, 1987)

Percent of subjects who responded that all adjectives of a given category were self-descriptive

Adjective content	Subject group			
	Normal	Anxious	Mildly depressed	Moderately depressed
Nondepressed–nonanxious	78	36	18	25
Anxious	0	18	12	36
Depressed	0	0	0	0

Percent of subjects who rejected all adjectives of a given category as self-descriptive

Nondepressed–nonanxious	0	0	0	6
Anxious	42	0	0	6
Depressed	80	75	54	25

when differences emerged, subjects ascribed fewer positive and more negative adjectives to people in general than to either themselves or their best friends. Yet, there were some very interesting exceptions to this generalization. For AR adjectives, depressives' view of people in general *and* of themselves was more negative than their best-friend concepts; moreover, moderately depressed subjects' self-schemata were even *worse* than their best-friend *and* their people-in-general schemata. This latter finding is important because it was the only case in which a group of subjects rated themselves more negatively than people in general.

Efficiency of Schemata

An examination of subjects' reaction times in processing self- and other-referent information is thought to provide evidence regarding the efficiency of self- and other-schemata for processing schema-relevant content.[6] Greenberg and Alloy (1987) obtained an intriguing set of findings with regard to processing speed. Inspection of Figure 4-2 shows that normal and anxious students were faster in responding "yes" to positive than to negative adjectives but were slower in responding "no" to positive than to negative items. The mean differences here were quite large, often exceeding 1,000 milliseconds. However, depressives' reaction times did not differ for either positive or negative adjectives when responding "yes" or "no," but instead were "evenhanded." Thus depressed subjects did not exhibit any facilitation when processing personal information, whereas normal and anxious subjects showed a clear pattern of "efficiency/inefficiency," depending upon the type of information they were processing about themselves.

This "balanced" pattern of reaction times displayed by depressed subjects was also found in the Vazquez and Alloy study. Interestingly, the severity of depression affected the speed of responding only to depressed-type adjectives, not to nondepressed–nonanxious adjectives. That is, moderately depressed subjects were slower than mildly depressed and normal subjects to decide whether or not depressed-type adjectives were self-descriptive, but both depressed groups were equally slow relative to normal subjects in deciding about nondepressed–nonanxious adjectives. Further, moderate depressives were *equally slow* for both types of decisions. Thus, similar to Greenberg and Alloy's finding, moderately depressed subjects did not process either positive or negative information efficiently in a self-referent judgment task. In addition, reaction times for "self" and "best-friend" questions were, in general, faster than times for "semantic" and "people-in-general" questions. However, moderately depressed subjects were also an exception to this finding: They did not show any facilitation in processing self-referent information; their reaction times for self-referent judgments were as slow as their times for "people-in-general" judgments.

Influence of Schemata on Memory

An analysis of subjects' recall (Greenberg & Alloy, 1987) and recognition (Vazquez & Alloy, 1987) of stimuli processed with reference to the self or others

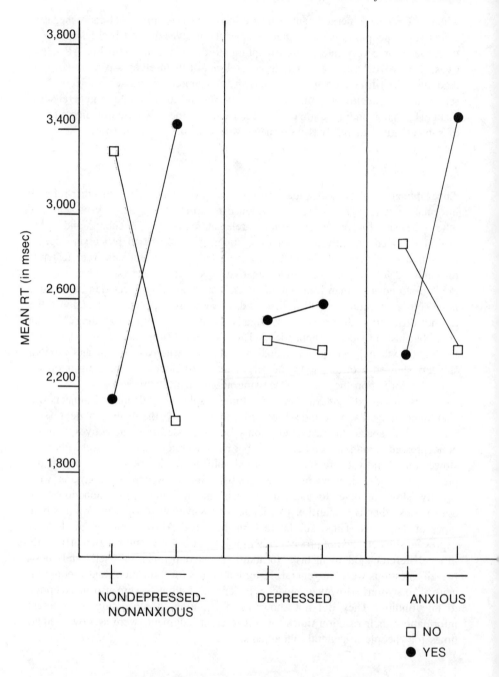

Figure 4-2. Mean reaction time (RT): Response times for positive (+) and negative (−) adjectives given "yes" and "no" ratings by nondepressed–nonanxious, depressed, and anxious subjects.

provides evidence regarding the facilitating and biasing effects of self- and other-schemata on memory for schema-relevant content. Following the typical procedure in depth-of-processing paradigms (e.g., Craik & Tulving, 1975), Greenberg and Alloy analyzed subjects' recall for "yes"- and "no"-rated adjectives separately.[7] For "yes"-rated adjectives, there were no significant effects involving the critical subject-group factor. In general, though, all subjects exhibited enhanced recall for positively valenced adjectives encoded in self- or other-referent versus semantic fashion. In addition, all subjects recalled more positive and fewer negative adjectives for their best friends than for themselves.

Differences in subjects' recall were found for the "no"-rated adjectives. Depressed subjects recalled more negative than positive DR adjectives, whereas normal and anxious subjects did not differ in their recall of positive and negative DR adjectives. There were no differences in subjects' recall for the AR adjectives. Thus only recall of the "no"-rated DR stimuli discriminated among the three groups.

Greenberg and Alloy also obtained some important group differences when the recall data were analyzed for each content type. There were no group effects on the C stimuli, but differences emerged for the DR and AR adjectives. Figure 4-3 shows that normal subjects recalled an equal number of DR items encoded in schematic and semantic fashion for both self and other. However, both depressed and anxious subjects recalled more schematically encoded than semantically encoded self-referent DR stimuli, but not other-referent stimuli. In addition, both depressed and anxious subjects recalled more schematically encoded DR adjectives for the self than did normal subjects, whereas the three groups did not differ in their recall for others. In sum, enhanced recall of DR adjectives was restricted primarily to the depressed group, and to a lesser extent, the anxious group, with schematic effects obtained for the self-referent items but with more or less equivalent schematic versus semantic recall for all groups on the other-referent items. For the AR adjectives, anxious subjects recalled more AR items encoded with reference to the self than did either depressed or normal subjects, who did not differ in their recall levels (see Figure 4-4). In addition, there were no group differences for recall of the other-referent AR items. Finally, only the anxious group recalled more schematically encoded than semantically encoded AR adjectives for the self.

Vazquez and Alloy (1987) employed a somewhat different strategy in examining recognition memory. Subjects' recognition performances were analyzed for different types of content processed under different types of questions, regardless of subjects' responses (i.e., "yes" or "no") to the cue questions. No significant differences were obtained among the various subject groups (see also Zuroff *et al.*, 1983). Nevertheless, as in many other studies (e.g., Derry & Kuiper, 1981; Greenberg & Alloy, 1987; Rogers *et al.*, 1977), the best memory was obtained for those adjectives processed in self-referent fashion. Adjectives processed with reference to the self were recognized more frequently than adjectives processed under either "people-in-general" or "semantic" cue questions. Memory for adjectives related to "best friends" did not differ significantly from that for any of these other three orienting questions. These differences in recognition accuracy were due

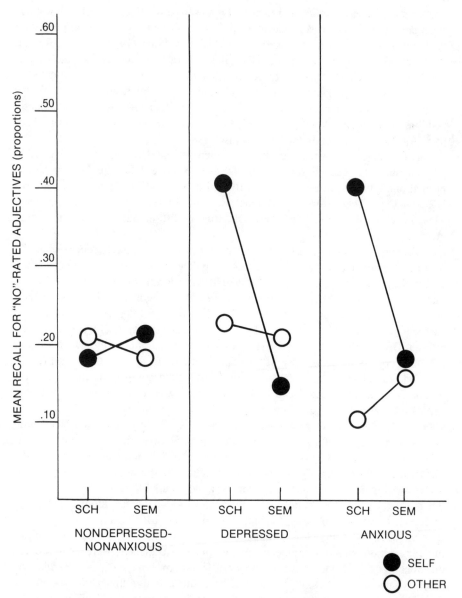

Figure 4-3. Mean recall for "no"-rated adjectives: Recall of depression-relevant adjectives under self- and other-schema (SCH) and semantic encoding (SEM) for nondepressed–nonanxious, depressed, and anxious subjects.

mainly to differences in "hits" (correct recognitions); the pattern of false alarms (distortions) was not different for the four different types of cue questions.

Unlike Rogers, Rogers, and Kuiper (1979), Vazquez and Alloy did not find an increase in false alarms on adjectives processed in self-referent fashion. One possible explanation for this discrepancy is that Rogers *et al.* (1979) obtained a false-alarm effect when a long time interval (i.e., 2.5 months) intervened between the judgment task and the recognition test. The probability of finding such an effect in the Vazquez and Alloy study was minimized because of the absence of delay

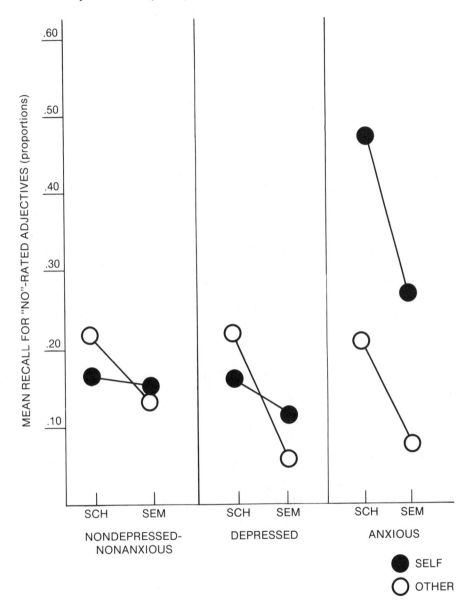

Figure 4-4. Mean recall for "no"-rated adjectives: Recall of anxiety-relevant adjectives under self- and other-schema (SCH) and semantic encoding (SEM) for nondepressed–nonanxious, depressed, and anxious subjects.

between the judgment task and the recognition test. Indeed, Zuroff *et al.* (1983), using a similar procedure, failed to find a false-alarm effect even with a 7-day interval between the encoding task and the recognition test. Further, Vazquez and Alloy obtained a "ceiling effect" in subjects' performances on the recognition test. In effect, subjects' global performances were very good, and therefore distortions in memory did not emerge.

One of the main reasons for using a recognition test in the Vazquez and Alloy study was to obtain a measure of subjects' response biases. The most interesting finding was a negative response bias for adjectives processed in a self-referent manner. That is, subjects had a tendency to be "liberal" in their recognition of synonyms of adjectives originally processed in a self-referent way.

Discussion

DEPRESSION, ANXIETY, AND SELF-SCHEMATA

Taken together, subjects' patterns of endorsements, reaction times, and recall for trait adjectives encoded in reference to themselves in both the Greenberg and Alloy (1987) and Vazquez and Alloy (1987) studies provided some support for a weak version of the content-specificity hypothesis.[8] In contrast, the recognition-memory findings of Vazquez and Alloy were not consistent with Beck's (1967, 1976; Beck & Emery, 1985) content-specificity hypothesis. Vazquez and Alloy obtained no group differences in recognition of different-content adjectives previously processed in self-referent fashion. However, as noted previously, the failure to find group differences in recognition memory may have been due to the recognition test's having been given immediately following the encoding of the adjective stimuli. With such a short delay between exposure to the adjectives and the memory test, group differences may have been attenuated. Indeed, several investigators have suggested that memory differences are minimized with recognition tests that are easy and that do not require much effort (Blaney, 1986; Isen, 1984; Roy-Byrne, Weingartner, Bierer, Thompson, & Post, 1986).

Replicating earlier findings (e.g., Derry & Kuiper, 1981; Ingram *et al.*, 1983; Kuiper & Derry, 1982), nondepressed/nonanxious individuals' self-referent processing in both studies provided relatively strong evidence that these individuals possess highly positive self-schemata. First, normal subjects were the only group that consistently judged more positive than negative adjectives as self-descriptive for all content types, and they endorsed more positive and fewer negative DR and AR adjectives than either depressed or anxious subjects. In addition, normal subjects gave very extreme self-descriptiveness judgments, with most of them endorsing *all* positive and rejecting *all* negative adjectives as self-descriptive. Second, as reflected in reaction times, normal subjects exhibited greater processing efficiency for positive than for negative self-referent information. That is, they endorsed positive adjectives as self-descriptive more quickly than negative adjectives, and rejected negative adjectives as not self-descriptive more rapidly than positive adjectives. Finally, although all subjects exhibited enhanced recall for positive adjectives judged as self-descriptive ("yes"-rated adjectives), only the normal subjects failed to show enhanced recall for "no"-rated DR and AR adjectives encoded in reference to the self. That nondepressed–nonanxious people appear to be characterized by positive-content self-schemata is consistent with other evidence documenting "optimistic" or "self-serving" cognitive biases and illusions on the part of nondepressed individuals (e.g., Abramson & Alloy, 1981; Alloy & Abramson, 1979; Lewinsohn, Mischel, Chaplain, & Barton, 1980; see Alloy & Abramson, Chapter 8, this volume). Indeed, several authors have suggested that positive self-schemata may provide a mechanism contributing to nondepressive positive biases in perceptions and inferences about the self (Alloy *et al.,* 1987; Dykman, Abramson, Alloy, & Hartlage, 1987; Kayne & Alloy, in press).

Anxious individuals' self-referent processing provided weak, and not completely consistent, evidence for content specificity. Only anxious subjects endorsed more negative than positive AR adjectives as self-descriptive (although depressives showed a similar but nonsignificant trend), and these subjects judged fewer negative DR stimuli as descriptive than did depressed subjects. In fact, in the case of DR and C adjectives, anxious subjects, like the normal subjects, accepted more positive than negative traits as characteristic of themselves, although their judgments were not quite as extreme as those of the normal subjects. Anxious individuals were also unique in exhibiting enhanced recall for "no"-rated AR adjectives encoded in self-referent fashion, and they recalled more self-referent AR adjectives than did depressed and nondepressed–nonanxious individuals. However, they did not differ from depressed subjects in recalling "no"-rated DR adjectives. Finally, like the nondepressed–nonanxious subjects, anxious individuals more rapidly judged that positive rather than negative traits described them and that negative rather than positive traits did not describe them. Overall then, anxious individuals' self-schemata appear to contain predominantly positive content, with the exception of one negative component embodying AR themes. Consistent with numerous theories of anxiety (e.g., Beck & Emery, 1985; Epstein, 1972, 1976; Mandler, 1972; Sarason, 1975; Spielberger, 1972), these themes include self-perceptions of threat, lack of confidence, and vulnerability.

Finally, depressed individuals also exhibited a unique pattern of judgments, reaction times, and recall. However, rather than being indicative of a strong negative, depressive-content self-schema, depressives' self-referent processing suggested the presence of a balanced, "mixed-content" schema, containing both positive and negative self-perceptions. Unlike the anxious and nondepressed–nonanxious subjects, depressives (both mild and moderate) showed no preference for ascribing either positive or negative DR and AR adjectives to themselves. That is, they were evenhanded and not very extreme in their self-descriptions. In addition, depressives were unique in exhibiting equivalent reaction times for rating positive and negative traits, and slow reaction times for both types of traits, thus failing to show especially efficient processing of either type of stimulus. Kuiper (1981) found that adjectives that are moderately self-descriptive are processed more slowly than either highly descriptive or highly nondescriptive traits. If depressives' self-schemata contain mixed positive and negative content, then both positive and negative adjectives would be moderately self-descriptive for depressives and would be expected to be processed relatively slowly. Finally, depressives were the only group to recall more negative than positive "no"-rated DR traits; however, they exhibited enhanced recall for DR adjectives in general (both positive and negative) when these adjectives were encoded in self-referent as compared to semantic fashion.

Depressives' evenhanded processing and recall of positive and negative self-referent information in our studies is consistent with previous findings (e.g., Ingram *et al.*, 1983; Kuiper & Derry, 1982; Kuiper & MacDonald, 1982; Kuiper *et al.*, 1985) suggesting that mildly depressed individuals may have relatively disorganized self-structures, incorporating both positive and negative content. It is possible that mild depression represents a "switch point" between the strong positive self-schemata exhibited by nondepressed people and the strong negative self-schemata hypothesized for clinically depressed persons by Beck (1967, 1976) and reported by Derry and Kuiper (1981). Indeed, Davis (1979b) and Lloyd and Lishman (1975) reported that severity of depression was related to greater biases in favor of efficient processing of negative self-referent information. However, an important issue concerns the severity level of depression at which the switch point from mostly positive to mostly negative content self-schemata occurs. Vazquez and Alloy (1987) found the most balanced, evenhanded self-schemata in moderate depressives (BDI scores of 16–23) rather than in mild depressives (BDI scores of 9–15). Clearly, these findings suggest the need for further research that explicitly examines in a fine-grained fashion the effects of severity of depression, as well as other variables such as chronicity or past history of depression and anxiety, on the schematic processing of self-referent information.

That mildly or moderately depressed individuals may possess mixed positive- and negative-content self-schemata is congruent with the body of work demonstrating that such individuals often provide more accurate and realistic personal judgments than do nondepressed individuals (Abramson & Alloy, 1981; Alloy & Abramson, 1979; Alloy & Ahrens, 1987; Golin, Terrell, & Johnson, 1977; Golin, Terrell, Weitz, & Drost, 1979; Lewinsohn *et al.*, 1980; Martin *et al.*, 1984; Tabachnik *et al.*, 1983; see Alloy & Abramson, Chapter 8, this volume). Although schemata facilitate the interpretation of environmental input, an important by-product of their operation is cognitive bias and distortion (e.g., Alloy & Tabachnik, 1984; Taylor & Crocker, 1980). If some depressed individuals possess mixed-content, relatively unstable self-schemata, then their processing of personally relevant situational information should be less biased by schema-based expectations (Alloy *et al.*, 1987; Dykman *et al.*, 1987; Kayne & Alloy, in press).

SELF- VERSUS OTHER-SCHEMATA

An important question addressed by the Greenberg and Alloy (1987) and Vazquez and Alloy (1987) studies was whether self-referent processing effects are specific to the self. Kuiper and Rogers (1979) presented evidence suggesting that the presence of superior schematic versus semantic recall is a function of the degree of familiarity of the targeted individual, with superior self-recall observed only when the targeted other was relatively unfamiliar. Therefore, to provide a stringent test of the content specificity of self-schema processing, we used both a highly familiar other (best friend) and a generalized, unfamiliar other (people in general) as the comparison targets in our studies.

The results of the trait-rating tasks clearly showed that subjects' self-descriptiveness judgments were not characteristic of their other-descriptiveness judgments. Regardless of group membership or content type, best-friend judgments were overwhelmingly positive, and for depressed and anxious subjects, more positive than their self-referent judgments. In contrast, normal and anxious subjects' ratings of people in general were more negative than their self-ratings, whereas in some cases, depressives rated people in general even more positively than themselves. Further, self–other differences were also obtained for the recall task (Greenberg & Alloy, 1987), where more positive and less negative "yes"-rated adjectives were recalled for best friends than for the self, and where depressed and anxious subjects exhibited enhanced schematic recall for DR and AR "No"-rated stimuli for themselves but not for their best friends. Finally, on the recognition test (Vazquez & Alloy, 1987), adjectives processed in reference to the self were recognized more frequently than those processed in reference to people in general.

These self–other differences contradict proposals that the self is important only so far as it leads to the accessing of a rich cognitive structure (Bellezza, 1984; Ganellen & Carver, 1985). According to this view, any advantage to self-referent processing would be minimized when compared to cognitive structures equivalent in richness and semantic elaboration (e.g., a highly familiar other). Thus the use of best friends as one of the comparison targets in our studies supports previous investigations (Greenwald & Pratkanis, 1984; Mueller, Thompson, & Davenport, 1984) demonstrating different schematic processing for self and other, and strengthens the conclusion that self-referent processing is unique to the self.

The self–other distinction also figures prominently in Beck's cognitive theory of depression and anxiety (Beck, 1967, 1976; Beck & Emery, 1985). A social-comparison hypothesis (Alloy *et al.*, 1987; Kuiper & MacDonald, 1982) suggested that depressed and anxious individuals would exhibit negative self-schemata but positive-content schemata for others, whereas nondepressed–nonanxious persons would exhibit more positive self- than other-schemata. In contrast, a self-consensus hypothesis (Fong & Markus, 1982; Markus & Smith, 1981) suggested that the presence of an organized self-schema biases an individual to perceive others in a fashion similar to the way in which they perceive themselves. The self-consensus hypothesis received little support in our studies. Clear self–other differences were found, as outlined previously, in the trait-rating task and in the recall and recognition of trait adjectives. Alternatively, the social-comparison hypothesis was corroborated. Depressed and anxious subjects' judgments for themselves were clearly more negative than their judgments for their best friends, particularly for the DR and AR traits, respectively. Moreover, moderately depressed subjects' self-ratings were even more negative than their ratings of a generalized other (people in general). In contrast, normal subjects judged their best friends as positively as themselves but did depreciate "people in general" relative to themselves, as expected (see also Tabachnik *et al.*, 1983). By possessing self-schemata that are at least as positive as their schemata for others (if not more so), nondepressed–nonanxious people, in contrast to depressed and anxious people, may be able to maintain high self-regard and may be less prone to social-comparison-induced threats to self-esteem (Alloy *et al.*, 1987).

LIMITATIONS OF THE STUDIES AND FUTURE DIRECTIONS

The Greenberg and Alloy (1987) and Vazquez and Alloy (1987) investigations go beyond prior studies of depression and schematic processing of self-referent information in two ways. First, by explicitly comparing the schematic processes of depressed individuals and anxious but nondepressed individuals, these studies provide information regarding the ways in which depressed persons' self-schemata are both similar to and different from those of anxious persons. Inasmuch as depressed individuals are not only more depressed, but also often more anxious, than nondepressed individuals, our findings suggest the importance of including an anxiety control group in studies comparing depressed and nondepressed people's schemata. Second, by including stimuli that differed in content as well as in valence, our experiments demonstrated some differences among depressed, anxious, and normal individuals' self-schemata that are in line with Beck's content-specificity hypothesis. These findings suggest that future research designed to investigate psychopathological individuals' schematic processes would do well to consider the specific content of the stimuli to be processed as well as whether these stimuli are positive or negative (Riskind & Rholes, 1984).

Despite these advances, some limitations in the current work suggest meaningful directions for further research. Although our findings provided support for a weak version of the content-specificity hypothesis, depressed and anxious subjects' self-referent processing exhibited some overlap as well as some differences. Of course, the overlap may reflect real underlying similarities in depressed and anxious persons' self-schemata; however, several factors in our designs may have contributed to less than perfect differentiation. First, subjects were separated into depressed and anxious groups on the basis of their scores on the BDI (Beck *et al.*, 1961) and the TAI (Spielberger *et al.*, 1970). Yet, an examination of the items on these two questionnaires reveals considerable overlap in their content. Use of different self-report inventories or other methods for selecting depressed and anxious groups may lead to greater specificity of the two groups' self-schemata (see Riskind *et al.*, 1986). In particular, a comparison of the schematic processing of individuals meeting DSM-III criteria for depressive versus anxiety disorders may be an especially profitable direction for further research in this area. Similarly, as noted previously, further work is needed in order to understand the relationship between severity and chronicity of depressive and anxious symptoms and self-schemata (Davis, 1979a, 1979b; Davis & Unruh, 1981; Kuiper & Derry, 1982; Kuiper & MacDonald, 1982).

Second, although considerable care was taken in selecting appropriate DR and

AR adjectives for use in our studies (see Selection and Matching of Task Stimuli section), the stimuli may not fully capture potential content differences in self-schemata associated with depression versus anxiety because they were validated against separate groups of depressed and anxious subjects also classified on the basis of BDI and TAI scores. Thus further work on the stimulus content included in studies of depressed and anxious people's schematic processes may also be needed.

Finally, an important direction for future research that may help to disentangle the schematic processes involved in depression and anxiety is the examination of schematic processes among normal individuals that contribute vulnerability to the development of depressive versus anxious symptoms. Several such research programs are already under way (Alloy, Clements, Kolden, & Tal, 1987; Hammen, Marks, de Mayo, & Mayol, 1985; Hammen, Marks, Mayol, & de Mayo, 1985; Kuiper *et al.*, 1985; Kuiper, Olinger, & MacDonald, Chapter 10, this volume).

In summary, the findings presented here support the differentiation of depression and anxiety as partially distinct phenomena. Normal, depressed, and anxious subjects each exhibited a unique pattern of schematic effects for information processed in reference to the self. These findings suggest that a cognitive–information-processing approach may provide a useful theoretical framework for understanding the similarities and differences between anxious and depressive states.

NOTES

1. The cutoff scores of 9 or above on the BDI and 38 or above on the TAI represent the upper quartiles of these inventories for Northwestern University students.
2. Each adjective was presented twice, in a different random order each time. Half of the adjectives in each content-by-valence combination were associated with the semantic orienting question and half were associated with either the self- or the other-referent orienting question on both presentations.
3. For the semantic orienting question, a list of synonyms and nonsynonyms was constructed so that half of subjects' responses would be "yes" and half would be "no."
4. To study the temporal consistency of memory for self- and other-referent information, Vazquez and Alloy (1987) gave a second, unexpected recognition test immediately following the first one. Although memory performance was worse on the second test, there were no interesting effects of subject group or adjective content, and thus the results from the second recognition test are not presented here.
5. The major difference was that anxious subjects ascribed more nondepressed–nonanxious-type adjectives to themselves than did anxious subjects in Greenberg and Alloy's (1987) study.
6. In both the Greenberg and Alloy (1987) and Vazquez and Alloy (1987) studies, there were a number of cases in which subjects failed to give any "yes" (or "no") responses to either positive or negative adjectives of particular content types. Consequently, those subjects had missing reaction times in such cases. To deal with this problem, Greenberg and Alloy conducted several "patch-up" analyses, collapsing over one or more factors of the experimental design (see Greenberg & Alloy, 1987, for details). Vazquez and Alloy adopted a somewhat different approach, combining subjects' "yes" and "no" responses for the purpose of analysis.

7. See Greenberg and Alloy (1987) for a discussion of the most appropriate dependent measures to use in analyzing recall data.

8. See Greenberg and Alloy (1987) and Vazquez and Alloy (1987) for some cautions in considering the findings of our two studies.

ACKNOWLEDGMENTS

Preparation of this chapter was supported by a grant from the John D. and Catherine T. MacArthur Foundation to Lauren B. Alloy. Carmelo V. Vazquez was supported by a Fulbright Fellowship during preparation of this chapter.

REFERENCES

Abramson, L. Y., & Alloy, L. B. (1981). Depression, nondepression, and cognitive illusions: Reply to Schwartz. *Journal of Experimental Psychology: General, 110,* 436–447.

Abramson, L. Y., Seligman, M. E. P., & Teasdale, J. (1978). Learned helplessness in humans: Critique and reformulation. *Journal of Abnormal Psychology, 97,* 49–74.

Alba, J. W., & Hasher, L. (1983). Is memory schematic? *Psychological Bulletin, 93,* 203–231.

Alloy, L. B., & Abramson, L. Y. (1979). Judgment of contingency in depressed and nondepressed students: Sadder but wiser? *Journal of Experimental Psychology: General, 108,* 441–485.

Alloy, L. B., & Ahrens, A. H. (1987). Depression and pessimism for the future: Biased use of statistically relevant information in predictions for self versus others. *Journal of Personality and Social Psychology, 52,* 366–378.

Alloy, L. B., Albright, J. S., & Clements, C. M. (1987). Depression, nondepression, and social comparison biases. In J. E. Maddux, C. D. Stoltenberg, & R. Rosenwein (Eds.), *Social processes in clinical and counseling psychology* (pp. 94–112). New York: Springer-Verlag.

Alloy, L. B., Clements, C., & Kolden, G. (1985). The cognitive diathesis–stress theories of depression: Therapeutic implications. In S. Reiss & R. Bootzin (Eds.), *Theoretical issues in behavior therapy* (pp. 379–410). New York: Academic Press.

Alloy, L. B., Clements, C., Kolden, G., & Tal, C. S. (1987). *Self-schemata, dysfunctional attitudes, and stressful life events in the classroom: Predicting depressive and anxious mood reactions.* Unpublished manuscript, Northwestern University, Evanston, IL.

Alloy, L. B., Greenberg, M. S., Clements, C., & Kolden, G. (1983, August). *Depression, anxiety, and self schemata: A test of Beck's theory.* Paper presented at the meeting of the American Psychological Association, Anaheim, CA.

Alloy, L. B., & Tabachnik, N. (1984). Assessment of covariation by humans and animals: The joint influence of prior expectations and current situational information. *Psychological Review, 91,* 112–149.

American Psychiatric Association. (1980). *Diagnostic and statistical manual of mental disorders* (3rd ed.). Washington, DC: Author.

Barlow, D. H. (1985). The dimensions of anxiety disorders. In A. H. Tuma & J. D. Maser (Eds.), *Anxiety and the anxiety disorders* (pp. 479–500). Hillsdale, NJ: Erlbaum.

Bartlett, F. C. (1932). *Remembering.* Cambridge, England: Cambridge University Press.

Beck, A. T. (1967). *Depression: Clinical, experimental, and theoretical aspects.* New York: Harper & Row.

Beck, A. T. (1976). *Cognitive therapy and the emotional disorders.* New York: International Universities Press.

Beck, A. T., & Emery, G. (1985). *Anxiety disorders and phobias: A cognitive perspective.* New York: Basic Books.

Beck, A. T., Ward, C. H., Mendelson, M., Mock, J., & Erbaugh, J. (1961). An inventory for measuring depression. *Archives of General Psychiatry, 4,* 561–571.

Bellezza, F. S. (1984). The self as a mnemonic device: The role of internal cues. *Journal of Personality and Social Psychology, 47,* 506–516.

Bibring, E. (1953). The mechanism of depression. In P. Greenacre (Ed.), *Affective disorders: Psychoanalytic contributions to their study* (pp. 13–48). New York: International Universities Press.

Biglan, A., & Dow, M. (1981). Toward a second generational model: A problem-specific approach. In L. Rehm (Ed.), *Behavior therapy for depression: Present status and future directions* (pp. 97–121). New York: Academic Press.

Blaney, P. H. (1986). Affect and memory: A review. *Psychological Bulletin, 99,* 229–246.

Bobrow, D. G., & Norman, D. A. (1975). Some principles of memory schemata. In D. G. Bobrow & A. Collins (Eds.), *Representation and understanding: Studies in cognitive science.* New York: Academic Press.

Bower, G. H., Black, J. B., & Turner, T. J. (1979). Scripts in memory for text. *Cognitive Psychology, 11,* 177–220.

Bower, G. H., & Gilligan, S. G. (1979). Remembering information related to one's self. *Journal of Research in Personality, 13,* 420–432.

Bransford, J. D., & Johnson, M. K. (1972). Contextual prerequisites for understanding: Some investigations of comprehension and recall. *Journal of Verbal Learning and Verbal Behavior, 11,* 717–726.

Bransford, J. D., & Johnson, M. K. (1973). Consideration of some problems of comprehension. In W. G. Chase (Ed.), *Visual information processing* (pp. 383–438). New York: Academic Press.

Brown, J. (Ed.). (1976). *Recall and recognition.* New York: Wiley.

Cantor, N., & Mischel, W. (1977). Traits as prototypes: Effects on recognition memory. *Journal of Personality and Social Psychology, 35,* 38–48.

Clements, C., Alloy, L. B., Kolden, G., & Greenberg, M. S. (1987). *Depression, anxiety, and self-schemata: A test of Beck's theory of the emotional disorders.* Unpublished manuscript, Northwestern University, Evanston, IL.

Cloninger, C. R., Martin, R. L., Clayton, P., & Guze, S. B. (1981). A blind follow-up and family study of anxiety neurosis: Preliminary analysis of the St. Louis 500. In D. F. Klein & J. G. Rabkin (Eds.), *Anxiety: New research and changing concepts* (pp. 137–154). New York: Raven Press.

Costello, C. G., & Comrey, A. I. (1967). Scales for measuring depression and anxiety. *Journal of Psychology, 66,* 303–313.

Craighead, W. E. (1980). Away from a unitary model of depression. *Behavior Therapy, 11,* 122–128.

Craik, F. I. M., & Tulving, E. (1975). Depth of processing and the retention of words in episodic memory. *Journal of Experimental Psychology: General, 104,* 268–294.

Crowe, R. R., Noyes, R., Jr., Pauls, D. L., & Slyman, D. (1983). A family study of panic disorder. *Archives of General Psychiatry, 40,* 1065–1069.

Davis, H. (1979a). Self-reference and the encoding of personal information in depression. *Cognitive Therapy and Research, 3,* 97–110.

Davis, H. (1979b). The self-schema and subjective organization of personal information in depression. *Cognitive Therapy and Research, 3,* 415–425.

Davis, H. & Unruh, W. R. (1981). The development of self-schema in adult depression. *Journal of Abnormal Psychology, 90,* 125–133.

Depue, R. A., & Monroe, S. M. (1979). The unipolar–bipolar distinction in the depressive disorders. *Psychological Bulletin, 85,* 1001–1029.

Derogatis, L. R., Lipman, R. S., Covi, L., & Rickles, K. (1972). Factorial invariance of symptom dimensions in anxious and depressive neuroses. *Archives of General Psychiatry, 27,* 659–665.

Derry, P. A., & Kuiper, N. A. (1981). Schematic processing and self-reference in clinical depression. *Journal of Abnormal Psychology, 90,* 286–297.

Dobson, K. S., & Shaw, B. F. (1987). Specificity and stability of self-referent encoding in clinical depression. *Journal of Abnormal Psychology, 96,* 34–40.

Dykman, B. M., Abramson, L. Y., Alloy, L. B., & Hartlage, S. (1987). *Processing of ambiguous and unambiguous feedback by depressed and nondepressed college students: Schematic biases and their implications for depressive realism.* Manuscript submitted for publication.

Epstein, S. (1972). The nature of anxiety with emphasis upon its relationship to expectancy. In C. D. Spielberger (Ed.), *Anxiety: Current trends in theory and research* (Vol. 2, pp. 291–337). New York: Academic Press.

Epstein, S. (1976). Anxiety, arousal, and the self concept. In I. G. Sarason & C. D. Spielberger (Eds.), *Stress and anxiety* (Vol. 3, pp. 185–224). New York: Wiley.

Festinger, L. (1954). A theory of social comparison processes. *Human Relations, 7,* 117–140.

Foa, E. B., & Foa, U. G. (1982). Differentiating depression and anxiety: Is it possible? Is it useful? *Psychopharmacology Bulletin, 18,* 62–68.

Fong, G. T., & Markus, H. (1982). Self-schemas and judgements about others. *Social Cognition, 1,* 191–204.

Fowles, D. & Gersh, F. (1979). Neurotic depression: The endogenous–neurotic distinction. In R. Depue (Ed.), *The psychobiology of the depressive disorders: Implications for the effects of stress* (pp. 55–80). New York: Academic Press.

Ganellen, R. J., & Carver, C. S. (1985). Why does self-reference promote incidental encoding? *Journal of Experimental Social Psychology, 21,* 284–300.

Garber, J., Miller, S. M., & Abramson, L. Y. (1980). On the distinction between anxiety states and depression: Perceived control, certainty, and probability of goal attainment. In J. Garber & M. E. P. Seligman (Eds.), *Human helplessness: Theory and applications* (pp. 131–171). New York: Academic Press.

Gersh, R., & Fowles, D. (1979). Neurotic depression: The concept of anxious depression. In R. Depue (Ed.), *The psychobiology of depressive disorders: Implications for the effects of stress* (pp. 81–104). New York: Academic Press.

Gillund, G., & Shiffrin, R. M. (1984). A retrieval model for both recognition and recall. *Psychological Review, 91,* 1–67.

Golin, S., Terrell, F., & Johnson, B. (1977). Depression and the illusion of control. *Journal of Abnormal Psychology, 86,* 440–442.

Golin, S., Terrell, F., Weitz, J., & Drost, P. L. (1979). The illusion of control among depressed patients. *Journal of Abnormal Psychology, 88,* 454–457.

Gotlib, I. H. (1984). Depression and general psychopathology in university students. *Journal of Abnormal Psychology, 93,* 19–31.

Gray, M. (1978). *Neuroses: A comprehensive and critical view.* New York: Van Nostrand Reinhold.

Green, D. M., & Swets, J. A. (1966). *Signal detection theory and psychophysics.* Huntington, NY: Krieger.

Greenberg, M. S., & Alloy, L. B. (1987). *Depression versus anxiety: Schematic processing of self- and other-referent information.* Manuscript submitted for publication.

Greenwald, A. G. (1980). The totalitarian ego: The fabrication and revision of personal history. *American Psychologist, 35,* 603–618.

Greenwald, A. G., & Pratkanis, A. R. (1984). The self. In R. S. Wyer & T. Srull (Eds.), *Handbook of social cognition* (Vol. 3, pp. 129–178). Hillsdale, NJ: Erlbaum.

Grinker, R. R. (1966). The psychosomatic aspects of anxiety. In C. D. Spielberger (Ed.), *Anxiety and behavior* (pp. 129–142). New York: Academic Press.

Grinker, R. R., & Nunally, J. C. (1968). The phenomena of depressions. In M. Katz, J. O. Cole, & W. E. Barton (Eds.), *The role and methodology of classification in psychiatry and psychopathology.* Chevy Chase, MD: U.S. Public Health Service.

Gurney, C., Roth, M., Garside, M., Kerr, T. A., & Schapira, K. (1972). Studies in the classification of affective disorders: The relationship between anxiety states and depressive illness. 2. *British Journal of Psychiatry, 121,* 162–166.

Hammen, C., Marks, T., de Mayo, R., & Mayol, A. (1985). Self-schemas and risk for depression: A prospective study. *Journal of Personality and Social Psychology, 49,* 1147–1159.

Hammen, C., Marks, T., Mayol, A., & de Mayo, R. (1985). Depressive self-schemas, life stress, and vulnerability to depression. *Journal of Abnormal Psychology, 94,* 308–319.

Hammen, C., Miklowitz, D., & Dyck, D. (1986). Stability and severity parameters of depressive self-schema responding. *Journal of Social and Clinical Psychology, 4,* 23–45.

Hastie, R., & Carlston, D. (1980). Theoretical issues in person memory. In R. Hastie, T. M. Ostrom, E. B. Ebbesen, R. S. Wyer, Jr., D. L. Hamilton, & D. E. Carlston (Eds.), *Person memory: The cognitive basis of social perception* (pp. 1–53). Hillsdale, NJ: Erlbaum.

Ingram, R. E., Smith, T. W., & Brehm, S. S. (1983). Depression and information processing: Self-schemata and the encoding of self-referent information. *Journal of Personality and Social Psychology, 45,* 412–420.

Isen, A. M. (1984). Toward understanding the role of affect in cognition. In R. S. Wyer & T. K. Srull (Eds.), *Handbook of social cognition* (Vol. 3, pp. 179–236). Hillsdale, NJ: Erlbaum.

Jablensky, A. (1985). Approaches to the definition and classification of anxiety and related disorders in European psychiatry. In A. H. Tuma & J. D. Maser (Eds.), *Anxiety and the anxiety disorders* (pp. 735–758). Hillsdale, NJ: Erlbaum.

Jablensky, A., Sartorius, N., Gulbinat, W., & Ernberg, G. (1981). Characteristics of depressive patients contacting psychiatric services in four cultures. *Acta Psychiatrica Scandinavica, 63,* 367–383.

Kayne, N. T., & Alloy, L. B. (in press). Clinician and patient as aberrant actuaries: Expectation-based distortions in assessment of covariation. In L. Y. Abramson (Ed.), *Social cognition and clinical psychology.* New York: Guilford Press.

Kendell, R. E. (1976). The classification of depressions: A review of contemporary confusion. *British Journal of Psychiatry, 129,* 15–28.

Kerr, T. A., Roth, M., & Schapira, K. (1974). Prediction of outcome in anxiety states and depressive illnesses. *British Journal of Psychiatry, 124,* 125–127.

Kiloh, L. G., & Garside, R. F. (1963). The independence of neurotic depression and endogenous depression. *British Journal of Psychiatry, 109,* 451–463.

Klein, D. F. (1980). Anxiety reconceptualized. *Comprehensive Psychiatry, 21,* 411–427.

Klerman, G. (1977). Anxiety and depression. In G. Burrows (Ed.), *Handbook of studies on depression* (pp. 145–164). New York: Excerpta Medica.

Kraepelin, E. (1981). *Clinical psychiatry: A textbook for physicians* (A. Diefendorf, Trans). New York: Macmillan. (Original work published 1883)

Kuiper, N. A. (1981). Convergent evidence for the self as a prototype: The "inverted-U RT effect" for self and other judgments. *Personality and Social Psychology Bulletin, 7,* 438–443.

Kuiper, N. A., & Derry, P. (1982). Depressed and nondepressed content self-reference in mild depressives. *Journal of Personality, 50,* 67–79.

Kuiper, N. A., & MacDonald, M. R. (1982). Self and other perception in mild depressives. *Social Cognition, 1,* 223–229.

Kuiper, N. A., Olinger, L. J., MacDonald, M. R., & Shaw, B. F. (1985). Self-schema processing of depressed and nondepressed content: The effects of vulnerability to depression. *Social Cognition, 3,* 77–93.

Kuiper, N. A., & Rogers, T. B. (1979). Encoding of personal information: Self–other differences. *Journal of Personality and Social Psychology, 4,* 499–514.

Lang, K. A., Mueller, J. H., & Nelson, R. E. (1983). Test anxiety and self-schemas. *Motivation and Emotion, 7,* 169–178.

Lazarus, R. S., & Averill, J. R. (1972). Emotion and cognition: With special reference to anxiety. In C. D. Spielberger (Ed.), *Anxiety: Current trends in theory and research* (Vol. 2, pp. 241–283). New York: Academic Press.

Leckman, J. F., Merikangus, K. R., Pauls, D. L., Prusoff, B. A., & Weissman, M. M. (1983). Anxiety disorders and depression: Contradictions between family study data and DSM-III conventions. *American Journal of Psychiatry, 140,* 880–882.

Leckman, J. F., Weissman, M. M., Merikangus, K. R., Pauls, D. L., & Prusoff, B. A. (1983). Panic disorder and major depression: Increased risk of depression, alcoholism, panic, and phobic disorders in families of depressed probands with panic disorder. *Archives of General Psychiatry, 40,* 1055–1066.

Leonhard, K. (1979). *The classification of endogenous psychoses.* New York: Wiley.

Levitt, E., & Lubin, B. (1975). *Depression: Concepts, controversies, and some new facts*. New York: Springer-Verlag.

Lewinsohn, P. (1974). A behavioral approach to depression. In R. Friedman & M. Katz (Ed.), *The psychology of depression: Contemporary theory and research* (pp. 157–186). Washington, DC: Winston-Wiley.

Lewinsohn, P., Mischel, W., Chaplain, W., & Barton, R. (1980). Social competence and depression: The role of illusory self perceptions? *Journal of Abnormal Psychology, 89*, 203–212.

Lewis, A. J. (1934). Melancholia: A clinical survey of depressive states. *Journal of Mental Science, 80*, 277–278.

Lewis, A. J. (1938). States of depression and their clinical and aetiological differentiation. *British Medical Journal, 21*, 183–186.

Lloyd, G. G., & Lishman, W. A. (1975). Effect of depression on the speed of recall of pleasant and unpleasant experiences. *Psychosomatic Medicine, 5*, 173–180.

Lorr, M., Sonn, T., & Katz, M. (1967). Toward a definition of depression. *Archives of General Psychiatry, 17*, 183–186.

Mandler, G. (1972). Helplessness: Theory and research in anxiety. In C. D. Spielberger (Ed.), *Anxiety: Current trends in theory and research* (Vol. 2, pp. 359–374). New York: Academic Press.

Mandler, G., & Watson, D. (1966). Anxiety and the interruption of behavior. In C. D. Spielberger (Ed.), *Anxiety and behavior* (pp. 263–288). New York: Academic Press.

Markus, H. (1977). Self-schemata and processing information about the self. *Journal of Personality and Social Psychology, 35*, 63–78.

Markus, H., & Smith, J. (1981). The influence of self-schema on the perception of others. In N. Cantor & J. Kihlstrom (Eds.), *Personality, cognition, and social interaction* (pp. 233–262). Hillsdale, NJ: Erlbaum.

Martin, D. J., Abramson, L. Y., & Alloy, L. B. (1984). Illusion of control for self and others in depressed and nondepressed college students. *Journal of Personality and Social Psychology, 46*, 125–136.

Mathew, R. S., Swihart, A., & Weinman, M. L. (1982). Vegetative symptoms in anxiety and depression. *British Journal of Psychiatry, 141*, 162–165.

McNicol, D. (1972). *A primer of signal detection theory*. London: George Allen & Unwin.

Meites, K., Lovallo, T., & Pishkin, V. (1980). Comparison of four scales for anxiety, depression, and neuroticism. *Journal of Clinical Psychology, 36*, 427–431.

Mendels, J., Weinstein, N., & Cochrane, C. (1972). The relationship between depression and anxiety. *Archives of General Psychiatry, 27*, 649–653.

Miller, W. R., Seligman, M. E. P., & Kurlander, H. M. (1975). Learned helplessness, depression, and anxiety. *Journal of Nervous and Mental Disease, 161*, 347–357.

Minsky, M. (1975). A framework for representing knowledge. In P. H. Winston (Ed.), *The psychology of computer vision*. New York: McGraw-Hill.

Morse, S., & Gergen, K. J. (1970). Social comparison, self consistency and the concept of self. *Journal of Personality and Social Psychology, 16*, 148–156.

Mueller, J. H., & Curtois, M. R. (1980). Retention of self descriptive and nondescriptive words as a function of test anxiety level. *Motivation and Emotion, 4*, 229–237.

Mueller, J. H., Thompson, W. B., & Davenport, J. S. (1984, May). *Order of access to semantic content and self-schema*. Paper presented at the meeting of the Midwestern Psychological Association, Chicago.

Murray, L. G., & Blackburn, I. M. (1974). Personality differences in patients with depressive illnesses and anxiety neuroses. *Acta Psychiatrica Scandinavica, 50*, 189–190.

Nadich, M., Gargan, M., & Michael, L. (1975). Denial, anxiety, and the discrepancy between aspiration and achievements as components of depression. *Journal of Abnormal Psychology, 84*, 1–9.

Neisser, U. (1967). *Cognitive psychology*. New York: Appleton-Century-Crofts.

Nelson, J. C., & Charney, D. S. (1981). The symptoms of major depressive illnesses. *British Journal of Psychiatry, 138*, 1–13.

Nezu, A., Nezu, C., & Nezu, V. (1986). Depression, general distress, and causal attributions among university students. *Journal of Abnormal Psychology, 95,* 184–186.

Overall, J. E., & Zisook, S. (1980). Diagnosis and the phenomenology of depressive disorders. *Journal of Consulting and Clinical Psychology, 48,* 626–634.

Owens, J., Bower, G., & Black, J. (1979). The "soap opera" effect in story recall. *Memory and Cognition, 7,* 185–191.

Parkes, K. (1981). Field dependence and the differentiation of affective states. *British Journal of Psychiatry, 139,* 52–58.

Paykel, E. S. (1971). A classification of depressed patients: A cluster analysis derived grouping. *British Journal of Psychiatry, 118,* 275–288.

Paykel, E. S. (1972a). Correlates of a depressive typology. *Archives of General Psychiatry, 27,* 203–209.

Paykel, E. S. (1972b). Depressive typologies and response to amitriptyline. *British Journal of Psychiatry, 120,* 147–156.

Prusoff, B., & Klerman, G. (1974). Differentiating depressed from anxious neurotic outpatients: Use of discriminant function analysis for separation of neurotic affective states. *Archives of General Psychiatry, 30,* 302–309.

Riskind, J. E., Beck, A. T., Brown, G., & Steer, R. A. (1986). *Taking the measure of anxiety and depression: Validity of reconstructed Hamilton Scales.* Manuscript submitted for publication.

Riskind, J. H., & Rholes, W. S. (1984). Cognitive accessibility and the capacity of cognitions to predict future depression: A theoretical note. *Cognitive Therapy & Research, 8,* 1–12.

Rogers, T. B. (1981). A model of the self as an aspect of the human information processing system. In N. Cantor & J. F. Kihlstrom (Eds.), *Personality, cognition, and social interaction* (pp. 193–214). Hillsdale, NJ: Erlbaum.

Rogers, T. B., Kuiper, N., & Kirker, W. (1977). Self reference and the encoding of personal information. *Journal of Personality and Social Psychology, 35,* 677–688.

Rogers, T. B., Rogers, P. J., & Kuiper, N. A. (1979). Evidence for the self as a cognitive prototype: The "false alarm effect." *Personality and Social Psychology Bulletin, 5,* 53–56.

Rosch, E. (1975). Cognitive representation of semantic categories. *Journal of Experimental Psychology: General, 104,* 192–233.

Rosenberg, M. (1965). *Society and the adolescent self-image.* Princeton, NJ: Princeton University Press.

Rosenthal, S., & Klerman, G. L. (1966). Content and consistency in the endogenous depression problem. *British Journal of Psychiatry, 112,* 471–481.

Ross, L., Greene, D., & House, P. (1977). The false consensus phenomenon: An attributional bias in self-perception and social perception processes. *Journal of Experimental Social Psychology, 13,* 279–301.

Ross, M. J., & Mueller, J. H. (1983, May). *Consistency of the self-schema in depression.* Paper presented at the meeting of the Midwestern Psychological Association, Chicago.

Ross, M. J., Mueller, J. H., & de la Torre, M. (1986). Depression and trait distinctiveness in the self-schema. *Journal of Social and Clinical Psychology, 4,* 46–59.

Roth, M., Gurney, C., Garside, R. F., & Kerr, T. (1972). Studies in the classification of affective disorders: The relationship between anxiety states and depressive illness—1. *British Journal of Psychiatry, 121,* 147–161.

Roth, M., & Mountjoy, C. Q. (1982). The distinction between anxiety states and depressive disorders. In E. S. Paykel (Ed.), *Handbook of affective disorders* (pp. 70–92). Edinburgh: Churchill-Livingstone.

Roy-Byrne, P. D., Weingartner, H., Bierer, L. M., Thompson, K., & Post, R. M. (1986). Effortful and automatic processes in depression. *Archives of General Psychiatry, 43,* 265–267.

Sarason, I. G. (1975). Anxiety and self preoccupation. In I. G. Sarason & C. D. Spielberger (Eds.), *Stress and anxiety* (Vol. 2, pp. 27–44). New York: Wiley.

Sarason, I. G. (1985). Cognitive processes, anxiety, and the treatment of anxiety disorders. In A. H. Tuma & J. D. Maser (Eds.), *Anxiety and the anxiety disorders* (pp. 87–107). Hillsdale, NJ: Erlbaum.

Schachter, S. (1959). *The psychology of affiliation*. Stanford, CA: Stanford University Press.

Schank, R., & Abelson, R. (1975). Scripts, plans, and knowledge. *Advance Papers of the Fourth International Joint Conference on Artificial Intelligence* (pp. 151–157). Tbilisi, Georgia, USSR.

Schapira, K., Roth, M., Kerr, T. A., & Gurney, C. (1972). The prognosis of affective disorders: The differentiation of anxiety from depressive illness. *British Journal of Psychiatry, 121*, 175–181.

Schweitzer, L., & Adams, G. (1979). The diagnosis and management of anxiety for primary care physicians. In W. Fann, I. Karacan, A. Porkorny, & R. Williams (Eds.), *Phenomenology and treatment of anxiety* (pp. 19–42). New York: Spectrum.

Serra, A., & Pollitt, J. (1975). The relationship between personality and the symptoms of depressive illness. *British Journal of Psychiatry, 27*, 211–218.

Spielberger, C. D. (1972). Anxiety as an emotional state. In C. D. Spielberger (Ed.), *Anxiety: Current trends in theory and research* (Vol. 2, pp. 23–49). New York: Academic Press.

Spielberger, C. D., Gorsuch, R. L., & Luschene, R. E. (1970). *Manual for the State–Trait Anxiety Inventory*. Palo Alto, CA: Consulting Psychologists Press.

Spitzer, R. L., & Williams, J. B. W. (1985). Proposed revisions in the DSM-III classification of anxiety disorders based on research and clinical experience. In A. H. Tuma & J. D. Maser (Eds.), *Anxiety and the anxiety disorders* (pp. 759–773). Hillsdale, NJ: Erlbaum.

Tabachnik, N., Crocker, J., & Alloy, L. B. (1983). Depression, social comparison, and the false-consensus effect. *Journal of Personality and Social Psychology, 45*, 688–699.

Taylor, S., & Crocker, J. (1980). Schematic bases of social information processing. In E. Higgens, P. Hermann, & M. Zanna (Eds.), *The Ontario Symposium on Personality and Social Psychology* (Vol. 1, pp. 87–134). Hillsdale, NJ: Erlbaum.

Teja, J. S., Narang, R. L., & Aggarwal, A. K. (1971). Depression across cultures. *British Journal of Psychiatry, 119*, 253–260.

Tellegen, A. (1985). Structures of mood and personality and their relevance to assessing anxiety, with an emphasis on self-report. In A. H. Tuma & J. D. Maser (Eds.), *Anxiety and the anxiety disorders* (pp. 681–706). Hillsdale, NJ: Erlbaum.

Torgerson, S. (1983). Genetic factors in anxiety disorders. *Archives of General Psychiatry, 40*, 1085–1089.

Van Valkenburg, C., Akiskal, H. S., Puzantian, V., & Rosenthal, T. (1984). Anxious depression: Clinical, family history, and naturalistic outcome comparisons with panic and major depressive disorders. *Journal of Affective Disorders, 6*, 67–82.

Vazquez, C. V., & Alloy, L. B. (1987). *Schematic memory processes for self- and other-referent information in depression versus anxiety: A signal detection analysis*. Unpublished manuscript, Northwestern University, Evanston, IL.

Weissman, M. M. (1985). The epidemiology of anxiety disorders: Rates, risks, and familial patterns. In A. H. Tuma & J. D. Maser (Eds.), *Anxiety and the anxiety disorders* (pp. 275–296). Hillsdale, NJ: Erlbaum.

Weissman, M. M., Gershon, E. S., Kidd, K. K., Prusoff, B. A., Leckman, J. F., Dibble, E., Hamovit, J., Thompson, W. D., Pauls, D. L., & Guroff, J. J. (1984a). Psychiatric disorders in the relatives of probands with affective disorders: The Yale–NIMH collaborative family study. *Archives of General Psychiatry, 41*, 13–21.

Weissman, M. M., Leckman, J. F., Merikangus, K. R., Prusoff, B. A., & Gammon, G. D. (1983). Depression and anxiety disorders in parents and children: Results from the Yale family study. *Archives of General Psychiatry 38*, 139–152.

Weissman, M. M., Prusoff, B. A., Gammon, G. D., Merikangus, K. R., Leckman, J. F., & Kidd, K. K. (1984b). Psychopathology in the children (ages 6–18) of depressed and normal parents. *Journal of the American Academy of Child Psychiatry, 23*, 78–84.

Zuroff, D. C., Colussy, S. A., & Wielgus, M. S. (1983). Selective memory in depression: A cautionary note concerning response bias. *Cognitive Therapy and Research, 7*, 223–232.

5

Self-management and Cognitive Processes in Depression

LYNN P. REHM
University of Houston

The general premise of this chapter is that self-management concepts can provide a useful framework within which to discuss depression. This argument does not rely on adopting any single model of self-management. Self-management can be considered as a particular perspective or clinical paradigm within which clinical phenomena can be approached. A number of features of self-management models in general will be abstracted and shown to be relevant to the problems of depression. The chapter offers an overview of research in depressive psychopathology and attempts to abstract from recent research findings those characteristics of depression that appear to be central features and that would necessarily be described or accounted for in a comprehensive self-management theory of depression.

SELF-MANAGEMENT

Many different models of self-management have been proposed. Within the behavioral paradigm, Skinner (1957) suggested a number of strategies whereby individuals manipulate their environments in order to influence their own future behavior. Bandura has contributed in several ways to research and theory in self-management, most recently, with his self-efficacy model (Bandura, 1977). Kanfer (1970; Kanfer & Karoly, 1972a, 1972b) developed a three-stage feedback-loop model of self-control and applied it to a variety of problems in psychology. An elaborate revision of this model was recently proposed by Kanfer and Hagerman (1981), with specific application to depression. In 1977, I proposed a modification of the original Kanfer model and applied the model to depression (Rehm, 1977). Information-processing models have been applied to problems of self-control by Carver and Scheier (1982). Self-management as cognitive self-instruction strategies has been developed by Meichenbaum (e.g., Meichenbaum & Cameron, 1974) for applications with children and adults. Eric Klinger (1982) proposed a model involving cognitive structuring of plans and concerns. Richard Lazarus's (1974) work on stress and coping strategies should also be included as a perspective on self-management. Many of these models have been applied in one form or another to the phenomena of depression. These applications are facilitated by the fact that self-management models share certain common characteristics and concerns.

All models of self-management focus on control processes regulating behavior. Self-management of behavior assumes that people are capable of two coexisting levels of behavior. At the first level, the person is a behaving organism interacting with an external environment and its situations, contingencies, and consequences. At the second level, the same person is behaving in ways that influence the first level of behavior by overtly or covertly manipulating aspects of the situation and arranging alternative contingencies and consequences. This internal regulation or control supplements, or in some instances counteracts, the external control of behavior. We attribute self-control or self-management of behavior to individuals when they behave in ways that are not directly predictable from observations of current external influences. "Persistence" is self-control behavior in the face of current lack of reward or even current punishment (e.g., jogging). "Resistance to temptation" is failure to respond to current rewards (e.g., dieting). The external control influencing these behaviors is less obvious, but this does not deny that the goal of self-control behavior is to obtain rewards or avoid punishment in the long range (e.g., good health). "Self-management" simply refers to acquired skills that function to enhance behavior aimed at achieving long-range goals.

Self-management approaches focus on person variance in the person-by-situation interaction. This is in contrast to the more behavioral models, which stress external situational control. Self-management deals with acquired general skills that the individual may employ across similar situations. Again in contrast to the more behavioral approaches, self-management models deal more frequently with covert, cognitive processes, and occasionally with cognitive structures. Models vary considerably in the degree and sophistication with which they employ concepts and constructs from cognitive psychology. That covert processes are postulated, however, does not mean that these models necessarily rely upon or postulate a "structural self."

In one form or another, most of the self-management models incorporate the concept of a feedback loop. Homeostatic self-regulatory models from biology, mechanics, and information processing are here given psychological application. These models usually postulate steps in the feedback loop, such as input, processing, and output functions. The feedback-loop concept suggests a focus on ongoing adjustment, adaptation, and readaptation to changing environmental circumstances. Kanfer (1970), for instance, suggests that self-control behaviors are engaged in only under certain circumstances. These circumstances occur when the person perceives in a particular situation that well-practiced, routine behavior is no longer achieving the desired results. Self-management deals with strategies for behavior change in response to unfavorable environmental consequences. Such strategies typically have been applied to problems such as losing weight, quitting smoking, or controlling alcohol or drug use. In each instance, individuals must perceive that their behavior no longer produces a desirable balance of positive to negative consequences. Self-management concepts are also relevant and applicable to interpersonal situations where the individual is adapting or problem solving in response to behaviors of another person.

Individual differences in self-management skills exist apart from particular current needs for adaptation. Thus self-management can be seen in terms of vulnerability. Behavior pathology may arise when particular environmental demands occur and the individual does not have the self-management skills to cope with the change. Consistency of self-management skills would suggest that they could be assessed independently and prior to situational demand.

Another important focus of the self-management approach is temporal integration, or "time binding." Self-management is concerned mainly with behavioral strategies for accomplishing long-term as opposed to short-term goals. The aim of operating or control processes is temporal integration. Mature, confident, skilled behavior requires processes whereby long-term, delayed reinforcers may be obtained in the face of short-term influences promoting other behaviors.

These various features of self-management models make them particularly applicable to the problems of depression. Depression is a complex set of phenomena, with many factors contributing to cause, characteristics, maintenance, and recovery. Depression may be heterogeneous with regard to these factors. A broad overview of depression theory suggests that a number of major sets of factors influence depression and that self-management models may help us to think about some of these. Although this volume focuses on the psychological factors associated with depression, it is important to note that biological factors also influence this disorder. Biologic factors should be thought of as setting certain thresholds and parameters of response. They should be seen as interacting with environmental stress and with psychological coping skills. For example, individuals may vary in their physiological and biologic responses to certain stressors and in their ability to apply psychological strategies to control these physiological and emotional responses. Self-management models clearly deal more with the stress and coping elements of this interaction. Certain kinds of stressors, such as social exits and losses, are particularly important in precipitating depression. Thus skills in adapting to change are clearly relevant. Most current theories of depression focus on psychological coping factors that may interact with environmental stressors. Lewinsohn's (1974) model focuses on activity-level, social-skill, and anxiety factors that may contribute to depression. The helplessness theory (Abramson, Seligman, & Teasdale, 1978) focuses on attributional style, and Beck's theory (Beck, Rush, Shaw, & Emery, 1979), on the cognitive distortion of experience. Research on psychological vulnerability factors has frequently focused on these cognitive characteristics of individuals. Each of these models can be seen as focusing on aspects of self-management behavior.

In sum, the general argument here is that self-management models offer a particular perspective that is relevant to depression. This proposition can be examined in greater detail by reviewing current research on cognitive factors in depression. This review is organized under a variety of headings relevant to self-management.

SELF-MONITORING IN DEPRESSION

The concept of self-monitoring has been applied to studies of depression in a number of ways. Self-monitoring has to do with the degree and accuracy with which individuals observe their own behavior and experiences and their ability to report accurately on these.

One way in which self-monitoring concepts have been applied in the study of depression is to assume that all persons can act as veridical recorders of their own experiences and that the data thus collected can be related to other aspects of the person's behavior (e.g., depressed mood). One of the major thrusts of this research is to have individuals assess the occurrence of pleasant or unpleasant events in their lives and to relate this to self-reports of mood.

Instruments for assessing and recording the incidence of events have been developed by Lewinsohn and his colleagues. MacPhillamy and Lewinsohn (1982) developed a 320-item Pleasant Events Schedule. For self-monitoring purposes, the entire schedule or a subset of its items is used as a daily checklist for the occurrence of each event. The Pleasant Events Schedule is also used in a retrospective report format in which subjects are asked to indicate the frequency of occurrence of each of the events in the last 30 days and to rate its enjoyability. A similar instrument was constructed for unpleasant events by Lewinsohn and Talkington (1979). More recently, the Cognitive Events Schedule has been devised (Lewinsohn, Larson, & Munoz, 1982) to assess the occurrence of pleasant and unpleasant self-statements, that is, positive or negative statements made about oneself or thoughts about oneself. Correlations between positive mood and daily pleasant events have been well established (Grosscup & Lewinsohn, 1980; Lewinsohn & Graf, 1973; Lewinsohn & Libet, 1972; O'Hara & Rehm, 1979; Rehm, 1978). Positive mood also has been well demonstrated to correlate negatively with self-monitored unpleasant events (e.g., Grosscup & Lewinsohn, 1980; Lewinsohn & Talkington, 1979; O'Hara & Rehm, 1979; Rehm, 1978). In those studies in which both pleasant and unpleasant events have been monitored (Grosscup & Lewinsohn, 1980; O'Hara & Rehm, 1979; Rehm, 1978), it has generally been found that the number of pleasant events is not correlated with the number of unpleasant events and thus that they each contribute independently to mood variance.

Do Events Influence Mood?

Several additional studies have attempted to demonstrate a causal relationship between events and mood by manipulating self-monitoring processes. Kirschenbaum and Karoly (1977) instructed college students who were working on math problems to self-monitor either the number of problems answered correctly or the number of errors. Negative self-monitoring (errors) produced lower self-evaluation, decreased self-reinforcement, decreased accuracy, and increased anxiety. Although the dysphoric mood assessed here was anxiety rather than depression, the study did demonstrate that the strategy of self-monitoring can influence self-evaluation, self-reinforcement, and mood.

Another study (Hammen & Glass, 1975) reported two experiments on the effects of self-monitoring instructions. In the first experiment, a group that was instructed to increase pleasant events did so; however, no effects were found for mood. In the second experiment, subjects who were asked to increase their pleasant events ended up being slightly *more* depressed. Hammen and Glass argued that cognitive mediation regarding the significance of the events was critical for mood effects rather than just the number of events. Lewinsohn (1975) replied that no positive effect on mood was obtained possibly because (1) the experiment did not ensure that depressed subjects began with low levels of activity, (2) the events monitored were not necessarily enjoyable to those subjects, and (3) the initial correlation between mood and these activities was not obtained. It should also be pointed out that the subjects knew the experience was an experiment and did not see it as something from which they expected to benefit.

O'Hara and Rehm (1979) had normal community volunteers monitor pleasant events, unpleasant events, both, or neither. The valence of events monitored had no effect either on activity level or on mood, despite the fact that correlations between activity level and mood were found. This study also demonstrated that it was not activity level *per se* that mediated the effect, because activity level, as measured by pedometers, did not correlate with mood or with the number of daily events. O'Hara and Rehm speculated that no effect of monitoring strategy on mood was obtained partly because the subjects reported that they generally did not actively monitor themselves during the day as instructed but rather, waited until the end of the day to record their events and assess their mood.

Harmon, Nelson, and Hayes (1980) investigated this distinction. They had subjects monitor either mood or activity on a variable-interval 1-hour schedule for 11 recordings per day. In addition, all subjects filled out Depression Adjective Check Lists (Lubin, 1967) and a 139-item Pleasant Events Schedule at the end of the day. Self-monitoring of either mood or activity produced an increase in both positive mood and activity. Mood and activity were correlated. The authors concluded that activity and mood affect one another mutually. They also concluded that once-a-day global self-monitoring does not have reactive effects, whereas frequent self-monitoring during the day does. In this experiment, subjects were motivated to change because they were in treatment and because the task was presented as a treatment technique.

Finally, Evans and Hollon (1979) studied depressed and nondepressed college students who monitored their mood in what was described as either an immediate (hourly) monitoring condition or a delayed (daily) monitoring condition. In addition, subjects filled out Depression Adjective Check Lists each evening for 7 days. Depressed subjects differed from nondepressed subjects in daily but not in hourly ratings. Only in the daily monitoring was mood consistent with Depression Adjective Check List scores. The investigators suggested that delayed (daily) monitoring may be distorted, as all summary estimates may be, and recommended immediate or hourly monitoring as potentially more accurate. However, no criterial for accuracy exist in this study.

Self-Monitoring by Depressed Persons

A second set of studies has focused on the differences in self-monitoring behavior and strategies between depressed and nondepressed individuals. The earliest of these studies (Lewinsohn & Libet, 1972) found no differences between (1) depressed, (2) psychiatric control, and (3) normal subjects with regard to monitored events on the Pleasant Events Schedule. However, Lewinsohn and Graf (1973), using a similar design, found that depressed subjects did report engaging in fewer and less frequent pleasant events. MacPhillamy and Lewinsohn (1974), using the Pleasant Events Schedule in its retrospective format, found that depressed subjects, as compared to nondepressed psychiatric control and to normal subjects, reported engaging in fewer pleasant events, rated pleasant events as less enjoyable, and reported less obtained pleasure. Lewinsohn and Talkington (1979) found the expected reverse effect between depressed and control groups on the Unpleasant Events Schedule. Lewinsohn and Amenson (1978) found that depressed and nondepressed subjects differed more on items that had been found to be mood related in the general population than on items that were less mood related. Grosscup and Lewinsohn (1980) and Lewinsohn, Youngren, and Grosscup (1979) reported an improvement in activity scores on the Pleasant and Unpleasant Events Schedules by depressed subjects after treatment. They also reported a decrease in the aversiveness of items on the Unpleasant Events Schedule after treatment.

Distortion in Self-monitoring

The question of distortion in the self-monitoring of events has been addressed in a number of studies that have looked at differences between depressed and nondepressed individuals in their interpretation of ambiguous stimuli. It is a common clinical observation that depressed persons distort their experience in a negative direction, and this is frequently observed in clinical assessments.

For example, using projective techniques, Weintraub, Segal, and Beck (1974) had depressed and nondepressed patients give responses to story introductions. The stories of depressed subjects contained more expectations of discomfort and of failure and more negative perceptions of self. Funabiki and Calhoun (1979) had college students rate common problems. Depressed students rated interpersonal problems as more difficult to cope with than did nondepressed students, and depressed females rated problems as producing more concern. Finkel, Glass, and Merluzzi (1979) also used college students and had them rate statements from three categories—positive, negative, and neutral. Depressed subjects rated positive statements as less positive, and identified fewer of them as being positive, than did nondepressed students. On the other hand, they also rated the negative statements as less negative. This study offers some support for the idea of a negative bias in depression, but it also suggests that other response biases may be demonstrated by depressed individuals.

Hammen and Krantz (1976) devised a questionnaire to assess both negativity of interpretation and distortion. Mildly depressed college students chose more depressed–distorted and fewer nondepressed–nondistorted response alternatives than did nondepressed students. Hammen (1978) replicated this result and also found that depressed subjects who had a low number of adverse life events showed the greatest distortion. These depressed subjects were presumably less reactively depressed, and perhaps more chronically or characterologically depressed, and thus may have been most likely to demonstrate cognitive distortion. Krantz and Hammen (1979) summarized data demonstrating that scores on their questionnaire show improvement with psychotherapy.

The preceding studies demonstrate an interpretative bias in depression that is negative. It may not be accurate to call this bias "distortion," since in these studies the tasks were highly ambiguous, and there was no veridical response against which to compare answers. Some additional studies have looked more at the nature of the interpretative process and its veridicality.

Accuracy in Depression

Roth and Rehm (1980) had depressed and nondepressed psychiatric patients view videotapes of themselves role playing in a conversational interaction with an experimenter. Subjects were asked to identify and record instances of specific positive and negative behaviors while viewing the tape. As compared to nondepressed psychiatric patients, the depressed patients counted fewer positive and more negative behaviors. An objective observer found no differences between the two groups of patients. The events observed by the subjects were relatively objective, and the subjects were trained in order to ensure that they understood the response classes and the nature of the task. Distortion was unlikely at this relatively low level of interpretation or abstraction. It may have been that subjects had differential criteria for identifying and reporting a negative as opposed to a positive behavior. Alternatively, subjects may have distributed their attention differentially between detecting negative and detecting positive behaviors.

In a second study, Roth and Rehm (1980) had depressed and nondepressed psychiatric patients guess the most common associate to a series of ambiguous words. No immediate feedback was given during the task. Afterward, subjects were told that they had been right on half of the trials and that in a series of feedback trials, they would be given the opportunity to see either a stimulus word that they had gotten right or a stimulus word that they had gotten wrong. Depressed psychiatric patients more frequently chose to see items that they had gotten wrong, whereas nondepressed psychiatric patients chose to see items that they had gotten right. This study demonstrates that depressed and nondepressed subjects use different strategies in deploying attention.

Basic studies of the effects of mood on the distribution of attention have been conducted by Mischel, Ebbesen, and Zeiss (1973, 1976). In their first study, they found that following success, normal subjects spent more time attending to feedback information about their assets than to feedback information about their liabilities in comparison to subjects who had prior failure or neutral experience. They concluded that the success experience induced a positive affect, which subjects sought to maintain by attending to additional positive information about themselves. In their second study, they manipulated success and failure independent of a manipulation of expectancy for success or failure on a future test. They found no effect for success versus failure *per se* but did find that positive expectancy for a future test led to remembering less negative information about one's self. They concluded that positive expectancy leads to a "warm glow of success," which subjects attempted to maintain by minimizing their attention to negative information about themselves. Studies by Schiffman (1978), Zuroff (1980), and Hammen (1977) replicated the Mischel, Ebbesen, and Zeiss (1973) design, with the addition of using depressed and nondepressed subject groups. These three studies partially replicated the "warm glow" effect, but did not find strong evidence that depressed subjects were differentially affected. Overall, there is some scattered evidence that induced mood or individual differences in mood may affect time spent attending to positive versus negative information about oneself, but the effect is rather ephemeral and may be a function of subtle parameters of the manipulation.

Incidental Memory

Another series of studies has looked at the question of distortion in depression by assessing self-monitoring in the form of incidental memory about performance. Friedman (1964) asked severely depressed and normal subjects to estimate the number of times they tapped on trials of a tapping-speed task. Depressed subjects significantly underestimated their tapping speeds. To the extent that the subject was being asked to recollect the number of taps, this task was an incidental memory task. However, since this would be virtually impossible to do accurately, the number of taps would have to be considered an ambiguous stimulus. The same is true in other studies of this type, that is, incidental memory requires some estimation.

Wener and Rehm (1975) reported a secondary finding in a study where amount of positive feedback was manipulated in an attempt to influence mood. Depressed subjects consistently underestimated the amount of positive feedback that they were given in the experiment when they were asked to estimate this amount afterward. Other designs have been used just to study this incidental memory process. Buchwald (1977) had college students go through two trials on a rote learning test. At the end of each presentation of the 20-item word list, subjects were asked to estimate the number of words they had gotten correct. In general, all subjects underestimated this number. However, there was a correlation between depression and the subject's estimate when the actual number of correct answers was partialed out, confirming an underestimation related to the degree of depression.

Nelson and Craighead (1977) gave subjects a task in which level of positive feedback was manipulated. Depressed subjects recalled less positive and more negative feedback than controls, but this was significant only in the condition in which a high rate of positive and a low rate of negative feedback were given.

In a related study, De Monbreun and Craighead (1977) compared the performance of depressed psychiatric, nondepressed psychiatric, and nondepressed–nonpsychiatric patients. Depressed subjects again recalled less positive feedback, but only in the high-positive-feedback condition. The investigators assessed the trial-by-trial accuracy with which subjects perceived the feedback they were given and found that all subjects accurately perceived feedback on a trial-by-trial basis. This study was replicated by Craighead, Hickey, and De Monbreun (1979) in comparing three groups of college students: one that was high on depression and anxiety, a second that was low on depression but high on anxiety, and a third that was low on both scales. Once again, it was found that depressed subjects did not distort on a trial-by-trial basis. In this study, there was also no effect of depression on recall.

The preceding studies show that depressed individuals do not distort on a trial-by-trial basis, nor do they distort on feedback that is consistent with their expectancy. Anomalous findings related to these studies were reported by Gotlib (1979a). In a verbal recognition task with no objective feedback, depressed subjects *underestimated* the degree of self-punishment. The major difference in this study was that the feedback was self-generated. Since depressed patients gave high rates of self-punishment, it is unclear what it means to find that they underestimated this higher rate in comparison to another group.

Summary

Studies of self-monitoring in depression, though not always consistent, do suggest a number of specific facts about the ways in which depressed individuals observe themselves in their environments. It is clear that depressed individuals record fewer positive and more negative events in their daily experiences. It is important to note that this may, in part, reflect veridical differences in the environments of depressed persons. In individuals, the nature of events from one day to another does seem to influence mood. It is equally clear, however, that depressed individuals interpret and make inferences about events that make them less positive and more negative. This does not seem to be due to an actual distorted perception. Depressed subjects may distribute their attention differently between negative and positive events or may have different criteria for identifying positive and negative events. Research suggests that the negativity lies in inference or interpretation, and perhaps in recall.

These facts suggest two important areas of research in self-management that are relevant to depression. First, a great deal of research on depression has focused on inferential processes. Different researchers or theorists have identified different classes of inference as particularly important in, or central to, producing depression. This chapter will review inferences characterized as attributions, expectancies, self-efficacy, and self-evaluation. Second, memory studies have recently taken on increased importance in the study of depression. A review of these studies later in the chapter will help clarify the nature of self-monitoring and inference in depression. Third, performance factors in depression are important and will be briefly surveyed.

INFERENCE PROCESSES IN DEPRESSION

Attribution

Attribution of causality has been identified as an important form of inference in regard to depression. It is assumed that one of the natural inferences that people make about important events in their lives is that of inferring their cause. Inferences about the cause of prior events will presumably influence future behavior concerning similar events.

Social psychological research (Weiner *et al.*, 1971) suggests that causes can be classified according to a relatively simple dimensional structure. The dimensions most often identified are *internal* versus *external* causes, and *stable* versus *unstable* causes. An attribution to skill is internal–stable, an attribution to effort is internal–unstable, an attribution to a difficult or easy task is external–stable, and an attribution to luck is external–unstable. Attributions can also be classified as *global* versus *specific*, depending upon the breadth or generality of the inferred cause.

Seligman's learned helplessness model of depression in its revised form (Abramson, Seligman, & Teasdale, 1978) states that the nature of the attributions a person makes about a major aversive event will determine whether or not a depression is produced. Furthermore, the specific dimensions of attribution will determine the characteristics of the depression. An attribution to a global cause will yield a generalized depression influencing all areas of the person's life. An internal attribution will yield low self-esteem and guilt, and a stable attribution will yield enduring depression. The theory further postulates that individuals have consistent attributional styles and that a person may be prone to depression if he or she has a particular depressive attributional style. Depressed persons are generally assumed to make attributions for negative events to internal, stable, and global causes, and to make attributions for positive events to external, unstable, and specific causes.

A full review of research on attributional style in depression is beyond the scope of this chapter. However, an overview of some of these studies will suggest the tenor of findings in this area.

Learned helplessness theory suggests that people who are depressed show a depressive attributional style. This issue has been examined in a number of studies (Hammen, Krantz, & Cochran, 1981; Harvey, 1981; Klein, Fencil-Morse, & Seligman, 1976; Oliver & Williams, 1979; Raps, Peterson, Reinhard, Abramson, & Seligman, 1982; Rizley, 1978; Seligman, Abramson, Semmel, & von Baeyer, 1979; Zuroff, 1980, 1981). Overall, the results, although partially supporting the model by suggesting the existence of negative attributions in depression, have been somewhat inconsistent in showing the hypothesized pattern of attributions, and raise questions about the generality of the effect.

Another major assumption of the model is that individuals will show a traitlike attributional style that will be manifest independent of episodes of depression. Mukherji, Abramson, and Martin (1982) used a mood-induction procedure to assess the effect of induced mood on attributions. They found no effect on attributions and concluded that this finding was consistent with a traitlike rather than a statelike nature for attributions. Eaves and Rush (1984) assessed hospitalized psychiatric patients and found that attributional-style scores changed with symptomatic improvement. They concluded that attributional style was not traitlike in comparison to some of the other measures. A similar study by Hamilton and Abramson (1983) also found that attributional style and other measures of cognitive symptomatology all decreased at discharge. They noted that some patients never had a profile suggesting cognitive symptomatology. Overall, the evidence for a depressive attributional style as a consistent individual difference is not well supported. Some studies have suggested that only a minority of the general population displays consistency in style.

The learned helplessness model in its revised form would predict that a depressive attributional style would interact with a stressful life event to produce depression. Three studies of postpartum depression have tested this hypothesis with inconsistent results. O'Hara, Rehm, and Campbell (1982) found that the attributional style did contribute over and above prepartum depression to the prediction of postpartum depression. A similar study, however, by Manly, McMahon, Bradley, and Davidson (1982) found that attributional style did not predict postpartum depression. Cutrona (1983) found that attributional style predicted postpartum depression for those subjects who were not already depressed in the prepartum period. She also found that attributional style contributed to lack of recovery from postpartum depression.

Cochran and Hammen (1980) studied depression, life events, and attributional style in college students at two points in time 2 months apart. A causal modeling analysis resulted in the conclusion that globality attributions contributed to the prediction of the extent of depression at Time 2. Generally, they concluded that the model did not fit the data well. Miller and Norman (1981) attempted to assess the relationship between attribution and mood by direct manipulations of attributions. Helpless and depressed subjects who received internal attributions were less depressed at posttest. Depressed subjects who received global attributions tended to generalize the experimental effect better on a subsequent anagrams task. Both results would be predicted by the revised theoretical model.

As with some of the other inference factors, self- versus other-distortion is important. Sharp and Tennen (1983) gave depressed and nondepressed college students a manipulated failure experience on an experimental task and then had them observe a confederate who performed equally poorly. Depressed students made more internal attributions for their own failure than did nondepressed students, but they did not attribute failure of the confederate to similar internal causes.

In summary, the evidence for attributions as important cognitive mediators in producing depression has been scattered and somewhat inconsistent, although it certainly supports to some degree the basic hypothesis. A question could be raised as to the centrality of attributions in the cognitive processes that produce depression. The helplessness theory holds that attributions are of central importance at least for certain depressions, that is, reactive depressions. Other models of depression have suggested that attributions play an auxiliary or contributing role along with other cognitive factors. In the self-control model (Rehm, 1977), I saw the role of attribution as a moderator in self-evaluation. Positive or negative self-evaluations cannot occur without internal attributions of responsibility. Kanfer and Hagerman (1981) viewed attributions as playing a role in influencing self-management behavior at many points in self-control processes related to depression. One could also ask whether attributions might not simply be the epiphenomena of negative-self evaluation. That is, if one infers that one's performance has been poor, then attributions that are consistent with a poor performance might be inferred secondarily. Some of these issues will be addressed in subsequent sections of this chapter.

Expectancy and Self-efficacy

Expectancy is an important construct in a number of theoretical models of self-management and of depression. Basically, expectancies are predictions about future performances that are based on inferences from specific and general information about the task and about past performances. Many different factors may influence expectancies, and it may be important to consider specific components of expectancy.

Helplessness theory has examined the phenomenon of expectancy shift. Helplessness is a perception of response–outcome independence. It would be predicted that helpless depressed persons would be slower than nondepressed persons in changing their predictions of outcome based on accumulated experience. For example, if a person begins with an expectancy for a certain level of performance but consistently performs above that level, the person's expectancy will shift to the level of the actual performance. It would be predicted that the depressed person would be more sluggish in making this expectancy shift.

Results confirming this prediction were first reported by Miller and Seligman (1973). Miller and Seligman (1976) used their helplessness induction task as well as groups of depressed subjects to demonstrate that depression produced smaller decreases in expectancy after failure on a task described as one involving skill but not after failure on a task described as one involving chance. However, no expectancy effects for depression or induced helplessness were found after success, as would also have been predicted. Abramson, Garber, Edwards, and Seligman (1978) had depressed nonschizophrenic patients, depressed schizophrenic patients, nondepressed schizophrenic patients, and normal subjects perform a task with manipulated success and failure under instructions indicating that the task involved skill or chance. Compared to the other groups of subjects, depressed nonschizophrenic patients showed less expectancy shift in the skilled task following failure but not following success, a finding similar to that of Miller and Seligman (1976).

The results of other studies have been less consistent with regard to their support for the hypothesis. A failure to replicate an expectancy-shift deficit among depressed alcoholics was reported by O'Leary, Donovan, Krueger, and Cysewski (1978). Willis and Blaney (1978) failed to replicate differential expectancy-shift phenomena in two studies. Sacco and Hokanson (1978) tested the hypothesis in public versus private settings and found that depressed subjects showed less expectancy shift in the public setting and more in the private setting. McNitt and

Thornton (1978) found that with instructions indicating that a task involved chance, depressed subjects showed a larger expectancy shift than nondepressed subjects in a 75% success condition. They interpreted this result by suggesting the presence of overgeneralization in depression as opposed to helplessness. The expectancy-shift phenomenon in relationship to depression appears to be partially replicable, but the effect does not appear to be robust, and additional factors may be important. For example, the reversal of effects in the private setting in the Sacco and Hokanson (1978) study suggests that impression management may also be important in determining the self-report responses of depressed subjects in experimental situations.

Two studies have investigated the presumed motivational deficit in depression using the concept of motivation as the product of expectancy times value. This generic model suggests that the reinforcing value of a particular outcome is the product of its value times the expected probability of its occurrence. Layne, Merry, Christian, and Ginn (1982) found that depressed subjects had lower value ratings for positive outcomes and lower expectancies, resulting in lower motivation for reward. In a second part of this study depressed subjects undervalued punishment, but there were no differences in expectancies. Gurtman (1981), had college students fill out questionnaires regarding their expectancies and their needs (values) for sets of academic and peer-affection outcomes. Values did not correlate with either depression or hopelessness scores. Expectancies did correlate negatively with these scores, and the expectancy-need product correlated moderately with them in a regression analysis. The two studies are somewhat contradictory with regard to whether it is expectancy or value that differentiates depressed from nondepressed subjects.

Bandura (1977) made an important distinction regarding expectancy in his self-efficacy theory. He distinguished between outcome expectancy (the probability that an outcome will occur, given an appropriate response) and response expectancy, or self-efficacy (the probability that the particular individual is capable of performing the necessary response). Interpreting this model in terms of depression, Davis and Yates (1982) predicted that depression would be induced under conditions in which response expectancy (self-efficacy) was low and outcome expectancy high. This result was obtained for males only. A second prediction was that no depressive deficit would occur under conditions in which both self-efficacy and outcome expectancy were low. This prediction was validated again for males only. The latter finding of this study was held to be contrary to learned helplessness theory, which would have predicted that any condition in which response and outcome were perceived to be independent would produce depression.

Devins *et al.* (1982) studied self-efficacy and outcome expectancies among patients with end-stage renal disease. Self-efficacy and outcome expectancies were rated several general life and health areas. The results produced some scattered support for a relationship between these predictors and the criterion variables. However, the predicted interaction between self-efficacy and outcome expectancy was not found.

The distinction between self-efficacy and outcome expectancy is a useful one, which, to date, is only beginning to be applied in research. Another role of expectancy in self-evaluation is reviewed in the next section.

Self-evaluation

A number of theorists maintain that negative self-evaluation is a central factor in depression. Beck (1972), for example, holds that a negative view of self is one of the essential features of depression. In the self-control model of depression (Rehm, 1977), negative self-evaluation is held to be one of several critical factors in depression, a factor hypothesized to be based on the setting of high standards and influenced by negative self-monitoring and a depressive attributional style. It is evident that negative self-evaluation is a multidimensional concept.

That depressed individuals are negative in their evaluations of themselves is a commonly observed clinical fact and is well documented in the research literature. For example, Young, Moore, and Nelson (1981) found that when college students were given positive, negative, and neutral bogus personality descriptions, depressed students rated the negative statements as more valid about themselves than did nondepressed students. In a role-playing study, Lasher and Lynn (1981) reported that depressed college students expected to make a less favorable impression and were more negatively self-evaluating than nondepressed students.

Self-evaluation has also been assessed by looking at individuals' evaluations of themselves as they are (the real self) versus how they would ideally like to be (the ideal self). The ideal self can be seen as a generalized form of standard setting, and the real self, as a form of self-evaluation. Laxer (1964) had psychiatric patients assess themselves over the course of treatment. Changes in real-self ratings correlated with changes in clinical improvement. No changes were found in ideal-self ratings. Standards remained somewhat constant, while self-evaluations improved with treatment. Using a similar format, Wessman, Ricks, and Tyl (1960) found that daily changes in mood correlated with real-self but not with ideal-self ratings.

Fry (1976) measured positive- and negative-adjective self-ratings of normal subjects before and after success, failure, and control experiences. Following success, subjects demonstrated greater gains on positive adjectives as opposed to negative adjectives. Following failure, greater changes were shown on the negative adjectives rather than the positive adjectives. Thus the nature of the change in self-evaluation was a function of the valence of the rating dimensions. It may be that self-evaluative criteria for success are somewhat different from, and on slightly different dimensions than, self-evaluative criteria for failure. Gotlib (1979b) found that in comparison to normal subjects, depressed psychiatric patients showed a lower expectation for success, a lower expectation for performance, and a lower satisfaction with their performance. In this study, however, depressed patients did not differ from the nondepressed psychiatric patients in their self-evaluative criteria. Gotlib questioned whether negative self-evaluation is specific to depression or is generally an aspect of psychiatric disturbance.

A number of studies have compared self-evaluations of depressed and nondepressed subjects and have then looked at their actual performance. Lewis, Mercatoris, Cole, and Leonard (1980) looked at a number of self-control behaviors of college students on a concept-formation task. Depressed students evaluated their performance as poor, even though it was objectively the same as that of nondepressed students. Also, depressed students' recall of number correct was accurate and was equal to that of nondepressed students. Loeb, Beck, Diggory, and Tuthill (1967) assessed actual performance by depressed and nondepressed subjects on a card-sorting task and similarly found objectively equal performance despite lower self-evaluation by depressed subjects.

Lewinsohn, Mischel, Chaplin, and Barton (1980) had psychiatric patients interact with normal persons in a group setting. All subjects evaluated their social performance on a series of rating scales. Depressed subjects rated themselves as less skillful than did the other subjects, and they were rated as less skillful by the others. Interestingly, it was the nondepressed psychiatric and normal subjects whose self-evaluations were distorted; that is, they rated themselves as more skillful than others rated them. Depressed subjects' self-ratings more closely corresponded to the ratings given them by others. It should be noted here, however, that the criterion was social consensus, not an objective quantification. Each person may value a unique pattern of factors that typifies his or her own behavior and that comprises factors at which they are most skilled. Thus normal persons' self-evaluations may be higher than the average of ratings given them by others because the others may have used different combinations of factors in making their ratings. Depressed subjects engage in the same process but evaluate themselves lower and may merely appear to be more accurate. This study also found that ratings by self and by others improved with treatment but that the discrepancy between ratings did not change.

In the Lewinsohn *et al.* (1980) study, depressed subjects were more negative in their evaluations of themselves than they were in their evaluations of others. Several additional studies have addressed this theoretically important issue. Shrauger and Terbovic (1976) had college students assess themselves on a concept-formation task and then, 1 week later, assess a videotape either of themselves or of another subject, who in fact was a confederate replicating the subject's own responses. Low-self-esteem (depressed) subjects rated themselves lower than did high-self-esteem subjects. Low-self-esteem subjects also rated themselves as lower than the model, who was identical to the subject in performance. High-self-evaluation subjects rated themselves as equal to the model. In this study, it was the low-self-esteem subjects who distorted their self-evaluation. Similar evidence was obtained by Garber, Hollon, and Silverman (1979). In their study, depressed females (but not males) set higher standards for themselves, evaluated themselves lower, and rewarded themselves less in comparison to their aspirations for others, their evaluations of others, and their reward of others, respectively.

A final group of studies is relevant to the issue of what particular factors produce the negative self-evaluation. It has been noted that the actual perception of performance is not inaccurate. It may be distorted only when ambiguity exists. It is also important to distinguish between the expectation or prediction of performance and the standard that has been set for performance. Two individuals predicting the same performance may evaluate it differently. Golin and Terrell (1977) asked college students to predict their performance and to indicate their level of aspiration. Depressed students had expectancies for performance similar to those of nondepressed students but had higher levels of aspirations, especially in the skill task. Similar findings have been obtained by Craighead *et al.* (1979); Hammen and Krantz (1976); Mercatoris, Cole, Lewis, and Leonard (1980); Rizley (1978); Sacco and Hokanson (1978); and Smolen (1978). All studies have not been consistent, however. Schwartz (1974) found a relationship between depression and the discrepancy between predicted and actual exam scores in a college course. He reported that the depression effect was attributable to "a trend" of optimism (i.e., higher predicted/expected performance) for the more depressed subjects. Loeb *et al.* (1967) found that depressed subjects gave lower estimates of their probability of success on a card-sorting task than did nondepressed subjects. "Success," however, could be taken as evaluation and not as performance expectancy. O'Leary *et al.* (1978) found lower initial and final performance expectancies for depressed versus nondepressed alcoholics. However, using the same population, Donovan and O'Leary (1979) did not replicate this effect. A study in our labs (Rokke, Carter, & Rehm, 1983) failed to find differences related to depression among college students in their setting of standards for success or failure on several different tasks.

The majority of studies reviewed here suggest that expectancy or prediction of depressed subjects will be accurate and equivalent to that of nondepressed subjects. Results are fairly consistent in suggesting that depressed subjects set higher standards for themselves, which leads to more negative evaluations of themselves but not of others, even with equivalent performance.

MEMORY AND DEPRESSION

Memory problems constitute a typical symptom of depression. Several different models have been developed in order to explore the precise nature of memory deficits in depression.

Generalized Memory Deficit

One perspective that several researchers have investigated is the idea of a generalized memory deficit in depression. For example, Stromgren (1977) concluded that all aspects of memory are susceptible to depression, based on the fact that scores on various memory tasks improved with clinical improvement. Sternberg and Jarvik (1976) tested endogenous depressed patients and matched normal controls on paired-associate recall, figure recognition, and recall of facts about a fictitious person in both immediate and delayed (3-hour) memory conditions. The authors concluded that only short-term memory is impaired in depression and that it improved with clinical response to drugs. Henry, Weingartner, and Murphy (1973) assessed serial and free-recall learning in patients with unipolar and bipolar depression. They found memory improvement with certain drugs (L-dopa and L-tryptophan) but not with others (e.g., imipramine or lithium). Miller and Lewis

(1977) made an important methodological contribution to this literature by applying signal detection methods. They assessed elderly patients on a figure-recognition task. Both depressed patients and patients with dementia made more errors. However, when criteria were controlled, the memory of depressed patients was demonstrated to be equal to that of the normal subjects and better than that of the patients with dementia. The authors suggested that it was a conservative response strategy rather than any deficit in memory that produced the seemingly poor recall.

Weingartner and his associates (Weingartner, Cohen, Murphy, Martello, & Gerdt, 1981; Weingartner, Kaye, Smallberg, Ebert, Gillin, & Sitaram, 1981) have argued that the memory deficit in depression is due to depressed subjects' failing to generate effective encoding strategies. They demonstrated, for instance, that depressed subjects' recall performance suffers when words are unclustered in presentation, as opposed to the recall performance of normal subjects, who presumably are able to generate their own clustering strategy to aid in recall. Similarly, depressed subjects are helped less by semantic as opposed to acoustic association between words in presentation lists. A study by Russell and Beekhuis (1976) found that both schizophrenic and depressed patients showed a failure to use semantic clustering in comparison to normal subjects.

Cognitive Self-structure Effects on Encoding

Another strategy that has been used in exploring memory and depression has been to investigate cognitive self-structure as a biasing effect in memory. The basic argument here is that there exists in the structure of memory a cluster or schema made up of organized information about oneself. This schema can then be employed as an organizing strategy for encoding new information about oneself. If in depressed subjects this structure contains a great deal of negative information, then such subjects will show deficits in memory when the material to be encoded is positive but should show enhancement of memory for negative material.

Rogers, Kuiper, and Kirker (1977) and Kuiper and Rogers (1979) reported a series of experiments with various depth-of-processing conditions. They demonstrated that incidental recall of information processed according to self-reference is superior to recall of information under other processing conditions, such as semantic, phonemic, or structural similarities between words. Derry and Kuiper (1981) found that self-referent recall is superior to recall with structural or semantic encoding but that this enhancement is for words rated as referent to oneself only. There was an interaction such that depressive adjectives were recalled better by depressed subjects, and nondepressive adjectives, by nondepressed psychiatric and normal subjects. Depressed subjects were quicker to accept negative as opposed to positive adjectives. Kuiper and Derry (1982), using mildly depressed subjects, found similar differences, but in this instance, incidental recall by nondepressed subjects for positive self-referent adjectives was superior to recall with semantic encoding, and depressed subjects recalled both positive and negative self-referent information better than semantically organized information. In a second study (Kuiper & Derry, 1982) a distinction was made between self-referent and "other"-

referent adjective recall. Incidental recall by nondepressed subjects was enhanced for positive self-referent adjectives only. Depressives' recall was greater for negative self-referent as opposed to negative other-referent information, but positive self-referent information was encoded as well as positive other-referent information. The relative effects are basically in support of the hypothesis that a depressive self-schema will organize negative material, although not all the predicted differences were found, and absolute effects were not always as expected.

Replications in other laboratories have also led to somewhat mixed results. Mathews and Bradley (1983) took extreme positive and negative bias responders on a recall task involving self-referent adjectives and tested them 4 months later. They found that this response bias was unstable. A mood-induction procedure also did not produce changes in bias, suggesting that the effect was not due to transient mood state. Recall response bias did correlate with reported frequency and severity of depression. This study offers partial support for the concept of a negative self-schema, in that such a schema should not be an effect of transient mood. However, the evidence does not seem to support the idea of a self-schema that is stable over periods of time, as the theory would suggest.

Martin, Ward, and Clark (1983), using college students, studied the process of memory for positive and negative self-referent information. Both depression and neuroticism were assessed and were found to be intercorrelated, so that the results of the study are not necessarily specific to depression. The results suggested a negative encoding bias associated with neuroticism for the recall of personally relevant adjectives. A signal detection analysis suggested that the effect was not due simply to a criterion shift. The investigators concluded that attention and encoding, has opposed to retrieval strategies, may be involved in producing the effect.

Ingram, Smith, and Brehm (1983) tested depressed and nondepressed subjects, following success and failure conditions, on incidental recall of positive and negative adjectives. They found that in self-referent processing following success, nondepressed subjects recalled more positive than negative adjectives but that depressed subjects did not. They argued that depressed subjects failed to generate a positive self-schema following success that would aid in encoding other information. It is somewhat hard to imagine, however, that a self-schema could develop so rapidly, that is, within an experimental session.

Davis (1979a, 1979b; Davis & Unruh, 1981) has argued that depressed subjects may indeed develop a negative self-schema but that the process of developing such an organized self-schema takes a long time. He argues that initially an acutely depressed person will be confused about himself or herself. This person's self-schema should be in transition and thus be less structured or organized. In one study (Davis, 1979b), mildly depressed college students were found to do poorly on recall of personally relevant adjectives. Davis concluded that they have less structural organization available for aiding encoding. In a second study (Davis, 1979a), depressed psychiatric patients were found to be equal to control subjects in their performance on semantic memory tasks but inferior on tasks involving self-referent encoding. Interestingly, duration of depression correlated with improvement in self-referent memory in relation to semantic memory. Davis concluded that as subjects remain depressed for longer periods, their negative self-schemata become more organized and more useful in organizing new information. In a third study, Davis and Unruh (1981) compared short-term depressed patients and long-term depressed patients to nondepressed patients on free recall of self-descriptive adjectives. Only the short-term depressed patients showed a deficit in recall, supporting the hypothesis that they alone lacked organized self-schemata. None of these studies separately compared memory for positive and negative self-referent information. Therefore it is not possible to ascertain whether these effects are specific to certain kinds of self-referent information, for instance, positive self-referent information.

State-Dependent Learning Effects

Another perspective in exploring memory and depression has been to view depression as an emotional state and to employ the concept of state-related learning. The essential idea here is that when a person is in a specific emotional/physiological state, retrieval of information learned in a comparable state is enhanced. Affect is hypothesized to be a particularly important aspect of episodic memory, which may influence both encoding and retrieval.

Lishman (1972) had depressed inpatients make semantic differential ratings of 18 topics. Two weeks later, they were tested for recall of the topics. Of the 13 subjects who recalled 6 or more topics, 8 were still depressed and 5 were hypomanic or improved. Nondepressed subjects recalled positive topics more frequently than negative. Depressed subjects were more likely to recall information with a negative tone. Lloyd and Lishman (1975) had depressed inpatients recall pleasant memories associated with stimulus words from one list, and unpleasant memories, from a second list. Latencies for pleasant and unpleasant memories were related to depression and neuroticism. Nondepressed subjects were faster in recalling pleasant as opposed to unpleasant memories, and depressed subjects were faster in recalling unpleasant memories.

State-dependent learning effects have been found with a variety of experimental conditions and designs. Leight and Ellis (1981) studied the effect of induced mood states on recall and chunking of letter sequences. They found that depressed mood hindered both recall and chunking, and they identified a state-dependent retention effect with delayed recognition but not with recall. Bower (1981) described a series of studies demonstrating state-dependent learning effects using a hypnotic mood-induction procedure. In one study, he had subjects learn a first list of words in either a happy or a sad induced mood. Next, subjects learned a second list under the same or the opposite mood condition. On a third occasion, subjects were tested on the first list in either a happy or a sad induced mood. Recall for the first list was enhanced when testing was done in the same mood as that induced for first-list learning and when this mood contrasted with the mood induced for second-list learning. Testing in a mood that was consistent with the mood induced during second-list learning but inconsistent with the mood induced during first-list learning tended to lower the recall scores for the first list. In a second study reported by Bower (1981), subjects recorded pleasant and unpleasant events for a week and then recalled their list under a hypnotically induced happy or sad mood. Subjects tended to recall events that were rated more in the direction of the induced mood. In a third study, subjects recalled childhood memories and rated their affective tone while in a neutral mood. Later they were asked to recall these memories again, while in a hypnotically induced happy or sad mood, and a mood-matching effect was found. Bower proposes an associative network theory of memory and emotion: State-dependent retrieval occurs because the eliciting emotions sum with context variables to arouse specific associative connections.

In a series of studies, Teasdale and his colleagues have elaborated on the state-dependent learning effect and on its theoretical implications. Teasdale and Russell (1983) had subjects recall lists of positive, negative, and neutral personality-trait words under induced sad or elated mood conditions. Recall scores tended to be enhanced for mood-consistent adjectives. Using a within-subjects design, Teasdale and Fogarty (1979) had subjects, while in an induced happy or sad mood, recall either pleasant or unpleasant memories in response to constant stimulus words. Latency for production of memories was shorter when induced mood and type of memory were consistent. This study was followed up by Teasdale, Taylor, and Fogarty (1980), who had students on two different occasions and under depressed or happy mood-induction conditions produce real-life personal memories in response to stimulus words. On a third occasion, the students were asked to rate the happiness versus the unhappiness of the memories that they had described in the first two sessions. Memories described under the induced happy mood were rated as happier in general, and those under the induced depressed mood were rated as generally more unhappy. Again, latencies were shorter for mood-consistent memories. Clark and Teasdale (1982) replicated this design using 12 patients with unipolar depression who showed A.M. versus P.M. diurnal variation in their mood, with diurnal variation in mood replacing the mood-induction procedure. Again, in the more depressed period, patients recalled experiences that were rated by independent raters as sadder at the time they occurred. A similar clinical state-dependent mood effect was found by Weingartner, Miller, and Murphy (1977) using eight patients with bipolar (manic–depressive) disorder. Recall of verbal associations was found to be state dependent in that recall was better when the patient was in the same mood condition (even mania) as had existed during learning rather than when the patient had experienced disparate mood conditions during recall and learning.

In sum, the state-dependent learning effect has been found for depressed versus nondepressed subjects, for depressed versus elated mood using a variety of induction techniques, for diurnal variations in mood, and for manic versus depressed states. The effect has been demonstrated on recall and recognition in a variety of verbal learning tasks, on recall of recent personal episodes, and on recall of childhood memories. Teasdale (1983, in press-a,b) has integrated the state-dependent learning findings and has developed a theoretical model for considering depression. He argues that mood state acts as a context variable that influences both encoding and retrieval of experience. Accumulated experiences in periods of loss and disappointment may link depressed affective elements to thoughts of failure, low self-esteem, deprivation, and so forth. When new experiences of loss elicit depressed affect, there is an associative spread that facilitates recall of similar depressive experiences and associated cognitions. Individual differences in prior accumulated experiences with depression will influence the structure and extent of depressive associations to new depressive experiences, and thus the nature and course of a depressive episode. These ideas are relevant to self-management during episodes of depression.

PERFORMANCE FACTORS IN DEPRESSION

From a self-management perspective, self-monitoring would describe certain input variables, and both inference and memory would be related to internal processing. The output stage of the feedback loop would then include various aspects of performance that follow from and reflect the earlier stages.

Self-reinforcement

Kanfer's (1970) model of self-control identifies self-reinforcement as the third stage in the feedback loop that begins with self-monitoring and self-evaluation. This is the effective output of the process that is presumed to influence the individual's behavior by supplementing external reinforcement. The self-control model of depression (Rehm, 1977) states that the various self-control deficits that may exist in depression sum to produce low levels of contingent self-reward and high levels of self-punishment. Although the concept of self-reinforcement has been criticized in behavioral circles (e.g., Catania, 1975; Goldiamond, 1976), the concept also has its defenders (e.g., Bandura, 1976; Thoresen & Wilbur, 1976) and has been applied in a variety of behavioral therapy programs for diverse disorders (e.g., Karoly & Kanfer, 1982; Thoresen & Mahoney, 1974).

Rozensky, Rehm, Pry, and Roth (1977) compared the self-reinforcement and self-punishment behaviors of depressed and nondepressed VA psychiatric referrals on a recognition memory task. Depressed subjects used self-reinforcement less and self-punishment more, despite no actual differences in the accuracy of memory. Roth, Rehm, and Rozensky (1980) found that depressed college students used self-punishment more but found no differences in self-reward. Identical results were obtained by Rozensky, Kravitz, and Unger (1981) using a concept-learning task. Subjects who underwent a learned helplessness induction used self-punishment less, contrary to prediction. Nelson and Craighead (1977) found that depressed college subjects used self-reward less but found no differences in self-punishment. Ciminero and Steingarten (1978) used a task requiring translation of digits to symbols and found that depressed subjects both evaluated their performance as poorer and gave themselves fewer reward tokens than did nondepressed subjects. Nelson and Craighead (1981) used a marble maze task with depressed–anxious, nondepressed–anxious, and nondepressed–nonanxious college students. There were no main effect differences between them, but subjects who reached their goals used more self-reinforcement and made internal attributions that were less dysphoric.

Also, subjects who set more stringent standards used self-reinforcement less. Gotlib (1981, 1982) used a verbal recognition task and a social interaction task. In both studies, the depressed psychiatric subjects used self-reward less and self-punishment more than the normal controls, but the depressed psychiatric subjects did not differ from the nondepressed psychiatric patients. Gotlib concluded that the self-control deficits may be general among psychiatric patients. Sacco (1979) assessed self-reinforcement in public and private settings. The only significant result was a complex Subject Group × Public–Private Setting × Sequence interaction. In general, when the sequence of reinforcement was from a high rate to a low rate, both depressed and helpless subjects used self-reinforcement, more in the private setting, whereas nondepressed subjects used self-reinforcement less in the private setting. These results suggest that impression management may be an important determinant of depressive behavior.

In general, these studies have not experimentally differentiated between self-evaluation and self-reinforcement. In some studies, both have been measured, but as two dependent variables for the same manipulation (e.g., Ciminero & Steingarten, 1978). Rokke *et al.* (1983) gave college subjects a hypothetical distribution of outcomes for four different situations. They were asked to determine what their self-evaluative standards would be for excellent, good, fair, and poor performances. They were then asked how much they would reward or punish themselves if they had met each of these standards. Contrary to most of the preceding studies, no effects for depression were found on either self-evaluation or self-reinforcement. The tasks may have been excessively complex.

An assumption of the self-control model of depression is that positive self-statements function as rewards and negative self-statements as punishments. Four studies have demonstrated low rates of positive and high rates of negative self-statements by depressed subjects. Missel and Sommer (1983) gave clinic patients questionnaires that described situations of positive and negative outcomes. Subjects were asked to indicate which of three multiple-choice statements would be most typical of their own self-statements. Depressed subjects chose more negative and fewer positive self-statements. Vasta and Brockner (1979) had undergraduates self-monitor positive and negative overt and covert self-evaluative statements. They found that a self-esteem measure correlated with the number of negative self-statements and with the ratio of the number of negative self-statements to the total number of self-statements. High-self-esteem subjects recorded approximately equal numbers of positive and negative self-statements. Hinchliffe, Lancashire, and Roberts (1971) analyzed speech samples of depressed and control surgical patients. Depressed patients demonstrated a higher number of "negators," primarily negative references to the self or to others. Similarly, Fuchs and Rehm (1977) sampled the verbal behavior of depressed patients before and after therapy and found a decrease in the number of negative self-statements with more positive therapy outcome.

Overall, the results do suggest that depressed individuals use self-reward less and self-punishment more. A number of questions have been raised as to whether this phenomenon is specific to depression, whether it is a function of the public or private setting, and whether self-reinforcement is, indeed, at least partially independent of self-evaluation. Another issue that has not been directly addressed is whether self-administered reward and punishment actually function to increase and decrease, respectively, the probability of responses in depression. More research is necessary if the self-reinforcement concept is to be a central explanatory mechanism in the studies of depression.

Problem Solving

A number of researchers have investigated the problem-solving strategies of depressed individuals. Gotlib and Asarnow (1980) gave a series of questionnaires to groups of depressed and nondepressed college students and concluded that depressed students were, in general, poor in their interpersonal problem-solving skills. Billings, Cronkite, and Moos (1983) studied patients with unipolar depression who were entering treatment in comparison with matched nondepressed controls. The depressed patients showed more stressful life events and more severe chronic strains regarding their own and their families' physical illnesses, their family relationships, and their home and work situations. The depressed patients also showed less active problem-solving behavior and more emotion-focused coping. Coyne, Aldwin, and Lazarus (1981) studied the coping behavior of individuals who reported over the course of a year on their single greatest stress each month and on the ways in which they coped with it. The problem-solving behavior of depressed subjects was characterized as involving a greater need for additional information, a greater sense that the situation must be accepted, greater wishful thinking, greater seeking of help, and greater seeking of support from others. Klass and Tutin (1980) used a questionnaire concerning recent experience about which college students felt guilty. Compared to nondepressed students, depressed students were more negative in their evaluations of themselves, presented fewer self-justifications and more self-oriented content (as opposed to social content), and were less likely to see alternatives available to them.

A number of researchers have used laboratory problem-solving tasks in attempts to investigate the specific nature of problem-solving deficits among depressed individuals. Dobson and Dobson (1981) found that depressed college students took longer to solve problems and were less efficient in their problem-solving strategies than nondepressed college students. Hiroto and Seligman (1975) demonstrated that induced helplessness produced decrements in solving anagrams and in learning to avoid an aversive stimulus in a shuttle-box problem. Miller and Seligman (1975) replicated a portion of this study, using depressed and nondepressed college students. Depressed students behaved like helpless subjects. They were slower at solving anagrams and took longer to perceive an anagram pattern. Price, Tryon, and Raps (1978) replicated the same task with VA psychiatric and medical patients. Again, both depression and induced helplessness produced deficits in solving anagrams. In a laboratory task, Shrauger and Sorman (1977) assessed female college students who were high and low on self-esteem. Following initial failure, low-self-esteem subjects showed less persistence than did high-self-esteem subjects. Performance for low-self-esteem subjects was generally poor. Abramson,

Alloy, and Rosoff (1981) studied the hypothesis-generating behavior of depressed and nondepressed subjects on a concept-formation task. When lists of hypotheses to be tested were available to subjects, there were no differences in performance between depressed and nondepressed subjects. When subjects themselves had to generate hypotheses, the depressed subjects showed a deficit, relative to nondepressed subjects, in problem-solving ability. The authors argued for a motivational explanation of learned helplessness.

Generally, these studies suggest that depressed individuals do show deficits in problem solving. Depressed persons are less likely to generate efficient, active problem-solving strategies; they are poor at generating hypotheses; and they are more likely to focus on their emotional reactions to the situation and on coping with these feelings.

Social Skills

It has been suggested in the clinical literature that social skills are the core deficits in depression, and several studies (e.g., Hersen, Bellack, Himmelhoch, & Thase, 1984) have used social skill training as a treatment modality for depression. A couple of studies have assessed overall assertiveness in depressed and nondepressed subjects. Lea and Paquin (1981) found a relationship between self-reported depression and self-reported assertion on two scales. Barbaree and Davis (1984) gave college students an assertiveness role-playing test. Depressed students were rated as less assertive and also had more negative expectancies and self-evaluations than nondepressed students. Training led to greater increases in assertiveness for the depressed students.

A fairly extensive literature has developed on the assessment of bodily movements, paralinguistic behavior, and content analysis of the speech of depressed subjects (cf. Rehm, 1988). Although findings are mixed, the overt behavior of a depressed individual can, in general, be characterized by obvious signs of sadness (e.g., less smiling, more head hanging), by lower levels of expressive activity, and, in some instances, by higher levels of nonexpressive activity. In regard to paralinguistic behavior, depressive subjects in general have been found to speak with lower volume, less modulation, and for shorter periods. Content analyses have fairly consistently found more negative self-references and, in some instances, more references to the self generally.

A phenomenon that has recently received considerable attention is the finding by Coyne (1976) that the interpersonal behavior of depressed subjects produces negative reactions in those with whom they interact. For example, in a replication by Gotlib and Robinson (1982), depressed and nondepressed subjects were videotaped in conversations with college students. The college-student subjects who talked to the two sets of targets did not differ on mood or acceptance of the target. If they talked with a depressed subject, they were observed to smile less, with less arousal and pleasantness in their faces; they showed fewer positive- and more negative-content statements; and they were less supportive of the subject. Depressed targets also made fewer statements of support and showed more negative content.

Boswell and Murray (1981) had college students listen to taped interviews with depressed and schizophrenic psychiatric inpatients and to control interviews with staff members. Listening to the conversations of the depressed and schizophrenic patients produced more dysphoria in the listener and more rejection, but for males only. The study concluded that these findings did not support the specificity of these affects for depression.

Jacobson and Anderson (1982) attempted a somewhat finer grained analysis of the behavior of depressed subjects in interactions with a confederate in the experimental waiting room. Depressed subjects made more negative self-references and produced more unsolicited self-disclosures. Interestingly, there was also a time-sequence effect, whereby depressed subjects more frequently made self-disclosures after the confederate made a self-disclosure or a statement about the environment. The authors argue that it may be the inappropriate sequence of content rather than the content itself that influences the perception of others.

The social skill behavior of depressed persons has generally been evaluated as poorer than that of nondepressed persons. The explanation for this may be motivational; that is, depressed persons respond with less intensity, duration, and amplitude. They also have a negative effect on others, and this is partly due to their focusing on themselves and on negative self-statements.

CONCLUSIONS

Research on the psychopathology of depression covers diverse topics, and findings are sometimes mixed and contradictory. Certain themes and consistencies do emerge, and they suggest some ways for reorganizing the facts available and indicate some new directions for research and theory building.

The research on self-monitoring leads to several important conclusions. The life experience of depressed persons is different from that of nondepressed persons. Depressed persons are likely to be experiencing and to have experienced fewer positive and more negative life events, both small and large. This always needs to be kept in mind when considering the perceptions of depressives. One should always consider the possibility that perceptions are based on a different, yet veridical, set of generalizations.

It seems fairly clear that the perception of the objective world is not distorted in depression. Depressed individuals accurately report specific events in their lives. Distortion and bias do affect the *inferences about* and the *interpretations of* experience made by depressed people. When there is ambiguity in the information available, or when an abstract evaluation is required, depressed persons are more negative about themselves.

Self-monitoring has often included a variety of processes that seem to be quite distinguishable. First, objective perception can be differentiated. Second, one can talk about the observation strategy that the person adopts. Third, one can talk about the inferences, interpretations, and judgments made by the individual. Objective perception does not seem to be distorted in depression, though it may be of interest to study this behavior as it relates to assessment. There is some evidence that depressed persons may typically deploy their attention in an aberrant fashion. Depressed persons may choose to attend to more negative information about themselves. The reasons for this are unclear. Ferster (1973) suggested that depressed persons may be vigilant in searching for cues for aversive events that they believe are highly likely to occur. The nature of these processes deserves further attention and is relevant to intervention research.

Inferences, interpretations, and judgments should be viewed as internal processing variables rather than as input variables. Inference in judgmental processes has received a great deal of attention, but different theories have postulated different types of inferences as the core factors in determining depression. Although the evidence is somewhat mixed, there is a trend suggesting that depressed individuals make negative attributions about failures, and perhaps about successes. Depressed individuals are more negative in their estimates of their own ability to produce desired responses (self-efficacy). They do not, however, seem to be unrealistic in objectively making predictions or offering expectancies about their performance. This seems quite consistent with the idea that depressed persons are accurate in their perceptions. The only exceptions to accurate expectancy would be in those areas in which depressed persons may, in reality, perform more poorly (e.g., in social skills). It is quite clear that depressed persons evaluate themselves negatively, and it appears that a discrepancy between expectancy and standards is the determining factor. Negative interpretation is relatively specific to abstractions about oneself.

The important question to be asked here is, Can the various factors that have been postulated be reduced to some single factor characteristic of depressive inference? The likely candidate appears to be simply negativity about oneself. If persons assume that their behavior generally is poor, then, when asked, they may report that their performance is below their standard, that they are incompetent in their performance, that they are to blame for negative events, and that they are incapable of producing positive events. Each of these may be a logical derivative of negative self-evaluation.

The recent research on memory in depression is perhaps the most exciting because it provides some clues and suggestions for new ways of integrating the available information. Perhaps the most important findings have to do with state-related learning and with the importance of memory structures related to oneself. Models of depression of varying degrees of generality have been appearing recently that employ these concepts and that are drawn from cognitive psychology. Kuiper and Derry (1982) and Davis (1979a, 1979b) have suggested models that are relatively specific to memory processing in depression. Ingram (1984) and Teasdale (1983a, 1983b in press) have suggested models with broader clinical application to depression phenomena.

These models deal with many of the central processing aspects of self-management that are typical of depression. There is an assumption of a relatively automatic process by which certain life experiences, including various negative events, losses, and frustrations, produce the response of depressive affect. While the person is in this depressed state, events that were acquired by and organized in the memory during similar affective states are more easily accessed. Retrieval is facilitated by connections to affective features of pertinent memories. Affect is assumed to be a potent and salient organizing feature of certain kinds of memory. Episodic memory is that for specific experiences; it is the most affectively encoded kind of memory. (Tulving, 1983). A major portion of episodic memory could be expected to be devoted to memories about oneself. A current depressive state would facilitate access to negative thoughts and beliefs about oneself. These thoughts and beliefs would include a variety of past inferences, evaluations, and generalizations that would be relevant to current inference and self-evaluation. The extent and coherence of depressive affective organization of information about oneself would be a function of the frequency, duration, and intensity of previous depressive experiences. Thus childhood losses, frequent negative events, major negative life events, and prior episodes of depression would all increase the organizational structure of the depressive, affectively organized memory. Information accrued during neutral or other affective states would also be organized in memory but might be organized in semi-independence from information organized in depressive states. Such information could also be accessed, but only with greater difficulty when in a depressed state.

This general model would clearly explain various inferences and interpretation processes and would also be applicable, with some elaboration, to output processes. The depressed person would presumably show less persistence, because in the depressed mood, ideas of failure, futility, and lack of efficacy would be facilitated and easily accessed. Thoughts and strategies for positive striving and for the generation of hypotheses would be retarded. The depressed individual could then be expected to shift his or her attention from active self-management to self-consciousness and attempts to control emotionality in interactions with others. A depressive's well-structured and well-organized memory about the self would be a vulnerability factor for future depressions that would not be easily detected between episodes.

This general model would have implications for therapy, as suggested by Teasdale (1983b). When a person is depressed, he or she would need help in gaining access to more realistic interpretations and constructions of events. This could be done either directly, by guiding the person in confronting negative cognitions and in gaining access to alternative positive cognitions, or by attempting to modify the affective state, thus facilitating access to neutral and positive cognitions. Gaining access to realistic thought could be done either by encouraging the person to engage in activities that would, through automatic processes, create more positive affect, or by manipulating the affect directly with drugs. Cognitive therapy focuses on the direct guidance of cognitions, whereas many of the behavioral therapies focus on increasing activity level.

This general model is promising as a model of self-management in depression. We need to give more attention to the topic of temporal integration in depression, and to the cognitive self-management processes involved. The influence of negative retrieval on strategies for observing oneself and the world needs to be studied, to help us gain further understanding of the implication of depression for encoding strategies. The literature on memory and on the cognitive processes in depression needs to devote more attention to issues regarding the course of clinical depression. Much is known about the heritability, vulnerability, natural history, and typical course of depressions and about the life experiences that precede and that are concurrent with depression. An adequate model of self-management in depression needs to take these issues into account as well. The past 10 years have constituted an era during which behavioral and cognitive models of depression have emerged and have led to the generation of new data. It is time for these data to be reorganized and for new models to be developed.

REFERENCES

Abramson, L. Y., Alloy, L. B., & Rosoff, R. (1981). Depression and the generation of complex hypotheses in the judgment of contingency. *Behavior Research and Therapy, 19,* 35–47.

Abramson, L. Y., Garber, J., Edwards, N. B., & Seligman, M. E. P. (1978). Expectancy changes in depression and schizophrenia. *Journal of Abnormal Psychology, 87,* 102–109.

Abramson, L. Y., Seligman, M. E. P., & Teasdale, J. D. (1978). Learned helplessness in humans: Critique and reformulation. *Journal of Abnormal Psychology, 87,* 49–74.

Bandura, A. (1976). Self-reinforcement: Theoretical and methodological considerations. *Behaviorism, 4,* 135–155.

Bandura, A. (1977). Self-efficacy: Towards a unifying theory of behavior change. *Psychological Review, 84,* 191–215.

Barbaree, H. E., & Davis, R. B. (1984). Assertive behavior, self-expectations, and self-evaluations in mildly depressed university women. *Cognitive Therapy and Research, 8,* 153–172.

Beck, A. T. (1972). *Depression: Causes and treatment.* Philadelphia. University of Pennsylvania Press.

Beck, A. T., Rush, A. J., Shaw, B. F., & Emery, G. (1979). *Cognitive therapy for depression.* New York: Guilford Press.

Billings, A. G., Cronkite, R. C., & Moos, R. H. (1983). Social–environmental factors in unipolar depression: Comparisons of depressed patients and nondepressed controls. *Journal of Abnormal Psychology, 92,* 119–134.

Boswell, P. C., & Murray, E. J. (1981). Depression, schizophrenia, and social attraction. *Journal of Consulting and Clinical Psychology, 49,* 641–647.

Bower, G. H. (1981). Mood and memory. *American Psychologist, 36,* 129–147.

Brown, G. W., & Harris, T. (1978). *Social origins of depression: A study of psychiatric disorder in women.* New York: Macmillan.

Buchwald, A. M. (1977). Depressive mood and estimates of reinforcement frequency. *Journal of Abnormal Psychology, 86,* 443–446.

Carver, C. S., & Scheier, M. F. (1982). An information processing perspective on self-management. In P. Karoly & F. H. Kanfer (Eds.), *Self-management and behavior change: From theory to practice* (pp. 93–128). New York: Pergamon Press.

Catania, A. C. (1975). The myth of self-reinforcement. *Behaviorism, 3,* 191–199.

Ciminero, A. R., & Steingarten, K. A. (1978). The effects of performance standards on self-evaluation and self-reinforcement in depressed and nondepressed individuals. *Cognitive Therapy and Research, 2,* 179–182.

Clark, D. M., & Teasdale, J. D. (1982). Diurnal variation in clinical depression and accessibility of memories of positive and negative experiences. *Journal of Abnormal Psychology, 91,* 87–95.

Cochran, S. D., & Hammen, C. L. (1980, September). *Cognitive mediators of stress and depression: A test of theoretical predictions.* Paper presented at the meeting of the American Psychological Association, Montreal, Canada.

Coyne, J. C. (1976). Depression and the response of others. *Journal of Abnormal Psychology, 85,* 186–193.

Coyne, J. C., Aldwin, C., & Lazarus, R. S. (1981). Depression and coping in stressful episodes. *Journal of Abnormal Psychology, 90,* 439–447.

Craighead, W. E., Hickey, K. S., & De Monbreun, B. G. (1979). Distortion of perception and recall of neutral feedback in depression. *Cognitive Therapy and Research, 3,* 291–298.

Cutrona, C. E. (1983). Causal attributions and perinatal depression. *Journal of Abnormal Psychology, 92,* 161–172.

Davis, F. W., & Yates, B. T. (1982). Self-efficacy expectancies versus outcome expectancies as determinants of performance deficits and depressive affect. *Cognitive Therapy and Research, 6,* 23–35.

Davis, H. (1979a). Self-reference and the encoding of personal information in depression. *Cognitive Therapy and Research, 3,* 97–108.

Davis, H. (1979b). The self-schema and subjective organization of personal information in depression. *Cognitive Therapy and Research, 3,* 415–426.

Davis, H., & Unruh, W. R. (1981). The development of the self-schema in adult depression. *Journal of Abnormal Psychology, 90,* 125–133.

De Monbreun, B. G., & Craighead, W. E. (1977). Distortion of perception and recall of positive and neutral feedback in depression. *Cognitive Therapy and Research, 1,* 311–329.

Derry, P. A., & Kuiper, N. A. (1981). Schematic processing and self-reference in clinical depression. *Journal of Abnormal Psychology, 90,* 286–297.

Devins, G. M., Binik, Y. M., Gorman, P., Dattel, M., McCloskey, G., Oscar, G., & Briggs, J. (1982). Perceived self-efficacy, outcome expectancies, and negative mood states in end-stage renal disease. *Journal of Abnormal Psychology, 91,* 241–244.

Dobson, D. J. G., & Dobson, K. S. (1981). Problem-solving strategies in depressed and nondepressed college students. *Cognitive Therapy and Research, 5,* 237–250.

Donovan, D. M., & O'Leary, M. R. (1979). Depression, hypermania, and expectation of future success among alcoholics. *Cognitive Therapy and Research, 3,* 141–154.

Eaves, G., & Rush, A. J. (1984). Cognitive patterns in symptomatic and remitted unipolar major depression. *Journal of Abnormal Psychology, 93,* 31–40.

Evans, M. D., & Hollon, S. D. (1979, December). *Immediate vs. delayed mood self-monitoring in depression.* Paper presented at the meeting of the Association for the Advancement of Behavior Therapy, San Francisco.

Ferster, C. B. (1973). A functional analysis of depression. *American Psychologist, 28,* 857–870.

Finkel, C. B., Glass, C. R., & Merluzzi, T. V. (1979, December). *Differential discrimination of self-referent statements by depressives and nondepressives.* Paper presented at the meeting of the Association for the Advancement of Behavior Therapy, San Francisco.

Friedman, A. S. (1964). Minimal effects of severe depression on cognitive functioning. *Journal of Abnormal and Social Psychology, 69,* 237–243.

Fry, P. S. (1976). Success, failure, and self-assessment ratings. *Journal of Consulting and Clinical Psychology, 44,* 413–419.

Fuchs, C. Z., & Rehm, L. P. (1977). A self-control behavior therapy program for depression. *Journal of Consulting and Clinical Psychology, 45,* 206–215.

Funabiki, D., & Calhoun, J. F. (1979). Use of a behavioral-analytic procedure in evaluating two models of depression. *Journal of Consulting and Clinical Psychology, 47,* 183–185.

Garber, J., Hollon, S. D., & Silverman, V. (1979, December). *Evaluation and reward of self vs. others in depression.* Paper presented at the meeting of the Association for the Advancement of Behavior Therapy, San Francisco.

Goldiamond, I. (1976). Fables, armadyllics, and self-reinforcement. *Journal of Applied Behavior Analysis, 9,* 521–525.

Golin, S., & Terrell, F. (1977). Motivational and associative aspects of mild depression in skill and chance tasks. *Journal of Abnormal Psychology, 86,* 389–401.

Gotlib, I. H. (1979a, June). *Self-monitoring and self-reinforcement in clinically depressed psychiatric patients.* Paper presented at the Canadian Psychological Association, Quebec City, Canada.

Gotlib, I. H. (1979b, September). *Self-control processes in depressed and nondepressed psychiatric patients: Self-evaluation.* Paper presented at the meeting of the American Psychological Association, New York.

Gotlib, I. H. (1981). Self-reinforcement and recall: Differential deficits in depressed and nondepressed psychiatric inpatients. *Journal of Abnormal Psychology, 90,* 521–530.

Gotlib, I. H. (1982). Self-reinforcement and depression in interpersonal interaction: The role of performance level. *Journal of Abnormal Psychology, 91,* 3–13.

Gotlib, I. H., & Asarnow, R. F. (1980). Independence of interpersonal and impersonal problem-solving skills: Reply to Rohsenow. *Journal of Consulting and Clinical Psychology, 48,* 286–288.

Gotlib, I. H., & Robinson, L. A. (1982). Responses to depressed individuals: Discrepancies between self-report and observe-rated behavior. *Journal of Abnormal Psychology, 91,* 231–240.

Grosscup, S. J., & Lewinsohn, P. M. (1980). Unpleasant and pleasant events and mood. *Journal of Clinical Psychology, 36,* 252–259.

Gurtman, M. B. (1981). The relationship of expectancies for need attainment to depression and hopelessness in college students. *Cognitive Therapy and Research, 5,* 313–316.

Hamilton, E. W., & Abramson, L. Y. (1983). Cognitive patterns and major depressive disorder: A longitudinal study in a hospital setting. *Journal of Abnormal Psychology, 92,* 173–184.

Hammen, C. L. (1977). Effects of depression, feedback, and gender on selective exposure to information about the self. *Psychological Reports, 40,* 403–408.

Hammen, C. L. (1978). Depression, distortion, and life stress in college students. *Cognitive Therapy and Research, 2,* 189–192.

Hammen, C. L., & Glass, D. R., Jr. (1975). Depression, activity, and evaluation of reinforcement. *Journal of Abnormal Psychology, 84,* 718–721.

Hammen, C. L., & Krantz, S. (1976). Effect of success and failure on depressive cognitions. *Journal of Abnormal Psychology, 85,* 577–586.

Hammen, C., Krantz, S. E., & Cochran, S. D. (1981). Relationships between depression and causal attributions about stressful life events. *Cognitive Therapy and Research, 5,* 351–358.

Harmon, T. M., Nelson, R. O., & Hayes, S. C. (1980). Self-monitoring of mood versus activity by depressed clients. *Journal of Consulting and Clinical Psychology, 48,* 30–38.

Harvey, D. M. (1981). Depression and attributional style: Interpretations of important personal events. *Journal of Abnormal Psychology, 90,* 134–142.

Henry, G. M., Weingartner, H., & Murphy, D. L. (1973). Influence of affective states and psychoactive drugs on verbal learning and memory. *American Journal of Psychiatry, 130,* 966–971.

Hersen, M., Bellack, A. S., Himmelhoch, J. M., & Thase, M. E. (1984). Effects of social skill training, amitriptyline, and psychotherapy in unipolar depressed women. *Behavior Therapy, 15,* 21–40.

Hinchliffe, M. K., Lancashire, M., & Roberts, F. J. (1971). Depression: Defense mechanisms in speech. *British Journal of Psychiatry, 118,* 471–472.

Hiroto, D. S., & Seligman, M. E. P. (1975). Generality of learned helplessness in man. *Journal of Personality and Social Psychology, 31,* 311–327.

Holmes, T. H., & Rahe, R. H. (1967). The Social Readjustment Rating Scale. *Journal of Psychosomatic Research, 11,* 213–218.

Ingram, R. E. (1984). Toward an information-processing analysis of depression. *Cognitive Therapy and Research, 8,* 443–478.

Ingram, R. E., Smith, T. W., & Brehm, S. S. (1983). Depression and information processing: Self-schemata and the encoding of self-referent information. *Journal of Personality and Social Psychology, 45,* 412–420.

Jacobson, N. S., & Anderson, E. A. (1982). Interpersonal skill and depression in college students: An analysis of the timing of self-disclosures. *Behavior Therapy, 13,* 271–282.

Kanfer, F. H. (1970). Self-regulation: Research, issues and speculations. In C. Neuringer & J. L. Michael (Eds.), *Behavior modification in clinical psychology* (pp. 178–220). New York: Appleton-Century-Crofts.

Kanfer, F. H., & Hagerman, S. (1981). The role of self-regulation. In L. P. Rehm (Ed.), *Behavior therapy for depression: Present status and future directions* (pp. 143–180). New York: Academic Press.

Kanfer, F. H., & Karoly, P. (1972a). Self-control: A behavioristic excursion into the lion's den. *Behavior Therapy, 2,* 398–416.

Kanfer, F. H., & Karoly, P. (1972b). Self-regulation and its clinical application: Some additional conceptualizations. In R. C. Johnson, P. R. Dokecki, & O. H. Mowrer (Eds.), *Socialization: Development of character and conscience* (pp. 428–437). New York: Holt, Rinehart & Winston.

Karoly, P., & Kanfer, F. H. (Eds.). (1982). *Self-management and behavior change: From theory to practice*. New York: Pergamon Press.

Kirschenbaum, D., & Karoly, P. (1977). When self-regulation fails: Tests of some preliminary hypotheses. *Journal of Consulting and Clinical Psychology, 45,* 1116–1125.

Klass, E. T., & Tutin, J. A. (1980, April). *Guilt and self-criticism in depression.* Paper presented at the meeting of the Eastern Psychological Association, Hartford, CT.

Klein, D. C., Fencil-Morse, E., & Seligman, M. E. P. (1976). Learned helplessness, depression, and the attribution of failure. *Journal of Personality and Social Psychology, 33,* 508–516.

Klinger, E. (1982). On the self-management of mood, affect, and attention. In P. Karoly & F. H. Kanfer (Eds.), *Self-management and behavior change: From theory to practice* (pp. 129–164). New York: Pergamon Press.

Krantz, S., & Hammen, C. (1979). Assessment of cognitive bias in depression. *Journal of Abnormal Psychology, 88,* 611–619.

Kuiper, N. A., & Derry, P. A. (1982). Depressed and nondepressed content self-reference in mild depressives. *Journal of Personality, 50,* 67–80.

Kuiper, N. A., & Rogers, T. B. (1979). Encoding of personal information: Self–other differences. *Journal of Personality and Social Psychology, 37,* 499–514.

Lasher, B. J., & Lynn, S. J. (1981, August). *Depressed versus nondepressed college students' responses to evaluative personal feedback.* Presented at the meeting of the American Psychological Association, Los Angeles.

Laxer, R. M. (1964). Self-concept changes of depressive patients in general hospital treatment. *Journal of Consulting Psychology, 28,* 214–219.

Layne, C., Merry, J., Christian, J., & Ginn, P. (1982). Motivational deficit in depression. *Cognitive Therapy and Research, 6,* 259–273.

Lazarus, R. S. (1974). Psychological stress and coping in adaptation and illness. *International Journal of Psychiatry in Medicine, 5,* 321–333.

Lea, G., & Paquin, M. (1981). Assertiveness and clinical depression. *The Behavior Therapist, 4*(2), 9–10.

Leight, K. A., & Ellis, H. C. (1981). Emotional mood states, strategies and state-dependency in memory. *Journal of Verbal Learning and Verbal Behavior, 20,* 251–266.

Lewinsohn, P. M. (1974). A behavioral approach to depression. In R. M. Friedman & M. M. Katz (Eds.), *The psychology of depression: Contemporary theory and research* (pp. 157–185). New York: Wiley.

Lewinsohn, P. M. (1975). Engagement in pleasant activities and depression level. *Journal of Abnormal Psychology, 84,* 729–731.

Lewinsohn, P. M., & Amenson, C. S. (1978). Some relations between pleasant and unpleasant mood-related events and depression. *Journal of Abnormal Psychology, 87,* 644–654.

Lewinsohn, P. M., & Graf, M. (1973). Pleasant activities and depression. *Journal of Consulting and Clinical Psychology, 41,* 261–268.

Lewinsohn, P. M., Larson, D. W., & Munoz, R. F. (1982). The measurement of expectancies and other cognitions in depressed individuals. *Cognitive Therapy and Research, 6,* 437–446.

Lewinsohn, P. M., & Libet, J. (1972). Pleasant events, activity schedules, and depression. *Journal of Abnormal Psychology, 79,* 291–295.

Lewinsohn, P. M., Mischel, W., Chaplin, W., & Barton, R. (1980). Social competence and depression: The role of illusory self-perceptions. *Journal of Abnormal Psychology, 89,* 203–213.

Lewinsohn, P. M., & Talkington, J. (1979). Studies on the measurement of unpleasant events and relations with depression. *Applied Psychological Measurement, 3,* 83–101.

Lewinsohn, P. M., Youngren, M. A., & Grosscup, S. J. (1979). Reinforcement and depression. In R. A. Depue (Ed.), *The psychobiology of the depressive disorders: Implications for the effects of stress* (pp. 291–315). New York: Academic Press.

Lewis, L., Mercatoris, M., Cole, C. S., & Leonard, A. (1980, November). *The self-control process in episodic depression.* Paper presented at the meeting of the Association for the Advancement of Behavior Therapy, New York.

Lishman, W. A. (1972). Selective factors in memory, Part 2: Affective disorder. *Psychological Medicine, 2,* 248–253.

Lloyd, G. G., & Lishman, W. A. (1975). Effect of depression on the speed of recall of pleasant and unpleasant experiences. *Psychological Medicine, 5,* 173–180.

Loeb, A., Beck, A. T., Diggory, J. C., & Tuthill, R. (1967). Expectancy, level of aspiration, performance and self-evaluation in depression. *Proceedings of the 75th Annual Convention of the American Psychological Association,*

Lubin, B. (1967). *Manual for the Depression Adjective Check Lists.* San Diego: Educational and Industrial Testing Service.

MacPhillamy, D. J., & Lewinsohn, P. M. (1974). Depression as a function of levels of desired and obtained pleasure. *Journal of Abnormal Psychology, 83,* 651–657.

MacPhillamy, D. J., & Lewinsohn, P. M. (1982). The Pleasant Events Schedule: Studies on reliability, validity, and scale intercorrelation. *Journal of Consulting and Clinical Psychology, 50,* 363–380.

Manly, P. C., MacMahon, R. J., Bradley, C. F., & Davidson, P. O. (1982). Depressive attributional style and depression following childbirth. *Journal of Abnormal Psychology, 91,* 245–254.

Martin, M., Ward, J. C., & Clark, D. M. (1983). Neuroticism and the recall of positive and negative personality information. *Behaviour Research and Therapy, 21,* 495–504.

Mathews, A., & Bradley, B. (1983). Mood and the self-reference bias in recall. *Behaviour Research and Therapy, 21,* 233–240.

McNitt, P. C., & Thornton, D. W. (1978). Depression and perceived reinforcement: A reconsideration. *Journal of Abnormal Psychology, 87,* 137–140.

Meichenbaum, D., & Cameron, R. (1974). The clinical potential of modifying what clients say to themselves. In M. J. Mahoney & C. E. Thoresen (Eds.), *Self-control: Power to the person* (pp. 263–290). Monterey, CA: Brooks/Cole.

Mercatoris, M., Cole, C. S., Lewis, L., & Leonard, A. (1980, November). *Depression and the self-evaluation process.* Paper presented at the meeting of the Association for the Advancement of Behavior Therapy, New York.

Miller, E., & Lewis, P. (1977). Recognition memory in elderly patients with depression and dementia: A signal detection analysis. *Journal of Abnormal Psychology, 86,* 84–86.

Miller, I. W., & Norman, W. H. (1981). Effects of attributions for success on the alleviation of learned helplessness and depression. *Journal of Abnormal Psychology, 90,* 113–124.

Miller, W. R., & Seligman, M. E. P. (1973). Depression and the perception of reinforcement. *Journal of Abnormal Psychology, 82,* 62–73.

Miller, W. R., & Seligman, M. E. P. (1975). Depression and learned helplessness in man. *Journal of Abnormal Psychology, 84,* 228–238.

Miller, W. R., & Seligman, M. E. P. (1976). Learned helplessness, depression and the perception of reinforcement. *Behaviour Research and Therapy, 14,* 7–17.

Mischel, W., Ebbesen, E. B., & Zeiss, A. M. (1973). Selective attention to the self: Situational and dispositional determinants. *Journal of Personality and Social Psychology, 27,* 129–142.

Mischel, W., Ebbesen, E. B., & Zeiss, A. M. (1976). Determinants of selective memory about the self. *Journal of Consulting and Clinical Psychology, 44,* 92–103.

Missel, P., & Sommer, G. (1983). Depression and self-verbalization. *Cognitive Therapy and Research, 7,* 141–148.

Mukherji, B. R., Abramson, L. Y., & Martin, D. J. (1982). Induced depressive mood and attributional patterns. *Cognitive Therapy and Research, 6,* 15–21.

Nelson, R. E., & Craighead, W. E. (1977). Selective recall of positive and negative feedback, self-control behaviors, and depression. *Journal of Abnormal Psychology, 86,* 379–388.

Nelson, R. E., & Craighead, W. E. (1981). Tests of a self-control model of depression. *Behavior Therapy, 12,* 123–130.

O'Hara, M. W., & Rehm, L. P. (1979). Self-monitoring, activity levels and mood in the development and maintenance of depression. *Journal of Abnormal Psychology, 88,* 450–453.

O'Hara, M. W., Rehm, L. P., & Campbell, S. B. (1982). Predicting depressive symptomatology: Cognitive–behavioral models and postpartum depression. *Journal of Abnormal Psychology, 91,* 457–461.

O'Leary, M. R., Donovan, D. M., Krueger, K. J., & Cysewski, B. (1978). Depression and perception of reinforcement: Lack of differences in expectancy changes among alcoholics. *Journal of Abnormal Psychology, 87,* 110–112.

Oliver, J. M., & Williams, G. (1979). The psychology of depression as revealed by attribution of causality in college students. *Cognitive Therapy and Research, 3,* 355–360.

Price, K. P., Tryon, W. W., & Raps, C. S. (1978). Learned helplessness and depression in a clinical population: A test of two behavioral hypotheses. *Journal of Abnormal Psychology, 87,* 113–121.

Raps, C. S., Peterson, C., Reinhard, K. E., Abramson, L. Y., & Seligman, M. E. P. (1982). Attributional style among depressed patients. *Journal of Abnormal Psychology, 91,* 102–108.

Rehm, L. P. (1977). A self-control model of depression. *Behavior Therapy, 8,* 787–804.

Rehm, L. P. (1978). Mood, pleasant events and unpleasant events: Two pilot studies. *Journal of Consulting and Clinical Psychology, 46,* 849–853.

Rehm, L. P. (1988). The measurement of behavioral aspects of depression. In A. J. Marsella, R. Hirschfeld, & M. Katz (Eds.), *The measurement of depression: Clinical, biological, psychological, and psychosocial perspectives* (pp. 199–239). New York: Guilford Press.

Rizley, R. (1978). Depression and distortion in the attribution of causality. *Journal of Abnormal Psychology, 87,* 32–48.

Rogers, T. B., Kuiper, N. A., & Kirker, W. S. (1977). Self-reference and the encoding of personal information. *Journal of Personality and Social Psychology, 35,* 677–688.

Rokke, P. D., Carter, A. S., & Rehm, L. P. (1983, November). *Self-evaluation and self-reinforcement processes in depression.* Paper presented at the meeting of the Texas Psychological Association, San Antonio.

Roth, D., & Rehm, L. P. (1980). Relationships among self-monitoring processes, memory, and depression. *Cognitive Therapy and Research, 4,* 149–159.

Roth, D., Rehm, L. P., & Rozensky, R. A. (1980). Self-reward, self-punishment and depression. *Psychological Reports, 47,* 3–7.

Rozensky, R. A., Rehm, L. P., Pry, G., & Roth, D. (1977). Depression and self-reinforcement behavior in hospital patients. *Journal of Behavior Therapy and Experimental Psychiatry, 8,* 35–38.

Rozensky, R. A., Kravitz, S., & Unger, R. (1981). Learned helplessness and the self-control model of depression. *Psychological Reports, 48,* 987–994.

Russell, P. N., & Beekhuis, M. E. (1976). Organization in memory: A comparison of psychotics and normals. *Journal of Abnormal Psychology, 85,* 527–534.

Sacco, W. P. (1979, April). *Self-reinforcement by depressives under public and private measurement conditions.* Paper presented at the meeting of the Eastern Psychological Association, Philadelphia.

Sacco, W. P., & Hokanson, J. E. (1978). Expectations of success and anagram performance of depressives in a public and private setting. *Journal of Abnormal Psychology, 87,* 122–130.

Schiffman, T. S. (1978). *Effects of depression and feedback on selective self-monitoring.* Unpublished master's thesis, University of Pittsburgh, Pittsburgh, PA.

Schwartz, J. L. (1974). Relationship between goal discrepancy and depression. *Journal of Consulting and Clinical Psychology, 42,* 309.

Seligman, M. E. P., Abramson, L. Y., Semmel, A., & von Baeyer, C. (1979). Depressive attributional style. *Journal of Abnormal Psychology, 88,* 242–247.

Sharp, J., & Tennen, H. (1983). Attributional bias in depression: The role of cue perception. *Cognitive Therapy and Research, 7,* 325–332.

Shrauger, J. S., & Sorman, P. B. (1977). Self-evaluations, initial success and failure, and improvement as determinants of persistence. *Journal of Consulting and Clinical Psychology, 45,* 784–795.

Shrauger, J. S., & Terbovic, M. L. (1976). Self-evaluations and assessments of performance by self and others. *Journal of Consulting and Clinical Psychology, 44,* 564–572.

Skinner, B. F. (1957). *Verbal behavior.* New York: Appleton-Century-Crofts.

Smolen, R. C. (1978). Expectancies, mood, and performance of depressed and nondepressed psychiatric inpatients on chance and skill tasks. *Journal of Abnormal Psychology, 87,* 91–101.

Sternberg, D. E., & Jarvik, M. E. (1976). Memory functions in depression. *Archives of General Psychiatry, 33,* 219–224.

Stromgren, L. S. (1977). The influence of depression on memory. *Acta Psychiatrica Scandinavica, 56,* 109–128.

Teasdale, J. D. (1983a). Affect and accessibility. *Philosophical Transactions of the Royal Society of London, B302,* 403–412.

Teasdale, J. D. (1983b). Negative thinking in depression: Cause, effect, or reciprocal relationship? *Advances in Behaviour Research and Therapy, 5,* 27–49.

Teasdale, J. D. (in press). Change in cognition during depression: Psychopathological implications. *Journal of the Royal Society of Medicine.*

Teasdale, J. D., & Fogarty, S. J. (1979). Differential effects of induced mood on retrieval of pleasant and unpleasant events from episodic memory. *Journal of Abnormal Psychology, 88,* 248–257.

Teasdale, J. D., & Russell, M. L. (1983). Differential effects of induced mood on the recall of positive, negative and neutral words. *British Journal of Clinical Psychology, 22,* 163–172.

Teasdale, J. D., Taylor, R., & Fogarty, S. J. (1980). Effects of induced elation–depression on the accessibility of memories of happy and unhappy experiences. *Behaviour Research and Therapy, 18,* 339–346.

Thoresen, C. E., & Mahoney, M. J. (1974). *Behavioral self-control.* New York: Holt, Rinehart & Winston.

Thoresen, C. E., & Wilbur, C. S. (1976). Some encouraging thoughts about self-reinforcement. *Journal of Applied Behavior Analysis, 9,* 518–520.

Tulving, E. (1983). *Elements of episodic memory.* Oxford, England: Oxford University Press.

Vasta, R., & Brockner, J. (1979). Self-esteem and self-evaluative covert statements. *Journal of Consulting and Clinical Psychology, 47,* 776–777.

Weiner, B., Frieze, I., Kukla, A., Reed, L., Rest, S., & Rosenbaum, R. M. (1971). *Perceiving the causes of success and failure.* Morristown, NJ: General Learning Press.

Weingartner, H., Cohen, R. M., Murphy, D., L., Martello, J., & Gerdt, C. (1981). Cognitive processes in depression. *Archives of General Psychiatry, 38,* 42–47.

Weingartner, H., Kaye, W., Smallberg, S. A., Ebert, M. H., Gillin, J. C., & Sitaram, N. (1981). Memory failures in progressive idiopathic dementia. *Journal of Abnormal Psychology, 90,* 187–198.

Weingartner, H., Miller, H., & Murphy, D. L. (1977). Mood-state-dependent retrieval of verbal associations. *Journal of Abnormal Psychology, 86,* 276–284.

Weintraub, M., Segal, R. M., & Beck, A. T. (1974). An investigation of cognition and affect in the depressive experiences of normal men. *Journal of Consulting and Clinical Psychology, 42,* 911.

Wener, A. E., & Rehm, L. P. (1975). Depressive affect: A test of behavioral hypotheses. *Journal of Abnormal Psychology, 84,* 221–227.

Wessman, A. E., Ricks, D. F., & Tyl, M. M. (1960). Characteristics and concomitants of mood fluctuation in college women. *Journal of Abnormal and Social Psychology, 60,* 117–127.

Willis, M. H., & Blaney, P. H. (1978). Three tests of the learned helplessness model of depression. *Journal of Abnormal Psychology, 87,* 131–136.

Young, L. D., Moore, S. D., & Nelson, R. E. (1981, November). *Effects of depression on acceptance of personality feedback.* Paper presented at the meeting of the Association for the Advancement of Behavior Therapy, Toronto, Canada.

Zuroff, D. C. (1980). Distortions of memory and attribution in depressed, formerly depressed, and never depressed. *Psychological Reports, 46,* 415–425.

Zuroff, D. C. (1981). Depression and attribution: Some new data and a review of old data. *Cognitive Therapy and Research, 5,* 273–282.

6

Depression, Vulnerability, and World Assumptions

RONNIE JANOFF-BULMAN
BERNARD HECKER
University of Massachusetts, Amherst

Pessimism is often regarded as the element that changes simple sadness into depression (Arieti & Bemporad, 1978; Gutheil, 1959). Not only do depressives question whether they will ever get over their depression, but they typically have negative expectations about the future in general. Beck (1967), for example, found that 78% of the depressed patients he studied (and 87% of the severely depressed patients) reported negative expectations about the future, as compared with 22% of the nondepressed group.

> The patient's pattern of expecting the worst and rejecting the possibility of any improvement poses formidable obstacles in attempts to engage him in a therapeutic program. . . . Unlike the anxious patient, who tempers his negative anticipations with the realization that the unpleasant events may be avoided or will pass in time, the depressed patient thinks in terms of a future in which his present deficient condition (financial, social, physical) will continue or even get worse. (Beck, 1967, p. 23)

The significance of such beliefs becomes apparent when we recognize the extent to which people tend to be optimistic regarding personal future outcomes. We generally operate on the basis of an "illusion of invulnerability" or "unrealistic optimism" (Janoff-Bulman, Madden, & Timko, 1983; Janoff-Bulman & Lang-Gunn, 1988; Perloff, 1983; Weinstein, 1980; Weinstein & Lachendro, 1982). We regard ourselves as relatively safe and secure, more or less protected from negative outcomes.

Not only do most people report themselves as being happy (e.g., in the large Gurin, Veroff, and Feld [1960] study, only 10% rated themselves as "not too happy," the most negative category), but there are data demonstrating that people see the future as holding even more happiness for them personally, even if not for their own society or the world at large (Watts & Free, 1973). Matlin and Stang (1978) present empirical evidence in support of the "Pollyanna principle"; they claim that pleasant items are processed more efficiently and accurately than unpleasant or neutral items, and thus that "pleasantness predominates." Such biases operate not only in relation to present and past events but also in relation to future outcomes.

The tendency to be optimistic is particularly apparent in people's estimates of their own likelihood of being victimized. Janoff-Bulman, Madden, & Timko (1980) found that college students consistently underestimated their own chances of being victimized—by disease, accident, or crime—as compared to their estimates for the average person their age and in the same class. Similarly, Weinstein (1980; Weinstein & Lachendro, 1982) found that people underestimate the likelihood that they will experience negative events and overestimate the likelihood that they will experience positive events in their lives. Not only do people underestimate the likelihood that certain negative events will occur (Kunreuther, 1979; Perloff, 1983; Slovic, Fischhoff, & Lichtenstein, 1976), but they regard themselves as particularly invulnerable to negative events, including heart disease, cancer, crimes, and automobile accidents (Harris & Guten, 1979; Hindelang, Gottfredson, & Garofalo, 1978; Kirscht, Haefner, Kegeles, & Rosenstock, 1966; Knopf, 1976; Perloff, 1983; Robertson, 1977). Generally, we walk around with a belief that "It can't happen to me." We may recognize that bad events occur (e.g., that one out of four people will get cancer), but we nevertheless believe that they will happen to others. This perception of invulnerability, of unrealistic optimism, is one reason why victims experience such psychological upheaval following their misfortune (Bard & Sangrey, 1979; Janoff-Bulman & Frieze, 1983; Perloff, 1983; Scheppele & Bart, 1983).

Some have argued that optimism is inherent, evolutionarily "built in," because of a biological advantage that follows from a positive view of the future (e.g., see Tiger, 1979). Regardless of the accuracy of this position, it is nevertheless the case that optimism and perceived invulnerability are normative assumptions, whereas pessimism and perceived vulnerability represent more "deviant" beliefs about the future. For one who is depressed, the assumptions of protection and safety no longer operate, and he or she is overwhelmed by feelings of pessimism and despair.

ATTRIBUTIONS, SELF-BLAME, AND PESSIMISM

Theorists and researchers working in the area of depression have often identified pessimism and self-blame as primary symptoms of the phenomenon. As Arieti and Bemporad (1978) write, "Since the earliest description of depressive illness, distortions in cognition, such as extreme pessimism or unrealistic self-reproaches, have been noted by most authors as part of the symptom complex" (p. 45). It is the coincidence of these two symptom clusters—hopelessness and futility on the one hand, and self-blame and self-deprecation on the other—that led Abramson and Sackeim (1977) to discuss the "paradox in depression"; that is, how can depressives both blame themselves and regard events as uncontrollable?

In the personality and social psychological literature, much of the work on depression in recent years has been understood within the framework of learned helplessness (Abramson, Seligman, & Teasdale, 1978; Seligman, 1975), and consequently, the pessimism of depressed individuals has explicitly been treated as perceived helplessness, a belief in the uncontrollability of outcomes. In the reformulated model of learned helplessness, Abramson *et al.* (1978) proposed that attributions for events determine expectations of future noncontingency and that these attributions are therefore essential to an understanding of helplessness and depression. The generality, chronicity, and intensity of depression are presumed to be related to the particular causal attributions one makes in response to the question of why he or she is helpless. Abramson *et al.* (1978) have argued that those who make internal, global, and stable attributions are likely to be particularly prone to depression. To be depressed, according to the learned helplessness model, one must expect to be helpless; in other words, one must expect that outcomes are uncontrollable. Not surprisingly, most people operate on the basis of an "illusion of control" (Langer, 1975; also see Wortman, 1976), which is consistent with a general belief in invulnerability. Depressed individuals, however, are not likely to expect controllable outcomes. In fact, it has been demonstrated that depressives are not subject to an illusion of control but, rather, that they make relatively accurate assessments of response–outcome contingency as compared to nondepressed individuals; the latter have been shown to overestimate their control over successful outcomes and to underestimate their control over outcomes involving failure (Abramson, Alloy, & Rosoff, 1981; Alloy & Abramson, 1979). The contingency assessments of depressed individuals do not appear to be self-serving. According to the learned helplessness model, they do not expect controllability, and in this sense, it could be argued, they feel more vulnerable than their nondepressed counterparts.

In the literature on attribution theory, work in the area of self-blame has been most explicit in linking depression and perceived vulnerability/pessimism, for it has been argued that the maladaptiveness or adaptiveness of a particular type of self-blame lies in the attribution's implications for perceived future vulnerability or invulnerability, respectively (Janoff-Bulman, 1979; Wortman, 1976). In particular, one of us (Janoff-Bulman, 1979) has distinguished between two types of self-blame: characterological and behavioral. Although the former attribution focuses on one's character and the latter on one's behavior, the primary distinction between the two "is the perceived controllability (i.e., modifiability through one's own efforts) of the factor(s) blamed" (Janoff-Bulman, 1979, p. 1799). Research has demonstrated that behavioral self-blame attributions are generally made in the past tense ("I should or should not have done . . ."), whereas characterological self-blame attributions are generally made in the present tense ("I am or am not . . ."), reflecting implicit differences in the extent to which the attributional factor continues to define the person (Janoff-Bulman, 1979). It is characterological self-blame, and not behavioral self-blame, that is associated with depression and discussed by theorists such as Beck (1967, 1976). The "paradox in depression" is readily resolved when one recognizes that depressed individuals blame themselves characterologically, and not behaviorally; that is, they do not blame themselves for outcomes that they regard as controllable. Rather, as has been pointed out elsewhere, "In the case of personal failure, the characterological blamers will point to deficits in themselves that are believed to account for these failures. The deficits are likely to lie in the realm of characteristics that generally define them, characteristics that are relatively nonmodifiable, stable, and global" (Janoff-Bulman, 1979, p. 1801).

In accordance with the reformulated learned helplessness model (Abramson *et al.,* 1978), internal attributions for failure lead to low self-esteem and are associated with depression (e.g., see Metalsky, Abramson, Seligman, Semmel, & Peterson, 1982; Raps, Peterson, Reinhard, Abramson, & Seligman, 1982; Seligman, Abramson, Semmel, & von Baeyer, 1979). Work specifically on self-blame, however, has demonstrated that the nature of the self-attribution is important: Behavioral self-blame roughly coincides with an internal attribution that is unstable, controllable, and specific; characterological self-blame, on the other hand, coincides with an internal attribution that is stable, uncontrollable, and global. An important distinction to be drawn between behavioral and characterological self-blame is the different implication of each attribution for perceived vulnerability.

Characterological self-blame is related to self-esteem and is associated with a belief that one is personally deserving of past negative outcomes, whereas behavioral self-blame is related to control and is associated with a belief that one can, in the future, avoid a negative outcome (Janoff-Bulman, 1979; 1982). A person who can point to a particular past behavior in order to account for a negative outcome is able to maintain a belief in the future avoidability of a similar misfortune. On the other hand, a person who attributes the negative outcome to a more or less stable character trait will not be afforded a similar belief in future invulnerability. Just as the student who attributes failure to a lack of effort can expect to perform better next time, behavioral self-blamers can be optimistic about the future; the student who believes he or she failed because of a lack of ability will have negative expectations about future performance, as will the characterological self-blamer.

It is not always easy to readily distinguish between behavioral and characterological self-blame (Miller & Porter, 1983). The rape victim who says "I should not have hitchhiked" or "I should not have gone up to his apartment" is clearly engaging in behavioral self-blame, for she is pointing to a discrete behavior that she has defined as having occurred in the past. However, the self-blame expressed by the rape victim who says "I pick the wrong people to go out with" or "I give the wrong signals to men" is more difficult to type. Though the woman appears to be pointing to behaviors, she is actually engaging in characterological self-blame, for she is talking about continuing behaviors (i.e., they are phrased in the present tense) and is defining herself in terms of these behaviors; in other words, she regards herself as the kind of person who does the particular things in question, as a person with particular self-defining "flaws."

Behavioral self-blame affords a belief in future avoidability and thus minimizes a person's perceived vulnerability and pessimism about the future. Characterological self-blame does not provide a basis for optimism; rather, it reinforces a negative view of the self and negative expectations about the future. Empirically, characterological self-blame has been found to be positively associated with depression (e.g., see Janoff-Bulman, 1979; Major, Mueller, & Hildebrandt, 1985; Peterson, Schwartz, & Seligman, 1981). Behavioral self-blame has not been positively associated with depression (e.g., Janoff-Bulman, 1979; Major *et al.,* 1985) but, rather, has been negatively associated with poor coping and depression (e.g., Peterson *et al.,* 1981; Tennen, Affleck, Allen, McGrade, & Ratzan, 1984; Tennen,

Affleck, & Gershman, 1986; Timko & Janoff-Bulman, 1985; cf. Meyer & Taylor, 1986). It is behavioral self-blame in the absence of characterological self-blame that is adaptive. Care must be taken in ensuring that the behavioral self-blame in a given instance does not simply reflect characterological self-blame, which may be simultaneously exhibited. Thus people who believe they are stupid also probably believe they do stupid things, thus engaging in both characterological and behavioral self-blame; such persons would presumably be depressed, and the behavioral self-blame would be simply an extension of their low self-esteem. It is only when behavioral self-blame is manifested without characterological self-blame that one would expect the benefits of such an attribution to operate. Further, one would not expect characterological self-blame to be associated with depression if the characteristic blamed were held in high esteem by the person, such as when a divorced woman blames her valued "independence and personal strength" for her divorce (see Miller & Porter, 1983, for a discussion of this issue).

The importance of vulnerability assumptions as mediators of the self-blame–depression relationship was recently demonstrated in a study by Timko and Janoff-Bulman (1985). The researchers found that the adaptiveness of self-blame attributions was dependent upon the attributions' implications for perceived future vulnerability. Respondents in this study were women who had had mastectomies as a result of breast cancer. Using path-analytic techniques, the researchers found that the women's causal attributions for their disease were not differentially associated with depression; in fact, there was no direct association between attributions and depression, as has also been found by Taylor, Lichtman, and Wood (1984). However, behavioral and characterological self-blame attributions were indirectly associated with depression, for they represented the endpoints of two different causal paths that predicted perceived vulnerability to a recurrence of cancer, and perceived vulnerability, in turn, directly predicted depression. The characterological self-blame path was negatively associated with a belief that one would be free of cancer in the future, whereas the behavioral self-blame path was positively associated with such a belief. Given that the belief that one would be free of cancer was negatively associated with depression (and positively associated with positive emotions and self-esteem), the study provides empirical support for the importance of vulnerability beliefs as mediators in understanding the relationship between particular attributions and depression. In the Timko and Janoff-Bulman (1985) study, the adaptiveness of behavioral self-blame and the maladaptiveness of characterological self-blame were evident in light of their contribution to beliefs about future vulnerability. The association between perceived vulnerability/pessimism and depression was strong and direct, and suggested the importance of more fully understanding people's assessments of their future vulnerability.

PESSIMISM AND A MODEL OF RELEVANT WORLD ASSUMPTIONS

Although work on self-attributions may provide some insights into people's beliefs about personal vulnerability, a more complete picture of vulnerability-related beliefs would entail going beyond the beliefs about the self implied by self-attributions. Each day, we operate on the basis of assumptions we hold about ourselves and the world (see Janoff-Bulman & Frieze, 1983). Whether labeled "assumptive world" (Parkes, 1971, 1975), "world models" (Bowlby, 1969), "theory of reality" (Epstein, 1973, 1980), or "structures of meaning" (Marris, 1975), this basic conceptual system provides people with a means for understanding their world and ordering their behavior.

What are the basic assumptions or beliefs people hold that are associated with their pessimism or optimism? In attempting to formulate a heuristic model of people's world assumptions related to vulnerability, one of us (Janoff-Bulman, in press) proposed three general categories of beliefs that seem particularly central. The three categories are (1) assumptions about the malevolence or benevolence of the world, (2) assumptions about distributional principles for good and bad outcomes, and (3) assumptions about the self-relevance of the distributional principles. As shown in Table 6-1, each category comprises two or more subcategories, corresponding to the more specific assumptions people may hold within the general category. These categories and subcategories certainly do not exhaust all vulnerability-related assumptions, but they do provide a starting point for examining people's beliefs in this area.

Beliefs about the benevolence or malevolence of the world represent individuals' assumptions about the frequency of good or bad outcomes, respectively. In many ways, these seem to be similar to base-rate estimates (e.g., see Kahneman & Tversky, 1973) of positive and negative events. People differ in terms of how good or bad they perceive the world to be, and a distinction can be drawn between people's beliefs about the "goodness" of the impersonal world and their beliefs about the "goodness" of people (i.e., the personal world). This distinction provides the basis for the two subcategories of this assumptive dimension—the benevolence or malevolence of the impersonal world and the benevolence or malevolence of people.

The second category of relevant assumptions concerns people's beliefs about how good and bad outcomes are distributed; this category seems to represent assumptions about process. Given an individual's perception of the frequency of good and bad events (as represented by the benevolence–malevolence dimension),

Table 6-1. Categories and Subcategories of the Heuristic Model of Vulnerability-Related Assumptions

Category	Subcategories
Benevolence or malevolence of the world	Benevolence or malevolence of the impersonal world, benevolence or malevolence of people
Distributional principles	Justice, controllability, randomness
Self-relevant dimensions	Self-worth, self-controllability, luck

how are these events "distributed"? In other words, why do good things happen to some people and bad things to others, or why do good things happen at certain times and bad things at other times? Three distributional principles constitute the sub-categories of this dimension. First, people may believe that outcomes are distributed according to a principle of justice (cf. Rawls, 1971); that is, good or bad events happen on the basis of whether or not people deserve particular outcomes. This perspective is closely akin to beliefs about a "just world," as discussed by Lerner and his colleagues (e.g., Lerner, 1980; Lerner & Miller, 1978). These authors have written extensively about people's beliefs that individuals deserve what they get and get what they deserve; in other words, bad things happen to bad people, and good things happen to good people. The best way to guarantee positive outcomes for oneself (and avoid negative outcomes) is to be a good, moral, decent human being.

Individuals may also think about the distribution of good and bad outcomes in the world in terms of people's behaviors. Do people engage in behaviors so as to avoid misfortune and maximize positive outcomes for themselves? The principle embraced here is that of a controllable world, in which actions are determinants of outcomes. If misfortune strikes an individual, it is presumably because he or she had not engaged in the precautionary behaviors necessary to avoid the outcome. Related to this assumption is the work by Seligman and his colleagues (e.g., Abramson *et al.*, 1978; Seligman, 1975), who proposed that learned helplessness follows from a recognition of noncontingency between actions and outcomes; in other words, helplessness results from the invalidation of a belief in controllability. This assumption of controllability suggests that outcomes are distributed in accordance with one's actions and that therefore the best way to minimize one's own vulnerability is to engage in the "right" (e.g., careful, proper, precautionary, foresightful) behaviors. This assumption is distinguishable from beliefs about justice on the basis of its focus on one's actions rather than on one's moral character. Generally, beliefs in justice and controllability constitute the sense of "meaning" often discussed in psychological literature (e.g., Frankl, 1963; Lifton, 1967; Silver, Boon, & Stones, 1983; Silver & Wortman, 1980). An event is meaningful, or makes sense, to the extent that it is consistent with predictable social laws, and the social laws most often invoked in Western society are those of controllability and justice.

The final subcategory of process assumptions is the principle of randomness, or chance. From this perspective, good and bad outcomes occur on a seemingly random basis, and there is essentially nothing an individual can do to maximize positive outcomes and minimize negative ones. To the extent that people believe strongly in justice or controllability as a distributional principle, they would presumably believe less in chance. Nevertheless, individuals are likely to believe in all three assumptions, to a greater or lesser extent; in other words, we do not propose that the beliefs are mutually exclusive, for individuals can believe that chance operates to some extent, for example, while simultaneously holding strong beliefs in controllability and justice.

The third major category of vulnerability-related assumptions involves beliefs about qualities of the self. A person may assume that the frequency of negative events in the world is extremely high and that justice, or the degree to which the individual is deserving of a particular outcome, is the primary means by which outcomes are distributed. We still would not know the extent to which this person feels vulnerable, however, for we do not know the person's evaluation of what he or she "deserves." In this case, to the extent that one feels a great deal of self-worth, he or she will feel protected from negative outcomes. Similarly, an individual who believes that there is not a great deal of misfortune in the world and that people can avoid negative outcomes through their actions (i.e., the world is controllable) will probably feel optimistic about future outcomes to the extent that this individual believes he or she engages in precautionary behaviors (i.e., is the kind of person whose actions are "correct").

Thus, for the purpose of gaining insight into people's perceptions of vulnerability, beliefs about the benevolence of the world and about the distribution of outcomes are probably best understood in light of beliefs about the self. Certainly, to the extent that one truly believes in chance, beliefs about the self should be irrelevant. However, even in such cases, it appears that people hold implicit beliefs about their luck, and these may be related, however primitively, to assumptions about chance.

The three self-relevant assumptions proposed in our model, then, parallel the beliefs about the distribution of good and bad outcomes. The first subcategory is that of perceived self-worth, or the extent to which people perceive themselves as being moral, decent, and good, and therefore worthy of positive (and not negative) outcomes. The second subcategory is that of personal controllability, or, more specifically, the extent to which people perceive themselves as being the type of person who engages in "proper" behaviors. Do they see themselves as individuals whose actions are cautious, foresightful, well thought out, intelligent? Or do they engage in behaviors that are likely to effect negative outcomes and minimize positive ones? The third subcategory is perceived luck, that elusive self-perception that allows people to believe, even if illogically, that they may come out ahead (or behind, in the case of perceived bad luck), even when chance and randomness operate. To the extent that people see themselves as lucky, they believe that they will be protected from misfortune, even if misfortune is randomly distributed. However, they are not able to point to any particular aspect of themselves that can account for this protection, and they therefore label the quality "luck."

In general, one would expect the assumptive world of depressives to reflect greater vulnerability. However, it is unclear which vulnerability-related assumptions in particular would distinguish between depressed and nondepressed individuals. In recent studies, depressed and nondepressed respondents differed in their predictions of the likelihood of negative outcomes for themselves, with the depressed reporting greater pessimism (e.g., Alloy & Ahrens, 1987; Pietromonaco & Markus, 1985). Yet, in one case, the depressed did not differ from the nondepressed in their predictions of negative outcomes for others (Pietromonaco & Markus, 1985), whereas in another instance, the depressed were also more pessimistic than the nondepressed in their predictions for others (Alloy & Ahrens, 1987). We would expect the self-relevant components of the assumptive world to reflect more negative self-perceptions for depressed than for nondepressed individuals, based upon past work on depressives' low self-esteem (e.g., Abramson & Sackeim, 1977; Beck, 1967). Do depressives also perceive other people more negatively than nondepressed individuals? Do they perceive the world as more malevolent? Do they hold different assumptions about the operation of distributional principles? (One of us [Janoff-Bulman, 1979], for example, found that depressed respondents engaged in more characterological self-blame *and* believed more in chance outcomes.) Or do depressives perceive themselves as more vulnerable solely because they regard themselves as unworthy? Negative self-perceptions would certainly be a sufficient condition for feelings of increased vulnerability and pessimism. Yet, it is possible, given the non-mutually-exclusive nature of the assumptions, that depressives perceive all facets of their world—themselves, other people, the impersonal world, the principles by which outcomes are distributed—more negatively than nondepressed persons.

It is also interesting to speculate on forms of depression that are not consistent with the typical clinical picture of the individual with low self-esteem. The despair of existential philosophers (Barrett, 1958), for example, is a form of depression (e.g., sadness coupled with pessimism) in which the world is regarded as malevolent and in which there is no self-protection because randomness is the means by which the negative outcomes are distributed. From an existentialist's perspective, the world is not just, nor is it particularly controllable; rather, it is regarded as meaningless and random. The self-relevant dimensions of the assumptive world are essentially irrelevant to the pessimism of existential philosophers, yet their despair is readily comprehensible.

AN EMPIRICAL LOOK AT THE MODEL

Our proposed model consists of three general categories and eight subcategories of assumptions relevant to people's perceptions of vulnerability or invulnerability, optimism or pessimism. Given depressives' negative expectations and pessimism, we decided to investigate the extent to which depressed individuals would differ from nondepressed individuals on each of the eight subcategories.

To measure these assumptions, one of us developed a scale (see Janoff-Bulman, in press) composed of four items for each of the eight subcategories of assumptions:

1. Benevolent impersonal world (e.g., The world is a good place; There is more good than evil in the world)

2. Benevolent people (e.g., People are basically kind and helpful; Human nature is basically good)

3. Justice (e.g., By and large, good people get what they deserve in this world; Misfortune is least likely to strike worthy, decent people)

4. Controllability (e.g., If people took preventive actions, most mis-

fortune could be avoided; When bad things happen, it is typically because people have not taken the necessary actions to protect themselves)

5. Randomness (e.g., Bad events are distributed to people at random; The course of our lives is largely determined by chance)

6. Self-worth (e.g., I have reason to be ashamed of my personal character; I am very satisfied with the kind of person I am)

7. Self-controllability (e.g., I always behave in ways that are likely to maximize good results for me; I take the actions necessary to protect myself against misfortune)

8. Luck (e.g., I am basically a lucky person; Looking at my life, I realize that chance events have worked out well for me).

Respondents were to indicate their extent of agreement or disagreement with each statement on an 8-point scale, with endpoints "agree completely" and "disagree completely." Analyses indicated that each subscale of four items had a reliability between .68 and .88. A factor analysis was conducted in order to examine the factor structure of the overall scale (i.e., 32 items), for one can have excellent alpha coefficients and yet not be measuring independent factors. The factor structure was comparable to that which was proposed; in fact, it was identical, except for the Benevolent Impersonal World and Benevolent People factors, which emerged as a single factor. Not only did the three process assumptions and the three self-relevant assumptions emerge as six independent factors, but each was composed of precisely those four items intended for that factor, and only those items. Despite the single-factor structure of the Benevolent Impersonal World and Benevolent People dimensions, the two factors were nevertheless examined separately for heuristic purposes.

To determine whether depression was related to differences in the proposed assumptions, 352 undergraduates (143 men, 209 women) completed the 32-item World Assumptions Questionnaire and the Zung Self-Rating Depression Scale (Zung, 1965), which is sensitive to depression among college students. (As in Janoff-Bulman, 1979, a "none-of-the-time" response category was added, rendering the scale particularly sensitive to depression among college students.) Data were first analyzed using 3×2 analyses of variance. Depression scores were used to divide respondents into three groups (those with low, medium, and high scores), in the hope of providing a more fine tuned picture than that usually provided by a median split. Depression and gender were the independent variables used in analyzing the data.

Scores on the Zung Self-Rating Depression Scale ranged from 6 to 89. The least depressed group had scores that ranged from 6 through 18; the middle group, scores from 19 through 27; and the most depressed, scores from 28 through 89. The subscales (subcategories of assumptions) were scored such that a high score (possible range of 0 to 28) indicated a greater belief in that particular subscale. Thus a high score on the Randomness subscale indicated a greater belief that events are distributed randomly, and a high score on Controllability indicated a greater belief that the world is controllable.

Analyses of variance found a main effect for gender on one of the eight assumptions; women perceived other people as more benevolent than did men (19.34 vs. 18.13, $F(1, 350) = 9.27$, $p < .003$). There were no Gender × Depression interactions on any of the assumptions. As shown in Table 6-2, main effects for depression were found for seven of the eight assumption subscales; only the process assumption regarding justice was not significant, $F(2, 350) = 0.97$. Student-Newman-Keuls tests were conducted for each of the seven subscales with significant F values in order to determine specifically which of the groups differed from one another. Results indicated that for all seven subscales, there were significant differences between the least and the most depressed groups, and the differences were such that the depressed group's beliefs consistently indicated greater perceived vulnerability. As compared to the least depressed group (i.e., the nondepressed group), the most depressed respondents assumed that people and the impersonal world are more malevolent, that the world is less controllable, that chance operates to a greater extent, that their self-worth is less positive, that they are less likely to engage in proper behaviors, and that they are less lucky.

With one exception, these same differences emerged in the comparisons between the middle group and the most depressed group, for their subscale scores differed significantly for Benevolent Impersonal World, Benevolent People, Randomness, Self-worth, Self-controllability, and Luck. Of the seven subscales with significant F values, only Controllability did not emerge as significantly different for these two groups. Again, the scores of the most depressed group consistently indicated greater perceived vulnerability. On three subscales, scores for the middle group also differed from the least depressed group. The least depressed (i.e., nondepressed) group believed in a more controllable world, in greater self-worth, and in greater self-controllability (i.e., being engaged in proper behaviors) than the middle group of respondents.

Depressed males and females did not differ in their assumptive worlds; men

Table 6-2. Differences in Subscales of the World Assumptions Questionnaire for Groups Differing in Depression

	Group				
Subscale	X Nondepressed	X Middle	X Depressed	F value	P value
Benevolent Impersonal World	19.12	18.51	16.68	8.06	<.001
Benevolent People	19.65	19.36	17.55	9.58	<.001
Justice	12.77	12.57	12.63	0.97	n.s.
Controllability	15.52	14.07	14.58	3.23	<.05
Randomness	13.09	13.55	15.17	5.45	<.005
Self-worth	23.89	21.32	17.31	59.07	<.001
Self-controllability	19.93	18.18	16.99	14.37	<.001
Luck	18.55	18.51	15.89	12.74	<.001

and women (across all depression groups) differed in their beliefs about the benevolence of people, with women viewing people as more benevolent than did men. Nevertheless, the experience of depression as examined through the vulnerability-related assumptions did not differ for male and female undergraduates in this sample. However, with the exception of beliefs about the world as being a just place, depressed respondents differed from their nondepressed counterparts on all of the vulnerability-related assumptions tapped by the scale. Further, they differed from their less depressed counterparts (i.e., the middle group) on all of the subscales except Justice and Controllability (although it is interesting to note that the nondepressed and less depressed groups did differ on beliefs regarding controllability). In all cases, those in the most depressed group indicated the most pessimistic, vulnerable view of the world and themselves. Clearly, the largest difference appeared on the self-esteem scale. Yet, in addition to viewing themselves more negatively, the depressed respondents perceived other people and the world around them as more malevolent, and the distributional principles as most random and least controllable. In fact, the depressed respondents endorsed the distributional principle of randomness most strongly, as compared to the nondepressed respondents, who endorsed controllability most strongly. The lack of difference in beliefs about justice between these two groups was not accounted for by strong positive beliefs in justice by the two groups but, rather, by the negative assumptions about justice held by both; in this case, the nondepressed group also did not believe strongly in justice as a distributional principle. Those in the nondepressed group, however, would presumably not feel vulnerable as a result, for they saw negative outcomes as being far less likely to occur and further, that those that do occur are apt to be controllable through people's actions (those who engage in the "right" behaviors). In addition, any negative outcomes that do occur because of chance (even if relatively few in number) are not likely to happen to them, for they are lucky, and any negative outcomes that do occur because of principles of justice (even if relatively few in number) are not likely to happen to them because they are worthy individuals!

Depressed individuals are not similarly protected against feeling vulnerable. From their perspective, both the impersonal world and other people are likely to be seen as less benevolent, and the relatively common negative outcomes that occur are apt to be distributed randomly; that is, chance operates, and the world's events are not very controllable. Further, they perceive themselves as unworthy individuals and as ones who do not even act so as to bring about the greatest good for themselves. In this relatively malevolent, random world, they also see themselves as unlucky. Clearly, the pessimism of depressed individuals is deeply and broadly reflected in their assumptive worlds. Their feelings of vulnerability are reflected in assumptions that extend far beyond negative beliefs about themselves.

THE ROLE OF PESSIMISM IN DEPRESSION

It appears that depressed individuals make assumptions about themselves and the world that differ from those made by nondepressed people. What, specifically, is the role of such assumptions? Are they causally related to depression? Do they render a person more vulnerable to depression? Do they play a maintenance function? Recent reviews of cognitive factors in depression (e.g., Brewin, 1985; Coyne & Gotlib, 1983) should sensitize us to claims about the causal role of cognitions. Brewin (1985) specifically reviewed literature on attributions and depression, and Coyne and Gotlib (1983) reviewed five major areas of cognitive functioning (i.e., expectations and evaluations of performance, perception of environmental information, recall of information, cognitive biases, and attributional processes). Coyne and Gotlib (1983) wrote, "Considered collectively, these investigations have demonstrated little success in identifying a significant cognitive vulnerability to depression or depressive behavior in people who are not already in a depressed state" (p. 499). Brewin (1985) similarly ruled out such a vulnerability model but nevertheless concluded that attributions "do have considerable predictive value and may be involved in the processes of recovery and coping with depression. . . . There is little to suggest that attributions are important because of their relationship to specific events in people's lives; instead it is likely that they enjoy a more direct relationship to depressed mood and may reflect a positive or negative coping style" (p. 28).

At this point, it would be difficult and premature to make a strong claim for the causal antecedence of vulnerability-related assumptions. It is possible that such assumptions represent deeper, more pervasive belief systems than the cognitions reviewed by Brewin and by Coyne and Gotlib, and as such may play a greater causal role. Perhaps such beliefs sensitize individuals to negative events around them. To the extent that individuals assume that the world is malevolent, that randomness operates, and that they are worthless, they are more likely to overestimate the possibility of misfortune for themselves, and they are more likely to respond to the possibility of such misfortune with depression (i.e., hopelessness and despair) than with anxiety, which entails some belief (no matter how minimal) in avoidability. Certainly, one could make a stronger claim for the maintenance function of such pessimistic assumptions, for once an individual is depressed, the presence of such assumptions about the world and oneself would no doubt serve to maintain and even exacerbate the individual's negative affect. Further, to the extent that people truly feel hopeless about their situation, therapeutic intervention may not be sought, and such an outcome as suicide may become the chosen course of action.

The actual role of such cognitions remains an open question. Our personal aim in examining depressives' vulnerability-related assumptions, however, has not been to argue for their causal significance but has been to begin to understand the world as seen through the eyes of depressives. As Coyne and Gotlib (1983) wrote, "Undoubtedly, a viable model of depression will have to take into account how depressed people think. Current cognitive models of depression are correct in their claim that in order to understand the behavior and distress of depressed persons we need to understand how they experience their world and how they process new information that becomes available to them" (p. 500). Certainly, a questionnaire is not ideal as the sole means of obtaining information about how people experience their world, nor do vulnerability-related assumptions constitute the sole (or even the most important) area worthy of investigation. Nevertheless, our work is a basic step in the process of uncovering the specific experiences and perspectives of the depressive's inner world.

The depressive's inner world certainly seems to differ from that of the nondepressive. Are these differences in assumptions in some way justifiable in terms of the life experiences of depressed versus nondepressed individuals? As Coyne and Gotlib (1983) argue, "What people think probably depends more on what their external circumstances provide than these cognitive models assume" (p. 500). For example, have depressed individuals been exposed to more (or more salient) negative outcomes? In light of this perspective, it is interesting to note that traumatic life events may have a particularly devastating psychological impact (including depression) because they invalidate the assumptive world of victims (see Janoff-Bulman & Frieze, 1983, for a complete discussion of this perspective). Vulnerability-related assumptions are particularly affected by unexpected, extremely negative life events, and those who feel most invulnerable beforehand may in fact suffer the greatest depression following the victimizing event (Perloff, 1983; Scheppele & Bart, 1983).

Recognizing the role of environmental antecedents and life events—particularly, the relationship between such events and people's understanding of their world—remains an important task for researchers and theorists working in the area of depression. For the present, we have evidence suggesting specific differences in the nature of depressives' versus nondepressives' assumptive worlds. Our proposed heuristic model provides a means with which to begin to understand the inner world of depressed individuals, a world that is pervaded by perceptions of vulnerability.

REFERENCES

Abramson, L. Y., Alloy, L. B., & Rosoff, R. (1981). Depression and the generation of complex hypotheses in the judgment of contingency. *Behavior Research and Therapy, 19,* 75–86.
Abramson, L. Y., & Sackeim, H. A. (1977). A paradox in depression: Uncontrollability and self-blame. *Psychological Bulletin, 84,* 838–851.
Abramson, L. Y., Seligman, M. E. P., & Teasdale, J. (1978). Learned helplessness in humans: Critique and reformulation. *Journal of Abnormal Psychology, 87,* 49–74.
Alloy, L. B., & Abramson, L. Y. (1979). Judgment of contingency in depressed and nondepressed students: Sadder but wiser? *Journal of Experimental Psychology: General, 108,* 441–485.
Alloy, L. B., & Ahrens, A. H. (1987). Depression and pessimism for the future: Biased use of statistically relevant information in predictions for self versus others. *Journal of Personality and Social Psychology, 52,* 366–378.
Arieti, S., & Bemporad, J. (1978). *Severe and mild depression.* New York: Basic Books.
Bard, M., & Sangrey, D. (1979). *The crime victim's book.* New York: Basic Books.
Barrett, W. (1958). *Irrational man: A study in existential philosophy.* Garden City, NY: Doubleday.
Beck, A. T. (1976). Cognitive therapy and the emotional disorders. New York: Meridian.
Beck, A. T. (1967). *Depression: Clinical, experimental, and theoretical aspects.* New York: Harper & Row.
Bowlby, J. (1969). *Attachment and loss. Volume 1: Attachment.* London: Hogarth.
Brewin, C. R. (1985). Depression and causal attributions: What is their relationship? *Psychological Bulletin, 98,* 297–309.

Coyne, J. C., & Gotlib, I. H. (1983). The role of cognition in depression: A critical appraisal. *Psychological Bulletin, 94*, 472–505.

Epstein, S. (1973). The self-concept revisited: Or a theory of a theory. *American Psychologist, 28*, 404–416.

Epstein, S. (1980). The self-concept: A review and the proposal of an integrated theory of personality. In E. Staub (Ed.), *Personality: Basic issues and current research* (pp.). Englewood Cliffs, NJ: Prentice-Hall.

Frankl, V. E. (1963). *Man's search for meaning: An introduction to logotherapy.* New York: Washington Square Press.

Gurin, G., Veroff, J., & Feld, S. (1960). *Americans view their mental health.* New York: Basic Books.

Gutheil, E. A. (1959). Reactive depressions. In S. Arieti (Ed.), *American handbook of psychiatry* (Vol. 1, pp.). New York: Basic Books

Harris, D. M., & Guten, S. (1979). Health protective behavior: An exploratory study. *Journal of Health and Social Behavior, 20*, 17–29.

Hindelang, M. J., Gottfredson, M. R., & Garofalo, J. (1978). *Victims of personal crime.* Cambridge, MA: Ballinger.

Janoff-Bulman, R. (1979). Characterological versus behavioral self-blame: Inquiries into depression and rape. *Journal of Personality and Social Psychology, 37*, 1798–1809.

Janoff-Bulman, R. (1982). Esteem and control bases of blame: "Adaptive" strategies for victims versus observers. *Journal of Personality, 50*, 180–192.

Janoff-Bulman, R. (In press). *Understanding people in terms of their assumptive worlds.* In D. J. Ozer, J. M. Healy, & A. J. Stewart (Eds.), *Perspectives on personality: Self and emotion.* Greenwich, CT: JAI Press.

Janoff-Bulman, R., & Frieze, I. H. (1983). A theoretical perspective for understanding reactions to victimization. *Journal of Social Issues, 39*, 1–17.

Janoff-Bulman, R., & Lang-Gunn, L. (1988). Coping with disease and accidents: The role of self-blame attributions. In L. Y. Abramson (Ed.), *Social–personal inference in clinical psychology.* New York: Guilford Press.

Janoff-Bulman, R., Madden, M. E., & Timko, C. (1980). *The illusion of invulnerability.* Unpublished manuscript, University of Massachusetts, Amherst.

Janoff-Bulman, R., Madden, M. E., & Timko, C. (1983). Victims' reactions to aid: The role of perceived vulnerability. In A. Nadler, J. D. Fisher, & B. M. DePaulo (Eds.), *New directions in helping* (Vol. 3, pp. 21–42). New York: Academic Press.

Kahneman, D., & Tversky, A. (1973). On the psychology of prediction. *Psychological Review, 80*, 237–251.

Kirscht, J. P., Haefner, D. P., Kegeles, S. S., & Rosenstock, I. M. (1966). A national study of health beliefs. *Journal of Health and Human Behavior, 7*, 248–254.

Knopf, A. (1976). Changes in women's opinions about cancer. *Social Science and Medicine, 10*, 191–195.

Kunreuther, H. (1979). The changing societal consequences of risks from natural hazards. *The Annals of the American Academy of Political and Social Science, 443*, 104–116.

Langer, E. (1975). The illusion of control. *Journal of Personality and Social Psychology, 32*, 311–328.

Lerner, M. J. (1980). *The belief in a just world.* New York: Plenum.

Lerner, M. J., & Miller, D. T. (1978). Just world research and the attribution process: Looking back and ahead. *Psychological Bulletin, 85*, 1030–1051.

Lifton, R. J. (1967). *Death in life: Survivors of Hiroshima.* New York: Simon & Schuster.

Major, B., Mueller, P., & Hildebrandt, K. (1985). Attributions, expectations, and coping with abortion. *Journal of Personality and Social Psychology, 48*, 585–599.

Marris, P. (1975). *Loss and change.* Garden City, NY: Anchor-Doubleday.

Matlin, M. W., & Stang, D. J. (1978). *The Pollyanna principle: Selectivity in language, memory, and thought.* Cambridge, MA: Schenkman Books.

Metalsky, G. I., Abramson, L. Y., Seligman, M. E. P., Semmel, A., & Peterson, C. (1982). Attributional styles and life events in the classroom: Vulnerability and invulnerability to depressive mood reactions. *Journal of Personality and Social Psychology, 43*, 612–617.

Meyer, C. B., & Taylor, S. E. (1986). Adjustment to rape. *Journal of Personality and Social Psychology, 50,* 1226–1234.

Miller, D. T., & Porter, C. A. (1983). Self-blame in victims of violence. *Journal of Social Issues, 39,* 141–154.

Parkes, C. M. (1971). Psycho-social transitions: A field for study. *Social Science and Medicine, 5,* 101–115.

Parkes, C. M. (1975). What becomes of redundant world models? A contribution to the study of adaptation to change. *British Journal of Medical Psychology, 48,* 131–137.

Perloff, L. S. (1983). Perceptions of vulnerability to victimization. *Journal of Social Issues, 39,* 41–61.

Peterson, C., Schwartz, S. M., & Seligman, M. E. P. (1981). Self-blame and depressive symptoms. *Journal of Personality and Social Psychology, 41,* 253–259.

Pietromonaco, P. R., & Markus, H. (1985). The nature of negative thoughts in depression. *Journal of Personality and Social Psychology, 48,* 799–807.

Raps, C. S., Peterson, C., Reinhard, K. E., Abramson, L. Y., & Seligman, M. E. P. (1982). Attributional style among depressed patients. *Journal of Abnormal Psychology, 91,* 102–108.

Rawls, J. (1971). *A theory of justice.* Cambridge, MA: Harvard University Press.

Robertson, L. S. (1977). Car crashes: Perceived vulnerability and willingness to pay for crash protection. *Journal of Community Health, 3,* 136–141.

Scheppele, K. L., & Bart, P. B. (1983). Through women's eyes: Defining danger in the wake of sexual assault. *Journal of Social Issues, 39,* 63–81.

Seligman, M. E. P. (1975). *Helplessness: On depression, development and death.* San Francisco: W. H. Freeman.

Seligman, M. E. P., Abramson, L. Y., Semmel, A., & von Baeyer, C. (1979). Depressive attributional style. *Journal of Abnormal Psychology, 88,* 242–247.

Silver, R. L., Boon, C., & Stones, M. L. (1983). Searching for meaning in misfortune: Making sense of incest. *Journal of Social Issues, 39,* 83–103.

Silver, R. L., & Wortman, C. B. (1980). Coping with undesirable life events. In J. Garber & M. E. P. Seligman (Eds.), *Human helplessness* (pp. 279–340). New York: Academic Press.

Slovic, P., Fischhoff, B., & Lichtenstein, S. (1976). Cognitive processes and societal risk taking. In J. S. Carroll & J. W. Payne (Eds.), *Cognition and social behavior* (pp. 165–184). Hillsdale, NJ: Erlbaum.

Taylor, S., Lichtman, R. R., & Wood, J. V. (1984). Attributions, beliefs about control, and adjustment to breast cancer. *Journal of Personality and Social Psychology, 46,* 489–502.

Tennen, H., Affleck, G., Allen, D. A., McGrade, B. J., & Ratzan, S. (1984). Causal attributions and coping with insulin-dependent diabetes. *Basic and Applied Social Psychology, 5,* 131–142.

Tennen, H., Affleck, G., & Gershman, K. (1986). Self-blame among parents of infants with perinatal complications: The role of self-protective motives. *Journal of Personality and Social Psychology, 50,* 690–696.

Tiger, L. (1979). *Optimism: The biology of hope.* New York: Simon & Schuster.

Timko, C., & Janoff-Bulman, R. (1985). Attributions, vulnerability, and psychological adjustment: The case of breast cancer. *Health Psychology, 4,* 521–544.

Watts, W., & Free, L. A. (1973). *State of the nation, 1972.* New York: Universe Books.

Weinstein, N. D. (1980). Unrealistic optimism about future life events. *Journal of Personality and Social Psychology, 39,* 806–820.

Weinstein, N. D., & Lachendro, E. (1982). Egocentrism as a source of unrealistic optimism. *Personality and Social Psychology Bulletin, 8,* 195–200.

Wortman, C. B. (1976). Causal attributions and personal control. In J. H. Harvey, W. J. Ickes, & R. F. Kidd (Eds.), *New directions in attributions research* (Vol. 1, pp.). Hillsdale, NJ: Erlbaum.

Zung, W. K. (1965). A self-rating depression scale. *Archives of General Psychiatry, 12,* 63–70.

7

Depression and Self-directed Attention

ROBERT F. MUSSON
LAUREN B. ALLOY
Northwestern University

Depression has long been described as being a withdrawal into the self. External involvement is reduced in each area of functioning in depression and seems to reflect a turning inward of attention. Emotionally, there is a loss of involvement in activities or with other people. Cognitively, there is a preoccupation with self-critical thoughts. Behaviorally, there is a preference for solitary, nondemanding activities. Physically, there is a preoccupation with bodily functioning. Indeed, ever since the turn of the century—when psychological causes of depression were first proposed—preoccupation with the self has played an important part in many theories of depression, including psychodynamic (Abraham, 1911; Freud, 1917/1957), behavioral (Bandura, 1969, 1977; Rehm, 1977), cognitive (Beck, 1967), social (Coates & Wortman, 1980), phenomenological (Rogers, 1959), and dispositional (Eysenck, 1967) perspectives.

In recent years, a line of research has evolved on the effects of directing attention onto the self. This research, conducted by social and personality psychologists (e.g., Carver & Scheier, 1981; Duval & Wicklund, 1972; Fenigstein, Scheier, & Buss, 1975), shows that self-directed attention can—under certain circumstances—produce effects that are remarkably similar to many symptoms and characteristics of depression. The purpose of this chapter is to compare the research findings for these two phenomena: depression (nonpsychotic, nonbipolar) and self-directed attention. We hope that such a comparison will increase our understanding of some of the attentional processes that may contribute to a depressive episode.

SELF-DIRECTED ATTENTION: CONCEPT, MANIPULATION, AND ASSESSMENT

Before examining the parallels between depression and self-directed attention, it will be useful to discuss briefly the concept of self-directed attention and research investigating its manipulation and assessment. Wicklund and Duval (1971; Duval & Wicklund, 1972) were the first researchers to study experimentally the effects of attention focused on the self as compared with that focused on the environment. In their view, an increase in self-focused attention, or "objective self-awareness," as they originally called it, means an increase in the proportion of time that one's attention is directed toward the self. In general, the notion of attending to the self refers to a condition of heightened awareness of any aspect of oneself. Thus self-attention might involve focusing on one's own physical sensations, for example, or on one's own emotions, or even on the standards one has set for oneself.

Studies designed to investigate the effects of self-focus are based on the assumption that direction of attention can be manipulated systematically. Experiments based on this view differ from the majority of designs used in psychological research, according to Carver and Scheier (1981). Most experimenters vary the input to which their various subject groups are exposed. In this body of research, by contrast, "manipulations of attentional focus are intended to vary the *selective processing of information that is already available to all subjects*" (Carver & Scheier, 1981, p. 41; emphasis added). Manipulations used in self-awareness experiments are designed to push subjects into increasing the degree of attention focused on the self. Such methods include having subjects face their own mirror images or listen to a tape recording of themselves speaking. Methods used to decrease the degree of self-focus involve exposing subjects to an attention-demanding distractor (such as a dramatic television program) while they work on some experimental task.

The strongest evidence that a person is in a state of heightened self-awareness, according to researchers in this area, is an increase in the number of self-references that he or she makes. This has been the basis for validating many of the frequently used self-focusing manipulations (Carver & Scheier, 1978; Davis & Brock, 1975; Geller & Shaver, 1976). The typical method used in these validation experiments is to measure a subject's tendency to read self-referent content into ambiguous or incomplete verbal material (Wicklund & Hormuth, 1981) in the presence versus the absence of the self-focusing manipulation (e.g., a mirror).

To this point, we have discussed the manipulation of the *state* of self-directed attention. A parallel line of investigation conducted by personality psychologists has examined the *trait,* or disposition, to be self-focused. Fenigstein *et al.* (1975) developed a scale to measure individual differences in "self-consciousness," or the tendency to be self-focused. Three distinct factors have emerged from statistical analyses of the items contained in their Self-Consciousness Scale: Private Self-consciousness, Public Self-consciousness, and Social Anxiety. "Private self-consciousness" is the tendency to be attentive to the "covert" aspects of the self, such as one's own thoughts and attitudes. "Public self-consciousness" is the tendency to be attentive to aspects of the self that are potentially attended to by others, such as grooming and speech. "Social anxiety" seems to be a product of public self-consciousness for certain individuals, such that they tend to be uneasy about the way they are perceived by others; thus it is the tendency to react in a particular way to being focused on the public self. Private and public self-consciousness are not opposite tendencies. Correlations of the subscales for these two dispositions are consistently found to be positive, although typically they are low. This means that a person might be highly disposed to attend to only one or the other of these self-aspects, or to both or neither.

For our purposes, it is important to note that the tendency to be attentive to *private* self-aspects has been found to parallel closely the mirror-present manipulation of self-awareness (Carver & Scheier, 1978; Scheier, 1976; Scheier & Carver, 1977). However, other manipulations (e.g., audiences) must be used to obtain effects that closely resemble *public* self-consciousness. Carver and Scheier (1981) speculate that mirrors serve to focus attention on the private self (despite their function of reflecting public self-aspects) because they are usually encountered in circumstances where observation by others is unlikely; however, if a mirror is perceived by subjects as being a one-way window, "its private nature very likely disappears" (p. 50).

THEORETICAL MODELS OF SELF-DIRECTED ATTENTION

Much of the research on self-directed attention stems from Duval and Wicklund's (1972) theory of objective self-awareness and Carver and Scheier's (1981) theoretical model of self-regulation. In Duval and Wicklund's model, a state of self-awareness simply involves a situation in which a person spends an increased proportion of time thinking about some aspect of the self. According to these authors, for each self-aspect on which a person may focus attention, certain standards or ideal goals are developed. Just which aspect of the self becomes salient, in Duval and Wicklund's view, is typically influenced by situational factors. Thus, for example, a reminder notice to schedule an appointment with one's dentist might lead a person to focus on the current state of his or her dental hygiene. Duval and Wicklund argue that increased self-awareness naturally leads a person to compare the way he or she is with the way he or she would like to be. This comparison will most often reveal a negative discrepancy—a falling short of the goal—according to the model. Awareness of a negative discrepancy is said to produce self-criticism which, in turn, creates a state of tension and discomfort in the individual. This heightens the motivation to be more consistent with the relevant goals. However, it is often easier to relieve the discomfort by reducing the level of self-awareness. (It should be noted that the amount of discomfort that the person experiences is said to be a function of both the size of the discrepancy and the porportion of time he or she spends attending to it.) It will be most convenient for us to discuss the effects of discomfort and of reducing self-focus in other sections below.

Carver and Scheier's (1981) model also involves a discrepancy-reduction process in which self-directed attention plays a key role. Theirs is a kind of cybernetic or information-processing model of the human system of self-regulation. The main difference between their theory and that of Duval and Wicklund exists in the mechanism postulated by each model to underlie the behavior that follows increased awareness of a discrepancy. According to Duval and Wicklund, this behavior (i.e., behavior aimed at reducing either the discrepancy or the awareness of it) is *motivated* by a need to reduce the aversiveness of the recently created tension or drive state. According to Carver and Scheier's model, this behavior is simply the "negative feedback" (i.e., discrepancy-reducing) portion of a self-regulating system. Simply put, feedback used in the regulation of a system is said to be negative (or "corrective") when the *activation* of one component of the system leads to the *deactivation* of another component. The term "negative feedback" refers to its function of conveying information on the extent to which a discrepancy has been *negated*. The use of an illustration can help to clarify this further.

The illustration used most often to explain the concept of a self-regulating system is that of a thermostat connected to a furnace. The relevant standard in this situation is the temperature-level position that is set on the indicator of the thermostat. The role of the thermostat is to *monitor* the actual room temperature (through the thermometer that it contains) and *compare* it to the level set on its indicator. Thus, in this system, the *control* function resides in the thermostat. Consider the example of a situation in which the room temperature has dropped well below the level at which the thermostat has been set. Once it detects the deviation, the thermostat activates the furnace. The furnace then supplies additional heat, which is the system's *output* function. A negative feedback loop is completed when the thermostat detects that this additional heat is sufficient to eliminate the discrepancy (i.e., that the room temperature again matches that of the setting) and deactivates the furnace.

Carver and Scheier's (1981) model also involves a negative feedback loop. Their conceptualization is that people regulate their behavior through a series of feedback systems. As part of this process, perceived input about various aspects of the self is compared with certain reference standards. In their scheme, this comparison process results from focusing attention onto some aspect of the self (when some behavioral standard is salient). The overall function of this system is to keep sensed discrepancies to a minimum. When a discrepancy is perceived to be significant, then the functional output of the system—the person's behavior—is adjusted. In their view, then, behavioral self-regulation is a continual adjustment process. The role played by self-focus in this process is similar to that played by a thermostat in a heating system; it serves to monitor the match between the present state of the system and its intended state.

An additional aspect of Carver and Scheier's model—distinct from the loop we just described—is said to be engaged whenever a self-aware person either anticipates or experiences difficulty in matching a salient standard. According to these authors, such situations produce uncertainty in the person, which, in turn, triggers a process in which the probability of meeting the standard is assessed. When this occurs, behavior aimed at reducing the discrepancy is temporarily interrupted. If the assessment process results in a positive expectancy, the model predicts that the person will resume his or her attempt to reduce the discrepancy. If, however, the result is a negative expectancy, the person is predicted to withdraw from further attempts (cf. Klinger, 1975; Lewin, 1935). Unless the situation prevents it, this withdrawal will take the form of physical departure from the situation, according to the model. When physical withdrawal is not possible, however, Carver and Scheier predict that the person will withdraw mentally. It is assumed that self-focus will exaggerate the effects of expectancy on these predicted responses—enhancing the persistence of discrepancy-reducing efforts with positive expectancy and strengthening the urge to withdraw with negative expectancy. The theory also postulates that the expectancy-assessment process has affective consequences as well, depending on the nature and size of the discrepancy and the subjective importance of the dimension in question. Positive expectancy is presumed to lead to a certain amount of positive affect; negative expectancy should lead to negative affect.

In the sections that follow, we examine the parallels between the research findings on the consequences of being depressed and those related to being self-focused. In particular, we discuss six points of comparison, including cognitive, affective, and behavioral effects. When these findings are compared, a remarkable pattern emerges. Each of the effects produced by self-directed attention is characteristic of naturally occurring depression. An additional point of comparison suggests that attentional distraction away from the self has similar effects on both depression and self-awareness. Finally, we briefly review studies that have explicitly examined the relationship between depression and self-directed attention and suggest directions for future research that may serve to clarify their interrelation.

PARALLEL EFFECTS OF DEPRESSION AND SELF-DIRECTED ATTENTION

Increased Preoccupation with the Self

We have already noted that a consideration of the symptoms of depression suggests that self-preoccupation characterizes this disorder. More direct evidence, however, comes from a study by Hinchliffe, Lancashire, and Roberts (1971) indicating that depressed patients, relative to surgical controls, exhibited significantly higher numbers of personal references (and lower numbers of nonpersonal references) despite having lower overall rates of speech in 5-minute speech samples. More recently, Jacobson and Anderson (1982) found that depressed students could be distinguished from nondepressed students by their greater tendency to make unsolicited self-references in interactions with a confederate.

The effects of self-focus lead to a similar pattern of results. Carver and Scheier (1978), for example, found that subjects working with a mirror present made proportionately more self-centered sentence completions than when working without a mirror. Ickes, Layden, and Barnes (1978) also demonstrated that self-focus increases self-preoccupation. Subjects placed in a self-focusing condition gave more responses to a "Who am I?" questionnaire (describing the self) than did controls.

Increased Discomfort and Intensified Emotional Experience

Depression is, almost by definition, a negative emotional experience that is so intense it is painful. The discomfort connected with depression is well known and is reflected in the way in which depressed patients describe themselves. According to Beck (1967), many depressed individuals respond to the question "How do you feel?" with words such as miserable, hopeless, blue, sad, lonely, unhappy, useless, downhearted, humiliated, ashamed, worried, guilty. Further, he reports that 70% of a group of severely depressed patients indicated in a survey that they were "so sad that it was very painful; or that they were so sad they could not stand it" (Beck, 1967, p. 17). Coyne (1976) also views certain depressive symptoms, such as weeping and moping, as strong signals of a deep underlying misery, while among the physical symptoms of depression, sleep and appetite disturbance are probably the clearest signs of discomfort.

There is evidence that discomfort and intensified emotional experience are associated with self-directed attention as well. According to Duval and Wicklund (1972), the self-focused person has a heightened awareness of how he or she would like to be ("ideal self") as well as of how he or she really is ("real self"). Hence Duval and Wicklund argue that self-directed attention increases the salience of any perceived personal shortcoming[1] and, depending on the size of the discrepancy, produces discomfort. The self-focused person can seek relief by dealing with either component of the self-evaluative state—the self-focus or the discrepancy (Wicklund & Hormuth, 1981). Self-focus can be decreased either by avoiding stimuli that provoke self-attention or by seeking distractions. Discrepancies can be reduced either by changing the personal standard involved or by behaving in closer accordance with that standard. Wicklund (1975) theorizes that normally the self-focused person's immediate reaction to the discomfort of this state is avoidance of self-focusing stimuli because this eliminates the negative affect most quickly, even if only temporarily. Carver and Scheier (1981) disagree; they contend that self-focus produces discomfort *only* when a discrepancy cannot be reduced, not merely because it exists. Whatever the case may be, both sides agree that when a negative discrepancy is difficult to reduce, self-focus will produce discomfort.

One of the earliest experiments on the discomforting effects of heightened self-awareness was conducted by Duval, Wicklund, and Fine (1972). Just prior to the start of a sham experimental session, subjects were presented with feedback from a bogus personality evaluation that was either extremely favorable or extremely unfavorable. The experimental room in which subjects were individually placed contained both a large wall mirror and a TV camera that faced either toward or away from the subject. Before being left alone in the room, each subject was told that the experimenter had been delayed and that the subject was to wait about 5 minutes for his return. Subjects were told that they were free to leave if he did not appear within that time. It was expected that subjects with a large discrepancy (unfavorable feedback) whose self-attention was heightened (i.e., who faced their mirror images) would leave the experimental room sooner than any other group. Indeed, a significant avoidance effect of this kind was obtained. Further, Archer, Hormuth, and Berg (1979; also cited in Wicklund & Hormuth, 1981), in a study assessing discomfort through self-report, reported that subjects in a heightened self-awareness (mirror-present) condition found that talking out loud to themselves was less enjoyable when the topics were intimate and that they felt worse about themselves than did subjects in a "less self-aware" (mirror-absent) condition. There is also evidence to suggest that when a person meets or exceeds some personal standard, self-focused attention is not aversive (Gibbons & Wicklund, 1976; Greenberg & Musham, 1981); however, given a salient negative discrepancy, self-directed attention appears to produce discomfort.

Carver, Blaney, and Scheier (1979) suggested an additional factor that may influence the degree of discomfort experienced following self-focus: the expectancy of being able to reduce the discrepancy. Carver *et al.,* (1979) created a large negative discrepancy for all of their subjects on a bogus test of abstract reasoning. Half the subjects were given a negative expectancy by informing them that performance on the first task was highly predictive of performance on the second. The rest of the subjects were given a favorable expectancy. Carver *et al.* found that subjects with unfavorable expectancies were significantly less persistent on the second task in a mirror's presence than in its absence. However, subjects in the positive expectancy condition either were not affected by the presence of the mirror (Experiment 1) or were more persistent on the second task (Experiment 2). In sum, the evidence suggests that self-directed attention does indeed produce discomfort, but only in situations in which the person has little hope of being able to close the gap between his or her real and ideal selves.

Scheier (1976) reported evidence that self-directed attention is also associated with intensified emotional experience. He reasoned that to the degree an emotion is the salient aspect of oneself, attention directed to the self will gravitate to that emotion and intensify its subjective experience. To test this notion, Scheier conducted an experiment in which all the subjects engaged in aggressive behavior toward a confederate in either the presence or the absence of a mirror. Prior to this phase, Scheier attempted to increase the anger level of half the subjects by having the confederate provoke them. Scheier found that self-focused subjects who had been provoked gave significantly higher self-ratings of anger levels than did the provoked subjects who were not exposed to a mirror. This difference was also expressed behaviorally in that the provoked subjects were significantly more aggressive toward the confederate in the presence of a mirror than in its absence. Similarly, Scheier and Carver (1977) found that either the state of self-focus or the dispositional tendency to be high in private self-consciousness intensified the experience of attraction or repulsion, elation or depression.

An important question is whether self-focused attention intensifies an emotion directly or whether it accomplishes this by increasing awareness of one's internal state. Gibbons, Carver, Scheier, and Hormuth (1979) employed a placebo drug to investigate this issue. If self-attention provides greater awareness of one's internal state, then self-focused subjects should be less susceptible to experiencing placebo effects. In this study, all subjects ingested a small amount of baking soda. Some of the subjects were told that this substance was a drug that would produce arousal symptoms; the rest, who were not led to expect side effects, served as controls. Self-focus was manipulated through the use of a mirror when subjects responded to a checklist of symptoms later in the session. Gibbons *et al.* found that subjects in the placebo group who worked without a mirror reported having significantly more of the suggested symptoms than did controls. However, placebo-group subjects who worked in the presence of the mirror were far less likely to report having the suggested symptoms; the difference between this group and the controls was virtually eliminated, thus supporting the self-awareness interpretation. Gibbons and Gaeddert (1984) also concluded that self-focused attention increases awareness of an internal state, but not necessarily awareness of the cause of that state. These findings suggest that the increased salience of an internal state that is produced by self-directed attention is the result of increased awareness of that state.

Lowered Self-esteem

Low self-esteem is a hallmark among the cognitive symptoms of depression (Beck, 1967; Bibring, 1953; Freud, 1917/1957). In fact, Beck (1967) was so struck by the pervasiveness of low self-esteem among his depressed patients that he hypothesized a causal role for it in depression. Laxer (1964) found that relative to control subjects, a group of depressives gave low real-self ratings shortly after hospital admission. This produced a large gap between real-self and ideal-self ratings, suggesting a low level of self-esteem. However, this gap narrowed as the patients recovered from their depressions. Additional support for a relationship between depression and low self-esteem was obtained by Nadich, Gargan, and Michael (1975). These investigators found a small, but statistically significant, correlation between depression and the difference between subject ratings of aspirations (ideal self) and achievements (real self; see also Blatt, D'Affliti, & Quinlan, 1976).

In considering the effects of self-directed attention, recall that such attention is thought to elicit self-evaluation (Duval & Wicklund, 1972). Wicklund (1975) reasoned that the more time spent in the self-focused state, the more the various aspects of the self-dimension in focus will be examined. The longer a person engages in self-examination, the more likely he or she is to find a personal shortcoming. And, it is the awareness of a major shortcoming (i.e., a negative discrepancy between the real and ideal selves) that causes one to suffer loss in self-esteem.[2]

To test the notion that self-focus lowers self-esteem (given a negative discrepancy), Ickes, Wicklund, and Ferris (1973, Experiment 3) manipulated both evaluative feedback and self-attention. They found that following negative feedback on a fictitious trait, self-ratings on *familiar* trait dimensions (e.g., intelligence) were significantly reduced by self-focused (mirror-present) attention. Self-focus also served to increase self-ratings for familiar traits following positive feedback, although this tendency was not statistically significant. This finding fits with Wicklund's (1975) revision of self-awareness theory, suggesting that an increase in self-esteem results from a positive discrepancy made salient by an increase in self-attention. Another indication that self-directed attention may help reduce self-esteem is the finding that self-focusing stimuli can produce the same kinds of behavior that characterize people with low self-esteem. For example, Wicklund and Duval (1971) found that subjects were more conforming when their attention was focused on themselves. Several studies (e.g., Janis, 1954) have reported high levels of conformity for people with low self-esteem. Additionally, Turner, Scheier, Carver, and Ickes (1978) obtained a significant negative correlation between individual-difference measures of self-consciousness and self-esteem. Their results indicated that the more a person tends to be aware of himself or herself, the lower is his or her self-esteem.

Brockner (1979b) contends that people with low self-esteem exhibit impaired task performance because they tend to focus more of their attention on themselves than on the task. To investigate this notion, Brockner (1979a; 1979b) conducted a series of studies. Reasoning that those *high* in self-esteem (high SEs) typically are neither self-focused nor anxious during task performance, he predicted that increasing the self-attention of high SEs would not interfere with their task performance to the extent that it would for subjects with low self-esteem (low SEs). Brockner also expected that by attracting attention to the task (and thereby distracting it away from the self), he could improve the performance of low SEs. As predicted, Brockner's (1979b) first study showed that self-focusing stimuli tended to adversely affect the performance of low SEs but did not affect that of medium or high SEs. In addition, a *task*-focusing manipulation dramatically improved the performance of low SEs but had no effect on the performance of those with higher self-esteem.

These findings suggest that increasing the level of self-focus of individuals with low self-esteem impairs their task performance (unless an effective external distraction is available). However, Brockner (1979a) noted the Ickes *et al.* (1973) findings (described previously) and reasoned that it is not always necessary to reduce the self-focus of those with low self-esteem in order to improve their task performances. He argued that a recent success experience changes the effects of self-directed attention such that the person increases the attention given to his or her positive aspects. In terms of self-awareness theory, a positive discrepancy is produced, resulting in higher self-esteem, positive expectancy, and efficient task performance.

Thus, in a follow-up study, Brockner (1979a) gave high and low SEs either success or failure feedback in the presence or the absence of a mirror. As expected, the presence of the mirror facilitated the performance of low SEs who had received positive feedback, and impaired the performance of low SEs who had been given negative feedback. However, the type of feedback made no difference for low SEs working without a mirror; performance levels for these groups were not significantly different from each other. In addition, the feedback had little effect on high SEs. When compared with low SEs though, high SEs performed markedly better in the negative feedback condition; this was especially true for those working in the presence of the mirror, mainly because it impaired the performance of the low SEs so much. However, when coupled with positive feedback, the presence of the mirror facilitated the performance of low SEs such that they did *as well as* the high SEs. In a parallel finding, the performance of those high in dispositional self-consciousness (in the absence of the mirror) followed the same pattern as that of low SEs with a mirror: They performed well with positive feedback and poorly with negative feedback.

Higher Standards and Increased Salience of Standards

To this point, we have discussed the increased awareness of the real self produced by self-focused attention, and the potential effects this has on self-esteem. But an equally important role in theories of self-directed attention is played by standards. The higher or more inflexible a given behavioral standard, other things being equal, the more difficult it is to attain. This, too, would be conducive to creating a large negative discrepancy and hence to reducing self-esteem. It is possible that the low self-esteem characteristic of depression and of self-focus in the presence of negative discrepancies is produced by high standards, or by an increased awareness of unattainable standards, as well as by an increased awareness of one's real self on various behavioral dimensions.

Golin and Terrell (1977) examined the aspiration levels (i.e., standards) and expectancies for success of mildly depressed and nondepressed college students on a skill task and on a task involving chance. They found that the two groups did not differ in expectations for success but that the depressed students had significantly higher levels of aspiration, particularly for the skill task. Research done by LaPointe and Crandell (1980) and by Nelson (1977) also provides support for the view that depressed individuals maintain higher self-expectations relative to nondepressed individuals. In contrast, Kanfer and Zeiss (1983) did not find higher standards in depressed versus nondepressed students, but did find that the depressed students exhibited a larger discrepancy between interpersonal standards and actual behaviors than did the nondepressed students. There is also evidence to suggest that standards are more salient to depressives and that they place more weight on measuring up to their standards than nondepressives (Rehm, 1977; Chapter 5, this volume).

Higher standards and increased salience of standards are also characteristic of self-directed attention. This was well demonstrated in a study by Scheier and Wicklund (cited in Wicklund, 1975). Subjects were told that they had scored poorly on a test of psychological mindedness. These subjects then completed a real-self–ideal-self questionnaire that included a dimension of psychological mindedness. On that dimension, the experimenter marked in the real-self rating at the low end of the scale for all subjects, whereas the subjects were free to mark in their ideal on that dimension, either with a mirror present or without a mirror. Subjects who made their ratings in the presence of a mirror indicated a significantly higher ideal self for psychological mindedness than did subjects who rated themselves without a mirror being present. This implies that in conditions in which the real self is seen as being fixed, self-directed attention may lead to heightened standards.

Self-directed attention leads to an increased concern with matching one's behavior to a standard that has become salient, according to Scheier and Carver (1983, Experiment 1). In their study to investigate this notion, these authors hypothesized that self-focus would increase the amount of time subjects would spend referring to a performance standard in an experimental task. The task they used involved having subjects attempt to reproduce complex drawings of overlaid geometric figures. The standard for this task was the accuracy of the subjects' drawings. The prototype drawings were presented to the subjects via rear-projected slides on a screen positioned directly in front of their work stations. Although subjects were allowed to view each of the slides as often as they wished, they were not permitted to draw while the prototypes were on display. When a slide was not being projected, some subjects simply saw a blank screen (control condition) and the rest were exposed to a reflective screen (self-focusing condition). Scheier and Carver's (1983, Experiment 1) predictions were confirmed. Subjects in the self-focusing condition referred to the slides more often than did the subjects in the other group. These findings were later conceptually replicated on the basis of dispositional self-consciousness.

Froming, Walker, and Lopyan (1982) investigated the effects of manipulating the salience of conflicting—public and private—standards in an experimental situation. They selected subjects who reported believing both that (1) punishment is a relatively ineffective and inappropriate way to promote learning, and (2) most people hold the opposite view and endorse the use of punishment. Some time later, in what they thought was a different study, subjects were instructed to deliver shocks to a (confederate) co-subject as punishments for incorrect answers. Thus, their use of punishment was contrary to the belief that they had expressed earlier. For some of the subjects, the salience of *private* self-aspects was increased by having them work in front of a mirror. For other subjects, an attempt was made to increase the salience of *public* self-aspects in two separate groups, each of which involved having observers present during the sessions. Subjects in one of these latter groups were told that the observers were evaluating their effectiveness as teachers; those in the other group were merely told that some advanced students would be observing their performance.

Froming *et al.* (1982, Experiment 1) found that subjects who worked in the presence of a mirror adhered more closely to their previously expressed beliefs; they inflicted shocks of significantly lower intensity than did those in the other groups. Subjects who worked in the presence of evaluative observers inflicted shocks of significantly higher intensity than did those in the other groups. Subjects who worked in front of the nonevaluative observers inflicted shocks at a level midway between those used in these other two groups. Froming *et al.* concluded that the mirror-present subjects showed greater adherence to their privately held beliefs because their awareness of the *private* self was increased, which made their internal standards salient. Froming *et al.* also concluded that subjects in the evaluative-observer group showed greater conformity to the perceived group standard because their awareness of the *public* self was increased, which made salient their belief that most people are in favor of punishment. (Tabachnik, Crocker, & Alloy, 1983, suggest that a frequent basis of self-evaluative standards for depressives may be consensus information, i.e., comparison of themselves with similar others.)

Several inferences may be drawn from these findings. First, it appears that self-focus can increase the salience of a given standard, which may have the effect of making that standard higher or more inflexible. In addition, increasing the level of self-attention leads a person to compare his or her behavior more often with a salient standard. This suggests that self-focus promotes one's efforts to conform to a salient standard. However, this all seems to be dependent on having the standard in question be relevant to the self-aspect which is most in focus.

Increased Tendency to Attribute a Causal Role to the Self

A reliable phenomenon in social psychology is that people tend to attribute positive outcomes to internal causal factors and negative outcomes to external causal factors, a tendency referred to as the "self-serving attributional bias" or "attributional egotism" (e.g., Greenwald, 1980; Miller & Ross, 1975; Snyder, Stephan, & Rosenfield, 1978). Most people also tend to attribute positive events to more stable (chronic over time) and global (general across situations) causes than negative events (e.g., Peterson & Seligman, 1984; Sweeney, Anderson, & Bailey, 1986). Interestingly, recent evidence suggests that this "self-serving" attributional style only characterizes nondepressed individuals. In contrast, depressed individuals have been hypothesized (Abramson, Seligman, & Teasdale, 1978) and found to make internal, stable, and global attributions for negative outcomes, and external, unstable, and specific attributions for positive outcomes *relative to* nondepressed individuals (for reviews, see Miller & Moretti, Chapter 9, this volume; Peterson & Seligman, 1984; Sweeney *et al.*, 1986).

However, the attributional style of depressives can also be characterized as being more "evenhanded"—that is, similar for both positive and negative events—than that of nondepressives (e.g., Alloy, 1982c; Miller & Moretti, Chapter 9, this volume; Raps, Reinhard, Peterson, Abramson, & Seligman, 1982). Of particular interest for our purposes is that depressives' attributions are not only evenhanded but also relatively internal for both positive and negative outcomes (e.g., Klein, Fencil-Morse, & Seligman, 1976; Kuiper, 1978; Rizley, 1978). That is, depressives tend to ascribe relatively more causal responsibility for both positive and negative outcomes to themselves than to other possible causes.

The tendency to attribute a causal role to the self, regardless of outcome, is also associated with heightened self-attention. Duval and Wicklund (1973, Experiment 2) presented subjects with both negative and positive hypothetical outcomes and increased self-focus for half of the subjects by introducing a mirror. As predicted, the presence of the mirror produced more attributions to the self than did the no-mirror condition, regardless of whether the outcome was positive or negative. Buss and Scheier (1976) replicated Duval and Wicklund's finding with dispositional self-consciousness. They found that those who were high in private self-consciousness attributed a higher percentage of responsibility to the self for the situational outcomes than did those who were low in private self-consciousness. In addition, there was a triple interaction, such that subjects high in private self-consciousness tended to take less of the credit for positive outcomes and more of the blame for negative outcomes when a mirror was present than they did when a mirror was absent. It may be that a condition of greatly heightened self-focus, that is, a person high in private self-consciousness being confronted by his or her own mirror image, tends to intensify self-examination, which, in turn, makes a person more self-critical. Recall that depressives also take more responsibility for negative than for positive outcomes relative to nondepressives.

Duval, Duval, and Neely (1979) also investigated the effects of self-directed attention on the attribution process, in a study of helping behavior. They predicted that an increase in self-attention would lead to an increase in self-attribution of responsibility to provide help. Subjects viewed a videotape on poverty in Latin America. Of the five conditions included in the experimental design, two were intended to heighten self-focused attention and involved having subjects fill out a biographical questionnaire.[3] One condition had a 4-minute time delay between filling out the biographical questionnaire and viewing the videotape, whereas the other had no delay. Duval *et al.* (1979) predicted that subjects with no delay would feel more responsibility for, and be more willing to help, poverty-stricken Latin Americans than would subjects in the 4-minute-delay condition. This prediction was based on Heider's (1958) hypothesis that reducing the time interval separating an event and an agent increases the tendency to attribute responsibility to that agent. Duval *et al.* (1979) suggested that this principle also applies to the time interval that separates periods of increased awareness of event and agent. Hence they expected that the smaller the interval between heightened awareness of the self and heightened awareness of a situation (such as Latin American poverty), the greater the likelihood of a subject's connecting the self and the situation.

The results were as expected. Subjects who viewed the videotape right after completing the biographical questionnaire gave significantly higher ratings of personal responsibility on the average than did those with a 4-minute delay or any of those in the control groups. In addition, subjects with no delay exhibited greater willingness to expend time, effort, and money to help than did those in the 4-minute-delay condition or in the control groups.

Although several studies have supported Duval and Wicklund's (1973) contention that self-directed attention leads to an increase in causal attributions to the self, a finding by Federoff and Harvey (1976) indicates that there are some conditions in which this tendency does not operate. They suggested that when a situation is highly ego involving, self-focus may increase "self-defensive" tendencies and thus lead to internal attributions for positive outcomes but external attributions for negative outcomes, rather than increasing self-attributions for both kinds of outcomes. However, Carver and Scheier (1981) argued that the use of a camera in the Federoff and Harvey study to increase self-awareness probably had the effect of making self-presentational concerns the most prominent standard. This follows from their earlier finding that a TV camera tends to increase one's awareness of his or her *public* self-aspects. Therefore the bulk of the evidence continues to indicate that heightening private self-focus increases the tendency to assign a causal role to the self for a salient outcome.

Increased Accuracy of Self-reports

A problem that has bothered psychologists for a long time is that one frequently used source of information, the subject himself or herself, is often highly unreliable when reporting on his or her own behavior. Some theorists hold that people have very limited access to their own cognitive processes (e.g., Nisbett & Wilson, 1977). This, they argue, makes them poor self-observers. In this section, we review evidence on distortion versus accuracy in reporting information about the self.

In contrast to Beck's (1967) model of depression, which suggests that depressed people distort reality in a negative direction, recent research has indicated that depressives are often more accurate or realistic than nondepressives in making self-relevant judgments in a variety of situations (for review, see Abramson & Alloy, 1981; Alloy & Abramson, Chapter 8, this volume). For example, Alloy and Abramson (1979) found that depressed students were highly accurate in judging the amount of control they exerted over both positive and negative outcomes, whereas nondepressed students overestimated their control over good outcomes that were uncontrollable and underestimated their control over bad outcomes that were controllable.

Similarly, Golin and his colleagues (Golin, Terrell, & Johnson, 1977; Golin, Terrell, Weitz, & Drost, 1979) found that depressed students and psychiatric inpatients were more accurate than nondepressed students and patients in providing expectancies for success on a task involving chance into which elements of skill tasks (self-involvement) were introduced. Whereas nondepressives' reported expectations for success were inappropriately higher than the objective probabilities of success, depressives' expectations were in line with the objective probabilities. Lewinsohn, Mischel, Chaplain, and Barton (1980) also obtained evidence for the depressive realism effect among clinically depressed subjects. Depressed outpatients' self-perceptions of their social competence were in line with objective observers' perceptions of them, whereas nondepressed outpatients and normal controls overestimated their social competence as compared with the ratings of the observers (see Alloy & Abramson, Chapter 8, this volume, for many other examples of depressive realism).

It is interesting that almost all of the studies that have demonstrated depressive realism involved perceptions or judgments that were directly related to the self in some way. If it is assumed that depressives are preoccupied with themselves, as the parallels between depression and self-directed attention reviewed so far would suggest, then their greater accuracy in perceiving themselves may be the product of asking them to make judgments about the very object on which their attention is focused (see Alloy, 1982a). That is, if depressives are characterized by increased self-focus, then this may lead them to be more self-aware (cf., Gibbons, 1983). It would follow from this line of reasoning that depressives should be less accurate when asked to make judgments about others. In other words, the superiority depressives show over nondepressives in making accurate judgments as *actors* should disappear when they are in the position of *observer*. Support for this prediction was obtained recently in a study by Martin, Abramson, and Alloy (1984). Whereas depressed students were significantly more accurate than nondepressed students in judging their personal control over a positive, uncontrollable outcome, depressed students in the observer position tended to overestimate the level of control another person exerted (for similar findings, see also Alloy & Ahrens, 1987; Crocker, Alloy, & Kayne, in press; Golin *et al.*, 1977; Tabachnik *et al.*, 1983; for reviews of self–other differences in depressive realism, see Alloy & Abramson, Chapter 8, this volume; Alloy, Albright, & Clements, 1987).

A heightened level of self-attention also has been found to be associated with increased accuracy of self-reports. This was demonstrated in a study by Pryor, Gibbons, Wicklund, Fazio, and Hood (1977, Experiment 2). These researchers set out to investigate whether attention focused on the self would increase the accuracy of information reported about objective information recalled from memory. Subjects were asked to list their combined SAT scores and the percentile rank of their psychology midterm grades in either the presence or the absence of a mirror. Pryor *et al.* found that SAT scores reported in the presence of a mirror were much closer to the subjects' true scores than those reported in the mirror's absence. There was no significant effect for the percentile ranking on the psychology exam. In commenting on this finding, Carver and Scheier (1981) point out that it is unlikely that subjects had ever encoded their exam scores in memory in terms of percentile rank; it seems probable that self-focus enhances recall only for information that has been encoded. Similar to Pryor *et al.*'s findings for manipulated self-focus were the findings of Scheier, Buss, and Buss (1978), who demonstrated that subjects high in private self-consciousness gave more accurate ratings of their hostility as reflected in their behavior than subjects low in private self-consciousness.

Pryor *et al.* (1977, Experiment 1) also tested whether a person's self-reported behavior would correlate more highly with his or her observed behavior when completed under conditions of heightened self-focus. To test this, Pryor *et al.* had male subjects rate themselves on a measure of sociability in either the presence or the absence of a mirror. Each subject returned to the lab within a few days for a second session and was required to wait for the experimenter in the presence of an attractive female confederate. A recording was made of their conversation via a hidden tape recorder. From the recording, one rating of sociability was obtained by counting the number of words spoken by the subject. A second rating was made by the confederate. As expected, the correlation between self-report and behavior for subjects in the self-directed-attention condition was quite high (average $r = .66$), whereas the correlation for those whose self-focus was not heightened turned out to be quite poor (average $r = .16$). Pryor and his associates explained these results by indicating that increasing a person's self-focus increases his or her motivation to achieve behavioral and cognitive consistency. Hence the self-focused subjects were motivated to report their past behaviors accurately on the sociability questionnaire. Carver and Scheier (1981) had a different explanation, however. In their view, self-focused attention "caused subjects to assess more completely the memories of past behaviors that were relevant to the questionnaire items. By considering a more representative sample of information, they were able to give more accurate reports of their normal behavioral tendencies" (Carver & Scheier, 1981, p. 274). For further evidence of increased accuracy of self-reports associated with self-directed attention, see Gibbons, 1978; Gibbons & Gaeddert, 1984; Gibbons *et al.*, 1979; Scheier, Carver, & Gibbons, 1979.

Effects of Distraction

Another similarity between depression and self-directed attention is that distraction can attenuate certain of their consequences—at least temporarily. For example,

Miller (1975) reviewed evidence strongly suggesting that external distraction leads to improvement in depressives' performance on motor and speed tests. Foulds (1952) found that certain types of neurotics (depressive, anxious, and obsessional) were significantly slower on a paper-and-pencil maze test than others (hysterics and psychopaths). However, the first three groups showed such great improvement in retesting with a distraction that the performance differences among the groups disappeared. Foulds later showed that these improvements were not due to differential practice effects among the groups. Shapiro, Campbell, Harris, and Dewsbery (1958) generalized the facilitating effects of distraction to psychotic as well as neurotic depressives. Foulds hypothesized that the impaired motor performance found for depressives in a number of experiments resulted from "over-attention to *internal* stimuli and that distraction draws . . . attention away from internal, affective disturbances" (cited in Miller, 1975, p. 248, emphasis added). It is interesting that Eysenck (1970) identified each of the three neurotic types (depressive, high-anxious, and obsessional) that benefited from distraction in Foulds's study as tending to be introverted. Because introversion involves the tendency to turn attention inward, this is consistent with Foulds's hypothesis. Eysenck also found that hysterics and psychopaths tended to be extroverted, which is also consistent with Foulds's finding that neither of these groups benefited from distraction.

A second relevant finding is that motor activity interferes with the accuracy of self-ratings of performance for depressives. According to Duval and Wicklund (1973), motor activity distracts attention away from the self by directing it outward. In two studies (Friedman, 1964; Loeb, Beck, & Diggory, 1971), depressed and nondepressed subjects made self-ratings of speed or ability on their performance of some motor task. Depressive realism findings for other types of tasks have shown that depressed individuals are often more accurate than nondepressives in rating themselves, as discussed previously. In these studies involving motor activity, however, depressed subjects underestimated their test performances. Perhaps the motor activity decreased the self-awareness of the depressives to such an extent that they viewed themselves inaccurately.

Attentional deficits that accompany depression can also possibly be explained by the monopolizing effects that self-directed attention has on attentional resources. If depressives are chronically self-focused, few resources would be available for attending to external tasks. Thus self-directed attention may lead to cognitive interference in a variety of areas. This reasoning may explain the findings of three studies reported by Miller (1975) that indicate reversibility in intellectual impairment during a depressive episode (Callagan, 1952; Davidson, 1939; Fisher, 1949). In each case, IQ scores increased for depressives following clinical improvement.

Miller (1975) speculated that depressives experience cognitive interference because of the distracting intrusion of personal thoughts and worries. Building on this notion of cognitive interference, Pasahow (1976) reasoned that an external distraction would improve the cognitive performance of depressives by drawing their attention away from irrelevant thoughts and worries. He also investigated the effect of a distractor on the cognitive performance of subjects given a helplessness pretreatment. Using a learned helplessness paradigm, Pasahow had depressed and nondepressed college students work on solvable, unsolvable, or control discrimination problems. Subjects then worked on a solvable anagram task in the presence or absence of a distractor consisting of a tape recording of tones from a metronome. Among other results, Pasahow found that the average of the pooled depressed–control and nondepressed–unsolvable pretreatment (i.e., helpless) groups performed worse than the nondepressed–control group when working without a distraction. However, there were nonsignificant differences among these groups with a distraction. Also noteworthy is that nondepressed–control subjects reported significantly fewer task-irrelevant thoughts than did either the depressed–control or the nondepressed–unsolvable task subjects; however, the presence of the distraction was associated with considerably fewer irrelevant thoughts among the latter two groups. This led Pasahow to conclude that the presence of a distractor produced a therapeutic effect on the performance of both the depressed–control and the helpless groups by decreasing their focus on irrelevant personal thoughts.

Coyne, Metalsky, and Lavelle (1980) also took the approach that a distraction could alleviate the cognitive interference that hampers performance in helplessness. Although they discussed the interference itself in terms of anxiety, their basic view was similar to Pasahow's: "For susceptible subjects, failure experiences elicit a task-irrelevant, negative focus on self" (Coyne *et al.*, 1980, p. 350). These researchers reasoned that a relaxing imagination exercise would reduce the negative self-preoccupation of subjects given a helplessness (failure) experience. Consistent with their predictions, Coyne *et al.* found that subjects in the failure pretreatment (i.e., helpless) group significantly benefited from the imagination exercise when it was accompanied by a rationale. (For similar therapeutic effects of distraction for helpless subjects, see also Snyder, Smoller, Strenta, & Frankel, 1981).

As it does with depression, distraction also reduces the consequences of self-directed attention. Duval and Wicklund (1972) argued that self-evaluation is difficult when a person is externally focused. This led Ferris and Wicklund (cited in Wicklund, 1975) to predict that self-criticism would be reduced if attention were diverted away from the self. To test this, subjects were required to inspect a series of rug samples and to record the extent to which they liked themselves after examining each piece. Each subject was exposed to a different television image during each of the three times he or she went through the series: a dramatic western program, a test pattern, and the subject's own face. The dramatic program was predicted to decrease self-focus, the subject's own image was predicted to heighten self-focus, and the test pattern was intended to serve as a neutral control. As predicted, the self-ratings made in the dramatic-program condition were significantly more positive than were those made in either of the other conditions. Thus the program appeared to be effective in distracting attention away from the self. Moreover, there was a main effect across the three levels of self-focused attention such that even the self-ratings made with the test pattern were significantly higher than those made in the "own-image" condition. Recall that Brockner (1979b) similarly found that focusing the attention of low-self-esteem subjects onto a concept-formation task produced a significant improvement in their performance on that task. He argued that this manipulation had distracted them from focusing on their shortcomings and had thereby reduced their anxiety.

In addition to reducing self-evaluation, external focus has been found to have another consequence: It reduces the tendency to attribute outcomes to the self. Duval and Wicklund (1973, Experiment 1) tested this by having subjects engage in a distracting physical activity (pursuit rotor task) while making attributions in the task described previously in the Increased Tendency to Attribute a Causal Role to the Self section. These investigators reasoned that physical activity would draw attention outward onto the environment because it is a process of acting on the environment. The results were consistent with the prediction. The combined percentage of self-blame for the physical-activity condition was significantly lower than for the control (i.e., nonactive) condition. Recall that the addition of a self-focusing manipulation (a mirror) to the second phase of this experiment produced a significantly greater number of attributions to the self than were made by subjects in the control condition. So, once again, a form of distraction led to behavior that was opposite to that produced by heightened self-focus.

Summary

We have reviewed a number of remarkable parallels between the characteristic features of naturally occurring depression and the behavioral and emotional effects of self-directed attention. These parallels suggest that depressed individuals may be characterized by a greater degree of self-focus than nondepressed individuals. Interestingly, although Foulds (1952) was apparently the first investigator to actually manipulate the attention of depressed subjects, only recently has a significant degree of interest in the possible relationship between depression and self-directed attention emerged (Alloy, 1982a; Ganellen & Blaney, 1981; Musson, 1981; Smith & Greenberg, 1981). In the following section, we review the findings of studies that have directly examined the relationship of these two phenomena.

STUDIES INVOLVING BOTH DEPRESSION AND SELF-DIRECTED ATTENTION

Direction of attention in depressed subjects: Is it focused primarily on private aspects of the self? A number of studies have examined the correlation between depression and self-directed attention. With the exception of one (Exner, 1973), these studies have found that depression is associated with self-focus (most often in the form of private self-consciousness). For example, Smith and Greenberg (1981) found that scores on both the Private Self-consciousness and the Social Anxiety subscales of the Self-Consciousness Scale (Fenigstein *et al.*, 1975) were significantly correlated with scores on the D-30 Scale (Dempsey, 1964), a depression measure derived from the Minnesota Multiphasic Personality Inventory (MMPI) depression scale. However, only Private Self-Consciousness produced a reliable partial correlation with depression in a subsample of "more depressed" subjects, r (87) =

.26 (but see Sacco & Hokanson, 1978). Ingram and Smith (1984, Study 1) also found private self-consciousness to be significantly related to a different measure of depression (BDI; Beck, 1967) in three separate samples: $r(168) = .23$, $r(215) = .32$, and $r(201) = .28$. In a second study, using the Self-Focus Sentence Completion Task (Exner, 1973) instead of the Self-Consciousness Scale, Ingram and Smith (1984) observed that depressed subjects had significantly higher neutral and negative self-focus scores and lower external focus scores than nondepressed subjects (see also Strack, Blaney, Ganellen, & Coyne, 1985). Further, Smith, Ingram, and Roth (1985, Study 1) demonstrated that whereas depression (BDI scores) correlated significantly with Private Self-Consciousness, test anxiety was reliably related to public, but not Private Self-Consciousness. Finally, in an extension to clinically depressed subjects, Ganellen, Blaney, Costello, and Scheier (1987) found that private self-consciousness (with public self-consciousness partialed out) correlated significantly with severity of depression in both a psychiatric outpatient and an inpatient sample, $r = .47$ and .51, respectively, but that public self-consciousness (with private self-consciousness partialed out) did not (see also Ingram, Lumry, Cruet, & Sieber, 1987). On balance then, the evidence indicates rather strongly that depression is indeed associated with a tendency to focus on private aspects of the self.

Effect on comfort: Is self-focus aversive for depressed individuals? Recall that the paradigm typically used in studies designed to investigate the aversiveness of self-directed attention involves a measure of the extent to which subjects expose themselves to self-focusing stimuli (e.g., Duval et al., 1972). Using this approach, Pyszczynski and Greenberg (1985) presented subjects with the task of working on two sets of word puzzles, one of which was positioned in front of a mirror, following prior success or failure feedback on a set of anagrams (represented as a test of verbal intelligence). After spending 3 minutes working on each of the two puzzle sets, subjects rated the degree to which they liked them and indicated their preference should they be given additional time to work on them. Surprisingly, depressed subjects expressed more liking for self-focus following *negative* feedback than following *positive* feedback; by contrast, nondepressed subjects expressed more liking for self-focus following positive feedback than following negative feedback, consistent with earlier findings of preference for self-focus following success rather than failure (e.g., Duval et al., 1972; Gibbons & Wicklund, 1976).

In a follow-up investigation (Pyszczynski & Greenberg, 1986), these researchers allowed subjects to allocate 10 minutes between the two puzzles (after having 3 minutes of "practice time" with each of them) in order to provide a behavioral measure of preference. Second, they added a control group of subjects who did not receive any pretask feedback. Consistent with a "depressive self-focusing style," depressed–positive feedback subjects spent reliably less time at the mirror position than did the depressed–control group, whereas those in the depressed–negative feedback group spent more time there compared with controls. For nondepressed subjects, there were no significant differences among the three groups. In another study, Greenberg and Pyszczynski (1986) found that both depressed and nondepressed subjects may engage in more self-focus after failure than after success immediately, but that only depressives continue to self-focus after failure over time, whereas nondepressives revert to greater self-focus following success.

In attempting to explain depressives' tendency to self-focus more following failure than success, Pyszczynski and Greenberg (1985) noted that this style is consistent with a large body of research indicating that depressives fail to exhibit many of the defensive cognitions characteristic of nondepressed individuals (for reviews, see Abramson & Alloy, 1981; Alloy & Abramson, Chapter 8, this volume). To the extent that the aversion to self-focus following negative outcomes that is typically seen in nondepressed persons is motivated by concerns for maintenance of self-esteem, depressives' failure to find such self-focus aversive may be due to the breakdown of the ability or motivation to defend self-esteem (Abramson & Alloy, 1981; Alloy & Abramson, 1982, and Chapter 8, this volume; Pyszczynski & Greenberg, 1985). Alternatively, Pyszczynski and Greenberg (1985) suggest that depressives' self-focusing style may represent a maladaptive attempt to cope with negative life events. By not avoiding self-focus after failure, depressives may promote low expectations and thus guard against disappointments. Although the best explanation for depressives' self-focusing style is, as yet, unknown, Pyszczynski and Greenberg's studies suggest that self-directed attention may be aversive for depressed people following positive feedback but not after negative feedback. Research on the effects of self-focus on the intensity of negative affect and level of self-esteem for depressives may shed further light on its aversiveness for depressed persons.

Effect on emotion: Does self-focus intensify negative emotion for depressed individuals? Gibbons, *et al.* (1985, Study 2) investigated the effect of self-directed attention on mood in a study with psychiatric inpatients. Using the Multiple Affect Adjective Check List (Zuckerman & Lubin, 1965), they found that depressed patients responding in front of their mirror images endorsed a significantly higher number of negative adjectives than did those without the mirror on each of the three subscales: Depression, Anxiety, and Hostility (see also Smith *et al.*, 1985). Thus self-focus appears to enhance negative emotion for depressives, and may be aversive to them.

Effect on self-esteem: Does self-focus lead to lowered self-esteem in depressed individuals? Smith *et al.* (1985, Study 1) included ratings of real self and ideal self in their correlational study of depression and self-consciousness described earlier. As expected, they found that both depression and private self-consciousness were correlated with increased discrepancy between real and ideal self (i.e., lower self-esteem). Pyszczynski and Greenberg (1985) also had their subjects complete a self-esteem measure twice: once prior to performing the experimental tasks (Time 1) and again after completing all the other tasks (Time 2). Recall that subjects in this experiment received either positive or negative feedback and were subsequently exposed to a mirror for 3 minutes. In comparison with initial self-esteem ratings, only those depressed subjects who had received negative pretask feedback showed a significant drop in self-esteem at Time 2. Although this study does not provide direct evidence for the effects of self-attention on the self-esteem of depressed individuals, it does suggest that self-focus may function in combination with recent

negative feedback to reduce self-esteem. That self-focus appears to increase negative affect and decrease self-esteem in depressed individuals is consistent with the
idea presented earlier that depressives' style to self-focus after failure may reflect a
maladaptive and dysfunctional coping effort.

*Effect on standards: Does self-focus enhance the salience of situational stan-
dards for depressives?* Although we are aware of no study that directly addresses
this point, there is at least one that appears to have some relevant data. Gibbons *et
al.* (1985, Study 2) asked depressed and nondepressed medical and psychiatric
inpatients to complete a questionnaire, with the reflecting surface of a mirror facing
either toward them or away from them. Among other things, the questionnaire dealt
with aspects of the patient's problem, including ratings of its severity, causal
responsibility, and treatment responsibility. To provide a basis of comparison, the
psychiatric patients were evaluated on these same dimensions by two staff members
who were familiar with them. Earlier, we described evidence indicating that
self-directed attention tends to increase the salience of situational standards. For
psychiatric inpatients, "attitudinal" standards concerning useful ways of viewing
their problems are typically promoted by staff members. If it is assumed that staff
members would promote the notion that it is desirable for patients to take
responsibility for their treatment, then heightening self-focus should encourage an
increased degree of concurrence with this standard. Indeed, Gibbons *et al.* found
that the eight depressed patients who responded to the questionnaire while facing
their own reflection had a .53 correlation with staff ratings; the seven depressed
patients who were not in the self-focusing condition had a −.53 ($p < .10$) correlation
with staff ratings. In other words, depressed inpatients responding in front of a
mirror were more likely to endorse the view promoted by the staff than were those
who did not respond in front of a mirror.

*Effect on causal attributions: Does self-focus increase the tendency for de-
pressives to make internal attributions?* Gibbons *et al.* (1985, Study 2) concluded
that "self-focused attention did not increase patients' acceptance of responsibility
for the determination of their problem" (p. 672). However, examination of the data
for the depressive subsample alone appears to indicate that these patients were
significantly more likely to accept responsibility for their problems (i.e., make an
internal attribution for them) when their self-attention was heightened than when it
was not.

*Effect on accuracy: Does self-focus increase the accuracy of self-reports made
by depressives?* Recall that depressed individuals have been found to provide more
accurate or realistic self-relevant judgments than nondepressed individuals in a
variety of situations. Gibbons *et al.* (1985) demonstrated that self-focus can increase depressives' accuracy about the self even further. Depressed psychiatric
inpatients who filled out a questionnaire about their problems in front of a mirror
gave more accurate reports of the number of their previous hospitalizations, of the
length of their hospitalization, and of the duration of their problem, as compared
with hospital records, than did those who completed the questionnaire in the
absence of the mirror. In addition, depressed patients' evaluations of the seriousness
of their problems were also more in line with staff members' assessments in the

presence versus the absence of the mirror. (For a study of the effects of self-focus and external distraction on the accuracy of depressed and nondepressed students' judgments of control, see Musson & Alloy, 1987).

THE ROLE OF SELF-DIRECTED ATTENTION IN DEPRESSION AND DIRECTIONS FOR FUTURE RESEARCH

Taken together, a consideration of the evidence—that is, the parallels between the affective, behavioral, and cognitive characteristics of depression and the state of self-directed attention; the demonstrated association between these phenomena in subclinically and clinically depressed samples; and the preliminary evidence that distraction reduces the consequences of both depression and self-focus—suggests that attention directed inward to the self may play an important role in the etiology, maintenance, and/or symptomatology of depressive disorders. However, the precise nature of the role of self-directed attention in depression is still primarily a matter of speculation. Lewinsohn, Hoberman, Teri, and Hautzinger (1985) hypothesized that disruptions in an individual's normal behavioral patterns may produce increased self-focus, which, in turn, mediates the common behavioral and cognitive symptoms of depression. Similarly, Pyszczynski and Greenberg (1987) suggested that depressives may persist in a self-regulatory cycle following significant loss, which produces a constant state of self-directed attention and, consequently, intensified symptoms of depression (see also Alloy, 1982b; Ganellen & Blaney, 1981; Ingram *et al.,* 1985). Alternatively, Ingram *et al.* (1985) hypothesized that self-focused attention may serve as a triggering mechanism for the negative cognitive patterns characteristic of depression. They suggest that if certain cognitively vulnerable individuals possess negative self-schemata (Beck, 1967) that are latent and not normally active (see Alloy, Clements, & Kolden, 1985; Riskind & Rholes, 1984), self-focused attention may serve to trigger their activation by making the content of these dormant structures more salient. The effect of this process may be to intensify already existing depressive affect or to access depressive affect if it is not currently present (Ingram *et al.,* 1985).

Although these theoretical views differ in regard to the precise mechanisms by which self-directed attention promotes depression, they all postulate a causal role for self-focused attention in the onset or maintenance of depressive episodes. Yet, no studies to date have employed research designs that would be relevant to examining this causal hypothesis. Clearly, we need *prospective* longitudinal studies in which dispositional and situational self-focus and depressive affective, behavioral, and cognitive symptoms are assessed at multiple points in time in order to disentangle the function of self-focus as a cause, a concomitant, or a consequence of depression. Similarly, to test the causal role of internal attention in depression, we need additional experimental studies in which direction of attention is manipulated and its effects on features of depression are observed (e.g., Musson & Alloy, 1987), or in which depression is manipulated and its effects on self-focused attention are observed (i.e., mood-induction studies). Finally, treatment studies employing distraction or attentional redeployment techniques with depressed persons may also shed some light on the causal issue. (For treatment implications of the association between self-focus and depression, see Gibbons *et al.,* 1985; Gur & Sackeim, 1978; Ingram & Hollon, 1986; and Schmitt, 1983.)

A further issue is the exact nature of the self-focused attention processes associated with depression. Do depressives suffer from excessive or chronic self-focus *per se,* or do they engage in self-focus at inappropriate times or in maladaptive situations? (see also Ingram *et al.,* 1985). Pyszczynski and Greenberg's (1985, 1986; Greenberg & Pyszczynski, 1986) finding that depressed individuals tend to engage in and prefer self-focus more after failure than success suggests that their self-attentional processes may be inappropriately timed rather than excessive in amount. Further studies that examine the situational determinants versus cross-situational generality of self-focusing strategies in depression would be helpful in determining how self-directed attention may promote the onset or maintenance of depression. In sum, the remarkable parallels between depression and self-focused attention raise the exciting possibility that attentional processes play a contributory role in the onset or course of depressive episodes. We eagerly await the results of research designs such as those proposed here that may clarify the role of self-directed attention in depression.

NOTES

1. Note the similarity of this view with Rehm's (1977; Chapter 5, this volume) self-control model of depression. Rehm's position is also that a self-evaluation stage follows self-monitoring.
2. Wicklund (1975) acknowledges the occurrence of positive discrepancies and thus suggests that self-focused attention will not lead to lowered self-esteem following a success. However, he argues that "because aspirations rise and eventually surpass the individual's recently attained success re-creating negative discrepancies" (p. 470), self-focus will lead to lowered self-esteem when the immediate positive discrepancy-producing effects of recent successes fade with time.
3. Duval and Wicklund (1972) had found this procedure to be effective in increasing self-focus.

ACKNOWLEDGMENT

Preparation of this chapter was supported by a grant from the John D. and Catherine T. MacArthur Foundation to Lauren B. Alloy.

REFERENCES

Abraham, K. (1911). Notes on the psychoanalytic investigation and treatment of manic–depressive insanity and allied conditions. In D. Bryan & A. Strachey (Eds. & Trans.), *Selected papers on psycho-analysis* (pp. 137–156). New York: Brunner/Mazel.

Abramson, L. Y., & Alloy, L. B. (1981). Depression, nondepression, and cognitive illusions: A reply to Schwartz. *Journal of Experimental Psychology: General, 110,* 436–447.

Abramson, L. Y., Seligman, M. E. P., & Teasdale, J. (1978). Learned helplessness in humans: Critique and reformulation. *Journal of Abnormal Psychology, 87,* 49–74.

Alloy, L. B. (1982a, October). *Depression and social comparison: Illusory self or other perceptions?* Paper presented at the meeting of the Society of Experimental Social Psychology, Nashville, IN.

Alloy, L. B. (1982b, November). *Depression, nondepression, and cognitive illusions.* Paper presented at the meeting of the Association for the Advancement of Behavior Therapy, Los Angeles.

Alloy, L. B. (1982c, August). *Depression: On the absence of self-serving cognitive biases.* Paper presented at the meeting of the American Psychological Association, Washington, DC.

Alloy, L. B., & Abramson, L. Y. (1979). Judgment of contingency in depressed and nondepressed students: Sadder but wiser? *Journal of Experimental Psychology: General, 108,* 441–485.

Alloy, L. B., & Abramson, L. Y. (1982). Learned helplessness, depression and the illusion of control. *Journal of Personality and Social Psychology, 42,* 1114–1126.

Alloy, L. B., & Ahrens, A. H. (1987). Depression and pessimism for the future: Biased use of statistically relevant information in predictions for self versus others. *Journal of Personality and Social Psychology, 52,* 366–378.

Alloy, L. B., Albright, J. S., & Clements, C. M. (1987). Depression, nondepression, and social comparison biases. In J. E. Maddux, C. D. Stoltenberg, & R. Rosenwein (Eds.), *Social processes in clinical and counseling psychology* (pp. 94–112). New York: Springer-Verlag.

Alloy, L. B., Clements, C., & Kolden, G. (1985). The cognitive diathesis–stress theories of depression: Therapeutic implications. In S. Reiss & R. Bootzin (Eds.), *Theoretical issues in behavior therapy* (pp. 379–410). New York: Academic Press.

Archer, R. L., Hormuth, S. E., & Berg, J. H. (1979, August). *Self-disclosure under conditions of self-awareness.* Paper presented at the meeting of the American Psychological Association, New York.

Bandura, A. (1969). *Principles of behavior modification.* New York: Holt, Rinehart & Winston.

Bandura, A. (1977). Self-efficacy: Toward a unifying theory of behavioral change. *Psychological Review, 84,* 191–215.

Beck, A. T. (1967). *Depression: Clinical, experimental, and theoretical aspects.* New York: Harper & Row.

Bibring, E. (1953). The mechanism of depression. In P. Greenacre (Ed.), *Affective disorders: Psychoanalytic contributions to their study* (pp. 13–48). New York: International Universities Press.

Blatt, S. J., D'Affliti, P., & Quinlan, D. M. (1976). Experiences of depression in normal young adults. *Journal of Abnormal Psychology, 85,* 383–389.

Brockner, J. (1979a). The effects of self-esteem, success–failure, and self-consciousness on task performance. *Journal of Personality and Social Psychology, 37,* 1732–1741.

Brockner, J. (1979b). Self-esteem, self-consciousness, and task performance: Replications, extensions, and possible explanations. *Journal of Personality and Social Psychology, 37,* 447–461.

Buss, D. M., & Scheier, M. F. (1976). Self-awareness, self-consciousness, and self-attribution. *Journal of Research in Personality, 10,* 463–468.

Callagan, J. E. (1952). *The effect of electro-convulsive therapy on the test performances of hospitalized depressed patients.* Unpublished doctoral dissertation, University of London.

Carver, C. S., Blaney, P. H., & Scheier, M. F. (1979). Focus of attention, chronic expectancy, and responses to a feared stimulus. *Journal of Personality and Social Psychology, 37,* 1186–1195.

Carver, C. S., & Scheier, M. F. (1978). Self-focusing effects of dispositional self-consciousness, mirror presence, and audience presence. *Journal of Personality and Social Psychology, 36,* 324–332.

Carver, C. S., & Scheier, M. F. (1981). *Attention and self-regulation: A control theory approach to human behavior.* New York: Springer-Verlag.

Coates, D., & Wortman, C. B. (1980). Depression maintenance and interpersonal control. In A. Baum & J. Singer (Eds.), *Advances in environmental psychology* (Vol. 2, pp. 149–182). Hillsdale, NJ: Erlbaum.

Coyne, J. C. (1976). Toward an interactional description of depression. *Psychiatry, 39,* 28–40.

Coyne, J. C., Metalsky, G. I., & Lavelle, T. L. (1980). Learned helplessness as experimenter-induced failure and its alleviation with attentional redeployment. *Journal of Abnormal Psychology, 89,* 350–357.

Crocker, J., Alloy, L. B., & Kayne, N. T. (in press). Attributional style, depression and perceptions of consensus for events. *Journal of Personality and Social Psychology.*

Davidson, M. (1939). Studies in the application of mental tests to psychotic patients. *British Journal of Medical Psychology, 18,* 44–52.

Davis, D., & Brock, T. C. (1975). Use of first person pronouns as a function of increased objective self-awareness and prior feedback. *Journal of Experimental Social Psychology, 11,* 381–388.

Dempsey, P. (1964). A multidimensional scale for the MMPI. *Journal of Consulting Psychology, 28,* 364–370.

Duval, S., Duval, V. H., & Neely, R. (1979). Self-focus, felt responsibility, and helping behavior. *Journal of Personality and Social Psychology, 37,* 1769–1778.

Duval, S., & Wicklund, R. A. (1972). *A theory of objective self-awareness.* New York: Academic Press.

Duval, S., & Wicklund, R. A. (1973). Effects of objective self-awareness on attributions of causality. *Journal of Experimental Social Psychology, 9,* 17–31.

Duval, S., Wicklund, R. A., & Fine, R. L. (1972). Avoidance of objective self-awareness under conditions of high and low intra-self discrepancy. In S. Duval & R. A. Wicklund (Eds.), *A theory of objective self-awareness* (pp. 16–21). New York: Academic Press.

Exner, J. E. (1973). The self-focus sentence completion: A study of egocentricity. *Journal of Personality Assessment, 37,* 437–455.

Eysenck, H. J. (1967). *The biological basis of personality.* Springfield, IL: Charles C. Thomas.

Eysenck, H. J. (1970). *The structure of human personality.* London: Methuen.

Federoff, N. A., & Harvey, J. H. (1976). Focus of attention, self-esteem, and attribution of causality. *Journal of Research in Personality, 10,* 336–345.

Fenigstein, A., Scheier, M. F., & Buss, A. H. (1975). Public and private self-consciousness: Assessment and theory. *Journal of Consulting and Clinical Psychology, 43,* 522–527.

Fisher, K. A. (1949). Changes in test performance of ambulatory depressed patients undergoing electro-shock therapy. *Journal of General Psychology, 41,* 195–232.

Foulds, G. A. (1952). Temperamental differences in maze performance. Part 2. The effect of distraction and of electroconvulsive therapy on psychomotor retardation. *British Journal of Psychology, 43,* 33–41.

Freud, S. (1957). Mourning and melancholia. In J. Strachey (Ed. and Trans.), *The standard edition of the complete psychological works of Sigmund Freud* (Vol. 14, pp. 239–258). London: Hogarth Press. (Original work published 1917)

Friedman, A. S. (1964). Minimal effects of severe depression on cognitive functioning. *Journal of Abnormal and Social Psychology, 69,* 237–243.

Froming, W. J., Walker, G. R., & Lopyan, K. J. (1982). Public and private self-awareness: When personal attitudes conflict with societal expectations. *Journal of Experimental Social Psychology, 18,* 476–487.

Ganellen, R., & Blaney, P. H. (1981, August). *A cognitive model of depressive onset.* Paper presented at the meeting of the American Psychological Association, Los Angeles.

Ganellen, R., Blaney, P. H., Costello, E. J., & Scheier, M. F. (1987). *Depression and self-consciousness.* Unpublished manuscript, University of Miami, Miami, FL.

Geller, V., & Shaver, P. (1976). The cognitive consequences of self-awareness. *Journal of Experimental Social Psychology, 12,* 438–445.

Gibbons, F. X. (1978). Sexual standards and reactions to pornography: Enhancing behavioral consistency through self-focused attention. *Journal of Personality and Social Psychology, 36,* 976–987.

Gibbons, F. X. (1983). Self-attention and self-report: The "veridicality" hypothesis. *Journal of Personality, 51,* 517–542.

Gibbons, F. X., Carver, C. S., Scheier, M. F., & Hormuth, S. E. (1979). Self-focused attention and the placebo effect: Fooling some of the people some of the time. *Journal of Experimental Social Psychology, 15,* 263–274.

Gibbons, F. X., & Gaeddert, W. P. (1984). Focus of attention and placebo utility. *Journal of Experimental Social Psychology, 20,* 159–176.

Gibbons, F. X., Smith, T. W., Ingram, R. E., Pearce, K., Brehm, S. S., & Schroeder, D. (1985). Self-awareness and self-confrontation: Effects of self-focused attention on members of a clinical population. *Journal of Personality and Social Psychology, 48,* 662–675.

Gibbons, F. X., & Wicklund, R. A. (1976). Selective exposure to self. *Journal of Research in Personality, 10,* 98–106.

Golin, S., & Terrell, F. (1977). Motivational and associative aspects of depression in skill and chance tasks. *Journal of Abnormal Psychology, 86,* 389–401.

Golin, S., Terrell, F., & Johnson, B. (1977). Depression and the illusion of control. *Journal of Abnormal Psychology, 86,* 440–442.

Golin, S., Terrell, F., Weitz, J., & Drost, P. L. (1979). The illusion of control among depressed patients. *Journal of Abnormal Psychology, 88,* 454–457.

Greenberg, J., & Musham, C. (1981). Avoiding and seeking self-focused attention. *Journal of Research in Personality, 15,* 191–200.

Greenberg, J., & Pyszczynski, T. (1986). Persistent high self-focus after failure and low self-focus after success: The depressive self-focusing style. *Journal of Personality and Social Psychology, 50,* 1039–1044.

Greenwald, A. G. (1980). The totalitarian ego: Fabrication and revision of personal history. *American Psychologist, 35,* 603–618.

Gur, R. C., & Sackeim, H. A. (1978). Self-confrontation and psychotherapy: A reply to Sanborn, Pyke and Sanborn. *Psychotherapy: Theory, Research and Practice, 15,* 258–265.

Hinchliffe, M. K., Lancashire, M., & Roberts, F. J. (1971). Depression: Defense mechanisms in speech. *Journal of Psychiatry, 118,* 471–472.

Ickes, W., Layden, M. A., & Barnes, R. D. (1978). Objective self-awareness and individuation: An empirical link. *Journal of Personality, 46,* 146–161.

Ickes, W. J., Wicklund, R. A., & Ferris, C. B. (1973). Objective self-awareness and self-esteem. *Journal of Experimental Social Psychology, 9,* 202–219.

Ingram, R. E., & Hollon, S. D. (1986). Cleaning up cognition in depression: An information processing perspective on cognitive therapy of depression. In R. E. Ingram (Ed.), *Information processing approaches to psychopathology and clinical psychology* (pp. 259–281). New York: Academic Press.

Ingram, R. E., Lumry, A. E., Cruet, D., & Sieber, W. (1987). Attentional processes in depressive disorders. *Cognitive Therapy and Research, 11,* 351–360.

Ingram, R. E., & Smith, T. W. (1984). Depression and internal versus external focus of attention. *Cognitive Therapy and Research, 8,* 139–152.

Jacobson, N. S., & Anderson, E. A. (1982). Interpersonal skill and depression in college students: An analysis of the timing of self-disclosure. *Behavior Therapy, 13,* 271–282.

Janis, I. (1954). Personality correlates of susceptibility to persuasion. *Journal of Personality, 22,* 504–518.

Kanfer, R., & Zeiss, A. (1983). Depression, interpersonal standard setting and judgments of self-efficacy. *Journal of Abnormal Psychology, 92,* 319–329.

Klein, D. C., Fencil-Morse, E., & Seligman, M. E. P. (1976). Learned helplessness, depression, and the attribution of failure. *Journal of Personality and Social Psychology, 33,* 508–516.

Klinger, E. (1975). Consequences of commitment to and disengagement from incentives. *Psychological Review, 82,* 1–25.

Kuiper, N. (1978). Depression and causal attributions for success and failure. *Journal of Personality and Social Psychology, 36,* 236–246.

LaPointe, K. A., & Crandell, C. J. (1980). Relationship of irrational beliefs to self-reported depression. *Cognitive Therapy and Research, 4,* 247–250.

Laxer, R. (1964). Self-concept changes of depressed patients in general hospital treatment. *Journal of Consulting Psychology, 28,* 214–219.

Lewin, K. (1935). *A dynamic theory of personality.* New York: McGraw-Hill.

Lewinsohn, P. M., Hoberman, H., Teri, L., & Hautzinger, M. (1985). An integrative theory of depression. In S. Reiss & R. Bootzin (Eds.), *Theoretical issues in behavior therapy* (pp. 331–359). New York: Academic Press.

Lewinsohn, P., Mischel, W., Chaplain, W., & Barton, R. (1980). Social competence and depression: The role of illusory self-perceptions? *Journal of Abnormal Psychology, 89,* 203–212.

Loeb, A., Beck, A. T., & Diggory, J. (1971). Differential effects of success and failure on depressed and nondepressed patients. *Journal of Nervous and Mental Disease, 152,* 106–114.

Martin, D. J., Abramson, L. Y., & Alloy, L. B. (1984). Illusion of control for self and others in depressed and nondepressed college students. *Journal of Personality and Social Psychology, 46,* 125–136.

Miller, D. T., & Ross, M. (1975). Self-serving biases in the attribution of causality: Fact or fiction? *Psychological Bulletin, 82,* 213–225.

Miller, W. R. (1975). Psychological deficit in depression. *Psychological Bulletin, 82,* 238–260.

Musson, R. F. (1981). *Self-consciousness and depression.* Unpublished manuscript, Northwestern University, Evanston, IL.

Musson, R. F., & Alloy, L. B. (1987). *Depression, self-consciousness, and judgments of control: A test of the self-focused attention hypothesis.* Unpublished manuscript, Northwestern University, Evanston, IL.

Nadich, M., Gargan, M., & Michael, L. (1975). Denial, anxiety, locus of control, and the discrepancy between aspirations and achievements as components of depression. *Journal of Abnormal Psychology, 84,* 1–9.

Nelson, R. E. (1977). Irrational beliefs in depression. *Journal of Consulting and Clinical Psychology, 45,* 1190–1191.

Nisbett, R. E., & Wilson, T. D. (1977). Telling more than we can know: Verbal reports on mental processes. *Psychological Review, 84,* 231–259.

Pasahow, R. (1976). *Cognitive interference in depressed and helpless individuals.* Unpublished manuscript, University of Pennsylvania, Philadelphia.

Peterson, C., & Seligman, M. E. P. (1984). Causal explanations as a risk factor for depression: Theory and evidence. *Psychological Review, 91,* 347–374.

Pryor, J. B., Gibbons, F. X., Wicklund, R. A., Fazio, R. H., & Hood, R. (1977). Self-focused attention and self-report validity. *Journal of Personality, 45,* 514–527.

Pyszczynski, T., & Greenberg, J. (1985). Depression and preference for self-focusing stimuli following success and failure. *Journal of Personality and Social Psychology, 49,* 1066–1075.

Pyszczynski, T., & Greenberg, J. (1986). Evidence for a depressive self-focusing style. *Journal of Research in Personality, 20,* 95–106.

Pyszczynski, T., & Greenberg, J. (1987). Self-regulatory perseveration and the depressive self-focusing style: A self-awareness theory of reactive depression. *Psychological Bulletin, 102,* 122–138.

Raps, C. S., Reinhard, K. E., Peterson, C., Abramson, L. Y., & Seligman, M. E. P. (1982). Attributional style among depressed patients. *Journal of Abnormal Psychology, 91,* 102–108.

Rehm, L. P. (1977). A self-control model of depression. *Behavior Therapy, 8,* 787–804.

Riskind, J. H., & Rholes, W. S. (1984). Cognitive accessibility and the capacity of cognitions to predict future depression: A theoretical note. *Cognitive Therapy and Research, 8,* 1–12.

Rizley, R. (1978). Depression and distortion in the attribution of causality. *Journal of Abnormal Psychology, 87,* 32–48.

Rogers, C. R. (1959). A theory of therapy, personality, and interpersonal relationships, as developed in the client-centered framework. In S. Koch (Ed.), *Psychology: A study of a science* (Vol. 3, pp. 184–256). New York: McGraw-Hill.

Sacco, W. P., & Hokanson, J. E. (1978). Expectations of success and anagram performance of depressives in a public and private setting. *Journal of Abnormal Psychology, 87,* 122–130.

Scheier, M. F. (1976). Self-awareness, self-consciousness, and angry aggression. *Journal of Personality, 44,* 627–644.

Scheier, M. F., Buss, A. H., & Buss, D. M. (1978). Self-consciousness, self-report of aggressiveness, and aggression. *Journal of Research in Personality, 12,* 133–140.

Scheier, M. F., & Carver, C. S. (1977). Self-focused attention and the experience of emotion:

Attraction, repulsion, elation, and depression. *Journal of Personality and Social Psychology, 35,* 625–636.

Scheier, M. F., & Carver, C. S. (1983). Self-directed attention and the comparison of self with standards. *Journal of Experimental Social Psychology, 19,* 205–222.

Scheier, M. F., Carver, C. S., & Gibbons, F. X. (1979). Self-directed attention, awareness of bodily states, and suggestibility. *Journal of Personality and Social Psychology, 37,* 1576–1588.

Schmitt, J. P. (1983). Focus of attention in the treatment of depression. *Psychotherapy: Theory, Research and Practice, 20,* 457–463.

Shapiro, M. B., Campbell, D., Harris, A., & Dewsbery, J. P. (1958). Effects of E.C.T. upon psychomotor speed and the "distraction effect" in depressed psychiatric patients. *Journal of Mental Science, 104,* 681–695.

Smith, T. W., & Greenberg, J. (1981). Depression and self-focused attention. *Motivation and Emotion, 5,* 323–331.

Smith, T. W., Ingram, R. E., & Roth, D. L. (1985). Self-focused attention and depression: Self-evaluation, affect, and life-stress. *Motivation and Emotion, 9,* 381–389.

Snyder, M. L., Smoller, B., Strenta, A., & Frankel, A. (1981). A comparison of egotism, negativity, and learned helplessness as explanations for poor performance after unsolvable problems. *Journal of Personality and Social Psychology, 40,* 24–30.

Snyder, M. L., Stephan, W. G., & Rosenfield, D. (1978). Attributional egotism. In J. H. Harvey, W. J. Ickes, & R. F. Kidd (Eds.), *New directions in attribution research* (Vol. 2, pp. 91–117). Hillsdale, NJ: Erlbaum.

Strack, S., Blaney, P. H., Ganellen, R. J., & Coyne, J. C. (1985). Pessimistic self-preoccupation, performance deficits, and depression. *Journal of Personality and Social Psychology, 49,* 1076–1085.

Sweeney, P. D., Anderson, K., & Bailey, S. (1986). Attributional style in depression: A meta-analytic review. *Journal of Personality and Social Psychology, 50,* 974–991.

Tabachnik, N., Crocker, J., & Alloy, L. B. (1983). Depression, social comparison, and the false-consensus effect. *Journal of Personality and Social Psychology, 45,* 688–699.

Turner, R. G., Scheier, M. F., Carver, C. S., & Ickes, W. (1978). Correlates of self-consciousness. *Journal of Personality Assessment, 42,* 285–289.

Wicklund, R. A. (1975). Objective self-awareness. In L. Berkowitz (Ed.), *Advances in experimental social psychology* (Vol. 8, pp. 465–507). New York: Academic Press.

Wicklund, R. A., & Duval, S. (1971). Opinion change and performance facilitation as a result of objective self-awareness. *Journal of Experimental Social Psychology, 7,* 319–342.

Wicklund, R. A., & Hormuth, S. E. (1981). On the functions of the self: A reply to Hull and Levy. *Journal of Personality and Social Psychology, 40,* 1029–1037.

Zuckerman, M., & Lubin, B. (1965). *Manual for the Multiple Affect Adjective Check List.* San Diego: Educational and Industrial Testing Service.

DEPRESSIVE INFERENCE:
REALISM OR DISTORTION?

8

Depressive Realism: Four Theoretical Perspectives

LAUREN B. ALLOY
Northwestern University
LYN Y. ABRAMSON
University of Wisconsin-Madison

It is common knowledge that depressed people view themselves and their experiences negatively. According to Beck's (1967, 1976) cognitive model of depression, these negative evaluations are a core symptom and cause of depression. While it is well known that depressed persons' self-perceptions are negative in content, the relatively unique aspect of Beck's theory is that it hypothesizes that these negative self-evaluations are produced by specific logical errors in interpreting reality. That is, depressed individuals are seen as making inferences about themselves and their experiences that are unrealistic and distorted, whereas normal, nondepressed individuals are viewed as rational information processors who are logical, realistic, and free from systematic biases in their cognitions. Recently, however, a surprising paradox has come to the attention of depression researchers. Although cognitive theories of depression emphasize distortion in depressive inference, a large body of research suggests that depressed people's perceptions and inferences are often more accurate or realistic than those of nondepressed people (Abramson & Alloy, 1981).

The emerging findings of "depressive realism" (Mischel, 1979) and nondepressive biases and illusions have quickly captured the imagination of clinical, social, and personality psychologists alike (e.g., Abramson & Alloy, 1981; Alloy & Tabachnik, 1984; Coyne & Gotlib, 1983; Greenwald, 1980; Kruglanski & Jaffe, in press; Mischel, 1979; Nisbett & Ross, 1980; Taylor, 1983). Among theorists and researchers of psychopathology, and of depression in particular, the findings of depressive realism and their interpretation have been especially controversial (Abramson & Alloy, 1981; Alloy, Albright, & Clements, 1987; Coyne & Gotlib, 1983). For example, of the 12 chapters included in this volume, 10 address the issue of depressive realism. Why is the phenomenon of depressive realism so provocative?

We believe there are at least five reasons why the findings of depressive realism and nondepressive cognitive bias have provoked and captivated psychologists. First, these findings seem to violate our everyday intuitions and basic theoretical notions about psychopathology. A number of recent investigations have begun to discover systematic errors or irrationalities in people's cognitions and beliefs (e.g., Nisbett & Ross, 1980; Tversky & Kahneman, 1974). Both clinical theorists and lay people alike have supposed that such irrational beliefs would be exaggerated in individuals with psychopathology. Indeed, a growing number of theorists (e.g., Abramson & Alloy, 1980; Abramson, Metalsky, & Alloy, 1987, in press; Abramson, Seligman, & Teasdale, 1978; Beck, 1967, 1976; Beck & Emery, 1985; Ellis, 1962; Forgus & Shulman, 1979; Greenberg, Vazquez, & Alloy, Chapter 4, this volume; Kihlstrom & Nasby, 1981; Kuiper, Olinger, & MacDonald, Chapter 10, this volume; Langer, 1975; Rehm, Chapter 5, this volume; Seligman, 1975) have conceptualized psychopathology, including the emotional disorders, in terms of aberrant cognitions and cognitive processes. The findings of depressive realism and nondepressive cognitive biases suggest that at least one group of psychopathological individuals may be characterized by less, rather than more, cognitive bias and distortion.

Second, as will become clear later in this chapter, the phenomenon of depressive realism directly challenges the basic postulates of the major cognitive theories of depression (e.g., Beck, 1967, 1976; Seligman, 1975). Inasmuch as cognitive theories have been preeminent among psychological approaches to depression in the last two decades, challenges to these theories are of great theoretical interest.

Third, the phenomenon of depressive realism also questions the basic assumptions underlying cognitive therapies for depression (e.g., Beck, Rush, Shaw, & Emery, 1979). Cognitive therapy for depression is a demonstrably effective treatment (see Evans & Hollon, Chapter 12, this volume) and consists of strategies designed to challenge and modify depressives' negatively distorted perceptions of reality. The findings of depressive realism and nondepressive optimistic distortions suggest that the primary active ingredient in cognitive therapy may be the training of depressed clients to engage in the sort of optimistic biases and illusions that nondepressives typically construct rather than the enhancement of realistic self-appraisal as is currently assumed by Beck and his colleagues (Beck *et al.*, 1979; for further discussion of the implications of depressive realism for cognitive therapy, see Alloy, Clements, & Kolden, 1985; Evans & Hollon, Chapter 12, this volume; and Kayne & Alloy, in press).

Fourth, the phenomenon of depressive realism has the potential to build a bridge between clinical and experimental psychology. Historically, explanation of errors and abnormalities has led to general insights about psychological processes (e.g., Freud, 1920; Gregory, 1966, 1970). Although researchers in several areas of psychology (e.g., neuropsychology and visual perception) have utilized the strategy of studying abnormal individuals as a means of developing principles of normal psychological functioning, clinical psychologists rarely have pursued this line of inquiry. The comparison of depressive and nondepressive cognition may not only increase our understanding of depression but may also serve to illuminate the functions of pervasive and robust nondepressive biases in human cognition (Abramson & Alloy, 1980; 1981; Freud, 1917/1957; Greenwald, 1980; Tiger, 1979).

Finally, the phenomenon of depressive realism may be especially provocative because of its potential practical implications. A number of theorists (e.g., Abramson & Alloy, 1981; Alloy *et al.*, 1987; Alloy & Koenig, 1987; Greenwald, 1980; Scheier & Carver, 1985; Taylor, 1983; Tiger, 1979) have suggested that optimistic cognitive illusions of the sort typically displayed by nondepressives may have adaptive consequences, including positive affect, high self-esteem, behavioral persistence, improved coping with stress, and decreased vulnerability to depression, suicide, and physical illness. If taken at face value, the findings of depressive realism suggest that seeing oneself and the world as they really are may be threatening to one's psychological and physical health and well-being.

In the remainder of this chapter, we briefly describe the cognitive theories of depression and then review studies examining the relative realism of depressed and nondepressed persons' cognitions in a variety of situations and contexts. In reviewing these studies, we discuss their relevance to the concepts of distortion, bias, irrationality, and maladaptiveness. We then discuss possible boundary conditions on depressive realism, including situational and personal determinants of the phenomenon. Next, we evaluate the status of four cognitive and motivational hypotheses that have been proposed to explain depressive realism and nondepressive cognitive biases. We then present four theoretical perspectives for understanding the meaning of this body of research for depressed and nondepressed people's realism in everyday life. We conclude by considering the psychological and physical consequences that may be associated with depressive realism versus nondepressive cognitive biases and illusions.

THE COGNITIVE THEORIES OF DEPRESSION

According to the cognitive perspectives on depression, the major cognitive, motivational, and affective symptoms of depression result from depressives' idiosyncratic style of processing self-relevant information. For example, Beck's (1967, 1976) cognitive model assigns a central role to negative and distorted interpretations of oneself and the environment in the etiology, maintenance, and treatment of depression. In particular, depressives' inferences are hypothesized to be characterized by a "systematic bias against the self," in which they selectively abstract negative details of environmental events, overgeneralize others, and make arbitrary inferences based on information insufficient to justify their conclusions. According to Beck, depressives' distorted and illogical inferences are produced by certain primitive, rigid preconceptions, or schemata, which are activated automatically during environmental stress (e.g., failure, loss, rejection). These schemata consist of pervasive negative beliefs and dysfunctional assumptions about the self and its relation to the world and the future. The schemata are conceptualized as relatively enduring cognitive organizing structures that guide the processing of situational information (Beck *et al.*, 1979; Rush & Giles, 1982). Once activated by stress, these negative self-schemata become prepotent and dominate the cognitions of depressed individuals, leading to the systematic distortions in interpreting reality. It is important to note that implicit in Beck's (1967, 1976) theory is the idea that normal, nondepressed individuals do not exhibit biases and distortions in their self-relevant inferences.[1]

Similarly, although the learned helplessness theory of depression (Abramson, Seligman, & Teasdale, 1978; Alloy & Seligman, 1979; Seligman, 1975) allows for the possibility of distortion in both depressed and nondepressed people's cognitions, both the reformulated and the original models of helplessness and depression focus on depressive biases in inferences about personal control. According to helplessness theory, depressed individuals are characterized by the general expectation that they cannot control personally important life events. Among other symptoms of depression, this expectation leads to a cognitive symptom in which depressives' perceptions of subsequent response–outcome relationships are biased, so that they consistently underestimate their personal control over events.

Recently, Abramson, Metalsky, and Alloy (1987; in press; Chapter 1, this volume) suggested that it may be inappropriate to draw predictions from the reformulated helplessness theory—revised and called the "hopelessness theory" by Abramson *et al.* (1987; in press)—and from Beck's theory concerning depressed individuals as a group versus nondepressed individuals as a group. The problem is that depression may be a very heterogeneous disorder, composed of a number of functional or etiological subtypes (e.g., Craighead, 1980; Depue & Monroe, 1978). Indeed Abramson, Metalsky, and Alloy (1987, in press; Chapter 1, this volume) argued that the logic of the causal pathways specified in the hopelessness theory and in Beck's theory predicts the existence in nature of a subtype of depression—"negative cognition depression." Strictly speaking, predictions derived from the cognitive theories of depression about depressive cognitive biases and distortions would apply only to negative cognition depressives and not to individuals suffering from other forms of depression. However, because all of the empirical studies reviewed here that have investigated the relative realism of depressed and nondepressed people's inferences have compared depressed and nondepressed subjects in general, we continue to speak of depressives and nondepressives as a group in the remainder of this chapter.

THE CONCEPTS OF ERROR/DISTORTION, BIAS, IRRATIONALITY, AND MALADAPTIVENESS

In considering the implications of studies examining the judgments of depressed and nondepressed individuals, it is useful to distinguish among the concepts of error or distortion, bias, irrationality, and maladaptiveness (see also Abramson & Alloy, 1981; Alloy & Tabachnik, 1984). An "erroneous" or "distorted" inference would consist of a judgment or conclusion that disagrees or is inconsistent with some commonly accepted measure of objective reality. Thus, to determine the accuracy or realism of an individual's inference in any given situation, one would need to know the objective state of affairs—that is, the "correct" answer—in that situation. In the remainder of this chapter, we use the terms "erroneous" and "distorted" synonymously, and likewise, the terms "accurate" and "realistic," to refer to the degree of accuracy of people's judgments and perceptions. Only some of the studies we review employed tasks in which the objective reality of the situation was known, and therefore only these studies are relevant for drawing conclusions about the relative accuracy or realism of depressed and nondepressed people's inferences.

In contrast, the concept of inferential "bias" refers to a tendency to make judgments in a systematic and consistent manner across specific times and situations (e.g., a tendency to draw negative conclusions about oneself, regardless of the particular circumstances). It is important to note that an individual with an inferential bias can make *either* accurate or erroneous judgments in particular situations. Reliance on a biased inferential process will lead to realistic judgments when the objective circumstances happen to be congruent with the content of the bias, but to distorted conclusions when the objective reality is at odds with the content of the bias. Thus, even those studies reviewed that do not include a measure of objective reality against which to compare the accuracy of individuals' judgments are relevant to determining the nature and degree of bias associated with depressed and nondepressed people's inferences.

The relative "irrationality" of depressed and nondepressed people's judgments is much more difficult to determine, however. In determining the relative rationality of a person's inferential strategies, it is important to consider whether those strategies lead to accuracy in the person's everyday environment as well as to accuracy in the short run in particular laboratory situations. Thus "rationality" may be defined as realism over the long run. Abramson and Alloy (1981) and Alloy and Tabachnik (1984) have argued that if an individual's inferential biases accurately reflect the contingencies in his or her usual environment, it would not be irrational for him or her to utilize these biases in interpreting current situational information, even if the current information is at odds with the content of the bias and leads to errors in the short run. Because current information encountered in one particular situational context may represent one piece of conflicting evidence against the background of the large body of data summarized by an inferential bias, it may be rational for people to weight their generalized biases and expectations more heavily than the current information in the judgment process. If, however, the usual contingencies and information provided by their everyday environments were to change permanently, it would be rational for people to revise their inferential biases so that they would accurately reflect the contingencies of their new environments. Unfortunately, none of the studies reviewed here on depressed and nondepressed people's judgments has used a research design that is appropriate for determining the relative realism of the two groups' inferences over the long run in their daily environments. However, later in this chapter (see the section The Meaning of Depressive Realism and Nondepressive Bias: Four Theoretical Perspectives), we discuss the possible implications of these studies for the long-term rationality of the two groups' inferences.

Finally, the concept of "maladaptiveness" refers to the negative physical and psychological consequences that may occur as a function of the kinds of inferences or judgments a person makes. Regardless of whether depressed or nondepressed persons' inferential strategies turn out to be more realistic, less biased, or more rational in the senses we have described, what are the affective, behavioral, and physical sequelae of their judgmental strategies? We use the term "maladaptive" to denote inferences that have negative consequences for an individual's physical and psychological health and well-being; we discuss the issue of adaptiveness in the last section of this chapter.

DEPRESSIVE REALISM: EMPIRICAL STUDIES

In this section, we review studies comparing the judgments, inferences, and information processing of depressed and nondepressed individuals.[2] Our review focuses on studies falling into six categories: judgment of contingency, expectancy/ prediction, attribution, perception and recall of feedback, self-evaluation, and self–other/social-comparison studies.

Judgment-of-Contingency Studies

We begin with judgment-of-contingency studies for two reasons. First, it was a study of depressed–nondepressed differences in contingency judgments (Alloy & Abramson, 1979) that first brought the phenomenon of depressive realism to the attention of depression researchers. Second, because the judgment-of-contingency studies contain an objective measure of reality (the actual degree of contingency between subjects' responses and study outcomes), they allow for an examination of the relative accuracy of depressed and nondepressed persons' judgments.

Alloy and Abramson (1979, Experiments 1 through 4) presented depressed and nondepressed college students with one of a series of contingency learning problems varying in the actual degree of contingency between students' responses (pressing or not pressing a button) and an experimental outcome (onset of a green light) as well as in the frequency and valence of the outcome. Surprisingly, and in contrast to the predictions of the learned helplessness theory and to Beck's views on cognitive distortions in depression, depressed students accurately judged the degree of control their responses exerted over green-light onset in all conditions of all problems, both for contingent and for noncontingent response–outcome relations. It was only nondepressed students who systematically erred in judging their control. Non-depressives exhibited an "illusion of control" and overestimated their control over uncontrollable outcomes that occurred with high frequency (Experiment 2) or that were associated with success (winning money; Experiment 3). In addition, non-depressives showed an "illusion of no control" and underestimated their impact on controllable outcomes associated with failure (losing money; Experiment 4). Non-depressives also underestimated their control over controllable outcomes when the passive response of not pressing was associated with greater success (Experiment 4). It is important to point out that depressed students' accuracy in judging their control in the Alloy and Abramson (1979) experiments is not attributable to a tendency of depressives to always judge that they exert little control (as predicted by helplessness theory) or a tendency to believe that they are incompetent and have low ability (Bryson, Doan, & Pasquali, 1984) because they also accurately judged that they exerted control over positive, controllable outcomes (Experiments 1 & 4). In addition, nondepressives' illusions of control appeared to be due to difficulty or bias in organizing the information needed to make a judgment of contingency rather than to a difficulty in perceiving the information itself. In general, across all four experiments, both depressed and nondepressed students perceived the conditional probabilities of green-light onset given pressing and not pressing accurately. Moreover, both groups engaged in the two response alternatives equivalently.

Since the original Alloy and Abramson (1979) investigation, a number of studies have replicated the findings of each of their four experiments when using similar conditions (e.g., Alloy & Abramson, 1982; Alloy, Abramson, & Kossman, 1985, Experiment 3; Alloy, Abramson, & Viscusi, 1981, neutral and no-mood-induction conditions; Benassi & Mahler, 1985, Experiments 1 & 2; Dresel, 1984, many-trials condition; Martin, Abramson, & Alloy, 1984, self condition; Musson & Alloy, 1987, Experiments 1 & 2, neutral conditions), including a replication in a Spanish sample (Vazquez, 1987, Experiments 1 through 3). In contrast, Bryson *et al.* (1984) were unable to replicate Alloy and Abramson's (1979) Experiment 2; however, it is unclear how to interpret this finding inasmuch as Bryson *et al.* also failed to obtain the more basic finding that people's judgments of control are influenced by the frequency of noncontingent outcomes (e.g., Jenkins & Ward, 1965). In sum, depressive realism and nondepressive illusions of control appear to be robust phenomena under usual conditions.

Further evidence that depressed individuals make accurate judgments of non-contingency was provided by Alloy and Abramson (1982). Depressed and nonde-pressed students were exposed to controllable, uncontrollable, or no noises in a typical helplessness triadic design (cf. Maier & Seligman, 1976) and were then asked to judge their control for one of two problems in which the outcome was objectively uncontrollable but associated with success or failure (winning or losing money). In direct opposition to the predictions of helplessness theory (see Alloy & Abramson, 1982), nondepressed students exposed to either uncontrollable or no noises greatly overestimated their subsequent control over the outcome in the noncontingent-win problem, whereas nondepressives exposed to controllable noises judged the noncontingency accurately. Depressed subjects also gave accurate judg-ments of noncontingency, regardless of their prior experience. Alloy and Abramson (1982) suggested that their findings were consistent with a self-esteem-maintenance account of depressive realism and nondepressive optimistic illusions (see the section Motivational and Cognitive Hypotheses of Depressive and Nondepressive In-ference). Similar to Alloy and Abramson (1982), Ford and Neale (1985) also recently found that unselected subjects (who presumably were mostly nondepres-sed) exposed to a typical helplessness induction judged (accurately) that they exerted a high degree of control over a subsequent contingent outcome rather than underestimating their control, as predicted by helplessness theory.

Based upon an observation in Alloy and Abramson's (1979) experiments that depressed students were less likely to generate complex hypotheses for exerting control over green-light onset than were nondepressed students, Abramson, Alloy, and Rosoff (1981) hypothesized that depressives might underestimate their control over an outcome if a complex hypothesis were required for exerting control. Consistent with this prediction, Abramson *et al.* (1981) found that relative to nondepressed students and to the *potential* amount of control available, depressed students underestimated their control when they were required to generate the controlling complex hypothesis themselves but not when it was generated for them. In addition, as predicted, depressives' underestimation of their control was due to a decreased probability of performing the correct complex hypothesis and therefore to a failure to sample adequately the potential contingency between their responses and the outcome. Indeed, depressives' judgments of control accurately mirrored the degree of control they actually exerted over the outcome (as opposed to the potential control available over the outcome). Therefore it would seem that depressives may not typically distort response–outcome contingencies when they have had sufficient opportunity to perceive these contingencies. Consistent with this idea, Dresel (1984) found that when exposed to a noncontingent outcome for many (48) trials, depressed students judged their lack of control accurately, whereas nondepressed students succumbed to an illusion of control, replicating Alloy and Abramson (1979). However, when exposed to the noncontingent outcome for only a few (16) trials, depressed students' judgments of control were higher than those of nondepressed students. That is, whereas nondepressives exhibited an equally large illusion of control with both brief and lengthy exposure to the noncontingency, depressives' judgments of control became more accurate with increasing experience with the response–outcome noncontingency.

Alloy *et al.* (1981) investigated the directionality of the relationship between depression and accuracy in judging response–outcome contingencies by inducing depressive mood in nondepressed students and elated mood in depressed students and by evaluating the impact of these transient mood states on students' judgments of control over an objectively uncontrollable, but positive, outcome. Alloy *et al.* found that depressed students who were induced to be temporarily elated judged that they had significantly more control over the noncontingent positive outcome than did depressed students who received no or neutral mood induction or who simulated elation. Nondepressed students who were induced to be temporarily depressed judged accurately that they exerted less control than nondepressed students who received no or neutral mood induction or who simulated depression. Although Alloy *et al.*'s (1981) results suggest that the accuracy of control judgments may be a function of current mood state, they do not rule out the alternative possibility that individual differences may exist in susceptibility to illusions of control and that those persons who are less susceptible to such illusions may be more vulnerable to developing depressive episodes (see the section The Adaptiveness of Depressive and Nondepressive Inferences).

Recently, a number of judgment-of-contingency studies have begun to investigate more specifically the conditions under which depressive realism and nondepressive illusions of control occur. For example, Martin *et al.* (1984) asked depressed and nondepressed students to judge either their own or another person's (a male or female confederate's) control over an uncontrollable, but positive, outcome. Replicating Alloy and Abramson (1979, Experiment 3), depressed students judged their personal control accurately, whereas nondepressed students succumbed to their typical illusion of control. However, with only one exception (depressed males judging a male other's control), depressives overestimated another person's control, whereas nondepressives (particularly, nondepressed males) were more likely to judge accurately that the other person did not exert much control. Thus Martin *et al.* (1984) suggested that depressive realism and nondepressive illusions in judging control may be specific to the self. (For further discussion of self–other differences, see the sections Self–Other/Social-Comparison Studies and Situational Constraints.) Consistent with this line of reasoning, Alloy, Abramson & Kossman (1985, Experiments 1 through 3) found that nondepressed students were as accurate as depressed students in judging both positive and zero contingencies between two stimulus events, neither of which involved students' own responses, regardless of the events' frequencies or valence. However, when subjects' own responses were one of the two events in the contingency learning problem (Experiment 3), nondepressives displayed their usual illusions of control, whereas depressives' judgments were accurate.

Other recent studies have suggested that even depressives' judgments of personal control may show illusions under certain circumstances. Vazquez (1987, Experiments 3 & 4) used either positive- or negative-content sentences as the outcomes in the Alloy and Abramson (1979) contingency judgment task. He found that when the sentences were contingent on students' responses (Experiment 3), nondepressed students overestimated their control over positive-content sentences but not negative-content sentences, whereas depressed students gave equivalent and relatively accurate control judgments for both types of sentences. When the occurrence of the sentences was noncontingently related to students' responses (Experiment 4), however, nondepressives exhibited an illusion of control for positive-but not negative-content sentences, whereas depressives exhibited an illusion of control for negative- but not positive-content sentences. These effects obtained only when the sentences were self-referent. Benassi and Mahler (1985) found that when depressed and nondepressed students performed a judgment-of-contingency task alone, depressives accurately judged that they exerted little control over a noncontingent, high-frequency outcome, whereas nondepressives exhibited an illusion of control (Experiment 1), replicating Alloy and Abramson (1979, Experiment 2). However, when subjects performed the task with an observer watching them, depressed students gave higher judgments of control than did nondepressed students (Experiments 1 & 3). Finally, Alloy, Abramson, and Musson (1987) examined personal and situational predictors of the illusion of control among students for a noncontingent, positive outcome. They found that larger illusions of control were predicted by younger age, being female, higher grade-point average, positive mood, higher trait anxiety, a positive self-schema, low self-consciousness, higher perceived frequency of positive outcomes, and greater experience with and liking for logic and math problems. This set of nine predictors discriminated "realists"

(judgment of control ≤ 16) from "illusionists" (judgment of control ≥ 60) with 84%
accuracy in a discriminant function analysis, and discriminated these two groups
with 80% accuracy in a cross-validation sample.

In summary, the judgment-of-contingency studies suggest that depressed individuals generally may be less susceptible to illusions of personal control than
nondepressed individuals. However, two important boundary conditions on depressive realism and nondepressive illusions of control may be specificity to the self
and private judgment.

Expectancy/Prediction Studies

Three major kinds of expectancy/prediction studies have been conducted. Expectancy-of-success studies have examined depressed and nondepressed subjects'
expectancies of success for their performance on chance-determined tasks that are
made to appear controllable or skill determined. Langer (1975) reported that people
succumb to an "illusion of control"[3] and give expectancies of success inappropriately higher than the objective probability of success on chance-determined
tasks when factors characteristic of skill-determined tasks, such as personal involvement, are introduced into the situation. Based on Langer's work, Golin, Terrell, and
Johnson (1977) asked depressed and nondepressed students to provide expectancies
of success for a dice game in which either students rolled the dice themselves
(player-control condition) or the dice were thrown by the experimenter (croupier-
control condition). Dice rolls of 2, 3, 4, 9, 10, 11, and 12 were defined as
successful outcomes, and thus the objective, chance-determined probability of
success was 44%. Similar to Martin *et al.'s* (1984) findings for judgments of control
for self and other conditions, *Golin et al.'s* (1977) findings showed that depressed
students' expectancies of success were accurate reflections of the objective probability of success when they rolled the dice themselves, whereas nondepressed
students' expectancies were inappropriately higher than the objective probability of
success for the self condition. When the experimenter rolled the dice, however,
nondepressed students' expectancies were accurate, whereas depressives' expectancies were inappropriately high. Golin, Terrell, Weitz, and Drost (1979)
subsequently replicated these findings in depressed versus nondepressed (primarily
schizophrenic) psychiatric patients.

A second group of expectancy-of-success studies, originally conducted to test
the learned helplessness theory, examined changes in depressed and nondepressed
subjects' expectancies of success over a series of trials following prior successes
and failures in chance-determined and ostensible "skill" tasks. (For reviews of these
chance–skill studies,[4] see Abramson, Seligman, & Teasdale, 1978; Alloy &
Abramson, 1980; and Alloy & Seligman, 1979). In fact, subjects' objective probability of success on both the chance and the "skill" tasks was 50% and was
randomly determined by the experimenter. The "skill" task was merely made to
appear skill determined. In general, these studies found that depressed students and
psychiatric inpatients showed smaller expectancy changes across trials than nondepressed students and patients on "skill" tasks but that the two groups' expectancy

changes did not differ from each other on the chance tasks (e.g., Abramson, Garber, Edwards, & Seligman, 1978; Klein & Seligman, 1976; Miller & Seligman, 1973, 1976; Miller, Seligman, & Kurlander, 1975). Although not reported in these publications, a finding of particular interest here is that depressed subjects' *final* expectancies of success on the "skill" tasks more accurately reflected the objective probability of success than did nondepressed subjects' expectancies (personal communication, Seligman, 1981). That is, after exposure, for ten trials, to the random reinforcement schedule used in the "skill" tasks, depressives appeared to perceive their objective chances for success more accurately than did nondepressives.

Interestingly, self–other and public–private manipulations that have been found to influence depressed and nondepressed persons' judgments of contingency have also been reported to affect their expectancy changes in these chance–skill studies. Garber and Hollon (1980) found that depressed students gave smaller changes in expectancies of success than did nondepressed students on a "skill" task only when they performed the task themselves (self condition). There were no depressed–nondepressed differences in expectancy change for the "skill" task when they provided expectancies for another student who performed the task (other condition). Sacco and Hokanson (1978) found smaller expectancies of success for depressed students on a "skill" task in a public measurement setting but not in a private one. In fact, in the private setting, depressed students gave larger expectancy changes than nondepressed students. In sum, depressed individuals appear to be less susceptible to "illusions of success" than nondepressed individuals for themselves (and perhaps in private) but more susceptible to "illusions of success" for others.

A third set of studies investigated depressed and nondepressed people's predictions of the likelihood of future positive and negative events both for themselves and for others. Alloy and Ahrens (1987) found that depressed students were more pessimistic than nondepressed students in their forecasts of the likelihood of a future academic success or failure for both themselves and others. In addition, though, nondepressives exhibited a self-enhancing bias in which they overestimated their own probability of success and underestimated their own probability of failure relative even to their forecasts for others who were identical to themselves on the predictor variables. Depressives' forecasts for self relative to others were completely unbiased. Similarly, Crocker, Alloy, and Kayne (1987a) found that nondepressed students judged that positive events were more likely, and negative events less likely, to happen to themselves than to the average college student in both the past and the future, whereas depressed students' estimates of the likelihood of occurrence of positive and negative events for self versus other were unbiased (see also Drake, 1986, for similar depressed–nondepressed differences, and Weinstein, 1980, 1982, and 1986, for similar findings among normal subjects). Pietromonaco and Markus (1985) observed that although depressed and nondepressed students did not differ in their estimates of the likelihood of occurrence of happy events for the self, depressed students predicted that sad events were more likely to happen to them than did nondepressed students. In addition, whereas nondepressives predicted that sad events were less likely to happen to them than to an acquaintance, depressives predicted that they were more likely to happen to them than to an acquaintance.

Attribution Studies

Attribution studies have examined depressed and nondepressed individuals' causal attributions for either hypothetical or real positive and negative events. Consistent with the reformulated helplessness theory (Abramson, Seligman, & Teasdale, 1978) and the revised hopelessness theory (Abramson *et al.*, 1987; in press; Chapter 1, this volume) of depression, these attribution studies have generally found that depressed individuals, *relative* to nondepressed individuals, make internal, stable, and global attributions for negative events, and external, unstable, and specific attributions for positive events (see Sweeney, Anderson, & Bailey, 1986, for an extensive meta-analytic review of these studies, and Peterson & Seligman, 1984, for a conceptual review).

The attribution studies have not employed methods that allow them to assess the degree of distortion in depressed and nondepressed persons' causal inferences because they contain no measures of the objectively correct causes of the relevant events. It is of interest for our purposes, however, that a number of these studies have demonstrated that whereas nondepressed individuals exhibit a strong and systematic tendency to make more internal, stable, and global attributions for positive than for negative outcomes—a tendency referred to as the "self-serving attributional bias" (e.g., Bradley, 1978; Miller & Ross, 1975) or "beneffectance bias" (Greenwald, 1980)—depressed individuals exhibit this bias to a lesser extent or provide quite "evenhanded" (similar) attributions for positive and negative events (e.g., Alloy, 1982b; Kuiper, 1978; Raps, Reinhard, Peterson, Abramson, & Seligman, 1982; Sackheim & Wegner, 1986). For example, Alloy (1982b) conducted a small meta-analysis of nine studies that provided means for depressed and nondepressed subjects' attributions for positive and negative events. The nine studies examined a total of 11 samples of depressed and nondepressed college students, children, or psychiatric inpatients or outpatients. For each study, Alloy (1982b) calculated the degree of self-serving bias exhibited by depressed versus nondepressed subjects by subtracting their attributions for negative events from their attributions for positive events along the internality, stability, and globality dimensions. Alloy found that nondepressives exhibited a significantly greater self-serving bias than depressives on each of the attributional dimensions and that the overall pattern was quite representative of the findings of the individual studies. In 10 of 11, 9 of 11, and 7 of 7 comparisons between depressed and nondepressed samples for each of the three attributional dimensions, respectively, nondepressives exhibited a greater self-serving bias than depressives. Moreover, not only did depressives show less self-serving bias than nondepressives, but, in fact, they showed no evidence of attributional bias at all. Depressives' difference scores for positive and negative events for each dimension did not differ significantly from a score of 0, indicating perfect evenhandedness.

Interestingly, even several studies that have examined severely depressed (unipolar) psychiatric inpatients have observed that these subjects show smaller self-serving attributional biases or greater attributional evenhandedness than do nondepressed psychiatric controls or normal controls (e.g., Hamilton & Abramson, 1983; Raps *et al.,* 1982; Sackheim & Wegner, 1986). An exception to this occurred, however, for ratings of praise and blame, where Sackheim and Wegner (1986, Study 2) found that unipolar depressed inpatients and outpatients actually showed a self-derogating pattern, taking more blame for bad events than praise for good events.

As was the case in the judgment-of-contingency and expectancy-of-success studies, the attribution studies also revealed that depressive attributional evenhandedness and nondepressive self-serving bias may be specific to the self. Sweeney, Shaeffer, and Golin (1982) found that depressed students' attributions for positive and negative events were more evenhanded than those of nondepressed students for themselves but that the two groups' attributions did not differ for others. Finally, Tennen and Herzberger (1987) have suggested that depressive attributional evenhandedness may be a function of low self-esteem rather than of depression *per se*. They found that when self-esteem was controlled, depression had only a small relation to attributional style, but that when depression was controlled, self-esteem remained strongly related to attributional style. However, when Crocker, Alloy, & Kayne (1987b) replicated Tennen and Herzberger's analyses with a different sample of depressed and nondepressed students, depression was a significantly better predictor of attributional evenhandedness than was self-esteem. In sum, it appears that depression is associated with attributional evenhandedness for the self but not for others.

Studies of Perception and Recall of Feedback

A number of studies have examined depressed and nondepressed individuals' immediate perception and later recall of experimenter-provided evaluative feedback. The feedback provided to subjects in these studies is generally either about their task performances or about their personalities and is designed to be either relatively ambiguous or unambiguous. Because the nature of the feedback provided to subjects in these studies is determined by the experimenter, the findings from the studies are relevant to the issue of bias *and* to the issue of distortion.

First, we review studies of the immediate perception of evaluative feedback. Two studies have examined perception of task-performance feedback. DeMonbreun and Craighead (1977) found that depressed psychiatric outpatients (military veterans) did not differ from nondepressed psychiatric outpatients and normal controls (also veterans) on their immediate perception of positive and neutral (ambiguous) performance feedback and that the perceptions of all three groups were accurate. Similarly, Craighead, Hickey, and DeMonbreun (1979) found that depressed–anxious, nondepressed–anxious, and nondepressed–nonanxious college students all perceived neutral (ambiguous) performance feedback accurately and did not differ from one another. Thus both depressed and nondepressed persons appear to perceive ambiguous (neutral) performance feedback in an accurate, nondistorted manner.

Five studies have investigated depressed and nondepressed subjects' perception of evaluative personality feedback. Gotlib (1983) gave depressed and nondepressed psychiatric inpatients and nondepressed hospital employees personality feedback about themselves on 13 dimensions that overall was evaluatively neutral. The subjects in all three groups perceived the feedback to be equally accurate in describing themselves, but depressed patients perceived it to be less favorable than did the other two groups. This appeared to be due to an underestimation of the feedback's favorableness by the depressed patients and to an overestimation of its favorableness by the nondepressed patients and controls. Similarly, Vestre and Caulfield (1986) found that mildly depressed and nondepressed college students did not differ in their ratings of the accuracy with which neutral (ambiguous) personality feedback described themselves but that depressed students perceived the feedback as less favorable than did nondepressed students. However, depressives' perceptions were more accurate (closer to the neutral point) than were those of nondepressives, who overestimated the feedback's favorableness.

Dykman, Abramson, Alloy and Hartlage (1987, Study 2) gave moderately depressed and nondepressed students *both* ambiguous and unambiguous personality feedback either on dimensions that differentiated the two groups' self-schemata or on dimensions on which the two groups had similar self-schemata (as determined in Study 1). No group or condition differences were obtained on immediate perceptions of unambiguous feedback. However, depressives perceived ambiguous feedback more negatively than nondepressives on the schema-discriminating dimensions, whereas the two groups' perceptions did not differ on the schema-nondiscriminating dimensions. However, compared to an accurate, unbiased perception, all groups showed significant positive biases, with depressives in the schema-discriminating condition being the least positively biased (most accurate), nondepressives in the same condition being the most positively biased, and depressed and nondepressed subjects in the schema-nondiscriminating condition falling in between. In general, the more positive an individual's self-schema, the more positive the degree of bias he or she showed in ambiguous-feedback perception. In addition, a more detailed analysis of subjects' perceptions for each ambiguous-feedback cue showed that all groups sometimes engaged in positively biased, sometimes in negatively biased, and sometimes in accurate feedback encoding, with bias and accuracy being a function of the relative positioning of the content of each group's self-schema and the valence of the particular ambiguous-feedback cue being processed.

Finally, two self–other studies on perception of personality feedback have been conducted. Wenzlaff and Berman (1985) gave mildly depressed and nondepressed students favorable or unfavorable personality feedback about themselves or another person. Nondepressives overestimated the favorableness of unfavorable feedback about themselves relative to depressives' perceptions (which were more accurate). No depressed–nondepressed differences occurred in perceptions of unfavorable feedback for others or in perceptions of favorable feedback for both self and others.

Similarly, Hoehn-Hyde, Schlottmann and Rush (1982) had female unipolar depressed inpatients, remitted depressives, and normal controls observe and evaluate the favorableness of a set of videotaped interactions in which a male actor directed positive, neutral, or negative comments toward either the subject (self condition) or another person (other condition). No depressed–nondepressed differences in perception of feedback for self or other were obtained for the positive or neutral comments. For the negative interactions, depressed patients gave more negative evaluations than the normal controls, but only when the comments were directed toward the self. However, this appeared to be due to the normal controls' distortion of the self-directed negative comments in a positive direction, because the normal controls evaluated the same negative comments less negatively if directed toward themselves than toward another person. In sum, the studies on perception of personality feedback suggest that depressed individuals perceive evaluative feedback about themselves, but not others, to be more unfavorable than do nondepressed individuals; however, much of the time (but *not* always) this is because nondepressives overestimate the favorableness of their feedback, whereas depressives' perceptions are more accurate. However, the Dykman *et al.* (1987) study suggests that both depressed and nondepressed persons may exhibit positive biases, negative biases, and accurate perceptions at different times, depending on the relative match of their self-schemata to the feedback content.

Studies of recall of task-performance feedback have tended to find that depressed students underestimate positive or "correct" performance feedback (Buchwald, 1977; Wener & Rehm, 1975), whereas nondepressed students tend to overestimate such feedback (Buchwald, 1977). Depressed students' and psychiatric outpatients' recall of positive performance feedback is especially likely to show underestimations if the positive feedback occurs at a high rate, but it is likely to be accurate if the positive feedback occurs at a low rate (DeMonbreun & Craighead, 1977; Nelson & Craighead, 1977). Nondepressed psychiatric outpatients tended to overrecall the amount of positive task feedback they received at both high and low rates of positive feedback (DeMonbreun & Craighead, 1977). In contrast, Dennard and Hokanson (1986) found that moderately depressed students[5] underestimated their positive feedback only in a low-rate-of-positive-feedback condition, whereas nondepressed students overestimated only in a high-rate-of-positive-feedback condition. Mildly depressed students recalled their positive feedback accurately for both low- and high-rate conditions. However, Nelson and Craighead (1977) found that in recalling negative performance feedback, depressed students were accurate, whereas nondepressed students underrecalled their negative feedback in a low-rate-of-negative-feedback condition. Finally, for neutral, ambiguous task-performance feedback, two studies have found no differences in depressed and nondepressed students' and outpatients' recall (DeMonbreun & Craighead, 1977; Craighead *et al.*, 1979). In sum, both depressed and nondepressed persons appear to recall neutral, ambiguous performance feedback accurately, whereas depressives tend to underestimate positive performance feedback, and nondepressives tend to overestimate positive and underestimate negative performance feedback (see also Gotlib, 1981, for a study of recall of self-reinforcement).

Four studies have examined recall of evaluative personality feedback. Gotlib (1983) found that depressed psychiatric inpatients recalled a personality evaluation as being more negative than it actually was, whereas nondepressed patients and normal controls tended to recall the feedback as being more positive than it was (although this positive bias was not significant). Dykman *et al.* (1987) obtained no depressed–nondepressed differences in recall of unambiguous personality feedback, although depressed students' recall in the schema-discriminating condition was negatively biased. Wenzlaff and Berman (1985), in contrast, found that depressed students' recall of both favorable and unfavorable personality feedback was accurate for both themselves and others, although they showed some tendency to overestimate the positivity of unfavorable feedback for another person. However, nondepressed students recalled unfavorable feedback about themselves as being more positive than it was, and unfavorable feedback about another as being less positive than it was. Finally, Loewenstein and Hokanson (1986) found that mildly and moderately depressed students (see Note 5) recalled less evaluative personality feedback about themselves than did nondepressed students, but there was no positive or negative recall bias on the part of any of the subject groups. No depressed–nondepressed differences occurred in recall of personality information about another person. In sum, recall of personality feedback for the self appears sometimes to be accurate and sometimes negatively distorted for depressives, and sometimes accurate and sometimes positively distorted for nondepressives. Less distortion and bias appears to occur in both depressives' and nondepressives' recall of personality feedback for others.

Also of some relevance to our discussion are studies of depressed and nonde-pressed people's processing and recall of self-referent, positive and negative events, trait adjectives, or phrases. We do not review these studies here because they have recently been reviewed elsewhere (e.g., Blaney, 1986; Greenberg, Vazquez, & Alloy, Chapter 4, this volume, Isen, 1984; Kuiper, Olinger, & MacDonald, Chapter 10, this volume). In general, though, these studies find that depressed subjects recall less positive and more negative self-referent information than do nonde-pressed subjects. Interestingly, however, these studies tend to find that although depressives' processing and recall of self-relevant information is more negative than is nondepressives', depressives' processing and recall of positive and negative information actually tends to be balanced, rather than truly negative (e.g., Blaney, 1986; Greenberg, Vazquez, & Alloy, Chapter 4, this volume).

Self-evaluation Studies

We review four types of self-evaluation studies in this section: self-reinforcement studies, self-evaluation studies that contain no standard of comparison, self-evaluation studies that compare subjects' self-evaluations with others' evaluations of them, and self-evaluation studies that provide subjects with social comparison information about others' performance.

As Bandura (1971) and Kanfer and Duerfeldt (1968) have noted, self-reinforcement involves the process of self-evaluation as well as self-reward. In self-reinforcement studies, subjects perform a task, and after providing a response on each trial of the task, they are asked to reward or punish themselves, depending on their own evaluation of how "correct" (Rozensky, Rehm, Pry, & Roth, 1977) or "good" (Gotlib, 1981; Lobitz & Post, 1979; Nelson & Craighead, 1977; Sacco & Hokanson, 1982) their responses were. Three of the self-reinforcement studies contained a measure of subjects' objectively correct task performance with which to compare self-reinforcements. Nelson and Craighead (1977) found that mildly depressed college students rewarded themselves less than nondepressed students in a 30% experimenter-provided reinforcement condition but that the two groups did not differ in their self-reward in the 70% reinforcement condition or in their self-punishment in either a 30% or a 70% experimenter-provided punishment condition. Although depressed students rewarded themselves less than nondepressed students in the low-rate-of-reinforcement condition, their self-reward was closer to the actual rate of reinforcement than was that of nondepressives, who greatly overrewarded themselves. Similarly, Rozensky *et al.* (1977) found that highly depressed psychiatric patients (veterans) rewarded themselves less and punished themselves more than nondepressed patients or normal controls but that this was attributable to greater accuracy on the part of highly depressed patients and to overrewarding of self compared to objective performance by the nondepressed patients and normal controls. Gotlib (1981) observed less self-reinforcement and more self-punishment by both depressed and nondepressed psychiatric inpatients relative to normal controls, with the two psychiatric groups underrewarding themselves but more accurately punishing themselves, relative to their objective performances, as compared to the normal controls.

Sacco and Hokanson (1982) suggested that depressives' tendency to self-reward less than nondepressives may be specific to public measurement conditions. These authors found that among subjects who received a high–low reinforcement rate sequence, depressed students self-rewarded less than nondepressed students in a public setting but more than nondepressed students in a private setting, a finding similar to their earlier findings for expectancies of success (Sacco & Hokanson, 1978). No depressed–nondepressed differences were obtained among subjects in a low–high reinforcement rate condition. Finally, Lobitz and Post (1979) compared depressed and nondepressed psychiatric inpatients' levels of expectation, evaluation, and reward for themselves and others. Depressed patients were lower than nondepressed patients on each of these measures for themselves. However, depressives' ratings on each of the measures for others tended to be higher than nondepressives' ratings. This occurred because depressed patients tended to evaluate and reward others' performances higher than their own, whereas nondepressed patients tended to evaluate and reward their own performances higher than those of others (see also Shrauger & Terbovic, 1976, for similar self–other differences in subjects with high and low self-esteem). Thus depressives self-reward less and self-punish more than nondepressives, but they may be more likely to do so in public situations and for the self rather than for others. In addition, depressives' self-reinforcement and punishment are often in closer accord with their objective performances than are those of nondepressives.

Among the studies that have examined depressed and nondepressed people's self-evaluations in the absence of any standard of comparison, a highly consistent finding is that depressives' self-perceptions tend to be "evenhanded" and balanced between positive and negative content, whereas nondepressives' self-perceptions are biased toward positive evaluations. Vazquez (1987, Experiments 3 & 4) found that nondepressed students made extreme appraisals of themselves, showing a great acceptance of positive self-descriptive sentences and a great rejection of negative self-descriptive sentences, whereas depressed students made more balanced appraisals and accepted both kinds of sentences equally (see also Finkel, Glass, & Merluzzi, 1982, and Karoly & Ruehlman, 1983, for similar findings). Dennard and Hokanson (1986) also obtained evenhandedness on the part of depressed students (see Note 5) in their self-ascriptions and in their later correct recognitions of positive and negative trait adjectives, whereas nondepressed students endorsed and correctly recognized more positive than negative adjectives (see also Vazquez & Alloy, 1987, for similar results). Tabachnik, Crocker, and Alloy (1983; see also Crocker, Kayne, & Alloy, 1985) found that whereas nondepressed students judged that positive personal attributes were truer and negative personal attributes less true of themselves than of the average college student, depressed students gave evenhanded judgments and saw positive and negative attributes as equally true of themselves and the average college student (see also Campbell, 1986, for highly similar findings). Likewise, Ahrens, Zeiss, and Kanfer (in press) observed that nondepressed students rated themselves higher than others on personal standards and self-efficacy expectations, and also placed their standards well above the level of performance they felt others could attain. No self–other differences were obtained for depressed students on these measures.

Of the five studies comparing depressed and nondepressed subjects' self-evaluations to others' ratings of them, three have used "objective" observers (Gibbons *et al.*, 1985; Lewinsohn, Mischel, Chaplain, & Barton, 1980; Roth & Rehm, 1980), while two have used other nondepressed subjects who interacted with the depressed or nondepressed targets (Siegel & Alloy, 1987; Strack & Coyne, 1983). It should be noted, however, that both "objective" observers' and interactive observers' ratings of depressed and nondepressed subjects do not necessarily constitute a measure of objective accuracy or reality, inasmuch as observers exhibit systematic cognitive biases of their own (e.g., Jones & Nisbett, 1971; Nisbett & Ross, 1980). Certainly though, the use of observer evaluations allows one to compare depressed and nondepressed persons' self-evaluations with how they are perceived by others and thus with the type of social feedback they may receive from others in everyday life (Siegel & Alloy, 1987; Strack & Coyne, 1983).

Lewinsohn *et al.* (1980) found that depressed outpatients rated their social skills in agreement with independent and "blind" observers' ratings of them, whereas nondepressed outpatients and normal controls significantly overestimated their social skills in comparison to the observer ratings. Further, as the depression subsided over the course of psychotherapy, depressed patients began to overrate themselves in comparison to the observer ratings like the nondepressed subjects did. Roth and Rehm (1980) had depressed and nondepressed psychiatric inpatients (military veterans) observe videotapes of themselves in a social interaction and monitor one positive and one negative class of their own behavior. Compared to the ratings of objective observers who also coded the videotapes, depressed patients accurately monitored their negative behaviors, whereas nondepressed patients underestimated their negative behaviors. Both depressed and nondepressed patients underestimated their positive behaviors relative to the objective observers, although depressives' underestimation was greater than that of nondepressives. Gibbons *et al.* (1985, Study 2) demonstrated that depressed subjects' self-ratings could be brought into even closer agreement with both objective records and observers by placing the subjects in a state of heightened self-focused attention. Depressed psychiatric patients who filled out a questionnaire about their problems in front of a mirror gave more accurate reports of their previous hospitalizations, length of their current hospitalization, and duration of their problems, as compared with hospital records, than did those who completed the questionnaire in the absence of the mirror. In addition, depressed patients' evaluations of the seriousness of their problems were also more in line with staff members' assessments in the presence versus the absence of the mirror. (See Musson & Alloy, Chapter 7, this volume, for a review of other studies showing increased accuracy of self-reports with heightened self-focused attention.)

In Strack and Coyne (1983), depressed and nondepressed female student targets engaged in a brief social interaction with another nondepressed student. Depressed targets correctly anticipated more rejection from the subjects with whom they interacted than did nondepressed targets. In Siegel and Alloy's (1987) study, depressed, anxious but nondepressed, and nondepressed–nonanxious student targets and their nondepressed–nonanxious, same-sex roommates rated the affective and behavioral impact on themselves of interactions with their roommates and judged their own interpersonal impact on their roommates. Depressed males realistically perceived the negative effect they produced in their roommates, whereas depressed females judged their interpersonal impact to be worse than it actually was. However, depressed females' overestimation of their negative impact appeared to be due to overly positive ratings of them by their normal roommates rather than to overly negative ratings of their own impact by the depressed females. In contrast, the normal roommates of depressed targets perceived their interpersonal impact as better than it actually was. In general, these effects were specific to depression as opposed to anxiety. In sum, the self-evaluation studies that also measure others' evaluations suggest that most of the time, depressives' self-evaluations are in closer accord with others' ratings of them than are nondepressives' self-evaluations, because nondepressives tend to evaluate themselves more positively than they are evaluated by others.

Two studies have examined depressed and nondepressed individuals' self-evaluations relative to others in either the presence or the absence of comparison information about these others. Zich and Zeiss (1987) gave depressed and nondepressed students favorable, unfavorable, or no social comparison information prior to a "creative empathy test." Subjects were asked to rate the percentage of people they believed would perform worse than they did. Depressives exhibited a selfdisfavoring expectancy; that is, when no social comparison information was available, depressives acted "as if" they had received unfavorable information regarding their performances. In contrast, nondepressives exhibited a self-favoring expectancy, acting "as if" they had received favorable social comparison information, although no information was actually provided. Depressives and nondepressives did not differ in their self-evaluations relative to others when actual favorable or unfavorable social comparison information was provided. In a similar study, Ahrens (1986) gave depressed and nondepressed students mixed information about their performances relative to others. Depressives seemed to ignore information about another who had failed and compared themselves to a successful other. This was reversed for nondepressives, who ignored the successful other and compared themselves to the unsuccessful other.

Self–Other/Social-Comparison Studies

In our review of empirical studies in the previous five sections, we have already described a number of studies that compared depressed and nondepressed individuals' perceptions and judgments for themselves and for others. Therefore, in this section, we do not repeat these descriptions but, rather, summarize the findings of the studies taken as a whole.

One group of self–other studies employed *between-subjects* designs, in which subjects provided *either* self *or* other judgments, but not both (Ahrens, 1986; Garber & Hollon, 1980; Golin *et al.*, 1977; Hoehn-Hyde *et al.*, 1982; Martin *et al.*, 1984; Pietromonaco & Markus, 1985; Vazquez, 1987; Wenzlaff & Berman, 1985; Zich & Zeiss, 1987). These between-subjects studies found that nondepressives consistently exhibit self-enhancing social comparison biases, perceiving the self more positively than others, and that in contrast, depressives, with one exception (Hoehn-Hyde *et al.*, 1982), exhibit other-enhancing biases, perceiving others more positively than the self. A second set of self–other studies used *within-subjects* designs, in which subjects provided *both* self and other judgments (Ahrens *et al.*, in press; Alloy & Ahrens, 1987; Campbell, 1986; Crocker *et al.*, 1985, 1987a; Drake, 1986; Lobitz & Post, 1979; Loewenstein & Hokanson, 1986; Siegel & Alloy, 1987; Sweeney *et al.*, 1982; Tabachnik *et al.*, 1983; Weinstein, 1980, 1982, 1986). In the within-subjects studies, nondepressives again show consistent self-enhancing social comparison biases, whereas depressives, with one exception (Lobitz & Post, 1979), are evenhanded and unbiased in their judgments of self relative to others.

What could explain the differing findings for depressives? Differences in the ambiguity of the judgment task inherent in between- versus within-subjects designs may account for the discrepant findings (see Alloy *et al.*, 1987). In between-subjects designs, there is no explicit reference point or standard of comparison by which to make inferences about either the self or the other; thus the judgment context is ambiguous. Social psychological research has suggested that subjective biases are enhanced in ambiguous situations (e.g., Ickes, 1984; McGregor, 1938; Metalsky & Abramson, 1981; Nisbett & Ross, 1980). If it is assumed that nondepressives possess a *strong* self-enhancing bias and that depressives possess a much *weaker* other-enhancing bias, then in ambiguous between-subjects studies, nondepressives' strong self-enhancing bias will appear even stronger and depressives' weak other-enhancing bias may become apparent. In within-subjects designs, subjects make judgments for *both* self and other; thus *explicit* social comparison occurs. Given the reduced ambiguity of the judgment context in within-subjects designs, nondepressives may still exhibit a self-enhancing bias, but less strongly than in between-subjects designs. Similarly, depressives' weak other-enhancing bias may be weakened further by the clarity of the judgment context, and thus they may appear evenhanded in their social comparisons in within-subjects designs (see Albright, Alloy, & Barch, 1987, for a test of this hypothesis).

BOUNDARY CONDITIONS ON DEPRESSIVE REALISM

Our review of empirical studies comparing depressed and nondepressed individuals' inferences suggests that although the perceptions and judgments of depressives are more accurate or less biased than those of nondepressives much of the time, this is not always the case. Some studies have found nondepressives' inferences to be more accurate or less biased than depressives' inferences under certain conditions, while other studies suggest that the two groups' cognitions may be equally susceptible to certain biases or distortions of opposite content.

In this section, we consider some of the situational and personal factors that may influence the degree of inferential distortion or bias shown by depressed versus nondepressed persons. We point out, however, that our suggestions regarding some of these possible factors are based on the findings of only a few studies or on theoretical speculation; thus such suggestions are intended to serve as points of departure for additional research aimed at further investigation of the factors in question. Moreover, our discussion may suggest factors that will need to be considered in proposing theoretical mechanisms or explanations of differences in depressive and nondepressive cognition.

Situational Constraints

Self- versus Other-reference. As indicated earlier, a rather consistent finding across many studies is that nondepressed individuals exhibit optimistic biases and illusions in their perceptions and judgments about themselves but not in their inferences about others. Likewise, depressed individuals are often (though not always) more realistic and less biased in their self-relevant perceptions and inferences but succumb to optimistic biases or distortions in their other-referent judgments. These studies suggest that a critical determinant of the degree and nature of inferential bias or distortion exhibited by depressed and nondepressed people is whether judgments are made about the self or others. The potential importance of the self–other distinction is consistent with the predictions of the cognitive theories of depression (Abramson, Seligman, & Teasdale, 1978; Abramson *et al.*, 1987; Beck, 1967, 1976) as well as with basic research in social cognition documenting differing biases characteristic of actor (self) and observer (other) perspectives (e.g., Jones & Nisbett, 1971; Nisbett & Ross, 1980).

Private versus Public Conditions. Three studies have found that depressed–nondepressed differences in personal judgments of control, changes in expectancies of success, and rates of self-reinforcement (Benassi & Mahler, 1985; Sacco & Hokanson, 1978, 1982, respectively) that occur in public situations are reversed when assessed in private situations. In two of the three studies (Sacco & Hokanson, 1978, 1982), nondepressives exhibited more optimistic cognitions in public than in private, whereas depressives showed less-optimistic cognitions in public than in private. These studies suggest that depressed and nondepressed people's personal cognitions may not be the same as those they express in the presence of others. Clearly, further work is needed to determine the generality of public–private differences in depressive and nondepressive cognition to the other kinds of inferential tasks reviewed previously.

Immediate versus Delayed Inference. A number of the studies we have reviewed examined depressed and nondepressed people's inferences about performance or personality feedback either immediately after presentation or after a delay (recall of feedback). A generally consistent finding was that depressed subjects' immediate perceptions were typically accurate or unbiased (Craighead *et al.,* 1979; DeMonbreun & Craighead, 1977; Hoehn-Hyde *et al.,* 1982; Nelson & Craighead, 1977; Vestre & Caulfield, 1986; and Wenzlaff & Berman, 1985; for exceptions, see Dykman *et al.,* 1987; and Gotlib, 1983), whereas their delayed memories of the feedback were more subject to bias or distortion (Buchwald, 1977; DeMonbreun & Craighead, 1977; Dennard & Hokanson, 1986; Dykman *et al.,* 1987; Gotlib, 1981, 1983; Nelson & Craighead, 1977; and Wener & Rehm, 1975; for an exception, see Wenzlaff & Berman, 1985). Nondepressives tended to show bias or distortion in both their immediate perceptions and their delayed recall of the feedback. These studies suggest that whereas cognitive and/or motivational processes that lead to biases and distortions (optimistic ones) may operate early in the information-processing sequence for nondepressives, such processes may act later among depressives, whereby after time or additional processing, initially accurate or unbiased judgments are transformed into negatively biased or erroneous inferences. Fruitful directions for further research would be an examination of the generality of such immediate versus delayed differences in depressive inference to other types of judgment tasks and an investigation of the types of psychological processes that would be likely to produce cognitive bias and distortion only after a delay in the presentation of feedback.

Ambiguous versus Unambiguous Information. The studies we have reviewed can also be classified in terms of whether they ask subjects to make judgments or inferences about ambiguous or unambiguous information. Interestingly, nondepressed subjects exhibited optimistic biases or distortions about themselves in 20 of 23 (87%) studies involving relatively ambiguous information or events (e.g., Ahrens *et al.,* in press; Hoehn-Hyde *et al.,* 1982; Lewinsohn *et al.,* 1980; Roth & Rehm, 1980; Vestre & Caulfield, 1986) but in only 11 of 18 (61%) studies using unambiguous information (e.g., Dykman *et al.,* 1987; Gotlib, 1981; Wener &

Rehm, 1975). In contrast, depressed subjects showed pessimistic, self-referent biases or distortions in only 6 of 23 (26%) studies providing ambiguous information (e.g., Ahrens, 1986; Dykman *et al.*, 1987; Gotlib, 1983) but in 8 of 18 (44%) studies using unambiguous information (e.g., Buchwald, 1977; Dennard & Hokanson, 1986; Gotlib, 1981; Vazquez, 1987). Thus, although depressives are less likely to exhibit cognitive biases and distortions for the self than nondepressives overall, depressives appear to be more susceptible to bias in situations involving unambiguous information (e.g., clear positive or negative outcomes or feedback), whereas nondepressives appear more susceptible to bias in situations involving ambiguous information (e.g., neutral or no information). Studies that directly compare depressed and nondepressed people's inferences for ambiguous and unambiguous information on *equivalent* tasks are needed in order to investigate this issue further (see Albright *et al.*, 1987).

Social versus Nonsocial Information. Based on the interpersonal perspectives of depression (e.g., Coyne, 1976; Gotlib & Asarnow, 1979), one might speculate that depressives' inferences would be more likely to be negatively biased in social than in nonsocial situations. However, in comparing seven studies in which subjects provided self-perceptions in the context of engaging in a social interaction or receiving feedback from others (Gotlib, 1983; Hoehn-Hyde *et al.*, 1982; Lewinsohn *et al.*, 1980; Loewenstein & Hokanson, 1986; Roth & Rehm, 1980; Siegel & Alloy, 1987; Strack & Coyne, 1983) with five studies in which they provided self-perceptions following nonsocial feedback (Craighead *et al.*, 1979; DeMonbreun & Craighead, 1977; Dykman *et al.*, 1987; Vestre & Caulfield, 1986; Wenzlaff & Berman, 1985), we find that depressives' self-perceptions are equally likely to be accurate or unbiased for both social and nonsocial information (five of seven versus four of five studies). Similarly, nondepressives' self-perceptions are equally likely to *show* positive biases or distortions for both social and nonsocial information (six of seven versus three of five studies). Although depressives appear to be no more biased, and nondepressives no less biased, in processing social versus nonsocial information about themselves, none of the "depressive realism" studies conducted to date has directly compared the two groups' processing of social and nonsocial information with equivalent tasks or situations. Further research needs to address this issue.

Personal Constraints

Severity of Depression. In considering the findings of studies on depressive realism and nondepressive biases and illusions, several theorists (e.g., Beck, 1986; Evans & Hollon, Chapter 12, this volume; Ruehlman, West, & Pasahow, 1985) have suggested that the degree and nature of cognitive biases may be a function of the severity of depression. That is, nondepressed individuals may be characterized by consistent optimistic biases and distortions; mildly depressed individuals, by a breakdown of these optimistic biases, thus exhibiting unbiased and often realistic cognitions; and severely depressed individuals, by the negative biases and distortions originally hypothesized by Beck (1967, 1976).

Of the studies we have reviewed, 14 included clinical samples of depressives, that is, psychiatric inpatients or outpatients, or individuals seeking treatment for depression (Abramson, Garber, Edwards, & Seligman 1978; DeMonbreun & Craighead, 1977; Gibbons *et al.*, 1985; Golin *et al.*, 1979; Gotlib, 1981, 1983; Hamilton & Abramson, 1983; Hoehn-Hyde *et al.*, 1982; Lewinsohn *et al.*, 1980; Lobitz & Post, 1979; Raps *et al.*, 1982; Roth & Rehm, 1980; Rozensky *et al.*, 1977; Sackheim & Wegner, 1986). If it is assumed that clinical samples are likely to be relatively severely depressed (at least as compared to samples of college students), then a consideration of depressives' judgments in these studies is relevant to an evaluation of the severity hypothesis. In 8 of these 14 studies, depressed subjects' perceptions and judgments were completely unbiased or accurate, and in another 4 studies, depressives' inferences were accurate or unbiased for some of the tasks or conditions (e.g., DeMonbreun & Craighead, 1977, accurate perception of feedback; Gotlib, 1981, accurate self-punishment; Roth & Rehm, 1980, accurate monitoring of negative behavior; Sackheim & Wegner, 1986, unbiased attributions). Two studies have directly addressed the severity issue by comparing mildly and moderately depressed college students' inferences. Dennard and Hokanson (1986) found that both moderately and mildly depressed students gave accurate recognitions and perceptions of reward, the only exception being that moderately depressed students underestimated a low reinforcement rate. Loewenstein and Hokanson (1986) found that while both moderately and mildly depressed students displayed less recall of self-referent feedback than did nondepressed students, neither depressed group exhibited biased recall.

In sum, the severity hypothesis does not appear to be strongly supported by the studies conducted to date, but clearly this issue requires further empirical attention. We need studies that directly investigate the degree of inferential bias or error across a wide range of severities of depression as well as studies that examine whether realism or distortion is differentially associated with different subtypes or chronicities of depression.

Self-concept/Self-esteem. An intriguing possibility is that it is not depression *per se* that is associated with inferential realism or evenhandedness about the self but rather some other personal attribute that is correlated with depression and that more directly underlies the absence of self-referent cognitive biases. Tennen and Herzberger (1987) suggested low self-esteem or a negative self-concept as a prime candidate. They found that an evenhanded attributional style was more strongly associated with low self-esteem than with depression, although it should be noted that Crocker *et al.* (1987b) obtained precisely the opposite result in a replication of Tennen and Herzberger's analyses with a different sample. Alloy *et al.* (1987) also suggested that a number of predictors that they found discriminated "realists" from "illusionists" on a judgment-of-control task could be interpreted as indicative of a low versus a high self-concept. More generally, a number of behaviors and cognitions associated with depression are also exhibited by individuals with low self-esteem (e.g., Ickes & Layden, 1978; Shrauger & Terbovic, 1976). Thus an important direction for future research would be an examination of the relative contributions of depression versus low self-esteem/self-concept to inferential realism. Studies of depressed individuals with high self-esteem and nondepressed individuals with low self-esteem may be particularly enlightening in this regard.

MOTIVATIONAL AND COGNITIVE HYPOTHESES OF DEPRESSIVE AND NONDEPRESSIVE INFERENCE

An important question concerns the origins of differences in the nature and degree of cognitive bias and distortion exhibited by depressed and nondepressed people. Although a variety of potential mechanisms have been proposed (Alloy *et al.*, 1987, Kayne & Alloy, in press), we limit our discussion here to two motivational accounts (self-esteem maintenance and impression management) and two cognitive explanations (self-schema processing and self-directed attention) of depressed–nondepressed differences in inferential bias and distortion. An adequate account of these differences in cognitive bias must address why nondepressed individuals consistently display optimistic, self-enhancing biases and illusions, whereas depressed individuals are less susceptible to biases in their self-assessments. Moreover, it should be noted that the various motivational and cognitive hypotheses discussed in this section need not be mutually exclusive (see Tetlock & Levi, 1982). Rather, nondepressive self-enhancing biases and the relative absence of these biases among depressives may be multiply determined and result from a number of motivational and cognitive mechanisms, perhaps with different mechanisms operating in different situations.

Self-esteem Maintenance

In explaining the finding that people generally attribute successes to internal factors but attribute failures to external factors, several social psychologists have posited a motivation to maintain or protect self-esteem (Bradley, 1978; Miller & Ross, 1975; Snyder, Stephan, & Rosenfield, 1978). More generally, a consistent tendency to perceive oneself optimistically and to enhance oneself relative to others may also be the consequence of concerns regarding self-esteem maintenance. Thus nondepressives' "self-serving" optimistic biases and illusions may be adaptive and may function to protect them against assaults to their self-esteem that would be engendered by a more objective or unbiased view of their personal successes and failures, strengths and weaknesses. According to the hypothesis of self-esteem maintenance, depressives are relatively unbiased in their self-perceptions and inferences because they have suffered a breakdown in this motivation. This breakdown may occur for a number of reasons. Depressives, who often possess low self-esteem (e.g., Beck, 1967; Laxer, 1964; Nadich, Gargan, & Michael, 1975), may be unable to generate or utilize self-enhancing strategies that would serve to defend against assaults on self-esteem (Bibring, 1953; Freud, 1917/1957). Alternatively, preexisting low levels of self-esteem may leave the depressed person with little that he or she would be motivated to protect (Abramson & Alloy, 1981).

The hypothesis of self-esteem maintenance is consistent with the finding that depressive realism and nondepressive optimistic bias appear to be specific to the self (see Self- versus Other-reference.) If nondepressive self-enhancing biases reflect needs for self-esteem maintenance, one would expect such biases to be less likely in nondepressives' judgments about others, because misperceiving others would have a smaller effect on self-esteem than misperceiving oneself. Similarly, if the relative absence of cognitive illusions about the self in depressives is the result of a breakdown in the mechanisms of self-defense, such dysfunction should not apply to perceptions of others. Similarly, the hypothesis of self-esteem maintenance can account for why low self-esteem or self-concept is also often found to be associated with balanced, unbiased inferences and high self-esteem with optimistic biases (see Self-concept/Self-esteem). It can also explain why nondepressives' tendency to self-enhance is accentuated under conditions of high ego involvement (e.g., Alloy, Abramson, & Kossman 1985; Miller, 1976) or direct threats to self-esteem (e.g., Alloy & Abramson, 1982), whereas depressives' judgments remain accurate or unbiased under conditions of both high and low ego involvement or threat (e.g., Alloy & Abramson, 1982; Alloy, Abramson, & Kossman, 1985).

More problematic for the hypothesis of self-esteem maintenance are the results of three studies (Benassi & Mahler, 1985; Sacco & Hokanson, 1978, 1982) suggesting that depressed and nondepressed individuals' relative susceptibility to cognitive illusions or distortions may be reversed in public versus private situations. Presumably, the motivation of nondepressives to maintain self-esteem and the breakdown of this motivation in depressives would be independent of the presence or absence of others' knowledge of their responses. However, Tetlock and Manstead (1985) have argued that public–private manipulations cannot adequately distinguish between impression management and such intrapsychic hypotheses as self-esteem maintenance because public–private manipulations may have implications for self-esteem as well as for maintaining the approval of others. Thus the hypothesis of self-esteem maintenance remains a viable explanation of differences in depressive and nondepressive inference.

Impression Management

In almost all of the studies we have reviewed that examine depressive and non-depressive inference, subjects' judgments were public—that is, they were observed by the experimenter, or sometimes by others. Several social psychologists (e.g., Arkin, Appleman, & Burger, 1980; Bradley, 1978; House, 1980) have suggested that the public nature of individuals' inferences may be the critical factor underlying self-serving biases. Thus nondepressives' optimistic, self-enhancing biases may be viewed as public self-presentations motivated by a desire to increase or maintain the esteem in which they are held by others, rather than by a desire to maintain self-esteem. Indeed, recent social psychological research demonstrates that at least under some conditions, positive, self-enhancing biases of the kind exhibited by nondepressed people are effective in generating favorable impressions in others (e.g., Schlenker & Leary, 1982). From this perspective, depressives' relative insusceptibility to self-serving biases may reflect a breakdown in the mechanisms for maintaining others' approval rather than a loss of self-protective mechanisms.

The notion that depressives' failure to exhibit self-enhancing cognitive biases represents dysfunctional impression-management strategies is consistent with the interpersonal theories of depression (e.g., Coates & Wortman, 1980; Coyne, 1976; Youngren & Lewinsohn, 1980). According to interpersonal theorists, depression is mediated by an inability to obtain positive reinforcement from the social environment. This inability may, in turn, originate partly from depressives' failure to engage in self-enhancement as a result of a breakdown in their impression-management strategies. The logic of the impression-management hypothesis suggests that depressives would be more likely to exhibit optimistic, self-serving biases in private situations than in public ones, whereas nondepressives would be less likely to self-enhance in private, because there would be no motive for self-aggrandizement when others are not present. The results of the two public–private studies by Sacco and Hokanson (1978, 1982) are consistent with this prediction; however, Benassi and Mahler (1985) obtained the opposite result, with depressives exhibiting optimistic distortions in public but not in private, and nondepressives showing greater positive distortions in private than in public. Of course, the impression-management hypothesis predicts public–private differences in depressive and nondepressive inference, but it also can explain why nondepressive optimistic illusions and depressive realism are specific to the self (see Self- versus Other-reference). If nondepressives' biases and depressives' lack of bias are a function of the presence and absence, respectively, of impression-management motives, such motives and strategies to maintain the approval of others would not be relevant in making judgments about other people. The impression-management hypothesis would have a more difficult time accounting for the relation between level of self-esteem and degree of optimistic bias discussed previously (but see Tetlock & Manstead, 1985, for how this hypothesis might explain self-esteem effects).

Self-schema Processing

Among cognitive explanations for nondepressive optimistic biases and illusions and depressive realism in inferences about the self, the self-schema hypothesis is one of the most promising. "Self-schemata" have been defined as organized representations in memory that embody an individual's generalized beliefs, attitudes, and assumptions about the self and its relation to the environment as well as specific self-relevant thoughts and behaviors (Markus, 1977). Basic research in cognitive and social psychology suggests that all types of schemata facilitate the perception, interpretation, and memory of situational information but that at the same time, schematic processing produces systematic biases and distortions in inference and memory (e.g., Abramson & Martin, 1981; Alloy & Tabachnik, 1984; Markus, 1977; Nisbett & Ross, 1980; Taylor & Crocker, 1980). According to Beck (1967, 1976), depressed people's self-schemata contain negative content as compared to those of nondepressed people. Functionally, depressives' self-schemata should act as a conceptual filter, leading them to interpret and remember personal information in a relatively negative, schema-consistent manner.

According to the hypothesis of self-schema processing then, nondepressives' optimistic, self-enhancing biases and illusions are the product of the operation of self-schemata with strong and consistent positive content. In contrast, to explain depressives' relative insusceptibility to such optimistic distortions and their tendency to make unbiased, evenhanded judgments about themselves, depressives' self-schemata would have to be less differentiated than those of nondepressives and, instead, contain negative content in addition to positive content (Kayne & Alloy, in press). Consistent with this hypothesis, a number of studies comparing the self-schemata of depressed and nondepressed individuals have shown that nondepressives possess strong, positive self-schemata, whereas mildly and moderately depressed subjects' self-schemata appear to contain mixed and rather balanced positive and negative content (e.g., Davis, 1979a, 1979b; Greenberg & Alloy, 1987; Ingram, Smith, & Brehm, 1983; Kuiper & Derry, 1982; Kuiper & MacDonald, 1982; and Vazquez & Alloy, 1987; for reviews, see Greenberg, Vazquez, & Alloy, Chapter 4, this Volume; and Blaney, 1986). One study (Derry & Kuiper, 1981) has suggested that more severely depressed persons may possess self-schemata with more consistent negative content, although this finding is not yet well established (see Blaney, 1986; Vazquez & Alloy, 1987). If severely depressed people do possess strong and consistent negative self-schemata, one would expect their processing of self-referent information to be pessimistically biased. Our review earlier of studies that included more severely depressed subjects indicated that their inferences may be as unbiased as those of mildly depressed subjects, although, clearly, more evidence is needed on this point.

A clear prediction of the hypothesis of self-schema processing is that even though depressives' mixed-content self-schemata may lead them to be less biased than nondepressives overall, *both* depressives and nondepressives should exhibit both biased and unbiased processing, depending on the relative match between the information to be processed and each group's self-schema. Consistent with this prediction, Dykman *et al.* (1987) found that both depressed and nondepressed subjects showed positive biases, negative biases, and accurate encoding of ambiguous feedback at different times, depending on the relative positioning of the content of each group's self-schema and the valence of the feedback cue being processed. Of course, the hypothesis of self-schema processing also readily explains the specificity of nondepressive optimistic biases and depressive evenhandedness to the self and the association between self-esteem or self-concept and the degree and nature of inferential bias (see Self– versus Other-reference and Self-concept/Self-esteem). Interestingly, the hypothesis may also be able to account for the finding that nondepressives' inferences are more biased for ambiguous information, whereas depressives are more likely to exhibit biases for unambiguous information. If nondepressives' self-schemata possess strong positive content, then information that is ambiguous may be interpreted as positive under the operation of these self-schemata. In contrast, if depressives' self-schemata contain mixed positive and negative content, then ambiguous information will be pulled equally in positive and negative directions by the operation of the self-schemata and thus be processed in a relatively unbiased fashion. Clear-cut, unambiguous positive or negative information, on the other hand, may serve to "activate" or "prime" the positive or negative portions of depressives' self-schemata, respectively (see Alloy, Clements, & Kolden, 1985; Riskind & Rholes, 1984), thereby leading to more biased processing of the unambiguous information. Like the hypothesis of self-esteem maintenance, however, self-schema processing does not readily explain public–private differences in depressive and nondepressive inference (but see Tetlock & Manstead, 1985, for a possible explanation).

Self-directed Attention

Another cognitive explanation for greater realism and decreased bias in depressives' judgments than in nondepressives' judgments about the self derives from social psychological research on self-directed attention, or "objective self-awareness," as it was originally called (e.g., Duval & Wicklund, 1972; Carver & Scheier, 1981). "Self-directed attention" refers to the proportion of time that one's attention is directed toward some aspect of the self rather than toward the environment. Experimental methods used to increase self-focused attention include exposing a person to his or her own mirror image or voice. Musson and Alloy (Chapter 7, this volume) reviewed a number of remarkable parallels between the characteristic features of depression and the behavioral, cognitive, and emotional effects of self-directed attention. Of particular interest here are the findings that the state of self-focused attention increases the accuracy of self-reports (Gibbons, 1978, 1983; Gibbons & Gaeddert, 1984; Gibbons *et al.*, 1985; Pryor, Gibbons, Wicklund, Fazio, & Hood, 1977; Scheier, Carver, & Gibbons, 1979) and that individuals high in "private self-consciousness," the dispositional tendency to be self-focused, give more accurate self-referent judgments than those low in private self-consciousness (Scheier, Buss, & Buss, 1978). The striking parallels between features of depression and self-directed attention suggest that depressed individuals may be more self-focused than nondepressed individuals, and, in fact, depression has been found to correlate with private self-consciousness (see Musson & Alloy, Chapter 7, this volume).

Attention is an important factor in producing bias in cognitive functioning because people more efficiently process information that they attend to. If depressives tend to be more self-focused than nondepressives, then their generally greater accuracy and decreased bias in perceiving themselves may be the product of asking them to make judgments about the very object on which their attention is focused (see Alloy, 1982a). That is, if depressives are characterized by increased self-directed attention, then this may lead them to be more self-aware (Gibbons, 1983). In contrast, nondepressives, who are presumably more externally focused, would exhibit greater biases or distortion in self-relevant judgments.

No studies to date have directly tested the hypothesis of self-directed attention in depressive and nondepressive inference (but see Musson & Alloy, 1987, for a test in progress). However, the hypothesis is consistent with the specificity of non-depressive optimistic biases and depressive realism to the self. It would follow from the hypothesis of self-directed attention that depressives should be less accurate and more biased when making judgments about others, whereas more externally focused nondepressives should be more accurate and less biased in their inferences about others. Inasmuch as it is private self-consciousness that is thought to increase the accuracy of self-reports, the hypothesis of self-directed attention may also be able to explain why nondepressives' self-referent judgments *may* be less biased in private than in public settings (Sacco & Hokanson, 1978, 1982). Depressives' greater bias in private than in public would be inconsistent with this hypothesis, although, as indicated earlier, the effects of public versus private settings are still unclear (see Benassi & Mahler, 1985, vs. Sacco & Hokanson, 1978, 1982; and the discussion earlier in this chapter).

THE MEANING OF DEPRESSIVE REALISM AND NONDEPRESSIVE BIAS: FOUR THEORETICAL PERSPECTIVES

Clearly, studies are needed that directly test each of the motivational and cognitive hypotheses proposed here; such studies will ultimately help us understand the bases of depressive and nondepressive inference. Of greater conceptual and practical significance than the issue of which psychological mechanisms underlie depressive and nondepressive cognition, however, is the meaning, for everyday life, of the differences in depressed and nondepressed individuals' susceptibility to cognitive biases and distortions. Earlier we distinguished among the concepts of error or distortion, bias, and irrationality. We argued that rationality involves the consideration of whether people's inferential strategies lead to accuracy or realism over the long run in their daily environments as opposed to accuracy in the short run in specific situations. In this section, we briefly discuss four theoretical perspectives regarding the meaning of the findings of depressive realism and nondepressive bias for depressives' and nondepressives' rationality in their everyday environments (see also Evans & Hollon, Chapter 12, this volume, and Kayne & Alloy, in press). We also point out some of the implications of each perspective and outline the type of research program that is needed in order to distinguish among the perspectives.

The Naive Perspective

It is possible that the judgments and perceptions observed in depressed and nondepressed persons in many of the laboratory studies we have reviewed are representative of their inferences in daily life. If this is so, then depressed people's cognitions would be realistic or unbiased much of the time, whereas nondepressed people's cognitions would be optimistically biased or distorted over the long run. Depressive rationality and nondepressive irrationality would be the case if any one or a combination of the motivational and cognitive mechanisms underlying depressive and nondepressive inference in the empirical studies is also operative in the everyday environment. If, for example, depressives are characterized by a generalized breakdown in the motivation to maintain self-esteem and/or the approval of others, or by weaker, less differentiated self-schemata or greater self-awareness, then rationality over the long run should be the consequence. We refer to this perspective as "naive" because it involves taking the findings of the depressive realism studies at face value and generalizing them to the everyday physical and social environment.

If the naive perspective is correct, then three intriguing implications may follow. First, the perspective would suggest that Beck's (1967, 1976) cognitive model of depression, with its emphasis on negative depressive distortions, is wrong and that at least one psychopathological group is less rather than more susceptible than normals to cognitive irrationality and distortion. Second, this perspective raises the possibility that a realistic and unbiased perception of oneself and one's relation to the world contributes to the cause or maintenance of depression (see Kayne, Alloy, Romer, & Crocker, 1987). Finally, the naive perspective suggests that cognitive therapy for depression (Beck *et al.,* 1979), a demonstrably effective program for treating depression (see Evans & Hollon, Chapter 12, this volume), may work *not* by enhancing the realism of depressives' cognitions, as is currently assumed, but by training depressives to construct for themselves the kinds of optimistic biases and distortions typically exhibited by nondepressed people (see Alloy, Clements, & Kolden, 1985; Alloy *et al.,* 1987; Evans & Hollon, Chapter 12, this volume; Kayne & Alloy, in press).

The Ironic Perspective

Alternatively, it may be premature to conclude on the basis of the laboratory studies conducted to date that over the long run depressives are less likely to succumb to cognitive distortions and biases than nondepressives. From an ironic perspective, nondepressives' optimistic errors and biases in the laboratory may be indicative of rationality in everyday life, while depressives' relative insusceptibility to such errors and biases may reflect irrationality over the long run (see Abramson & Alloy, 1981; Alloy & Tabachnik, 1984). This could be the case if nondepressives' optimistic biases and illusions in the laboratory are the product of inferential heuristics that accurately reflect the usual contingencies they face and the feedback they receive in their everyday lives. For example, nondepressives may actually cause good outcomes, experience success, and receive positive feedback about themselves frequently in their daily lives. Insofar as nondepressives' optimistic biases accurately reflect the contingencies and feedback in their usual environments, it would not seem irrational for them to use these biases in interpreting new personally relevant information in particular situations. Reliance on such inferential strategies would yield realistic perceptions and judgments except in short-run circumstances, such as some of the laboratory studies in which the experimental contingencies or feedback happened to be inconsistent with nondepressives' biases. From the ironic perspective, depressives may frequently give more accurate and less biased judgments, not because their inferential strategies are more rational, but because their strategies happen to fit more closely the contingencies or feedback programmed in the laboratory studies.

An analogy from visual perception may help to illustrate the ironic perspective. Researchers in perception have discovered that people are very susceptible to a number of visual illusions associated with depth, size, or perspective (Gregory, 1966). Few, if any, perceptual psychologists, however, would infer from these findings that people's susceptibility to illusions results from an irrational or inferior strategy of processing visual information. Instead, perceptual psychologists emphasize that the inappropriate application of a visual strategy that normally leads to veridical perceptions in the everyday physical world can give rise to visual illusions under special conditions. For example, when cues normally associated with depth are superimposed on a figure without real depth, people inappropriately use these cues and see depth where it does not exist. Similarly, nondepressives' optimistic biases and illusions may reflect a misapplication of inferential heuristics, which, over the long run, generally lead to realistic judgments in everyday life. Ironically, depressives' relative insusceptibility to these biases and distortions in the laboratory may represent the breakdown or absence of generally rational strategies for self-assessment in the complexities of their everyday environments. If the ironic perspective accurately represents the nature of depressive and nondepressive inference over the long run, then this would be consistent with Beck's notion of the importance of cognitive distortion in depression and with the current assumption of cognitive therapy that the cognitive treatment program enhances the reality-testing skills of depressives.

The Comic Perspective

A third possibility is that the perceptions and judgments of both depressed and nondepressed individuals are realistic assessments of the contingencies and the feedback they experience in their everyday environments. This could occur if depressed and nondepressed people make their respective worlds conform to their perceptions and inferences through their own behavior. Essentially, the comic perspective is based on the notion of self-fulfilling prophecy. Several investigators have demonstrated that a perceiver's initially erroneous preconceptions about the environment may lead him or her to behave in ways consistent with those conceptions. These belief-consistent behaviors in turn channel subsequent environmental interaction in ways that cause life experiences to confirm the perceiver's beliefs (e.g., Abramson et al., 1981; Rosenthal & Rubin, 1978; Snyder & Swann, 1978a, 1978b; Snyder, Tanke, & Berscheid, 1977; see also Wachtel, 1977). For example, if depressives perceive that they are incompetent, such perceptions may lead them to try fewer problem-solving behaviors or to engage in less coping effort, and thus they may actually experience failure and confirm the incompetence they originally inferred. Similarly, nondepressives' belief in their abilities may lead to extended efforts to exert control and find solutions, and these efforts may eventuate in the success that the nondepressives expected, thus confirming their competence. Nondepressives may have shown optimistic errors and biases in many of the laboratory studies because the situational contingencies and information in these studies were programmed by the experimenters in a fixed manner. Consequently, these contingencies were not susceptible to influence by nondepressives' behaviors, and thus behavioral confirmation of nondepressives' perceptions could not occur.

If the comic perspective most closely describes the realism that exists in the daily lives of depressed and nondepressed persons, this would suggest that Beck's emphasis on cognitive distortions in depression is incorrect but that his concept of negative self-schemata in depression may be important. According to the comic perspective, it is such negative self-schemata that lead to dysfunctional behaviors, which end up realistically confirming the negative schemata. The implications for therapy deriving from the comic perspective are that one must either aid depressives in developing more optimistic self-schemata or train them to engage in more active and effective problem-solving behaviors in order to prevent the fulfillment of their self-concepts (Beck *et al.*, 1979).

The Tragic Perspective

Finally, both depressed and nondepressed people's inferences may be unrealistic over the long run in the natural environment. Both groups may exhibit erroneous inferences distorted in opposite directions, with nondepressives distorting environmental information optimistically and depressives distorting it pessimistically. The tragic perspective could obtain if both groups engage in schema-driven or motivationally based biases of opposite content that are inconsistent with the environmental feedback each group typically confronts (Dykman *et al.*, 1987). From this perspective, depressed subjects' self-relevant judgments are often accurate or unbiased in many laboratory studies because the situational cues in these studies happened to match their biases, even though these biases may not be in accord with environmental cues over the long run in their daily lives. The tragic perspective would imply that Beck's theory is correct in describing the negatively distorted personal inferences of depressives over the long run but incorrect in assuming that nondepressives' self-referent inferences are realistic in everyday life. Therefore, from this view, cognitive therapy for depression could be directed toward enhancing the reality-testing skills of depressives or toward training depressives to engage in optimistic biases and illusions like those of nondepressives.

Distinguishing among the Four Perspectives

Essentially, determining which of the four theoretical perspectives best describes the rationality of depressed and nondepressed persons' inferences in their daily lives will require an assessment of the content and strength of each group's inferential biases and of the relative fit of these biases to the environmental cues or feedback each group experiences on a day-to-day basis (Abramson & Alloy, 1981; Alloy & Tabachnik, 1984). The first requirement—assessing the two groups' biases—can be accomplished by conducting (1) a wide-ranging series of laboratory studies that examine depressive and nondepressive inference under conditions designed to be incongruent with the presumed nature of the biases and thus capable of revealing these biases and (2) studies designed to uncover the psychological mechanisms underlying the two groups' inferential strategies. However, determining the fit, or match, between the inferential strategies of depressives and nondepressives and the information provided by their everyday environments can be achieved only through a research program that also assesses comprehensively the nature of the contingencies, feedback, and cues depressives and nondepressives confront in their daily interactions with the social and nonsocial world (Coyne, 1982; Coyne & Gotlib, 1983). Such a program could include naturalistic studies of the kinds of life events the two groups experience, the kinds of feedback they receive from others in their social spheres, the types of environmental contingencies they usually confront, and the kinds of cues that predict each group's successes and failures in both achievement and interpersonal domains.

THE ADAPTIVENESS OF DEPRESSIVE
AND NONDEPRESSIVE INFERENCES

The final issue we raise concerns the relative adaptiveness of depressed and nondepressed people's inferential strategies. Regardless of whether the two groups' perceptions and judgments are realistic or unrealistic over the long run in the natural environment, what are the psychological and physical consequences associated with each type of strategy? A number of researchers have suggested that optimistic biases and illusions in self-perception of the sort typically displayed by nondepressed individuals are highly adaptive (e.g., Abramson & Alloy, 1981; Alloy & Koenig, in press; Greenwald, 1980; Taylor, 1983; Tiger, 1979).

One adaptive consequence of optimistic, self-enhancing biases may be the protection they afford against threats to self-esteem (Abramson & Alloy, 1981; Alloy & Abramson, 1979, 1982; Ickes & Layden, 1978; Taylor, 1983). Such biases may also increase liking and approval from others (Alloy, 1982b; Schlenker & Leary, 1982). A second adaptive consequence of the nondepressive style of inference may be the maintenance of positive expectations of success, leading to increased behavioral persistence toward desired goals and thus, ultimately, to a greater likelihood of eventually attaining such goals (Alloy, 1982a; Greenwald, 1980). Indeed, Scheier, Weintraub, and Carver (1986) found that optimists engage in more active and elaborate problem-focused coping strategies than do pessimists. Finally, optimistic, self-enhancing biases or illusions appear to promote invulnerability to depression when individuals are confronted with stressful life events (Abramson & Alloy, 1981; Alloy et al., 1987; Carver & Gaines, 1987; Kayne et al., 1987; Metalsky, Abramson, Seligman, Semmel, & Peterson, 1982; Metalsky, Halberstadt, & Abramson, 1987) and to decrease the potential for suicide (e.g., Beck, Kovacs, & Weissman, 1975; Kazdin, French, Unis, Esveldt-Dawson, & Sherick, 1983; Minkoff, Bergman, Beck, & Beck, 1973; Petrie & Chamberlain, 1983). More generally, optimistic illusions may also decrease susceptibility to stress-related physical symptoms (e.g., Scheier & Carver, 1985) and enhance successful coping with life-threatening events (e.g., Silver & Wortman, 1980; Taylor, 1983). Along these lines, Tiger (1979) suggested that optimism has become relatively pervasive in human cognition through natural selection processes in humans' evolutionary history because of its adaptive significance. Of course, if taken to the extreme, possibly as in mania, optimistic, self-enhancing biases may be maladaptive if they interfere with the achievement of desired goals or decrease successful coping with stress because a person is not sensitive to the actual environmental contingencies or his or her true strengths and weaknesses (e.g., Abramson & Alloy, 1981). In fact, optimistic biases, particularly if they are unrealistic, may reduce people's likelihood of engaging in risk-preventing behaviors because of their illusions of personal strength and invulnerability (e.g., Weinstein, 1982, 1984, 1986).

Although much additional research and sophisticated thinking are needed in order to fully understand the boundary conditions of depressive realism and nondepressive biases and distortions, the psychological mechanisms producing depressive and nondepressive inferences, and the ultimate meaning of these different inferential strategies in the real world, one point appears clear: Depressed individuals may be suffering from the absence or breakdown of normal optimistic biases and distortions. Maladaptive symptoms of depression, such as low self-esteem, social skills deficits, negative affect, decreased persistence, poor coping with stress, and suicidal thoughts and attempts, may be consequences, in part, of the absence of healthy personal illusions.

NOTES

1. More recently, Beck (1986) has acknowledged the possibility that nondepressed people may also engage in schema-based optimistic distortions.
2. In reviewing the empirical studies, we only include studies that explicitly examine depressed–nondepressed differences in judgments or inferences or other individual differences that may be related to depression (e.g., helplessness, self-esteem). We do not review studies on the judgmental strategies of people in general or studies on individual differences whose relationship to depression is unclear (e.g., differences between Type A and Type B personalities).
3. Although Langer (1975) refers to this phenomenon as an "illusion of control," we believe that it is better characterized as inappropriately high expectancies of success, because subjects' judgments of control are not actually assessed.
4. The chance–skill studies have been criticized for not providing adequate tests of the helplessness theory's hypothesis that depressed and helpless subjects perceive response–outcome independence (the associative deficit—see Alloy & Abramson, 1980, and Alloy & Seligman, 1979, for these criticisms). However, the appropriateness of the chance–skill studies for testing the associative deficit of helplessness theory is not our major concern here. We discuss the chance–skill studies here in terms of their relevance to understanding the relative realism and bias of depressed and nondepressed persons' expectancies of success.
5. Dennard and Hokanson (1986) and Loewenstein and Hokanson (1986) classified subjects into groups on the basis of BDI (Beck, 1967) scores but actually use the terms "dysphoric" and "nondysphoric" to describe their subjects, rather than "depressed" and "nondepressed."

REFERENCES

Abramson, L. Y., & Alloy, L. B. (1980). Judgment of contingency: Errors and their implications. In A. Baum & J. Singer (Eds.), *Advances in environmental psychology* (Vol. 2, pp. 111–130). Hillsdale, NJ: Erlbaum.

Abramson, L. Y., & Alloy, L. B. (1981). Depression, nondepression, and cognitive illusions: A reply to Schwartz. *Journal of Experimental Psychology: General, 110,* 436–447.

Abramson, L. Y., Alloy, L. B., & Rosoff, R. (1981). Depression and the generation of complex hypotheses in the judgment of contingency. *Behaviour Research and Therapy, 19,* 35–45.

Abramson, L. Y., Garber, J., Edwards, N. B., & Seligman, M. E. P. (1978). Expectancy changes in depression and schizophrenia. *Journal of Abnormal Psychology, 87,* 102–109.

Abramson, L. Y., & Martin, D. (1981). Depression and the causal inference process. In J. Harvey, W. Ickes, & R. Kidd (Eds.), *New directions in attribution research* (pp. 117–168). Hillsdale, NJ: Erlbaum.

Abramson, L. Y., Metalsky, G. I., & Alloy, L. B. (1987). *The hopelessness theory of depression: A metatheoretical analysis with implications for psychopathology research.* Manuscript submitted for publication.

Abramson, L. Y., Metalsky, G. I., & Alloy, L. B. (in press). The hopelessness theory of depression: Does the research test the theory? In L. Y. Abramson (Ed.), *Social cognition and clinical psychology: A synthesis.* New York: Guilford Press.

Abramson, L. Y., Seligman, M. E. P., & Teasdale, J. (1978). Learned helplessness in humans: Critique and reformulation. *Journal of Abnormal Psychology, 87,* 49–74.

Ahrens, A. H. (1986). *Choice of social comparison targets by depressed and nondepressed students.* Unpublished doctoral dissertation, Stanford University, Stanford, CA.

Ahrens, A. H., Zeiss, A. M., & Kanfer, R. (in press). Depressive deficits in interpersonal standards, self-efficacy, and social comparison. *Cognitive Therapy and Research.*

Albright, J. S., Alloy, L. B., & Barch, D. (1987). *Depression and social comparison: The role of implicit versus explicit comparison sets.* Research in progress, Northwestern University, Evanston, IL.

Alloy, L. B. (1982b, August). *Depression: On the absence of self-serving cognitive biases.* Paper presented at the meeting of the American Psychological Association, Washington, DC.

Alloy, L. B. (1982a, October). *Depression and social comparison: Illusory self or other perceptions?* Paper presented at the meeting of the Society of Experimental Social Psychology, Nashville, IN.

Alloy, L. B., & Abramson, L. Y. (1979). Judgment of contingency in depressed and nondepressed students: Sadder but wiser? *Journal of Experimental Psychology: General, 108,* 441–485.

Alloy, L. B., & Abramson, L. Y. (1980). The cognitive component of human helplessness and depression: A critical analysis. In J. Garber & M. E. P. Seligman (Eds.), *Human helplessness: Theory and application* (pp. 59–70). New York: Academic Press.

Alloy, L. B., & Abramson, L. Y. (1982). Learned helplessness, depression, and the illusion of control. *Journal of Personality and Social Psychology, 42,* 1114–1126.

Alloy, L. B., Abramson, L. Y., & Kossman, D. (1985). The judgment of predictability in depressed and nondepressed college students. In F. R. Brush & J. B. Overmier (Eds.), *Affect, conditioning and cognition: Essays on the determinants of behavior* (pp. 229–246). Hillsdale, NJ: Erlbaum.

Alloy, L. B., Abramson, L. Y., & Musson, R. F. (1987). *Who distorts?: Predictors of the illusion of control.* Unpublished manuscript, Northwestern University, Evanston, IL.

Alloy, L. B., Abramson, L. Y., & Viscusi, D. (1981). Induced mood and the illusion of control. *Journal of Personality and Social Psychology, 41,* 1129–1140.

Alloy, L. B., & Ahrens, A. H. (1987). Depression and pessimism for the future: Biased use of statistically relevant information in predictions for self versus others. *Journal of Personality and Social Psychology, 52,* 366–378.

Alloy, L. B., Albright, J. S., & Clements, C. (1987). Depression, nondepression, and social comparison biases. In J. E. Maddux, C. D. Stoltenberg, & R. Rosenwein (Eds.), *Social processes in clinical and counseling psychology* (pp. 94–112). New York: Springer-Verlag.

Alloy, L. B., Clements, C., & Kolden, G. (1985). The cognitive diathesis–stress theories of depression: Therapeutic implications. In S. Reiss & R. Bootzin (Eds.), *Theoretical issues in behavior therapy* (pp. 379–410). New York: Academic Press.

Alloy, L. B., & Koenig, L. (in press). Hopelessness: On some of the antecedents and consequences of pessimism. *Behaviour Research and Therapy.*

Alloy, L. B., & Seligman, M. E. P. (1979). On the cognitive component of learned helplessness and depression. In G. H. Bower (Ed.), *The psychology of learning and motivation* (Vol. 13, pp. 219–276). New York: Academic Press.

Alloy, L. B., & Tabachnik, N. (1984). Assessment of covariation by humans and animals: The joint influence of prior expectations and current situational information. *Psychological Review, 91,* 112–149.

Arkin, R. M., Appelman, A. J., & Burger, J. M. (1980). Social anxiety, self-presentation, and the self-serving bias in causal attribution. *Journal of Personality and Social Psychology, 38,* 23–35.

Bandura, A. (1971). Vicarious and self-reinforcement processes. In R. Glaser (Ed.), *The nature of reinforcement* (pp. 228–278). New York: Academic Press.

Beck, A. T. (1967). *Depression: Clinical, experimental, and theoretical aspects.* New York: Harper & Row.

Beck, A. T. (1976). *Cognitive therapy and the emotional disorders.* New York: International Universities Press.

Beck, A. T. (1986). Cognitive therapy, behavior therapy, psychoanalysis, and pharmacotherapy: The cognitive continuum. In J. B. W. William & R. L. Spitzer (Eds.), *Psychotherapy research: Where are we and where should we go?* (pp. 114–134). New York: Guilford Press.

Beck, A. T., & Emery, G. (1985). *Anxiety disorders and phobias: A cognitive perspective.* New York: Basic Books.

Beck, A. T., Kovacs, M., & Weissman, A. (1975). Hopelessness and suicidal behavior: An overview. *Journal of the American Medical Association, 234,* 1146–1149.

Beck, A. T., Rush, A. J., Shaw, B. F., & Emery, G. (1979). *Cognitive therapy of depression: A treatment manual.* New York: Guilford Press.

Benassi, V. A., & Mahler, H. I. M. (1985). Contingency judgments by depressed college students: Sadder but not always wiser. *Journal of Personality and Social Psychology, 49,* 1323–1329.

Bibring, E. (1953). The mechanism of depression. In P. Greenacre (Ed.), *Affective disorders: Psychoanalytic contributions to their study* (pp. 13–48). New York: International Universities Press.

Blaney, P. H. (1986). Affect and memory: A review. *Psychological Bulletin, 99,* 229–246.

Bradley, G. W. (1978). Self-serving biases in the attribution process: A reexamination of the fact or fiction question. *Journal of Personality and Social Psychology, 36,* 56–71.

Bryson, S. E., Doan, B. D., & Pasquali, P. (1984). Sadder but wiser: A failure to demonstrate that mood influences judgments of control. *Canadian Journal of Behavioral Science, 16,* 107–119.

Buchwald, A. M. (1977). Depressive mood and estimates of reinforcement frequency. *Journal of Abnormal Psychology, 86,* 443–446.

Campbell, J. D. (1986). Similarity and uniqueness: The effects of attribute type, relevance, and individual differences in self-esteem and depression. *Journal of Personality and Social Psychology, 59,* 281–294.

Carver, C. S., & Gaines, J. G. (1987). Optimism, pessimism, and postpartum depression. *Cognitive Therapy and Research, 11,* 449–462.

Carver, C. S., & Scheier, M. F. (1981). *Attention and self-regulation: A control theory approach to human behavior.* New York: Springer-Verlag.

Coates, D., & Wortman, C. D. (1980). Depression maintenance and interpersonal control. In A. Baum & J. Singer (Eds.), *Advances in environmental psychology* (Vol. 2, pp. 149–182). Hillsdale, NJ: Erlbaum.

Coyne, J. C. (1976). Toward an interactional description of depression. *Psychiatry, 39,* 28–40.

Coyne, J. C. (1982). A critique of cognitions as causal entities with particular reference to depression. *Cognitive Therapy and Research, 6,* 3–13.

Coyne, J. C., & Gotlib, I. H. (1983). The role of cognition in depression: A critical appraisal. *Psychological Bulletin, 94,* 472–505.

Craighead, W. E. (1980). Away from a unitary model of depression. *Behavior Therapy, 11,* 122–128.

Craighead, W. E., Hickey, K. S., & DeMonbreun, B. G. (1979). Distortion of perception and recall of neutral feedback in depression. *Cognitive Therapy and Research, 3,* 291–298.

Crocker, J., Alloy, L. B., & Kayne, N. T. (1987a). *Attributional style, depression and perceptions of consensus for events*. Manuscript submitted for publication.

Crocker, J., Alloy, L. B., & Kayne, N. T. (1987b). *Self-esteem, depression, and attributional style*. Manuscript submitted for publication.

Crocker, J., Kayne, N. T., & Alloy, L. B. (1985). Comparing the self to others in depressed and nondepressed college students: A reply to McCauley. *Journal of Personality and Social Psychology, 48*, 1579–1583.

Davis, H. (1979a). Self-reference and the encoding of personal information in depression. *Cognitive Therapy and Research, 3*, 97–110.

Davis, H. (1979b). The self-schema and subjective organization of personal information in depression. *Cognitive Therapy and Research, 3*, 415–425.

DeMonbreun, B. G., & Craighead, W. E. (1977). Distortion of perception and recall of positive and neutral feedback in depression. *Cognitive Therapy and Research, 1*, 311–329.

Dennard, D. O., & Hokanson, J. E. (1986). Performance on two cognitive tasks by dysphoric and nondysphoric students. *Cognitive Therapy and Research, 10*, 377–386.

Depue, R. A., & Monroe, S. M. (1978). Learned helplessness in the perspective of the depressive disorders. *Journal of Abnormal Psychology, 87*, 3–20.

Derry, P., & Kuiper, N. A. (1981). Schematic processing and self-reference in clinical depression. *Journal of Abnormal Psychology, 90*, 286–297.

Drake, R. A. (1986). *Optimism, consistency, and control: Effects of manipulated cerebral hemisphere activation*. Manuscript submitted for publication.

Dresel, K. M. (1984). *Effects of the Type A behavior pattern, depression, and the duration of noncontrol on the illusion of control*. Unpublished master's thesis, University of Manitoba, Winnipeg.

Duval, S., & Wicklund, R. A. (1972). *A theory of objective self-awareness*. New York: Academic Press.

Dykman, B. M., Abramson, L. Y., Alloy, L. B., & Hartlage, S. (1987). *Processing of ambiguous and unambiguous feedback by depressed and nondepressed college students: Schematic biases and their implications for depressive realism*. Manuscript submitted for publication.

Ellis, A. (1962). *Reason and emotion in psychotherapy*. Secaucus, NJ: Lyle Stuart.

Finkel, C. B., Glass, C. R., & Merluzzi, T. V. (1982). Differential discrimination of self-referent statements by depressives and nondepressives. *Cognitive Therapy and Research, 6*, 173–183.

Ford, C. E., & Neale, J. M. (1985). Learned helplessness and judgments of control. *Journal of Personality and Social Psychology, 49*, 1330–1336.

Forgus, R., & Schulman, B. H. (1979). *Personality: A cognitive view*. Englewood Cliffs, NJ: Prentice-Hall.

Freud, S. (1920). *A general introduction to psychoanalysis*. New York: Pocket Books.

Freud, S. (1957). Mourning and melancholia. In J. Strachey (Ed. and Trans.), *The standard edition of the complete psychological works of Sigmund Freud* (Vol. 14, pp. 239–258). London: Hogarth Press. (Original work published 1917)

Garber, J., & Hollon, S. D. (1980). Universal versus personal helplessness in depression: Belief in uncontrollability or incompetence. *Journal of Abnormal Psychology, 89*, 56–66.

Gibbons, F. X. (1978). Sexual standards and reactions to pornography: Enhancing behavioral consistency through self-focused attention. *Journal of Personality and Social Psychology, 36*, 976–987.

Gibbons, F. X. (1983). Self-attention and self-report: The "veridicality" hypothesis. *Journal of Personality, 51*, 517–542.

Gibbons, F. X., & Gaeddert, W. P. (1984). Focus of attention and placebo utility. *Journal of Experimental Social Psychology, 20*, 159–176.

Gibbons, F. X., Smith, T. W., Ingram, R. E., Pearce, K., Brehm, S. S., & Schroeder, D. (1985). Self-awareness and self-confrontation: Effects of self-focused attention on members of a clinical population. *Journal of Personality and Social Psychology, 48*, 662–675.

Golin, S., Terrell, F., & Johnson, B. (1977). Depression and the illusion of control. *Journal of Abnormal Psychology, 86*, 440–442.

Golin, S., Terrell, F., Weitz, J., & Drost, P. L. (1979). The illusion of control among depressed patients. *Journal of Abnormal Psychology, 88*, 454–457.

Gotlib, I. H. (1981). Self-reinforcement and recall: Differential deficits in depressed and nondepressed psychiatric patients. *Journal of Abnormal Psychology, 90,* 521–530.

Gotlib, I. H. (1983). Perception and recall of interpersonal feedback: Negative bias in depression. *Cognitive Therapy and Research, 7,* 399–412.

Gotlib, I. H., & Asarnow, R. F. (1979). Interpersonal and impersonal problem-solving skills in mildly and clinically depressed university students. *Journal of Consulting and Clinical Psychology, 47,* 86–95.

Greenberg, M. S., & Alloy, L. B. (1987). *Depression versus anxiety: Schematic processing of self- and other-referent information.* Manuscript submitted for publication.

Greenwald, A. G. (1980). The totalitarian ego: Fabrication and revision of personal history. *American Psychologist, 35,* 603–618.

Gregory, R. L. (1966). *The psychology of seeing.* New York: McGraw-Hill.

Gregory, R. L. (1970). *The intelligent eye.* New York: McGraw-Hill.

Hamilton, E. W., & Abramson, L. Y. (1983). Cognitive patterns in major depressive disorder: A longitudinal study in a hospital setting. *Journal of Abnormal Psychology, 92,* 173–184.

Hoehn-Hyde, D., Schlottman, R. S., & Rush, A. J. (1982). Perception of social interactions in depressed psychiatric patients. *Journal of Consulting and Clinical Psychology, 50,* 209–212.

House, W. C. (1980). Effects of knowledge that attributions will be observed by others. *Journal of Research in Personality, 14,* 528–545.

Ickes, W. J. (1984). Personality. In A. S. Bellack & M. Hersen (Eds.), *Research methods in clinical psychology* (pp. 157–178). New York: Pergamon Press.

Ickes, W. J., & Layden, M. A. (1978). Attributional styles. In J. Harvey, W. Ickes, & R. Kidd (Eds.), *New directions in attribution research* (Vol. 2, pp. 119–152). Hillsdale, NJ: Erlbaum.

Ingram, R. E., Smith, T. W., & Brehm, S. S. (1983). Depression and information processing: Self-schemata and the encoding of self-referent information. *Journal of Personality and Social Psychology, 45,* 412–420.

Isen, A. M. (1984). Toward understanding the role of affect in cognition. In R. S. Wyer & T. K. Srull (Eds.), *Handbook of social cognition* (Vol. 3, pp. 179–236). Hillsdale, NJ: Erlbaum.

Jenkins, H. M., & Ward, W. C. (1965). Judgment of contingency between responses and outcomes. *Psychological Monographs, 79* (1, Whole No. 594).

Jones, E. E., & Nisbett, R. E. (1971). The actor and the observer: Divergent perceptions of the causes of behavior. In E. E. Jones, D. E. Kanouse, H. H. Kelley, R. E. Nisbett, S. Valins, & B. Weiner (Eds.), *Attribution: Perceiving the causes of behavior* (pp. 79–94). Morristown, NJ: General Learning Press.

Kanfer, F. H., & Duerfeldt, P. H. (1968). Comparison of self-reward and self-criticism as a function of types of prior external reinforcement. *Journal of Personality and Social Psychology, 3,* 261–268.

Karoly, P., & Ruehlman, L. (1983). Affective meaning and depression: A semantic differential analysis. *Cognitive Therapy and Research, 7,* 41–50.

Kayne, N. T., & Alloy, L. B. (in press). Clinician and patient as aberrant actuaries: Expectation-based distortions in assessments of covariation. In L. Y. Abramson, (Ed.), *Social cognition and clinical psychology: A synthesis.* New York: Guilford Press.

Kayne, N. T., Alloy, L. B., Romer, D., & Crocker, J. (1987). *Predicting depression and elation reactions in the classroom: A test of an attributional diathesis–stress theory of depression.* Manuscript submitted for publication.

Kazdin, A. E., French, N. H., Unis, A. S., Esveldt-Dawson, K., & Sherick, R. B. (1983). Hopelessness, depression, and suicidal intent among psychiatrically disturbed inpatient children. *Journal of Consulting and Clinical Psychology, 51,* 504–510.

Kihlstrom, J. F., & Nasby, W. (1981). Cognitive tasks in clinical assessment: An exercise in applied psychology. In P. C. Kendall & S. D. Hollon (Eds.), *Assessment strategies for cognitive–behavioral interventions* (pp. 287–317). New York: Academic Press.

Klein, D. C., & Seligman, M. E. P. (1976). Reversal of performance deficits and perceptual deficits in learned helplessness and depression. *Journal of Abnormal Psychology, 85,* 11–26.

Kruglanski, A. W., & Jaffe, Y. (in press). Curing by knowing: The epistemic approach to cognitive therapy. In L. Y. Abramson (Ed.), *Social cognition and clinical psychology: A synthesis*. New York: Guilford Press.

Kuiper, N. A. (1978). Depression and causal attributions for success and failure. *Journal of Personality and Social Psychology, 36,* 236–246.

Kuiper, N. A., & Derry, P. (1982). Depressed and nondepressed content self-reference in mild depressives. *Journal of Personality, 50,* 67–79.

Kuiper, N. A., & MacDonald, M. R. (1982). Self and other perception in mild depressives. *Social Cognition, 1,* 223–229.

Langer, E. J. (1975). The illusion of control. *Journal of Personality and Social Psychology, 32,* 311–328.

Laxer, R. (1964). Self-concept changes of depressive patients in general hospital treatment. *Journal of Consulting Psychology, 28,* 214–219.

Lewinsohn, P. M., Mischel, W., Chaplain, W., & Barton, R. (1980). Social competence and depression: The role of illusory self-perceptions? *Journal of Abnormal Psychology, 89,* 203–212.

Lobitz, W. C., & Post, R. D. (1979). Parameters of self-reinforcement and depression. *Journal of Abnormal Psychology, 88,* 33–41.

Loewenstein, D. A., & Hokanson, J. E. (1986). The processing of social information by mildly and moderately dysphoric college students. *Cognitive Therapy and Research, 10,* 447–460.

Maier, S. F., & Seligman, M. E. P. (1976). Learned helplessness: Theory and evidence. *Journal of Experimental Psychology: General, 105,* 3–46.

Markus, H. (1977). Self-schemata and processing information about the self. *Journal of Personality and Social Psychology, 35,* 63–78.

Martin, D. J., Abramson, L. Y., & Alloy, L. B. (1984). The illusion of control for self and others in depressed and nondepressed college students. *Journal of Personality and Social Psychology, 46,* 125–136.

McGregor, D. (1938). The major determinants of the prediction of social events. *Journal of Abnormal and Social Psychology, 33,* 179–204.

Metalsky, G. I., & Abramson, L. Y. (1981). Attributional styles: Toward a framework for conceptualization and assessment. In P. C. Kendall & S. D. Hollon (Eds.), *Cognitive–behavioral interventions: Assessment methods* (pp. 13–58). New York: Academic Press.

Metalsky, G. I., Abramson, L. Y., Seligman, M. E. P., Semmel, A., & Peterson, C. (1982). Attributional styles and life events in the classroom: Vulnerability and invulnerability to depressive mood reactions. *Journal of Personality and Social Psychology, 43,* 612–617.

Metalsky, G. I., Halberstadt, L. J., & Abramson, L. Y. (1987). Vulnerability to depressive mood reactions: Toward a more powerful test of the diathesis–stress and causal mediation components of the reformulated theory of depression. *Journal of Personality and Social Psychology, 52,* 386–393.

Miller, D. T. (1976). Ego involvement and attributions for success and failure. *Journal of Personality and Social Psychology, 34,* 901–906.

Miller, D. T., & Ross, M. (1975). Self-serving biases in the attribution of causality: Fact or fiction? *Psychological Bulletin, 82,* 213–225.

Miller, W. R., & Seligman, M. E. P. (1973). Depression and the perception of reinforcement. *Journal of Abnormal Psychology, 82,* 62–73.

Miller, W. R., & Seligman, M. E. P. (1976). Learned helplessness, depression, and the perception of reinforcement. *Behaviour Research and Therapy, 14,* 7–17.

Miller, W. R., Seligman, M. E. P., & Kurlander, H. M. (1975). Learned helplessness, depression, and anxiety. *Journal of Nervous and Mental Disease, 161,* 347–357.

Minkoff, K., Bergman, E., Beck, A. T., & Beck, R. (1973). Hopelessness, depression and attempted suicide. *American Journal of Psychiatry, 130,* 455–459.

Mischel, W. (1979). On the interface of cognition and personality: Beyond the person–situation debate. *American Psychologist, 34,* 740–754.

Musson, R. F., & Alloy, L. B. (1987). *Depression, self-consciousness, and judgments of control: A test of the self-focused attention hypothesis*. Unpublished manuscript, Northwestern University, Evanston, IL.

Nadich, M., Gargan, M., & Michael, L. (1975). Denial, anxiety, locus of control, and the discrepancy between aspirations and achievements as components of depression. *Journal of Abnormal Psychology, 84,* 1–9.

Nelson, R. E., & Craighead, W. E. (1977). Selective recall of positive and negative feedback, self-control behaviors and depression. *Journal of Abnormal Psychology, 86,* 379–388.

Nisbett, R., & Ross, L. (1980). *Human inference: Strategies and shortcomings of social judgment.* Englewood Cliffs, NJ: Prentice-Hall.

Peterson, C., & Seligman, M. E. P. (1984). Causal explanations as a risk factor for depression: Theory and evidence. *Psychological Review, 91,* 347–374.

Petrie, K., & Chamberlain, K. (1983). Hopelessness and social desirability as moderator variables in predicting suicidal behavior. *Journal of Consulting and Clinical Psychology, 51,* 485–487.

Pietromonaco, P. R., & Markus, H. (1985). The nature of negative thoughts in depression. *Journal of Personality and Social Psychology, 48,* 799–807.

Pryor, J. B., Gibbons, F. X., Wicklund, R. A., Fazio, R. H., & Hood, R. (1977). Self-focused attention and self-report validity. *Journal of Personality, 45,* 514–527.

Raps, C. S., Reinhard, K. E., Peterson, C., Abramson, L. Y., & Seligman, M. E. P. (1982). Attributional style among depressed patients. *Journal of Abnormal Psychology, 91,* 102–108.

Riskind, J. H., & Rholes, W. S. (1984). Cognitive accessibility and the capacity of cognitions to predict future depression: A theoretical note. *Cognitive Therapy and Research, 8,* 1–12.

Rosenthal, R., & Rubin, D. B. (1978). Interpersonal expectancy effects: The first 345 studies. *Behavioral and Brain Sciences, 3,* 377–386.

Roth, D., & Rehm, L. P. (1980). Relationships among self-monitoring processes, memory, and depression. *Cognitive Therapy and Research, 4,* 149–157.

Rozensky, R. H., Rehm, L. P., Pry, G., & Roth, D. (1977). Depression and self-reinforcement behavior in hospitalized patients. *Journal of Behavior Therapy and Experimental Psychiatry, 8,* 35–38.

Ruehlman, L. S., West, S. G., & Pasahow, R. J. (1985). Depression and evaluative schemata. *Journal of Personality, 53,* 46–92.

Rush, A. J., & Giles, D. E. (1982). Cognitive therapy: Theory and research. In A. J. Rush (Ed.), *Short-term psychotherapies for depression.* New York: Guilford Press.

Sacco, W. P., & Hokanson, J. E. (1978). Expectations of success and anagram performance of depressives in a public and private setting. *Journal of Abnormal Psychology, 87,* 122–130.

Sacco, W. P., & Hokanson, J. E. (1982). Depression and self-reinforcement in a public and private setting. *Journal of Personality and Social Psychology, 42,* 377–385.

Sackheim, H. A., & Wegner, A. Z. (1986). Attributional patterns in depression and euthymia. *Archives of General Psychiatry, 43,* 553–560.

Scheier, M. F., Buss, A. H., & Buss, D. M. (1978). Self-consciousness, self-report of aggressiveness, and aggression. *Journal of Research in Personality, 12,* 133–140.

Scheier, M. F., & Carver, C. S. (1985). Optimism, coping, and health: Assessment and implications of generalized outcome expectancies. *Health Psychology, 4,* 219–247.

Scheier, M. F., Carver, C. S., & Gibbons, F. X. (1979). Self-directed attention, awareness of bodily states, and suggestibility. *Journal of Personality and Social Psychology, 37,* 1576–1588.

Scheier, M. F., Weintraub, J. K., & Carver, C. S. (1986). Coping with stress: Divergent strategies of optimists and pessimists. *Journal of Personality and Social Psychology, 51,* 1257–1264.

Schlenker, B. R., & Leary, M. R. (1982). Audiences' reactions to self-enhancing, self-denigrating, and accurate self-presentations. *Journal of Experimental Social Psychology, 18,* 89–104.

Seligman, M. E. P. (1975). *Helplessness: On depression, development, and death.* San Francisco: W. H. Freeman.

Shrauger, J. S., & Terbovic, M. L. (1976). Self-evaluation and assessments of performance by self and others. *Journal of Consulting and Clinical Psychology, 44,* 564–572.

Siegel, S. J., & Alloy, L. B. (1987). *Interpersonal perceptions and consequences of depressive–significant other interactions: A naturalistic study of college roommates.* Manuscript submitted for publication.

Silver, R. L., & Wortman, C. B. (1980). Coping with undesirable life events. In J. Garber & M. E. P.

Seligman (Eds.), *Human helplessness: Theory and applications* (pp. 279–375). New York: Academic Press.

Snyder, M. L., Stephan, W. G., & Rosenfield, D. (1978). Attributional egotism. In J. H. Harvey, W. J. Ickes, & R. F. Kidd (Eds.), *New directions in attribution research* (Vol. 2, pp. 91–117). Hillsdale, NJ: Erlbaum.

Snyder, M., & Swann, W. B., Jr. (1978b). Hypothesis-testing processes in social interaction. *Journal of Personality and Social Psychology, 36,* 1202–1212.

Snyder, M., & Swann, W. B., Jr. (1978a). Behavioral confirmation in social interaction: From social perception to social reality. *Journal of Experimental Social Psychology, 14,* 148–162.

Snyder, M., Tanke, E. D., & Berscheid, E. (1977). Social perception and interpersonal behavior: On the self-fulfilling nature of social stereotypes. *Journal of Personality and Social Psychology, 35,* 656–666.

Strack, S., & Coyne, J. C. (1983). Social confirmation of dysphoria: Shared and private reactions. *Journal of Personality and Social Psychology, 44,* 798–806.

Sweeney, P. D., Anderson, K., & Bailey, S. (1986). Attributional style in depression: A meta-analytic review. *Journal of Personality and Social Psychology, 50,* 974–991.

Sweeney, P. D., Shaeffer, D., & Golin, S. (1982). Attributions about self and others in depression. *Personality and Social Psychology Bulletin, 8,* 37–42.

Tabachnik, N., Crocker, J., & Alloy, L. B. (1983). Depression, social comparison, and the false-consensus effect. *Journal of Personality and Social Psychology, 45,* 688–699.

Taylor, S. E. (1983). Adjustment to threatening events: A theory of cognitive adaptation. *American Psychologist, 38,* 1161–1173.

Taylor, S. E., & Crocker, J. (1980). Schematic bases of social information processing. In E. T. Higgins, C. P. Herman, & M. P. Zanna (Eds.), *Social cognition: The Ontario symposium* (Vol. 1, pp. 87–134). Hillsdale, NJ: Erlbaum.

Tennen, H., & Herzberger, S. (1987). Depression, self-esteem, and the absence of self-protective attributional biases. *Journal of Personality and Social Psychology, 52,* 72–80.

Tetlock, P. E., & Levi, A. (1982). Attribution bias: On the inconclusiveness of the cognition–motivation debate. *Journal of Experimental Social Psychology, 18,* 68–88.

Tetlock, P. E., & Manstead, A. S. R. (1985). Impression management versus intrapsychic explanations in social psychology: A useful dichotomy? *Psychological Review, 92,* 59–77.

Tiger, L. (1979). *Optimism: The biology of hope.* New York: Simon & Schuster.

Tversky, A., & Kahneman, D. (1974). Judgment under uncertainty: Heuristics and biases. *Science, 185,* 1124–1131.

Vazquez, C. V. (1987). Judgment of contingency: Cognitive biases in depressed and nondepressed subjects. *Journal of Personality and Social Psychology, 52,* 419–431.

Vazquez, C. V., & Alloy, L. B. (1987). *Schematic memory processes for self- and other-referent information in depression versus anxiety: A signal detection analysis.* Unpublished manuscript, Northwestern University, Evanston, IL.

Vestre, N. D., & Caulfield, B. P. (1986). Perception of neutral personality descriptions by depressed and nondepressed subjects. *Cognitive Therapy and Research, 10,* 31–36.

Wachtel, P. L. (1977). *Psychoanalysis and behavior therapy: Toward an integration.* New York: Basic Books.

Weinstein, N. D. (1980). Unrealistic optimism about future life events. *Journal of Personality and Social Psychology, 39,* 806–820.

Weinstein, N. D. (1982). Unrealistic optimism about susceptibility to health problems. *Journal of Behavioral Medicine, 5,* 441–460.

Weinstein, N. D. (1984). Why it won't happen to me: Perceptions of risk factors and illness susceptibility. *Health Psychology, 3,* 431–457.

Weinstein, N. D. (1986). *Unrealistic optimism about susceptibility to health problems: Conclusions from a community-wide sample.* Manuscript submitted for publication.

Wener, A. E., & Rehm, L. P. (1975). Depressive affect: A test of behavioral hypotheses. *Journal of Abnormal Psychology, 84,* 221–227.

Wenzlaff, R. M., & Berman, J. S. (1985, August). *Judgemental accuracy in depression.* Paper presented at the meeting of the American Psychological Association, Los Angeles.

Youngren, M. A., & Lewinsohn, P. M. (1980). The functional relation between depression and problematic interpersonal behavior. *Journal of Abnormal Psychology, 89,* 333–341.

Zich, J. M., & Zeiss, A. M. (1987). *Social comparison biases in depressed versus nondepressed subjects.* Manuscript submitted for publication.

9

The Causal Attributions of Depressives: Self-serving or Self-disserving?

DALE T. MILLER
Princeton University

MARLENE M. MORETTI
University of Waterloo

The question of why people's perceptions, recollections, and evaluations of social life are often distorted fascinates cognitive and social psychologists. The search for an answer to this question has generally followed one of two approaches (Miller & Porter, in press; Nisbett & Ross, 1980). The first has led to a consideration of various psychological needs or motives that are presumed to subvert otherwise rational cognitive processes. The need to promote a positive image of oneself is the most protean of these forces. In the words of Gordon Allport (1937), "The defense of the ego is nature's eldest law" (p. 170). The need to think well of ourselves has been linked to such features of information processing as the tendencies to attend to and remember positive information about ourselves more readily than negative information (Greenwald, 1980; Greenwald & Pratkanis, 1984; Shrauger, 1982).

The second, and currently more popular, approach to understanding cognitive biases was inspired by a model of man emerging from the literature on human judgment. According to this model, people are rational, but their rationality is bounded (Simon, 1957). The principles and heuristics they use to process and simplify information, though generally serving them well, predispose them to certain biases or errors (Kahneman, Slovic, & Tversky, 1982; Nisbett & Ross, 1980). The conviction that errors and biases need not reflect motivationally induced distortion is a distinguishing feature of contemporary social and cognitive psychology (Fiske & Taylor, 1984).

Throughout its history, clinical psychology has been interested in the cognitive errors or disturbances of thought associated with various forms of psychopathology, especially depression (Abramson, Seligman, & Teasdale, 1978; Beck, 1967, 1976). Recent evidence suggesting that depressives may actually exhibit *fewer* cognitive distortions than nondepressives has intensified interest in this topic (see Alloy & Abramson, 1979, 1982; Lewinsohn, Mischel, Chaplin, & Barton, 1980; Taylor & Brown, 1986).

In this chapter, we examine the differences between depressives and nondepressives in one of the most extensively investigated facets of information processing: causal attribution. In particular, we focus on causal attributions for outcomes of different valences. It is now well established that there is a tendency for people to take more causal responsibility for success than for failure (Zuckerman, 1979). That this asymmetry appears to maximize the positive affect a person derives from outcomes led Miller and Ross (1975) to term this the "self-serving attributional bias." The pervasiveness of this bias may no longer be in doubt, but debates over its origins continue to generate interest (see Tetlock & Levi, 1982). Historically, this bias has been assumed to reflect motivational distortion (Hastorf, Schneider, & Polefka, 1970). Heider (1958) contended that we engage in such attributions because they "flatter us and put us in a good light" (p. 172). Alfred Adler (1956) espoused an even more extreme motivational position when he stated that "a major benefit of causalistic thinking for the individual is that it excuses him from blame and frees him from responsibility" (p. 270).

Over a decade ago, Miller and Ross (1975) challenged the motivational account of the self-serving attributional bias. They argued that three informational processing factors operating in isolation or combination may cause individuals to take more personal responsibility for success than for failure. First, individuals are more likely to accept responsibility for expected outcomes than for unexpected outcomes, and, in general, people expect success rather than failure. Second, individuals discern a closer covariation between behavior and outcomes in the case of increasing success than in the case of constant failure, where changes in behavior are not perceived to be associated with changes in outcomes. Third, individuals tend to hold an erroneous conception of contingency, which leads them to associate control primarily with the occurrence of the desired (successful) outcome.

The objectives of our chapter are twofold: (1) to review evidence on the differences between the causal attributions of depressives and nondepressives and (2) to consider the relevance of this evidence to an understanding of both self-serving attributions and the etiology of depression. We begin with a review of the relevant literature. For the purposes of our review, we organize studies comparing the causal attributions of depressed and nondepressed individuals into three categories: (1) attributions for hypothetical events, (2) attributions for stressful life experiences, and (3) attributions for performances on experimental tasks.

STUDIES OF CAUSAL ATTRIBUTIONS

Attributions for Hypothetical Events

A number of studies have compared the causal attributions that depressed and nondepressed individuals offer for hypothetical events. The most popular instrument used in this research is the Attributional Style Questionnaire (ASQ), developed by Seligman, Abramson, Semmel, and von Baeyer (1979). The ASQ presents individuals with a combination of 12 hypothetical interpersonal and achievement-oriented situations that yield either positive or negative outcomes. For example, a respondent is asked to imagine, "You meet a friend who compliments you on your appearance" (positive interpersonal item), or "You can't get all the work done that others expect of you" (negative achievement item). For each situation, subjects are requested to identify the cause most responsible for the occurrence of the event. Having done this, they are asked to use 7-point Likert scales to assess three dimensions of the cause: (1) its internality (Is the cause of . . . due to something about you or something about the other person or circumstances?), (2) its stability (In the future when . . ., will this cause again be present?), and (3) its globality (Is the cause something that just affects . . ., or does it also influence other areas of your life?). These measures yield three attributional indices (internality, stability, globality) for both positive and negative outcomes.

COLLEGE POPULATIONS

Most ASQ studies have used college populations. In the first of these studies, Seligman *et al.* (1979) found that self-rated depression on the BDI (Beck, 1967) correlated positively with the internality, stability, and globality of attributions for negative outcomes, and with the externality, instability, and specificity of attributions for positive outcomes. Subsequent studies have replicated this pattern of results (Feather, 1983; Nezu, Nezu, & Nezu, 1986).

Other ASQ studies have not provided as clear a picture of the relation between attributional patterns and depression. Golin, Sweeney, and Shaeffer (1981) only partially replicated the earlier findings of Seligman and his colleagues. They did find that self-reported depression correlated positively with the internality, stability, and globality of attributions for negative outcomes, but in the case of positive outcomes, only the internality measure showed the predicted relation to depression. Moreover, Golin *et al.* noted that their results generally were less robust than those of Seligman *et al.* (1979). Cutrona, Russell, and Jones (1984) also reported a weak relationship between responses on the ASQ and depression. In their sample of more than 1,000 students, they found that responses on the ASQ accounted for only 4% of the variance in depression scores. The results of Blaney, Behar, and Head (1980) are similarly mixed. Consistent with the earlier research, depression was positively correlated with the stability and globality of attributions for negative outcomes, but, in contrast to the earlier research, the internality of attributions for negative outcomes was not associated with depression.

More recent studies using the ASQ continue to produce mixed results. Carver, Ganellen, and Behar-Mitrani (1985) report a negative relationship between attributions of internality and stability for positive events and depression. In contrast, Zautra, Guenther, and Chartier (1985) found no evidence that attributions for positive events predict depression. Similarly, Tennen and Herzberger (1987) found that strength of self-serving attributional bias was unrelated to depression level, although it was positively correlated with self-esteem level.

Peterson, Schwartz, and Seligman (1981) used the ASQ and 12 negative events selected from the Life Events Questionnaire (Marx, Garrity, & Bower, 1975) to study the relation between depression and characterological as well as behavioral self-blame (Janoff-Bulman, 1979). Characterological blame implicates enduring, global characteristics of the self, whereas behavioral blame focuses on unstable and specific characteristics. The results indicated that scores on the BDI correlated negatively with the degree of behavioral self-blame for negative events, but positively with the degree of characterological self-blame for such outcomes. The responses to neither the behavioral nor the characterological attributional probes were associated with depression in the context of positive outcomes. Janoff-Bulman's (1979) study assessed the causal attributions of depressed and nondepressed students for four negative hypothetical situations. The two groups did not differ in behavioral self-blame, but depressives did take more characterological self-blame. In other words, depressives were more likely than nondepressives to blame stable and global aspects of their core "self" for negative events.

CLINICAL POPULATIONS

Studies using the ASQ in clinical populations have yielded mixed results. Raps, Peterson, Reinhard, Abramson, and Seligman (1982) reported that depressed psychiatric patients attributed negative outcomes to internal and stable factors more readily than either nondepressed psychiatric patients or nondepressed controls. Depressives also considered external and unstable factors to be more responsible for positive outcomes than did nondepressed controls, although not more than nondepressed psychiatric controls.

Eaves and Rush (1984) noted that the attributions of clinically depressed patients were more internal, stable, and global for negative events than were the attributions of nondepressed controls. Interestingly, this relationship held even for those patients whose symptomatology was in remission. The attributions of depressives and nondepressives for positive events did not differ significantly. Persons and Rao (1985) also found that attributions of stability and globality made significant and independent contributions to explaining the variance in BDI scores within a sample of psychiatric inpatients. As predicted, global attributions for negative events were associated with higher BDI scores. Contrary to the attributional model, however, stable attributions for negative events were associated with lower BDI scores. An additional finding of interest in this study was that there was a temporal shift in attributions over the course of the study: The tendency to make internal, stable, and global attributions for negative events decreased as depression remitted. The results of Hamilton and Abramson (1983) confuse the issue even further. These researchers found that depressives provided fewer self-serving attributions for positive ASQ events than did nondepressed psychiatric patients, but they found no differences between the two groups in their attributions for negative ASQ events.

The inconsistency in the findings of Hamilton and Abramson (1983), Eaves and Rush (1984), and Persons and Rao (1985) raises questions about the role that attributions play in chronic depression. Further skepticism is raised by Miller, Klee, and Norman's (1982) failure to find any differences between depressed and nondepressed patients on the ASQ.

Attributions for Stressful Life Experiences

Relatively few studies have examined the nature of depressive attributions for actual past events. Those that do exist provide moderate support for the hypothesis that depressives explain stressful experiences less self-servingly than do nondepressives. In one study, Barthe and Hammen (1981) elicited students' mood ratings and causal attributions for self-rated success or failure on their midterm exams. As predicted, students characterized by depressed mood were more likely to attribute failure to lack of ability than were nondepressed students. However, the mood ratings and attributions of successful students were not related. Consistent with these findings, Zautra *et al.* (1985) reported a significant relationship between attributions of internality, stability, and globality for negative life events and depression. The relationship between attributions for positive life events and depression was not significant.

In a recent study, Tabachnik-Kayne, Alloy, Romer, and Crocker (1986) had students complete attributional measures and indicate their aspirations and expectations for performance on a midterm exam both prior to taking the exam and upon receipt of their grades. As predicted, a significant interaction between attributional style and exam outcome emerged, indicating that students with depressive attributional style experienced greater depression following an exam outcome that was negative (achieving a grade lower than expected) than did students with a neutral or nondepressive attributional style. When the exam outcome was positive (achieving a grade higher than expected), students with depressive attributional style experienced less elation than did students with a neutral or nondepressive attributional style. Further, latent-variable analysis revealed the critical finding that increased depression following a negative exam outcome was mediated by specific attributions for this event (see also Metalsky, Halberstadt, & Abramson, 1987).

The attenuated self-servingness of depressives was also demonstrated in Harvey's (1981) study of causal attributions for recalled positive and negative personal events. Although depressives did not differ from nondepressives in their attributions for recalled positive events, they did perceive negative events as more internally caused and controllable. Subsequent analysis indicated that the depressive–nondepressive difference emerged because the causal attributions of depressives did not differ across positive and negative outcomes. These results are consistent with those noted by Raps *et al.* (1982) and suggest that the depressed individual's perception of causality may be impervious to the valence of the event.

Hammen, Krantz, and Cochran (1981) also found a relationship between depression and causal attributions in their investigations of people's responses to five recent stressful life experiences. Specifically, they found that the tendency to explain stressful experiences by reference to controllable and global factors was positively correlated with depressed affect. Similar findings were reported by Cochran and Hammen (1985). In this study, subjects' attributions for stressful life experiences were elicited at the beginning of the study (Time 1) and at a 2-month follow-up (Time 2). Analyses of the concurrent relationship between attributions and depression at Time 1 indicated that only global attributions were directly related to depression. At Time 2, however, both the globality and the externality of subjects' attributions were related to depression. In contrast, Hammen and Cochran (1981), using both interview and questionnaire methods to probe causal attributions for recent stressful events, found no evidence that the causal attributions of depressives and nondepressives differed in any respect. Similarly, Hammen and de Mayo (1982) noted that depression in high school teachers was not related to their causal attributions for stressful experiences, although it was negatively related to their perceptions of control over the occurrence of such events. The latter finding directly contradicts the studies of Harvey (1981) and Hammen *et al.* (1981), in which depression was found to be positively correlated with perceived control over negative events.

Three studies have evaluated the causal attributions of clinically depressed individuals for stressful life experiences. In a sample of depressed elderly psychiatric patients, Cochran and Hammen (1985) found that both external and global attributions for negative life events predicted depression. The most impressive finding in this study, revealed through latent-variable analysis, was that attributions accounted for 42% of the variance in depression scores. Gong-Guy and Hammen (1980) found that clinically depressed patients blamed internal factors more for their most recent stressful experience than did nondepressives. Miller *et al.* (1982) also reported that depressives provided less self-serving causal attributions for their most stressful recent experience than did nondepressed psychiatric patients. Yet, as previously noted, these same two groups of patients did not differ in their responses to the ASQ. At the very least, this result raises doubts about the cross-situational consistency of causal ascriptions and the construct validity of the ASQ.

Attributions for Task Performance

Considerable attention has been given to the hypothesis that depressives and nondepressives differ in their attributions for their performance on experimental tasks involving achievement and interpersonal relations. Such research typically creates success and failure conditions through manipulation of performance feedback (noncontingent feedback) and instructs subjects to answer a variety of causal questions about these outcomes.

ATTRIBUTIONS FOR ACHIEVEMENT TASKS

There is reasonably strong evidence to suggest that depressives are less likely than nondepressives to provide self-serving explanations for negative experimental outcomes. The picture with respect to positive outcomes is equivocal.

College Populations. In one of the first investigations in this tradition, Rizley (1978) compared the attributions of depressed and nondepressed students for noncontingent success or failure on a simple number-guessing task. Depressives reported more internal attributions for failure than did nondepressives, but the two groups did not differ in their explanations for success. Once again, an inspection of the results indicates that the causal attributions of depressives simply do not differ across positive and negative outcomes. Unlike nondepressives, they were "evenhanded" in their explanations of success and failure. In a similar experiment, Kuiper (1978) also found that depressives made more internal attributions for failure than nondepressives but did not differ from nondepressed controls in their causal perceptions regarding success. The tendency for depressives to attribute failure on achievement-related tasks to internal factors such as lack of ability is also evident in the results of Oliver and Williams (1979) and Zemore and Johansen (1980). Here, too, there was no evidence that depressives are less self-serving than nondepressives in their causal attributions for success.

   Clinical Populations. Two studies have examined the nature of clinically depressed peoples' causal attributions for task performance. Abramson, Garber, Edwards, and Seligman (1978) compared the attributions of depressed psychiatric patients, nondepressed schizophrenics, and a nondepressed, normal control group for successful or failing outcomes on tasks of skill and of chance. In contrast to the research that employed nonclinical populations, no differences were found among the various groups on either attributional internality or perceived control. Gotlib and Olson (1983) argued that Abramson *et al.*'s failure to find group differences may have been because experimental manipulation of outcomes did not produce differences in subjects' *perceptions* of the outcomes. To check this possibility, they compared the attributions of depressed and nondepressed psychiatric inpatients and nondepressed nonpsychiatric controls for *self-judged* success and failure experiences. The results indicated that subjects who perceived their performance to be a success were more likely to attribute this outcome to internal factors than were subjects who perceived their performance to be a failure. Conversely, subjects who perceived their performance as a failure were more likely to attribute this outcome to external factors than were subjects who perceived their performance as a success. The effect of outcome valence was not qualified by psychiatric status; all subjects manifested self-serving biases in their causal ascriptions.

ATTRIBUTIONS FOR INTERPERSONALLY RELEVANT TASKS

In one of the relatively few studies to focus on interpersonal tasks, Rizley (1978, Experiment 2) found that depressives were more likely than nondepressives to report feelings of control over interpersonal relations when their influence was negative. Depressives did not differ from nondepressives, however, in the internality of their attributions or in their self-ascribed responsibility for the negative effects. Moreover, when feedback indicated that their interpersonal influence was positive, depressed and nondepressed individuals did not differ in their ratings of control or causal attributions.

   An intriguing study by Sharp and Tennen (1983) also demonstrated a weakened self-serving bias in depressives. Depressed and nondepressed subjects in this study were provided with failure feedback following completion of an empathy task. Nondepressives blamed external factors, such as the confederate and the task, more than did depressives. Finally, Zuroff (1981) provided mixed results with respect to the link between depression and self-servingness. Depressed students endorsed more internal attributions for task failure than did nondepressives, but they also endorsed more internal attributions for successful outcomes than did non-depressives.

ASSESSING THE EVIDENCE

More than 30 studies have compared the causal attributions of depressed and nondepressed individuals. It is clear from our review of these studies that the relation between depression and causal attribution is far from invariant. The most reliable finding is that depressives take more personal responsibility for negative outcomes than do nondepressives. The two groups generally do not differ in their attributions for positive outcomes; both prefer internal over external attributions. That depressives take more responsibility for negative outcomes than do nondepressives is consistent with a weak version of the self-disserving hypothesis. The strong version of the hypothesis, which states that depressives take more responsibility for negative than for positive outcomes, received virtually no support from these studies. The picture of a depressive that emerges is that of somebody who takes considerable responsibility for all outcomes, whether positive or negative. It is by assuming personal responsibility in the latter circumstance that the depressive distinguishes himself or herself most clearly from the nondepressive. Sweeney, Anderson, and Bailey's (1986) recent meta-analytic review corroroborates this conclusion.

Methodological Caveats

Before discussing the implications these findings have for understanding depression, a few comments are in order on the nature of the experimental tasks and subject populations that have been used. As this review documents, the positive and negative events that are the focus of causal attributions in the reported studies differ considerably. Some involve hypothetical events, which require subjects to role play; some involve real-life events that the subjects define as stressful; and some involve experimenter-controlled tasks.

One of the most popular measurement instruments is the ASQ. Although Peterson and Seligman's (1984) review of the ASQ suggests that it is both valid and reliable, Cutrona *et al.* (1984) report some problems with the measure. First, they reported reliability coefficients for the ASQ that are considerably lower than previous estimates (Peterson *et al.*, (1982). Second, their factor analyses of the ASQ indicated considerable situational specificity. Third, they found ASQ scores to be poor predictors of women's causal attributions for actual negative events, suggesting either that the ASQ is a poor measure of attributional style or that the hypothesized trait of attributional style is a questionable construct.

In addition to a high degree of cross-study variation in stimulus events, dependent measures also vary considerably, ranging from open-ended questions about the causes of events to requests to distribute a 100% causality across a variety of potential sources. Given the diversity of measurement procedures employed in the reviewed studies, the observed inconsistency is perhaps not surprising. The research of Watson and Dyck (1984) highlights the importance of measurement techniques in evaluating depressive attributional style. These researchers found support for a depressive attributional style when subjects provided dimensional ratings of spontaneous attributions, but not when raters assessed the dimensionality of subjects' attributions. Krantz and Rude (1984) also recently reported poor convergence among existing measures of causal attributions.

The range of the subject populations used in the reviewed studies is another, perhaps more serious, impediment to the achievement of empirical consistency and conceptual clarity in this area. Although virtually all the reviewed studies drew inferences about the clinical disorder of depression, only eight of them actually employed subjects who were clinically depressed. This fact could lead to an underestimation of the differences between depressives and nondepressives in causal attributions. This is especially likely to be true if depression is a unitary dimension, such that clinically depressed and mildly depressed individuals differ only in degree. There appears to be good reason to question this assumption, however (Buchwald, Coyne, & Cole, 1978; Coyne & Gotlib, 1983; Depue & Monroe, 1978). To the extent that clinically depressed individuals differ qualitatively as well as quantitatively from mildly depressed individuals, generalization from one group to the other becomes problematic. We can only add our voices to the call for additional research comparing the mildly and the clinically depressed.

It is difficult to assess the role that methodological factors have played in attribution studies. In a review of 61 tests of the attributional model, Peterson, Raps, and Villanova (1985) identified three highly correlated factors that distinguished studies that produced support for the model from those that did not. A significant relationship between attributions and depression was more likely to emerge in studies that employed a large, rather than a small, sample; that elicited attributions for hypothetical, rather than actual, life events; and that elicited attributions for a large, rather than a small, number of events. Unfortunately, it is not clear why these particular factors characterize studies supporting the attributional model.

IMPLICATIONS OF THE EVIDENCE FOR UNDERSTANDING DEPRESSION

Methodological issues notwithstanding, the extant research does indicate that there are some interesting and reliable differences between depressed and nondepressed people. We will now consider the significance of these differences as we address, in turn, two questions: (1) Are the causal attributions of depressives more or less accurate than those of nondepressives? and (2) How do the causal attributions of depressives relate to the etiology and maintenance of depression?

Depression and the Veridicality of Causal Attributions

The position that psychologically disturbed individuals have more insight into reality than normal people has been voiced sporadically for centuries. Until recently, however, such arguments have not come from members of the scientific community. The dominant scientific view of depression has been that it is a consequence of cognitive distortion and error, not cognitive veridicality (Beck, 1969, 1976; Seligman *et al.,* 1979). In the last decade, this position has begun to change as evidence emerges suggesting that depressives may indeed be less biased in various judgmental activities (Taylor & Brown, 1986).

One such activity is the perception of control. For nondepressives, the perception of control is influenced by the valence of the outcome: Estimates of control are lower when outcomes are negative than when they are positive (Langer, 1975). Neither depressed students nor depressed psychiatric patients, however, appear to be influenced by the valence of the outcome in estimating the degree of contingency between their actions and outcomes (Golin, Terrell, & Johnson, 1977; Golin, Terrell, Weitz, & Drost, 1979).

In a fascinating series of studies, Alloy and Abramson (1979) pursued the hypothesis that the perceptions of control held by depressives not only are *less* self-serving than those held by nondepressives, but are *more* accurate. In a series of four experiments, these researchers compared the response–outcome contingency estimates of depressed and nondepressed individuals. When there was contingency between subjects' responses and their outcomes on the experimental task, the estimates of depressed subjects closely approximated the objective degree of contingency. On the other hand, nondepressed subjects, while estimating accurately in the high-reinforcement (success) condition, underestimated control in the low-reinforcement (failure) condition. When the experimental tasks were objectively uncontrollable, nondepressives both overestimated control in high-reinforcement (success) conditions and underestimated control in low-reinforcement (failure) conditions. In contrast, depressives provided relatively accurate contingency estimates in both conditions. Consistent with these findings, Ford and Neale (1985) reported that subjects exposed to helplessness-induction procedures made more accurate judgments of control on Alloy and Abramson's (1979) task than did control subjects.

The findings of Lewinsohn *et al.* (1980) are also pertinent to the issue of depressive realism. In this research, depressed and nondepressed psychiatric patients, as well as nondepressed controls, participated in four 45-minute group interactions that were observed through one-way mirrors and rated by blind judges on several dimensions of social ability. Subjects also rated themselves on these dimensions. As predicted, depressed patients initially perceived themselves as less socially skilled than did nondepressed patients and controls. Of more interest is that although all groups tended to rate themselves more positively than they were rated by observers, depressed patients' self-ratings were more consistent with observer ratings than were those of either of the nondepressed groups. Lewinsohn, Steinmetz, Larson, and Franklin (1981) conclude that depression is characterized more by the absence of an illusory "warm glow" than by the presence of a distorted world view.

The most provocative explanation of these various results is that the judgments and inferences of depressives are less biased (more accurate) than those of non-depressives. This logic could easily be extended to the domain of causal attribution: The greater asymmetry in the attributions of nondepressives suggests that they are *less* accurate in their explanations of outcomes than are depressives. As tantalizing as this inference is, it can be drawn only if we assume that it is possible to assess self-servingness and accuracy. To identify causal bias, researchers traditionally have tended to compare the attributions of one group of subjects to those of other subjects for whom outcomes or perspectives differ. Without normative models for assessing the potency of causal factors, it is impossible to conclude that the attributions of one group are more or less accurate than those of another, but the fact that groups differ in their attributions for the *same* behavior would seem to suggest that some bias is involved. Applying the same logic, it could be deduced that asymmetrical explanations for positive and negative outcomes reflect inaccuracy because the factors influencing positive and negative outcomes are the same. This would seem to be especially true in the laboratory, where the experimenter manipulates the outcomes and where subjects' actions and outcomes are completely independent. Pursuing this line of analysis, it would seem possible to go even further and argue that depressives, because they show fewer differences in their explanations of positive and negative outcomes, are more accurate than nondepressives.

There are problems with this reasoning, however. Kahneman and Miller (1986) have recently proposed that people do not explain events *per se* but, rather, contrasts between events and alternatives that are considered more normal or less surprising than the event in question. The corollary of this point is that the same event can suggest many different effects to be explained, and consequently can yield many different (but equally accurate) attributions. If we accept that it is contrasts between events and expected or imagined alternatives that people explain, the question of attributional accuracy assumes added complexity. Neither the presence nor the absence of differences in attributions across outcomes is sufficient to demonstrate inaccuracy or accuracy. Without knowing what the comparison alternative is, we cannot know what is being explained.

The relevance of this analysis to the issue before us is twofold. First, it suggests that the self-serving attributional bias need not reflect distortion, either motivated or nonmotivated. Positive and negative events may evoke different contrasts (effects) and thus produce different causal analyses. This point was anticipated by Miller and Ross (1975), who noted that people generally expect success and thus account for it by internal, stable, and global factors, whereas failure, like any unexpected outcome, is accounted for by external, unstable, and specific factors. The second implication of this analysis is that negative outcomes may not evoke the same effects for depressed and nondepressed individuals. Negative outcomes may constitute an expected, unsurprising result for depressed individuals, which leads them to look toward internal, and possibly stable, causal factors. That depressives are less optimistic about success on performance tasks than are nondepressives is well documented, as we noted earlier (see also Pyszczynski, Holt, & Greenberg, 1987).

Outcomes are often compared to the real or imagined outcomes of others as well as to expectations. When the performance of nondepressives violates their expectations, they tend to assume that others have done comparably poorly, but this is not true of depressives (Coates & Peterson, 1982). Nondepressives thus have two reasons, not shared by depressives, for attributing a failure experience to external factors. First, it generally will be inconsistent with their expectancy and past experience. Second, they generally will not assume it to be unique to themselves. The point here is that the principal difference between depressive and nondepressive individuals may reside more in their expectancies, and in the contrasts that their experiences evoke, than in their attributional style. Moreover, these differential expectancies and contrasts may reflect different social histories rather than differential assessments of comparable social histories.

In summary, the question of whether the causal attributions of depressives are more or less accurate than those of nondepressives seems currently unanswerable. We have no normative models to use in evaluating causal attributions of this type, and the proposal that people explain contrasts rather than effects suggests that the expectancies of depressed and nondepressed individuals must be considered. In fact, the question may be stated more properly as, "Whose expectancies are more rational, those of depressives or nondepressives?" Researchers are only beginning to realize that the differential experiences of depressives and nondepressives must be assessed and considered if we are to understand the self-schemata of depressives and their reactions in our experiments (see Coyne & Gotlib, 1983).

How Do Causal Attributions Relate to Depression?

The impetus behind research on differences in the causal attributions of depressives and nondepressives is the hope that this research may provide some insight into factors that contribute to and maintain depression. What can we now say about this issue? We address it by considering three possible relationships between causal attributions and depression: (1) causal attributions induce depressive affect; (2) causal attributions are effects of depressive affect; (3) causal attributions and depressive affect are linked by virtue of their relation to a third variable.

CAUSAL ATTRIBUTIONS AS DETERMINANTS OF DEPRESSIVE AFFECT

The central assumption in both Beck's (1967) and Seligman *et al.*'s (1979) models of depression is that the thoughts, beliefs, and inferences of depressives are causally related to their depressive state. According to the reformulated helplessness model of depression (Abramson, Seligman, & Teasdale, 1978), depressed affect results from the perception of noncontingency between one's actions and important outcomes. Depressives tend to assume both that desirable outcomes are unobtainable and that undesirable outcomes are unavoidable. Abramson *et al.* contend that depressives differ from nondepressives not only in their tendency to perceive events as uncontrollable but also in their bias toward internal, stable, and global explanations for this lack of control. This "depressogenic" attributional style interacts with stress to precipitate depression (Abramson, Metalsky, & Alloy, 1986).

As our review indicates, evidence on the link between depressive affect and causal attributions is mixed. The most robust finding is that depressives make fewer self-serving (i.e., more internal, global, and stable) attributions for negative outcomes than do nondepressives. One interpretation of this finding is that the tendency to attribute negative outcomes to internal, stable, and global causes renders people susceptible to depression. A study by Tabachnik-Kayne et al. (1986) is suggestive in this regard. In this study, depression following receipt of a low grade was strongly predicted by students' specific attributions for exam performance. Similar results were reported in a study using the ASQ (Metalsky, Abramson, Seligman, Semmel, & Peterson, 1982). In this study, both the internality and the stability of attributions for negative events were predictive of mood following receipt of a low grade on a midterm exam. However, as Williams (1985) points out, the analyses completed by Metalsky et al. do not provide an adequate test of the diathesis–stress hypothesis. Additional analyses completed by Williams (1985) revealed that the relationship between attributions and depression was *not* moderated by the receipt of a low grade. Further difficulty for the depressogenic hypothesis is raised by Cochran and Hammen's (1985) report that assessments of students' attributional styles elicited 2 months prior to an exam did not predict reactions to exam performance.

Other studies that have addressed this question have also produced equivocal findings. Using a cross-correlational panel analysis, Golin et al. (1981) found that although the stability and globality of attributions for negative events were predictive of depression 1 month later, the internality of attributions for such events did not predict later depression. Moreover, although the stability and globality attribution dimensions were significant predictors, they accounted for a limited amount of the variance in depression. Peterson et al. (1981) reported that depression was associated with characterological self-blame in responses on the ASQ but that the degree of self-blame was not predictive of depression at 6- and 12-month follow-ups. Similarly, Lewinsohn et al.'s (1981) longitudinal study of a community population indicated that causal attributions for hypothetical events predicted neither the development of depression in nondepressed subjects nor the course of the disorder in depressed ones.

Four studies have explored the ability of the ASQ to predict the onset of postpartum depression. The results of these studies are contradictory. Cutrona (1983) found that prenatal ASQ scores predicted postpartum depression among women who were not depressed during pregnancy. Similar results were reported by O'Hara, Rehm, and Campbell (1982), although the contribution of ASQ responses as a predictor variable in this analysis was small, accounting for only 2.3% of the variance. In contrast, Manly, McMahon, Bradley, and Davidson (1982) found that responses on the ASQ did not predict postpartum depression. A recent study by O'Hara, Neunaber, and Zekoski (1984) also noted that responses on the ASQ were not predictive of postpartum depression.

Another approach to assessing the causal potency of attributions is to observe the effects that attempts to modify causal attributions have on experienced affect. Intervention studies of this nature have provided some evidence that manipulating the attributions of depressives can reduce previously demonstrated behavioral deficits (Dweck, 1975; Klein, Fencil-Morse, & Seligman, 1976), but few studies have evaluated the consequences of these manipulations on depressed affect. One study that did examine this issue was reported by Miller and Norman (1981). These researchers wished to see if the negative affect produced by helplessness training would be diminished by a subsequent success experience for which subjects were encouraged to make internal attributions. Intervention was successful for both clinical and remitted depressives. These results are promising, but to date no researchers have evaluated the impact that an emphasis on external attributions has on depressed mood following negative outcomes. This type of research is particularly pertinent to the issue of attributional potency, since it appears that depressives differ most from nondepressives in their causal attributions for negative events.

To summarize, the evidence offers only limited support for the hypothesis that attributions play a causal role in the development of depression. A similar conclusion was reached by Brewin (1985). In reviewing the relevant literature, Brewin organized evidence according to several possible causal models of the relation between attributions and depression. Rather than providing support for models that cast depressive attributions in a causal role (e.g., onset model or vulnerability model), Brewin's (1985) review supported models in which depressive attributions were seen as either symptoms of depression (symptom model) or as influential factors in the course of the depressive episode (recovery model or coping model). Brewin (1985) concluded his review by noting that methodological problems make it difficult to draw any confident conclusions about a causal relation between attributions and depression.

The failure of current research to provide an adequate test of the attributional model is also emphasized in a critical review by Abramson *et al.* (1986). The central point of this review is that research strategies have failed to realize the full implications of the diathesis–stress component of the attributional model by not assessing whether the influence of attributions on depression is moderated by the occurrence of negative life events. As a consequence of this omission, these authors conclude that the evaluation of the causal role of attributions in depression is premature.

CAUSAL ATTRIBUTIONS AS EFFECTS OF DEPRESSED MOOD

The existence of a relationship between causal attributions and depressed mood could reflect the influence of mood on attributions. Such a possibility becomes more and more plausible as evidence accumulates concerning the influence that mood has on memory (Bower, 1981; Bower, Monteiro, & Gilligan, 1978), attentional processes (Mischel, Ebbesen, & Zeiss, 1973), and attitudes and behaviors (Isen, 1970; Isen & Levin, 1972). At this point, there are only a few studies that have investigated the effects of mood-induction techniques on causal attributions. Furthermore, their findings are mixed.

    Alloy, Abramson, and Viscusi (1981) evaluated the effects of mood induction on estimated control over noncontingent outcomes. Depressives in whom positive mood was induced exhibited an "illusion of control" on noncontingent tasks. Conversely, nondepressives in whom negative mood was induced failed to show the customary self-serving biases in contingency estimation. Negative mood induction thus appeared to improve the accuracy of nondepressed individuals. In another relevant study, Mukherji, Abramson, and Martin (1982) found that inducing negative mood in nondepressed subjects did not affect either their self-serving attributional biases or their subsequent depression.

    Despite the absence of strong empirical support, there are at least two reasons why negative affect might lead to the acceptance of responsibility for negative outcomes. First, negative affect may make people focus inward, and as research on objective self-awareness indicates, people who are made to focus on themselves make more internal attributions (Duval & Wicklund, 1972). Second, people experiencing negative affect may think more about other negative experiences than those in a positive mood. Both Bower (1981) and Isen (1970) have suggested that affect can act as a cue that facilitates the recall of mood-congruent information. The greater availability of prior negative experiences may, in turn, make the occurrence of future negative events seem less surprising and thus more congruent with stable, internal characteristics.

CAUSAL ATTRIBUTIONS AND DEPRESSION AS NONCAUSALLY
RELATED VARIABLES

One explanation for the absence of compelling evidence for a causal link between attributions and affect is that their relationship is mediated by a third variable. If this were the case, causal attributions might well be epiphenomenal to the etiology of depression. One candidate for the role of third variable is a cognitive schema. Beck (1967) originally used this term to refer to the relatively stable cognitive representations in depressives that influence many facets of their information processing. The research of Kuiper and his colleagues (Derry & Kuiper, 1981; Kuiper, Olinger, MacDonald, & Shaw, 1985) has done much to clarify and delineate the significance of a negative self-schema in depression. In an interesting series of experiments, Kuiper and Derry demonstrated that the negative self-schema that characterizes depressives facilitates the processing of self-descriptive information with negative content. Moreover, the processing advantage of depressive over nondepressive content increased with the severity of depression. It seems a possibility, therefore, that both depressed mood and causal attributions are products of pathological information-processing proclivities that originate in a negative self-schema. The self-schema, like an expectancy set, may operate to determine the nature of contrasts evoked during the processing of information.

    Biochemical factors constitute another candidate for the role of third variable. Depressive characteristics, including causal attributions, may result from some underlying physiological or biochemical disturbance. In this regard, it would be interesting to evaluate the effects that somatic treatments (e.g., tricyclic antidepressants) have on causal attributions.

To question the role of causal attributions in determining affective states is to challenge a powerful zeitgeist. Nevertheless, there is increasing evidence that the tide may be changing. The strongest evidence for a causal link between attributions and affective states comes from laboratory studies focusing on events of low hedonic relevance (see Miller & Porter, 1983) and from questionnaires asking for subjects' imagined responses to hypothetical events (Weiner, Russell, & Lerman, 1978). Attempts to link causal attributions to affective states in populations experiencing more powerful affect have generally been unsuccessful (Miller & Porter, 1983; Taylor, Wood, & Lichtman, 1983). At this time, it seems most prudent to say simply that it remains to be proven that causal attribution plays a large role in either causing or maintaining severe depressive affect.

FINAL REMARKS

The research reviewed in this chapter indicates that the causal attributions of depressives are less self-serving than those of nondepressives. At the least, the former take more personal responsibility for negative outcomes than do the latter. The two groups do not differ in their attributions for positive outcomes. It is difficult to determine whether depressives are more or less accurate in their causal attributions than are nondepressives. On the basis of the available evidence, it is also impossible to say whether or not the attributional pattern exhibited by depressives contributes to the etiology or maintenance of their depression. In our analysis, we speculated that differences in the causal attributions of depressives and nondepressives may be traceable to more basic differences in information processing. One such difference may be the standards by which the two groups evaluate experience. Evaluative standards include past experiences, idealized goals, and imagined "possible worlds" (Kahneman & Miller, 1986). Support for the speculation that evaluative standards have important affective consequences comes from Higgins, Klein, and Strauman's (1985) finding that discrepancy between the actual-self and "ideal" standards (e.g., hopes, wishes, aspirations) is associated with depression, whereas discrepancy between the actual-self and "ought" standards (e.g., responsibilities, obligations) is associated with anxiety.

When considering investigations of the link between causal attributions and depression, it is also important to realize that these investigations focused on elicited, not spontaneous, attributions. Attributions that have been elicited by researchers' probes may or may not be the same as those the individuals spontaneously generate. Kahneman and Miller (1986) have recently identified a number of problems associated with the assumption that elicited inferences can provide a model for spontaneous inferences. Foremost among these is the possibility that the focus on elicited attributions may have yielded an exaggerated estimate of the degree of spontaneous causal analysis. People have little trouble in responding to causal questions, but this fact need not imply that they have engaged in analysis before they were questioned. The significance of this point for our discussion is that the elicited-attribution methodology used in the research discussed here prohibits the discovery of any difference between depressives and nondepressives in the extent of their causal analyses. It is possible that the most significant difference between depressives and nondepressives lies in the presence or absence of the tendency to ask "Why?" questions and to seek explanations for the events in their lives. We know that there are individual differences in the inclination to ponder causal questions (Wortman, 1983), and this may be one of the differences between depressives and nondepressives. Indeed, recent studies (Alloy & Ahrens, 1987; McCaul, 1983; Weary, Elbin, & Hill, 1987; Weary, Jordan, & Hill, 1985) have demonstrated that depressives differ from nondepressives in their use of attributional information.

Finally, we would be remiss if we ended our discussion without raising the issue of motivational explanations for depressives' lack of self-servingness in explaining negative events. Viewing depressive–nondepressive differences from this perspective suggests two possibilities: (1) Depressives may differ from nondepressives in their motivation to protect or enhance their self-esteem, and/or (2) depressives may differ from nondepressives in their understanding of how causal attributions can serve the self and its needs. Unfortunately, there is little evidence relevant to these different possibilities. That depressives take more personal responsibility for failure than nondepressives is consistent with both possibilities. It does appear, however, that the hypothesis that depressives are motivated to maintain a negative image of themselves can be ruled out. If this were the case, we would expect depressives to take less responsibility for success than for failure, and less responsibility for success than do nondepressives. Neither of these differences emerged. Their "evenhandedness" in explaining positive and negative events is more consistent with the hypothesis that either they have little motivation to protect or enhance their self-esteem or they have not learned how causal attributions can serve them in this regard.

REFERENCES

Abramson, L. Y., Garber, J., Edwards, N. B., & Seligman, M. E. P. (1978). Expectancy changes in depression and schizophrenia. *Journal of Abnormal Psychology, 87,* 102–109.

Abramson, L. Y., Metalsky, G. I., & Alloy, L. B. (1986). *The hopelessness theory of depression: A metatheoretical analysis with implications for psychopathology research.* Manuscript submitted for publication.

Abramson, L. Y., Seligman, M. E. P., & Teasdale, J. D. (1978). Learned helplessness in humans: Critique and reformulation. *Journal of Abnormal Psychology, 87,* 49–74.

Adler, A. (1956). *The individual psychology of Alfred Adler.* New York: Basic Books.

Alloy, L. B., & Abramson, L. Y. (1979). Judgments of contingency in depressed and nondepressed students: Sadder but wiser? *Journal of Experimental Psychology: General, 108,* 441–485.

Alloy, L. B., & Abramson, L. Y. (1982). Learned helplessness, depression, and the illusion of control. *Journal of Personality and Social Psychology, 42,* 1114–1126.

Alloy, L. B., Abramson, L. Y., & Viscusi, D. (1981). Induced mood and the illusion of control. *Journal of Personality and Social Psychology, 41,* 1129–1140.

Alloy, L. B., 7 Ahrens, A. H. (1987). Depression and pessimism for the future: Biased use of statistically relevant information in predictions for self versus others. *Journal of Personality and Social Psychology, 52,* 366–378.

Allport, G. W. (1937). *Personality: A psychological interpretation.* New York: Holt.

Barthe, D. G., & Hammen, C. L. (1981). The attributional model of depression: A naturalistic extension. *Personality and Social Psychology Bulletin, 7*, 53–58.

Beck, A. T. (1967). *Depression: Clinical, experimental, and theoretical aspects*. New York: Harper & Row.

Beck, A. T. (1976). *Cognitive therapy and the emotional disorders*. New York: International Universities Press.

Blaney, P. H., Behar, V., & Head, R. (1980). Two measures of depressive cognitions: Their association with depression and with each other. *Journal of Abnormal Psychology, 89*, 678–682.

Bower, G. H. (1981). Mood and memory. *American Psychologist, 36*, 129–148.

Bower, G. H., Monteiro, K. P., & Gilligan, S. G. (1978). Emotional mood as a context of learning and recall. *Journal of Verbal Learning and Verbal Behavior, 17*, 573–585.

Brewin, C. R. (1985). Depression and causal attributions: What is their relation? *Psychological Bulletin, 98*, 297–309.

Buchwald, A. M., Coyne, J. C., & Cole, C. S. (1978). A critical evaluation of the learned helplessness model of depression. *Journal of Abnormal Psychology, 87*, 180–193.

Carver, C. S., Ganellen, R. J., & Behar-Mitrani, V. (1985). Depression and cognitive style: Comparisons between measures. *Journal of Personality and Social Psychology, 49*, 722–728.

Coates, D., & Peterson, B. A. (1982). Depression and deviance. In G. Weary & H. Mirels (Eds.), *Integration of social and clinical psychology* (pp. 154–170). New York: Oxford University Press.

Cochran, S. D., & Hammen, C. L. (1985). Perceptions of stressful life events and depression: A test of the attribution models. *Journal of Personality and Social Psychology, 48*, 1562–1571.

Coyne, J. C., & Gotlib, I. H. (1983). The role of cognition in depression: A critical appraisal. *Psychological Bulletin, 94*, 472–505.

Cutrona, C. E. (1983). Causal attributions and perinatal depression. *Journal of Abnormal Psychology, 92*, 161–172.

Cutrona, C. E., Russell, D., & Jones, R. D. (1984). Cross-situational consistency in causal attributions: Does attributional style exist? *Journal of Personality and Social Psychology, 47*, 1043–1058.

Depue, R. A., & Monroe, S. M. (1978). Learned helplessness in the perspective of the depressive disorders: Conceptual and definitional issues. *Journal of Abnormal Psychology, 87*, 3–20.

Derry, P. A., & Kuiper, N. A. (1981). Schematic processing and self-reference in clinical depression. *Journal of Abnormal Psychology, 90*, 286–297.

Duval, S., & Wicklund, R. A. (1972). *A theory of objective self-awareness*. New York: Academic Press.

Dweck, C. S. (1975). The role of expectations and attributions in the alleviation of learned helplessness. *Journal of Personality and Social Psychology, 31*, 674–685.

Eaves, G., & Rush, J. A. (1984). Cognitive patterns in symptomatic and remitted unipolar major depression. *Journal of Abnormal Psychology, 93*, 31–40.

Feather, N. T. (1983). Some correlates of attributional style: Depressive symptoms, self-esteem, and Protestant ethic values. *Personality and Social Psychology Bulletin, 9*, 125–135.

Fiske, S., & Taylor, S. E. (1984). *Social cognition*. Reading, MA: Addison-Wesley.

Ford, C. E., & Neale, J. M. (1985). Learned helplessness and judgments of control. *Journal of Personality and Social Psychology, 49*, 1330–1336.

Golin, S., Sweeney, P. D., & Schaeffer, D. E. (1981). The causality of causal attributions in depression: A cross-lagged panel correlational analysis. *Journal of Abnormal Psychology, 90*, 14–22.

Golin, S., Terrell, T., & Johnson, B. (1977). Depression and the illusion of control. *Journal of Abnormal Psychology, 86*, 440–442.

Golin, S., Terrell, T., Weitz, J., & Drost, P. L. (1979). The illusion of control among depressed patients. *Journal of Abnormal Psychology, 88*, 454–457.

Gong-Guy, E., & Hammen, C. (1980). Causal perceptions of stressful events in depressed and nondepressed outpatients. *Journal of Abnormal Psychology, 89*, 662–669.

Gotlib, I. H., & Olson, J. M. (1983). Depression, psychopathology, and self-serving attributions. *British Journal of Clinical Psychology, 22*, 309–310.

Greenwald, A. G. (1980). The totalitarian ego: Fabrication and revision of personal history. *American Psychologist, 35*, 603–608.

Greenwald, A. G., & Pratkanis, A. R. (1984). The self. In R. S. Wyer & T. K. Srull (Eds.), *The handbook of social cognition* (Vol. 3, pp. 129–178). Hillsdale, NJ: Erlbaum.

Hamilton, E. W., & Abramson, L. Y. (1983). Cognitive patterns and major depressive disorder: A longitudinal study in a hospital setting. *Journal of Abnormal Psychology, 92,* 173–184.

Hammen, C., & Cochran, S. D. (1981). Cognitive correlates of life stress and depression in college students. *Journal of Abnormal Psychology, 90,* 23–27.

Hammen, C., & de Mayo, R. (1982). Cognitive correlates of teacher stress and depressive symptoms: Implications for attributional models of depression. *Journal of Abnormal Psychology, 91,* 96–101.

Hammen, C., Krantz, S., & Cochran, S. (1981). Relationship between depression and causal attributions about stressful life events. *Cognitive Therapy and Research, 5,* 351–358.

Harvey, D. (1981). Depression and attributional style: Interpretation of important personal events. *Journal of Abnormal Psychology, 90,* 134–142.

Hastorf, A., Schneider, D., & Polefka, J. (1970). *Person perception.* Reading, MA: Addison-Wesley.

Heider, F. (1958). *The psychology of interpersonal relations.* New York: Wiley.

Higgins, E. T., Klein, R., & Strauman, T. (1985). Self-concept discrepancy theory: A model for distinguishing among different aspects of depression and anxiety. *Social Cognition, 3,* 51–76.

Isen, A. M. (1970). Success, failure, attention and reaction to others: The warm glow of success. *Journal of Personality and Social Psychology, 15,* 294–301.

Isen, A. M., & Levin, P. F. (1972). On helping: Cookies and kindness. *Journal of Personality and Social Psychology, 21,* 384–388.

Janoff-Bulman, R. (1979). Characterological versus behavioral self-blame: Inquiries into depression and rape. *Journal of Personality and Social Psychology, 37,* 1798–1809.

Kahneman, D., & Miller, D. T. (1986). Norm theory: Comparing reality to its alternatives. *Psychological Review, 93,* 126–153.

Kahneman, D., Slovic, P., & Tversky, A. (Eds.). (1982). *Judgment under uncertainty: Heuristics and biases.* New York: Cambridge University Press.

Klein, D. C., Fencil-Morse, E., & Seligman, M. E. P. (1976). Learned helplessness, depression, and the attribution of failure. *Journal of Personality and Social Psychology, 33,* 508–516.

Krantz, S. E., & Rude, S. (1984). Depressive attributions: Selection of different causes or assignment of dimensional meaning? *Journal of Personality and Social Psychology, 47,* 193–203.

Kuiper, N. A. (1978). Depression and causal attributions for success and failure. *Journal of Personality and Social Psychology, 36,* 236–246.

Kuiper, N. A., Olinger, L. J., MacDonald, M. R., & Shaw, B. F. (1985). Self-schema processing of depressed and nondepressed content: The effects of vulnerability to depression. *Social Cognition, 3,* 77–93.

Langer, E. J. (1975). The illusion of control. *Journal of Personality and Social Psychology, 32,* 311–328.

Lewinsohn, P. M., Mischel, W., Chaplin, W., & Barton, R. (1980). Social competence and depression: The role of illusory self-perceptions. *Journal of Abnormal Psychology, 89,* 203–212.

Lewinsohn, P. M., Steinmetz, J. L., Larson, D. W., & Franklin, J. (1981). Depression-related cognitions: Antecedents or consequence? *Journal of Abnormal Psychology, 90,* 213–219.

Manly, P. C., McMahon, R. J., Bradley, C. F., & Davidson, P. O. (1982). Depressive attributional style and depression following childbirth. *Journal of Abnormal Psychology, 91,* 245–254.

Marx, M. B., Garrity, T. F., & Bower, F. R. (1975). The influence of recent life experiences on the health of the college freshman. *Journal of Psychosomatic Research, 19,* 87–98.

McCaul, K. D. (1983). Observer attributions of depressed students. *Personality and Social Psychology Bulletin, 9,* 74–82.

Metalsky, G. I., Abramson, L. Y., Seligman, M. E. P., Semmel, A., & Peterson, C. (1982). Attributional styles and life events in the classroom: Vulnerability and invulnerability to depressive mood reactions. *Journal of Personality and Social Psychology, 43,* 612–617.

Metalsky, G. I., Halberstadt, L. J., & Abramson, L. Y. (1987). Vulnerability to depressive mood reduction: Toward a more powerful test of the diathesis–stress and causal mediation components of the reformulated theory of depression. *Journal of Personality and Social Psychology, 52,* 386–393.

Miller, D. T., & Porter, C. A. (1983). Self-blame in victims of violence. *Journal of Social Issues, 39,* 139–152.

Miller, D. T., & Porter, C. A. (in press). Errors and biases in the attribution process. In L. Abramson (Ed.), *Social Cognition and Clinical Psychology.* New York: Guilford Press.

Miller, D. T., & Ross, M. (1975). Self-serving biases in the attribution of causality: Fact or fiction? *Psychological Bulletin, 82,* 213–225.

Miller, I. W., Klee, S. H., & Norman, W. H. (1982). Depressed and nondepressed inpatients' cognitions of hypothetical events, experimental tasks, and stressful life events. *Journal of Abnormal Psychology, 91,* 78–81.

Miller, I. W., & Norman, W. H. (1981). Effects of attribution for success on the alleviation of learned helplessness and depression. *Journal of Abnormal Psychology, 90,* 113–124.

Mischel, W., Ebbesen, E. B., & Zeiss, A. M. (1973). Selective attention to the self: Situational and dispositional determinants. *Journal of Personality and Social Psychology, 27,* 129–142.

Mukherji, B. R., Abramson, L. Y., & Martin, D. J. (1982). Induced depressive mood and attributional patterns. *Cognitive Therapy and Research, 6,* 5–21.

Nezu, A. M., Nezu, C. M., & Nezu, V. A. (1986). Depression, general distress, and causal attributions among university students. *Journal of Abnormal Psychology, 95,* 184–186.

Nisbett, R. E., & Ross, L. (1980). *Human inference: Strategies and shortcomings in social judgment.* Englewood Cliffs, NJ: Prentice-Hall.

O'Hara, M. W., Neunaber, D. J., & Zekoski, E. M. (1984). Prospective study of postpartum depression: Prevalence, course and predictive factors. *Journal of Abnormal Psychology, 93,* 158–171.

O'Hara, M. W., Rehm, L. P., & Campbell, S. B. (1982). Predicting depressive symptomatology: Cognitive–behavioral models and postpartum depression. *Journal of Abnormal Psychology, 91,* 457–461.

Oliver, J. M., & Williams, G. (1979). The psychology of depression as revealed by attribution causality in college students. *Cognitive Therapy and Research, 3,* 355–360.

Persons, J. B., & Rao, P. A. (1985). Longitudinal study of cognitions, life events, and depression in psychiatric inpatients. *Journal of Abnormal Psychology, 94,* 51–63.

Peterson, C., Raps, C. S., & Villanova, P. (1985). Depression and attributions: Factors responsible for inconsistent results in the published literature. *Journal of Abnormal Psychology, 94,* 165–168.

Peterson, C., Schwartz, S. M., & Seligman, M. E. P. (1981). Self-blame and depressive symptoms. *Journal of Personality and Social Psychology, 41,* 253–259.

Peterson, C., & Seligman, M. E. P. (1984). Causal explanations as a risk factor for depression: Theory and evidence. *Psychological Review, 91,* 347–374.

Peterson, C., Semmel, A., von Baeyer, C., Abramson, L. Y., Metalsky, G. I., & Seligman, M. E. P. (1982). The Attributional Style Questionnaire. *Cognitive Therapy and Research, 6,* 287–300.

Pyszczynski, T., Holt, K., & Greenberg, J. (1987). Depression, self-focused attention, and expectancies for positive and negative future life events for self and others. *Journal of Personality and Social Psychology, 52,* 994–1001.

Raps, C. S., Peterson, C., Reinhard, K. E., Abramson, L. Y., & Seligman, M. E. P. (1982). Attributional style among depressed patients. *Journal of Abnormal Psychology, 91,* 102–108.

Rizley, R. (1978). Depression and distortion in the attribution of causality. *Journal of Abnormal Psychology, 87,* 32–48.

Seligman, M. E. P., Abramson, L. Y., Semmel, A., & von Baeyer, C. (1979). Depressive attributional style. *Journal of Abnormal Psychology, 88,* 242–247.

Sharp, J., & Tennen, H. (1983). Attributional bias in depression: The role of cue perception. *Cognitive Therapy and Research, 7,* 325–332.

Shrauger, J. S. (1982). Selection and processing of self-evaluative information: Experimental evidence and clinical implications. In G. Weary & H. L. Mirels (Eds.), *Integration of clinical and social psychology* (pp. 128–153). New York: Oxford Press.

Simon, H. A. (1957). *Models of man.* New York: Wiley.

Sweeney, P. D., Anderson, K. A., & Bailey, S. (1986). Attributional style in depression: A meta-analytic review. *Journal of Personality and Social Psychology, 50,* 974–991.

Tabachnik-Kayne, N., Alloy, L. B., Romer, D., & Crocker, J. (1986). *Predicting depression and elation reactions in the classroom: A test of the attributional diathesis–stress theory of depression.* Manuscript submitted for publication.

Taylor, S. E., & Brown, J. (1986). *Illusion and well-being: Some social psychological contributions to a theory of mental health.* Unpublished manuscript.

Taylor, S. E., Wood, J. V., & Lichtman, R. R. (1983). It could be worse: Selective evaluation as a response to victimization. *Journal of Social Issues, 39,* 19–40.

Tennen, H., & Herzberger, S. (1987). Depression, self-esteem and the absence of self-protective attributional biases. *Journal of Personality and Social Psychology, 52,* 72–80.

Tetlock, P., & Levi, A. (1982). Attribution bias: On the inconclusiveness of the cognition–motivation debates. *Journal of Experimental Social Psychology, 18,* 68–88.

Watson, G. M. W., & Dyck, D. G. (1984). Depressive attributional style in psychiatric inpatients: Effects of reinforcement level and assessment procedure. *Journal of Abnormal Psychology, 93,* 312–320.

Weary, G., Elbin, S., & Hill, M. (1987). Attributional and social comparison processes in depression. *Journal of Personality and Social Psychology, 52,* 605–610.

Weary, G., Jordan, J. S., & Hill, M. G. (1985). The attributional norm of intentionality and depressive sensitivity to social information. *Journal of Personality and Social Psychology, 49,* 1283–1293.

Weiner, B., Russell, D., & Lerman, D. (1978). Affective consequences of causal attributions. In J. Harvey, W. Ickes, & R. Kidd (Eds.), *New directions in attribution research* (Vol. 2, pp. 59–90). Hillsdale, NJ: Erlbaum.

Williams, J. M. G. (1985). Attributional formulation of depression as a diathesis–stress model: Metalsky *et al.* reconsidered. *Journal of Personality and Social Psychology, 48,* 1572–1575.

Wortman, C. B. (1983). Coping with victimization: Conclusions and implications for future research. *Journal of Social Issues, 39,* 195–221.

Zautra, A. J., Guenther, R. T., & Chartier, G. M. (1985). Attributions for real and hypothetical events: Their relation to self-esteem and depression. *Journal of Abnormal Psychology, 94,* 530–540.

Zemore, R., & Johansen, L. Y. (1980). Depression, helplessness and failure attributions. *Canadian Journal of Behavioural Science, 12,* 167–174.

Zuckerman, M. (1979). Attribution and success and failure revisited: Or the attributional bias is alive and well in attribution theory. *Journal of Personality, 47,* 245–247.

Zuroff, D. D. (1981). Depression and attribution: Some new data and a review of old data. *Cognitive Therapy and Research, 5,* 273–281.

COGNITIVE VULNERABILITY FACTORS IN DEPRESSION AND THEIR REMEDIATION

10

Vulnerability and Episodic Cognitions in a Self-worth Contingency Model of Depression

NICHOLAS A. KUIPER
University of Western Ontario

L. JOAN OLINGER
Brescia College at University of Western Ontario

MICHAEL R. MACDONALD
St. Mary's Hospital, London, Ontario

Depression is one of the most common and serious mental health problems encountered by our society (Wing & Bebbington, 1985). Epidemiological studies in North America indicate that one in eight individuals will require psychiatric attention for depression at some point in his or her life (Secunda, Katz, Friedman, & Schuyler, 1973). Furthermore, research indicates that the effects of depression are not always fully reversible or time limited. Of individuals who are clinically depressed, 8% do not fully recover to their premorbid level of functioning within 2 years. Even for individuals who do fully recover, most of them will again experience a clinical depression within 10 to 20 years (Beck, 1967).

The widespread incidence and prevalence of depression is especially problematic when considered in light of the known relationship between depression and suicide. Approximately 1 in every 200 depressives commits suicide, and of those shown to have committed suicide, 80% suffered depressions within a few months prior to their deaths (Minkoff, Bergman, Beck, & Beck, 1973). Overall, then, the impact of depression on individuals, families, and society is enormous. As one example, in the early 1970s, the National Institute of Mental Health concluded that depression accounts for 75% of psychiatric hospitalizations (Secunda *et al.*, 1973).

Given the enormity of this problem, depression researchers have expended considerable energy over the past decade investigating various facets of this disorder. As one illustration, a number of investigators have described symptomatic aspects of depression in both general and psychiatric populations. Typically, these symptoms include cognitive, emotional, motivational, behavioral, and vegetative components (Shaw, Vallis, & McCabe, 1985). Cognitive components of depression relate to such factors as a negative view of the self, perceptions of hopelessness, loss of self-esteem, guilt, and self-castigation. The emotional components refer to feelings of dysphoria, anxiety, and sadness. Motivationally and behaviorally, the depressed individual is characterized by a lowered activity level and lethargic responding, which some investigators have attributed to a "paralysis of the will"

(Beck, 1967). Finally, depression is often characterized by the presence of somatic or vegetative complaints, such as irregular and dysfunctional sleeping and eating patterns.

Depression investigators have also advanced various etiological models to account for this disorder. These theoretical perspectives have ranged from behaviorally based models to those postulating an important role for cognitive factors. Representative of the former are approaches that have attempted to link the onset and maintenance of depression to deficits in social skills and/or reinforcer effectiveness (Costello, 1976; Hoberman & Lewinsohn, 1985). Examples of the latter are Beck's cognitive model of depression (Sacco & Beck, 1985) and the reformulated learned helplessness model, which emphasizes the possible role of causal attributions in the etiology of depression (Peterson & Seligman, 1985).

We intend in this chapter to provide an overview of the recent social cognition research conducted in our laboratory that has explored the nature of personal and social information processing in depressed and nondepressed individuals. After describing several studies outlining self-schema content and processing effects in these individuals, we present a self-schema model of depression. This model considers both the content and the consolidation components of the self-schema and relates these characteristics to the degree of depression exhibited by the individual. After outlining this self-schema model, we discuss the possible role of cognitions in the etiology and maintenance of depression and present a self-worth contingency model of depression. This model incorporates the self-schema model by suggesting that certain individuals may display a cognitive vulnerability to depression centering around their dysfunctional attitudes for evaluating self-worth. The self-worth contingency model also provides for a distinction between vulnerability and episodic cognitions. "Vulnerability cognitions" are cognitive structures that may play a role in the onset of depressive symptoms. Conversely, "episodic cognitions" are maladaptive cognitive structures that become activated only after the onset of other depressive symptoms, such as negative affect. Based on empirical data, it is proposed that dysfunctional attitudes, increased public self-consciousness, and heightened levels of social anxiety may represent the type of cognitions evident in vulnerable individuals. In contrast, further findings presented in this chapter suggest that negative self-schema content and increased self-focused attention are concomitants of a depressive episode, and as such should be considered episodic cognitions.

A SELF-SCHEMA MODEL OF DEPRESSION

Content and Consolidation Components

Over the past several years, it has often been proposed that dysfunctional cognitions may play an important role in depression (Beck, Rush, Shaw, & Emery, 1979; Hammen, Marks, de Mayo, & Mayol, 1985; Kuiper & Higgins, 1985; Kuiper & Olinger, 1986; Ruehlman, West, & Pasahow, 1985; Sacco & Beck, 1985). These depressive cognitions have generally been defined in terms of negative cognitive schemata that influence how an individual processes both personal and social information. As one example, Beck and his colleagues suggested that the content of depressive schemata centers around themes of personal deficiency, self-blame, and negative expectations. In turn, these negative schemata determine not only what stimuli an individual attends to but also how these stimuli are integrated and evaluated.

One source of evidence for a negative schema in depression comes from several of our studies, which have focused on self-referent processes in normal and depressed individuals. Using a self-reference incidental recall paradigm, Derry and Kuiper (1981) documented the content represented in a depressive self-schema. This paradigm required clinical depressives and nondepressed controls to rate whether each adjective in a list of depressed- and nondepressed-content words (e.g., hopeless, inferior, etc. vs. capable, sociable, etc.) described themselves. Following this, subjects were unexpectedly asked to recall as many of the personal adjectives as possible. A self-schema model predicted that adjectives congruent with content represented in the self-schema would be better recalled than adjectives incongruent with an individual's view of self. In confirmation of these predictions, Derry and Kuiper (1981) reported that clinical depressives displayed enhanced recall for depressed-content personal adjectives receiving a prior self-referent judgment (compared to their recall for nondepressed-content adjectives given the same prior judgment). In contrast, nondepressed subjects displayed an entirely opposite self-referent pattern, recalling far more nondepressed- than depressed-content adjectives. Overall, then, these systematic differences suggested that the self-schema of clinical depressives consists primarily of pathological or depressed content, whereas the nondepressive's self-schema consists primarily of normal or nonpathological content.

A second important aspect of the self-schema model pertains to the degree of consolidation of self-referent material. Rating times of self-referent personality decisions have been used as one empirical indicator of self-schema consolidation (i.e., a processing-efficiency measure). In particular, Derry and Kuiper (1981) proposed that personal information that is congruent with content represented in a self-schema should be processed more quickly or efficiently than information that is incongruent. Employing this rating time (RT) measure, Derry and Kuiper (1981) found that clinical depressives were no less efficient in their speed of processing than normal controls. This RT pattern was replicated in a further clinical study by MacDonald and Kuiper (1985), suggesting that clinical depressives and normal subjects both employ an efficient and a well-consolidated self-schema to assist them in self-referent information processing (albeit for different content).

Additional research using this self-reference paradigm has established the effects of severity of depression on both self-schema content and consolidation. In one study by Kuiper and Derry (1982), mildly depressed and normal subjects made self-referent judgments concerning the depressed and nondepressed personal adjectives. Subjects were tested in groups, which precluded the assessment of RTs. The incidental recall data, however, revealed several patterns of interest. As in Derry

and Kuiper (1981), normal controls recalled far more nondepressed- than depressed-content adjectives, again suggesting a positive view of self. Mildly depressed subjects, in contrast, displayed equivalent self-referent recall for both types
of content. In turn, this finding hints that the self-schema of mildly depressed
persons may incorporate both pathological and normal content.

Further evidence for this latter proposal was obtained by Kuiper and MacDonald (1982). This study again examined self-reference effects in mildly depressed
and normal subjects, but in a paradigm that also allowed for the collection of RTs.
In accord with the self-schema model, normal subjects recalled significantly more
positive than negative information about themselves and also displayed quicker RTs
for schema-consistent positive material. Conversely, mildly depressed subjects
recalled equal amounts of positive and negative self-referent material. In combination with their longer RTs for both types of self-referent judgments, these findings
point to a view of self in mildly depressed persons that incorporates both positive
and negative personal content, but at the expense of the efficient processing of
either.

Self-schema consolidation has also been measured in terms of decision consistency across independent sets of self-referent judgments (MacDonald & Kuiper,
1984; MacDonald, Kuiper, & Olinger, 1985). Consolidation can be thought of as a
product of the specific organization of content within an individual's self-schema.
As such, greater consolidation (and therefore greater consistency) can be predicted
for content congruent with information already represented in a person's self-
schema. In other words, since self-schema-congruent information is thought to be
more deeply and elaborately encoded, and more easily retrieved from memory, it
was postulated that these cognitive assets would yield greater consistency for
congruent personal information.

To test these consistency predictions empirically, MacDonald and Kuiper
(1984) first had clinical depressives, nondepressed psychiatric controls, and normal
subjects make a series of self-referent yes-or-no decisions concerning the depressed-
and nondepressed-content adjectives used in previous research. Following this,
each subject rated each adjective on a 9-point degree-of-self-reference scale. On this
scale, 1 indicated "extremely unlike me," and 9 indicated "extremely like me." An
inconsistency represented either an adjective rated "yes" in the first part of the
experiment and later rated in the 1–4 range of the 9-point scale, or an adjective first
rated "no" and later rated in the 6–9 range of the scale.

Employing this measure, MacDonald and Kuiper (1984) found that decisions
concerning content congruent with information already represented in the self-
schema were made more consistently than decisions concerning incongruent content. To take one example, clinical depressives displayed significantly fewer
inconsistencies for depressed-content adjectives given a prior "yes" decision
(schema-congruent responding for these subjects) compared to their ratings for
depressed-content adjectives given a previous "no" decision (schema-incongruent
responding for these subjects). In contrast, both normal and nondepressed psychiatric controls displayed precisely the opposite pattern: Their decision inconsistency
was markedly higher for depressed-content adjectives given a prior "yes" rating
(schema-incongruent responding for these subjects) relative to their decision in-

consistency for the same type of adjectives given a "no" decision (schema-congruent responding for these subjects). In general, all subjects in this study exhibited greater consistency for self-schema-congruent than for self-schema-incongruent material. For clinical depressives, these findings highlight the stable, consolidated nature of their negative self-schemata. For nondepressives, on the other hand, these findings point to well-consolidated and stable positive self-schemata. Finally, the mildly depressed subjects tested in a second study by MacDonald *et al.* (1985) revealed the highest degree of decision inconsistency, which is consistent with the proposal that their self-schemata are poorly consolidated for both positive and negative content.

When combined, the findings of the preceding studies permit the formulation of a self-schema model of depression. A major tenet of this model is that depth of depression is a primary factor in determining both the content and the consolidation aspects of the self-schema. As shown in Table 10-1, normal persons and clinical depressives are both characterized by highly efficient self-schema processing of personal material, albeit for positive and negative content, respectively. In fact, work by MacDonald and Kuiper (1985) suggests that for clinical depressives and normal persons, this processing may proceed in an automatic fashion, with minimal awareness. Mildly depressed persons, however, incorporate both types of content in their view of self, but with inefficient processing for either type. Specifically, the self-referent RT pattern of mildly depressed persons suggests a poorly consolidated self-schema, which no longer facilitates the efficient processing of either positive or negative content (see also MacDonald *et al.*, 1985, for comparable results with the decision-consistency consolidation measure). Mild levels of depression might be marked by a period of uncertainty and confusion surrounding one's view of self.

Table 10-1. A Self-schema Model of Depression

Depression level	Self-schema content[a]	Self-schema consolidation[b]
Nondepressed	Positive	Strong: Normal persons display a highly consolidated self-schema that processes positive self-referent material efficiently and consistently.
Mildly depressed	Positive and negative	Weak: Mildly depressed persons display uncertainty about the validity of both positive and negative self-referent attributes, leading to a poorly consolidated schema. As such, both positive and negative self-referent material is processed in inefficiently and inconsistently.
Clinically depressed	Negative	Strong: Clinical depressives display a highly consolidated negative-content self-schema. Negative personal information is processed consistently and efficiently.

[a]Self-schema content can be measured in several ways—for example, by "yes" responses to depressed- and nondepressed-content adjectives and by recall patterns for these adjectives.

[b]Self-schema consolidation can be measured in terms of both processing efficiency (RTs for self-referent personality judgments) and processing consistency (congruence across sets of self-referent judgments).

Although the person may have already begun to experience some depressive symptoms, the mild nature of these symptoms may prohibit their precise identification and complete assimilation into the self-schema. At the same time, however, the mildly depressed individual may begin to question the validity of positive self-referent content. Together, these processes may serve to reduce the overall degree of consolidation of the mildly depressed person's self-schema.

Further Effects Associated with a Depressive Self-schema

The preceding studies have generally employed the same set of stimulus materials and dependent measures (e.g., recall, RT, and decision consistency) to determine self-schema content and consolidation. It should be possible, however, to use different dependent measures and stimuli to document further negative effects that may be associated with this schema. Accordingly, Kuiper and MacDonald (1983) employed a paradigm that departed considerably from the self-referent decision tasks used in many of our previous experiments. Instead of measuring recall and RT performance, these investigators required depressed and nondepressed subjects to provide estimates concerning the general frequency of occurrence of various negative situations, and of depressive responses to these situations, in the population at large.

Previous research in social cognition has suggested that individuals may rely extensively on self-based knowledge and experiences when required to generate frequency estimates (Nisbett & Ross, 1980). Since highly self-referent material is quite accessible in memory (Kuiper, 1981), it was reasoned by Kuiper and Mac-Donald (1983) that the negative content represented in a depressive's self-schema may be overutilized, relative to normals, in providing frequency estimates.

The results reported by Kuiper and MacDonald (1983) offered general support for this self-schema accessibility effect. One negative scenario, for instance, involved failure at school. Here, a student was described as contemplating leaving a university after poor performance on some midterm exams. Depressives, as predicted, offered a much higher estimate than did nondepressives for the occurrence of this particular negative scenario (68% vs. 46%, respectively). Furthermore, when asked to estimate the percentage of individuals who would display a rather severe depressive reaction to this situation, depressives again provided a much higher estimate than nondepressives (80% vs. 64%, respectively).

This self-schema accessibility effect was also noted for several other portions of the Kuiper and MacDonald (1983) data. As one example, depressives systematically overestimated their chances of becoming depressed, compared to their own concept of the average person. Nondepressed individuals, on the other hand, rated themselves as less likely to become depressed in these negative situations, compared to their concept of the average person. In turn, Kuiper and MacDonald suggested that this self-perceived superiority for normal persons represented a variant of the "illusory glow" phenomenon, in which nondepressives tend to perceive themselves more positively than others see them (Lewinsohn, Mischel, Chaplin, & Barton, 1980).

COGNITIONS AND THE ETIOLOGY OF DEPRESSION

The self-schema studies reviewed thus far have been primarily descriptive in nature. In other words, these studies have succeeded in mapping out the content and consolidation components of the self-schema at various levels of depression. Although this research does offer mechanisms to help explain how individuals might become depressed, it does not focus directly on the possible etiological role of cognitive schemata in depression. This etiological issue might be addressed in a number of ways, such as by the longitudinal study of depressives and former depressives (Dobson & Shaw, 1986; Hammen *et al.*, 1985; Rholes, Riskind, & Neville, 1985), the use of mood-induction techniques (Mitchell & Madigan, 1984), the examination of cognitive characteristics of remitted depressives (Altman & Wittenborn, 1980), and the identification of cognitive attributes associated with individuals vulnerable to depression but currently nondepressed (Kuiper, Olinger, MacDonald, & Shaw, 1985; Kuiper & Olinger, 1986, in press; Wilbert & Rupert, 1986). The research reported in the remainder of this chapter relies extensively on the last strategy, since it outlines more precisely the cognitive characteristics associated with individuals postulated to be vulnerable to depression.

A second consideration for etiological models of depression relates to the broader context of social information processing (Kuiper & Higgins, 1985; Swallow & Kuiper, in press). Here, the emphasis is on how individuals process information about other people in their environment, and on the social milieu in which these people interact (Dance & Kuiper, in press; Swallow & Kuiper, 1987). This broader perspective is important, because previous research has generally indicated that problems with social interaction are fairly typical among depressed individuals. Coyne (1976), for example, found that depressives engage their environment in a manner such that social support is lost and negative reactions are elicited from others. Similarly, Youngren & Lewinsohn (1980) report that depressed individuals give and receive less positive reinforcement in social interactions than do nondepressives. These difficulties in social interaction often result in isolation and problematic interpersonal relationships, and thus may contribute to both the etiology and maintenance of depression.

Of special interest to the cognitive investigator is the possible role of social information processing in contributing to the depressed person's expression of social skills deficits. In this examination, it may prove useful to divide the social skills problem into two components. On the one hand, there are the actual behaviors exhibited in the interaction. As one example, Gotlib and Robinson (1982) report that depressives exhibit more adapters (fidgeting, nonuseful behaviors) and fewer illustrators (useful aids in expression, such as hand movements) than do nondepressives. These behavioral social skills deficits would seem to work to the disadvantage of the depressed individual in maintaining a normal interaction. On the other hand, one can also think of cognitive components associated with the social interaction sequence. Previous literature indicates that depressed individuals evaluate their interactions with others more negatively than do nondepressed individuals, both for immediate evaluations following the interactions (Lewinsohn *et al.,* 1980) and for the more global recalled evaluations (Lunghi, 1977). Further-more, Kuiper and MacDonald (1982) found that depressed individuals have more positive conceptions of others than do nondepressed individuals.

Several of the social cognition findings just described can be labeled as preinteractional in nature. In other words, these cognitions are socially relevant assumptions, attitudes, opinions, and expectations that the individual possesses prior to a social interaction or engagement. Of course, individuals display additional social cognitions both during and after social interactions. The research documented in the following sections of this chapter, however, focuses primarily on the pre-interactional cognitions of depressed, nondepressed, and vulnerable individuals. A preinteraction focus was selected as an initial starting point because social cognition investigators have demonstrated that what transpires during a social interaction is often contingent upon the participant's attitudes and expectations prior to that interaction (Kuiper & Higgins, 1985).

VULNERABILITY AND A SELF-WORTH CONTINGENCY MODEL OF DEPRESSION

Considerable attention has been devoted in the past few years to the possible role of cognitive processes in the onset of depressive symptomatology. As one example, Kuiper and Olinger (1986, in press) recently developed a self-worth contingency model of depression. In this model, it is proposed that excessively rigid and inappropriate rules for guiding one's life constitute a cognitive predisposition or vulnerability to depression. Examples of such rules or dysfunctional attitudes are "If I do not do well all of the time, people will not respect me" or "If someone disagrees with me, it probably indicates that he does not like me." A number of these attitudes have been identified by Beck and his colleagues (Beck *et al.,* 1979) and can be measured by the DAS (Dobson & Shaw, 1986; Oliver & Baumgart, 1985).

Kuiper and Olinger (1986) noted that these dysfunctional attitudes are char-acterized by a contractual basis for self-worth or happiness. As one example, in the dysfunctional attitude "My value as a person depends upon what others think of me," the implicit condition for self-worth is approval from others. In the self-worth contingency model it is proposed that individuals with dysfunctional attitudes can remain nondepressed so long as their self-worth contingencies are being met. However, such vulnerable individuals will likely begin to experience depressive symptomatology if, for some reason, these contingencies are no longer perceived as being fulfilled. To return to the preceding example, so long as the vulnerable individual perceives that significant others are in fact approving, depressive symp-toms would not likely occur. If, however, the individual began to perceive that he or she was not well thought of, then depressive symptoms might emerge.

Vulnerability, Life Events, and Self-worth Contingencies

Empirical support for the self-worth contingency model has been advanced by Olinger, Kuiper, and Shaw (1987). In this research, participants completed the

DAS, the BDI, and the DAS-Contractual Conditions Scale (DAS-CC). The DAS-CC is a modified version of the DAS, designed to measure the presence or absence of life events that impinge on an individual's dysfunctional attitudes. For example, for the dysfunctional attitude "If you don't have other people to lean on, you are bound to be sad," the contractual condition for happiness is having other people to lean on. If individuals reported that they had other people to lean on, then they would be fulfilling the contractual conditions of their dysfunctional attitude and would thus not likely exhibit depressive symptoms. If they reported, however, that they did not have other people to lean on, then this was considered a failure in fulfilling the contractual conditions of their dysfunctional attitudes, and it was expected that they would show depressive symptoms.

As predicted by Olinger and her colleagues, vulnerability to depression moderated the relationship between impinging life events and depression. For those low on dysfunctional attitudes, impinging events had only a modest impact on depression scores. For those high on dysfunctional attitudes, the relationship was significant. Here, an increase in impinging events produced a substantial increment in depression scores. This pattern was obtained not only for the specific DAS-CC events relating to dysfunctional attitudes but also for a wider range of life events assessed in a second study.

The Olinger, Kuiper, and Shaw (1987) study also provided several further sources of data that converge on the potential importance of the vulnerability notion. In particular, it was proposed that attitudinal vulnerabilities may contribute to heightened levels of self-generated stress. In line with this proposal, individuals scoring high on the DAS did provide higher stress appraisals of actual or potential life events than individuals scoring low on the DAS. Furthermore, vulnerable individuals also reported increased perceptions of feeling overwhelmed and out of control.

Vulnerability and Self-schema Content

Research in our laboratory has also focused on the self-schema content exhibited by vulnerable individuals. One study by Kuiper et al. (1985), for example, used the self-reference incidental recall paradigm employed in previous research. Consistent with earlier findings and with the self-schema model of depression, Kuiper et al. (1985) found that normal subjects (i.e., those scoring low on both the DAS and the BDI) displayed a positive-content base for their view of self. Specifically, these subjects recalled far more nondepressed-content adjectives given a previous "yes" self-reference decision than depressed-content adjectives. Also in accord with the self-schema model of depression, mildly depressed subjects recalled equal amounts of depressed- and nondepressed-content material about themselves.

Of special interest in the Kuiper et al. (1985) study was the type of self-referent content that might be recalled by vulnerable subjects (i.e., those scoring high on the DAS but low on the BDI). In terms of the recall measure, vulnerable subjects recalled far more nondepressed- than depressed-content adjectives, as had normal subjects. Similarly, a tally of the number of "yes" responses to self-referent judgments concerning the depressed- and nondepressed-content adjectives revealed strong consistencies between the vulnerable and normal groups. Subjects in both of these groups said "yes" to far fewer of the depressed-content adjectives than did subjects in the depressed group (see also Kuiper, Olinger, & Swallow, in press, and Dance & Kuiper, 1987, for replications of these findings).

Further evidence for positive self-schema content in vulnerable individuals was obtained by Kuiper and Cole (1983). Instead of self-referent trait judgments, participants in this study made estimates of the frequency and intensity of their own prior depressive episodes. Results indicated that both normal controls and vulnerable subjects gave significantly lower estimates than currently depressed subjects. Stated differently, vulnerability *per se* did not lead to an increase in negative self-referent content regarding the reported frequency or intensity of prior depressive episodes. As such, these findings offer additional empirical support for the proposal that negative self-schema content is a concomitant of depression (and therefore not a vulnerability marker).

In further accord with findings from our laboratory, research conducted with formerly depressed subjects has also shown that a negative-content self-schema is not evident during remission (Laxer, 1964; Wilkinson & Blackburn, 1981). This pattern was also found by Hammen, Miklowitz, and Dyck (1986), in a longitudinal study. Here, subjects completed a self-reference recall task twice, once when depressed and later when nondepressed. Of particular interest was the finding that recall for negative self-schema content decreased significantly when the individual became nondepressed. This pattern is consistent with the findings reported by Kuiper *et al*. (1985) and suggests that negative self-schema content is an episodic marker of depression.

Vulnerability and Self-schema Consolidation

Although the self-worth contingency model proposes that vulnerable individuals have a positive view of self when nondepressed, it also suggests that this self-schema is poorly consolidated (Kuiper & Olinger, 1986). In particular, it is proposed that vulnerable individuals often engage in assessments of their self-worth, as determined by their dysfunctional contingencies. In turn, these frequent reevaluations contribute to increased uncertainty about self-referent attributes, and thus to a poorly consolidated self-schema.

In line with this proposal, research by MacDonald *et al*. (1985) revealed that vulnerable subjects display a lower level of decision consistency across independent sets of self-referent judgments than do normal controls. Furthermore, vulnerable subjects display significantly longer RTs for self-referent judgments, compared to normal controls (Dance & Kuiper, 1987). Thus, taken together, the preceding findings offer converging empirical support for the notion that vulnerable individuals who are currently nondepressed display a positive-content self-schema, though it is poorly consolidated.

INTEGRATION OF THE SELF-SCHEMA AND SELF-WORTH CONTINGENCY MODELS

An overview of the proposed integration between the self-schema and self-worth models of depression is presented in Table 10-2. As described previously for the self-worth model, individuals endorsing a large number of dysfunctional attitudes are considered to be cognitively vulnerable to depression. For these individuals, dysfunctional attitudes establish rigid and externally based contingencies for determining self-worth. These contingencies relate to a heightened concern over performance evaluation and an excessive need for approval by others; they may have developed, in part, as a function of a parenting style that fosters high levels of dependency and self-criticism (Carver & Ganellen, 1983; McGranie & Bass, 1984). When circumstances hamper the vulnerable individual's attempts to fulfill approval-based contingencies, this individual responds by attempting to modify or eliminate these stressful conditions. Mild threats to self-worth occur frequently for the vulnerable individual, who is highly dependent upon social and environmental feedback for self-esteem evaluation. Depressive symptoms might thus be provoked by major stressors (e.g., loss of employment) and/or culminating minor stressors (e.g., chronic interpersonal conflicts). In any case, these stressors all have their impact through an actual or perceived lack of fulfillment of self-worth contingencies. With each failed attempt to meet these contingencies, an increase in depressive types of responding is expected. Thus vulnerable individuals may rely increasingly

Table 10-2. A Self-worth Contingency Model of Depression

Type of individual	Self-schema content	Self-schema consolidation
Nonvulnerable– nondepressed	Positive	Strong: Normal persons exhibit a well-integrated positive-content self-schema.
Vulnerable– nondepressed	Positive	Weak: These vulnerable individuals often engage in self-worth assessments. As such, their positive view of self is relatively fragile and poorly consolidated. The content of this self-schema is still positive, however, because these individuals perceive that they are still meeting their dysfunctional self-worth contingencies.
Vulnerable– mildly depressed	Positive and negative	Weak: As the vulnerable individual increasingly perceives that self-worth contingencies are not being met, coping attempts and self-focused attention increase. Positive aspects of self are de-emphasized as negative components become more salient. Further depressive symptoms emerge (e.g., negative affect, social withdrawal).
Vulnerable– clinically depressed	Negative	Strong: Over time, the vulnerable individual's attempts to reinstate the conditions necessary to fulfilling dysfunctional self-worth contingencies may fail. Once the coping repertoire has been exhausted, a consolidated negative-content self-schema dominates personal information processing.

on emotional coping responses rather than direct problem-solving attempts (Billings & Moos, 1983). Furthermore, as detailed in Table 10-2, vulnerable individuals are expected to increase their self-focused attention, thereby shifting from a positive to a negative view of self.

VULNERABILITY VERSUS EPISODIC COGNITIONS

In light of our findings, it seems that further cognitive research on depression might distinguish more clearly between vulnerability and episodic cognitions (Kuiper *et al.*, 1985). Episodic cognitions are maladaptive cognitive structures that become activated only after the onset of other depressive symptoms (e.g., increased negative affect). Thus episodic cognitions or schemata may facilitate the maintenance of depression by enhancing the pervasiveness of the individual's negative information-processing style. In contrast, vulnerability cognitions or schemata are presumed to play an important role in the onset of depressive symptomatology. Thus vulnerability schemata may be actively employed to process information by a "high-risk" individual prior to the onset of a depressive episode. In turn, the negative product of this processing may then assist in triggering the onset of depressive symptoms. It should be noted, of course, that both these types of schemata are related, in that they are representational in nature. Furthermore, both vulnerability and episodic schemata involve organized cognitive structures that serve to influence how individuals perceive, process, and evaluate information about their environment. In general, then, vulnerability schemata are seen as bearing on both the etiology and the maintenance of depression, whereas episodic schemata are viewed primarily as concomitant features of this disorder. The critical point is that episodic schemata are not envisioned to play a central role in the onset of depressive symptomatology. Rather, their effects can be viewed as further symptomatic aspects of depression.

The content of episodic schemata may be largely negative and self-referential in nature. One example would be the depressive self-schema content documented in previous research. In line with an episodic notion, this research indicates that negative self-schema content is not characteristic of vulnerable individuals but is evident only in currently depressed individuals. Thus it would appear that the negative content associated with a depressive self-schema is apparent only after the onset of other depressive symptomatology (e.g., negative affect).

In contrast to episodic schemata, the content of vulnerability schemata includes the more general beliefs and assumptions that the individual holds. These may range from the dysfunctional attitudes described by Beck *et al.* (1979) to the irrational beliefs outlined by Ellis (1962). Other content represented in vulnerability schemata may include the individual's general social perceptions (Dance & Kuiper, in press) as the appropriateness of discussing various topics in social interactions (Kuiper & McCabe, 1985), or the relative capabilities of one's own and others' social skills (Swallow & Kuiper, 1987; Swallow & Kuiper, in press).

VULNERABILITY AND EPISODIC COGNITIONS IN THE SELF-WORTH MODEL

If the content we have described reflects the type of material incorporated in vulnerability schemata, then it should be possible to demonstrate that vulnerable individuals display effects for these content domains that are similar to those experienced by currently depressed individuals. In other words, the negative impact of vulnerability schemata should be apparent in "at-risk" persons, even when they are in a nondepressed state. Conversely, the self-worth model predicts that episodic cognitions should not be evident in vulnerable individuals when nondepressed. As outlined in the remainder of this section, several of our studies have empirically tested various aspects of these predictions.

Social Topic Appropriateness

Kuiper and McCabe (1985) investigated the effects of cognitive vulnerability to depression on judgments concerning the appropriateness of discussing various topics in typical social interactions. In this study, subjects made both self- and other-referent ratings concerning a wide range of positive and negative self-disclosure topics, including personal views toward one's work, financial status, personality, and health, and personal attitudes, opinions, tastes, and interests.

As predicted, it was found that currently depressed subjects viewed the negative self-disclosure topics as more appropriate for discussion (by themselves and by others) in social interactions than did normal subjects. This pattern may have important implications for the maintenance of depressive episodes. To illustrate, an interaction involving a depressed and a normal individual might proceed in the following manner: First, the normal individual might make some tangential reference to an inappropriate topic. The depressed individual may interpret this verbalization as quite appropriate, however, and view this as justification for further discussion on this topic. In turn, the normal individual may interpret the depressive's increasing verbalizations on this topic as inappropriate. As a result, the normal individual may begin to emit negative behavioral and/or verbal responses to the depressive, thus producing further rejection and isolation (Coyne, 1976).

Turning to the vulnerable individuals who were currently nondepressed, Kuiper and McCabe (1985) found that these subjects displayed the same pattern of topic appropriateness ratings as depressed subjects. Thus, in line with a vulnerability-schema interpretation, vulnerable subjects rated several of the negative self-disclosure topics as more appropriate for discussion (by either themselves or others) than did normal subjects. This finding suggests that vulnerable (but currently nondepressed) individuals may interact socially with normal people in a fashion similar to that just described for depressed individuals. The vulnerable individual's different concept of topic appropriateness may result in the at-risk individual's participating in increasingly negative social interactions. In particular, the vulnerable individual's expression of inappropriate social topics may lead to greater rejection and avoidance by others, and thus may play an important role in enhancing the possibility of ensuing depressive symptoms.

Assertion Difficulties

Over the past several years, considerable research has established that currently depressed individuals exhibit many deficits in social skills and assertion abilities (Barbaree & Davis, 1984). Depressed persons either may fail to express an opinion or viewpoint about potential issues of conflict or may do so in an ineffective and whining manner (Weissman & Paykel, 1974). Furthermore, depressed individuals often report high levels of subjective discomfort when attempting to behave in an assertive manner (Youngren & Lewinsohn, 1980).

The past literature clearly indicates a relationship between current depression level and assertion difficulties, which has often lead researchers to suggest that such difficulties may contribute to the maintenance of depressive episodes. Much less is known, however, about the assertion skills of vulnerable individuals and about how these skills may relate to the onset of depressive symptoms. To investigate this issue, Olinger, Shaw, and Kuiper (1987) recently conducted a study in which subjects at varying levels of cognitive vulnerability and depression completed both the Assertion Inventory (Gambrill & Richey, 1975) and the Conflict Resolution Scale (McFall & Lillesand, 1971).

Of particular interest for this study was the large number of conceptual similarities that have been postulated to exist between the cognitive patterns displayed by individuals with dysfunctional attitudes and those displayed by individuals with assertion difficulties. Ludwig and Lazarus (1972) have postulated that nonassertive persons are characterized by (1) the desire to be liked by everyone, (2) perfectionism and self-criticism, (3) unrealistic expectations and excessive criticism of others, and (4) the labeling of assertive behavior as inappropriate. Rich and Schroeder (1976) have speculated that assertive behavior may be cognitively inhibited by the nonassertive individual's excessive desire for approval. Thus the cognitive similarities between dysfunctional attitudes and nonassertiveness may involve excessive approval seeking and perfectionism. Attitudinally vulnerable persons may consider assertive behavior to be inappropriate. In this respect, dysfunctional attitudes stress self-denial, in that the approval or happiness of others is more important than the individual's own approval or happiness (Kuiper & Olinger, 1986). Furthermore, differences in opinion are viewed as indicators of dislike. Overall, then, these dysfunctional attitudes would certainly appear to be in opposition to the assertive expression of one's thoughts, feelings, and rights.

Given these similarities, Olinger, Shaw, & Kuiper (1987) reasoned that the vulnerable individual's attempts to guide and evaluate social interactions via dysfunctional attitudes would hamper the development and/or use of necessary assertion skills. When the needs and desires of the attitudinally vulnerable person conflict with those of others, the vulnerable person may experience a threat to self-esteem. To cope with this threat or loss of approval from others, the vulnerable person may deny his or her own desires. Thus, when an attitudinally vulnerable person does behave assertively, he or she is likely to experience subjective discomfort. Furthermore, the failure to resolve interpersonal conflicts assertively is likely to interfere with the quality of ongoing interpersonal relationships. In particular, nonassertiveness may yield relationships characterized by tension and unresolved conflicts.

In general, the results obtained by Olinger, Shaw, & Kuiper (1987) support the hypothesized co-occurrence of nonassertiveness and attitudinal vulnerabilities for depression. Compared to normal controls, vulnerable subjects failed to use appropriate strategies for dealing with interpersonal conflicts and also experienced significantly greater subjective discomfort when behaving assertively. Of particular importance is the finding that vulnerable subjects who were currently nondepressed displayed the same assertion deficits that characterize depressed individuals (Weissman & Paykel, 1974; Youngren & Lewinsohn, 1980). These deficits may well reflect the effects of attempting to direct one's interpersonal relationships via self-denying and passivity-enhancing dysfunctional attitudes. As such, the assertion difficulties documented in both of the above studies may well contribute to both the etiology and the maintenance of depressive episodes. For vulnerable individuals, dysfunctional attitudes would serve as cognitive mediators that disrupt normal interpersonal relationships both prior to and during depressive episodes (see also Wilbert & Rupert, 1986, for a discussion of the relationships between dysfunctional attitudes, loneliness, and depression).

Self-consciousness and Social Interaction Perceptions

In a recent study, Kuiper, Olinger, and Swallow (in press) proposed that a further source of internal stress for vulnerable individuals may relate to self-presentational concerns. The vulnerable individual's strong need for approval by others, coupled with an increased fear of rejection, may foster an exaggerated concern with the adequacy of personal social performance. As such, these researchers postulated that vulnerable individuals would display heightened social anxiety and evaluative concerns, even when in a nondepressed state.

One means of assessing these social evaluation concerns is the Self-consciousness Questionnaire (Buss, 1980). This questionnaire contains three subscales: Public Self-consciousness, Social Anxiety, and Private Self-consciousness. "Public self-consciousness" refers to the degree to which an individual attends to the same aspects of behavior and appearance that might be observed by others. Representative items include "I usually worry about making a good impression" and "I'm concerned about my style of doing things." Stated differently, this scale provides a measure of the degree to which an individual views oneself as a social object.

Based on the self-worth model, it was predicted by Kuiper, Olinger, and Swallow (in press) that vulnerable individuals, even when nondepressed, would score significantly higher on the Public Self-consciousness subscale than individuals scoring low on the DAS. This pattern would reflect the vulnerable individual's overriding concern with evaluation and approval by others and suggests that this source of internally generated stress may serve as an additional vulnerability aspect for depression. Furthermore, a similar pattern was predicted for the Social Anxiety subscale of the Self-consciousness Questionnaire (i.e., "I have trouble when someone is watching me" or "It takes me time to overcome my shyness in new situations"). Again, because of their strong evaluative concerns, it was expected that vulnerable individuals at any level of depression would be significantly more socially anxious than individuals scoring low on the DAS.

Different predictions were made by Kuiper, Olinger, and Swallow (in press), however, for the degree of private self-consciousness exhibited by vulnerable individuals. The Private Self-consciousness subscale includes such items as "I reflect about myself a lot" and "I'm always trying to figure myself out." Buss (1980) suggested that individuals scoring high on this subscale are preoccupied with scrutinizing themselves, trying to figure themselves out, and examining their personal motives. This tendency to focus on inner thoughts and feelings has also been employed as a measure of self-focused attention. Not unexpectedly, depressed individuals exhibit increased self-focused attention relative to nondepressed controls (Ingram & Smith, 1984). The self-worth model predicts, however, that vulnerable individuals who are not currently depressed would *not* exhibit increased levels of private self-consciousness. This prediction stems from the proposal that vulnerable individuals who perceive that they are currently meeting their dysfunctional self-worth contingencies would have a generally positive view of self. In turn, this positive evaluation would minimize the need for a *pervasive* self-focus on inner attributes and motives. If, however, a vulnerable individual began to perceive difficulties in fulfilling dysfunctional self-worth contingencies, then the self-worth model would predict a concomitant increase in self-focused attention. Here, the vulnerable individual might begin to ruminate increasingly on personal inadequacies and presumed shortcomings (Kuiper & Olinger, 1986). This increase is undesirable because such self-focused attention generally serves to heighten negative affect, increase social interaction problems, and increase levels of self-criticism and self-blame (Brockner, 1979; Ingram & Smith, 1984). In summary, then, it was expected by Kuiper, Olinger, and Swallow (in press) that increased public self-consciousness and social anxiety would be vulnerability cognitions, whereas increased private self-consciousness (i.e., self-focused attention) would be a concomitant or episodic cognition.

Congruent with the self-worth model, the findings from the first study reported by Kuiper, Olinger, and Swallow (in press) indicated that even when nondepressed, subjects scoring high on the DAS displayed heightened levels of public self-consciousness and social anxiety. This pattern is consistent with the proposal that vulnerable individuals display strong social evaluative concerns, which are tied to their dysfunctional self-worth contingencies, even when nondepressed. Furthermore, this pattern is also consistent with the proposal that increased social anxiety and public self-consciousness may contribute to enhanced levels of internally generated stress for the vulnerable but currently nondepressed individual (Olinger, Kuiper, & Shaw, 1987).

In contrast to these predicted vulnerability cognitions, this first study also provided empirical evidence for the proposed concomitant variables. In particular, increases in private self-consciousness and negative self-schema content were not evident in vulnerable individuals when nondepressed. This pattern is consistent with the proposal that vulnerable individuals who are currently nondepressed perceive that they are meeting their dysfunctional self-worth contingencies. As such, these individuals display a primarily positive view of self, which then limits their need to engage in increased self-reflection. According to the self-worth model, it is only when these individuals perceive a failure in meeting self-worth contingencies that increases in self-focused attention and negative self-schema content become apparent.

A second study reported by Kuiper, Olinger and Swallow (in press) provided further evidence relating to vulnerability cognitions and the self-worth model. In this study, participants completed the BDI, the DAS, the Assertion Inventory (Gambrill & Richey, 1975), the Social Support Questionnaire (which provides measure of both perceived availability of and perceived satisfaction with social support; Sarason, Levine, Basham, & Sarason, 1983), and a modified self-report version of Lewinsohn's social skills rating form (Lewinsohn *et al.,* 1980; Youngren & Lewinsohn, 1980). As expected in this study, increasing levels of depression were associated with increased perceptions of assertion problems, poorer social skills, and diminished available social support and satisfaction. Also as predicted, high DAS scorers, regardless of their current level of depression, reported increased subjective discomfort and lower response probability for assertive responses compared to subjects scoring low on the DAS (replicating the pattern reported by Olinger, Shaw, & Kuiper, 1987). Vulnerability cognitions were also evident in terms of the social support and social skills measures. Here, vulnerable subjects who were currently nondepressed perceived less satisfaction in their social relationships and indicated a lower level of perceived social skills compared to subjects scoring low on the DAS. Interestingly, these vulnerable subjects did not indicate that they had fewer individuals in their social network than nonvulnerable subjects. Instead, vulnerable subjects, compared to subjects scoring low on the DAS, rated the equivalent number of relationships as less satisfying.

Further aspects of the data reported by Kuiper, Olinger, and Swallow (in press) were also congruent with the self-worth model. In particular, a factor analysis of the social skills rating form yielded two major factors. Factor 1 was labeled Perceived Social Skills, with obtained findings as reported previously. Factor 2 consisted of items relating to popularity and attractiveness, and was labeled Perceived Popularity. Consistent with past research, a regression analysis revealed that Perceived Popularity diminished as depression level increased. Of special interest, however, was the significant interaction between depression and vulnerability scores. Here, subjects scoring high on the DAS exhibited the greatest downward shift in Perceived Popularity as depression level increased. Thus, consistent with the self-worth model, subjects scoring high on the DAS but low on the BDI rated their Perceived Popularity as quite high (in fact, even higher than subjects scoring low on both the DAS and the BDI). This pattern again fits the notion that vulnerable individuals who are currently nondepressed perceive that they are meeting their self-worth contingencies and thus are popular (i.e., have the approval of others). As depression level increased, however, vulnerable subjects displayed a marked decrease in Perceived Popularity. This decrease is consistent with the proposal that self-worth contingencies relating to the approval of others are no longer perceived as being met. Finally, for individuals scoring low on the DAS, dysfunctional self-worth contingencies should be of limited concern. Accordingly, these subjects exhibited relatively little change in Perceived Popularity ratings across levels of depression.

Further support for these proposals has been obtained in a recent study by Swallow and Kuiper (1987). In this research, subjects rated their similarity to others on a 7-point rating scale, with a regression analysis again indicating a significant interaction between depression and vulnerability scores. As was the case with Perceived Popularity ratings, vulnerable subjects who were nondepressed provided the highest Perceived Similarity ratings. Vulnerable subjects also displayed the largest decrease in similarity ratings as depression level increased. In contrast, those with low levels of vulnerability actually showed a slight increase in Perceived Similarity as depression scores increased. Overall, then, this pattern of similarity ratings offers further empirical support for the self-worth contingency model of depression. In this model, it is proposed that unfulfilled self-worth contingencies lead to an increased focus on negative aspects of self, enhancing the further expression of depressive symptomatology. In line with this model, vulnerable subjects in the Swallow and Kuiper (1987) study perceived themselves as increasingly dissimilar to others as depression level increased.

CONCLUDING COMMENTS

This chapter has documented some of our social cognition research concerning the processing of personal and social information in depressed, vulnerable, and nondepressed individuals. One of the first steps in this examination was the elaboration of self-schema processing effects in currently depressed individuals. Across several of our studies, it appears that there is now sufficient empirical evidence to formulate a self-schema model of depression. This model considers both content and consolidation components of the self-schema and relates these characteristics to the degree of depression exhibited by the individual.

Our subsequent work has focused more generally on the possible role of cognitive schemata in the etiology and maintenance of depression. To help guide this research, we have developed a self-worth contingency model of depression. In addition to incorporating the self-schema components of content and consolidation, this model offers a potentially important distinction between vulnerability and episodic schemata. As one example, the findings reported thus far suggest that negative self-schema content may be a symptomatic aspect of depression, and thus part of an episodic schema. In contrast, dysfunctional attitudes, general social knowledge, and normative expectations may constitute the content of vulnerability schemata. As such, vulnerability schemata may play an important role in both the etiology and the maintenance of depressive episodes.

Finally, several limitations of our current research program should be clearly acknowledged. Much of our work has been correlational and/or self-report in nature and thus should be considered only the first step in documenting vulnerability cognitions in depression. Although this research does offer preliminary construct validity for the use of the DAS as a cognitive vulnerability measure, it should be noted that remitted depressives do not always score higher on the DAS than appropriate controls (Hamilton & Abramson, 1983; Silverman, Silverman, & Earley, 1984). Consequently, further research is clearly required. In particular, longitudinal research focusing on the nature of stressful events, depression, and the coping styles exhibited by individuals with varying levels of dysfunctional attitudes may be extremely important. Using the Ways of Coping Questionnaire, we are currently exploring these issues (Kuiper, Olinger, & Air, 1987). In sum, although our findings to date do provide some initial evidence for a self-worth contingency model of depression, additional research is certainly required.

REFERENCES

Altman, J. H., & Wittenborn, J. R. (1980). Depression-prone personality in women. *Journal of Abnormal Psychology, 89,* 303–308.

Barbaree, H. E., & Davis, R. B. (1984). Assertive behavior, self-expectations, and self-evaluations in mildly depressed university women. *Cognitive Therapy and Research, 8,* 153–172.

Beck, A. T. (1967). *Depression: Clinical, experimental, and theoretical aspects.* New York: Harper & Row.

Beck, A. T., Rush, A. J., Shaw, B. F., & Emery, G. (1979). *Cognitive therapy of depression.* New York: Guilford Press.

Billings, A. G., & Moos, R. H. (1983). Psychosocial theory and research on depression: An integrative framework and review. *Clinical Psychology Review, 2,* 213–237.

Brockner, J. (1979). Self-esteem, self-consciousness, and task performance: Replications, extensions, and possible explanations. *Journal of Personality and Social Psychology, 37,* 447–461.

Buss, A. H. (1980). *Self-consciousness and social anxiety.* San Francisco: W. H. Freeman.

Carver, C. S., & Ganellen, R. J. (1983). Depression and components of self-punitiveness: High standards, self-criticisms and overgeneralization. *Journal of Abnormal Psychology, 92,* 330–337.

Costello, C. G. (1976). *Anxiety and depression: The adaptive emotions.* Montreal: McGill-Queens University Press.

Coyne, J. C. (1976). Depression and the response of others. *Journal of Abnormal Psychology, 85,* 186–193.

Dance, K. A., & Kuiper, N. A. (1987). *Self-schema content and consolidation: The impact of depression level and cognitive vulnerability to depression.* Manuscript submitted for publication.

Dance, K. A., & Kuiper, N. A. (in press). Self-schemata, social roles, and a self-worth contingency model of depression. *Motivation and Emotion.*

Derry, P. A., & Kuiper, N. A. (1981). Schematic processing and self-reference in clinical depression. *Journal of Abnormal Psychology, 90,* 286–297.

Dobson, K. S., & Shaw, B. F. (1986). Cognitive assessment with major depressive disorders. *Cognitive Therapy and Research, 10,* 13–30.

Ellis, A. (1962). *Reason and emotion in psychotherapy.* New York: Lyle Stuart.

Gambrill, E. D., & Richey, C. A. (1975). An assertion inventory for use in assessment and research. *Behavior Therapy, 6,* 550–561.

Gotlib, I. H., & Robinson, L. A. (1982). Responses to depressed individuals: Discrepancies between self-report and observer-rated behavior. *Journal of Abnormal Psychology, 91,* 231–240.

Hamilton, E. W., & Abramson, L. Y. (1983). Cognitive patterns and major depressive disorder: A longitudinal study in a hospital setting. *Journal of Abnormal Psychology, 92,* 173–184.

Hammen, C., Marks, T., de Mayo, R., & Mayol, A. (1985). Self-schemas and risks for depression: A prospective study. *Journal of Personality and Social Psychology, 49,* 1147–1159.

Hammen, C., Miklowitz, D. J., & Dyck, D. G. (1986). Stability and severity parameters of depressive self-schema responding. *Journal of Social and Clinical Psychology, 4,* 23–45.

Hoberman, H. M., & Lewinsohn, P. M. (1985). The behavioral treatment of depression. In E. E. Beckham & W. R. Lebe (Eds.), *Handbook of depression: Treatment, assessment, and research* (pp. 39–81). Chicago: Dorsey Press.

Ingram, R. E., & Smith, T. W. (1984). Depression and internal versus external focus of attention. *Cognitive Therapy and Research, 8,* 139–152.

Kuiper, N. A. (1981). Convergent evidence for the self as a prototype: The "inverted-U RT effect" for self and other judgments. *Personality and Social Psychology Bulletin, 7,* 438–443.

Kuiper, N. A., & Cole, J. (1983). Knowledge about depression: Effects of depression and vulnerability levels on self and other perceptions. *Canadian Journal of Behavioral Science, 15,* 142–149.

Kuiper, N. A., & Derry, P. A. (1982). Depressed and nondepressed content self-reference in mild depressives. *Journal of Personality, 50,* 67–79.

Kuiper, N. A., & Higgins, E. T. (1985). Social cognition and depression: A general integrative perspective. *Social Cognition, 3,* 1–15.

Kuiper, N. A., & MacDonald, M. R. (1982). Self and other perception in mild depressives. *Social Cognition, 1,* 223–239.

Kuiper, N. A., & MacDonald, M. R. (1983). Schematic processing in depression: The self-based consensus bias. *Cognitive Therapy and Research, 7,* 469–484.

Kuiper, N. A., & McCabe, S. B. (1985). The appropriateness of social topics: Effects of depression and cognitive vulnerability on self and other judgments. *Cognitive Therapy and Research, 9,* 371–379.

Kuiper, N. A., & Olinger, L. J. (1986). Dysfunctional attitudes and a self-worth contingency model of depression. In P. C. Kendall (Ed.), *Advances in cognitive–behavioral research and therapy* (Vol. 5, pp. 115–142). New York: Academic Press.

Kuiper, N. A., & Olinger, L. J. (in press). Stress and cognitive vulnerability to depression: A self-worth contingency model. In R. W. J. Neufeld (Ed.), *Advances in the investigation of psychologial stress.* New York: Wiley.

Kuiper, N. A., Olinger, L. J., & Air, P. A. (1987). *Stressful events, dysfunctional attitudes, coping styles, and depression.* Manuscript submitted for publication.

Kuiper, N. A., Olinger, L. J., MacDonald, M. R., & Shaw, B. F. (1985). Self-schema processing of depressed and nondepressed content: The effects of vulnerability to depression. *Social Cognition, 3,* 77–93.

Kuiper, N. A., Olinger, L. J., & Swallow, S. R. (in press). Dysfunctional attitudes, mild depression, views of self, self-consciousness, and social perceptions. *Motivation and Emotion.*

Laxer, R. M. (1964). Self-concept changes of depressive patients in general hospital treatment. *Journal of Consulting Psychology, 28,* 214–219.

Lewinsohn, P. M., Mischel, W., Chaplin, W., & Barton, R. (1980). Social competence and depression: The role of illusory self-perceptions. *Journal of Abnormal Psychology, 90,* 213–219.

Ludwig, L. D., & Lazarus, A. A. (1972). A cognitive and behavioral approach to the treatment of social inhibition. *Psychotherapy: Theory, Research, and Practice, 9,* 204–206.

Lunghi, M. E. (1977). The stability of mood and social perception measures in a sample of depressive in-patients. *British Journal of Psychiatry, 130,* 598–604.

MacDonald, M. R., & Kuiper, N. A. (1984). Self-schema decision consistency in clinical depressives. *Journal of Social and Clinical Psychology, 2,* 264–272.

MacDonald, M. R., & Kuiper, N. A. (1985). Efficiency and automaticity of self-schema processing in clinical depressives. *Motivation and Emotion, 9,* 171–184.

MacDonald, M. R., Kuiper, N. A., & Olinger, L. J. (1985). Vulnerability to depression, mild depression, and degree of self-schema consolidation. *Motivation and Emotion, 9,* 369–379.

McFall, R. M., & Lillesand, D. B. (1971). Behavior rehearsal with modeling and coaching in assertion training. *Journal of Abnormal Psychology, 77,* 313–323.

McGranie, E. W., & Bass, J. D. (1984). Childhood family antecedents of dependency and self-criticism: Implications for depression. *Journal of Abnormal Psychology, 93*, 3–8.

Minkoff, K., Bergman, E., Beck, A. T., & Beck, R. (1973). Hopelessness, depression, and attempted suicide. *American Journal of Psychiatry, 130*, 455–459.

Mitchell, J. E., & Madigan, R. J. (1984). The effects of induced elation and depression on interpersonal problem solving. *Cognitive Therapy and Research, 8*, 277–285.

Nisbett, R. E., & Ross, L. D. (1980). *Human inferences: Strategies and shortcomings of informal judgment.* Englewood Cliffs, NJ: Prentice-Hall.

Olinger, L. J., Kuiper, N. A., & Shaw, B. F. (1987). Dysfunctional attitudes and stressful life events: An interactive model of depression. *Cognitive Therapy and Research, 11*, 25–40.

Olinger, L. J., Shaw, B. F., & Kuiper, N. A. (1987). Nonassertiveness, dysfunctional attitudes, and mild levels of depression. *Canadian Journal of Behavioral Science, 19*, 40–49.

Oliver, J. M., & Baumgart, E. P. (1985). The Dysfunctional Attitude Scale: Psychometric properties and relation to depression in an unselected adult population. *Cognitive Therapy and Research, 9*, 161–167.

Peterson, C., & Seligman, M. E. P. (1985). The learned helplessness model of depression: Current status of theory and research. In E. E. Beckham & W. R. Leber (Eds.), *Handbook of depression: Treatment, assessment, and research* (pp. 914–939). Chicago: Dorsey Press.

Rholes, W., Riskind, J. H., & Neville, B. (1985). The relationship of cognitions and hopelessness to depression and anxiety. *Social Cognition, 3*, 36–50.

Rich, A. R., & Schroeder, H. E. (1976). Research issues in assertiveness training. *Psychological Bulletin, 83*, 1081–1096.

Ruehlman, L. S., West, S. G., & Pasahow, R. J. (1985). Depression and evaluative schemata. *Journal of Personality, 53*, 46–92.

Sacco, W. P., & Beck, A. T. (1985). Cognitive therapy of depression. In E. E. Beckham & W. R. Leber (Eds.), *Handbook of depression: Treatment, assessment, and research* (pp. 3–38). Chicago: The Dorsey Press.

Sarason, I. G., Levine, H. M., Basham, R. B., & Sarason, B. R. (1983). Assessing social support: The Social Support Questionnaire. *Journal of Personality and Social Psychology, 44*, 127–139.

Secunda, S. K., Katz, M., Friedman, R., & Schuyler, D. (1973). *Special report: The depressive disorders* (National Institute of Mental Health) Washington, DC: U.S. Government Printing Office.

Shaw, B. F., Vallis, T. M., & McCabe, S. B. The assessment of the severity and symptom patterns in depression. In E. E. Beckham & W. R. Leber (Eds.), *Handbook of depression: Treatment, assessment, and research* (pp. 372–407). Chicago: Dorsey Press.

Silverman, J. S., Silverman, J. A., & Earley, D. A. (1984). Do maladaptive cognitions cause depression? *Archives of General Psychiatry, 41*, 28–30.

Swallow, S. R., & Kuiper, N. A. (1987). The effects of depression and cognitive vulnerability to depression on judgments of similarity between self and other. *Motivation and Emotion, 11*, 157–167.

Swallow, S. R., & Kuiper, N. A. (in press). Social comparison and negative self-evaluations: An application to depression. *Clinical Psychology Review.*

Weissman, M., & Paykel, E. S. (1974). *The depressed women: A study of social relationships.* Chicago: University of Chicago Press.

Wilbert, J. R., & Rupert, P. A. (1986). Dysfunctional attitudes, loneliness, and depression in college students. *Cognitive Therapy and Research, 10*, 71–78.

Wilkinson, I. M., & Blackburn, I. M. (1981). Cognitive style in depressed and recovered patients. *British Journal of Clinical Psychology, 20*, 283–292.

Wing, J. K., & Bebbington, P. (1985). Epidemiology of depression. In E. E. Beckham & W. R. Leber (Eds.), *Handbook of depression: Treatment, assessment, and research* (pp. 765–794). Chicago: Dorsey Press.

Youngren, M. A., & Lewinsohn, P. M. (1980). The functional relation between depression and problematic interpersonal behavior. *Journal of Abnormal Psychology, 89*, 333–341.

11

Interactional and Cognitive Strategies for Affect Regulation: Developmental Perspective on Childhood Depression

PAMELA M. COLE
University of Houston
NADINE J. KASLOW
Yale University

Quite early in the unfolding of our personal dramas, we encounter distress and discomfort. Such encounters are frequent in early experience and may serve the developing abilities in differentiating, categorizing, remembering, and understanding a complex world (Izard, 1977; Lewis & Michalson, 1983; Sroufe, 1979). Although the precise manner in which early affective experiences are intertwined with cognitive and social development is yet a puzzle, one fact is clear: Human beings encounter negative feeling states from the outset and throughout the life span.

For some individuals, these encounters with negative feeling states can take the form of enduring, persistent, and intense affective experiences, or clinical depression. We typically associate such a condition with adulthood, but what of the experiences of discomfort, distress, unhappiness, frustration, shame, doubt, or despair that are encountered prior to adulthood? Can these states develop into enduring, persistent, intense conditions in children? Can a child experience hopelessness, depression?

Previous attempts to answer these questions have been controversial. The central conceptual issue underlying the controversy is whether children of a given age are capable of experiencing or generating depression. For example, traditional psychoanalytic thinkers maintained that the young child could not be depressed until the superego was sufficiently developed to induce guilt and aggression turned against the self (e.g., Rie, 1966). In contrast, Spitz (1945, 1946) argued that the loss of the emotional relationship between a mother and an infant was sufficient to produce depression in infants.

More recent discussions have argued that (1) childhood depression is basically identical to adult depression, with some symptom variation (for reviews, see Anthony, 1975; Bemporad, 1978a, 1978b; Kashani, Husain, Shekim, Hodges, Cytryn, & McKnew, 1981; Kovacs & Beck, 1977); (2) depression is "masked" by behavioral symptomatology in children (Bakwin, 1972; Cytryn & McKnew, 1972; Malmquist, 1977); or (3) depression is not a clinical condition in children because of its transient, frequent, and spontaneously remitting nature (Lefkowitz & Burton, 1978).

Many of these authors have invoked the importance of considering developmental features in forming an adequate conceptualization of childhood depression, but efforts to articulate specific models have not emerged. In this chapter, we discuss the development of interactional and cognitive strategies involved in the regulation of affect, and developmental differences in the nature of childhood depression. We chose the perspective of affect regulation because we view depression, at any age, as a failure in the regulation of negative affect. Therefore, if we understand the usual ontogeny of affect regulation processes, we can more readily realize the sources of such failures and the manifestation of these failures at different ages.

If one adopts the perspective of cognitive models of depression (Abramson, Seligman, & Teasdale, 1978; Beck, 1967; Rehm, 1977; Seligman, 1975), the question of childhood depression might be stated thus: At what point are children cognitively capable of the negative expectancies, internal attributions, and causal reasoning that have been identified as core components of depression? From this perspective, one would conclude that Spitz's "depressed" infants were not clinically depressed, because no infant is capable of internal attributions and causal inferences. However, if we take the cognitive models of depression as investigating *one* source of the depressive disorder, that is, ideation that maintains and/or intensifies negative affect, and if we realize that one's social system is another source of affect regulation—or misregulation—then we can discuss both interpersonal and intrapersonal sources of affect regulation developmentally and clinically and can provide a more integrated, conceptual framework for depression.

In this chapter, we first discuss the major contemporary cognitive models of adult depression, to demonstrate their emphasis upon affect regulation. We then survey representative research in developmental psychology that describes the role of the parent–child interaction in affect regulation and the acquisition of cognitive, self-regulating strategies in the expanding repertoire of affect regulation strategies. In this way, we highlight the significance of both interactional and cognitive strategies in adaptive affective functioning and the importance of parenting in the development of self-regulatory abilities. With this perspective in mind, we review the research on childhood depression, identifying the symptomatic features—interactional and individual—in children of different ages in terms of dysfunctions in parent–child interactions and in children's thinking.

We use the term "affect regulation" to indicate our belief that a person's affective state fluctuates over time in interaction with various elements of human experience. We wish to emphasize that human beings are able to make adjustments and modifications in their affective states; one measure of mental health is a person's ability to make such adjustments that are appropriate to the situation and adaptive for the individual. The well-adjusted adult can shift affectively as situations require, can access a range of emotions, and has strategies for modulating the experimental and expressive intensity of emotion. A successful actor needs to tap a variety of emotional intensities despite the artificiality of a stage; a successful business executive needs to dissimulate surprise, anger, or disappointment in the subtle negotiations of the trade. In our everyday routines, we experience a stream of emotional peaks and valleys, and for most of us, these stay within a normative, adaptive range.

We also believe that there are multiple factors that influence affective state and flow. Contemporary research continues to puzzle with the complex interrelationships of affect and various other components of human functioning. For our purposes here, we regard biologic, cognitive, and social influences as operative in affect regulation. We hope to promote a conceptual shift away from the question of a child's cognitive capacity for depressive thinking to the question of a child's intrapersonal *and* interpersonal resources for affect regulation at various points in development.

Prior to the development of self-regulating cognitive strategies for coping with affective experience, the child is emotionally dependent upon others to generate strategies for promoting positive affect, for diminishing negative affect, and, probably, for teaching affect regulation skills. A downward extension of an adult intrapersonal (whether psychoanalytic or cognitive) model of depression runs the danger of failing to consider the alternative sources individuals have for coping with negative affect, particularly the sources upon which children depend.

THE ADULT COGNITIVE MODELS

Expectancies, self-attributions, causal explanations, and self-awareness are all central mechanisms in the major cognitive theories of depression. Depressed adults are described as persistently sad or dysphoric individuals who expect that they should meet high standards, and yet who expect to fail to meet these standards; who evaluate themselves negatively; and who attribute their failures to global, stable, and negative aspects of themselves, thereby maintaining and prolonging their sad moods.

Learned Helplessness and Hopeless Attributions

According to Seligman's (1975) model of learned helplessness, the depressed individual characteristically expects that important outcomes in life and his or her own behavior are independent; a persistence in this expectational belief leads to the cognitive, motivational, and emotional symptoms that constitute the depressive syndrome. In their attributional reformulation of the original model, Abramson *et al.* (1978) argued that making an internal, stable, and global attribution for a negative event, and attaching importance to the event, increases the likelihood of the expectation of hopelessness and helplessness and, in turn, leads to the symptoms of depression. Research evidence has supported this hypothesis in that internal, stable, and global failure attributions and external, unstable, and specific success attributions are associated with depressive thinking (see Metalsky & Abramson, 1980, for a review).

Abramson *et al.* (1978) particularly emphasized "personal helplessness" as the key mechanism of depression, in which the outcomes of events are perceived as noncontingent upon one's instrumental behavior, and this is due to perceived deficits in oneself in comparison to others. These self-conscious inferences lead to a failure to experience personal control, which leads to lowered self-esteem, hopelessness, apathy, and dejection. In this sense, one's own cognitions can lead one to the doorstep of depression. Seligman (1975) felt that when an unexpected event occurs, an individual experiences a heightened state of arousal, which he termed "fear." This state persists until the individual discerns whether or not the negative event can be controlled. If one feels a sense of controllability, fear diminishes; if the negative event is viewed as beyond one's control, fear subsides, to be replaced by sadness and depression. It is interesting to note that depressives accurately estimate how much control they have over both controllable and uncontrollable events in both success and failure experiences (Alloy & Abramson, 1979, 1982). Nondepressives evidence more cognitive distortion, or an "illusion of control." Thus the affective experience is regulated by one's perceptions and explanations of the event, with inaccuracies perhaps having some adaptability.

However, affect and cognition have a complex relationship. Uncontrollable positive events, though they influence activity level, do not lead to an affective disturbance (Beach, Abramson, & Levine, 1981); only those uncontrollable negative events that are imbued with "current concern" lead to depression (Klinger, 1975). Therefore affect contributes to the selection of events to be explained, and the manner of explanation (attribution) serves to modulate the intensity and content of the affective experience. Perceived failures in important situations that are attributed to self-deficits produce greater negative affect (Weiner, 1974); thus one's interpretations serve to regulate affect.

Self-control Deficits

Rehm's (1977) self-control model of depression describes a three-stage feedback loop, involving self-monitoring, self-evaluation, and self-reinforcement. Depressed individuals are hypothesized to have deficits in one or more of these areas. In elaborating on this self-control model of depression, Rehm & O'Hara (1980) held that negative expectancies, more so than depressed attributional styles, are critical to depression; depressed attributions are merely extensions of a generalized negative expectancy about events in life. More important, negative expectancies lead to negative self-evaluation, high rates of self-punishment, low rates of self-reinforcement, and selective self-monitoring (attention to negative events), which constitute a characteristic style of self-control in the depressed individual. Research evidence supporting these self-control patterns in depressed adults is reviewed by Rehm in this volume (Chapter 5).

According to the self-control perspective, these self-conscious, self-critical thoughts lead to pessimism, poor self-image, and decreased behavior, from which the individual infers and experiences sadness. The depressed person's self-control patterns promote rather than diminish negative affective experience. Kanfer and

Hagerman (1981) have stated that increased self-consciousness is a critical phase in the development and maintenance of a depressive style of self-control behavior. Again, the cognitive processes of reflecting upon oneself and reasoning about events in relation to oneself influence how one feels.

Cognitive Distortions

Beck (1967, 1976) regarded depressed persons as those who developed negative views of themselves, the world, and the future, all of which can be discussed as negative expectancies. All experience is filtered through these biased expectancies, leading to distortions in perception and reasoning: arbitrary inference, selective abstraction, overgeneralization, magnification, minimization, and personalization (Beck, 1976). Although he does not specifically discuss attributions, Beck's emphasis on reasoning and inference errors is consistent with the previous two models in that the interpretation of why certain events have occurred is stylized in depressed persons.

Beck (1976) maintained that a negative bias toward oneself is central to depression; the depressed person "regards himself as lacking some element or attribute that he considers essential for happiness" (p. 105), and "his conviction of his presumed defects becomes so imperative that it infiltrates his every thought about himself" (p. 112). Again, preoccupied thinking about the self and certain explanations and inferences serve depression. Kovacs and Beck (1979) elaborated on the interplay between cognition and affect in depression. They claim that depressed persons' conceptualizations of situations are determined to a greater extent than are those of nondepressed persons by internal processes ("invoked schema"[1]) that distort the stimulus situation. The distorted conceptualization leads to excessive or inappropriate negative affect, which, in turn, is incorporated into the negative, internalized conceptualization. This cycle intensifies affect and leads to dysphoria as well as the other symptoms of depression. Therefore depressed individuals construe their worlds in such a way as to engender and maintain negative affect.

Summary

Although Abramson and colleagues, Beck, Rehm, and Seligman do not discuss affect regulation expressly as the primary factor in depression, we view their theories as landmarks in clarifying how cognition can serve affective experience in a debilitating, pathological manner. However, in focusing on adult depression, researchers have emphasized self-conscious causal thinking, cognitive activity that does not fully develop until middle childhood. Other sources of affect regulation, such as the behavior of significant others, are important to all persons, but may be critically important to the young child. In the following section, we review developmental research on affect regulation and on the emergence of self-awareness and the cognitive abilities, such as expectant and attributional thought, associated with the self-regulation of affective experience.

DEVELOPMENTAL ASPECTS OF AFFECT REGULATION

The term "affect regulation" denotes cognitive and behavioral processes by which the content and intensity of affect can be modified. Frustration may be reduced by a vigorous game of tennis, disappointment lessened by an optimistic thought. Sadness may be forgotten by going to a movie with a happy ending, by thinking about pleasant future plans, or by being hugged by a loved one. The possible and appropriate strategies for the regulation of affective experiences vary over the course of childhood, with the infant having the more limited repertoire and more dependency on others, and the maturing child developing a broader, more flexible repertoire and a greater degree of emotional independence.

Infancy and Toddlerhood (0–24 Months)

In its earliest form, the regulation of a child's affect is most clearly a mutual endeavor. The infant appears to have some innate tension-regulating capability and may use sucking behavior to self-soothe, or gaze aversion to reduce negative stimulation (Greenspan & Porges, 1984). Usually, the parent is equipped with a broader, more flexible repertoire of skills and assumes responsibility for alleviating infant distress. The success of parental attempts to regulate the child's affective state is somewhat dependent upon the infant, as in the case of the seemingly inconsolable colicky infant, and differences in infant temperament may contribute to the interactional quality of affect regulation (cf. Thomas, Chess, & Birch, 1965).

Parent and infant might be described as having an interdependent affective relationship. Infant displays of negative affect, for example, elicit emotional arousal in a parent, which requires the parent to regulate both his or her own affective state and the infant's (Frodi, Lamb, Leavitt, & Carson, 1978; Frodi, Lamb, Leavitt, Donovan, & Sherry, 1978). Likewise, the parent's emotional states influence the infant's state. Mothers who act depressed, passive, or rejecting elicit protest and wariness as well as behavioral disorganization in their infants (Cohn & Tronick, 1983; Main & Stadtman, 1981). Clearly, the ebb and flow of affective experiences is a complex interactional process for parent and infant.

Many have stated that infants develop an expectancy for a responsive, reactive quality of the environment and that this expectancy or "trust" is the cornerstone of social–emotional development and mental health (e.g., Erikson, 1963; Mahler, Pine, & Bergman, 1975). Research evidence on infant cognition supports the idea that infants are capable of expectant thinking; activities such as purposeful object manipulation, search for hidden objects, and playing peekaboo, all of which emerge in the first year, involve anticipatory or expectational thinking. Moreover, a relationship appears to exist between such expectancies and affect. The schema for events may be organized according to differential affective responses, or the match of schema and event may elicit an affective response. For example, Kagan (1971, 1975) argued that there is a relationship between affect and the degree of discrepancy between a stimulus and a schema. Recognition of familiar events is accompanied by positive affect in infants, whereas highly discrepant events elicit distress.

If the high degree of responsiveness and reactivity of the environment (e.g., the mother) comes to be expected by the infant, the acquisition of mobility must surely occasion many disconfirmations of this immediate responsivity assumption. As the infant comes to crawl and toddle, there is a reduction in the mother's proximity to, and direct physical regulation of, the child's activity; evidence suggests, however, that the mother's presence continues to be an important factor in the child's initiation and maintenance of autonomous activity (Ainsworth, Blehar, Waters, & Wall, 1978). Older infants display distress when they cannot locate their mothers, whereas they appear more comfortable, more happy, and more exploratory in their play when she is present, even though they may not interact with her during this time (Carr, Dobbs, & Carr, 1975; Kaplan, 1978). The physical presence of the mother may serve as a sufficient stimulus for the toddler to use his or her own cognitive processes (memory) to recall positive expectancies. Thus, in the first year, interactional processes are essential to the child's use of his or her own knowledge for maintaining affective balance.

Although this joint affective regulation characterizes infancy, children do acquire self-initiated strategies for regulating affect in their first 2 years. The earliest of these strategies can be described as passive: gaze aversion, social withdrawal, reduced activity, and vigilance (Field, 1981a, 1981b). These self-initiated strategies are, however, limited, and continued negative affect leads to behavioral disorganization (Greenspan & Porges, 1984).

At around 12 months, instrumental acts begin to influence the content and intensity of affect, as suggested by Gunnar's (1978, 1980) studies in which manipulation of a fear-inducing toy began to decrease distress in this age period. It is noteworthy that first "strategic" behaviors, if persistent, would be depressed behaviors; by the end of the first year, instrumental acts supplement such passive strategies. These early instrumental acts may form the roots of the relationship between one's own sense of agency and affect regulation.

During the second year, the disruption of the continuity between parent and infant relations is often described and experienced as the "terrible twos." Children's emotional reactions are often extreme (e.g., temper tantrums, uncontrolled laughing) and are less easily influenced by their parents. At the same time at which this emotional autonomy emerges, a clear awareness of self as a separate entity can be detected (Kagan, 1981; Lewis & Michalson, 1983). Most 2-year-olds recognize visual representations of themselves (e.g., in mirrors, pictures, videotapes) and have self-referential speech, most notably, self-referential pronoun usage (e.g., words like "me," "my," "I"). This latter ability is particularly noteworthy, because self-referential pronouns involve shifting reference: When child and parent say "Baby," each is referring to the child, but when child and parent say "I," each is referring to different persons. Thus the acquisition of a physically located, verbally identified sense of self entails some cognitive sophistication.

Sroufe (1979) stated that the toddler is gaining control over emotional experience largely because of developing memory and language abilities. He provides descriptive examples:

When, for example, the 18-month-old is told by mother, "I'll be right back; you play with dolly," and the infant looks at the door, fighting back the tears, then turns to the doll and repeats "Momma go, play dolly," and plays with occasional long looks at the door, it seems apparent that language and play are helping the child modulate or control emotional experience. . . . A final example illustrates the elaboration of the child's methods for control as well as the impact of emotion on the organization of complex behavior. The child, having been left alone, was mildly upset but not at all disorganized. He picked up the teddy bear and patted it; then, still holding the bear, picked up mother's purse and put it over his shoulder. He then waved "bye bye" to the mother's chair and walked out the door! (Sroufe, 1979, pp. 490–491)

Thus the first 2 years of affect regulation can be briefly summarized by a primary dependence upon the parent–child relationship and by an emergence of behavioral and cognitive strategies for the self-regulation of affective experience. These initial strategies appear to develop within the context of a strong, predictable emotional relationship between parent and child. In fact, the early mother–child attachment relationship has been associated with the quality of affective self-regulation and social competence in preschoolers (Arend, Gove, & Sroufe, 1979; Lieberman, 1977; Matas, Arend, & Sroufe, 1978; Vaughn, Egeland, Sroufe, & Waters, 1979).

Preschool Years (2–5 Years)

If the first 2 years can be characterized by the child's transition from emotional dependence to emerging emotional separateness, the preschool years might be characterized by further development in self-initiated affective regulation. The rage and resistance of the "terrible twos" subside as the preschooler gains increased control over emotional displays. Recent research suggests that preschoolers utilize some behavioral and cognitive strategies in affective situations, although the efficacy of these strategies is limited.

Children at this age have clear expectancies for mirthful and distressing situations, and actively seek the former while avoiding the latter (Sroufe, 1979). In experiments designed to induce sadness, preschoolers have been observed to spontaneously engage in distracting activities or generate statements that make a negative event seem positive (McCoy & Masters, 1985). A tendency for preschoolers to deny the experience of sadness has also been noted (Glasberg & Aboud, 1981, 1982). Preschoolers appear able to regulate the display of negative emotion in order to conform to social display rules (Cole, 1986). The effect of preschoolers' strategies for managing affect on their subsequent acts has not been studied, but in general, their strategies for behavior self-control are not as effective as those provided by adults for them (Patterson & Mischel, 1976).

Although there is some evidence that preschoolers generate strategies for managing their affective experience and that they become increasingly more socialized in their affective displays, evidence also exists that preschoolers will depend upon an adult if they can. One ethologist (and many a mother) has observed increases in the intensity of negative affective displays in preschoolers when an adult is present (e.g., Blurton-Jones, 1972). Maccoby (1980) provides an apt example:

> Parents during this period frequently become aware of willful elements in children's intense crying, and they recognize that children are capable of turning their tears on and off. When she noticed a cut on her four-year-old son's hand, one mother said, "Why, honey, you've hurt yourself! I didn't hear you crying." Said the boy, "I didn't know you were home!" (p. 178)

Thus young children are predominantly reliant upon adults for the management of negative affective experiences while they are acquiring a progression of behavioral and cognitive strategies. The degree to which a preschooler can self-regulate affect in a negative situation is probably a function of various situational dimensions (e.g., familiarity of the situation, intensity of the affect). They have, probably, some expectancy that adults are reliable sources of assistance when they are experiencing distress and discomfort, and in the protected context of those relationships, they can practice their own attempts at handling moderately negative affect and so develop the expectancy that they can cope with distress.

However, preschoolers differ from adults and older children in some important respects that bear on the discussion of affect regulation and depression. Preschoolers are only on the threshold of self-conscious thinking and the causal logic of explaining events and their own roles in them. Basically, they appear not to have developed either the cognitive schema by which one can abstract oneself from immediate experience and witness multiple aspects of a situation, or the symbolic ability to call on a stored representation of an event and reflect on the thoughts and actions of the situation.

This is not to say that preschoolers do not try to explain events. With a sufficient stimulus, preschoolers attempt to explain the causes of outcomes, although their explanations may appear less "logical" by adult standards.

Recent efforts have been focused on children's developing knowledge about emotions, and it appears that preschool-age children do have knowledge of emotion and can verbalize this knowledge (see Bretherton, Fritz, Zahn-Waxler, & Ridgeway, 1986, for a review). Preschoolers appear to understand the basic emotions, their situational antecedents, and behavioral consequences, and to infer emotionality on the basis of emotional expression. Complicated or atypical emotional situations (e.g., conflicting emotional cues) may confuse them; they nonetheless attempt to resolve such situations, and these attempts can lead them to incorrect conclusions.

Social cognition research has suggested that preschoolers also engage in attributional thinking but that it differs from that of adults. They are more likely to attribute greater motivation to individuals who are externally induced to perform (Karniol & Ross, 1976), greater effort to more able persons (Nicholls, 1978), and they tend not to differentiate luck from skill (Nicholls & Miller, 1984). Thus the differentiation of internal and external factors implied in adult thinking seems blurred in preschoolers' explanatory schema.

Less differentiated reasoning and differences in inferential reasoning may also lead preschoolers to incorrect conclusions about causality. For example, they tend to employ imperfect covariation (*x* sometimes occurs with *y*) or temporal contiguity (*x* and *y* occur simultaneously) in their judgments of causality (Sedlak & Kurtz, 1981). In addition, Piaget (1926) described preschoolers' thinking as pre-operational, to indicate their lack of mastery over flexible cognitive operations. He described their reasoning as both syncretic (disparate elements are incorporated into a confused whole) and egocentric (single perspectives or elements vs. coordinated multiple elements are used to draw conclusions).

Although the generalizability of laboratory studies of cognition may be limited, these studies suggest that preschoolers' interpretations and memories of novel, complicated emotional events may be subject to patterns of understanding and reasoning different from those of adults. These young children are, however, trying to understand and reason about such events; it is possible that such efforts may lead them to conclusions that contribute to persistent feelings of sadness.

Harter (1980) argued that the egocentric thinking of preschoolers may restrict their ability to "decenter" from one emotional perspective and to experience a second—and particularly, different—emotion at the same time. Therefore, once sad, the preschooler may feel "all bad" or "all sad" and be unable to generate or consider the possibility of feeling good or happy at the same time. Preschoolers also tend not to verbalize strategies for managing emotion when asked.

In sum, preschoolers appear to have some behavioral and cognitive strategies for coping with affective experiences and to engage in emotional behavior that implies some self-regulatory ability. The efficacy of their strategies is probably limited. Differences in the manner with which they discriminate or interpret self–other perspectives, regard intrinsic factors such as motivations and dispositions, select factors to understand a complicated situation, and conceptualize emotional experiences can possibly lead preschoolers to "illogical" beliefs (cf. Beck, 1976). So, for example, the self-attributions of blame, badness, worthlessness, and responsibility reported by children of divorce (Hetherington, Cox, & Cox, 1978; Wallerstein & Kelly, 1980) appear to be logical consequences of such reasoning. Preschoolers do continue to rely on adults and can have the experience that negative situations cannot be handled alone. They can feel overwhelmed by negative emotions that tax their emerging affect regulation skills and can draw conclusions that may foster confusion, sadness, and even hopelessness in the immediate situation. On the other hand, the lack of self-reflective skills that permit reflection about one's own thoughts and feelings may make preschoolers less vulnerable to persistent cognitive patterns that reinforce helplessness and hopelessness.

Middle Childhood (6–12 Years)

By the time children enter elementary school, they are expected to have sufficient self-control to sit quietly in class, to attend to relevant stimuli, and to engage in groups without requiring individual adult attention. In addition, they are expected to have developed sufficient control of their emotions such that intense or prolonged displays of negative emotion (in most circumstances) are inappropriate. The social expectations of middle childhood include taking more responsibility for one's behavior than had been true in the preschool years, and included among those behaviors are emotional reactions.

Research evidence has shown that children in these years demonstrate spontaneous emotional control over their facial expressions in social contexts (Cole, 1986; Saarni, 1984) and have verbal awareness of their efforts to manage their emotions (Cole, 1985; Harris, Olthof, & Terwogt, 1981; Saarni, 1979; Selman, 1981). Although school-age children may not be sophisticated in their strategies to self-regulate emotion, the important step they have acquired during middle childhood is the ability to reflect upon their internal experience and to engage in self-monitoring, self-evaluation, and self-reinforcement (Barling, 1980; Flavell & Wellman, 1977). Whereas preschoolers may display pride in a physical accomplishment (a picture, a race), school-age children may experience pride in not having let a bully see their fear, and they may mask the felt pride as well. With increasing self-awareness and the ability to reflect on one's own thoughts and feelings, self-regulation of emotional behavior is enhanced (Cole, 1985).

These self-reflective skills emerge with changes in the conceptual sense of self (Selman, 1981). Middle childhood is marked by increased use of dispositional, internal descriptors of self, the clear realization of the constancy of oneself and the immutability of one's identity, and the ability to self-evaluate on the basis of identity as well as actions. Self-evaluations that may at first be global—"I got in trouble with the teacher and I'm just no good"—become more complicated and differentiated during this period—"I may be terrible at soccer, but I'm good at math." Increased and more differentiated awareness of one's internal life is also reflected in the attributional thoughts of school-age children (Shantz, 1975). They can invoke internal factors to explain events, reason that outer appearances may differ from inner experiences, and internally reason with themselves (Selman, 1981). Their attributions have more influence upon their subsequent behavior and expectations (Dweck & Reppucci, 1973; Rholes, Blackwell, Jordan, & Walters, 1980) and upon their beliefs about themselves (Parsons & Ruble, 1977).

These situational expectancies and attributions lead to beliefs about the future and the self that probably become organized into such stylized patterns as those tapped by constructs such as locus of control, learned helplessness/self-efficacy, and self-esteem. The many changes in such attributional processes during middle childhood are beyond the scope of this chapter (but see Frieze, 1981, and Kassin, 1981). For our discussion here, it is worth noting that these patterns of increasing consistency in children's understanding of events and future outcomes are associated with the development of self-reflection; knowledge of past events is more easily integrated with present situations, and the child experiences more choice and control over behavior.

In relation to emotional experiences, school-age children are able to recognize that a felt emotion may persist and may continue to affect a person (Harris, 1983). They understand that mood affects behavior (as do preschoolers) but they are better able to talk about the reasons for this relationship and about strategies for changing mood in order to prevent negative effects on behavior (Cole, 1985, 1986; Harris *et al.,* 1981).

In general, there appears to be a developmental relationship between the child's affect and the degree of internality in the attributions they make regarding negative outcomes (Weiner & Graham, 1984). For example, there is a developmental increase in the tendency to link the feeling of guilt to attributions which involve controllable causes of negative outcomes (Graham, Doubleday, & Guarino, 1984). We suggest that patterns of interpreting and resolving emotional situations become stylized and that children develop affective styles of coping and self-regulating during middle childhood.

Children who persist in the face of failure (mastery children) attribute their failures to their own lack of effort—an internal, unstable, and specific attribution (Dweck & Reppucci, 1973)—and do not make causal attributions for their failures (Diener & Dweck, 1978). Children whose performance deteriorates after failure (helpless children) attribute these outcomes to their own lack of ability—an internal, stable, and global attribution (Diener & Dweck, 1978; Dweck & Reppucci, 1973). This latter pattern is associated with depression. Mastery children engage in ways to change the failure situation and to prevent deteriorated performance, whereas helpless children deteriorate, demonstrate negative affect, and expect to do poorly in the future. Therefore children's stylized self-conscious thinking affects how they do, how they feel about how they do, and how they will perform in the future.

In terms of self-evaluation, Coopersmith (1967) hypothesized that self-esteem reflects the extent to which one's performance is perceived as being congruent with one's aspirations. Thus the school-age child's ability to reflect upon self and to compare self with others and to parental standards provides a basis for self-standards and evaluation (cf. Ruble, Boggiano, Feldman, & Loebl, 1980). Coopersmith felt that high- and low-self-esteem children differed markedly in these personal aspirations, with the former group setting high standards determined by their expectancies of success (vs. hope) and the latter group being more pessimistic, less motivated, and less hopeful.

These studies of individual stylized patterns of thinking, behaving, and feeling in school-age children all implicate the child's shift to a self-regulated style of functioning. During middle childhood, developing skills in self-reflectivity, reasoning, and behavioral management are associated with increasing emotional autonomy and active involvement in the management of one's affective experience. Hence middle childhood marks a clear transition from dependence upon interpersonal sources of affect regulation to more intrapersonal regulation.

Lest we have portrayed school-age children as amazingly independent and rational, it is worth noting how these children differ from adolescents. During the transition into adulthood, youths develop new cognitive skills that permit greater abstractness and flexibility of thought. Ideas can be entertained that cannot be physically represented, and much knowledge of self and the world is called into question. We observe heightened self-consciousness and abstract reasoning about one's existence and its meaning. The adolescent engages in many of the same aspects of self-thought and behavioral control as adults, although experience has not usually made them aware of the conclusions about existence that derive from an accumulation of experience as an adult. The rapid changes of adolescence appear to be associated with increases in emotionality, but we have not been at a loss to understand depression among adolescents. Rather, it is the younger child who has confused us. We note that it is during middle childhood that we can detect the patterns of affective self-regulation that have traditionally discriminated depressed and nondepressed persons—negative beliefs about oneself, guilt, inferences about motivation and aspirations, and self-worth.

Now that we have briefly reviewed the course of development in terms of affect regulation, we turn to a consideration of childhood depression and how various sources of affect regulation, both cognitive and interpersonal, can fail in such a way as to engender depression. In the course of our discussion, we consider research on depressed children and on the parent–child interaction of "depressed" families.

THE DEPRESSED CHILD

Research on depressed children is strikingly scarce. This dearth is due to traditional beliefs that children are incapable of depression, to the confusion about developmental differences in the nature of depressive reactions, and to the view that depression in children is a transient phenomenon. Although good epidemiological data are minimal, the data that exist suggest that currently, the prevalence of major and minor depressive disorder is 1.8% and 2.5%, respectively (Kashani *et al.*, 1983). Survey research of nonclinical populations has suggested that 20%–33% of children between the ages of 5 and 15 years evidence depressive symptoms (Albert & Beck, 1975; Rutter, Graham, Chadwick, & Yule, 1976) and that 33%–50% of children seen in mental health facilities are deemed to be significantly depressed (Brumback, Dietz-Schmidt, & Weinberg, 1977; Carlson & Cantwell, 1980; Cass & Thomas, 1979; Hudgens, 1974). However, the actual use of a depression diagnosis is extremely rare in children under age 14 (1%–2%). The discrepancy between research findings on children's symptoms and the clinical use of depression as a diagnosis may be due in part to the adult status of the depression diagnosis and in part to the fact that evidencing some depressive symptoms is not a sufficient basis for diagnosing one as having clinical depression as a syndrome. Several clinicians have commented on the strong likelihood that depression in children is underdiagnosed (Carlson & Cantwell, 1980; Costello, 1980; Malmquist, 1977; Philips, 1979). Although some authors have argued that depression in children is a transient developmental phenomenon that dissipates with time, data from a prospective, longitudinal study reveal that while the depressive episodes of most children naturally remit, they tend to be of longer duration than was previously thought, and they tend to recur (Kovacs, Feinberg, Crouse-Novak, Paulauskas, & Finkelstein, 1984). The four components of the clinically depressed syndrome are (1) mood disturbance; (2) a pattern of negativistic thinking, including self-depreciation and suicidal ideation; (3) loss of interest and diminished activity; and

(4) disturbances in basic functions such as eating and sleeping. In the remainder of this section, we discuss the symptomatological picture of childhood depression in developmental terms.

Infancy and Toddlerhood (0–24 Months)

Depressive behavior has been reported in infants separated from their parents and residing in emotionally deprived settings (e.g., Spitz, 1945, 1946). These infants were seen as unhappy, apathetic, and showing no pleasure or curiosity in their environments, characteristics that are markedly different from those of the typical infant. These children also had difficulties in sleeping and eating, sometimes to the degree of failing to thrive. Because of the absence of the cognitive and language skills to self-reflect and self-report thoughts associated with depression, many authors prefer not to label this infant condition as depression (e.g., Anthony, 1975; Kovacs & Beck, 1977).

Although self-reflective thought is absent in infancy, our review of developmental research indicates that infants are nonetheless aware of their environments, although they may not distinguish themselves from their environments in the sense of self–other differentiation; furthermore, infants are clearly capable of forming expectations. Their awareness and expectations entail sensorimotor schema (i.e., cognitive processes bound by the actual tangible stimulation of events and their own movements). Although a discussion of the phenomenology of the infant is speculative, we must consider the possibilities that (1) the infant develops an expectation of some routine or regularity in event sequences and associates sequences with smells, sounds, sights, and physical contacts of interactions with the mother and familiar surroundings, and (2) the infant develops expectancies about the tactile or kinesthetic sensations of comfort and nurturance that follow sensations of discomfort or distress.

Piaget (1954) provided detailed observations of his own children, depicting the speed with which very young infants anticipate sequences such as feeding; in days, their behavior becomes more purposeful, more accurate, and more efficient as they seek, rather than react reflexively to, the nipple. At some level, the loss of this expected sensorimotor sequence must be experienced by the infant, and vague, undifferentiated feelings of distress might accompany this experience.

Infants who experience the loss of an "attached" relationship (i.e. a relationship in which attachment, or an emotional bond to a distinct person, has been formed) appear to react with expressions of anger and disruption of the organized behavior patterns they had acquired; this pattern then subsides, and the infants withdraw from social contact, appearing apathetic, disinterested, listless, and unhappy (Bowlby, 1969; Engel & Reichsman, 1956; Spitz, 1945, 1946). These observations have been criticized because the confounded effects of loss of parent and presence in an institutionalized, presumably less optimal, environment obfuscate clear cause for the infants' depressive reaction. Sander (1975) studied two groups of young infants who had had 10 days' experience with their mothers; half were separated from their mothers and placed in the care of a highly qualified but new caretaker. When the separated infants were compared with the nonseparated infants, it was found that the former cried more often and longer from the first day of separation. Cohn and Tronick (1983) described distress and disorganization of learned behavior patterns in 3-month-olds whose mothers were coached to be unresponsive to them. These studies suggest that very young children are aware of and reactive to losses of expected events.

In the framework of a developmental perspective, we believe that infant cognition, which is not as naive or minimal as was once believed, provides the infant with sufficient capability to quickly differentiate types of experiences, particularly along affective dimensions (cf. Sroufe, 1979), and to develop sensorimotor expectations for regularities in their routines. They react instrumentally to disruptions in these expected routines with purposeful social behavior, such as reaching out and crying, but when their responses fail, both expectancies and instrumental behaviors can be extinguished, leading to a decrease in activity and to apathy. If the environment fails to restore an order and to regulate experience, the child cannot generate his or her own care and pleasure; affect can flatten, curiosity can wane, and eating, sleeping, and eliminating can be disturbed. We view this as depression. The infant lacks the cognitive ability to reflect upon the circumstances and upon his or her helpless role, but chronic environmental (social) failures violate established expectancies and leave the infant helpless, not in a mentally represented sense, but certainly in a concrete behavioral sense. We expect that learning that your reaching, crying, and kicking have no impact on the environment leads to a debilitating behavioral disturbance involving losses of expected environmental sequences, or affective relief, and of acquired behavioral patterns, or depression.

Because our culture generally provides immediate care in some minimally acceptable form for infants whose mothers can no longer respond to them, most opportunities to observe and study infant depression are precluded. However, in less severe, less blatant situations in which mothers are functioning but are not able to manage their own affective experience and are emotionally unresponsive to their infants, infants may experience depression in less severe forms than we have just described. Such infants would be distinguished from nondepressed infants by their showing significantly more disinterest in people and objects, less exploration and positive affect, more irritability, and more sleeping and eating problems. These children would most likely be seen by pediatricians, if help is sought at all, rather than by mental health professionals. Clearly, our discussion is speculative, but it is based on a body of literature suggesting that infant depression is a possibility, that it can be understood as an interactional process, and that it can be systematically studied.

Preschool Years (2–5 Years)

There are scattered reports of depression in preschool-age children (Bakwin, 1972; Davidson, 1968), and the research suggests either that major depressive disorder is rare among preschoolers or that DSM-III (APA, 1980) criteria are not appropriate for diagnosing depression among preschoolers (Kashani & Ray, 1983; Kashani,

Ray, & Carlson, 1984). Depression during these years appears to be manifested by mood disturbance (increased irritability, excessive crying, hyperactivity or hypoactivity, loss of interest) and vegetative disturbance (insomnia, loss of appetite; Kashani, Carlson, Horwitz, & Reid, 1985; Ossofsky, 1974). Because most preschoolers cannot abstract and reflect upon inner experience, and do not verbalize statements about inner experience, self-reports of self-depreciation, hopelessness, and sadness are rare. Consequently, children displaying mood and vegetative disturbances may be seen by pediatricians who may judge the condition as transient. Depressed preschoolers may not be referred to mental health specialists, and thus clinical reports of depression in these youngsters are rare, and the incidence of depression is unknown.

Although preschoolers, like infants, are not capable of self-reflective thinking, our review established that preschoolers have definite, concrete senses of self and clear expectations that are less bound to the sensorimotor stimulation of the moment. A negatively toned experience can be an object of thought; preschoolers often persist in questioning a parent about the prolonged absence of the other parent, who may have left because of divorce or who may have died. They express worry and persist in asking when that person will return, although the parent may constantly explain that the lost parent will not return.

Developmental research indicates that preschoolers have concrete awareness of their own agency; in the case of the lost parent, the preschooler can see that his or her thoughts, expressions, and actions are not successful at regaining that parent. They may well try to explain their circumstances to themselves, but their cognitive schemata for reasoning about the causes of these circumstances may lead them to make incorrect conclusions. An egocentric, syncretic attributional schema might lead a child to conclusions that his or her own behavior effected the departure of the parent, and the negative feelings related to the loss could easily become associated with self.

A less dramatic situation than parental loss can be used to illustrate the preschooler's thinking. A 4-year-old girl does not fall asleep as quickly as usual one evening and becomes interested in the light and sounds outside the bedroom door. She has some sense that she should not go outside, and some expectation that her parents will scold her, but being pretty new at using expectations to inhibit an activity as compelling as getting to the light and sounds, she warily proceeds through the bedroom door. As she reaches the living room, she hears her parents yelling loudly and angrily (having a fight, which they delayed until the child was put to bed). In this novel, confusing, and upsetting situation, can the 4-year-old distinguish her own negative feeling related to the violation of a rule (getting out of bed) from her affective reactions to hearing her parents' yelling and their open angry feelings? Again, we speculate, but it seems conceivable, based on what is known about preschoolers' thinking, that the child may become confused, may feel responsible for these negative events, and may feel unable to attenuate her feelings. Being unable to decenter, or remove her own perspective of wrongness from her parents' independent problem, she may need her parents to help her sort through this affectively upsetting set of events.

Blatant failures in adults' management of children's affective experiences are usually accompanied by general failures in child care and are frequently remediated by families, friends, or agencies. Less obvious deficiencies, such as parental depression, however, may contribute to the development of dysfunctions or deficits in young children's affect regulation skills. Chronic feelings of badness and inefficacy (Johnny tries to make Mommy smile by showing her his painting, and Mommy turns away, cries, and still doesn't fix him lunch) may lead to reduced efforts, perceived failures, negative expectations, and feelings of discomfort and distress. Difficulties in sleeping, eating, and toileting may develop. The child is unable to rectify these situations alone, and depression can develop. Again, the basic dysfunction in the affect regulation is in an external, interactional source and not in self-reflective, depression-perpetuating thought.

Preschoolers cannot use accurate logic or defensive rationalizations to reason themselves out of distressing states. Research evidence suggests that their best effort is denial (Glasberg & Aboud, 1981, 1982). This may further contribute to the perception of transience in the depressed behavior of preschoolers (cf. Lefkowitz & Burton, 1978), as negative states are pushed from thought. Although this may preclude certain children from manifesting a full-blown depressed syndrome, we should consider the possibility that the memory of these events could be stored in a vague, unsophisticated manner, which may serve as a seed for later depression. Events in later life may stimulate access to a past memory that is vague and affectively toned but not sufficiently articulated to be understood and recategorized. Evidence for affect serving as an organizer of memory has been provided in both cognitive and developmental research (e.g., Bower, 1981; Sroufe, 1979); older, more vague, tacit expectations may interact with more current affective experiences.

Again, our culture generally spares children from chronic failure in their parenting, and thus children may be less susceptible to depression in their preschool years. Additionally, they may have some self-regulating capability for distancing themselves from feelings of sadness or depression. On the other hand, we should investigate the possibilities that certain environmental failures, such as parental depression, can lead to preschoolers' depression and that negative experiences in these years that are not adequately managed by the child or by adults may serve as seeds for later depression. The depressed preschooler might manifest disinterest in school activities and peers, dependent behavior upon adults, attention-getting behavior problems, eating and sleeping problems, and, occasionally, sad affect and negative self-expectations. Again, a pediatrician is more likely to be contacted, because listlessness and vegetative problems are seen as physical problems. The child's tendencies to distract himself or herself from sadness-inducing events may minimize open displays of persistent sadness (tearfulness); greater irritability and apathy might better differentiate the depressed and nondepressed preschooler.

Middle Childhood (6–12 Years)

When we discuss depression in children 6 years and older, we can move from speculation based on our reading of developmental psychology and clinical reports to research with depressed children. Between the ages of 6 and 8 years, depression is typified by prolonged sadness, separation anxiety, physical complaints, and disturbances in sleep, appetite, and elimination (Arajarvi & Huttunen, 1972; Brumback *et al.*, 1977; Geller, Chestnut, Miller, Price, & Yates, 1985; Leon, Kendall, & Garber, 1980; Ling, Oftedal, & Weinberg, 1970). Children at this age are less likely than children older than 8 years to verbalize feelings of self-deprecation or hopelessness. These children may, however, engage in attention-getting behavior. Several authors have discussed behavior problems as age-specific depressive symptoms in children who manifest all of the major components of depression except self-reported attitudes of depression (Bemporad, 1978a; Kovacs & Beck, 1977; Poznanski, 1979). This is not to say that depression is "masked," but that the "self-report,"instead of being an inner experience of sadness or hopelessness, is a behavioral effort to gain adult attention.

Depressed children, aged 8 and older, are said to manifest "self-esteem or guilt" depressions, characterized by low self-esteem, self-deprecatory ideas, and feelings of badness (McConville, Boag, & Purohit, 1973; Nissen, 1971); to exhibit psychosomatic symptoms and decreased energy, interest, and motivation (Nissen, 1971); and to have school problems (Ossofsky, 1974). Self-reports of dysphoria, helplessness, hopelessness, and low self-esteem have also been documented in these children (McConville *et al.*, 1973; Nissen, 1971; Schwartz, Friedman, Lindsay, & Narrol, 1982). Depressive symptoms of middle childhood have been found to be stable over time (3–6 months) as measured by self-report, peer report, and teacher report (Seligman *et al.*, 1984; Tessiny & Lefkowitz, 1982).

The assessment of depressive cognitive patterns requires self-awareness of internal states and verbal expressive ability to report these thoughts. Research on depressed children aged 6 and upward has been possible. For the most part, the cognitive patterns observed in these children are similar to those observed in depressed adults. Children who endorse more depressive symptoms on the Children's Depression Inventory (Kovacs & Beck, 1977) perform more poorly on a block design task and an anagram task (Kaslow, Tanenbaum, Abramson, Peterson, & Seligman, 1983) and on the Matching Familiar Figures Test (Schwartz *et al.*, 1982). These findings suggest that, consistent with the learned helplessness theory, depressed children show deficits in instrumental responding. A recent study (Weisz, Weiss, Wasserman, & Rintouli, 1987) directly addressed the question "Does childhood depression involve a perceived lack of control?" Results from this study suggest that depression in children is associated with perceived incompetence and "contingency uncertainty," but not perceived noncontingency. The authors argue from this finding that children may be more susceptible to "personal helplessness" than to "universal helplessness."

As would be predicted on the basis of Beck's cognitive model of depression, depressed children have lower self-esteem (Butler, Miezitis, Friedman, & Cole, 1980; Kaslow, Rehm, & Siegel, 1984; Kazdin, French, Unis, & Esveldt-Dawson, 1983; Kazdin, French, Unis, Esveldt-Dawson, & Sherick, 1983; Moyal, 1977; Saylor, Finch, Baskin, Furey, & Kelly, 1984; Schwartz *et al.*, 1982; Tesiny & Lefkowitz, 1982) and feel more hopeless (Kazdin, French, Unis, & Esveldt-Dawson, 1983; Kazdin, French, Unis, Esveldt-Dawson, & Sherick, 1983; Kazdin,

Rodgers, & Colbus, 1986) than do their nondepressed counterparts. Using the Cognitive Bias Questionnaire for Children, Haley and co-workers (Haley, Fine, Marriage, Moretti, & Freeman, 1985) found that depressed–distorted cognitions do correlate significantly with psychiatric and self-reported ratings of depression in children. Further, this cognitive bias was found to discriminate children with affective disorders from those with nonaffective disorders. In a study examining the self-schema processing in relatively depressed and nondepressed children, Hammen and Zupan (1984) found that, as predicted, nondepressed children had a tendency to recall positive self-descriptive traits but not negative self-descriptive traits. However, the predicted opposite results for depressed children were not obtained.

To examine the applicability of the reformulated model of learned helplessness, a number of studies have been conducted that examine attributions in children. Most of these studies use the KASTAN Children's Attributional Style Questionnaire (Seligman *et al.*, 1984) to assess the attributions children make for both positive and negative events. Similar to depressed adults, mildly depressed children make more internal, stable, and global attributions for failure and more external, unstable, and specific attributions for success (Blumberg & Izard, 1985; Kaslow *et al.*, 1984, Leon *et al.*, 1980; Saylor *et al.*, 1984; Seligman *et al.*, 1984). A related finding is that higher levels of depression are associated with an external locus of control (Lefkowitz, Tesiny, & Gordon, 1980; Mullins, Siegel, & Hodges, 1985; Tesiny & Lefkowitz, 1982). Attributional patterns in these children were found to be stable across a 3-month period (Seligman *et al.*, 1984). In addition, helplessness-inducing attributional patterns have been identified in a nonclinic population of school-age children (Diener & Dweck, 1978; Dweck & Repucci, 1973).

In support of Rehm's (1977) self-control model of depression, depressive self-control styles, such as higher rates of negative expectancies, negative self-evaluations, stringent standards, and beliefs in punishment as a more effective way to control children, have been noted in mildly depressed children (Kaslow *et al.*, 1984).

Intellectual task performance has been examined in depressed elementary school children. Depressed children perform significantly worse than normal children on the Block Design subtest of the Wechsler Intelligence Scale for Children-Revised (WISC-R) but score no differently on the Vocabulary subtest (Blumberg & Izard, 1985; Kaslow *et al.*, 1984; Seligman *et al.*, 1984). Similarly, Tesiny, Lefkowitz, and Gordon (1980) found that peer-related depression is negatively correlated with IQ scores in depressed children. Remission of major depression is associated with significant improvement in WISC-R Verbal IQ and Performance IQ (Staton, Wilson, & Brumback, 1981). School functioning is also impaired in depressed children (Puig-Antich *et al.*, 1985a); however, following remission from a depressive episode, school functioning is normalized (Puig-Antich *et al.*, 1985b).

The affective characteristics of depressed children are similar to those seen in depressed adults. Depressed children report experiencing a pattern of emotions including sadness, anger, self-directed hostility, and shame (Blumberg & Izard, 1985). However, both clinical impressions and empirical data suggest developmental variations in the affective picture of depressed children, (Izard & Schwartz, 1986). For example, older children who are classified as depressed report feeling more sadness than do younger children who are depressed (Kaslow & Wamboldt, 1986). Kazdin and colleagues (Kazdin, Esveldt-Dawson, Sherick, & Colbus, 1985; Kazdin, Sherick, Esveldt-Dawson, & Rancurello, 1985) reported that based on direct observation, depressed inpatients exhibited sad affect (e.g., tearfulness) and less affect-related expression (e.g., smiling, frowning) than did their nondepressed peers. It is interesting to note that the major disagreement in rating a child's symptoms is the difference between the clinician's rating of dysphoria, based on the child's nonverbal behavior, and the child's and parents' verbal report of no dysphoria (Poznanski, Mokros, Grossman, & Freeman, 1985). The nonverbal rating of dysphoria correlated the most significantly with a diagnosis of depression and was the best predictor of severity of depression.

A few studies have examined the interpersonal functioning of depressed children. Unpopular children are more depressed than popular children (Jacobsen, Lahey, & Strauss, 1983; Lefkowitz & Tesiny, 1980, 1985; Vosk, Forehand, Parker, & Rickard, 1982) and are seen by teachers as less socially skilled (Lefkowitz & Tesiny, 1980). Children rate their depressed peers as less likeable and attractive, as involved in less positive behaviors, and as needing therapy more than their nondepressed peers (Peterson, Mullins, & Ridley-Johnson, 1985). Depressive reactions in children are often difficult for teachers to handle because they enjoy working with these children less, feel more frustrated when working with these children, and keep a greater distance from them (Morris, 1980). Sacco and Graves (1984) reported that depressed children rated themselves lower on items assessing self-satisfaction with interpersonal problem-solving performance and showed deficits in interpersonal problem solving. However, other researchers have not replicated this finding (Mullins *et al.*, 1985). On the basis of semistructured interview data, Puig-Antich and co-workers (1985a) reported that during a major depressive episode, prepubertal children have deficits in social functioning with their peers, their parents, and their siblings, and that deficits in children's intrafamilial and extrafamilial relationships remain somewhat impaired after sustained recovery from an affective episode (Puig-Antich *et al.*, 1985b). In an observation study, Kazdin, Moser, Colbus, and Bell (1985) found that depressed children engage in significantly less social activity than do their nondepressed peers.

A relationship exists between depression and adverse environmental circumstances (e.g., Lefkowitz *et al.*, 1980), and consistent with this, depressed children report increased levels of stress, based on their ratings of significant life events (Mullins *et al.*, 1985). Children tend to rate more positively their depressed peers who are encountering a significant amount of external stress than they rate those peers with low life stress (Peterson *et al.*, 1985).

In general, several authors now believe that school-age children, particularly those over age 8, can manifest the affective, cognitive, motivational, and vegetative symptoms of a major depressive episode (Bemporad, 1978a; Kashani *et al.*, 1981; Kovacs & Beck, 1977). Furthermore, there is increasing support for using the DSM-III (APA, 1980) criteria for affective disorder in adults when diagnosing children (Cytryn, McKnew, & Bunney, 1980), even though these criteria overlook the unique developmental characteristics of children (Garber, 1981).

In sum, research on depressed children provides clear evidence that children under age 14 and as young as 8 manifest depression in ways that are comparable to those of adults. As we have reiterated frequently, children of these ages are generally capable of the self-reflectivity and inferential reasoning associated with adult depressed cognitive patterns, although there are still developmental differences in the quality of these patterns. These school-age children can generate the negatively toned self-oriented and event-oriented statements in addition to exhibiting the affective, behavioral, and vegetative symptoms of the depressed clinical syndrome. The 6- to 8-year-old will reveal such statements less often than the 12- to 14-year-old. Moreover, the content of these depressive thoughts in 6- to 8-year-olds can include verbalizations, ("I can't do nothing right" or "I'm all bad"), or communication through drawings or play, of negative outcomes. The older the child, the greater the tendency toward more verbalization of depressive thinking with the use of constructs such as self-worth and meaningfulness.

For children younger than 7 or 8 years, these cognitive processes are less developed or undeveloped, and thus depressive thinking patterns can neither be reported nor assessed. However, patterns of prolonged negative mood, decreases in activity level, apathy, and such basic functioning disturbances as sleeplessness, loss of appetite, enuresis, and encopresis have been observed even in very young children. These children are not capable of self-perpetuating patterns of depressive thought, but they are susceptible to chronic interactional failures; they are cognitively equipped to be aware of and to expect regularities in relationships, and they are reactive to disruptions in these regularities. Therefore we must also discuss interactional patterns that could be depression inducing. Though not capable of thought-perpetuated sad affect, young children are dependent upon the environment for maintaining a positive—or a negative—state of affairs.

Interactional Patterns and Depression

As discussed in our developmental section, early experience with affect regulation occurs in the context of the parent–child interaction. Throughout the life span, the social systems of individuals are integrally involved in their affect regulations Coyne, 1976). This involvement of the social system is most salient for the youngest child, and it appears that the relative degree of dependence upon social sources is what evolves developmentally (Cole, 1985).

In infancy, the mother generally provides a high degree of responsiveness to the infant's emotional signals of distress and discomfort. Sroufe and his colleagues maintain that the quality of this early mother–infant attachment is predictive of *later* (preschool) self-regulation of affect and coping (Sroufe, 1983). Thus an emotionally impoverished mother–infant relationship (e.g., one involving physical care but inconsistent or unresponsive socioemotional relations) may place the infant at risk for the later development of self-regulatory skills. On the other hand, ongoing or current parent–child interactional patterns may be equally, if not more, important to the child's functioning. If the mother is unresponsive to her infant despite the infant's use of its repertoire of signals (i.e., crying, disorganization), activity reduction and apathy may follow and may lead to severe infant pathology (Cohn & Tronick, 1983; Greenspan & Porges, 1984).

A likely candidate for such unresponsive mothering is the depressed mother. In fact, depressed mothers of infants express feelings of being helpless, overwhelmed, and ill-equipped to handle their infants' demands and their own standards for mothering (Weissman, Paykel, & Klerman, 1972). In general, parents who have difficulty managing their own affect have difficulty being adequate caretakers (Brunquell, Crichton, & Egeland, 1981). In identifying depressed infants, then, we expect to witness difficulties in the caretaker–infant interaction, specifically, a lack of maternal responsiveness to the infant's emotional signals. Furthermore, lacking the cognitive ability to symbolically maintain negative expectations of the environment, the infant must experience persistent unresponsiveness in its interactions with its primary caregiver in order to develop a depressive pattern.

Although physical loss of a parent creates risk for the pattern of social regulation of infant affect and for the infant's functioning (cf. Spitz's [1945] observations of depressed, institutionalized infants), emotional dyssynchrony can occur in the intact mother–infant relationship. Depressed women provide one example of maternal unresponsiveness in an intact mother–child relationship. Although modifications in the level of responsiveness of caretaker to infant should be particularly helpful to infants who are largely dependent on others for affect regulation, chronic unresponsiveness may place the infant at risk for utilizing new relationships. As discussed previously, the preschool years appear to mark a crucial period in the child's developing self-regulatory ability. Parental practices in rearing preschool-age children have been associated with the quality of preschoolers' affective functioning. For example, parents who employ inductive methods for disciplining their preschoolers (i.e., explaining situations, teaching children about causes and consequences of situations) and who model self-control and enforce rules consistently appear to foster self-regulation of affect and behavior (Baumrind, 1971; Block, 1971; Patterson, 1982) as well as positive self-esteem in middle childhood (Coopersmith, 1967). Reliance on punishment or withdrawal of love as contingencies for misbehavior, inconsistency in delivering consequences for misbehavior, and expectancies that children can be responsible for a parent's emotional needs are less effective in promoting self-control.

Hoffman (1970) provided a molecular analysis of the affective and cognitive aspects of the transmission of self-regulating behavior and moral reasoning. He reported that parents who focused on children's angry affect in a conflict situation rather than accepting the child's anger and focusing on the causes of the conflict situation were more likely to have children whose moral reasoning was conventional and rigid; the lack of flexibility, the harshness, and the "shoulds" in these children's reasoning are comparable to the depressed person's strict, rigid, critical self-judgments. Parents who draw attention to the causes of the problem rather than criticizing the child's angry expressions tended to have children with more flexible and humanistic levels of moral reasoning.

Parental responses that structure situations in a way in which the child can understand them appear to promote positive self-regulated behavior in preschool and school-age children. Moreover, a combination of parental acceptance and tolerance of a child's feelings and the provision of rules and expectations that are comprehensible to the child may better prepare a child to develop self-generated strategies for regulating behavior. Parents who have difficulty in tolerating negative affect and in having the energy to provide such reasoning about events fail to provide models and rules for young children. Again, the depressed parent may fit the latter description. Weissman & Paykel (1974) examined the parenting practices of depressed women and found four areas of dysfunction: insufficient emotional involvement, communication problems, lack of affection, and increased hostility. Depressed mothers of young children have been observed to be irritable, withdrawn, emotionally uninvolved with their children, and inconsistent in their parenting; their children manifested mild, overt depressive symptoms (Radke-Yarrow, Cummings, Kuczynski & Chapman, 1985; Weissman *et al.*, 1972).

In retrospective studies of depressed adults, a general pattern emerges in which parents are remembered as intrusive, rejecting, controlling, inadequate caretakers (Crook, Raskin, & Elliott, 1981; Lamont, Fischoff, & Gottlieb, 1976; Parker, 1979). Although several alternative explanations are possible (see Parker, 1979), our own belief is that parenting practices significantly affect the emotional competency of children and that parents' inadequacies in regulating their own affect and in helping a child to manage his or her feelings are transmitted to their children.

Indeed, there is suggestive evidence that children of parents with an affective disorder are at higher risk for depression than children in the general population (Anthony, 1975; Beardslee, Bemporad, Keller, & Klerman, 1983; Conners, Himmelhoch, Goyette, Ulrich, & Neil, 1979; McKnew, Cytryn, Efron, Gershon, & Bunney, 1979; Morrison, 1983; Orvaschel, Weissman, & Kidd, 1980; Weissman *et al.*, 1980; Welner, Welner, McCrary, & Leonard, 1977). Studies of depressed children and their parents indicate a higher incidence of depression in these parents when contrasted to parents of nondepressed children (see Orvaschel *et al.*, 1980, for a review).

Additionally, there are some recent findings regarding the characteristics of the families of depressed children. Marital discord is commonly reported in these families (Bemporad & Won Lee, 1984; Poznanski & Zrull, 1970). Many of the depressed childrens' parents are described as hostile and as alternately rejecting and overinvolved (Bemporad & Won Lee, 1984; Poznanski & Zrull, 1970). Serious family discord and child maltreatment have also been reported in some of these families (Kazdin, Moser, Colbus, & Bell, 1985; Puig-Antich, Blau, Marx, Greenhill, & Chambers, 1978). Finally, there appears to be a "poorness of fit," or discrepancy, between the demands and expectations of the environment and the child's capacities, motivation, and behavioral style (Chess & Thomas, 1984).

Although loss of a parent has been the traditional focus in discussions of causes or risk factors for depression (e.g., Beck, 1967; Bowlby, 1969; Spitz, 1945, 1946)—and, indeed, there is a high incidence of depression (31%) in children entering residential schools subsequent to a parent's death, a divorce, or a separation (Handford, Mattison, Humphrey, & McLaughlin, 1986)—our attention has been drawn to the interactional flow between the physically present but emotionally dysfunctional parent and her child. What are the implications of the finding that the more depressed the parents are, the more negatively they view their children, regardless of their children's actual behavior (Rogers & Forehand, 1983)? How might a parent fail to provide a context in which the child can develop self-regulatory skills that are adaptive rather than depressive? Might the overindulgent, overprotective mother fail to allow the child opportunities to experience and cope with negative affect? Might certain mothers who have difficulty tolerating negative affect interfere with their children's skill development? Might mothers who are emotionally unregulated create feelings of fear, hopelessness, and sadness in their children, and might these feelings, managed as best as can be by the child of a certain age, lead to depression at the time—or later? We suspect that the self-regulated mother is able to read and respond to her infant's emotional demands, to adjust her expectations and demands for the child in age-appropriate increments, to facilitate self-regulation in the child by using age-appropriate parenting strategies, and to know and accept that we all need others' help at one time or another in coping with our disappointments, frustrations, fears, and furies.

The cognitive theorists who have emphasized the role of cognitive strategies in regulating behavior and affect, as well as those who have emphasized the role of cognition in affective disturbances like depression, have also looked to the parent–child relationship in order to understand the development of depression, although none has developed a specific theory. Rehm (1977) posited that maladaptive modeling or reinforcement schedules should be found in the histories of depressed adults. The individual who has encountered intense negative, noncontingent experiences, and who has experienced a lack of ability to control such events, may develop the negatively biased monitoring strategies underlying depression. Kanfer and Hagerman (1981) provide two detailed discussions of the development of depression in adulthood. Certainly, parental patterns of monitoring children's behavior and of coping with their own and their child's negative experiences serve as vehicles for the transmission of coping skills for negative affect.

Seligman (1975) has described the "dance of development" in which children develop a mastery or a helplessness sense of their control over events, an interactional flow with its roots in the synchronies of the responsiveness of the mother–infant relationship. The mother's responsiveness to the infant instills the experience of response–outcome relationships. Loss of the mother or unresponsive mothering interfere with the early experience of mastery. Later in childhood, the parental establishment of rules and standards provides the context within which children will strive to meet parental approval, to earn the esteem of their parents, and to develop their own self-esteem. It should be quite possible (1) to study the interactional flow of parents' responsiveness to their children's affect, (2) to contrast depressed and nondepressed parents' patterns, and (3) to study the explicit or implied attributions for their own or their children's failures, their monitoring and discipline strategies, their tendencies to focus on the nature of the problem or on the child's affect, and so forth.

IMPLICATIONS OF A DEVELOPMENTAL PERSPECTIVE

In our attempt to understand the possibility, the nature, and the development of childhood depression, we argue that a synthesis of developmental and clinical research provides a developmental framework for understanding much of the past and present literature on the subject. Both intrapersonal and interpersonal sources of affect regulation operate over the life span, and the relative importance of each of these sources varies as a function of developmental phase and probably also as a function of the severity of current circumstances. An adult mourning the death of a spouse can be overcome with sadness and despair and stop functioning at an adult level of adequacy. Neighbors, relatives, and friends may provide food, comfort, finances, cleaning services, and child care; interpersonal resources operate to regulate the experience of the bereaved adult. If, after a certain length of time, the adult does not recuperate and resume responsibility for managing his or her experience, the condition (including affective experience) can be regarded as depression. Thus, even in adulthood, there are appropriate contexts for interpersonal, rather than self, regulation of affect to be the primary means of coping with negative affect. For the child younger than 6, interpersonal sources are necessary much of the time, and, in this social context, the child develops the ability to self-regulate affect.

If we can shift our models of depression to include not only the conscious, cognitive self-regulation processes articulated by theorists such as Abramson *et al.* (1978), Beck (1976), Rehm (1977), and Seligman (1975) but also the interpersonal sources, especially the family, then a broader, more unifying framework for studying the manifestation and development of depression over the life span is possible. A shift to a developmental framework with an emphasis on affect regulation as a constant feature over time, marked by age-specific strategies and changes in interpersonal relations, will provide a context for the identification of depression even in very young children. On the basis of normative data, we know that infants develop positive expectations of the interpersonal world, are reactive to violations of those expectations, and engage in help-seeking behavior and limited self-soothing. We expect depressed infants to drop these behaviors from their repertoires when they meet with persistent unresponsiveness and inconsistency and to become chronically sad, listless, apathetic, and unresponsive. The loss in regulating negative affect should be accompanied by disturbances in sleeping and eating patterns. Thus the DSM-III diagnosis for major depressive disorder, with the exception of the cognitive criteria is applicable to all children. Cases of childhood depression can be very serious, even life threatening, and the underreporting and underestimation of such depression is due in part to the lack of an adequate framework for conceptualizing how childhood depression can be possible.

We feel that an integrative analysis of developmental and clinical research related to aspects of childhood psychopathology is long overdue. As our viewpoints evolved, it was quite apparent that much of what we hypothesized could be operationalized and studied systematically. Although the research on the development of affect and self in very young children is quite recent and still confined in many respects, there is much fertile information that could be applied to the study of the conditions under which children's affective experiences are inadequately managed, the nature of the depressive experience in young children, and, perhaps most important, the factors involved in the development of depression in children and adults.

Finally, our conclusions reinforced for us that the treatment of depression in both children and adults should focus both on the individual's cognitive self-regulatory processes and on the interpersonal system involved in affect regulation. There is some literature that describes cognitive approaches for treating depressed children (Kaslow & Rehm, 1983, 1985; Petti, 1981), there are a few studies that demonstrate the efficacy of cognitive–behavioral treatments for depressed children (Butler *et al.,* 1980; Stark, Kaslow, & Reynolds, 1987), and there are models that attempt to focus on both intrapersonal (cognitive) and interpersonal processes of depression (Feldman, 1975; Pollack, Kaslow, & Harvey, 1982). However, a more complete and more testable approach would be one that focuses on the self-regulatory abilities of individuals in the depressed family, on the manner in which individuals attempt to respond to each other's affective states, and on the ability of individuals to use both internal and external sources.

NOTE

1. Both Beck (1976) and Piaget (1926, 1954) use the term "schema." Beck appears to refer to the content of one's thought, whereas Piaget refers to the structure of cognitive operations. In our discussion, we use the word "schema" in the Piagetian sense, to specify underlying forms of thought independent of specific types of thoughts. The thought "I'm dumb" is derived from a self-conscious reflective process, or schema for self-reflective thought, in the same way one can think "I'm athletic."

REFERENCES

Abramson, L. Y., Seligman, M. E. P., & Teasdale, J. (1978). Learned helplessness in humans: Critique and reformulation. *Journal of Abnormal Psychology, 87,* 49–74.

Ainsworth, M. D. S., Blehar, M., Waters, E., & Wall, S. (1978). *Patterns of attachment.* Hillsdale, NJ: Erlbaum.

Albert, N., & Beck, A. T. (1975). Incidence of depression in early adolescence: A preliminary study. *Journal of Youth and Adolescence, 4,* 301–308.

Alloy, L. B., & Abramson, L. Y. (1979). Judgment of contingency in depressed and nondepressed students: Sadder but wiser? *Journal of Experimental Psychology: General, 108,* 441–485.

Alloy, L. B., & Abramson, L. Y. (1982). Learned helplessness, depression, and the illusion of control. *Journal of Personality and Social Psychology, 42,* 1114–1126.

American Psychiatric Association. (1980). *Diagnostic and statistical manual of mental disorders* (3rd ed.). Washington, DC: Author.

Anthony, E. J. (1975). Childhood depression. In E. J. Anthony & T. Benedek (Eds.), *Depression and human existence* (pp. 231–277). Boston: Little, Brown.

Arajarvi, T., & Huttunen, M. (1972). Encopresis and enuresis as symptoms of depression. In A. L. Annell (Ed.), *Depressive states in childhood and adolescence* (pp. 212–217). Stockholm: Almqvist & Wiskell.

Arend, R., Gove, F., & Sroufe, L. A. (1979). Continuity in early adaptation: From attachment theory in infancy to resiliency and curiosity at age five. *Child Development, 50,* 950–959.

Bakwin, H. (1972, June). Depression—A mood disorder in children and adolescence. *Maryland State Medical Journal, 55–61.*

Barling, J. (1980). Performance standards and reinforcement effects on children's academic performance: A test of social learning theory. *Cognitive Therapy and Research, 4,* 409–418.

Baumrind, D. (1971). Current patterns of parental authority. *Developmental Psychology Monographs, 1,* 1–103.

Beach, S. R. H., Abramson, L. Y., & Levine, F. M. (1981). Attributional reformulation of learned helplessness and depression. In J. F. Clarkin & H. I. Glazer (Eds.), *Depression: Behavioral and directive intervention strategies* (pp. 131–165). New York: Garland.

Beardslee, W. R., Bemporad, J., Keller, M. B., & Klerman, G. L. (1983). Children of parents with major affective disorder: A review. *American Journal of Psychiatry, 140,* 825–832.

Beck, A. T. (1967). *Depression: Clinical, experimental, and theoretical aspects.* New York: Harper & Row.

Beck, A. T. (1976). *Cognitive therapy and emotional disorders.* New York: International Universities Press.

Bemporad, J. (1978a). Manifest symptomatology of depression in children and adolescents. In S. Arieti & J. Bemporad (Eds.), *Severe and mild depression: The psychotherapeutic approach* (pp. 87–106). New York: Basic Books.

Bemporad, J. (1978b). Psychodynamics of depression and suicide in children and adolescents. In S. Arieti & J. Bemporad (Eds.), *Severe and mild depression: The psychotherapeutic approach* (pp. 185–207). New York: Basic Books.

Bemporad, J., & Won Lee, K. (1984). Developmental and psychodynamic aspects of childhood depression. *Child Psychiatry and Human Development, 14,* 145–157.

Block, J. H. (1971). *Lives through time.* Berkeley, CA: Bancroft Books.

Blumberg, S. H., & Izard, A. E. (1985). Affective and cognitive characteristics of depression in 10- and 11-year-old children. *Journal of Personality and Social Psychology, 49,* 194–202.

Blurton-Jones, N. (1972). *Ethological studies of child behavior.* London: Cambridge University Press.

Bower, G. H. (1981). Mood and memory. *American Psychologist, 36,* 129–148.

Bowlby, J. (1969). *Attachment and loss* (Vol. 1). New York: Basic Books.

Bretherton, I., Fritz, J., Zahn-Waxler, C., & Ridgeway, D. (1986). Learning to talk about emotions: A functionalist perspective. *Child Development, 57,* 529–548.

Brumback, R. A., Dietz-Schmidt, S. G., & Weinberg, W. A. (1977). Depression in children referred to an educational diagnostic center: Diagnosis and treatment and analysis of criteria and literature review. *Diseases of the Nervous System, 38,* 529–535.

Brunquell, D., Crichton, L., & Egeland, B. (1981). Maternal personality and attitude in disturbances of childrearing. *American Journal of Orthopsychiatry, 51,* 680–691.

Butler, L., Miezitis, S., Friedman, R., & Cole, E. (1980). The effect of two school-based intervention programs on depressive symptoms in preadolescents. *American Education Research Journal, 17,* 111–119.

Carlson, G. A., & Cantwell, D. P. (1980). A survey of depressive symptoms, syndrome, and disorder in a child psychiatric population. *Journal of Child Psychology and Psychiatry, 21,* 19–25.

Carr, S. J., Dobbs, J. M., & Carr, T. S. (1975). Mother–infant attachment: The importance of the mother's visual field. *Child Development, 46,* 331–338.

Cass, L. K., & Thomas, C. B. (1979). *Childhood psychopathology and later adjustment.* New York: Wiley.

Chess, S., & Thomas, A. (1984). *Origins and evolution of behavior disorders: From infancy to early adult life.* New York: Brunner/Mazel.

Cohn, J. F., & Tronick, E. Z. (1983). Three-months-old infants' reaction to simulated maternal depression. *Child Development, 54,* 185–193.

Cole, P. M. (1985). Display rules and the socialization of affective displays. In G. Zivin (Ed.), *The development of expressive behavior: Biology–environment interactions* (pp. 269–290). New York: Academic Press.

Cole, P. M. (1986). Children's spontaneous control of facial expression. *Child Development, 57,* 1309–1321.

Conners, C. K., Himmelhoch, J., Goyette, C. H., Ulrich, R., & Neil, J. (1979). Children of parents with affective illness. *American Academy of Child Psychiatry, 18,* 600–607.

Coopersmith, S. (1967). *The antecedents of self-esteem.* San Francisco: W. H. Freeman.

Costello, C. G. (1980). Childhood depression: Three basic but questionable assumptions in the Lefkowitz and Burton critique. *Psychological Bulletin, 87,* 185–190.

Coyne, J. C. (1976). Toward an interactional description of depression. *Psychiatry, 39,* 28–40.

Crook, T., Raskin, A., & Elliott, J. (1981). Parent–child relationships and adult depression. *Child Development, 52,* 950–951.

Cytryn, L., & McKnew, D. H. (1972). Proposed classification of childhood depression. *American Journal of Psychiatry, 129,* 149–155.

Cytryn, L., McKnew, D. H., & Bunney, W. E. (1980). Diagnosis of depression in children: A reassessment. *American Journal of Psychiatry, 137,* 22–25.

Davidson, J. (1968). Infantile depression in a "normal" child. *Journal of the American Academy of Child Psychiatry, 7,* 522–535.

Diener, C. I., & Dweck, C. S. (1978). An analysis of learned helplessness: Continuous changes in performance, strategy, and achievement cognitions following failure. *Journal of Personality and Social Psychology, 36,* 451–462.

Dweck, C. S., & Reppucci, N. D. (1973). Learned helplessness and reinforcement responsibility in children. *Journal of Personality and Social Psychology, 25,* 109–116.

Engel, G., & Reichsman, F. (1956). Spontaneous and experimentally induced depression in an infant with gastric fistula. *Journal of the American Psychoanalytic Association, 4,* 428–456.

Erikson, E. H. (1963). *Childhood and society.* New York: W. W. Norton.

Feldman, L. B. (1975). Depression and marital interaction. *Family Process, 15,* 389–395.

Field, T. (1981b). Infant arousal, attention, and affect during early interactions. *Journal of the American Academy of Child Psychiatry, 20,* 308–317.

Field, T. (1981a). Affective displays of high-risk infants during early interactions. In T. Field & A. Fogel (Eds.), *Emotion and early interaction.* Hillsdale, NJ: Erlbaum.

Flavell, J., & Wellman, H. (1977). Metamemory. In R. Kail & J. Hagen (Eds.), *Perspectives on the development of memory and cognition* (pp. 3–33). Hillsdale, NJ: Erlbaum.

Frieze, I. H. (1981). Children's attributions for success and failure. In S. S. Brehm, S. M. Kassin, & F. X. Gibbons (Eds.), *Developmental social psychology: Theory and research* (pp. 57–71). New York: Oxford University Press.

Frodi, A. M., Lamb, M. E., Leavitt, A., & Carson, W. C. (1978). Fathers' and mothers' responses to infant smiles and cries. *Infant Behavior and Development, 1,* 187–198.

Frodi, A. M., Lamb, M. E., Leavitt, A., Donovan, C. N., & Sherry, D. (1978). Fathers' and mothers' responses to the faces and cries of normal and premature infants. *Developmental Psychology, 14,* 490–498.

Garber, J. (1981, August). Issues in the diagnosis of depression in children. In L. P. Rehm (Chair), *Empirical studies of childhood depression.* Symposium conducted at the meeting of the American Psychological Association, Los Angeles.

Geller, B., Chestnut, E. C., Miller, D., Price, D. T., & Yates, E. (1985). Preliminary data on DSM-III associated features of major depressive disorder in children and adolescents. *American Journal of Psychiatry, 142,* 643–644.

Glasberg, R., & Aboud, F. (1981). A developmental perspective on the study of depression: Children's evaluative reactions to sadness. *Developmental Psychology, 17,* 195–202.

Glasberg, R., & Aboud, F. (1982). Keeping one's distance from sadness: Children's self-reports of emotional experience. *Developmental Psychology, 18,* 287–293.

Graham, S., Doubleday, C., & Guarino, P. A. (1984). The development of relations between perceived controllability and the emotions of pity, anger, and guilt. *Child Development, 55,* 561–565.

Greenspan, S. I., & Porges, S. W. (1984). Psychopathology in infancy and early childhood: Clinical perspectives on the organization of sensory and affective–thematic experience. *Child Development, 55,* 17–29.

Gunnar, M. (1978). Changing a frightening toy into a pleasant toy by allowing the infant to control its actions. *Developmental Psychology, 14,* 157–162.

Gunnar, M. (1980). Control, warning signals, and distress in infancy. *Developmental Psychology, 16,* 281–289.

Haley, G. M. T., Fine, S., Marriage, K., Moretti, M. M., & Freeman, R. J. (1985). Cognitive bias and depression in psychiatrically disturbed children and adolescents. *Journal of Consulting and Clinical Psychology, 53,* 535–537.

Hammen, C., & Zupan, B. A. (1984). Self-schemas, depression, and the processing of personal information in children. *Journal of Experimental Child Psychology, 37,* 598–608.

Handford, H. A., Mattison, R., Humphrey, F. J., & McLaughlin, R. E. (1986). Depressive syndrome in children entering residential school subsequent to parent death, divorce, or separation. *Journal of the American Academy of Child Psychiatry, 25,* 409–414.

Harris, P. L. (1983). Children's understanding of the link between situation and emotion. *Journal of Experimental Child Psychology, 36,* 490–509.

Harris, P. L., Olthof, T., & Terwogt, M. M. (1981). Children's knowledge of emotion. *Journal of Child Psychology and Psychiatry, 22,* 247–261.

Harter, S. (1980). A cognitive–developmental approach to children's understanding of affect and trait labels. In T. Serafica (Ed.), *Social cognition in context* (pp. 417–432). New York: Guilford Press.

Hetherington, E. M., Cox, M., & Cox, R. (1978). The aftermath of divorce. In J. H. Stevens & M. Mathews (Eds.), *Mother–child, father–child relations* (pp. 149–154). Washington DC: National Association for the Education of the Young.

Hoffman, M. L. (1970). Moral development. In P. H. Mussen (Ed.), *Carmichael's manual of child psychology (Vol. 2, pp. 261–359).* New York: Wiley.

Hudgens, R. W. (1979). *Psychiatric disorders in adolescents.* Baltimore: Williams & Wilkins.

Izard, C. E. (1977). *Human emotions.* New York: Plenum.

Izard, C. E., & Schwartz, G. M. (1986). Patterns of emotion in depression. In M. Rutter, C. E. Izard, & P. B. Read (Eds.), *Depression in young people: Developmental and clinical perspectives* (pp. 33–70). New York: Guilford Press.

Jacobsen, R. H., Lahey, B. B., & Strauss, C. C. (1983). Correlates of depressed mood in normal children. *Journal of Abnormal Child Psychology, 11,* 29–40.

Kagan, J. (1971). *Change and continuity in infancy.* New York: Wiley.

Kagan, J. (1975). Discrepancy, temperament, and infant distress. In M. M. Lewis & L. Rosenblum (Eds.), *The origins of fear* (pp. 143–179). New York: Wiley.

Kagan, J. (1981). *The second year: The emergence of self-awareness.* Cambridge, MA: Harvard University Press.

Kanfer, F. H., & Hagerman, S. (1981). The role of self-regulation. In L. P. Rehm (Ed.), *Behavior therapy for depression: Present status and future directions* (pp. 143–180). New York: Academic Press.

Kaplan, L. (1978). *Oneness and separateness: From infant to individual.* New York: Simon & Schuster.

Karniol. R., & Ross, M. (1976). The development of causal attributions in social perception. *Journal of Personality and Social Psychology, 34,* 455–464.

Kashani, J. H., Carlson, G. A., Horwitz, E., & Reid, J. C. (1985). Dysphoric mood in young children referred to a child development unit. *Child Psychiatry and Human Development, 15,* 234–242.

Kashani, J. H., Husain, A., Shekim, W. O., Hodges, K. K., Cytryn, L., & McKnew, D. H. (1981). Current perspectives on childhood depression: An overview. *American Journal of Psychiatry, 138,* 143–153.

Kashani, J. H., McGee, R. O., Clarkson, S. E., Anderson, J. C., Walton, L. A., William, S., Silva, P. A., Robins, A. J., Cytryn, L., & McKnew, D. H. (1983). Depression in a sample of 9-year-old children: Prevalence and associated characteristics. *Archives of General Psychiatry, 40,* 1217–1223.

Kashani, J. H., & Ray, J. S. (1983). Depressive related symptoms among pre-school children. *Child Psychiatry and Human Development, 13,* 233–238.

Kashani, J. H., Ray, J. S., & Carlson, G. A. (1984). Depression and depressive-like states in preschool-age children in a Child Development Unit. *American Journal of Psychiatry, 141,* 1397–1402.

Kaslow, N. J., & Rehm, L. P. (1983). Childhood depression. In R. J. Morris & T. Kratochwill (Eds.), *The practice of child therapy: A textbook of methods* (pp. 26–51). New York: Pergamon Press.

Kaslow, N. J., & Rehm, L. P. (1985). Conceptualization, assessment, and treatment of depression in children. In A. E. Kazdin & P. Bornstein (Eds.), *Handbook of clinical behavior therapy with children* (pp. 599–657). Chicago: The Dorsey Press.

Kaslow, N. J., Rehm, L. P., & Siegel, A. W. (1984). Social cognitive and cognitive correlates of depression in children. *Journal of Child Psychology, 12,* 605–620.

Kaslow, N. J., Tanenbaum, R. L., Abramson, L. Y., Peterson, C., & Seligman, M. E. P. (1983). Problem-solving deficits and depressive symptoms among children. *Journal of Abnormal Child Psychology, 11,* 497–502.

Kaslow, N. J., & Wamboldt, F. S. (1986). Childhood depression: Current perspectives and future directions. *Journal of Social and Clinical Psychology, 3,* 416–424.

Kassin, S. M. (1981). From laychild to "layman": Developmental causal attribution. In S. S. Brehm, S. M. Kassin, & F. X. Gibbons (Eds.), *Developmental social psychology: Theory and research* (pp. 169–190). New York: Oxford University Press.

Kazdin, A. E., Esveldt-Dawson, K., Sherick, R. B., & Colbus, D. (1985). Assessment of overt behavior and childhood depression among psychiatrically disturbed children. *Journal of Consulting and Clinical Psychology, 53,* 201–210.

Kazdin, A. E., French, N. H., Unis, A. S., & Esveldt-Dawson, K. (1983). Assessment of childhood depression: Correspondence of child and parent ratings. *Journal of the American Academy of Child Psychiatry, 22* 157–164.

Kazdin, A. E., French, N. H., Unis, A. S., Esveldt-Dawson, K., & Sherick, R. B. (1983). Hopelessness, depression, and suicidal intent among psychiatrically disturbed inpatient children. *Journal of Consulting and Clinical Psychology, 51,* 504–510.

Kazdin, A. E., Moser, J., Colbus, D., & Bell, R. (1985). Depressive symptoms among physically abused and psychiatrically disturbed children. *Journal of Abnormal Psychology, 94,* 298–307.

Kazdin, A. E., Rodgers, A., & Colbus, D. (1986). The hopelessness scale for children: Psychometric characteristics and concurrent validity. *Journal of Consulting and Clinical Psychology, 54,* 241–245.

Kazdin, A. E., Sherick, R. B., Esveldt-Dawson, K., & Rancurello, M. D. (1985). Nonverbal behavior and childhood depression. *Journal of the American Academy of Child Psychiatry, 24,* 303–309.

Klinger, E. (1975). Consequences of commitment to and disengagement from incentives. *Psychological Review, 82,* 1–25.

Kovacs, M., & Beck, A. T. (1977). An empirical–clinical approach toward a definition of childhood depression. In J. G. Schulterbrandt & A. Raskin (Eds.), *Depression in childhood: Diagnosis, treatment, and conceptual models* (pp. 1–25). New York: Raven Press.

Kovacs, M., & Beck, A. T. (1979). Cognitive–affective processes in depression. In C. E. Izard (Ed.), *Emotions in personality and psychopathology* (pp. 417–442). New York: Plenum.

Kovacs, M., Feinberg, T. L., Crouse-Novak, M. A., Paulauskas, S., & Finkelstein, R. (1984). Recovery in childhood depressive disorders: A longitudinal prospective study. *Archives of General Psychiatry, 41,* 229–237.

Lamont, J., Fischoff, S., & Gottlieb, H. (1976). Recall of parental behaviors in female neurotic depressives. *Journal of Clinical Psychology, 32,* 762–765.

Lefkowitz, M. M., & Burton, N. (1978). Childhood depression: A critique of the concept. *Psychological Bulletin, 85,* 716–726.

Lefkowitz, M. M., & Tesiny, E. P. (1980). Assessment of childhood depression. *Journal of Consulting and Clinical Psychology, 48,* 43–50.

Lefkowitz, M. M., & Tesiny, E. P. (1985). Depression in children: Prevalence and correlates. *Journal of Consulting and Clinical Psychology, 53,* 647–656.

Lefkowitz, M. M., Tesiny, E. P., & Gordon, N. H. (1980). Childhood depression, family income, and locus of control. *Journal of Nervous and Mental Disease, 168,* 732–735.

Leon, G. R., Kendall, P. C., & Garber, J. (1980). Depression in children: Parent, teacher, and child perspectives. *Journal of Abnormal Child Psychology, 8,* 221–235.

Lewis, M., & Michalson, L. (1983). *Children's emotions and moods.* New York: Plenum.

Lieberman, A. F. (1977). Preschoolers' competence with a peer: Influence of attachment and social experience. *Child Development, 48,* 1277–1287.

Ling, W., Oftedal, G., & Weinberg, W. (1970). Depressive illness in childhood presenting as severe headache. *American Journal of Diseases in Children, 120,* 122–124.

Maccoby, E. E. (1980). *Social development: Psychological growth and the parent–child relationship.* New York: Harcourt Brace Jovanovich.

Mahler, M., Pine, F., & Bergman, A. (1975). *The psychological birth of the human infant.* New York: Basic Books.

Main, M., & Stadtman, L. (1981). Infant response to rejection of physical contact by the mother: Aggression, avoidance, and conflict. *Journal of the American Academy of Child Psychiatry, 20,* 292–307.

Malmquist, C. P. (1977). Childhood depression: A clinical and behavioral perspective. In J. G. Schulterbrandt & A. Raskin (Eds.), *Depression in childhood: Diagnosis, treatment, and conceptual models* (pp. 33–59). New York: Raven Press.

Matas, L., Arend, R., & Sroufe, L. A. (1978). Continuity of adaptation in the second year: The relationship between quality of attachment and later competence. *Child Development, 49,* 547–556.

McConville, B. J., Boag, L. C., & Purohit, A. P. (1973). Three types of childhood depression. *Canadian Psychiatric Association Journal, 18,* 133–138.

McCoy, C. L., & Masters, J. C. (1985). The development of children's strategies for the social control of emotion. *Child Development, 56,* 1214–1222.

McKnew, D. H., Cytryn, L., Efron, A. M., Gershon, E. S., & Bunney, W. E. (1979). Offspring of patients with affective disorders. *British Journal of Psychiatry, 134,* 148–152.

Metalsky, G. I., & Abramson, L. Y. (1980). Attributional styles: Toward a framework for conceptualization and assessment. In P. C. Kendall & S. C. Hollon (Eds.), *Cognitive–behavioral interventions: Assessment methods* (pp. 13–58). New York: Academic Press.

Morris, M. L. (1980). Childhood depression in the primary grades: Early identification, a teacher consultation remedial model, and classroom correlates of change. *Interchange, 11,* 61–75.

Morrison, H. L. (Ed.). (1983). *Children of depressed parents: Risk, identification, and intervention.* New York: Grune & Stratton.

Moyal, B. R. (1977). Locus of control, self-esteem, stimulus appraisal, and depressive symptoms. *Journal of Consulting and Clinical Psychology, 45,* 951–952.

Mullins, L. L., Siegel, L. J., & Hodges, K. (1985). Cognitive problem-solving and life event correlates of depressive symptoms in children. *Journal of Abnormal Child Psychology, 24,* 305–314.

Nicholls, J. G. (1978). The development of the concepts of effort and ability, perception of academic attainment, and the understanding that difficult tasks require more ability. *Child Development, 49,* 800–814.

Nicholls, J. G., & Miller, A. T. (1984). Reasoning about the ability of self and others: A developmental study. *Child Development, 55,* 1990–1999.

Nissen, G. (1971). *Depressive syndrome im kindes-und jugendalter.* Berlin: Springer-Verlag.

Orvaschel, H., Weissman, M. M., & Kidd, K. K. (1980). Children and depression: The children of depressed parents; the childhood of depressed patients; depression in children. *Journal of Affective Disorders, 2,* 1–6.

Ossofsky, H. J. (1974). Endogenous depression in infancy and childhood. *Comprehensive Psychiatry, 15,* 19–25.

Parker, G. (1979). Parental characteristics in relation to depressive disorders. *British Journal of Psychiatry, 134,* 138–147.

Parsons, J. E., & Ruble, D. N. (1977). The development of achievement related expectancies. *Child Development, 48,* 1075–1079.

Patterson, C., & Mischel, W. (1976). Effects of temptation-inhibiting and task-facilitating plans on self-control. *Journal of Personality and Social Psychology, 33,* 209–217.

Patterson, G. R. (1982). *Coercive family processes*. Eugene, OR: Castilia.

Peterson, L., Mullins, L. L., & Ridley-Johnson, R. (1985). Childhood depression: Peer reactions to depression and life stress. *Journal of Abnormal Child Psychology, 13*, 597–609.

Petti, T. A. (1981). Active treatment of childhood depression. In J. F. Clarkin & H. I. Glaser (Eds.), *Depression: Behavioral and intervention strategies* (pp. 311–343). New York: Garland.

Piaget, J. (1926). *The language and thought of the child*. New York: Harcourt Brace.

Piaget, J. (1954). *The construction of reality in the child*. New York: Basic Books.

Piersel, W. C., & Kratochwill, T. R. (1979). Self-observation and behavior change: Applications to academic and adjustment problems through behavioral consultation. *Journal of School Psychology, 17*, 151–161.

Pollack, S. L., Kaslow, N. J., & Harvey, D. M. (1982). Symmetry, complementarity, and depression: The evolution of a hypothesis. In F. W. Kaslow (Ed.), *The international book of family therapy* (pp. 170–183). New York: Brunner/Mazel.

Poznanski, E. O. (1979). Childhood depression: A psychodynamic approach to the etiology of depression in children. In A. French and I. Berlin (Eds.), *Depression in children and adolescents* (pp. 46–68). New York: Human Sciences Press.

Poznanski, E., Mokros, H. B., Grossman, J., & Freeman, L. N. (1985). Diagnostic criteria in childhood depression. *American Journal of Psychiatry, 142*, 1168–1173.

Poznanski, E. O., & Zrull, J. P. (1970). Childhood depression: Clinical characteristics of overtly depressed children. *Archives of General Psychiatry, 23*, 8–15.

Puig-Antich, J., Blau, S., Marx, N., Greenhill, L. L., & Chambers, W. (1978). Prepubertal major depressive disorder. *Journal of the American Academy of Child Psychiatry, 17*, 695–707.

Puig-Antich, J., Lukens, E., Davies, M., Goetz, D., Brennan-Quattrock, J., & Todak, G. (1985a). Psychosocial functioning in prepubertal major depressive disorders. *Archives of General Psychiatry, 42*, 500–507.

Puig-Antich, J., Lukens, E., Davies, M., Goetz, D., Brennan-Quattrock, J., and Todak, G. (1985b). Psychosocial functioning in prepubertal major depressive disorders. *Archives of General Psychiatry, 42*, 511–517.

Radke-Yarrow, M., Cummings, E., Kuczynski, L., & Chapman, M. (1985). Patterns of attachment in two- and three-year-olds in normal families and families with parental depression. *Child Development, 56*, 884–893.

Rehm, L. P. (1977). A self-control model of depression. *Behavior Therapy, 8*, 787–804.

Rehm, L. P., & O'Hara, M. W. (1980). The role of attributions theory in understanding depression. In I. H. Frieze, D. Bar-Tal, & J. S. Carroll (Eds.), *Attribution theory: Applications to social problems* (pp. 209–236). San Francisco: Jossey-Bass.

Rholes, W. S., Blackwell, J., Jordan, C., & Walters, C. (1980). A developmental study of learned helplessness. *Developmental Psychology, 16*, 616–624.

Rie, H. E. (1966). Depression in childhood: A survey of some pertinent contributions. *Journal of the American Academy of Child Psychiatry, 5*, 653–685.

Rogers, T., & Forehand, R. (1983). The role of parent depression in interactions between mothers and their clinic-referred children. *Cognitive Therapy and Research, 7*, 315–324.

Ruble, D. N., Boggiano, A. K., Feldman, N. S., & Loeble, J. H. (1980). Developmental analysis of the role of social comparison in self-evaluation. *Developmental Psychology, 16*, 105–115.

Rutter, M., Graham, P., Chadwick, O. F. D., & Yule, W. (1976). Adolescent turmoil: Fact or fiction? *Journal of Child Psychiatry and Psychology, 17*, 35–36.

Saarni, C. (1979). Children's understanding of display rules for expressive behavior. *Developmental Psychology, 15*, 424–429.

Saarni, C. (1984). Observing children's use of display rules: Age and sex differences, *Child Development, 55*, 1504–1513.

Sacco, W. P., & Graves, D. J. (1984). Childhood depression, interpersonal problem-solving, and self-ratings of performance. *Journal of Clinical Child Psychology, 13*, 10–15.

Sander, L. (1975). Infant and caretaking environment. In E. J. Anthony (Ed.), *Explorations in child psychiatry* (pp. 129–166). New York: Plenum.

Saylor, C. F., Finch, A. J., Baskin, C. H., Furey, W., & Kelly, M. M. (1984). Construct validity for measures of childhood depression: Application of multi-trait multimethod methodology. *Journal of Consulting and Clinical Psychology, 52,* 977–985.

Schwartz, M., Friedman, R., Lindsay, P., & Narrol, H. (1982). The relationship between conceptual tempo and depression in children. *Journal of Consulting and Clinical Psychology, 50,* 488–490.

Sedlack, A. J., & Kurtz, S. T. (1981). A review of children's use of causal inference principles. *Child Development, 52,* 759–784.

Seligman, M. E. P. (1975). *Helplessness: On depression, development and death.* San Francisco: W. H. Freeman.

Seligman, M. E. P., Peterson, C., Kaslow, N. J., Tanenbaum, R. L., Alloy, L. B., & Abramson, L. Y. (1984). Explanatory style and depressive symptoms among school children. *Journal of Abnormal Psychology, 93,* 235–238.

Selman, R. L. (1981). What children understand of intrapsychic processes. In E. K. Shapiro & E. Weber (Eds.), *Cognitive and affective growth* (pp. 187–215). Hillsdale, NJ: Erlbaum.

Shantz, C. U. (1975). The development of social cognition. In E. M. Hetherington (Ed.), *Review of child development research (Vol. 5,* pp. 257–354). Chicago: University of Chicago Press.

Spitz, R. (1945). Hospitalism: An inquiry into the genesis of psychiatric conditions in early childhood. *Psychoanalytic Study of the Child, 1,* 53–74.

Spitz, R. (1946). Anaclitic depression. *Psychoanalytic study of the Child, 2,* 313–342.

Sroufe, L. A. (1979). Socioemotional development. In J. D. Osofsky (Ed.), *Handbook of infant development* (pp. 462–516). New York: Wiley Interscience.

Sroufe, L. A. (1983). Infant–caregiver attachment and patterns of adaptation in preschool: The roots of maladaptation and competence. In M. Prelmutter (Ed.), *Minnesota Symposium in Child Psychology (Vol. 16,* pp. 47–83). Hillsdale, NJ: Erlbaum.

Stark, K. D., Kaslow, N. J., & Reynolds, W. M. (1987). A comparison of the relative efficacy of self-control therapy and a behavioral problem-solving therapy for depression in children. *Journal of Abnormal Child Psychology, 15,* 91–113.

Staton, R. D., Wilson, H., & Brumback, R. A. (1981). Cognitive improvement associated with tricyclic antidepressant treatment of childhood major depressive illness. *Perceptual and Motor Skills, 53,* 219–234.

Tesiny, E. P., & Lefkowitz, M. M. (1982). Childhood depression: A six-month follow-up study. *Journal of Consulting and Clinical Psychology, 50,* 778–780.

Tesiny, E. P., Lefkowitz, M. M., & Gordon, N. H. (1980). Childhood depression, locus of control, and school achievement. *Journal of Educational Psychology, 72,* 506–510.

Thomas, A., Chess, S., & Birch, N. J. (1965). *Temperament and behavior disorders in children.* New York: New York University Press.

Vaughn, B., Egeland, B., Sroufe, L. A., & Waters, E. (1979). Individual differences in infant–mother attachment at twelve and eighteen months: Stability and change in families under stress. *Child Development, 50,* 971–975.

Vosk, B., Forehand, R., Parker, J. B., & Rickard, K. (1982). A multimethod comparison of popular and unpopular children. *Developmental Psychology, 18,* 571–575.

Wallerstein, J. S., & Kelly, J. B. (1980). *Surviving the breakup: How children and parents cope with divorce.* New York: Basic Books.

Weiner, N. (1974). *Achievement motivation and attribution theory.* Morristown, NJ: General Learning Press.

Weiner, B., & Graham, S. (1984). An attributional approach to emotional development. In C. E. Izard, J. Kagan, & R. B. Zajonc (Eds.), Emotions, cognition, and behavior. New York: Cambridge University Press.

Weissman, M. M., & Paykel, E. S. (1974). *The depressed woman: A study of social relationships.* Chicago: University of Chicago Press.

Weissman, M. M., Paykel, E. S., & Klerman, G. L. (1972). The depressed woman as mother. *Social Psychiatry, 7,* 98–102.

Weissman, M. M., Prusoff, B. A., Gammon, G. D., Merikangas, K. R., Leckman, J. F., & Kidd, K.

K. (1984). Psychopathology in children (ages 6–18) of depressed and normal parents. *Journal of the American Academy of Child Psychiatry, 23,* 78–84.

Weisz, J. R., Weiss, B., Wasserman, A. A., and Rintouli, B. (1987). Control-related beliefs and depression among clinic-referred children and adolescents. *Journal of Abnormal Psychology, 96,* 58–63.

Welner, Z., Welner, A., McCrary, M. D., & Leonard, M. A. (1977). Psychopathology in children of inpatients with depression: A controlled study. *The Journal of Nervous and Mental Disease, 164,* 408–413.

12

Patterns of Personal and Causal Inference: Implications for the Cognitive Therapy of Depression

MARK D. EVANS
University of Minnesota and St. Paul-Ramsey Medical Center
STEVEN D. HOLLON
Vanderbilt University

Beck's cognitive theory of depression posits that systematic errors in thinking may be the cardinal feature in clinical depression (Beck, 1963, 1967, 1976). According to Beck, the thinking of depressed individuals is dominated by prepotent schematic knowledge organizations best exemplified as representing a negative cognitive triad. This triad consists of negative views of the self, the world, and the future. Incoming information is seen as being transformed by distorting mechanisms, which results in an undue rigidity and maintenance of those negative belief systems despite the occurrence of potentially corrective experiences.

Cognitive therapy is predicated on the notion that correcting these negative schemata and cognitive distortions can produce profound relief from the affective, behavioral, motivational, and vegetative components of the syndrome of depression (Beck, 1964, 1970; Beck, Rush, Shaw, & Emergy, 1979). Cognitive therapy combines cognitive and behavioral-activation procedures in an effort to train depressed clients to systematically test their beliefs and change their purportedly depressogenic beliefs and distortions. Controlled-outcome trials have supported the efficacy of cognitive therapy, with regard to producing change in the acute syndrome (Beck, Hollon, Young, Bedrosian, & Budenz, 1985; Blackburn, Bishop, Glen, Whalley, & Christie, 1981; Hollon, DeRubeis, Evans, Tuason, Wiemer, & Garvey, 1986; Murphy, Simons, Wetzel, & Lustman, 1984; Rush, Beck, Kovacs, & Hollon, 1977; Shaw, 1977; Taylor & Marshall, 1977), and to preventing subsequent relapse or recurrence (Blackburn, Eunson, & Bishop, 1986; Evans *et al.*, 1986; Kovacs, Rush, Beck, & Hollon, 1981; Simons, Murphy, Levine, & Wetzel, 1986).

Recent work in basic cognitive psychology (e.g., Kahneman, Slovic, & Tversky, 1982) and social cognition (e.g., Nisbett & Ross, 1980) has enriched our understanding of the ways in which nonpsychopathological populations organize knowledge about the world and process new information in the context of prior knowledge. In brief, a strong case can be made that the thinking of relatively nonpsychopathological populations is dominated by the same type of schematic knowledge representations and information-processing heuristics alleged by Beck to govern the thinking of depressives. In short, normals may not think very accurately, and often, when they arrive at the "right" response, it may be for the wrong reasons.

Closely related has been recent work suggesting that, in contrast to Beck's cognitive theory, depressives may actually be more accurate than nondepressives in many situations (Alloy & Abramson, 1979; Lewinsohn, Mischel, Chaplin, & Barton, 1980). This phenomenon, labeled "depressive realism," is reminiscent of Freud's classic thesis that it is only the psychopathological depressive who truly comprehends the baseness of the human spirit.

The dilemma posed by this recent work for a cognitive theory of therapy is twofold: (1) If normals do not think normatively, yet are not depressed, must depressed clients be trained to distort reality in a nondepressive way in order to stop being depressed? (2) If depressives are really more realistic than nondepressives, would not efforts to enhance reality testing, which cognitive therapists believe constitutes the main active ingredient in cognitive therapy, make people more depressed rather than less? Clearly, if the depressive realism account is accurate, the positive results observed with cognitive therapy cannot be attributed to the "reality-testing" process preferred by cognitive intervention theorists.

In this chapter, we address these issues from the perspective of their implications for the theory and practice of cognitive therapy. We will argue that schematic knowledge representations and heuristic information-processing "shortcuts" dominate the cognitive processes of all human beings, depressed and nondepressed alike, with the main distinction residing in the inaccurate negativity of content for the depressives and the unrealistic positivity of content for the nondepressives. Further, we will argue that cognitive therapy does indeed sharpen reality-testing skills, much as training in statistics and mathematics sharpens the inference-generation skills of trained scientists; this training in careful reality testing is, we believe, the primary means by which cognitive therapy produces its effect. In short, we will argue that cognitive therapy works by virtue of training depressed clients to be more systematic and normative in their information processing than are most nondepressives. In the sections that follow, we present the various competing models of inference in depressed and nondepressed individuals, discuss the cognitive content and processes of depressed and nondepressed individuals, and outline the changes that are thought to occur as a result of cognitive therapy.

COMPETING MODELS OF INFERENCE

There are several possible explanatory models that may represent the patterns of personal and causal inference in depressed versus nondepressed populations and the mechanisms of change in cognitive therapy. These models can be described in the following terms:

Model 1: Distorted depression, nondistorted nondepression, cognitive therapy that corrects depressive distortions. In this model, depressed patients are seen as holding inaccurately negative beliefs maintained by nonnormative information-processing heuristics (distortions). Conversely, nondepressives are seen as holding relatively accurate beliefs maintained by nondistorted, normative information-processing strategies. Cognitive therapy is seen as producing change in the depressives by means of enhancing their reality-testing skills, in effect, teaching them to think like normal persons. This model, depicted in Figure 12-1, comprises the set of propositions typically ascribed to Aaron Beck and his cognitive theory of therapy. In fact, though, it is not clear that Beck or his colleagues have attempted to specify the nature of thinking in nondepressives relative to some type of "Platonic truth" or reality. Similarly, it is not clear that Beck and his colleagues have ever proposed that cognitive therapy teaches depressed clients to think like nondepressives. To the best of our knowledge, cognitive theorists like Beck argue only that the therapy changes the way in which depressives think, not that it makes them more or less like nondepressives in their thought patterns.

Model 2: Distorted depressives, distorted nondepressives, cognitive therapy that corrects depressive distortions. This model, as depicted in Figure 12-2, retains the key elements of Beck's model with respect to depressed individuals. Depressives are seen as holding unnecessarily negative belief systems maintained by nonnormative information-processing heuristics, which are modified by cognitive therapy. In contrast to, Model 1, however, this one considers the belief systems and information processing of nondepressives to be both inaccurately positive and maintained by equally nonnormative information-processing heuristics. This model, which we favor, appears to be consistent with Beck's earlier theories and with recently emerging observations regarding thinking in nondepressives.

Model 3: Nondistorted depressives, distorted nondepressives, cognitive therapy that may work, but not by making depressives more accurate. Our third model is implied by recent research supportive of the depressive realism phenomenon (cf. Alloy & Abramson, 1979; Lewinsohn *et al.*, 1980). In this model, as depicted in

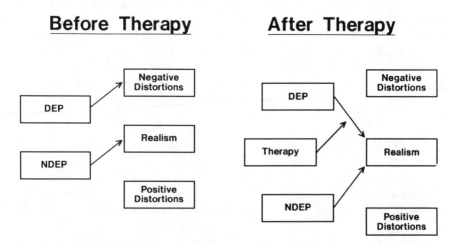

Figure 12-1. Distorted depressives and accurate nondepressives, with cognitive therapy working to make depressives more like nondepressives.

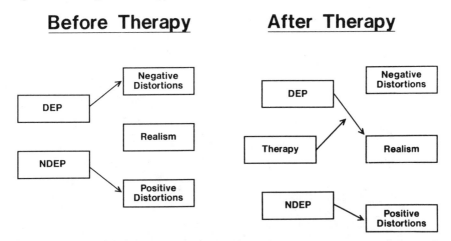

Figure 12-2. Distorted depressives and distorted nondepressives, with cognitive therapy working to make depressives more normative in their thinking, but not necessarily more like nondepressives.

Figure 12-3, depressives are seen as being relatively accurate in their perceptions of the state of nature. However, as in Model 2, nondepressives are seen as being unrealistically positive in their perceptions of the state of nature. Although little of the work on depressive realism has been directly concerned with therapy or its outcomes, the implication of this line of thinking is that either (1) cognitive therapy should not work, if it works through the enhancement of reality testing, or (2) cognitive therapy works, not by enhancing reality testing, but by the converse

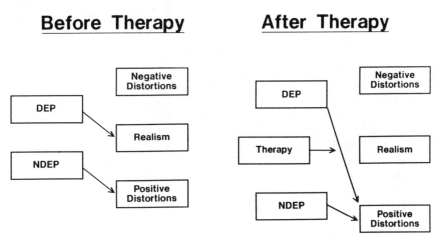

Figure 12-3. Nondistorted depressives and distorted depressives, with cognitive therapy working (if it works) to make depressives more unrealistically positive in their thinking and more like nondepressives.

mechanism, that is, by teaching depressives to be unrealistically positive in their evaluation of themselves, their worlds, and their futures.

In the next two sections, we review, respectively, the basic nature of personal and causal inference generation in nondepressives, and the efforts to explore such processes in depressed populations. Throughout this review, we will refer to the three models just postulated in an effort to see if any one is better supported by the existing data than the other two.

COGNITIVE CONTENT AND PROCESSES IN NONDEPRESSIVES

Intuitive Scientist or Fallible Information Processor?

Work over the last decade has strongly suggested that the thought content and the information processing of nonpsychopathological populations are strongly dominated by schematic knowledge representations and the operation of heuristic information-processing "shortcuts" (Kahneman *et al.*, 1982; Nisbett & Ross, 1980). This view is in contrast to Kelley's (1971) earlier assertion that the lay person "generally acts like a good scientist, examining covariation between cause and effect" (p. 2). Whereas Kelley viewed individuals as acting like "intuitive scientists," more recent work has suggested that lay persons (and, all too frequently, trained scientists) may be highly fallible information processors (e.g., see Ross, 1977). Existing beliefs appear to distort the processing of new information and to bias the retrieval of prior information from memory; information processing itself may rely more on intuitive heuristics that only haphazardly produce accurate inferences.

Ross (1977) suggested that there are three main types of inferences of particular interest to the student of human cognition: (1) inferences regarding the causes of events, or "causal attributions"; (2) inferences regarding the ascription of characteristics to various objects, situations, or persons, or "ascriptions of attributes"; and (3) inferences about the nature of events to come, or "predictions." For each of these types, it is theoretically possible (although pragmatically far more complex than one might first imagine) to specify what constitutes a normative inference under states of less than total certainty. One can ascertain what information ought to be available to an individual, process that information in accordance with conventional rules of logic, and specify the inference one would expect the individual to reach. Such an inference, based on known empirical laws and on the application of logical principles while taking into account the limits on the information available to the individual, has been referred to as a "normative inference."

Heuristics in Information Processing

In an intriguing program of research, Kahneman, Tversky, and their colleagues demonstrated that the inferences generated under states of uncertainty by both lay persons and trained scientists frequently do not correspond to the inferences we would expect if these individuals were operating in accordance with normative strategies. Tversky and Kahneman (1974) have described the operation of several heuristics in the way most individuals process information. "Heuristics" are information-processing strategies that reduce complex judgmental tasks to a set of simpler operations. Tversky and Kahneman describe three types of heuristics: availability, representativeness, and anchoring with adjustment. These heuristics are seen as "shortcut" strategies that can frequently facilitate efficient information processing. Under some conditions, however, these strategies can lead to "biases": particular tendencies or inclinations resulting in inferences at variance with those produced by normative processes.

A useful analogy to information-processing heuristics would be those processes that mediate visual perception. Visual perception proceeds not by transforming external objects into direct internal representations of those objects, but by contrasting images through a series of nonrepresentative strategies integrated at higher cortical centers. Continuing the analogy, although most perception yields reliable and veridical images of external events, it is quite possible to "fool" the senses in ways that highlight the operation of those nonrepresentative mechanisms. When we "see" water standing on a road on a hot day, or faces that become a vase, or a cube that alternately protrudes from the page and then retreats into it, we are experiencing visual illusions; these misperceptions of reality are consensually elicited from universal processing strategies. In effect, the information-processing heuristics described by Tversky and Kahneman function in the same fashion. That is, they typically facilitate efficient, accurate information processing, but, because they represent nonnormative shortcuts, they can occasionally produce inaccurate inferential "illusions," or biases.

The three types of heuristics cited are relevant to our discussion of cognition in depression. The first, "availability," refers to the tendency, when generating inferences, to rely on the ease with which information can be recalled rather than on its more formal logical properties. Such factors as the familiarity of relevant instances and the salience of those instances for an individual affect the ease with which they can be recalled. Nisbett and Borgida (1975) provided a classic example—that of the individual who bases his or her decision regarding what type of car to buy on a vivid description given by an acquaintance who bought a "lemon" rather than on the far more solid evidence provided by a respected consumer magazine.

The second heuristic, "representativeness," refers to the tendency to base judgments on perceived similarity rather than on more formal logical principles. An example drawn from Ross (1977) involves inferring that an individual described as an avid collector of Chinese art is more likely to be a professor of Chinese studies than a professor of psychology. In this instance, the ascription of attribute (belongingness) was based more on the perceived similarity of interest and profession than on a normative understanding of the far greater numbers of psychology professors relative to Chinese art professors.

The third type of heuristic, "anchoring and adjustment," refers to the apparent tendency for people to fail to revise (adjust) existing beliefs (anchors) as much as might be expected when they acquire new information. A common example is the phenomenon of developing an impression about someone on the basis of a first contact and then only slowly modifying that impression after subsequent, contrary experiences.

This listing of heuristics is far from exhaustive. As we shall see in a subsequent section, many of the distortions in information processing described by Beck for depressed populations may be recognizable as variations of one or more of the preceding heuristics. What is clear is that the information-processing strategies followed by nondepressed individuals appear frequently to operate in nonnormative ways.

There is also a tendency for all individuals to perceive *covariation* between events only poorly (for a review, see Nisbett & Ross, 1980). In brief, most people attend to, recall, and utilize only instances of co-occurrence in evaluating covariation (cf. Jenkins & Ward, 1965; Smedslund, 1963) rather than following the more appropriate strategy of evaluating all pairings of occurrence/nonoccurrence between two classes of events. In addition, the presence of an *a priori* theory relating two events appears to increase the likelihood that an individual will perceive covariation between them. These investigations of the detection of covariation provide a bleak picture of the capacity of the average individual to detect covariation accurately.

Schematic Knowledge Representations

The other major factor in information processing appears to be the role played by the presence of schematic knowledge representations. "Cognitive schemata" are thought to be naive theories organizing information concerning some stimulus domain. These knowledge representations are seen as playing a major role in determining (1) what information is retrieved from long-term memory, (2) what new information is perceived and how that information is processed, and (3) how the most critical types of inferences, that is, causality, attribute, and prediction, are generated.

Neisser (1976) has been perhaps the most active recent proponent of the schema concept in modern cognitive psychology. He defined schemata as that portion of the entire perceptual cycle which is internal to the perceiver, modifiable by experience, and somewhat specific to what is being perceived. The schema accepts information as it becomes available at sensory surfaces and is changed by that information; it directs movements and exploratory activities that make more information available, by which it is further modified" (Neisser, 1976, p. 54). The key aspect for our purposes is that while schemata may indeed be modified by experience, they in turn modify our perception of that experience. This latter process, referred to as "assimilation," describes the case in which incoming information is differentially recognized, processed, and, in fact, distorted in a manner compatible with existing knowledge representations. Furthermore, as Neisser points out, information search may be guided by existing schematic organizations.

Kihlstrom and Nasby (1981) noted that the schema concept is hardly a unitary one, with different theorists defining the construct in subtly different ways.

Although this conceptual variance clearly will need to be addressed, the basic commonalities appear to outweigh the differences. Markus (1977) provided a particularly thoughtful set of operations for detecting in a nontautological fashion, the manner in which schematic processes function, and Cantor and Mischel (Cantor, 1980a, 1980b; Cantor & Mischel, 1977, 1979) extended these operations to person and situation perception.

Kelley (1972, 1973) and Tversky and Kahneman (1980) described the operation of schematic organizations in the causal attribution process. Of greatest interest for our purposes is the proclivity described by Tversky and Kahneman that most people have for generating theories based on patently inadequate data. This proclivity, combined with a reticence to revise those existing theories based on disconfirming data, results in the generation and perpetuation of inaccurate beliefs. In essence, most nondepressives appear to be liberal theory generators and conservative theory revisers. These theories, particularly when organized into larger schemata, take on a life of their own; they are buttressed by the operation of heuristics in the face of new information.

Overall, a strong case can be made that the thought processes of nondepressed populations are dominated by nonnormative information-processing strategies. The operation of these heuristics and schemata need not produce biases and inaccurate beliefs, but it easily does; once generated, these biases and inaccuracies usually prove quite difficult to rectify. As Nisbett and Ross (1980) observe, all of these statements appear to be relatively true, even before one considers the operation of motivational factors. That is, people may generate and hold inaccurate beliefs and schemata in the absence of a desire to do anything other than process information efficiently. Motivational factors, such as a desire to make oneself look or feel better, undoubtedly complicate information processing even further, but a wide range of biases, distortions, and inaccuracies can be accounted for solely on the basis of what we know about the operation of purely cognitive processes.

In evaluating our three models, this literature, which points out the noncorrespondence of nondepressives' beliefs and processing to external reality and to normative strategies, appears to speak against Model 1. It appears that nonpsychopathological populations frequently rely on nonnormative strategies, which may lead to the adoption and maintenance of inaccurate, if benign, beliefs.

COGNITIVE CONTENT AND PROCESSES IN DEPRESSIVES

Schemata and Distortions in Depressive Information Processing: Beck's Classical View

In the early 1960s, Aaron Beck began asserting the primacy of cognitive errors and information processing in the affective disorders (Beck, 1963, 1967). On the basis of clinical observation, Beck argued that depressive belief systems appear to be dominated by negative cognitive schemata; he defined these schemata in a manner strikingly consistent with definitions held in the cognitive literature. According to

Beck, these schematic processes are particularly organized in accordance with the negative cognitive triad, that is, negative beliefs about the self and negative views of the world and of the future. Beck also asserted that these negatively valenced cognitive schemata are frequently erroneous, at least in part, if not in whole. This inaccuracy is most clearly evident in psychotic depressives, who may hold frankly delusional beliefs (e.g., that they have died, that they are responsible for all of the evil in the world, that evil odors emanate from their bodies). Less fantastic but similarly inaccurate beliefs are also thought to be present in the less severely depressed.

Beck is not the only theorist to posit that negative, false beliefs play a role in the etiology and maintenance of depression. Seligman's (1975) original learned helplessness theory essentially argued for the role of the erroneous perception of noncontingency between one's own efforts and important outcomes. The reformulated attributional helplessness model (Abramson, Seligman, & Teasdale, 1978) is even more explicitly cognitive in nature; idiosyncratic variability in the causal attributions made for undesirable and desirable outcomes is posited to largely determine who develops the erroneous perception of noncontingency.

In addition to positing the operation of schematic knowledge representations in depression, Beck (1963, 1967, 1976) argued for the existence of identifiable distorting processes. Chief among these are "selective abstraction," in which an individual attends to, stores, or recalls only those instances that are consistent with existing belief systems; "arbitrary inference," in which an individual generates causal explanations, ascribes characteristics, or makes predictions that are unwarranted in terms of any existing information (but that are consistent with that individual's schematic knowledge representations); and "all-or-none thinking," in which an individual ignores the subtleties of complex information and instead engages in superficial analyses of situations that fit with existing belief systems. Each of these "distortions" actually operates in a manner totally analogous to the operation of Tversky and Kahneman's heuristics. At present, our working thesis is as follows: *The distortions in information processing described by Beck as operating in depressives are actually representatives of the ubiquitous class of events labeled "heuristics" by Tversky and Kahneman.* In discriminating between the accuracy of beliefs and the normativeness of information processing, we would argue that both depressives and nondepressives may be inaccurate in many of their beliefs, although typically in opposite ways; at the same time, both may share the same general nonnormative heuristics. We know of no empirical evidence that speaks either for or against this premise, but we think the parallels between heuristics in nondepressives and "distortions" in depressives are so striking as to merit study.

If these speculations are valid, then the distortions identified by Beck as nonnormative processes serving to maintain the depressive schema may not be unique to depression. When, as happens in therapy, the therapist seeks to offset the pernicious influence of such distortions in information processing, he or she may be working against information-processing strategies universally employed by all humans, depressed or not.

The major challenges to Beck's model and to that of Abramson *et al.* come from two sources. First, the recent research on depressive realism suggests that while depressives may be negative, they are not necessarily inaccurate (Alloy & Abramson, 1979; Lewinsohn *et al.*, 1980). The second challenge derives from recent research by Davis and colleagues (Davis, 1979a, 1979b; Davis & Unruh, 1981), which suggested that depressives, unlike nondepressives, do not evidence schematic organization in their information processing. In the next two sections, we explore these two bodies of research, respectively.

Depressive Realism

A recent article by Alloy and Abramson (1979), subtitled "Sadder but Wiser," cast doubt on the claim that depressives are inaccurate when they are negative. In a series of studies assessing the capacity of depressed and nondepressed college students to detect contingencies between their own behavior and subsequent positive outcomes, these researchers found that the depressives were more accurate than the nondepressives, who consistently overestimated the degree of control they exerted. On tasks in which the outcomes were bad, the depressives more accurately judged the amount of control they exerted than did the nondepressives, who underestimated the amount of control they had. Based on these findings, Alloy and Abramson suggested that depressives may be more accurate in the inferences they draw across a variety of situations. Harking back to Freud's (1917/1957) classic observation in *Mourning and Melancholia,* the suggestion is that depressives are the only accurate perceivers of the true nature of the human condition—that it is depraved—and of the universe—that it is perverse.

Alloy and Abramson's depressive realism phenomenon was observed on a specific task in which individuals were asked to judge the degree of contingency between responses and outcomes. Consistent with the classical position, depressives typically inferred a lower response–outcome contingency for good outcomes and a higher response–outcome contingency for bad outcomes than did nondepressives. In a finding directly at variance with the classical position, however, the depressives' estimates were closer to a normatively calculated baseline than were the nondepressives'. Initially, it was surprising to many (including us) that nondepressed, "normal" individuals would be as inaccurate in their judgments of contingencies as they were in this study. Given the wealth of other data documenting the operation of schematic knowledge structures and heuristic strategies in the inferential processes of normal individuals (cf. Kahneman *et al.*, 1982; Nisbett & Ross, 1980), it appears that the anomalous finding that requires explanation is the depressives' apparent accuracy, not the nondepressives' relative inaccuracy.

The implication of these findings—that depressives are accurate information processors—is at odds with our experience in using cognitive therapy with depressed patients to identify and test their beliefs. On the other hand, there are no evident flaws in Alloy and Abramson's design or logic that would lead us to question the internal validity of their findings. The dilemma posed by these apparently discrepant pieces of information may suggest a more complex interaction between accuracy of judgment and level of depression. Specifically, it raises the possibility that whereas mildly depressed individuals may be more accurate than nondepressed individuals, more severely depressed individuals are not. This view holds that whereas nondepressives appear to distort information in a positive direction, moderately to severely clinically depressed patients distort information in a negative direction. Mildly depressed individuals may not distort information in either direction, or if they do, the distortion may not be readily detectable.

Ruehlman, West, and Pasahow (1985) recently published a review of empirical studies on judgment of contingency, attributions of causality, expectancy estimates, and self-schemata/self-reference that appear to support this tripartite distinction. They noted that in these studies nondepressives consistently displayed evaluative responses that were biased in a positive direction. They also noted a consistent tendency for mildly depressed individuals to be "relatively accurate across a wide range of conditions" (p. 81); mild depressives evidenced neither positive nor negative biases. Both of these conclusions are consistent with those of Alloy & Abramson (1979). In addition, however, they concluded that there was evidence of a tendency for severely depressed patients to be negatively biased in their evaluative responses. This evidence would help to account for why Alloy and Abramson, as well as others, have found mildly depressed individuals to be bias free, whereas clinical experience (including our own) suggests that more severely depressed persons evidence negative biases.

Ruehlman *et al.*'s evidence for a depressive negative bias, however, comes mainly from studies that they classified as being in the area of self-schemata/self-reference. Several studies suggested the presence of negative self-schemata and negative self-referent judgments in severely depressed patients. Neither was found in mildly depressed patients, and nondepressed patients evidenced positive self-schemata and positive self-referent judgments. Ruehlman *et al.* reported that there were no studies of severely depressed individuals' judgment of contingency and that the evidence for a negative expectancy or attributional style for severe depressives was mixed. Thus, though there is some evidence to suggest that severely depressed persons differ cognitively from mildly depressed persons in evidencing the negative thinking errors hypothesized by cognitive intervention theorists, this evidence is hardly conclusive. In the next section, we will examine the question of whether there are depressive schemata. But first, we shall consider a study that appears to provide evidence of depressive realism among clinically depressed individuals.

Lewinsohn and his colleagues (Lewinsohn *et al.*, 1980) videotaped the interactions in social groups of clinically depressed and nondepressed individuals. The participants then viewed their own videotaped interactions and rated their behavior with regard to the levels of social skills exhibited. These tapes were also rated on the same social skills variables by trained independent observers.

The results indicated that although the depressives typically rated their own social skills lower than the nondepressives rated theirs, it was the nondepressives who did not agree with the independent judges. Although the two groups did not differ with regard to their levels of social skills as rated by independent judges, the depressives provided self-ratings that were similar to those provided by the judges, whereas the nondepressives rated their social skills levels more benignly than did the judges. Accepting the independent judges' rating as reflecting normative "reality," the authors argued that the nondepressives were unrealistically positive in their evaluation of their own levels of social skills, whereas the depressives were brutally honest (and accurate) in their self-ratings.

As with the Alloy and Abramson (1979) study, the results of the Lewinsohn *et al.* study appear to be at least suggestive of a depressive realism phenomenon. Nonetheless, there are two factors that might mitigate against such an interpretation. First, it is not clear that the ratings of the independent observers can or should be taken as representing the "true" state of nature. Any judgments are subject to their own sources of artifact (e.g., see Landy & Farr's [1980] review of the literature on job performance rating, and it is quite possible that nondepressives in the observer mode had a tendency to underestimate others' social skills. The authors clearly preferred the interpretation that it was the nondepressives in the self-observation condition who were benignly inaccurate, but it is not clear why nondepressives should be accurate when making judgments about others and inaccurate when making judgments about themselves. Clearly, more research is needed on this issue before we can comfortably agree as to what constitutes *valid* measurement of the social skills construct.

Second, and clearly related, is the potential confound created by the distinction between actor and observer rating perspectives. A considerable literature has accrued suggesting that actors make very different inferences and judgments than do observers for the same events (Jones & Davis, 1965). Taylor and colleagues suggested that these differences may be best understood as deriving from different foci of attention (Taylor & Fiske, 1975). Although all ratings in the Lewinsohn *et al.* (1980) design were generated by individuals in the observer mode, the actual participants had prior access to information available only to actors. Specifically, participants knew what it was like to be in the experimental situation, most likely had opinions about their social skills based on previous experience, and, as a consequence of those two factors, probably had different ideas about what could be inferred from observations of their behavior in that situation. Before concluding that depressives were necessarily more accurate than nondepressives, it would have been interesting to see how each set of participants rated others' social behavior as well as their own. Our expectation is that depressives would rate their own behavior lower than the behavior of others and that nondepressives would do the converse. In addition, we expect that depressives would be universally benign in their ratings of others (whether those others were depressed or not). In essence, we predict that neither depressives nor nondepressives would be universally accurate. Rather, we suggest that depressives typically view their own actions negatively and the actions of others less negatively (whether those others are depressed or not), whereas nondepressives evidence the opposite tendencies. Rather than being universally accurate, we predict that depressed and nondepressed judgments would be dominated by schematic-governed processes equal in strength but opposite in content. The results we would expect to observe in an experimental situation like the one we just discussed would be a function of these processes and self–other perceptual anomalies.

Not all studies that have employed mildly depressed and nondepressed subjects have demonstrated a consistent accuracy in the judgments of depressed subjects. Garber and Hollon (1980) found that whereas nondepressives used feedback to adjust their expectations for future success on a task on which they were told they had control, depressives did not. Despite other indications that the depressives believed that the task required skill on their part, they did not change their expectations for success following feedback any more than they did on tasks whose outcomes they knew depended on chance. This finding suggests that whereas depressives may appear to make reasonable, accurate judgments in one situation, the same schemata and heuristics may result in unreasonable judgments in a different situation.

Overall, though we are not confident that the depressive realism phenomenon will survive subsequent investigation, most of the available experimental literature appears to support this interpretation, at least for mildly depressed individuals. (For a more complete review of the literature on depressive realism, see Chapter 8, this volume.) We suspect, however, that the information processing of both depressives and nondepressives will ultimately be found to be dominated by existing schemata and processing heuristics that lead to predictable and opposing inaccuracies in judgment.

It is possible that mildly depressed individuals will often appear to make relatively unbiased judgments as a result of the presence of competing depressive and nondepressive schemata, which offset each other. An alternative possibility is that though depressed individuals will be accurate in some situations, they will be inaccurate in others; this could occur as a result of an interplay of cognitive processes that are thus far poorly understood. We cannot, however, rule out the possibility that at least mild depressives are universally accurate, while nondepressives are optimistically inaccurate. Individuals who evidence low levels of depression may do so as a result of viewing themselves and their environments more critically, and hence accurately.

In a subsequent section, we will discuss the implications of depressive realism for cognitive therapy. For now, it is clear that we cannot choose between our Models 1 and 2 on the one hand versus Model 3 on the other solely on the basis of this literature.

Depressive Schemata: Differences between Depressives and Nondepressives

As crucial to our understanding of judgmental processes as the issue of whether depressive distortions function like nondepressive heuristics is Beck's other assertion—that depressives' thinking is dominated by schematic knowledge representations. Initially, the evidence, provided by Davis and colleagues, suggested an absence of schematic knowledge representations in depressed populations (Davis, 1979a, 1979b; Davis & Unruh, 1981). Applying a depth-of-processing paradigm to clinical depressives and nondepressed controls, Davis (1979a) found evidence for schematic knowledge representations among the nondepressives but not among the depressives. In this paradigm, subjects were asked to make structural, semantic, and self-referent decisions for sets of adjectives. Following these tasks, subjects engaged in an incidental recall task in which they were to list as many of the adjectives as they could remember. Greater recall of self-referent-rated adjectives was taken to be indicative of the operation of schematic processes. In subsequent studies, Davis (1979b) and Davis and Unruh (1981) replicated this basic phenomenon for short-term depressives but found evidence suggesting the presence of schematic processing in longer term depressives. Based on these findings, Davis and Unruh (1981) argued that "some depressives show nonschema based self-reference" and that "the self-schema of the short-term depressive is not a strong organizer of personal information" but that those self-schema are "a stronger information processor for long-term depressives" (pp. 125–126, 130).

Kuiper and Derry (1980; Derry & Kuiper, 1981) criticized Davis and colleagues for selecting only nondepressive adjectives for their stimulus materials. Such a limited array of stimulus materials is alleged to work against detecting depressive schemata, if such schemata exist.

To test this hypothesis, Derry and Kuiper (1981) carefully selected adjectives so that both depressive and nondepressive stimuli were present in the full array. Three sets of subjects (clinically depressed persons, clinical controls, and nonclinical controls) were exposed to these adjectives under each of three conditions (structural, semantic, and self-referent judgment tasks). Subjects were then tested again on an incidental recall task. As predicted, both depressives and nondepressives evidenced schematic processing but for different content domains. That is, depressives were more likely to recall *depressive* adjectives that they had endorsed as being "like me" in the self-referent task, whereas nondepressives were more likely to recall *nondepressive* adjectives that they had endorsed as being "like me" on the same self-referent task. The authors interpreted these findings as providing support for a "content-specificity" hypothesis, in which schematic organizations differing in their content are seen as operating in both depressives and nondepressives.

Overall, it appears that, as with nondepressives, the thinking of depressed individuals may be best described as being organized around schematic structures and frequently functioning through heuristic strategies rather than normative processes. There is strong evidence that the content and/or organization of the schemata differ between depressives and nondepressives. Note that the evidence for this difference is derived from a study in which the depressives were more severely (clinically) depressed individuals. It is possible that mildly (nonclinically) depressed individuals would not evidence these depressive schemata.

There is, to date, no clear evidence as to whether or not such schematic organizations are stable over time when depressives move from depressed to nondepressed states. Recent work by Hammen and colleagues (Hammen, Marks, de Mayo, & Mayol, 1985) appears to suggest that these schemata do not remain intact or that if they do, they are certainly less accessible. Hammen and colleagues reported following depressed individuals from depressed to nondepressed states with a depth-of-processing paradigm and finding that the presence of depressive schemata appeared to be state dependent. This finding is consistent with parallel work done by Lewinsohn, Steinmetz, Larson, and Franklin (1981) and by Hollon,

Kendall, and Lumry (1986), who found that other measures of allegedly depressive cognition also appear to be state dependent.

Although the findings of Hammen and her colleagues rule out the characterization of depressive schemata as stable, *active traits,* they do not rule out the possibility that these schemata continue to exist. It remains possible that depressive schemata are, in fact, present but are not detectable unless they are evoked by appropriate stimuli. The classical view espoused by Beck has always been a diathesis–stress model (e.g., see Beck, 1967 or 1976). In fact, Beck has long argued that depressotypic schemata should be propensities emerging in particular (i.e., stressful) situations, not traitlike phenomena that are always evident.

Researchers of biologic processes in depression have also considered a diathesis–stress model. Several promising biologic variables that differentiate depressed from nondepressed populations have turned out to be state dependent in nature, meaning that they may simply be symptomatic correlates of depression rather potential causes. In recent work, Depue and colleagues (Depue & Kleinman, 1979) suggested that biochemical processes can be identified that are *not* state dependent if remitted former depressives or currently asymptomatic individuals at risk are first stressed prior to assessment of the biochemical diathesis.

It is not clear that we can chose among the three competing models on the basis of the available literature, although we can probably reject aspects of each. In Figure 12-4, we present our best guess, based on the available literature, of what the probable state of nature is. In this figure, we have added two features. First, we have distinguished between "normativeness" and "realism." Thought processes can be more or less normative, that is, representative of the application of rational, logical information-processing strategies, as opposed to being nonrepresentative and dependent on processing heuristics. In either event, the inference drawn can be more or less accurate, that is, realistic.

In general, nondepressives are seen as relying on nonnormative processes and

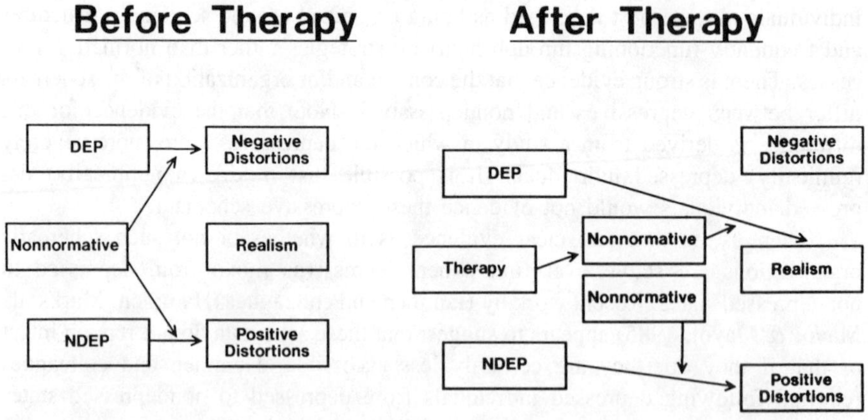

Figure 12-4. Probable relationships between cognition in depressives and cognition in nondepressives before and after treatment of depressives.

being distorted in a positive, or optimistic, fashion. However, they are not seen as being high on "realism." This does not change over time, since these individuals do not receive treatment. Depressives, at least those who manifest clinical levels of symptomatology, are seen as being as nonnormative as the nondepressives, perhaps in a remarkably similar way stylistically. They clearly differ from normals in the content of their beliefs and in their schematic organizations, being just as prone to distortion, but in a far more negative fashion. The depressives are not, as a result, any more accurate than the nondepressives. They are, however, clearly more pessimistic.

It remains to be seen where more mildly depressed individuals will fall on these two dimensions. They may exhibit nonnormative processes like those of the nondepressives and depressives, and may also evidence depressive schemata. On the other hand, they may differ from both of these other groups in exhibiting normative processes and in evidencing schemata that are neither overly positive nor overly negative. Where these groups fall on these dimensions raises critical issues for our theories of change. During treatment with cognitive therapy, depressives are seen as increasingly relying on compensatory strategies that affect the operation of information-processing heuristics, more and more closely approximating normative information-processing strategies. We will return later to how and why we think this occurs. These more normative strategies are used to alter the content of the negative systems and either to alter depressive schemata or to forment a switch to more benign, preexisting nondepressive schemata. In essence, we argue that cognitive therapy works, when it works, by teaching depressives to think in a very atypical fashion, *normatively,* in an effort to alter belief systems and structuring organizations that maintain the depressive symptomatology.

Cognitive therapists tend to believe that they are teaching their clients to think more realistically. This may or may not be true, depending on the validity of the depressive realism hypothesis. They do, we believe, teach their clients to think more normatively, something the typical "person on the street" usually does not do; we believe that it is this careful attention to information-processing strategies that produces the therapy-specific changes observed. In the sections that follow, we lay out a model of the therapeutic change process, describe the major processes and procedures of cognitive therapy, and discuss the model and these procedures in light of the recent cognitive and social cognitive literature.

MODELS OF CHANGE

Cognitive therapy, despite its name, integrates cognitive and behavioral procedures in an effort to alter existing belief systems and facilitate problem solving (see Beck *et al.,* 1979, for the most up-to-date and comprehensive description of this approach). As such, it is only one of several variants on a basically cognitive–behavioral theme. (For descriptions of other cognitive–behavioral approaches, see, for example, Foreyt & Rathjen, 1978; Goldfried & Davison, 1976; Kendall & Hollon, 1979; Mahoney, 1974; or Meichenbaum, 1977.)

The essence of cognitive therapy, as practiced by Beck and colleagues, is the process of treating beliefs as hypotheses to be tested rather than as established facts. The process of testing beliefs involves a careful review of evidence already available and/or prospective hypothesis testing, in which the client is encouraged to plan and execute empirical tests of his or her beliefs (Beck, 1970; Beck *et al.,* 1979). This process has been summarized by the term "collaborative empiricism" (Hollon & Beck, 1979), which is intended to reflect the purposive, experimental, evidential focus of therapy. Perhaps the best analogy that can be used to describe the progress of therapy is that the client and therapist function much like a talented graduate student and his or her advisor. The student supplies his or her own hypotheses and energies, while the advisor provides consultation regarding how to turn ideas into testable propositions.

Major Elements in the Change Process

In Figure 12-5, we present an overview of what we consider to be the major elements of the clinical change process. In this model, expanded only slightly from a model originally presented elsewhere (Hollon, DeRubeis, & Evans, 1981a, 1981b; Hollon & Kriss, 1984), we attempt to delineate the important processes that occur in therapeutic interventions. The "*descriptive*/differential components" element refers to all of the distinctive elements in any given treatment package, with "differential" in parentheses because some elements are unique to a given approach, whereas others are shared with one or more alternate interventions. The "active components" element is intended to highlight the fact that some, but by no means all, of the components of treatment play an active role in the change process. Therapist variables are of little interest for our discussion here, but this element

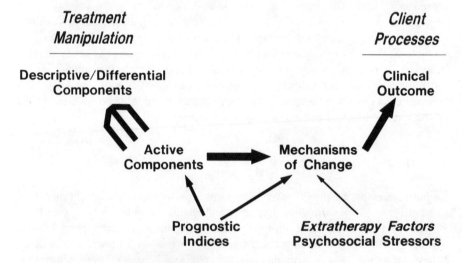

Figure 12-5. A model for the change process in the treatment of depression.

could easily have been included to convey a recognition that each therapist doubtless adds variance to the treatment package he or she delivers over and above those aspects specified by the therapeutic "school" being adhered to. These elements constitute the major sources of input in the treatment package.

On the "patient" side of the ledger are patient "prognostic indices," pretreatment individual-difference variables that influence the course of treatment (e.g., age, sex, intelligence, psychological mindedness); "mechanisms of change"; and "clinical outcomes." The mechanisms of change are conceptualized as those patient processes that mediate change in important clinical variables. In general, "mechanisms" are processes that derive their importance from their hypothesized causal mediation status, "clinical outcome" variables are typical indices of change by which the effectiveness of treatments is measured. Those latter processes are deemed sufficiently important in their own right; they are important enough to lead some people into treatment in order to change their status, and others into devising and testing therapies that purport to do so. "Extra therapy factors" are included, but not further discussed, since we recognize that important determinants of the change process occur outside of treatment. For our discussion, we will focus on cognitive content and processes as the potential mechanisms of interest and on the clinical syndrome of depression as the clinical outcome variable.

The arrows in the model represent presumed directions of causality. If we analyze the theory behind cognitive therapy for depression, it is evident that the differential components of the therapy are its integrated cognitive and behavioral change processes. Other nonspecific factors, such as the classic Rogerian facilitative conditions of warmth, genuinenness, and empathy, are also believed to be important accompaniments of these techniques (Beck *et al.,* 1979). These same differential components (integrated cognitive and behavioral components) are also considered most likely to be the specific active components producing change. A cognitive theory of therapy would specify that it is the process of empirical hypothesis testing, operationalized through those cognitive and behavioral techniques, that produces those therapeutic changes unique to cognitive therapy.

The mechanisms of interest are largely cognitive in nature and may well prove to be the schematic knowledge structures and heuristic processes described in earlier sections. We are unaware of any studies regarding the role of schemata and heuristics as potential causal mediators in which they are manipulated by active treatment procedures and, in turn, mediate changes in clinical depression; this is clearly an area that deserves exploration. The studies to date exploring schematic structures and heuristic processes in depression have all been descriptive psychopathology studies (e.g., Davis, 1979a, 1979b, Davis & Unruh, 1981, Derry & Kuiper, 1981). Only Hammen, Marks, de Mayo, and Mayol (1985) examined longitudinal changes in the same populations, but their study did not interpose treatment.

Research evaluating schemata and heuristics as potential differential mechanisms of change appears to hold great promise. In essence, if cognitive therapy works in the way its originators believe it works, the adequate implementation of the cognitive and behavioral change procedures (components) should produce measurable changes in key cognitive measures (mechanisms) as well as in levels of depression (outcome). Furthermore, levels of change within each of these three types of variables should be correlated. Given that the technologies now exist for assessing both therapy components (e.g., see DeRubeis, Evans, Hollon, Tuason, & Garvey, 1986; DeRubeis, Hollon, Evans, & Bemis, 1982; Evans *et al.*, 1983; Hollon, Evans, Auerbach, DeRubeis, Kriss, Piasecki, Grove, Elkin, Lowery, & Tuason, 1986; Luborsky, Woody, McLellan, O'Brien, & Rosenzweig, 1982; Young, 1979) and potential cognitive mechanisms, such research will doubtless be conducted.

Issues Relating to Models of Change

It is important to recognize that though schemata and/or heuristics may well be the cognitive mechanisms of interest, they are not necessarily the *only* such potential cognitive processes, nor will they necessarily prove to be easy to assess. Indeed, Beck has long talked of schematic structuring principles and information-processing distortions (which we have equated with heuristics) as mechanisms. It may be, however, that the end products of information processing, the inferences and judgments made by the patient, will be the actual mechanisms directly participating in the causal chain resulting in depression (if, indeed, the cognitive model of depression is even partially valid). Thus the causal attributions an individual entertains for events, the characteristic ascriptions he or she makes, and the predictions he or she generates may be most directly related to depressed mood and to deficits in behavioral response initiation. Hollon and Garber (1980) argued for the importance of each of these processes: Causal attributions are viewed as being most critically involved in the etiology of a given episode; ascriptions, in the formation of self-concept; and disconfirmations of predictions, in treatments. Schematic knowledge organizations and heuristics (distortions) may play a role in the generation of those end products, but, if it is not a sufficient causal role, we may well have misspecified the specific cognitive mediators. For example, two depressed individuals may evidence comparable depressive schematic organizations, but the first may leave his or her depressive cognitive end products unchallenged, whereas the second, presumably benefiting from skills acquired during cognitive therapy, may go the extra step and reality test those beliefs. Both individuals might evidence depressotypic schemata and heuristics when tested, yet the latter, by virtue of exercising additional unmeasured cognitive mechanisms further "downstream" in the causal chain, might evidence fewer depressotypic inferences and judgments and lower levels of clinical depression. This issue, which can be labeled the "mechanism misspecification issue," must be considered in efforts to identify the mechanisms by which treatments produce their effect.

Another state of nature that may well complicate efforts at theory testing is the possibility that some "final common pathway" exists for treatment-related change, analogous to that proposed by Akiskal and McKinney (1973, 1975) for the etiology of the affective disorders. For example, it is clearly the case that any of several disparate interventions is effective in the treatment of depression. (For reviews of the outcome literature, see, for example, DeRubeis & Hollon, 1981; Hollon, 1981; Hollon & Beck, 1978, 1979.) Although it seems unlikely that such disparate interventions as tricyclic pharmacotherapy and cognitive therapy work through the same active components, it may prove to be that each mobilizes the same mechanisms *but in different orders*. Thus tricyclic pharmacotherapy may work by virtue of altering amine-mediated transmission in the limbic region, but changes at the synapse may produce changes in cognitive structures and processes. Conversely, cognitive therapy may work by changing cognitive structures and processes, which subsequently produces changes in neurotransmitter processes at the synapse. Studies looking for change in specific mechanisms following specific interventions may produce evidence of universal change in all mechanisms with *any* treatment. (For an expanded discussion of this issue, see Hollon, DeRubeis, & Evans, 1986.) The interpretative problem raised by this pattern of results is that while it is compatible with a "common mechanism" hypothesis, it is also compatible with a model in which some or all of the purported mechanisms are causally inert, epiphenomenal consequences of some other unspecified active mechanism. We can refer to this interpretative confound generated by universal change mechanisms as the "common mechanisms issue." Causal modeling strategies (e.g., Heise, 1975; Kenny, 1979) or extremely fine grained experimental studies, far more sophisticated than any currently in the literature, may be required in order to clarify this issue.

Is there any existing evidence that speaks to any of the preceding hypotheses? As yet, the area is so new that little information is currently available. In our recently completed research trial (Hollon, DeRubeis, *et al.*, 1986; DeRubeis *et al.*, 1986), we attempted to collect both component and mechanism measures at least partially relevant to the preceding hypotheses, although our efforts now strike us as being relatively crude and conceptually naive. In this design, primary unipolar depressed patients were treated with cognitive therapy, imipramine pharmacotherapy, or combined cognitive therapy–pharmacotherapy during a 3-month acute treatment phase. Half of the pharmacotherapy-treated patients were continued on maintenance medication for the first year of a 2-year follow-up; all other patients were followed without scheduled treatment for 2 years. Patients evidencing a clinical relapse were reassigned to a treatment of their choice.

All treatment groups showed marked clinical improvement, with the group receiving combined cognitive therapy–pharmacotherapy evidencing the greatest response. On a composite measure of depression that combined all symptomatic outcome information available to us, patients in the combined-treatment group (1) experienced significantly more improvement than did patients in pharmacotherapy alone and (2) evidenced a trend toward a significant difference from patients who received cognitive therapy alone. Patients who received cognitive therapy alone or pharmacotherapy alone did not differ in the improvement they experienced. With regard to the components issues cited earlier, measures of explicit modality-specific components (cognitive and behavioral techniques in cognitive therapy, and blood plasma imipramine/desipramine levels in pharmacotherapy) were elevated in the appropriate cells (DeRubeis *et al.*, 1986).

With regard to the mechanism issue, cited earlier, cognitive end products, as measured by the Automatic Thoughts Questionnaire (ATQ; Hollon & Kendall, 1980), the DAS (Weissman & Beck, 1978), the Hopelessness Scale (Beck, Weissman, Lester, & Trexler, 1974), and the ASQ (Seligman, Abramson, Semmel, & von Baeyer, 1979), evidenced change in all conditions, including pharmacotherapy. Change in the DAS and the ASQ, however, was greater among those patients who experienced improvement in cognitive therapy than among those who did not improve in their depression level or who did improve but who did not receive cognitive therapy. In other words, improvement in depression was accompanied by major changes in the DAS and the ASQ only among patients who received cognitive therapy. With respect to biochemical mechanism measures, urinary MHPG, a metabolite of norepinephrine, did not change differentially in patients who received pharmacotherapy versus those who received cognitive therapy. These data suggest that whereas MHPG and some cognitive processes appear to be state dependent, other cognitive processes, including those measured by the ASQ and the DAS, may be mechanisms by which cognitive therapy exerts its effect.

With regard to clinical relapse[1] after active treatment, differences appeared favoring either continued maintenance medication or cognitive therapy, with or without medication, over pharmacotherapy alone without subsequent maintenance (Evans *et al.*, 1986). Cognitive measures obtained at the completion of treatment appeared to offer good predictive ability as to who would eventually relapse during the 2-year follow-up. Among patients who received cognitive therapy, the best predictor of subsequent relapse was the "quality" of the cognitive therapy they received; those patients who received cognitive therapy that was rated as having adhered closely to prescribed cognitive therapy techniques and as having been expertly delivered were less likely to relapse than patients who received less adequate cognitive therapy. Since most of those techniques are in the service of identifying, testing, and correcting inaccurate beliefs, these data support the importance of cognitive therapy's focus on depressive distortions.

Overall, this study provided strong support for the component theories implicit in both cognitive and pharmacological approaches. The results with regard to the purported mechanisms were less conclusive, although results on at least two of the cognitive measures were suggestive of a differential mechanism for cognitive therapy. Had we employed a mechanism measurement paradigm that was not primarily cross-sectional and diathesis focused (rather than diathesis–stress focused), and had we also measured schematic and heuristic processes as well as cognitive end products, the results may have been even more interesting. Nonetheless, these data suggest that further investigations of these processes may be fruitful.

Other investigations of potential mechanisms have been less encouraging. Rush, Beck, Kovacs, Weissenberger, and Hollon (1982), in a further analysis of data collected in the Rush *et al.* (1977) comparison of cognitive therapy and imipramine pharmacotherapy, did find evidence of greater change in pessimism, as measured by the Hopelessness Scale (Beck *et al.*, 1974). However, the differential changes evident were weak in magnitude and apparent only during midpoints in treatment, not at the end of therapy. Zeiss, Lewinsohn, and Munoz (1979) attempted to measure specific cognitive, behavioral, and interpersonal mechanisms of change as a function of each of those three specific treatments and found universal change, undifferentiated with respect to treatment. Although these authors concluded that change occurred because of nonspecific factors, the absence of any differential manipulation checks (i.e., differential components) and the unvalidated, *ad hoc* nature of the mechanism measures they used preclude drawing any firm conclusions from that study.

In a treatment outcome study similar in design to the study by Hollon, DeRubeis *et al.* (1986) reported on previously, Simons, Garfield, and Murphy (1984) found no evidence of differential change on cognitive measures between depressed patients who received cognitive therapy and those who received pharmacotherapy alone. The cognitive measures that were employed in this study included the ATQ and the DAS, the latter of which did evidence differential change in our own outcome study (DeRubeis *et al.*, 1986). The ASQ, which also changed more in the cognitively treated patients in our study, was not obtained by Simons *et al.*

Much of the existing evidence suggests that if the measures of end products currently in use are tapping the cognitive constructs of interest, then those constructs are *eventually* likely to be altered by noncognitive as well as cognitive interventions, suggesting the presence of indirect, reciprocal causal pathways. However, findings such as those reported by DeRubeis *et al.* (1986) suggest that if reciprocal changes inevitably occur, we may be able at least to observe different patterns of change among treatments; our ability to do this is an important step in identifying mechanisms. Designs with carefully validated measures, carefully implemented (and documented) differential interventions, and carefully specified temporal lags will probably be needed in order to clarify these issues. As an example of efforts in this direction, Evans (1985) is currently conducting an investigation that might shed more light on the relationship among components of cognitive therapy, cognitive changes, and changes in depressive symptomatology.

Finally, we will need to come to grips with the issues raised earlier regarding the proper specification of the theoretical models to be tested. As noted, Beck's model is best described as a diathesis–stress model in which prepotent cognitive organizations are triggered by real or symbolic environmental stressors. Once triggered, these cognitive organizations function to guide further information search, information processing, and inference generation. The process is analogous to that which occurs when an adult returns to his or her parents' home for a holiday visit. Old patterns of interaction, including clusters of attitudes about oneself and one's role in the world, seem to surface after having lain dormant for years.

The issue is whether those cognitive organizations, if they exist, can readily be assessed outside of the context of the appropriate "stressful" situations. Longitudinal efforts to date, whether tied to treatment or not, have typically involved cross-sectional assessments of cognitive styles, organizations, or end products *without* any effort to ensure that the triggering "stressor" agent is present (e.g., Hammen *et al.*, 1985). It is possible that such a single-component, cross-sectional assessment strategy may fail to identify the presence of existing but dormant differential organizational structures. This issue, which could be referred to as the "theory misspecification issue," has important ramifications for the identification of mechanisms.

In the sections that follow, we first describe in greater detail the actual components of cognitive therapy and then attempt to relate those components to purported mechanisms and probable outcomes with such therapy. It is important to note that the remaining sections are largely speculative in nature. *Empirical* research regarding the actual components of therapy and their theoretical underpinnings is relatively new, and efforts to identify mechanisms of change are practically nonexistent. Although we regard these as being extremely promising areas for future work, most of our comments here are based on clinical speculation rather than on empirical findings.

COGNITIVE THERAPY

As noted, the essence of cognitive therapy is that clients are trained to actively (and more systematically) test the accuracy of their beliefs (cf. Beck *et al.*, 1979; Hollon & Beck, 1979). In actual practice, the approach appears to consist of six major aspects: (1) providing a cognitive rationale; (2) training the client in careful self-monitoring procedures; (3) utilizing behavioral change strategies; (4) identifying, testing, and modifying various specific beliefs, self-statements (automatic thoughts) and distortion processes; (5) identifying, testing, and modifying broad, general patterns of information processing (underlying assumptions); and (6) preparing the patient for termination.

In general, these six aspects unfold in the temporal sequence as listed, although there may be considerable overlap. (It is not unusual, for example, for the therapist to start referring to the eventual termination process in the first treatment session.) Thus this temporal ordering refers to a primary, not an exclusive, emphasis. Further, processes are typically presented within the context of a cognitive rationale. Rather than simply assigning a behavioral task, such as increasing the frequency of "pleasurable" activities, the task is structured so as to test (1) the client's belief that he or she could not do an activity being considered or (2) the client's belief that even if he or she did engage in that activity, it would not be enjoyed.

In an extremely interesting article examining the change process from a social–cognitive perspective, Ross (1977) argues that there appear to be three major ways of producing change in belief systems. The first, which he refers to as the "weight of brute evidence" approach, involves simply exposing an individual to numerous and repeated instances of belief disconfirmation. This approach largely involves overwhelming existing beliefs with the sheer weight of contrary evidence. Given the apparent tendency for normal individuals to distort new information in the direction of existing beliefs (assimilation; Nisbett & Ross, 1980), their greater proclivity to generate theories than to revise them (Tversky & Kahneman, 1980), and the possible *polarizing* impact of disconfirming evidence on existing beliefs (Lord, Ross, & Lepper 1979), reliance on such a mechanism alone appears questionable.

The second major way to change belief systems, according to Ross, involves providing an alternative belief system that accounts for many of the facts currently explained via existing systems. In the extreme, this appears to be the main process behind such phenomena as brain washing or religious conversion.

The third process involves educating the client regarding the nature of distorting processes, which work to assimilate new information into existing belief systems. Ross refers to this type of training as cognitive "process" training.

In essence, cognitive therapy has, quite independently, long utilized each of the three processes Ross identified in the general attitude-change literature. These three processes—identifying evidential disconfirmation, providing alternative explanatory systems, and generating insight into distorting processes—are all major components of cognitive therapy. (For a more extensive components analysis of cognitive therapy from the perspective of Ross's three processes, see Hollon and Garber, in press. In the sections that follow, we provide a brief overview of the main components of cognitive therapy.

Providing a Cognitive Rationale

We believe that it is important to introduce the client to a basic cognitive rationale and to ensure that he or she thoroughly understands it. This rationale holds that what a person believes or thinks (cognition), although it may not necessarily be accurate, can influence how that person feels (affect) and what he or she subsequently does (behavior). The therapist emphasizes that affective distress and behavioral impoverishment may in part reflect inaccurate or dysfunctional beliefs rather than a veridical reading of the true state of external reality.

Training in Self-monitoring

There is considerable reason to believe that most individuals, depressed or otherwise, are not particularly adept at noting, encoding, and retrieving information in a way that facilitates the accurate assessment of covariation (e.g., see Nisbett & Ross, 1980, pp. 90–112). Considerable attention is paid in cognitive therapy to training the client to keep systematic records of events in key domains, both to facilitate communication with the therapist and as a check on distortions in information retrieval and inference generation. Although which systems are actually used may vary with client need and therapist proclivity, most involve some attempt to monitor events and/or activities, affects (or moods), and, typically later, cognitions (see Beck *et al.*, 1979, or Hollon & Kendall, 1981, for a description).

Behavioral Strategies

Cognitive therapy makes use of a number of behavioral activation strategies designed to overcome lethargy and to test belief systems. In general, these strategies are most heavily relied on early in therapy, when clients are the most severely depressed. With particularly retarded or nonfunctioning clients, several of these components might well constitute the major initial emphasis of therapy.

Examples of frequently used behavioral strategies are (1) activity scheduling, in which therapist and client collaboratively plan the client's activities in advance for periods between sessions; (2) pleasurable or mastery activity scheduling, in which specific types of activities (e.g., pleasurable activities like dining out, or masterful activities like arranging to complete some long-avoided project) are executed; (3) "chunking," in which some complex and subjectively overwhelming task is broken into a series of more manageable component steps; and (4) "success therapy," in which some readily accomplishable task is scheduled prior to a more difficult task as a means of priming the client for activity. These and various other behavioral management components are typically presented within the context of a cognitive rationale and for the purpose of providing evidence suitable for testing various beliefs.

Identifying, Testing, and Modifying Specific Beliefs

Perhaps the single most important set of components in cognitive therapy consists of the identification and reality testing of specific beliefs in specific situations and the modification of those beliefs when necessary. This process involves at least five main subcomponents:

1. Identifying potentially inaccurate beliefs that should be subjected to reality-testing procedures. This identification is often guided by targeting beliefs that produce negative affect in the client. In addition, clients are sometimes alerted to specific types of distortions (e.g., thinking about things in black-and-white, "all-or-nothing" terms) that might be particularly prevalent in their thinking.

2. "Distancing" oneself from one's belief, that is, recognizing that any given belief is only a representation of external reality, which can be subjected to efforts to ascertain its accuracy, and not an established fact simply because it is entertained.

3. Exploring the connotative meanings associated with a specific belief. This is important, because affect and behavior typically covary with a larger implicit network of beliefs rather than with a specific accessible cognition. (For example, the simple thought "I'll be fired" is associated with a wide array of additional and idiosyncratic connotations, ranging from "How will I support my family?" to "I've utterly failed as a human being.")

4. Testing the validity of both the specific belief and its associated meaning structure.

5. Modifying beliefs in order to make them more accurate and less dysfunctional.

With regard to the hypothesis-testing process, at least three queries are frequently brought to bear: (1) What's your evidence for that belief? (the evidence question); (2) Is there any other way of looking at it? (the alternative explanation question); and (3) What are the realistic implications of that belief, if it is true? (the implications question).

The evidence question is directly and immediately related to hypothesis testing, since it immediately calls forth a review of the evidence upon which a belief is based and suggests additional evidence that can be gathered on a prospective basis.

The alternative explanation question refers to the introduction of additional plausible explanations for an event or observation beyond the personal or causal attributions generated initially by the client. This step is not actually a reality-testing step in itself. Rather, it approximates the generation of rival plausible hypotheses as a prelude to subsequent reality testing.

The final query, the implications question, involves having the client carefully examine what the realistic implications of a belief would be if it proved to be accurate. In other words, the purpose of this question is to examine the plausibility of additional predictions, which are generated once a given premise is granted.

Often, the process of reality testing beliefs will lead to their modification without any additional attention being paid to doing so. At times, however, it may be necessary for the therapist to review with the client the results of the client's testing and evaluation in order to help him or her arrive at a modified set of beliefs that more accurately reflects reality.

Identifying, Testing, and Modifying Underlying Assumptions

Closely related to the attention paid to specific belief in the previous section is the interest directed later in therapy to more general patterns of assumptive systems. Although it is frequently possible to identify discrete beliefs in specific situations, it often appears that the same types of beliefs recur across apparently disparate situations. Further, examination of the associated connotative meaning systems often elicits consistent themes at a more abstract level. Beck refers to these generic beliefs as "underlying assumptions" (Beck, 1967). These underlying assumptions frequently take the form of general statements that hold across a multitude of situations. The same strategies as those discussed previously are used to address underlying assumptions after they have been identified.

In terms of social cognitive principles, these underlying assumptions may represent prototypical beliefs at the center of connotative meaning structures. In our experience, these underlying assumptions are typically acquired early in life and are rarely, if ever, clearly articulated or consciously experienced, but they are consistent with and basic to a wide range of beliefs across a multitude of situations.

Termination

As noted earlier, the termination process is typically begun in the first session. Throughout treatment, the therapist refers to the client's preparation for termination. In particular, efforts are made to treat the accentuated reality-testing principles as skills to be learned with the therapist's assistance but to be retained long after therapy is over and employed independently of any ongoing intervention. In essence, this practice indicates that there has been an implicit assumption that depressed clients do not naturally utilize these skills when generating inferences. As was discussed earlier, it is questionable whether nondepressed individuals practice these skills as a matter of course. Our suspicion, based on our reading of the social cognitive literature (Kahneman *et al.*, 1982; Nisbett & Ross, 1980), is that they do not.

IMPLICATIONS OF SOCIAL COGNITIVE THEORIES FOR COGNITIVE THERAPY: CHANGING PATTERNS OF PERSONAL AND CAUSAL INFERENCE

Given the hypothesized reliance of cognitive therapy on empirical hypothesis testing as the main differential active component in therapy, what can be said about the probable mechanisms of change? We believe that specification of these mechanisms can progress only as rapidly as our understanding of basic cognitive processes. In general, we predict that the primary detectable changes produced by cognitive therapy will prove to be the introduction of formal reality-testing procedures that go beyond those in which most people typically engage. Specifically, we anticipate that subsequent research will find that depressives are taught to double-check the accuracy of their cognitive end products, that is, their causal attributions, ascriptions of characteristics, and predictions. In this regard, we are predicting that of the three models we presented earlier, Model 2 will ultimately be supported. This represents a change from the position we once held but never fully articulated: that cognitive therapy worked by virtue of leading depressives to think like nondepressives.

Figure 12-6 represents what we think is the likely course of change in therapy.

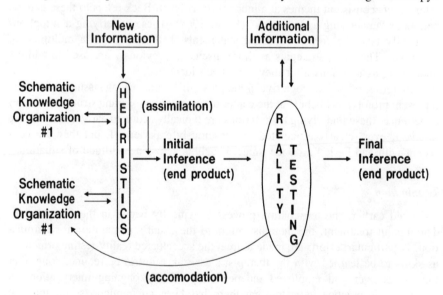

Figure 12-6. Predicted information processes in the treatment of depression.

As new information is encountered, it is processed in the context of whatever schematic system is currently operative (some information may, by its very nature, elicit some other schema). The resulting end product, or inference (e.g., causal attribution, characteristic ascription, or prediction), will be a product of the information, the processing heuristics, and the operative schema. We do *not* anticipate major differences between depressives and nondepressives in the nature of the information-processing heuristics, but we do anticipate big differences in the nature of the operating schemata for depressives versus nondepressives. We do not anticipate that most nondepressives will have even latent depressive schematas, but we do expect that most depressives, at least those with nonchronic histories, will also hold relatively intact nondepressive schemata.

The distortion of incoming information in ways that are consistent with the operating schema and that result from the operation of heuristic processes is consistent with the process of assimilation. The next step in the chain, reality testing, essentially involves the application of various skills that presumably go beyond the operation of heuristic processes. These reality-testing procedures would include, but not be limited to, those skills emphasized in cognitive therapy. We predict that depressives treated with cognitive therapy will exhibit far greater reliance on these reality-testing procedures than will nondepressives, currently depressed individuals, or formerly depressed individuals treated by other means. We stress that we have not yet conducted such tests because we know of no currently existing measures of such reality-testing processes.

Over time, we anticipate that the repeated application of these more normative reality-testing approaches will eventually produce some accommodation in the depressotypic schematic organizations. At the very least, the application of these procedures should increase the probability that a nondepressive schema would override a currently active depressive schema or retard the emergence of one.

CONCLUSIONS

Overall, this chapter raises far more questions than it answers. We have attempted to evaluate cognitive therapy from the perspective of recent advances in social cognition and cognitive psychology but have been frustrated by the fact that little attention has yet been paid to ascertaining what mechanisms actually mediate the change process. Nonetheless, some initial conclusions can be drawn and some suggestions for future research generated.

First, there seems to be considerable evidence that nondepressives are far from normative in their information-processing strategies and that their thinking is heavily influenced by the existence of schematic principles. It is not so clear that the same can be said about depressives; while the evidence clearly supports the existence of depressive schemata, it is mixed regarding the normativeness of depressives' information processing. The possibility was raised that whereas more severely depressed individuals evidence negatively distorted thinking, mildly depressived individuals may be relatively accurate. We suggested that although nondepressives and at least clinical depressives use similarly nonnormative heuristic processes, the content of their schemata is different.

Second, we have yet to specify to our satisfaction precisely what goes on in cognitive therapy, although it appears that training in various reality-testing processes consists of both differential and active treatment components. Again, recent advances in measurement technology should make more careful efforts at theory testing possible. Some models (e.g., depressive realism) might predict that an emphasis in careful reality testing will induce depression, not ameliorate it. Nonetheless, the evident success of cognitive therapy in reducing depression suggests that whatever the active component may be, it is clearly not depressogenic. If the active component is an emphasis on reality testing, that would argue against the depressive realism thesis. Clearly, far more research needs to be conducted in this area.

Third, though it is not yet clear precisely what mechanisms mediate change, we can speculate that our depressed clients acquire skills in therapy that, though not unique, are very different from those employed by most nondepressed individuals. Our best guess is that these skills first appear as checks on the inference-generation process, with existing depressotypic schemata and universal heuristic processes intact. Elsewhere (Hollon, Evans, & DeRubeis, in press) we have described this process in terms of "compensatory skills," which are applied by the client in order to modify the consequences of still active depressotypic schemata- and heuristic-related distortions. Over time, the continued application of these skills may produce changes in the depressotypic schemata through a process of accommodation. In essence, we believe that depressives treated with cognitive therapy do not come to think like nondepressives but that they come to think in ways that are more careful and more normative than those of typical nondepressed persons.

We close by stressing the importance of continued efforts to integrate basic cognitive and social cognitive research with more strictly clinical findings. Our impression has been that much basic research has developed that could well be applied to answering issues related to clinical change. Similarly, many of the recent advances in clinical cognitive-change procedures have not yet received sufficient attention with regard to their theoretical underpinnings. The technologies and paradigms for such evaluations are currently being developed. We anticipate that major strides will soon be made with regard to the articulation and testing of cognitive theories of change.

NOTE

1. The term "relapse" is used here to refer to either a relapse (which may be used more specifically to refer to a return of symptoms from the *same* episode) or a recurrence (which refers to the onset of a *new* episode). Operationally, "relapse" has been variously defined as a return of symptoms following less than 2 months of symptom remission (Spitzer, Endicott, & Robins, 1978) or within 6–9 months of the onset of the index episode (Klerman, 1978). Conversely, "recurrence" has been defined by these same authors as a return of symptoms following a symptom-free period of 2 months (Spitzer *et al.*, 1978) or 6–12 months

(Klerman, 1978). In the study referred to here, patients who experienced a return of symptoms did so as early as the first month after the end of treatment and as late as 19 months following treatment. Thus it may be more accurate to say that some of these patients experienced a recurrence rather than a relapse.

ACKNOWLEDGMENTS

The authors thankfully acknowledge the support of the Department of Psychiatry, St. Paul-Ramsey Medical Center, as well as individuals who have given private donations for the purpose of advancing our knowledge about the treatment of depression. In addition, we extend special thanks to Sherri Zacharias, Bea Lundell, and Diane Vitulli for typing our manuscript.

REFERENCES

Abramson, L. Y., Seligman, M. E. P., & Teasdale, J. D. (1978). Learned helplessness in humans: Critique and reformulation. *Journal of Abnormal Psychology, 87,* 49–74.

Akiskal, H. S., & McKinney, W. T. (1973). Depressive disorders: Toward a unified hypothesis. *Science, 182,* 20–29.

Akiskal, H. S., & McKinney, W. T. (1975). Overview of recent research in depression: Ten conceptual models. *Archives of General Psychiatry, 32,* 285–305.

Alloy, L. B., & Abramson, L. Y. (1979). Judgment of contingency in depressed and nondepressed students: Sadder but wiser? *Journal of Experimental Psychology: General, 108,* 441–485.

Beck, A. T. (1963). Thinking and depression: 1. Idiosyncratic content and cognitive distortions. *Archives of General Psychiatry, 9,* 324–333.

Beck, A. T. (1964). Thinking and depression: 2. Theory and therapy. *Archives of General Psychiatry, 10,* 561–571.

Beck, A. T. (1967). *Depression: Clinical, experimental, and theoretical aspects.* New York: Harper & Row.

Beck, A. T. (1970). Cognitive therapy: Nature and relation to behavior therapy. *Behavior Therapy, 1,* 184–200.

Beck, A. T. (1976). *Cognitive theory and the emotional disorders.* New York: International Universities Press.

Beck, A. T., Hollon, S. D., Young, J., Bedrosian, R. C., & Budenz, D. (1985). Treatment of depression with cognitive therapy and amitriptyline. *Archives of General Psychiatry, 42,* 142–148.

Beck, A. T., Rush, A. J., Shaw, B. F., & Emery, G. (1979). *Cognitive therapy of depression: A treatment manual.* New York: Guilford Press.

Beck, A. T., Weissman, A., Lester, D., & Trexler, L. (1974). The measurement of pessimism: The hopelessness scale. *Journal of Consulting and Clinical Psychology, 42,* 861–865.

Blackburn, I. M., Bishop, S., Glen, A. I. M., Whalley, L. J., & Christie, J. E. (1981). The efficacy of cognitive therapy in depression: A treatment trial using cognitive therapy and pharmacotherapy, each alone and in combination. *British Journal of Psychiatry, 139,* 181–189.

Blackburn, I. M., Eunson, K. M., & Bishop, S. (1986). A two-year naturalistic follow-up of depressed patients treated with cognitive therapy, pharmacotherapy, and a combination of both. *Journal of Affective Disorders, 10,* 67–75.

Cantor, N. (1980a). A cognitive–social analysis of personality. In N. Cantor & J. F. Kihlstom (Eds.), *Personality, cognition, and social interaction* (pp. 23–44). Hillsdale, NJ: Erlbaum.

Cantor, N. (1980b). Perceptions of situations: Situation prototypes and person–situation prototypes. In

D. Magnusson (Ed.), *The situation: An interactional perspective*. Hillsdale, NJ: Erlbaum.

Cantor, N., & Mischel, W. (1977). Traits as prototypes: Effects on recognition memory. *Journal of Personality and Social Psychology, 35*, 38–48.

Cantor, N., & Mischel, W. (1979). Prototypes in person perception. In L. Berkowitz (Ed.), *Advances in experimental social psychology* (Vol. 12, pp. 3–52). New York: Academic Press.

Davis, H. (1979a). Self-reference and the encoding of personal information in depression. *Cognitive Therapy and Research, 3*, 97–110.

Davis, H. (1979b). The self-schema and subjective organization of personal information in depression. *Cognitive Therapy and Research, 3*, 415–425.

Davis, H., & Unruh, W. R. (1981). The development of the self-schema in adult depression. *Journal of Abnormal Psychology, 90*, 125–133.

Depue, R. A., & Kleinman, R. M. (1979). Free cortisol as a peripheral index of central vulnerability to major forms of polar depressive disorders: Examining stress–biology interactions in sub-syndromal high-risk persons. In R. A. Depue (Ed.), *The psychobiology of the depressive disorders: Implications for the effects of stress* (pp. 177–204). New York: Academic Press.

Derry, P. A., & Kuiper, N. A. (1981). Schematic processing and self-reference in clinical depression. *Journal of Abnormal Psychology, 90*, 286–297.

DeRubeis, R. J., Evans, M. D., Hollon, S. D., Tuason, V. B., & Garvey, M. J. (1986). *Components and mechanisms in cognitive therapy and pharmacotherapy for depression: 3. Processes of change in the CPT project.* Unpublished manuscript, University of Minnesota and St. Paul-Ramsey Medical Center, Minneapolis-St. Paul.

DeRubeis, R. J., & Hollon, S. D. (1981). Behavioral treatment of the affective disorders. In L. Michelson, M. Hersen, & S. M. Turner (Eds.), *Future perspectives in behavior therapy* (pp. 185–213). New York: Plenum.

DeRubeis, R. J., Hollon, S. D., Evans, M. D., & Bemis, K. M. (1982). Can psychotherapies in depression be discriminated? A systematic investigation of cognitive therapy and interpersonal therapy. *Journal of Consulting and Clinical Psychology, 50*, 744–756.

Evans, M. D. (1985). *Measurement of components of treatments for depression.* Unpublished grant prospectus, University of Minnesota and St. Paul-Ramsey Medical Center, Minneapolis-St. Paul.

Evans, M. D., Hollon, S. D., DeRubeis, R. J., Piasecki, J., Tuason, V. B., & Garvey, M. J. (1986). *Relapse/recurrence following cognitive therapy and pharmacotherapy for depression: 4. Two-year follow-up in the CPT project.* Unpublished manuscript, University of Minnesota and St. Paul-Ramsey Medical Center, Minneapolis-St. Paul.

Foreyt, J. P., & Rathjen, D. P. (1978). *Cognitive behavior therapy: Research and application.* New York: Plenum.

Freud, S. (1957). Mourning and melancholia. In J. Strachey (Ed. and Trans.), *The standard edition of the complete psychological works of Sigmund Freud* (Vol. 14, pp. 243–258). London: Hogarth Press. (Original work published 1917).

Garber, J., & Hollon, S. D. (1980). Universal versus personal helplessness: Belief in uncontrollability or incompetence? *Journal of Abnormal Psychology, 89*, 56–66.

Goldfried, M. R., & Davison, G. C. (1976). *Clinical behavior therapy.* New York: Holt, Rinehart & Winston.

Hammen, C., Marks, T., de Mayo, R., & Mayol, A. (1985). Self-schemas and risk for depression: A prospective study. *Journal of Personality and Social Psychology, 49*, 1147–1159.

Heise, D. R. *Causal analysis.* (1975). New York: Wiley.

Hollon, S. D. (1981). Comparisons and combinations with alternative approaches. In L. P. Rehm (Ed.), *Behavior therapy in depression: Present status and future directions.* New York: Academic Press.

Hollon, S. D., & Beck, A. T. (1978). Psychotherapy and drug therapy: Comparisons and combinations. In S. L. Garfield & A. E. Bergin (Eds.), *The handbook of psychotherapy and behavior change* (2nd ed., pp. 437–490). New York: Wiley.

Hollon, S. D., & Beck, A. T. (1979). Cognitive therapy of depression. In P. C. Kendall & S. D. Hollon (Eds.), *Cognitive–behavioral interventions: Theory, research, and procedures* (pp. 153–203).

Hollon, S. D., DeRubeis, R. J., & Evans, M. D. (1981a). *A model for studying the change process in the context of the treatment outcome study.* Unpublished manuscript, University of Minnesota and St. Paul-Ramsey Medical Center, Minneapolis-St. Paul.

Hollon, S. D., DeRubeis, R. J., & Evans, M. D. (1981b, August). *Toward a history of therapy in depression: Concepts and operations.* Paper presented at the meeting of the American Psychological Association, Los Angeles.

Hollon, S. D., DeRubeis, R. J., & Evans, M. D. (in press). Causal mediation of treatment for disposition: Discriminating between nonspecificity and noncausality. *Psychological Bulletin, 102.*

Hollon, S. D., DeRubeis, R. J., Evans, M. D., Tuason, V. B., Wiemer, M. J., & Garvey, M. (1986). *Cognitive therapy, pharmacotherapy, and combined cognitive therapy–pharmacotherapy in the treatment of depression: 1. Differential outcome.* Unpublished manuscript, University of Minnesota and St. Paul-Ramsey Medical Center, Minneapolis–St. Paul.

Hollon, S. D., Evans, M. D., Auerbach, A., DeRubeis, R. J., Kriss, M., Piasecki, J. M., Grove, W., Elkin, I., Lowery, A., & Tuason, V. B. (1986). *Development of a system for rating therapies for depression: Differentiating cognitive therapy, interpersonal psychotherapy, and clinical management pharmacotherapy.* Unpublished manuscript, University of Minnesota and St. Paul-Ramsey Medical Center, Minneapolis–St. Paul.

Hollon, S. D., Evans, M. D., & DeRubeis, R. J. (in press). Preventing relapse following treatment for depression: The Cognitive–Pharmacotherapy project. In T. Field, P. McCabe, & N. Schneiderman (Eds.) *Stress and coping across development.* Hillsdale, NJ: Erlbaum.

Hollon, S. D., & Garber, J. (1980). A cognitive–expectancy theory of therapy for helplessness and depression. In J. Garber & M. E. P. Seligman (Eds.), *Human helplessness: Theory and applications* (pp. 173–195). New York: Academic Press.

Hollon, S. D., & Garber, J. (in press). Cognitive behavior therapy: A social–cognitive perspective. In L. Y. Abramson (Ed.), *Social–personal inferences in clinical psychology.* New York: Guilford Press.

Hollon, S. D., & Kendall, P. C. (1980). Cognitive self-statements in depression: Development of an automatic thoughts questionnaire. *Cognitive Therapy and Research, 4,* 383–395.

Hollon, S. D., & Kendall, P. C. (1981). In vivo assessment techniques for cognitive–behavioral processes. In P. C. Kendall & S. D. Hollon (Eds.), *Assessment strategies for cognitive–behavioral interventions* (pp. 319–362). New York: Academic Press.

Hollon, S. D., Kendall, P. C., & Lumry, A. (1986). Specificity of depressotypic cognitions in clinical depression. *Journal of Abnormal Psychology, 95,* 52–59.

Hollon, S. D., & Kriss, M. R. (1984). Cognitive factors in clinical research and practice. *Clinical Psychology Review, 3,* 35–76.

Jenkins, H. M., & Ward, W. C. (1965). Judgment of contingency between responses and outcomes. *Psychological Monographs, 79* (1, Whole No. 594).

Jones, E. E., & Davis, K. E. (1965). From acts to dispositions: The attribution process in person perception. In L. Berkowitz (Ed.), *Advances in experimental social psychology* (Vol. 2, pp. 219–266). New York: Academic Press.

Kahneman, D., Slovic, P., & Tversky, A. (1982). *Judgment under uncertainty: Heuristics and biases.* Cambridge: Cambridge University Press.

Kelley, H. H. *Attribution in social interaction.* (1971). Morristown, NJ: General Learning Press.

Kelley, H. H. (1972). *Causal schemata and the attribution process.* Morristown, NJ: General Learning Press.

Kelley, H. H. (1973). The process of causal attribution. *American Psychologist, 28,* 107–128.

Kendall, P. C., & Hollon, S. D. (Eds.). (1979). *Cognitive–behavioral interventions: Theory, research, and procedures.* New York: Academic Press.

Kenny, D. A. (1979). *Correlation and causality.* New York: Wiley.

Kihlstrom, J. F., & Nasby, W. (1981). Cognitive tasks in clinical assessment: An exercise in applied psychology. In P. C. Kendall & S. D. Hollon (Eds.), _Assessment strategies for cognitive–behavioral interventions_ (pp. 287–317). New York: Academic Press.

Klerman, G. L. (1978). Long-term maintenance of affective disorders. In M. A. Lipton, A. DiMascio, & K. Killam (Eds.), _Psychopharmacology: A generation of progress_ (pp. 1303–1311). New York: Raven Press.

Kovacs, M., Rush, A. J., Beck, A. T., & Hollon, S. D. (1981). Depressed outpatients treated with cognitive therapy or pharmacotherapy: A one-year follow-up. _Archives of General Psychiatry, 38,_ 33–39.

Kuiper, N. A., & Derry, P. A. (1980). The self as a cognitive prototype: An application to person perception and depression. In N. Cantor & J. F. Kihlstrom (Eds.), _Personality, cognition, and social interaction_ (pp. 215–232). Hillsdale, NJ: Erlbaum.

Landy, F. J., & Farr, J. L. (1980). Performance rating. _Psychological Bulletin, 87,_ 72–107.

Lewinsohn, P. M., Mischel, W., Chaplin, W., & Barton, R. (1980). Social competence and depression: The role of illusory self-perceptions. _Journal of Abnormal Psychology, 89,_ 203–212.

Lewinsohn, P. M., Steinmetz, J. L., Larson, D. W., & Franklin, J. (1981). Depression-related cognitions: Antecedent or consequence? _Journal of Abnormal Psychology, 90,_ 213–219.

Lord, C., Ross, L., & Lepper, M. R. (1979). Biased assimilation and attitude polarization: The effects of prior theories on subsequently considered evidence. _Journal of Personality and Social Psychology, 37,_ 2098–2109.

Luborsky, L., Woody, G. E., McLellan, A. T., O'Brien, C. P., & Rosenzweig, J. (1982). Can independent judges recognize different psychotherapies? An experience with manual-guided therapies. _Journal of Consulting and Clinical Psychology, 50,_ 49–62.

Mahoney, M. J. (1974). _Cognition and behavior modification._ Cambridge, MA: Ballinger.

Markus, H. (1977). Self-schemata and processing information about the self. _Journal of Personality and Social Psychology, 35,_ 63–78.

Meichenbaum, D. H. (1977). _Cognitive–behavior modification: An integrative approach._ New York: Plenum.

Murphy, G. E., Simons, A. D., Wetzel, R. D., & Lustman, P. J. (1984). Cognitive therapy and pharmacotherapy: Singly and together in the treatment of depression. _Archives of General Psychiatry, 41,_ 33–41.

Neisser, U. (1976). _Cognition and reality: Principles and implications of cognitive psychology._ San Francisco: W. H. Freeman.

Nisbett, R. E., & Borgida, E. (1975). Attribution and the psychology of prediction. _Journal of Personality and Social Psychology, 32,_ 932–943.

Nisbett, R. E., & Ross, L. (1980). _Human inference: Strategies and shortcomings of social judgment._ Englewood Cliffs, NJ: Prentice-Hall.

Ross, L. (1977). The intuitive psychologist and his shortcomings. In L. Berkowitz (Ed.), _Advances in experimental social psychology_ (Vol. 10, pp. 173–220). New York: Academic Press.

Ruehlman, L. S., West, S. G., & Pasahow, R. J. (1985). Depression and evaluative schemata. _Journal of Personality, 53,_ 46–92.

Rush, A. J., Beck, A. T., Kovacs, M., & Hollon, S. D. (1977). Comparative efficacy of cognitive therapy versus pharmacotherapy in outpatient depressives. _Cognitive Therapy and Research, 1,_ 17–37.

Rush, A. J., Beck, A. T., Kovacs, M., Weissenberger, J. A., & Hollon, S. D. (1982). Effects of cognitive therapy and pharmacotherapy on hopelessness and self-concept. _American Journal of Psychiatry, 139,_ 862–866.

Seligman, M. E. P. (1975). _Helplessness._ San Francisco: W. H. Freeman.

Seligman, M. E. P., Abramson, L. Y., Semmel, A., & von Baeyer, C. (1979). Depressive attributional style. _Journal of Abnormal Psychology, 88,_ 242–247.

Shaw, B. F. (1977). Comparison of cognitive therapy and behavior therapy in the treatment of depression. _Journal of Consulting and Clinical Psychology, 45,_ 543–551.

Simons, A. D., Garfield, S. L., & Murphy, G. E. (1984). The process of change in cognitive therapy and pharmacotherapy for depression. _Archives of General Psychiatry, 41,_ 45–51.

Simons, A. D., Murphy, G. E., Levine, J. L., & Wetzel, R. D. (1986). Cognitive therapy and pharmacotherapy for depression: Sustained improvement over one year. *Archives of General Psychiatry, 43,* 43–48.

Smedslund, J. (1963). The concept of correlation in adults. *Scandinavian Journal of Psychology, 4,* 165–173.

Spitzer, R. L., Endicott, J., Robins, E. (1978). Research diagnostic criteria: Rationale and reliability. *Archives of General Psychiatry, 35,* 77–82.

Taylor, F. G., & Marshall, W. L. (1977). Experimental analysis of a cognitive–behavioral therapy for depression. *Cognitive Therapy and Research, 1,* 59–72.

Taylor, S. E., & Fiske, S. T. (1975). Point of view and perceptions of causality. *Journal of Personality and Social Psychology, 32,* 439–445.

Tversky, A., & Kahneman, D. (1974). Judgment under uncertainty: Heuristics and biases. *Science, 185,* 1124–1131. (Reprinted in D. Kahneman, P., Slovic, & A. Tversky (Eds.), *Judgment under uncertainty: Heuristics and biases* (pp. 3–20). Cambridge, England: Cambridge University Press, 1982.)

Tversky, A., & Kahneman, D. (1980). Causal schemas in judgments under uncertainty. In M. Fishbein (Ed.), *Progress in Social Psychology.* Hillsdale, NJ: Erlbaum. (Reprinted in D. Kahneman, P. Slovic, & A. Tversky (Eds.), *Judgment under uncertainty: Heuristics and biases* (pp. 117–128). Cambridge, England: Cambridge University Press, 1982)

Weissman, A. R., & Beck, A. T. (1978, November). *Development and validation of the Dysfunctional Attitude Scale.* Paper presented at the meeting of the Association for the Advancement of Behavior Therapy, Chicago.

Young, J. (1979). *The cognitive therapy scale.* Unpublished manuscript, Center for Cognitive Therapy, Philadelphia.

Zeiss, A. M., Lewinsohn, P. M., & Munoz, R. F. (1979). Nonspecific improvement effects in depression using interpersonal skills training, pleasant activity schedules, or cognitive training. *Journal of Consulting and Clinical Psychology, 47,* 427–439.

Index